The Art of Editing

The Art of Editing

SECOND EDITION

Floyd K. Baskette

University of Colorado

Jack Z. Sissors

Medill School of Journalism, Northwestern University

Macmillan Publishing Co., Inc.
New York

Collier Macmillan Publishers
London

COPYRIGHT © 1977, MACMILLAN PUBLISHING CO., INC.

PRINTED IN THE UNITED STATES OF AMERICA

MACMILLAN PUBLISHING CO., INC.
866 Third Avenue, New York, New York 10022

COLLIER MACMILLAN CANADA, LTD.

Library of Congress Cataloging in Publication Data

Baskette, Floyd K
  The art of editing.

  Includes index.
  1. Journalism. I. Sissors, Jack Zanville,
(date)   joint author. II. Title.
PN4778.B3 1977   070.4'1   76-7972
ISBN 0-02-306270-3

Printing: 1 2 3 4 5 6 7 8   Year: 7 8 9 0 1 2 3

Foreword

The very title of *The Art of Editing* constitutes a comprehensive grasp of what goes on around copydesks, small and big alike.

Copyediting indeed is an art. Principles contained here, buttressed by countless examples of "do do" and "don't do," will be helpful alike to the frightened cub and to the deadline-scarred pro. This is because the authors are pros and educators.

The appearance of the first edition coincided with the beginning of the surge from "hot metal" to "cold type" printing. Editing on the "tubes" has now become part of the new technology and is covered in the revised edition.

The burden on editing to help insure accuracy—of facts as well as language—has never been greater if credibility of the news media is to survive. And the burgeoning of the variety of messages clamoring for attention demands better packaging of the news product.

No text on editing can be an ironclad compendium, workable on all newspapers in all situations. Local ground rules always will prevail.

But *The Art of Editing* does provide goal posts applicable on all newspapers and in all situations.

HOWARD B. TAYLOR
Editorial Consultant (Emeritus)
Copley Newspapers
La Jolla, California

v

Preface

A handbook can describe the mechanics of editing, but few books or even a set of books can tell a copyeditor how to edit fast and accurately. Editing demands judgment, imagination, dedication and some creativity—all qualities derived from experience rather than from principles and formulas. In fact, most formulas for writing or editing are shunned in the newsroom.

To help beginners recognize some of the many kinds of errors that get into print or are "nailed on the rim" before they appear in print, the authors have relied on scores of examples recited in critiques compiled by editors for their staffs. In many instances, the editors' comments are as priceless as the examples themselves. The teacher may find these examples more realistic and more stimulating than contrived ones as laboratory exercises.

Because credit cannot be given for all the examples as they appear throughout the text, the authors gratefully acknowledge these sources: Chicago *Tribune, English 1;* Cleveland *Press, Tips and Slips;* Indiana *Daily Student, Us Last Week;* Flint (Mich.) *Journal, Journalisms;* Hackensack (N.J.) *Record, Second Look;* Louisville (Ky.) *Times, Better Late Than Never;* Louisville *Courier-Journal, After the Fact;* Minneapolis *Star, Stars and Gripes;* Wilmington (Del.) *News-Journal, Hits and Misses;* Richmond (Va.) *Times-Dispatch, T-D Topics;* San Bernardino (Calif.) *Sun-Telegram, Feedbag;* St. Paul *Dispatch* and *Pioneer Press, Hits & Errors;* Winston-Salem (N.C.) *Journal and Sentinel, Pats and Paddles;* Chattanooga (Tenn.) *Times, Sum of the Times;* Indianapolis *News, "How We're Doin'";* and New London (Conn.) *Day, Cares That Infest the Day.*

Other sources from which examples have been used are Carl Byoir & Associates, Inc., *Ripples in the Copy Stream;* U.P.I.

Reporter; AP *Log;* APME *News;* ASNE *Bulletin;* the International Council of Industrial Editors *Reporting; Editor & Publisher; The Quill; Publishers' Auxiliary;* the Baltimore *Evening Sun Blue Book;* and numerous stylebooks.

The authors are indebted to their colleagues, students and professional workers who read chapters and gave many helpful suggestions. Special gratitude is extended to the Boulder (Colo.) *Daily Camera* for editing TTS, to the Huntington (W. Va.) *Advertiser* for VDT editing, to the Longmont (Colo.) *Times-Call* and Denver *Rocky Mountain News* for OCR copy preparation, to the Denver *Post* for picture and magazine editing, to the Denver bureaus of the AP and UPI for wire editing and to radio station KBOL in Boulder and television station KMGH-TV for broadcast news editing. Other credits are given within the text.

As the title suggests, editing is an art, but editing itself needs the skills of many—writer, photographer, artist, printer and engineer—to fulfill its purpose. These, and others, all have a hand in shaping the message for the media.

Practices and terms may vary from one newsroom to another. The new technology of the computer in some phases of editing is creating even more differences. Basically, however, editing is the same art no matter where or by whom it is practiced. To all who will accept the challenge of careful editing, this volume is dedicated.

Boulder, Colorado   F. K. B
Evanston, Illinois   J. Z. S.

Contents

1

The Copyeditor As Editor

Every editor edits. That is, the editor decides what shall and what shall not go into his publication on the basis of what he conceives to be the publication's mission and philosophy.

Of the various subeditors who help the editor carry out his job, one is the copyeditor, the man or woman who makes raw copy palatable for the reader.

Although each editor works at different levels, all have to edit. Adolph Ochs of the New York *Times* insisted that copyreading is editing. "A good copyreader," he said in a talk at the Pulitzer School of Journalism in 1925, "is truly and in the full meaning an editor. The most useful man on the newspaper is one who can edit."[1]

One may describe the duties of the editor, but no one can analyze how an editor works, any more than one can describe how a poet composes a poem. Norman Podhoretz, editor of *Commentary* magazine, came close to defining one obligation of the editor—"to improve an essentially well-written piece or to turn a clumsily written one into, at the very least, a readable and literate article, and, at the very most, a beautifully shaped and effective essay which remains true to the author's intention, which realizes that intention more fully than he himself was able to do. He cares about the English language; he cares about clarity of thought and of grace of expression; he cares about the traditions of discourse and of argument."[2]

---

[1] Adolph Ochs, as quoted by Stanley Walker in *City Editor* (New York: Stokes, 1934), p. 90.
[2] Norman Podhoretz, "In Defense of Editing," *Harper's*, p. 143 (October 1965).

Describing a publisher's editor in the Trade Winds column in the *Saturday Review* (February 10, 1968, p. 12), Herbert R. Mayes gave some attributes that apply equally well to the copydesk expert: "An editor, like a gardener with a green thumb, has a knack. There is no specific training involved. There is no college to offer a doctorate in editing, because editing is an empirical art. There is nothing scientific about it. There are no statistics, except after the fact, that can be relied on. Editing is intuitive. Experience confirms intuition but does nothing to develop it. Intuition is for what is the right writing for a given audience, of course, but no less for what makes the members of any audience laugh and cry, love and hate, be decent or vulgar, vengeful or sympathetic, greedy or generous, brave or cowardly."

The copyeditor has been called the midwife to the story, the reporter's best critic. The copyeditor is like the unsung craftsmen in a dramatic production whose skills put the quality into the material that draws the applause for the stars. Rudolph Burke of the Atlanta *Journal*, in a letter to *Editor & Publisher* (July 8, 1967, p. 7) has said that the byline lures the enthusiastic beginner, but every managing editor knows there is often a great deal of difference between what the reporter writes and what the reader reads after the story has gone through the hands of anonymous editors.

A few reporters grouse because the copyeditors "butcher all their good stuff." But most writers respect their collaborator on the desk, the ever-alert copyeditor who gives the copy a final look before it goes to the composing room and then to the reader. "It was the small author who ever resented the touch of the editorial pencil upon his precious effusions," said Edward Bok in *The Americanization of Edward Bok*.[3]

The term *copyeditor* is more apt than the traditional word *copyreader* because it connotes the essential job of editing copy. It suggests the art of correcting, refining and polishing a piece of copy. Editing, as crossword-puzzle fans know, means redacting, or bringing back, getting together, collecting, arranging, reducing, composing, framing, translating, selecting or adapting for publication. A redactor, therefore, is an editor. One aspect of redacting is copyediting, the British equivalent of subediting.

Editing begins the moment a reporter composes a story. If the writer has been trained in editing as well as in reporting, he or she will double-check the copy for errors of fact and style before submitting the story. The reporter may even have the responsibility of writing a headline for the story.

An excellent staff without a copydesk conceivably might produce a fair newspaper. A mediocre staff with a competent copydesk can produce an acceptable newspaper. But an excellent staff, backed by an excellent desk, guarantees an excellent paper. Such is the testament of a former executive, L. R. Blan-

---

[3] Edward Bok, *The Americanization of Edward Bok* (New York: Scribner, 1922), p. 382.

chard of the Gannett Newspapers, who added, "No man is qualified to be his own copyeditor. No matter what his reputation, his writing will benefit from another's look."[4] And another—this from Stan Amisov of *Newsday*—"There are many elements that go into the making of a fine newspaper, but one of the least heralded and most important is an outstanding copydesk. It can make a good newspaper better. It can make a better newspaper the best."[5]

The new technology is making it almost imperative for even the small daily newspaper to place a copyeditor, or some other executive, in charge of processing and moving copy. Automation is providing more copy from more sources than ever before, thereby demanding a greater degree of selectivity. Also, as will be explained later, the newsroom is becoming increasingly involved with the processes of production so that much of the responsibility that once belonged to the printer now rests with the editor.

The copydesk may be viewed as the newspaper's clearinghouse. Here the flow of copy is sorted, corrected, measured, headlined, scheduled and moved on to compositors. The vision of what the paper will contain and how the pages will look materializes on the copydesk.

Automation may not radically change content and presentation. As pointed out by Nathaniel M. Gerstenzang of the New York *Times*, new methods may change red ink to black on newspaper balance sheets, but they won't assure publishers of the best and fullest use of the most valuable commodity—the news column. "The assurance," Gerstenzang said, "can be given, in the last analysis, only by human brains—specifically by competent copyeditors."[6]

The copyeditor has talents that cannot be replaced by computers. One of these talents is the ability to edit copy; another is the ability to compose headlines. The first is as important as the second, if not more so, because editing demands many intangibles—judgment, scholarliness, background, memory, aggressiveness, motivation, curiosity, imagination, discretion, cynicism, skepticism and even some genius.

Almost all critics lead lonesome lives, but at least they have the respect of those they have taught. One of the most demanding of all editors was Harold Ross of the *New Yorker*, of whom Ogden Nash wrote in a letter quoted in James Thurber's *The Years with Ross*, "He was an almost impossible man to work for—rude, ungracious and perpetually dissatisfied with what he read; and I admire him more than anyone I have met in professional life."[7]

[4] L. R. Blanchard, *Editor & Publisher*, p. 44 (August 9, 1964).
[5] Stan Amisov, *Editor & Publisher*, p. 66 (February 6, 1965).
[6] Nathaniel M. Gerstenzang, "The Newspaper's Biggest Personnel Problem," *Columbia Journalism Review*, 4:40 (Winter 1966).
[7] James Thurber, *The Years with Ross* (Boston: Little, Brown, 1957), p. 123.

The copyeditor is a diamond cutter who refines and polishes, removes the flaws and shapes the stone into a gem. He searches for the ills in copy and meticulously scans the product for flaws and inaccuracy, ever searching for the maximum power of words. He knows when to prune the useless, the redundant, the unnecessary qualifiers. He gets movement in the piece by substituting active verbs for inactive ones, specifics for generalities. He obtains color by changing faraway words to close-up words. He keeps sentences short enough so that readers can grasp one idea at a time and still not suffer primer prose. He strives for pacing. If the sentence clothes several ideas majestically and in good order, he has the good sense to let the writer have his way. He realizes he is not the storyteller. His talent is in what he can do with another's copy to make it sparkle.

Lest this description suggest that the copyeditor is like a bored teacher correcting English themes, consider that the copydesk is one of the exciting places in the newsroom. On the desk tumbles all the copy of the day—the major battles, the moon landings, robberies, the cure for cancer, the election of a president, the Kentucky Derby winner, the rescue of a lost child. The desk is the heart that throbs with all the news from near and far, waiting for someone to shape it, size it, display it and send it to the reader.

"Because copyediting is an art," said J. Edward Murray of the Boulder (Colo.) *Camera*, "the most important ingredient, after training and talent, is strong motivation. The copyeditor must care. Not only should he know his job. He must love it. Every story. Every edition. Every day. No art yields to less than maximum effort. The copyeditor must be motivated by a fierce professional pride in the high quality of editing."[8] No one can tell copyeditors how to edit—they have to experience it for themselves.

A newspaper without a circle of geniuses around the copydesk would have been unthinkable to the sage of American journalism, Carl Lindstrom, formerly of the Hartford *Times*. He regarded the desk as the backbone of the paper. "The copydesk," he once observed, "is the abiding place of curiosity, discretion, cynicism, sympathy—all those human instincts personified in men who give your paper its flavor; newshounds all, with noses in the air for the scent of human interest and for libel. I salute the copydesk, the sacrificial altar of the sacred cow."[9]

Ask youngsters fresh out of a journalism school what they are looking for in their professional lives. The thoughtful ones will reply, "I want a job that offers an opportunity for growth. I want a chance to continue to expand my education. I want a place where I can, by my own incentive, advance to the higher echelons of responsibility." Mention the copydesk and they are

[8] J. Edward Murray, "Editing Artists: The Men Around the Rim," *The Quill*, p. 12 (March 1964).
[9] Carl Lindstrom, as quoted in *Journalism Quarterly*, **42:4**:638 (Autumn 1965).

likely to repeat the stereotypes of the desk as the haven for tired, worn-out newsmen who spend their days marking paragraphs and hurriedly composing commonplace headlines so they can get back to their crossword puzzles. The great and the near-great are those of the editors, the reporters, the columnists, the news commentators. Whoever heard of a hero of the copydesk?

Yet, no place on a publication offers a greater opportunity for growth, a chance to continue an education, an incentive to reach the higher places of responsibility. Copyeditors, even if mediocre, must of necessity accumulate a warehouse full of facts, facts they have gleaned from the thousands of stories they are compelled to read and edit or from the references they have had to consult to verify information.

Think of them as superdetectives, who incessantly search the story for clues that could transform a mediocre piece into an epic. Let them study ocean charts and maps and astronomical formulas, as did Carr Van Anda of the New York *Times*, to find the missing links in the routine story. Think of them as lawyers conducting a cross-examination. Let them study Harold Ross, who, as noted previously, made life miserable for writers on the *New Yorker* but who never let a piece escape him unless the meaning was crystal clear.

The greatness of both Ross and Van Anda was that they were mentally curious, a trait that should characterize all copyeditors. Few copyeditors today would correct an Einstein formula, as Van Anda did, but—if they are willing—they can probe, question, authenticate and exercise their powers of deduction.

If copyeditors are blessed with a good copydesk chief, they will learn. Day by day they will improve. If in college they worked under a wise and experienced professor on the staff, rather than under a graduate assistant who regarded a copydesk lab as a chore, they will probably love editing. The tradition that the copydesk is a man's domain is dying. Some of the best copyeditors are women. On some metropolitan papers, women with editing skill have risen to important positions, in charge of copyediting and layout of sections that run to many pages.

Whether copyeditors, as a class or a craft group, are a vanishing breed is debatable. Some editors think they are. A typical comment might be: A few very good ones exist here and there, but as individuals and not as part of a great fraternity that was with us thirty or forty years ago. Newspapers are poorer because of this, and I suspect that those who survive are lonesome. They were "swifts" and could handle large piles of copy with an unerring eye for big and little errors, misspelled words, factual faults.

If, in fact, good copyeditors are hard to come by, publishers might start paying more attention to the experts on the desk. A copyeditor with a good education and the opportunity to advance his knowledge will benefit the newspaper more than a reporter will. Let management recommend a copyeditor as a Nieman

---

The Copyeditor As Editor 5

Fellow, or give him an opportunity to attend the American Press Institute at Columbia University, or give him a leave of absence to ground himself at the London School of Economics, or give him a chance to trade jobs for a year with a copyeditor in another part of the country or invite him to sit in on office conferences where policy and philosophy are discussed.

Editors might keep trainees or interns on the copydesk at least long enough to find out whether the trainee will make a good copyeditor. By rotating good reporters on the desk, editors might find that both the desk and the reporters will profit.

The emphasis in this book is on copydesk work. It is not intended solely for those who will edit copy for a newspaper, a wire service, a magazine, a broadcast newsroom or even an advertising department or agency. Rather, it is designed to aid the reporter as well as the copyeditor. Editing should start with the reporter's own copy.

2

The Copyeditor and the Reader

Copyeditors can perceive copy as stories that come from machines and flow along an assembly line to the press. Or, they can view copy as messages destined for readers and thus concern themselves not only with copy but with audiences as well.

The Nature of Audiences

Newspapers in the past knew little about their readers—who they were, what they read, what really interested them. Editors relied on traditional news patterns evolved primarily from guesswork. Much of the news was concerned mainly with accident, crime and politics.

Today's editors may have to revise their definition of news, in the opinion of H. L. Stevenson, editor-in-chief and vice president of United Press International. "There is an increasing flow of information, a floodtide of facts and phrases and new jargon to master," he said.

Remember the space age and the moon landings and the new terms and technology suddenly thrust upon us? Now the big story is the economy and we are being treated to new terms like recession, consumer price index, petrodollars and stagflation. And the same is true in many other areas—civil rights, women's rights, changing lifestyles, work habits and educational priorities.

There are indications that stories which perform a service, telling people how to cope, are among the most popular and best read today. How do you make your dollar stretch farther? How do you repair your own automobile? How do you add a room to your house? How do you stay healthy? [1]

[1] "Collard Greens and the Future of Journalism" (speech at Greater Orlando Press Club, February 1, 1975).

Reader service, then, should be near the top of today's news priorities.

Newspapers have always covered violent changes such as war and disaster but in the past neglected what James B. Reston calls the quiet revolutions—changes of the family, the scientific laboratory and the electronic computer that are changing the fabric of the world.

Audiences as well as news definitions also change. The Census Bureau predicts that by the year 2000 a majority of the American populace will be over the age of 30. As projected by the bureau in 1975, the median age of the population is expected to rise from 28.6 years to between 31.4 and 37 by the year 2000. ("Median age" means that half of the population is above that figure and half below.) In the 35 to 44 age group, the increase is expected to reach 81 per cent with the proportion of blacks and the number of people 65 or older rising considerably (UPI release, October 20, 1975).

Editors have several ways of determining the nature of audiences. They can subscribe to a service such as Carl J. Nelson Research, Inc., and have a survey made of the paper. They can ring doorbells or eavesdrop in bars and cafes to find out what people are talking about, or find out why potential readers refuse to subscribe to the local paper. Or they can study the summaries of readership surveys found in the News Research Bulletins published by the American Newspaper Publishers Association (ANPA) and in a series of booklets titled *News Research for Better Newspapers.*[2]

Most readership research is intended to test hypotheses that editors have about the nature of news and audience behavior. But, said Dr. Bush, research itself does not create; editors create (Bush, I:5). He said editors may use some results of readership surveys to help take the guesswork out of editing. They may determine from a survey what readers read on a certain day. But a survey cannot tell editors what readers will read because newspapers change every day and the reading of news content also changes from day to day and from paper to paper. The selection of timely, interesting news articles is still very much the editor's art.

The effort to help readers identify themselves with the news is the first principle in good editing. But even if editors could know precisely what readers read or might want to read, it is doubtful that editors would limit news content to "best-read" types. If they did, they would get a paper described by one editor as "the most flamboyant, sensational and frivolous newspaper ever published—because the best-read stories, day in and day out, are usually those heavily vested with violence, sex, controversy and so-called human interest qualities." It was his opinion that editors will continue to use their own professional judgment of what is important, consequential and significant

---

[2] Seven volumes and an index were compiled from 1965 through 1975. Citations are to volume and page under the title of Bush, the original editor, and are used with permission. The late Dr. Chilton R. Bush was formerly head of the Department of Communication at Stanford University.

in the day's news (Bush, I:147).

Newspapers will have to offer more stories than they have in the past to get more variety of content and thus satisfy diverse tastes. This does not mean, necessarily, that readers will read more items or will spend more time reading newspapers. What they read may be more satisfying to them. The majority of adult readers now spend an average of 40 minutes with each weekday paper, whereas less than one fourth of teenage readers spend that much time reading weekday papers (Bush, I:16, 17, 18).

Newspapers reach out for a mass audience. That is their basic strength. They must try to meet the reading needs of all readers, not just a special group, observed Alan S. Donnahoe, president of Media General of Richmond, Va. "But because what will please or interest another—some dissatisfaction among readers is virtually guaranteed" (ANPA, Newspaper Information Service Newsletter, September 1975).

Nor can the habits of regular readers of newspapers be determined accurately. One executive suggested, "We don't know enough about the lightning-fast process in the reader's mind that causes him to read an item on the top of column two on page 47—but reject, or skip, adjacent news items in columns one and three" (Bush, I:10).

Past studies have demonstrated that most readers read their newspaper intensively, page by page. They expose themselves to everything in their paper to make sure they are not missing anything of interest.

Perhaps not all readers are as ecstatic about their newspapers as is Leo Rosten who said:

I love newspapers. I read them with delight—even with passion. To me a newspaper is a gorgeous daily "bazar of wonders and follies, a forum, a college, a freak show, a stage."

The best stories on earth parade through the columns of newsprint: stories with plots beyond what any writer in his senses would dare to contrive and with characters only God, in his infinite variety and amusement, could possibly concoct. Where but from the cooky carnival of life could one possibly find a woman as the one in Memphis who entered an elevator and, en route to Room 1263, proceeded to push buttons 12, 6, and 3?

Some news items, of course, can drive you up the wall—because they have been garbled by typesetters or emasculated by copyeditors or amputated unto pointlessness by robots who are concerned only with making lines fit available space without bothering to read the remnants they cut out.[3]

Readership studies have shown that the old ideas about readership in relation to the sex of the reader and to position in the paper or on the page should not be regarded as strictly as they once were. Men and women tend to read much the same things, although there are obvious statistical differences. The left-hand page is as well-read as the right-hand page. Small items at the bottoms of pages may attract as much attention as big displays at the tops of pages. Frequently, the best-read stories

[3] Leo Rosten, "Diversions," *Saturday Review*, p. 58 (April 19, 1975).

are not those displayed prominently on page 1.

Differences in reading are determined more by age, education and economic status than by sex or race. Of course, more women than men read the family pages and more men than women read the sports pages, but readership research suggests that the quality of stories, rather than their placement, is what attracts and holds the audience.

Neither the reporter nor the copyeditor can assume that everyone out there is panting to read every word the rising star journalist produces. No matter how much is offered or how it is presented, less than 20 per cent of the general news content will be read by adult men and women (Bush, I:143). That readers are highly selective in what they read is shown by the fact they will read no more than 10,000 words each weekday, regardless of the total offered (Bush, I:143). The kinds of things that people want and get out of a newspaper are much the same regardless of how much time they spend reading it (Bush, I:10, 11, 12).

A key question for most readers is, "What's in it for me?" Perhaps one answer can be found in the hypothesis formulated in 1949 by Dr. Wilbur Schramm that a reader selects news in expectation of a reward. Said Dr. Schramm, "Leaving out chance, conflicting mental sets, and the qualities of presentation which call attention to one item over others or make one item easier to read than others, we can hypothesize that a person chooses the items which he thinks are likely to give him the greatest reward.

". . . In general, there seems to be greater expectation of reward when there appears to be greater possibility of the reader identifying himself with the news" (Bush, II:13–18).

Studies have indicated that, so far, radio and television have not diminished newspaper reading. In fact, exposure to events by the broadcast media tends to increase reader interest in those events. The pattern may change if the trend toward reluctance to read or the inability to read continues or if news in newspapers is not presented more interestingly. The studies have suggested that shorter items suffer less loss of readers than do longer ones, but this may be because of story content and style rather than length. Also, stories written in the conventional inverted pyramid structure suffer a readership drop-off of 11.3 per cent in the first five paragraphs, 3.46 in the second five, 1.74 per cent in the third five and .54 per cent in the fourth five (Bush, III:15). Further, the practice of jumping stories from one page to another may have to be reevaluated because only about half the readers who start a story on one page will follow the story to the jump page (Bush, III:9).

Among questions that will continue to occupy newspaper editors are: How do readers perceive of news and news sources? How do readers see the paper? What do they expect from it?

Watergate proved what an effective weapon news can be. It also raised questions as to the credibility of the news media. Readers could well question institutions that seemed to prefer bad news to good news, that were prone to be one-sided, were apparently accountable to no one, that made mistakes, that were not content to tell the story but overkilled it.

Specifically, consumers protested that the media did not confine opinion to the editorial page but mixed it with news. They said too much attention was given to gloom news—violence, conflict, racial unrest, crime, drug abuse. They suspected that news could be manipulated by politicians and advertisers. Almost daily they could count errors in meaning, names and titles, misspelled names or places, wrong addresses, typographical errors. In one survey one third of the readers said typographical errors raised a serious question about credibility (Bush, V:79).

If stories are unclear and unreadable they likewise are unbelievable.

To enhance the newspaper's image, today's editors readily admit errors. One paper runs a daily notice, prominently displayed, inviting and encouraging readers to call attention to errors in the paper. Another editor regularly runs an accuracy check of its locally written news stories. A clipping of the story is mailed to the source along with a brief query on the accuracy of facts in the story and headline. Another invites persons involved in controversy to present amplifying statements when they feel their position has not been fully or fairly represented.

More corrections are being printed, even though this practice is distasteful to editors. When the Minneapolis *Star* had to print four corrections on one day, the editor warned the staff, "Let's hope it is a record that is never equalled—or something beside the sky will fall." The Boca Raton (Fla.) *News* candidly tells its readers of its corrections under the heading, "Dumb Things We Did."

More balance in opinion is noted in the use of syndicated columnists whose opinions differ from those of the newspaper

SHORT RIBS by Frank Hill

[*Reprinted by permission of Newspaper Enterprise Association.*]

and in an expanded letters column.

Some newspapers are using ombudsmen to hear readers' complaints or they subscribe to local, regional or national press councils. More are providing reader service columns to identify newspapers with readers' personal concerns. More attention is being given to internal criticism, in employe publications or at staff conferences.

Despite these measures, a newspaper's credibility depends essentially on its accuracy and balance. In the endeavor to assure accuracy both in fact and in language, the copyeditor's role is paramount.

Readability Measurements

Readership measures the extent to which an item is read. Readability measures the ease with which an item can be read, or, more accurately, it tries to measure some of the things that make reading difficult.

A readability measurement is no formula for writing, nor was it ever intended to be. Rather, it is a tool that may be used in rewriting or editing to improve the writing or to check the writing style from various departments of a paper or from the wire services.

Most readability formulas are based on concepts long familiar to newspaper editors. Short sentences generally are easier to read than long ones and short words generally are more likely to be comprehended than long ones. Two of the better-known formulas developed by readability experts use sentence and word lengths. The Flesch formula, devised by Dr. Rudolph Flesch, uses 100-word samples to measure average sentence length and number of syllables. The formula multiplies the average number of words in the sentence by 1.015 and the total syllable count by .846. The two factors are then added, subtracted from 206.835 to arrive at a readability score.[4] Some newspapers use computers periodically to test readability of news stories.

Robert Gunning uses a similar procedure to determine the *fog index*. He adds the average sentence length in words and the number of words of three syllables or more (omitting capitalized words; combinations of short, easy words like *butterfly*; and verb forms made into three syllables by adding –ed, –es, or –ing.) The sum is multiplied by .4 to get the *fog index*.[5]

Suppose the sample contains an average of 16 words to the sentence and a total of 150 syllables. By the Flesch formula the sample would have a readability score of 64, which Flesch rates as standard or fitting the style of *Reader's Digest*. In the same sample and assuming the hard words at 10 per cent, the *fog index* of the Gunning scale would be 10, or at the reading level

---

[4] Rudolph Flesch, *The Art of Readable Writing* (New York: Harper & Row, 1949), p. 197.
[5] Robert Gunning, *The Technique of Clear Writing* (New York: McGraw-Hill, 1952), pp. 36, 37.

of high school sophomores and fitting *Time* magazine style.

The wire services thought enough of both formulas to get an evaluation of their news reports. Gunning conducted the evaluation for United Press and Dr. Flesch did two measurements for the Associated Press.

Neither Flesch nor Gunning tests content or word familiarity. All they suggest is that if passages from a story or the whole story average more than 20 words to the sentence and the number of hard words in a sample of 100 words exceeds 10 per cent, a majority of readers will find the passages difficult to understand.

Nor would the formula designers recommend that copyeditors pare all long sentences to 20 words or less and all long words to monosyllables. Long sentences, if they are graceful and meaningful, should be kept intact. Mixed with shorter sentences, they give variety to style. A long word may still be a plain word.

An editorial executive of the New York *Times* preferred to measure density of ideas in sentences rather than sentence length itself and came up with a pattern of "one idea, one sentence." A special issue of the newsroom publication *Winners & Sinners* No. 79 (February 4, 1955) was devoted to this pattern, with reports of reading tests on two versions of the same articles. One tested the comprehension of the articles as they were written originally. Another tested the articles when rewritten to lower the density of ideas in the sentence. The "one idea, one sentence" dictum is not taken literally even at the *Times*, but, the editors insist, "Generally it speeds reading if there is only one idea to a sentence."

The number of unfamiliar words in passages has also been found to be an element in readability. Edgar Dale and Jeanne S. Chall at Ohio State University prepared a list of 3,000 words known to 80 per cent of fourth-graders. The word-load factor in the Dale-Chall formula consists of a count of words outside the list. Only 4 per cent of the words on the Dale-Chall list are words of three or more syllables.[6]

Editing stories to reduce the number of words outside the word-familiarity list would be time-consuming and probably impractical because the lists would have to be revised periodically to take out words that no longer are familiar and to add new words that have become part of everyday language—even to fourth-graders.

Most readability formulas use a few fundamental elements but neglect context or story structure. Thus, a passage in gibberish could rate as highly readable on the Flesch, Gunning and Dale-Chall scales. This was demonstrated by Dr. Wilson L. Taylor at the University of Illinois Institute of Communications Research. Dr. Taylor developed the *cloze* procedure (from "close" or "closure" in Gestalt psychology to test context). In

[6] Edgar Dale and Jeanne S. Chall, "A Formula for Predicting Readability," *Education Research Bulletin*, 27:45–55 (Feb. 18, 1948).

this procedure he omitted certain words—usually every fifth word—and asked respondents to fill in the missing words, then graded them on the number of correct words they could fill in. Of passages from eight writers, the Taylor method ranked samples of Gertrude Stein's semi-intelligible prose as next to the most difficult. The most difficult was a passage from James Joyce.[7] Both the Dale-Chall and the Flesch scales rated the Stein passage as the easiest to read and the Joyce passage in a tie for fourth with a passage from Erskine Caldwell (Bush I:92, 93). To test for human interest, Flesch measures personal words and sentences. Sentences that mention persons and have them saying and doing things increase readability.

The *cloze* procedure suggests that unfamiliar words may be used and understood if they are placed in a context where the reader can guess the word's meaning.

Few copyeditors will apply any of the readability formulas described because editing is an art, not a science. Still, beginning copyeditors might profit from testing story passages by formula to help them see where and how the structure can be tightened or broken up into more easily digestible bits.

Common-sense editing applies many of the elements used in readability tests. The skilled copyeditor knows when to break a long sentence into two and when to substitute a simple word for a hard one. The copyeditor is under constant pressure to simplify and clarify. Educational attainment may be increasing but evidence suggests that the ability to read is not improving. Today most news content has to be edited so that even the eighth-grade reader can understand it.

[7] Wilson L. Taylor, "'Cloze Procedure'; A New Tool for Measuring Readability," *Journalism Quarterly*, **30**:415–33 (Fall 1953).

3

The Tools and How to Use Them

The size of a newspaper and the production system it uses determine the main functions of copyeditors as well as the tools and symbols they use. Copyeditors once were limited to two main jobs—to edit copy and create headlines. But today copyeditors are as much involved in production as in editorial responsibilities.

Desk Functions

Desk editors likewise have the traditional chores of controlling the amount and flow of copy, supervising the work of reporters and copyeditors and designing page layouts. Desk editors also are assuming responsibilities once reserved exclusively to the production department. They may direct all typesetting and place stories and illustrations on news pages with hardly any assistance from printers.

The new technology gives the editorial function back to reporters, copyeditors and desk editors where it belongs. It bypasses Linotype operators, proofreaders and makeup personnel. The new system reduces errors and puts the news as much as 90 minutes closer to the printing press. Now more time can be given to better writing, better editing and better page designing. Not all the advances will make the work of reporters and editors easier, as will be explained later, but eventually more time can be devoted to editorial refinement and less time to production.

The physical arrangement for handling copy may be as varied as the production system. The copydesk may be a huge, horseshoe-shaped desk with the editor occupying the inside or slot of the desk and the copyeditors on the rim (Figure 3–1). Or copyeditors may have their own desks, some with standard type-

Figure 3–1. Traditional copydesk. This H-shaped copydesk, serving both The Louisville (Ky.) *Courier-Journal* and The Louisville *Times*, provides working space for more than twenty copyeditors. The center arm of the H is occupied by the news editor, assistant news editor, managing editor and assistant managing editor. The news room has since been redesigned to accommodate the hardware of the new technology. [*Photo courtesy of the* Courier-Journal *and the Louisville* Times.]

writers or electric typewriters or video display terminals (VDT)[1] (Figure 3–2).

The copydesk may be departmentalized, handling copy only from specialized departments such as local, wire, pictures, business, sports, family pages and special sections such as Sunday and zone editions. Or the desk may be semidepartmentalized, responsible for copy from some departments but not from others. Finally, the desk may be universal, one that processes copy from all departments, usually with the exception of the locally produced Sunday magazines.

Traditional Methods

Here is a step-by-step description of what happens in the traditional system when a story leaves the reporter's typewriter.

The story (called copy or "hard copy" in computer parlance) goes to the city editor. If the story is about the mayor's resignation it likely will be titled or slugged "Mayor." The city editor decides to give the reporter a byline, place the story on page 1 for the home edition and give the story a two-column, one-line head in 30-point Futura Medium type. The story will be indented

[1] A glossary of some of the terms used in the new technology is given at the end of this chapter.

Figure 3-2. Computerized newsroom—all news stories are written and edited on Video Display Terminals at the Huntington (W. Va.) *Advertiser.* [*Photo courtesy of Huntington Publishing Co.*]

to provide for a half-column (thumbnail) face shot (mug shot) of the mayor. The story will be set in one column or $14\frac{1}{2}$-pica measure. All this the city editor notes at the top of the story before passing the story to the copydesk.

The desk editor scans the story, noting the instructions supplied by the city editor, then releases the story to a copyeditor.

Routine of the copyeditor:

First read the story. Then go back and, using editing symbols (Figure 3-3), pencil in needed corrections, deletions and additions. On deletions, close up space to aid the compositor in following the copy (Figure 3-4).

If paragraphs are to be moved around, use shears and paste, not arrows.

With that part of the editing completed, go back over the story to indicate typographical instructions. This may start with the byline:

$$\text{\textit{bf} } -\|\text{ BY SALLY JONES}$$

Next indicate the lines to be indented for the half-column picture:

$$\textit{Indent for 7-pica cut}$$

The Tools and How to Use Them   17

Take out word and ~~and~~ close up space

Add word

Retain ~~crossed out~~ portion

Transpose letters words or

capitalize word: lower-case letter

Indent for paragraph

Don't indent

Insert period: ...John said

Insert comma: John who...

Insert apostrophe: Johns other wife

Insert quotation marks: John said, I'll go.

Insert hyphens: Jack and Jill School

Insert parentheses: John is his last name.

Use a circle to indicate:

Abbreviation: Colonel Smith

No abbreviation: the col. said

Use figure: six hundred

Spell out figure: He had 5 boys

Directions to compositors:

bf — Set boldface. Wavy line also denotes boldface: At the Alladin

lf — Set lightface

bc — Set boldface capitals

bfclc — Set boldface capital and lower-case

sc — Set small capitals. Two lines under letters denote small capitals: Macky

sh — Subhead. Write the subhead between lines of copy

ital. — Set in italic type. Underscore denotes italic: fog index

Rom. — Set in Roman type

dc / 15-pica — Set type in double-column measure or in measure indicated

Note: If a paragraph is to be deleted, draw a box around that paragraph, then draw a line to connect the last word of the preceding paragraph with the first word of the following paragraph.

Figure 3–3. Copyediting symbols.

If the story runs more than half a column deep, insert sub-heads between every third or fourth paragraph:

bfc // SALARY DISPUTE

Now determine the length of the edited story by counting the lines of copy, including the subheads. Assume there are 54 lines. That means the story will occupy 9 inches of type (if six copy lines are used to constitute an inch) and not including space for the headline. Write the length at the top of the page along with the copyeditor's name or initials. Reread the story.

Write the headline on a separate half-sheet, including the slug-line and type designation:

MAYOR - 2/30-FM

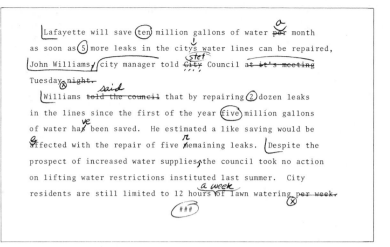

Lafayette will save (ten) million gallons of water per month as soon as (5) more leaks in the city's water lines can be repaired, John Williams, city manager told City Council at it's meeting Tuesday night. Williams told the council that by repairing (2) dozen leaks in the lines since the first of the year (five) million gallons of water has been saved. He estimated a like saving would be effected with the repair of five remaining leaks. Despite the prospect of increased water supplies, the council took no action on lifting water restrictions instituted last summer. City residents are still limited to 12 hours a week of lawn watering per week.

###

Figure 3–4. An example of edited copy.

If the slug is to consist of the first two words of the head, revise the original slug on the copy after the head has been written. The slug is then not necessary on the head copy.

If the story is to jump from page 1 to an inside page, write a jump head on a separate sheet or on the main head copy. The jumpline may contain no more than the key word "Mayor" or the action "Mayor resigns." It would be marked "Jump" or "R.O" for runover.

Return the edited story along with the head copy to the desk editor. If the editor rejects the head, write another, but change the story slug on the copy if the slug is to conform to the first two words of the headline.

Before releasing the story and head to the composing department, the desk editor catalogs the story on a slug sheet (Figure 3–5). If the story has been trimmed drastically, the desk editor notifies the makeup editor who may be responsible for designing page dummies (see Figure 14–5).

From this point on, the story is practically out of the hands of the editorial department. The headline goes to an operator of

Figure 3–5. Slug sheet for copy control—enables editors to keep account of copy handled and headlines used.

PAGE	SLUG	HEAD	LENGTH	PICTURES	COMMENTS
6	Curbs	1/36=	10	3 x 5½	10
4	Tin cup	1/24 = FML	3		13
1	Mayor	2/30 - FM	9	Thumb	22

one linecasting machine, the story to another. When the story has been set into type, the metal slugs are placed on a tray and a galley proof is pulled. The proof goes to a proofreader for typographical corrections.

If corrections are necessary, the proof goes to an operator of a ring machine (another linecaster) where corrected lines are re-set. Another worker (sometimes called "dump boy") replaces the incorrect line with corrected ones.

Now the galley of type is moved to a makeup table where the story, along with headline and picture, are placed in a metal frame. Unless the persons on makeup have a detailed page, dummy to follow or are supervised by a makeup editor, the makeup personnel use their own judgment on the placement and fitting of stories. If the type is too long for the space on the page, the makeup person may pull the subheads, reduce the normal spacing between head and story or may even lop off the final paragraph.

Note the number of hands through which the story has had to pass from the time it left the reporter until it was locked into a page form. Each handling adds to the chances for error. The new systems reduce much of this excessive copy-handling.

Teletypesetter* Beginning in the early 1950s, perforated tape came along to control the machinery. But in the letterpress (or "hot metal" system) it didn't eliminate the need for manual composition. Someone still had to set manually the sluglines, headlines and corrections. When wire services began transmitting stories by tape (Teletypesetter or TTS) (Figures 3–6 and 3–7), editors lost even more control of copy. Since the prime purpose of using tape was to reduce manual operation and thus save time and expense, the full tape had to be used the way the agencies sent it. If the story ran longer than the editor desired, the full story had to be set and the superfluous type then discarded. If heavy editing was done on the monitor copy accompanying the tape, such changes had to be set manually.

Copyeditors could use editing symbols to edit monitor TTS copy (see Figure 3–7) or they could use proof symbols (see Proofreading, Appendix II) since the monitor copy, in effect, served as proof.

Before the end of the 1960s computerized photocomposition was perfected, permitting many newspapers to convert from "hot metal" to "cold-type" production. Various systems are used to take advantage of this new technique.

System A Local copy is written and edited in the traditional manner, then given to tape punchers who perforate an idiot tape (unhyphen-

* Further description of composition methods is given in Chapter 13.

m157

~~d zzwyyfeess~~

639

TIN CUP

DENVER (AP) - Tin Cup,
Colo., is still alive today.
Secretary of State Mary Es-
till, Buchanan has ruled that the
town, incorporated in Gunnison
County in 1880, has a stable
population "more resembling
permanent residents than summer residents," and has a gov-
erning association that functions as a city government.
Therefore, she decided after
an emotional hearing in Gunnison Friday, that the town
cannot be declared abandoned.
Fourteen other towns were
not so lucky, however. They are ~~in-~~
~~clude~~ Anthracite, Bowerman,
Crystal City, Gothic, Irwin,
Moscow, North Star, Ohio City,
Petersburg, Ruby, Scofield,
Spencer, Tomichi, and White
Pine.
All are now declared officially abandoned.
Residents of Tin Cup packed (etc.)

Figure 3–6. Edited TTS monitor copy.

ated and unjustified, or with an uneven right margin). The idiot tape is fed into a computer to produce another tape correctly hyphenated and justified. This tape, in turn, goes to a photocomposition unit to produce camera-ready type.

Wire copy is delivered by tape and is edited on the monitor copy as described previously. The key to TTS handling is the book number or code number visible on the tape (see Figure 3–6). The tapes are strung on pegs corresponding to the book or computer number (peg 1 for tapes 1, 11, 21, etc.). The monitor copy is edited and sent to the composing room where an operator selects the proper tape and feeds it directly into a photocompositor. Sluglines, headlines and editing changes are manually punched on other tapes. Because of the time used, and the chances for errors in perforating the tape, heavy editing on TTS wire copy is discouraged.

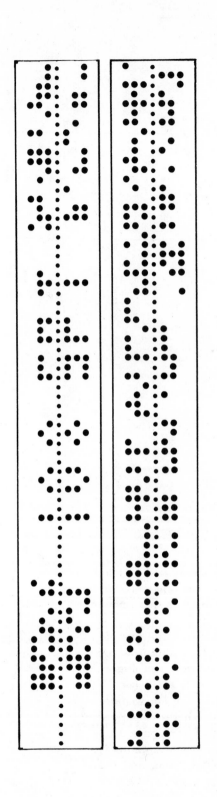

THE ASSOCIATED PRESS PRINTER CODE CHART

The Art of Editing

Copy from the syndicated news and feature services may be delivered to the newspaper by Teletype in several forms. If it is in all-capital letters, the copyeditor assumes the letters are all in lowercase and marks the letters to be capitalized (Figure 4–3). If the copy is in cap and lowercase or full cap and small cap, the copyeditor handles it as local copy. If the copy is delivered in tape form the copyeditor handles it the same as TTS.

To avoid the confusion in using tape from several sources, newspapers simply select different colored tapes for the reperforators—red for one wire service, green for another, yellow for the syndicate service, for instance.

System B

Same as System A except that tapes from the wire services and syndicates are fed into a VDT unit where the story is displayed on a screen and can be edited on the VDT keyboard at will (Figure 3–8).

Several methods may be used in editing wire story tapes. These include:

1. Select the wire story and direct the corresponding tape to the computer file. Edit the monitor copy in the traditional manner (see Figure 3–7) but write at the top of the copy the column set and the head and its size. Submit the edited copy to a VDT operator who will then call the story to the screen and keyboard the editing indicated by the copyeditor.

2. Send the wire story tape to the computer, call up the story on the VDT screen and use the keyboard to edit the story.

3. Feed the tape of the wire story directly into a paper tape reader on the VDT and edit on the keyboard. A new tape will be produced which can be directed on-line to the typesetter.

Scanner Copy

A scanner or OCR (optical character recognition) is a machine that can read or recognize either typewritten characters or a bar code representing the characters (Figures 3–9, 3–10). The machine has an electro-optical device that looks at the lines of typewritten copy and sends an electric signal to a mini-computer. The mini-computer identifies the signal as representing a certain letter or number and automatically cuts a TTS tape or feeds another computer with the signal.

Because an OCR is a computer, all instructions first have to be programmed into the unit, usually by code. The various codes

Figure 3–7. Teletypesetter tape. At the top is a six-level, justified Teletypesetter tape. In the second and third groups of perforations the number 100 and the letters SPT are visible. The second tape is a six-level, unjustified or "idiot" tape to be fed into a computer for justification and hyphenation. At bottom is a code chart for a five-level tape in all capital letters, showing combinations used to achieve the visible.

Figure 3-8. OCR with CRT and keyboard. Story is fed into the scanner (left), then may be displayed on the CRT screen (right) and revised or edited, using the keyboard, then relayed to the paper tape punch (shown at bottom of scanner). The paper tape reader, shown just above the copy holder on the scanner, permits the editing of paper tapes, including wire service tapes. [*Photo courtesy of DATATYPE Corporation.*]

then become important tools for the copyeditor, as will be explained later. (Figure 3-11.)

The reporter uses an electric typewriter to type the story on scanner paper. The reporter may correct typing errors either by using a correction tape on the machine or by writing in corrections with a nonscannable pastel pen. Editing can be done by several methods.

1. The copyeditor may edit with a pastel pen. The edited copy first goes through the scanner, then to a VDT operator. Tape from the OCR is relayed to the VDT where an operator makes changes indicated on the original scanner copy.

2. The copyeditor may put the reporter's copy through the scanner, then edit on a cathode ray tube (CRT) or VDT screen.

3. The copyeditor may do all the editing by using a black pen and an electric typewriter. The black pen can be used only to delete a letter, words or a line. Additions or changes have to be made on the copy by using an electric typewriter (see Figure 3-11). Since the changes are typed beneath the lines of the

williams

weekend

-°Here is a story as it is now written by a reporter to enable comput□

-ers to hasten production of the newspaper.

-°Instead of manual typewriters, each reporter uses an IBM electric

-typewriter that automaticĐally prints a bar code beneath each letter.

-Other codĐng is added for line starts and paragraphs.

-°At the editing desk, changes and corrections are added by pastel pen.

-The story then is dropped onto a conveyor to be taken to the composing

-room.

-°In the composing room, a comĐputer reads the ''bar codes'' and then

-prints out a punched tape. This tape is then displayed on a TV-scree□

-n-like ''editing terminal'', or visual display terminal (VDT). Here

-final changes are made.

-°The VDT operator then creates a corrected tape that is placed in anot□

-her computer to produce th type Đthat is placed in page form to be made

-into the final printing image that goes onto the press.□-

ĐĐ

Codes:

(-) line start

(°) paragraph

(□-) end of story

(Đ) rub out

ĐĐĐ(∧ΔBy Sally Williams∧#) byline

Other codes are used to begin and end cutlines, etc.

Figure 3–9. Scanner copy with visible bar code.

original copy, reporters usually triple-space copy. If the copy contains too many typing errors or too much editing, the scanner will reject it. The reporter or copyeditor may clip out and rearrange paragraphs provided correct alignment of the sheets is maintained. The unit will not recognize lines that are not parallel.

After editing the copy, the copyeditor types the headline and instructions for typesetting. For instance, Δ F 240 instructs the unit to set the text in 9 point, 10.6 picas wide; Δ F 245 would call for 9 point in 16 picas.

For headlines the code could be Δ F 403 for 24 point in a certain type family, Δ F 404 for 30 point, Δ F 405 for 36 point and the like.

All commands start with a code symbol. In the foregoing example, Δ is the code symbol and F defines the format. "More" is indicated by Δ M and ΔΔ defines the end of the story.

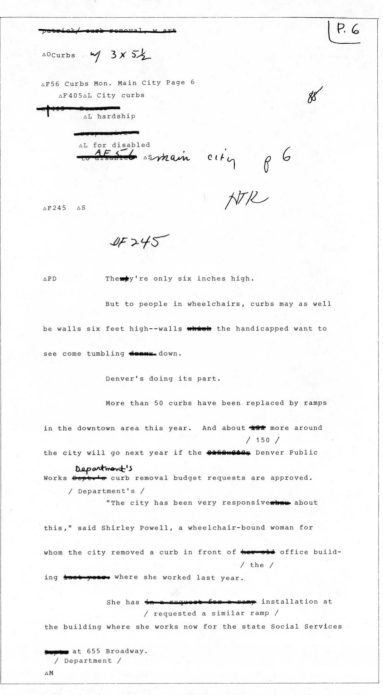

Figure 3–10. Edited scanner copy. Written notations on the copy are made by nonscannable pen. Letter, word and line deletions may be made by black pen or pencil but editing changes have to be typed beneath the lines of the reporter's copy. In Figure 3–9 the editing marks are also made with a nonscannable pen and corrections are then made when copy is displayed on a VDT.

VDT Systems   Video display terminals can be used for writing and editing copy and for making up pages, thus eliminating pencils, pens, per-

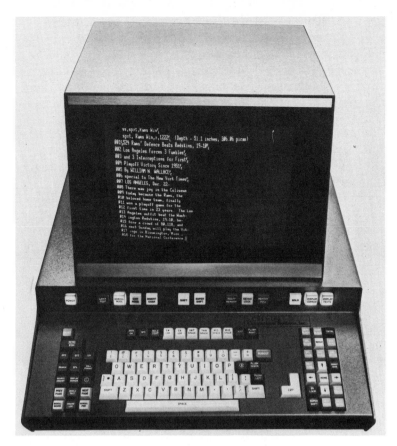

Figure 3–11. Video Display Terminal. This unit has a 102 Selectric Keyboard in addition to five single key button commands. The message is displayed on a green phosphorus screen in 20-point character size. Two wire service stories may be displayed simultaneously. Depth of the story is given in both inches and picas. FL and FC, shown on the screen, refer to flush left and flush center, respectively. On some models the keyboard can be separated from the screen to give editors more latitude in using the unit. [*Photo courtesy of Composition Systems, Inc.*]

forators and manual typewriters (see Figure 3–8). Eventually the same story displayed on a VDT in a newspaper office may appear on a home television screen.

To compose a story on a VDT keyboard, the reporter uses five basic commands. As described by the Huntington (W. Va.) System (used on the Huntington *Advertiser* and the *Herald-Dispatch*), the commands are:

1. Abort. When you are ready to write your story, be sure the terminal is in command mode, indicated by an asterisk in the home position (start of story). If there is a slash in the home position or if the screen is blank, use the abort command by placing the cursor (a blinking rectangular light) in home position, then type ab on the keyboard and hit the enter key. An asterisk will appear in home position and a READY will appear nearby on the screen.

The Tools and How to Use Them   27

2. Open. Now you are ready to tell the computer you are going to write a story and you want it to prepare a place for it within the system. You open a file by picking a number from the ones assigned to you and call the story by this file number. The file number will always consist of a letter and three numerals. Suppose you want to call your story x001. Move the cursor home and then type op (for open) on the keyboard, hit the space bar, type x001 (for the file number) and hit the enter key. The computer now knows you are going to write a story.

3. Next. When you see a small white block appear on the terminal screen, you must end your segment, or take, after a few more words. The terminal can hold only so many characters. If you have more to write, move the cursor home, type ne (for next) and hit the enter key. The computer removes the first segment from the screen, stores it and allows you to continue. You can have up to 26 segments.

4. Close. When you are finished with the story you must let the computer know this is the end. Take the cursor home, type cl (for close) and hit the enter key. The computer now has the story on file and the terminal is automatically returned to command mode and you are ready to write another story. A copy of the story you have written can be shown almost instantly to an editor. The command mode is pr which queues the story to a teleprinter.

5. Edit. Either the reporter or the copyeditor can call up the story for editing. Place the terminal in command position, take the cursor home, type ed (for edit), hit the space bar, type the story number and hit the enter key. When the editing is completed, close the story.

To remove a character, move the cursor to that character and strike the DEL CHAR button. To delete a word, strike the DEL WORD key, to remove a line, strike the DEL LINE key and to remove a complete paragraph, strike DEL PAR. To move one block of text to another position, use the MOVE BLK key. Or insert new text in the displayed section with the INS key.

If the VDT has a dual screen, the operator may call up two stories simultaneously and merge the selected elements of each into a single piece of copy, including the addition of any new copy.

Tapes from the wire services and syndicates may first be filed into a computer, then called up for editing on the VDT. Or the tapes may be fed directly into the editing terminal. Line justification is no problem since the computer can justify and hyphenate lines or can eliminate all hyphenation through letter and word spacing.

The system allows the story to be set in one form for one edition and another form for a later edition, all without a second keyboarding or second editing.

When the editing has been completed, the operator may ask for the length of the story—in characters, type lines or column inches. The computer keeps a file of all stories that have been edited, enabling an editor to consult the file for page makeup.

As described in the OCR system, the headline and other instructions as to column set, boldfaced lines, indentions and the like are keyboarded at the top of the story. Then, with a final flourish of another code combination, the copyeditor sends the story directly to the photocompositor.

Copyeditors can learn to operate a VDT quickly, especially if they have an instruction booklet. On some newspapers, instructions for editing are programmed into the computer so that if the beginners get stuck they can read the instructions on the screen. Further, the computer itself helps confused operators with questions such as: Already queued, queue again? Are you sure? File status checked—proceed anyway?

In a few days copyeditors can feel comfortable at the terminal. In a few weeks, having mastered the beast, they can forget about copy pencils, pastel pens and manual typewriters.

All the capabilities of the components previously described, plus many more functions, may be combined in a multi-task system. These capabilities include:

1. A storage and edit system with off-line editing using both paper tape and OCR equipment and on-line editing using video display terminals.

2. On-line and off-line wire service system including stripping, storage and editing.

3. Automatic formatting and makeup.

4. Ganged corrections. Corrections are ganged together in an edit tape which is then passed against the original story file. Only the words or lines that contain errors are corrected. After the copy is corrected, the entire story is rejustified and a clean file is produced and stored, ready for typesetting.

5. Multiple edit commands for combining stories.

New Leads, Inserts, Takes

After copy has left the copydesk, changes sometimes have to be made because of new developments, corrections or additional information (Figure 3–12).

Under the traditional system, the routine for new leads and inserts is as follows.

Obtain a proof of the story from the composing room. This proof has several designations, including "marker" "Cx" or "fixer." Draw a block around the portion of the lead to be deleted and write in the margin: "Kill for new lead." On the remaining portion, write in the margin: "Get pickup" (Figure 3–13).

The copy will be marked "New lede MAYOR" plus the slug-line. At the end of the new lead, write "pickup" and indicate the paragraph where the story resumes: "The council acted . . ." (2nd graf).

Assume two insertions are to be made, one between the fourth

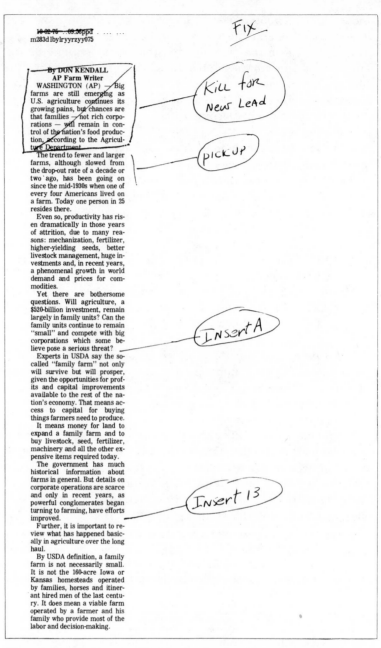

Figure 3–12. Marking proof for new lead and two insertions.

and fifth paragraphs, the other between the seventh and eighth paragraphs. Use the proof to show where the inserts are to go, marking one "insert A" in the margin, the other "insert B" or use the notation "TR (turn rule) for insert A," "TR for insert B."

The copy would be marked "insert A fourth graph MAYOR" and "insert B seventh graph MAYOR" and each would close with "end insert."

Return both the copy and the proof to the composing room.

The Art of Editing

```
m290

FARM 2nd lead 110

  WASHINGTON (AP)--Urban sprawl, highways, parks, airports....
The trend: 2nd graf m283

m295

FARM Insert 70

  WASHINGTON FARM m283, updating, insert after 4th graf:
threat?

  Meanwhile, the total land area in farms also has been....
Experts in USDA, etc. 5th graf.

m299

FARM  Insert 40

  WASHINGTON FARM m283, further updating, insert after 7th graf:
improved.

  Economic recovery and further industrialization during....
Further, etc. 8th graf.
```

Figure 3–13. Copy for new leads and inserts. m290 is the book number on the new lead (110 words) of the original story (book number m283). The story picks up at the second paragraph of the original, beginning "The trend . . ." Copy for the two inserts (70 and 40 words long) indicates the positions of the inserts.

If more information is to be added to the end of the story, the copyeditor simply uses the notation "Add MAYOR" on the copy. No proof or marker is necessary.

On VDT editing terminals, new leads and inserts, whether from the wires or local generation, are handled at first as separate stories under their own file number if the earlier version has already been typeset. Copyeditors set it in the same measure as the earlier story, retain the pickup line so those in the pasteup department can see it, and typeset the later revision—whether add, insert or lead. If the new lead comes in before the story has been typeset, the copyeditor can call the lead to the screen, insert the old story into that file, delete what should come out and typeset the story as a unit.

If the story has been sent to the typesetter but a copy of the story is in the storage file, the story can be recalled and corrected on a VDT. On OCR systems, new leads and inserts can be typed on separate sheets. The original story is then put on the screen and merging is accomplished by using the CRT paragraph insert feature. Finally, a copy of the typeset strip can be obtained and indications for new leads and inserts can be made on that proof.

A local story breaking near deadline may have to be handled in small segments or "takes" to minimize the time needed for typesetting. The first take usually is no more than the lead. It would carry the slug word, for example, MAYOR. If the head size has not been determined, the slug would indicate that the head will come later—HTC or HTK.

The first take ends with "more." The second take is slugged "1st add MAYOR" and similarly is kept open with "more." The process is repeated until the final take, usually so indicated, as "sixth and final take MAYOR." This segment closes with an endmark.

The copyeditor keeps notes as the story is moving so that the headline can be written as soon as the final take is in.

With the new technology this procedure is no longer as important as it once was because of the speed with which copy can now be written, edited and set into type, as described in Chapter 4.

Glossary of Terms

Alphanumeric—pertaining to a character set that contains both letters and numerals and usually other characters.

Analog—data in the form of varying physical characteristics such as voltage, pressure, speed, etc.

Autofunctions—copy symbols or commands placed on copy. Used to instruct the computer on type sizes, column widths, etc.

Auxiliary storage—any peripheral devices (tape, disk, etc.) upon which data may be stored.

Baud—speed rate of transmission. News personnel speak in terms of 66 or 1050 words a minute. Computer personnel talk of 1200 bits (or 150 characters) a second.

Binary—a base 2 numbering system using the digits 0 and 1. Widely used in computer systems whose binary code may represent numbers, letters, and punctuation marks. Performs "in" and "out" or "on" and "off" function.

Bit—one eighth of a byte. Combinations of eight basic bits yield up to 256 characters.

Byte—in computer terms, one alphanumeric character.

Cathode ray tube (CRT)—an electronic vacuum tube containing a screen on which information may be stored or displayed by means of a multigrid modulated beam of electrons. Same as VDT.

Character—an alphanumeric or special symbol.

Character generator—a cathode ray tube or similar device used to display characters in high-speed photocomposition systems.

Code—assignment of a meaning to a character or a label to identify a routine or function.

Coding form—a "header sheet" or preprinted page on which program instructions are written. Run through the OCR in advance of copy to program the computer for type size, column widths, etc.

Computer—a device capable of accepting information, applying prescribed processes to the information, and supplying the results of these processes; a computer usually consists of input and output devices, storage, arithmetic and logical units and a control unit. Various types of computers are calculators, digital computers and analog computers.

Computer program—a set of stored instructions that controls all hardware.

Core—the main memory of a computer in which data may be stored. Also called "Core Memory."

CPU—an abbreviation for Central Processing Unit. That portion of the computer that handles input, output and memory.

Cursor—a mobile block of light the size of a single character on the VDT screen indicating position at which editing change is to be made.

Cycle time—the length of time used by a computer for one operation, usually measured in microseconds (millionths) or nanoseconds (billionths).

Data—any kind of information that can be processed by a computer.

Debug—eliminating problems in a new or revised program or system.

Digit—a character used to represent one of the non-negative integers smaller than the radix, e.g., in decimal notation, one of the characters 0 to 9.

Digital—pertaining to data in the form of digits, in contrast with analog.

Disk drive—a unit somewhat like a record turntable that contains a disk pack and rotates it at high speed.

Disk pack—a set of magnetic disks used for storing data or text. Also called disk cartridge.

Disk storage—a means of storing data on a magnetic disk, a technique similar to magnetic tape or record, so that data can be read into the computer, changed by the computer or erased.

Dump—a routine which causes the computer to dump data from storage to another unit.

EBCDIC—Extended Binary Coded Decimal Interchange Code. An eight-bit code which can represent 256 characters.

Edit—programs for inputting, storing, correcting and outputting editorial textual matter.

Fixed word length—pertaining to a machine word or operand that always has the same number of bits or characters. Contrast with variable word length.

Font—a type face and size.

Format—a series of alphas and/or numerics which cause a computer to function in certain special ways.

Full duplex—pertaining to the simultaneous, independent transmission of data in both directions over a communications link. It is synonymous with duplex. Contrast with half duplex and simplex.

Hardware—the physical equipment which is a part of the overall production system. (OCRs, computers, phototypesetting machines, etc.)

Hard-wired—electronically connected, as in the case of one or more pieces of hardware connected to others.

Header sheet—see Coding form.

Hyphenless justification—a system of justifying lines by inter-word and interletter spaces, without breaking any words at the end of lines. Usually accomplished by computers.

IMS (Information Management System)—a computer-managed base consisting of all the elements a newspaper prints—pictures, headlines, text, sketches, captions, art work, comics, line drawings—and all production control information to monitor the production of a newspaper.

Index—a file or table pointing to data in a disk pack or, on VDTs in some cases, of the first five lines of a story.

Input—bringing data or text from external sources (typewriters, paper tape, through interfaces, etc.) into core storage.

Interface—a device, normally an electrical impulse, by which one piece of hardware or equipment "speaks" to another. The translation of output to input.

K—thousands of units of core or computer storage referring to storage positions for bytes, usually in multiples of 16.

Keyboarding—using keystrokes to put letters, numbers and symbols into a system.

Key punch—a device to punch holes in paper tape or cards for use in input.

Line printer—an output unit capable of printing an entire line at one time rather than a character at a time. Prints at speeds of about 1,000 lines or more a minute.

Log—to record the occurrence of an event, such as beginning and end of a program, on some output device, usually the console's typewriter.

Machine language—a language used directly by a computer; a set of instructions which a computer can directly recognize and execute.

Macro instruction—a single instruction which is expanded to a predetermined sequence of instructions during the assembly of the program.

Magnetic storage—any device using magnetic materials as a medium for storage of data: magnetic disk, film, tape, drum, core, etc.

Memory storage—see Core.

Modem—a piece of hardware utilizing an interface between two other pieces of hardware in a system.

Multiplexor (MUX)—a device that allows the computer to handle input or output simultaneously from several different devices connected to it.

Nondestructive read—the ability to read data from an auxiliary device or core storage location without destruction of the data in its original location.

OCR—optical character recognition, or "scanner," which converts typewritten material to electronic impulses and transmits these to a tape punch or computer.

On-line—a unit "on-line" is interfaced in the computer system as opposed to units operating independently of the system.

Operand—that which is operated upon. An operand is usually identified by an address part of an instruction.

Output—data coming from the computer system, either in printed or tape form.

Paper tape reader—a device that translates holes in perforated paper tape into proper internal form for the computer. Used as an input unit when OCRs and other hardware are not interfaced or on-line with the computer.

Perforator—a keyboard unit used for the production of punched paper tape. Control of typesetting and filmsetting equipment requires 6, 7, 8, 15 or 31 level paper tape.

POD—page output device.

Purge—a method by which data or text is removed from storage by erasure from the disk.

Queue—directing a story file to another operation, such as a line printer or photocomposition machine.

Register—an area in the central processor, usually one word in length, used by the computer for accumulating, addressing, indexing, etc. Access to registers is usually faster than access to core.

Reperf—a tape perforator.

Scroll—a means of moving story text forward so it can be displayed on a VDT screen.

Software—the programs that make the hardware work.

Sort—to arrange records of data or text in proper sequence.

Storage—see Core and Disk storage.

System—a combination of computer programs.

Terminal—a point in a system or communication network at which data can either enter or leave.

Throughput—the time it takes for material to go through a system.

Variable length record—a record, the length of which is independent of the length of other records in the file.

Variable word length—pertaining to a machine word or operand that may consist of a variable number of bits or characters.

VDT—an acronym for Video Display Terminal which looks like a typewriter with a small television set sitting on top. Stories may be composed or corrected on these units.

Versatile editing terminal (VET)—same as VDT.

4

Handling the Wire

Abstracting the Wire Nowhere in the news industry has the age of the computer been more apparent than in the news agencies. Even in the smallest state bureau the typewriter is all but obsolete, replaced by the computer and VDT for story composition and filing.

The use of abstracts by the news services is hastening the end of the old Teletypes that once were important instruments in newsrooms.

Traditionally, the wire service has opened the news cycle with a news budget or summary, indicating to wire editors the dozen or so top national and international stories that were in hand or were developing.

Today's wire editors may get a four or five-line abstract of the complete offering—foreign, national, regional and state. From these abstracts the wire editors select the stories they think their readers are interested in, then by using computer codes ("DIP") symbols, receive those stories directly into the paper's computer at a rate of 1,200 or more words a minute.[1]

Using this system, the wire services can deliver up-to-the-minute stories that are better written and better edited than those in the past. Wire editors are spared the task of plowing through scores of stories they don't want; they have more time

[1] The Wichita (Kan.) *Eagle* and *Beacon* receives on a single circuit the equivalent of six conventional UPI news circuits: A-wire, B-wire, business wire, sports wire, Kansas wire and Oklahoma wire. UPI abstract wires print only the item number (to be used in retrieving the item from the computer), the wordage of the story, the slug-line, and the first paragraph of the story. The story, if requested, is displayed on a VDT terminal for editing, then returned to the databank for typesetting.

to consolidate the offerings from both wire services and other news syndicates.

Associated Press (AP) and United Press International (UPI) gather news from around the world to serve subscribers both at home and abroad. Both offer—in addition to general news— features, special interest news (sports, business, religion), analyses or interpretives and pictures.

For domestic subscribers, these agencies deliver their reports by leased wire, telephone and telegraph and by mail. They also produce scannable copy in any font as well as camera-ready copy in proof. The bulk of the report, however, is on tape by electronic feed that is computer compatible.

The prime wire ("A" wire) originates in New York City and carries top national and international news. A secondary national wire, or "B" wire, is similarly devoted to national and international news.

Separate national wires deliver sports, markets and pictures. Smaller dailies rely primarily on the state wire, a combination of the main news wires, sports, markets—and state or regional news. The state bureau also delivers pictures, both by facsimile transmission and by mail. Both services provide subscribers with individually requested stories. Broadcasting stations have access to special radio wires but may also have, if they desire, any of the other wires.

The old Teletypes or teleprinters delivered messages at a rate of 66 words a minute. Newer printers have a speed of 100 words or more a minute. They operate on 12-hour time cycles—PMs for afternoon papers, AMs for morning papers, with the cycles often overlapping so that stories breaking near the cycle change are offered to both cycles or stories early in one cycle are picked up on stories late in the other cycle. In each cycle the machines deliver approximately 200 items, but this includes advisories (messages to editors) and separate book or file numbers delivered in takes or segments. The cycle also includes new leads, inserts and adds.

Traditional System

For a morning paper, the wire news day begins around noon with the following:

a200
 d lbylczzcczzc
Starting AMs Report, a 201 Next
1202pED 03-07

Then follows the news digest (or budget), notifying editors of the dozen top news stories in sight (Figure 4–1). An addition to the first budget may come a short time later. The budget is used to give wire editors a glimpse of the major stories forthcoming and aids them in planning page dummies.

```
      d  1by1czzcczzc
Starting AMs Report, a201 Next
1202pED 03-07


     a201
         r  1by1czzcv
AP NEWS DIGEST
Saturday AMS
 Here are the top news stories in sight for AMs at this hour. The
General Desk supervisor is Ed Dennehy. He may be reached at 212
262-6093 if you have urgent questions about the spot news report.
ECONOMIC-ENERGY
 WASHINGTON - The unemployment rate remained stable at 8.2 per cent
last month, largely because 580,000 persons stopped looking for work,
the labor department reports. New material. With Wirephoto chart
NY15.
 WASHINGTON - The Social Security System is plunging into deficit, an
advisory panel tells Congress, and should be strengthened with
general tax revenues. New material. Wirephoto upcoming.
 DETROIT - With six plants closed this week, Ford soon may step up
production next week to keep pace with General Motors, Chrysler and
American Motors, all of which will have every plant in operation.
Developing, to be announced officially late in afternoon.
 UNDATED - Millions of Americans with visions of ripe red tomatoes
and leafy green lettuce at home-grown costs are planning vegetable
plots this summer. But there are plenty of pitfalls between garden and
table. New, Consumer Scorecard, by Louise Cook.
```

Figure 4–1. Wire service budget.

Major stories breaking after the budget has been delivered are designated:

FLASH—a two- or three-word statement alerting editors to a story of unusual importance: President shot. On the old teleprinter machines a warning bell signifying a flash brought editors running to the machine. Today a flash is seldom used because a bulletin serves the same purpose and is almost as fast.

BULLETIN (BUN)—a short summary, usually no more than a lead, of a major story. Again, it is used primarily to alert editors and is not intended for publication unless the bulletin arrives at deadline. A bulletin may also be used to signal corrections such as a mandatory "kill" on a portion of a story that could be libelous.

BULLETIN MATTER—expands the bulletin with more, but brief, details. Unless the deadline is a factor, the wire editor holds up the story for a more detailed account.

URGENT—calls editors' attention to new material or to corrections on stories sent previously.

95—signifies that the story may have special regional interest.

Sorting the Pieces

Wire editors have two considerations in selecting wire copy for publication—the significance of the stories and the space allotted for wire copy. If space is tight, fewer wire stories are used and heavier trims may be made on those that are used.

Budget stories usually, but not necessarily, get top priority. When stories listed on the budget arrive they are so indicated by BUDGET or BJT, together with the length in words. If such stories are developing or are likely to have additional or new material, the editor places each story in a folder and concentrates on stories that will stand.

Eventually the stories in the folders have to move. This is done by working backwards—taking the latest book number and latest time indicator. The fifth and last lead may eliminate the fourth lead but pick up on the third lead and so forth until the story is compact and in order.

Associated Press has added a feature called DataRecaps to aid wire editors in handling a breaking story. Previously, editors had to assemble the pieces from multiple leads, inserts, subs and adds or wait until space was cleared on the wire for a no-pickup lead. The service notifies wire editors a recap is coming, then delivers a complete story at a rate of 1,200 words a minute.

To illustrate how the system works, AP issued a 20-word bulletin at 2:03 p.m. on Chinese Prime Minister Chou En-lai's death. The bulletin was followed by an Urgent add at 2:08, a second add at 2:17, a third add at 2:21, a fourth add at 2:27, a new lead at 2:29, a fifth add at 2:32 and a new lead add at 2:34. Using DataRecap, the service retransmitted the complete 900-word story in seconds.

Starts and stops occur even on copy apparently wrapped up. The following is typical. A story arriving early in the morning describes a congressional appropriation of $5.9 billion to provide jobs for the unemployed. Fifty items later editors are informed that the figure should be changed to $6.4 million. Still later, New York sends the message that the original $5.9 million should stand. Eventually the service again corrects the figure to the original $5.9 billion. (Directions for handling copy after it has left the desk have been given earlier.)

High Speed Circuits

Some of the wire services' many changes in copy have been eliminated with high speed circuits, referred to variously as dataspeed, DataStream, DataNews. The new circuits permit the agencies to hold back stories until they can be wrapped up or be self-contained.

Dataspeed circuits originally were used to transmit tabular matter such as the stock market and sports boxscores. Today the services deliver the national wires as well as feature syndicated and supplemental copy on such circuits. To illustrate the advantage of the faster transmission (1,500 words a minute), AP was able to release for wire movement the President's State of Union message and the new Wholesale Price Index in the same time it took to move the initial bulletin on the A wire.

Portable CRT A communication tool, called *Teleram* by AP, consists of a compact CRT that enables a reporter to write and edit stories at any scene where a power outlet and a telephone are available.

The unit has a keyboard, a screen and a tape cassette which substitutes for the memory bank of a CRT-computer system. As the story is written, it is displayed on the screen then stored on electronic blocks of tape. Each block is capable of holding up to 300 words. The story is then called back on the screen for final editing before transmission.

An attachment fits over the receiver of a telephone for transmission at 300 words a minute.

Wire Service Glossary ADV.—abbreviation for advance. A story intended for later use.

Agate—TTS tape intended for agate-size type. Used on items such as sports boxes and market quotations. AG is visible on the tape.

AMS, PMS—morning newspapers, afternoon newspapers.

Budget (or BJT called "News Digest" by AP)—listing of the major stories expected to be delivered by the wire service.

BUN—abbreviation for bulletin.

Bureau code letters—each service uses its own code letters to designate a bureau. UPI uses WA for Washington, the AP uses WX.

BGNG—abbreviation for beginning.

Circuits—refers to wires used. The A wire is the main trunk news circuit. Regional news trunk systems carry letter designations such as B, G and E wires and the D wire, the nationwide business news circuit. The S wire usually refers to a state trunk circuit.

CQN—abbreviation for correction.

CQ—abbreviation for correct.

Cycle—complete news report for either morning or afternoon newspapers.

Fax—abbreviation for facsimile, a machine used to receive photos on flimsy paper.

FYI—for your information. An advisory.

Graf (also PGH)—Short for paragraph.

HFR—hold for release. Expected release time is indicated if known.

INTRO—abbreviation for introduction or lead.

LD—abbreviation for lead (lede).

NL—abbreviation for night lead.

Pickup—used to designate where story is to be picked up after a new lead or insertion.

No Pickup—revised story contains all material sent previously. Also, "includes previous."

Repeat—a rerun of a story for a member or client.

Roundup—an undated story involving more than one place of origin of the news. Frequently used on weather, election returns and holiday fatalities.

Sidebar—a short feature intended to accompany a main news dispatch.

Split—term used to designate a break in a news circuit to permit the filing of other material, such as regional news.

Sub—abbreviation for substitute.

TAB—indicates tabular matter.

Top—new lead.

TTY—designation used by UPI for page teleprinter circuits.

Undated—a wire story containing no dateline. Instead, the story carries the service as a byline: "By United Press International" or "By the Associated Press."

Visible—visible letters punched in TTS tape. Perforations for the letters eesswyyf show up as TA 5 on the tape.

Wrapup—a final, comprehensive story combining stories and segments delivered previously.

Stories delivered by the wire services originate from several sources:

How the System Works

1. Copy developed by the agencies' own large staffs of reporters, feature writers, analysts, columnists and photographers.

2. Rewrite of stories developed by subscribers to the agency service. Papers or broadcasting stations contracting with a wire service agree to make their own news files available to the service, either by providing proofs or carbon copies of stories (DUPES). Other wire service staffers rewrite from any source available—smaller papers, research reports and other publications.

3. Stringers or correspondents in communities outside the bureau. Such stringers frequently are news reporters and are called stringers because of the old practice of paying a correspondent by his string of stories represented in column inches.

4. Exchanges with other news agencies, such as foreign agencies.

A Baytown reporter telephones a story to the state bureau of UPI. If the story has statewide interest, UPI files the story on its state wire. If the story has regional interest, the state bureau offers it to a regional bureau, or, in some cases, the state office

Handling the Wire   41

may offer the story directly to the national office in New York City.

The head office thus becomes the nerve center for the entire operation of the news agency. New York collects news from all the state, regional and foreign bureaus, culls the material, then returns it to the regional and state bureaus or to subscribers directly.

The operation sometimes is referred to as a gatekeeping system. A Dutch story, for example, has to get by the Amsterdam office before it can be disseminated in Holland. The same story would have to clear the London bureau before it is relayed to New York. New York then decides whether the story will be distributed nationally. New York may send the story directly to newspapers or route it through regional and state bureaus. In the latter cases, the regional bureau judges whether to transmit the story to a state bureau and a state bureau has the option of relaying the story to subscribers. A wire editor may accept or reject the story. Finally, the reader becomes the ultimate gatekeeper.

Small- and medium-sized dailies usually subscribe to only one wire service and receive only the state TTS service. Because both agencies cover approximately the same news, the choice for smaller dailies usually rests with the service offering the better state report. But because enough difference exists between the two agencies, larger papers are compelled to subscribe to both services.

Editing the Wire

Even on desks where wire editors have access to abstracts, the editors are likely to order more stories than they can use. Abstracts may cue editors to stories they don't want but abstracts cannot give the flavor of the full story. Editors may reason that it is better to err by having too much copy than to run the risk of missing an important story.

On traditional wire desks, editing starts with stripping the machines. That means that on any circuit wire someone clears all copy from the Teletype and sorts the stories for the various departments—sports, family living, entertainment, business and the like.

The wire editor then rips the individual stories and arranges them for page 1 (usually the budget and urgent stories), some for inside pages and still others for future use. Stories for the inside pages usually are handled first because such stories seldom change. The final selection of stories for page 1 depends upon local copy, pictures and the design of the page.

On larger dailies using all the wires from the two major national news agencies, the flow of copy is monumental even though the wire editor does not have to confront some of the special wires such as sports and markets.

One way to handle this spate of copy is to categorize the news—

one folder or pile for stories from Washington, D.C., another for New York and international, another for national, another for regional, another for area copy and the like.

An advantage of the paper receiving more than one news service is that the editor can use the story from one service to check facts against the same story from another service, such as casualty figures, proper names and spellings. If there is a serious discrepancy in facts, the editor asks the state or regional bureau for verification.

Compiling Stories

The editor is free to use whichever version he chooses. On competing papers one paper may lean toward one wire service and the other paper toward the other service. Or the editor may combine or compile the stories. In such cases the credit line is removed and is replaced with an overline something like **News-wire Services.**

Compiling may be done several ways:

1. Combining into one story the versions of the same story by the wire services, or by syndicates or even a local account. Example:

From Press Dispatches

President Ford was told Friday by Transportation Secretary William T. Coleman Jr. that airport security had been tightened.

No specific details were provided. . . .

The task force would not tell reporters. . . .

Coin operated baggage lockers in at least some airports have been closed (including some at Milwaukee's Gen. Mitchell Field).

The passenger terminal at LaGuardia Airport. . . .

Early Saturday, police arrested three teenagers. . . .

The LaGuardia bombing is creating one of the biggest tangles in insurance history, the New York *Journal of Commerce* said Friday. The first suit—for $10 million—was filed. . .

The foregoing story, published in the Milwaukee *Journal,* was accompanied by a side story giving details of the closing of most of the coin-operated lockers at Mitchell Field.

2. Combining into one story the accounts of two wire services on related topics. Example:

NAIROBI, Kenya (AP)—President Idi Amin of Uganda said Friday the African summit conference on Angola next week would be decisive for Angola's world role. He urged Africans to bury their differences concerning the war-torn nation, Uganda radio reported.

Uganda Broadcasting Corp., monitored in Nairobi, quoted Amin as saying Angola would not be admitted to the United Nations unless the Organization of African Unity agreed to recognize a government in the former Portuguese colony, which gained independence last November, etc.

MOSCOW (UPI)—The Soviet Union called today for an end to military involvement in Angola by foreign powers.

"The Soviet Union comes out firmly for the termination of foreign armed intervention in An-gola," the newspaper Pravda said. "The people of Angola should be given the right to decide themselves the questions of building a new life in the conditions of peace and freedom."

Pravda said the Kremlin, etc.

The two may be combined by trimming some of the first account, then adding the second account with a transitional phrase such as "In Moscow. . . . Or, the main point of the second account can be blended into the lead of the first story:

From News Dispatches

President Idi Amin of Uganda said Friday the African summit conference on Angola next week would be decisive for Angola's world role. In Moscow, the Soviet Union called for an end to military involvement in Angola by foreign powers.

3. Combining into one story an account from a wire service concerning the same subject from various sources, such as weather, politics and the like. These carry no dateline but do include the wire service credit. Examples:

United Press International

Citrus growers in California, motorists in New York, and just people from northern Minnesota to southern New Mexico felt the bite of winter Saturday.

Temperatures in the nation's richest farm region, etc.

United Press International

Gov. George Wallace said Sunday this year's try for the presidency would be his last if he loses. Sen. Birch Bayh said he stayed out of the Florida Democratic primary to avoid muddying the waters for Jimmy Carter, Wallace's main challenger there. . . .

Bayh, Carter, Gov. Milton Shapp of Pennsylvania and former Sen. Fred Harris of Oklahoma appeared together on a national television show (NBC-TV's Meet the Press).

In a separate television interview (CBS-TV's Face the Nation, Wallace said the 1976 presidential campaign will be his last venture into national politics unless he wins, etc.

In editing the wire the editor remains alert for material that can be used later in the week when more space is available. The editor looks for stories that might be given a local angle. He also takes note of stories that have accompanying photos. Available photos are noted on the budget (Figure 4–1) as well as on the stories when they are delivered.

As previously noted, TTS was developed to save time and expense of composition. TTS tape furnished by the wire service is justified and is intended to run line-for-line in a standard width, with eight lines constituting an inch of type. Papers using this service discourage severe editing because of the cost of resetting the type manually (See Figure 3–7).

Although TTS is used primarily for the state wire, it is also used on a national wire. Tapes accompany all stories on all circuits and can be used on-line in computer typesetting. In the new technology the wire service tapes are fed into a VDT unit and edited on the screen in whatever typesize or column width to generate a new tape for the photocompositor.

Two points must be kept in mind in editing wire copy. The first is that neither wire service tailors copy for a particular newspaper. Abundant details are included but most stories are constructed so that papers may trim sharply and still have the gist of the report or they can use the full account (Figure 4–2).

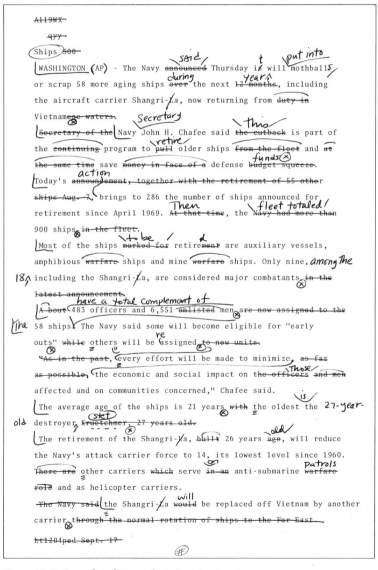

Figure 4–2. Sample editing of a wire story.

The second point is that the wire isn't sacred. Both AP and UPI have a deserved reputation for accuracy, impartiality and speed of delivery. They also make errors, sometimes colossal ones.

A source who turned out to be unreliable caused United Press to release a premature armistice story during World War I. A confused signal from a New Jersey courthouse caused AP to give the wrong penalty for Bruno Richard Hauptmann, convicted in the kidnaping and slaying of the Lindbergh child. The state wire, more often than not, is poorly written and poorly punched. Even the wire executives admit they still have bonehead editing and stories that don't jell. In both agencies, the stories abound with partial quotes, despite repeated protests from subscribers.

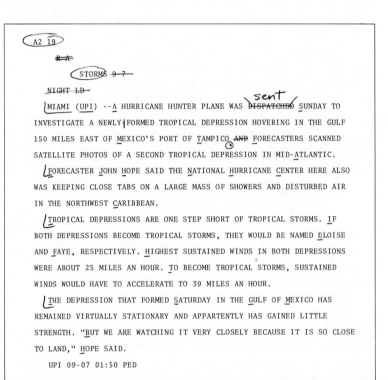

Figure 4–3. Editing the all-cap wire copy. The copyeditor assumes the story is in lower case, then marks the appropriate capital letters.

Perhaps more errors would go uncorrected but for the alertness of editors of subscribing newspapers. In an advance story on the Ali-Frazier prizefight the AP reported:

NEW YORK (AP)—Muhammed Ali and Joe Frazier slugged away at each other Thursday with tongues instead of fists—and the only damage was to 103 eardrums.

A sports editor figured it was possible that one of the people had only one eardrum but since the story didn't say so, the editor called New York. About an hour later came a sub-intro inserting "pairs of" in front of eardrums.

Both services have writing committees, usually composed of managing editors, who "ride herd" on writing performance. Here is one example from the APME (Associated Press Managing Editors) writing committee:

DETROIT (AP)—Two Detroit factory workers were killed Wednesday evening on their jobs, Detroit police said today. (*Clearly an industrial accident.*)

The two men, employes of the Hercules Forging Co., were identified as James H—, 51, the father of nine children, and M.C. Mc—, 37, both of Detroit. Mc—may have been struck accidentally, police reported. (*Oh, somebody struck him accidentally, but hit the other fellow on purpose.*)

Police said they had a man in custody and added he would probably be charged in connection with the deaths. (*Let's see, both of them were killed by the same man, but one death may have been an accident, but the suspect is charged with two murders?*)

Police say they interviewed 15 workers at the plant who could give no reason for the shootings. (*Now gunplay gets into this story.*)

Witnesses told police the man confronted H— with a carbine and shot him when he tried to run. He fired a second shot after H— fell, they said.

The third shot, apparently aimed at another workman, hit Mc—, police said. (*Now we are beginning to understand that what started out sounding like an industrial accident has become double murder.*)

Another criticism of wire services' performance is that, despite their ability to cover the national scene intensely, Eastern Seaboard cities (especially Washington and New York) get more attention than do Western cities, in part because of the differences in time zones.

Too Few Datelines

Editors of western points also complain that the West is neglected in roundup stories. (A roundup or undated story carries no dateline but has the service byline: **By the Associated Press, By United Press International.** Such stories concern items such as voting returns and weather reports. The credit line should remain. Whether bylines on other stories should be retained is a decision for the wire editor or the copyeditor.)

In reporting the foreign scene, the wire services can be faulted for concentrating heavily on some areas (the Middle East) at the expense of coverage of other areas (Latin America and Canada, for example) and for overplaying politics and the bizarre and underplaying economic and other changes.

The system can change if enough readers put enough pressure on editors to apply equal pressure on the wire services.

At least some attempt to balance the report from abroad has been made by one of the agencies in moving the European desk from London to Brussels and the Asian desk from Tokyo to Hong Kong.

Both AP and UPI are alert to the needs of the papers and stations they serve. If the wire editor feels that a story is confusing or incomplete, a telephone call to the nearest state bureau or regional hub will likely produce the information requested. Both services, on request but usually for a fee, will cover a story individually for a subscriber or put a wire editor in instant communication with almost any part of the world. The wire services can be utilized as an extension of a newspaper's staff and of its service to its readers.

Copyeditors generally like to handle wire copy because of its variety and significance. If they let errors go undetected, the consequences may not be as serious as if similar errors appeared in local copy. But copyeditors are hired to detect flaws in all copy placed before them. On the ideal desk, no goof—from whatever source—will go unchallenged.

Advances

Both agencies respect the newspapers' need to prepare as much copy as possible on days when the paper is light—to be used on days when the paper is heavy. Thus, copy intended for Sunday release may be delivered early in the week. Texts of speeches may arrive long before the speech actually has been delivered but an embargo is placed on the story until the speech has been given. If a prominent person becomes seriously ill, an advance obituary may be sent, with pictures.

Care must be taken in editing advance stories to make sure the stories do not get printed prematurely. Some editors use a colored pencil to underline or circle the ADVANCE notice. In most cases, the specific time and day for the release of the story will be given.

Release times on nonwire stories pose another problem. The device frequently is used to create good play for the story. So, a story arrives on Friday with a Sunday release saying that Joe Zilch has been named president of the XYZ corporation. The story might make a ripple in the Friday afternoon paper but would then have trouble attracting a good display in the Saturday morning paper. A Sunday release is indicated to get equal prominence in the Sunday editions of both papers, even if the news is three days old. Most editors prefer news while it is news and would ignore the embargo.

Other News Syndicates

Syndication of news by major metropolitan newspapers, a combination of such papers or a newspaper chain have made it possible for dailies to give readers a variety and depth of news coverage. Among such news syndicates are the New York *Times* News Service, Washington *Post*-Los Angeles *Times* Syndicate, Chicago *Daily News/Sun-Times*/Newhouse News Service, and Knight-Ridder, Copley and Gannett news services. By syndicating their news, the publishers participating in the supplemental services are able to recoup some of the costs of news gathering and, in fact, have been able to expand news coverage.

The wire services similarily offer their own feature syndicates that include news and features from other newspapers (London Express) or from parent corporations (Scripps-Howard News Service.)

The services mentioned are among the more than 200 syndicates offering publishers news, features, pictures, and special services. In addition to giving spot and secondary news, these services also provide sports, foods, fashions, bylined columns, and features ranging from amateur photography to zoo animals.

5

Creating the Headline

A copyeditor's first task is to correct and refine copy. This means, briefly, checking the copy for accuracy, clarity, conciseness, tone and consistency in style.

A second task is to create a headline that will capture readers' attention and provide enough information to help readers determine whether they wish to continue. A third task is to visualize the appearance of both story and headline of the page.

Because editing is a mixture of the three processes, it might be well to start with the headline because that's where readers start. A point to remember is that a headline is a digest, a condensation of a whole story in four or five words. Readers, using headlines as a guide, abstract the paper, searching for clues to stories that will interest them.

Copyeditors work in reverse. They first read the story, then compose the headline. This often leads to some muddled heads because copyeditors assume that if readers will but read the story they will understand what the headline is trying to convey. But the headline, standing alone, must be instantly clear. No reader will read the story to find out what the headline means unless his curiosity gets the better of him.

In an age when there was less demand on the readers' time and less competition for their attention, newspapers could afford to top stories with long, detailed headlines. Today's readers want their news in a hurry.

Headline Styles Change

Styles of headlines, like fashions, change constantly even though their function remains the same. Newspapers' first news display lines were short and slender, usually a single crossline giving little more than a topical label: **Latest from Europe.** By adding more lines or by varying the length of the lines, designers created the hanging indention, the inverted pyramid and the pyramid:

```
xxxxxxxxxxx          xxxxxxxxxxxx              xxxxxx
  xxxxxxxxxx            xxxxxxxxx             xxxxxxxxx
  xxxxxxxxx              xxxxxx            xxxxxxxxxxxx
```

Later, by indenting lines under the first line they achieved the stepped head, sometimes known as the drop head. It became one of the most popular styles of headlines and still is in use:

Heavy Rain
Shuts Down
All Beaches

The next move was to combine these elements—a stepped head, then an inverted pyramid, a crossline, then another inverted pyramid. The units under the introductory head became known as banks or decks. George Fitzpatrick, in an article in the October 1955 issue of *The Quill,* cited one he found in a western newspaper describing a reporter's interview with General Phil Sheridan in 1883:

FRISKY PHIL
Gazette Reporter Holds
Interesting Interview
With Hero of Winchester

The Great Warrior Receives the
Newspaperman with Open Arms;
He is More or Less Broken up on
the Craft Anyway

He Travels in a Special
Military Coach and Lives
On the Fat of the Land

Sheridan is Many Miles Away,
but the Champagne We Drank
with him Lingers with Us Still

We Feel a Little Puffed
Up Over Our Success At-
tending Our Reception by
Little Phil, But Man Is
Mortal

May He Who Watches Over the
Sparrows of the Field Never
Remove His Field Glasses from
the Diminutive Form and Great
Soul of Phil Sheridan

Throughout most of America's history newspaper headlines have tended to depict the mood of the times as well as the tone of the paper. **Jerked to Jesus** the Chicago *Times*, on November 27, 1875, shouted in headlining the account of a hanging. Other headlines are given in the following:

AWFUL EVENT
—
President Lincoln
Shot by an
Assassin.
—

The Deed Done at Ford's
Theatre Last Night
—
The Act of a Desperate Rebel
—
**The President Still Alive at
Last Accounts.**
—

No Hopes Entertained of His
Recovery
—

Attempted Assassination of
Secretary Seward
—
Details of the Dreadful Tragedy

The New York *Times*

AMERICA IS
MISTRESS
OF AIR
—
**Wright's Machine Is
Perfect; Uncle
Sam Buys.**
—
**Overland Trip With
Passenger Succeeds**
—
**"We Flew Eighty Miles an Hour
Coming Back," Says
Lieutenant.**

The Denver *Post*

The Art of Editing

PEARY WIRES HE HAS NAILED STARS AND STRIPES TO THE NORTH POLE AND IS ON HIS WAY HOME

OFFICIAL MESSAGE SENT ARCTIC CLUB

**Backers Were Momen-
tarily Expecting Veteran
Explorer to Report Suc-
cessful Quest of Goal
Reached by his Rival.**

**Latter Sends His Instru-
ments and Records to the
United States for Examin-
ation and Will Prove His
Claims Before a Jury of
Scientists of Two Conti-
nents—Dispells All Doubt.**

The Denver *Post*

Big type and clamoring messages still weren't enough. According to Gene Fowler, an executive told the owners of the Denver *Post*, "You've got to make this paper look different. Get some bigger headline type. Put red ink on Page 1. You've got to turn Denver's eyes to The Post every day, and away from the other papers." So the *Post* put the headlines in red to catch the readers' eyes. The message had to be gripping. According to Gene Fowler's version, Harry Tammen, co-owner of the Denver *Post*, was so incensed over a lifeless banner in the *Post* that he grabbed a piece of copy paper and composed one of his own: **Jealous Gun-Gal Plugs Her Lover Low.** When the copydesk protested that the headline wouldn't fit, Tammen snapped, "Then use any old type you can find. Tear up somebody's ad if necessary." Still the desk wasn't satisfied. "It isn't good grammar," the desk chief argued. But Tammen wouldn't budge. "That's the trouble with this paper," he is quoted as saying. "Too damned much grammar. Let's can the grammar and get out a live sheet."

The battle for circulation was hot. So were the headlines. Many also were colorful:

Demon of the Belfry Sent Through the Trap

Dons Planned to Skedaddle in the Night

Does It Hurt to Be Born?

Bless God—They're Safe
(On rescue of seaplane crew from the Pacific.)

Creating the Headline   53

Conductors Robbing Little Girls of Their Half Fare Tickets

Do You Believe in God?

During and after the Spanish-American War era some newspapers used as many as sixteen decks, or headline units, to describe the story. Frequently the head was longer than the story.

With improved presses and a greater variety of type and stereotyping available, designers were able to expand the headline. Eventually the head stretched across the page and became known as the banner, streamer or ribbon. On some papers it was called, simply, the line. This headline sometimes called for the largest type available in the shop. When metal type wasn't adequate for the occasion, printers fashioned letters from wood (called furniture). A 12-liner meant that the line was 12 picas, or 144 points (two inches).

Other headline designations are as follows: A story placed above the nameplate and banner headline is called a *skyline,* with the headline also known as a skyline head. Sometimes the skyline head stands alone but carries a notation as to where the story can be found.

A headline may have several parts—the main headline and auxiliary headlines known as *decks* or *banks*. These are not to be confused with subheads or lines of type (usually in boldface) placed between some paragraphs in the story.

A *kicker* headline is a short line of display type, usually no larger than half the point size of the main headline and placed over the main part of the headline. On some papers the kicker is termed the *eyebrow,* tagline or some other name.

The common newspaper abbreviation for headline is *hed.* HTK means "hed to kum."

A *stet* head is a standing headline such as **Today in history.**

A *reverse plate* headline is one that reverses the color values so that the letters are in white on a black background (Figure 5–1). A *reverse kicker,* in which one line in larger type is above the deck is called a *hammer* or a *barker* head.

Streamlining the Headline

As the tone of the newspaper was moderated, so were the headlines. Banner headlines still shout the news, sometimes in red ink, but gloom and doom headlines have virtually disappeared. Understating is more likely to be found in headlines today than overstating. Extra editions have been out of date for a long time And no longer do circulation managers hurry into the city room to demand a line that will increase the newspaper's street sales.

Between World Wars I and II the cult of simplification, known as streamlining, brought changes in the newspaper headline. Designers put more air or white space into the head by having each line flush left, with a zigzagged, or ragged, right margin.

Movies Are Better Than Ever

| 3 Big Hits Tonight At Vista View Drive-In | Two Comedies Slated Wednesday | 'The Perils Of Pauline' |

(A) BINDER HEAD

—SO DOES HITCH—
Boyer, Ritchie 'Revamp Team'

(B) THREE-WAY BROKEN OR SPLIT BOX OR HOOD

RATH TO RECOMMEND COUNTY AID FOR CITY IN TALKS WITH BILLS

Tells Sedita He'll Ask Board Approval Of Financial Assistance for Stadium Operation

(C) DROP OR STEPPED HEAD WITH INVERTED PYRAMID DECK

Washington Intensifies Diplomatic Efforts

(D) INVERTED PYRAMID HEAD

Status of Legislation

(E) SHADED OR BEN DAY HOOD

Bare Facts
Miniskirts, New Subway Seats Don't Mix

(F) BARKER HEAD

Today In History
By Associated Press

(I) REVERSED PLATE HEAD

Rubber Workers Strike Deadline Set at Goodyear

Union Tells Firm to Expect Walkout Early on Friday If No Agreement Reached

Tieup Would Close 11 Plants

(G) FLUSH-LEFT HEAD WITH HANGING INDENTATION AND CROSSLINE DECKS

Lottery Business Is Brisk as Sale Of Tickets Opens

Sellers, Buyers Share The Excitement as 425 WNY Outlets Service Customers

(H) FLUSH-LEFT HEAD WITH FLUSH-LEFT DECK

Writers Rap TV Antics In Soccer

(J) THREE-WAY BOX OR HOOD

Inside Today...

(K) RULED OR WICKET HEAD

Figure 5–1. Sample headline styles.

Urged by this spirit of simplification, they abolished the decorative gingerbread such as fancy boxes and reduced the number of banks or eliminated them altogether except for the deck reading out from a major head—called *readout* head. They argued that the *flush left* head was easier to read than the traditional head and that it was easier to write because the count was less demanding.

Another part of the streamlining process was the introduction of modern sans serif Gothic typefaces to challenge the traditional roman typefaces such as Century, Caslon, Goudy, Garamond and Helvetica (described in Chapter 13). Advocates of the new design contended that the sans serif faces were less ornate than the roman ones, gave more display in the smaller sizes, contained more thin letters (thus extending the count) and afforded greater mixture of faces because of the relative uniformity of the sans serifs.

Headlines in all-capital letters gradually gave way to capital and lower case letters. In modern headline design, only the first word of the headline and proper names are capitalized.

The wider columns in modern newspaper makeup give headline writers a better chance to make meaningful statements because of a better count in one-column heads. The trend away from vertical makeup and toward horizontal makeup provides more multicolumn headlines on the page. Such spread heads can be told effectively in one line.

Traditionally, the headline has headed the column and hence its name. But the headline need not necessarily go over the news column (see Figures 15–4, 15–5 and 15–6, Chapter 15).

Clever headlines continue to intrigue readers. Yet some readers tend to remember only the inept, the mixed-up, or the humorous ones. Some classics come to mind readily. One was the New York *Times* headline in 1916 proclaiming Charles Evans Hughes the winner over President Woodrow Wilson. Or *Life* magazine with a full-page shot of Gov. Thomas Dewey riding a ferry across San Francisco Bay, the cutline referring to "the next president of the United States." Or the banner in one edition of the Chicago *Tribune* proclaiming Dewey the victor over President Harry Truman. Still another was the amazing banner headline **Overhead Wins Indianapolis Race** that appeared in a small daily in Colorado. The editor, a racing car buff, had messaged the Associated Press to protect his paper on the winner of the Indianapolis Memorial Day race. In confirming the request, the AP wired the editor, WILL OVERHEAD (meaning AP would send by special telegram) INDIANAPOLIS MEMORIAL DAY RACE WINNER. The editor mistook the message for the bulletin and wrote the story and headline accordingly.

Whatever its style, the purpose of the headline is to urge the reader into the story. It gives an added dimension to the news story. It must get attention, then inform or titillate the reader. It has these major functions:

1. Attracts readers' attention to the story.
2. Summarizes or analyzes the story.
3. Depicts the mood of the story.
4. Helps readers index the contents of the page.
5. Helps set the tone of the newspaper.
6. Provides a major ingredient for page makeup.

Functions of the Headline

An editor's choice of size and style of the head is determined by the length and significance of the story, the position of the story on the page and the tone of the story.

Each newspaper has its own schedule showing headline designations and line count. Practice varies as to how headlines are designated. Here are four methods:

1. Number designation. Headlines of one or two columns are assigned a number. A 2 head, for example, might call for a one-column, two-line head in 24-point Bodoni, capitals and lower case. A 22 head would be the same as a 2 head but in two columns. Sometimes the number corresponds with the type size and style. A 24 head would be in 24 points, and a 25 would be in 24 points italic (Figure 5-2).

2. Letter designation. Here letters are used to show the type family and size. If C calls for 30-point Vogue extrabold, the head might be indicated as follows: 2C=. This means two columns, two lines of 30-point Vogue extrabold. The letter may also indicate the headline style. If D, for instance, means a one-column head in three lines of type, $\frac{1}{2}$D would be one column in two lines. Or if D is a headline with a deck, then $\frac{1}{2}$D would be the same head but without the deck.

3. Designation by numbers and type family. A designation such as 1-24-3 Bod. means one column, 24 points, three lines of Bodoni; 3-36-1 (or 3361) TBCI means three columns of 36-point, one line of Tempo bold condensed italic. On some papers, the first number designates the column width, the second number the number of lines and the third number the size of type (2/3/36).

4. Computer code designations. The code, F (for font) 406, could well mean the 400 series (Gothic) and 6 indicating size of type (48 point). The code numbers thus identify size and family of type, line width, number of lines and whether roman or italic.

The smallest headline may have no size indicated. A one-line head, set in the same size as the body copy but in boldface type, might be designated as BF or LCB (lower case bold). Such headlines are used on one-paragraph items.

L C B

Third Park Band Concert

14 MR

Star-Spangled Banner
Essay Contest Opens

18

Bronze Star Given
GI Killed In Viet

8

Car In Chase
Hits 3 Others

34

Freight Train
Draws Ticket
For Speeding

11

GOP Club Asks
Jury Probe Of
Walsh Case

2/2/24

Miss Grace Boardley To Do
Mission Work In Formosa

2/2/30

Fla. Crops Endangered
By Caribbean Fruit Fly

2/2/36

5,000-Mile Cruise
Begun By Manry

2/3/36

Arson Is Charged
To Man, 3 Youths
At Cambridge

Following are some of the common abbreviations used in headline designations:

X for extra (VXBI means Vogue extrabold italics).
x for italics (2302 SP *x* means two columns, two lines of Spartan italics).
It., I. or *ital.* for italics.
K for a kicker line or eyebrow (2302K).
H for hammer, an inverted kicker (3361H); also called barker head.
J for jump or runover head; also *RO*.
RO for readout, or a deck under a main multicolumn headline.
W for wicket head.
Sh for subhead.
R for roman (VXBR is Vogue extrabold roman)
Refer means lines directing the reader to a related story or picture on another page.

When a story reaches the copydesk, it bears some directions for handling, known as sluglines. The main part of the slug is the story's title, usually in one or two words (bank holdup). After the headline has been written, the story's slug is placed on the headline copy together with the headline designation.

On some newspapers the copyeditor writes the headline, then uses the first two words of the headline (plus the headline designation) to replace the original story slug. Suppose the story copy bears the slug "suspect." The copyeditor edits the copy and composes this headline: **Woman held / in slaying / released.** He then changes the "suspect" slug on the copy to "Woman held—1-30-3.

Counting the Headline

The easiest way to count a headline is by the typewriter system—one unit for all letters, figures, punctuation and space between words. If a line has a maximum of 18 units and the head shows a unit count of 15, the head will fit, unless it contains several fat letters (M and W). In that case, the writer recounts the line by a standard system: one unit for all lower case letters and numerals except f, l, i, t, and j ($\frac{1}{2}$), and m and w ($1\frac{1}{2}$); $1\frac{1}{2}$ for all capital letters except two units for cap M and W; $1\frac{1}{2}$ units for lower case m and w; $\frac{1}{2}$ unit for f, l, i, t and j; and $\frac{1}{2}$ unit for each space, for punctuation, for upper case I and for numeral 1.

Because of the variation in the widths of letters in different families of type or even within the same family, the standard system is not always correct. The letter i, for instance, is thinner than lower case t; in some faces r is thinner than d or g and a string of zeroes likely will make the line too long.

All headline writers are expected to keep within the maximum count allowable. It is costly and time-consuming to have heads

Figure 5–2. Headline schedule.

Creating the Headline   59

reset. If it appears that the desired head is slightly over the maximum count, the writer may provide an optional word as a substitute for a long word. The compositor then can try to fit the head as originally written. If it won't fit, he can use the optional word.

Some desk editors insist that each line of the head, even in a flush left head, take nearly the full count. Others argue there is merit in a ragged right edge. In a stepped head the lines cannot vary more than two or three units or the head will not step. Unless a special effect is desired, each line should fill more than half the maximum type-line width.

Ideally, the kicker should extend no more than half the width of the main head. As its name suggests, the kicker should be terse. A simple phrase, aptly put, will suffice, and a verb is not necessary. It should not rob the main head of key words or repeat words used in the main head. It should stand on its own and not depend on the main head for its meaning. The main head should not depend on the kicker for its meaning. The kicker may set the tone of the main head or supply information the writer would have used in the main head if space had been available. Sometimes it is used as a standing head: **Window of the world.**

The inverted kicker, or hammer head, carries the main idea of the story. The line underneath the hammer head supplements the hammer head. Sometimes the hammer head is a short line; more often, it fills the line.

The copyeditor does not write several heads for the same story and invite the editor to take his pick. He submits what he considers to be the best head he can write.

Creating the Headline

Occasionally the desk editor or some other executive will suggest an angle that should go into the head or call attention to an angle that should be avoided. Usually, however, headline writers are on their own. They know that within a matter of minutes or even seconds they must edit the copy and create a headline that will epitomize the story, that will make a statement in an easy-to-digest capsule.

By the time copyeditors have edited the copy they should have an idea brewing for the head. They begin by noting key words or phrases. These are their building blocks. With them they try to structure a headline. The first effort in headline writing starts with an answer to the question, "Who's doing what?" More than likely, the answer will provide some of the blocks for the structure: **Jets bomb ... Brothers split ... Boys convicted ... Allen vetoes. ...**

Key blocks may be a proper name or a reference to a name (Wilson, mayor, president), the setting (in Cambodia, Pueblo man), the age (baby, 100-year-old man, student), the occupation (janitor, actress, doctor) or the topic itself (accident, taxes, divorce).

With these blocks copyeditors try to make an accurate and co-herent statement. First they may try to phrase the statement in the active voice. If that fails, they use the passive. If possible, they try to get key words and a verb in the top line.

Take a routine accident story:

Three Atlantans were killed Friday when their car collided with a garbage truck on Hwy. 85 at Thames Road in Clayton County.
Dead were:...
Patrolman C. F. Thornton said the truck was driven north on Hwy. 85 by...
The auto pulled into the highway from Thames road and was hit by the truck, Thornton said.

The headline designation is three lines in one column that allows a maximum of nine units. In this story the lead almost writes the head. The obvious statement is "Three Atlantans killed as car and truck collide." **3 Atlantans** won't fit, so the writer settles for **3 killed.** For the second line he tries **in truck,** and for the third line **car collision.** He discards **car collision** because it is too long. **car crash** will fit. By changing the second line from **in truck** to **as truck** he gains another verb in the third line. The head now reads **3 killed / as truck, / car crash.**

Key headline words are like signposts. They attract the read-er's attention and give him information. Such words, meaning-fully phrased, produce effective headlines.

Note how quickly the key words (*Dutch, prince, born*) emerge in the lead of a wire story: "Crown Princess Beatrix gave birth to a son last night and Dutchmen went wild with joy at the ar-rival of a king-to-be in a realm where queens have reigned since 1890." One copyeditor used the key words this way:

Dutch treat

**A prince is born,
first in century**

Many dull heads can be improved if the writer will make the extra effort. Sometimes the first idea for the head is the best; often it is not. If the editor rejects the lifeless heads and in-sists on better ones, he inspires everyone on the rim to try harder. Furthermore, a good performance on news heads is likely to generate better headlines in all departments of the paper.

The job of the person on the rim is to create effective head-lines for all copy that comes along. The big story often is easier to handle than the routine one because the banner story has more action and thus more headline building blocks.

The usual death and wedding stories offer little opportunity for bright, original headlines. There are only so many ways to announce a wedding or a death in a head, and the writer dare not try to be clever in handling these topics. The standing gag on the copydesk is, "Let's put some life in these obit heads." If Jonathan Doe dies, that is all the headline can say, except to include his age: **Jonathan Doe / dies at age 65** or **Jonathan Doe / dead at 65.** If he were a former mayor, that fact would be used: **Jonathan Doe, / ex-mayor, dies.** Get the story interest in the head: **Lillian Roe, former postmaster, dies** is less newsworthy than **Lillian Roe, mother of selectman, dies.**

The Title Lesson

Beginning headline writers might start with what Carl Riblet Jr., an expert in headline writing, calls the title lesson. The learner starts by listing the titles of all the books he has read. This is to demonstrate that readers can recall titles even if they have forgotten the contents. It also demonstrates the effectiveness of an apt title. A good title helps sell the product, as illustrated by those revised by alert publishers: "Old Time Legends Together with Sketches, Experimental and Ideal" (*The Scarlet Letter*), "Pencil Sketches of English Society" (*Vanity Fair*), "The Life and Adventures of a Smalltown Doctor" (*Main Street*), "Alice's Adventures Underground" (*Alice in Wonderland*).

Limiting the learner to a one-line head with a maximum of fifteen or twenty units forces him to pack action in a few words, to merge as many elements as possible from the story, to indicate the tone or mood of the story and, finally, to compose an interesting statement. Riblet gives this example:

A young man said he and a middle-aged business agent had been drinking in a saloon. They went to the older man's apartment. There they quarreled over a gambling debt. The younger man told the police he was threatened with a .30 caliber rifle. In self-defense, he picked up a bow and arrow and shot the older man in the stomach. The younger man tried to pull the arrow out but it broke and the wounded man died.

The copyeditor got the story with instructions to write a one-line 20-count head. He knew the paper's rule that every headline must contain a verb. He wrote: **Business agent slain.** In this instance it would seem wiser to bend the rule and get the key words in the headline: **Bow and arrow killing.** This lesson has practical value in writing the one-line head, such as the banner **Mayor censured** or **Steelers No. 1,** the kicker **Smelly problem** or **Circus magic,** the column heading **The goldkeepers,** the filler head, **Postal auction** or the magazine feature **Acrobat on skis,** or **Messy education** or **Ohio's hub city.**

Phrasing the Headline

Practices vary, but on some desks no headline writer is permitted to hang conjunctions, parts of verbs, prepositions or modifiers on the end of any line of a headline. Like many newspaper rules, this one can be waived, but only if an exceptionally better headline can be created.

Rigid rules can bring grief to copydesks. One newspaper chain has two ironclad rules: No head may contain a contraction. Every head must contain a verb. This leads to some dull and tortured heads, especially on offbeat feature stories.

The Los Angees *Times* evidently has no policy against splitting ideas in heads. It may be argued that in the one-column headline the reader sees the headline as a unit and does not have to read each line separately as he would in a multicolumn head. Eventually experiments may be designed to test whether a reader can comprehend a split head as easily as he can one that breaks on sense. Until the results of such tests are available, headline writers should phrase headlines by sense. The practice can't hurt them if they join a desk that tolerates splits. A talented copyeditor will take no longer on a phrased headline than on a split headline.

Good phrasing in a headline helps the reader grasp its meaning quickly. Each line should be a unit in itself. If one line depends on another to convey an idea, the headline loses its rhythm. It may cause the reader to grope for the meaning. Note the differences in the original and the revised heads:

Original	*Revised*
Thousands join Easter parade in Philadelphia	**Thousands join Easter parade**
Men need to sleep longer study reveals	**Men require more sleep, report shows**
West Virginia reveals new plan for Negro education	**West Virginians to provide schooling for 1700 Negroes**
Stay calm Browns, you'll soon know your title foe	**Just stay calm Browns, you'll know foe soon**
Football ticket exchange to be revised next fall	**Ticket exchange for football will be revised**
Jones loses new bid for freedom	**Jones again loses bid for freedom**
Four Russian women tour Denver area	**Four women from Russia tour Denver**
Snow removal serious project in Soviet Union	**Removing snow is task in Soviet Union**
Ordnance station to welcome commander	**Naval ordnance station to welcome commander**
U.S. eyeing New Mexico site for nuclear wastes	**U.S. favors New Mexico for nuclear waste burial**

Expanded California doctors' malpractice strike threatened

Doctors' malpractice strike in California may expand

Police work draws in Japanese women

Police work lures Japanese women

Use the Present Tense

Unless the story is about a current or future event, most news is concerned with past events. But the headline, to give the effect of immediacy, uses the present tense for past events: **British doctors vouch / for girth control bill; City has bumper crop of junk cars; Jonathan Doe / dies at age 65.**

Suppose the headline announces a future event in the present tense? The reader won't know whether the event has occurred or will occur. **Powell's / wife tells / everything** means that the wife has testified. But if the reader learns from the story that the testimony will not be given until the following day, he knows the head has misled him. The head should have read **Powell's / wife to tell / everything.** The present tense can never be used if the date is included on a past event: **Jonathan Doe / dies Wednesday.**

On future events the headline may use the future, *will be;* the infinitive, *to be;* or the present: **Traffic parley / opens Monday.** *Scheduled* is a hard headline word because of its length. Convenient substitutes are *set* and *slated* and consequently are worked to death in heads over stories of future events. It happens like this: **Two speakers set.** and the reader wonders, "On eggs?"

Headline Punctuation

The full stop is never used except after abbreviations. Use single quotes instead of full quotes because the single quote takes less space and may be more appealing typographically. The comma may replace *and* and a semicolon and may even indicate a complete break: **Tumbling spacecraft tangles chute, / cosmonaut plummets to death.** The semicolon also indicates a full stop. Unless it is a last resort, neither the dash nor the colon should be used as a substitute for *says.* When used, the colon comes after the speaker, and the dash after what was said: **McCoy: dual role too big; Dual role too big—McCoy.**

Use Abbreviations Sparingly

Few beginning headline writers have escaped the abbreviation addiction. It occurs when the writer tries to cram too much in the head. The story said a woman under hypnosis had imagined herself as a reincarnation of an eighteenth century Bridey Murphy in Ireland. The theory was discounted by a professor of psychology at a state university. This is how a student headlined the story: **CU psych. prof. / doubts B.M. story.** A simple head such as **Professor doubts / 'Bridey' claims** would have given readers enough information to lead them into the story.

The Art of Editing

Abbreviations clutter the headline: **Mo. village / U.S. choice / for Pan-Am.** It could have been written as **Missouri / favored as / Pan-Am site.**

An abbreviation that has more than one meaning leads to confusion, especially when the headline also is guilty of poor phrasing: **Ten girls are added to St. / Vincent Candy Striper unit** or **Ill. man asks / Pa. to join Miss. / in Mass. protest,** or **Nebron New / L. A. Muni / Asst. P.J.** (He was elected assistant presiding judge of the Los Angeles Municipal Court.)

Headline writers frequently overestimate the ability of readers to understand the initials used in headlines. Some are easily recognized, such as FBI, YWCA, UN, DAR. Others aren't, such as AAUW, NAACP, ICBM. On many newspapers the style calls for abbreviations without periods in headlines.

Some contractions are acceptable in heads; others aren't. *Won't, don't* and *shouldn't* give no trouble, but *she'll, he'll, who're,* and the "s" and "d" contractions do: **Triplets 'fine' / so's mother of 22** or **Mother'd rather / switch than fight.** Try to read this aloud: **Anymore service, the town hall'll collapse.**

Grammar in Headlines

Although headline writers must constantly compress statements, they have no license to abuse the language. A grammatical error emblazoned in 48-point type may be worse than a half-dozen language errors buried in body type. The writer normally would say **Russian girls urged / to stop copying Paris.** But the second line was too long so the writer settled for **Russian girls urged / 'stop copying Paris'.** A comma should have been used to introduce the quoted clause. Transposing the lines would have produced a better head. A headline read **HHH best / of 2 choices, / senator says.** He can't be the best if there are only two choices.

Couple needs help with their sex life. Not both singular and plural in the same head. **Woman reports she is robbed / by man posing as inspector.** The present tense "reports" is correct. However, the second verb should be "was" to show that she is reporting a previous event.

A standing rule on use of proper names in headlines is that names in headlines should be instantly recognizable to most readers. **Union under investigation / gave to Tiernan campaign.** Unless this headline is for a Rhode Island paper, most readers won't recognize the name of a former Rhode Island congressman.

A copyeditor who can't catch spelling errors has no place on the copydesk. He is a menace if he repeats the error in his headline, as some editors did in these: **Rodeo parade has / governor as marshall; Kidnap victim trys / to identify captors. Walter Lipmann dies.** The name of the famed columnist, Walter Lippmann, was used fifteen times in the story as well as in a cutline for a one-column cut accompanying the story.

Headlining Sports

Sports pages are concerned with contests, meaning action and drama. Headlines over contest stories should be the easiest in the paper to write. Yet, because of the jargon used by sports writers and the numerous synonyms signaling a victory of one team over another, the sports story headline has become a jumble.

A reader says to his companion, "I see where the Jayhawkers crunched the Cornhuskers." "Yeah," answers a University of Nebraska basketball fan, "how much?" "It says here 98 to 94," says the reader. If that's a crunching, what verb describes a 98 to 38 victory?

The struggle for substitutes for *wins, beats,* and *defeats* produces verbs such as *bests, downs, smears* and *swamps.* Presumably, the reader reads a sports page to find out who wins in what races. What matter, then, if the simple word like *wins* or *defeats* is used over and over? Certainly they are better than editorialized counterparts such as *clobbers, wallops, flattens* and *trounces.*

Avoid Slang

A straight head that tells the reader precisely what happened in dictionary words is always better than one in which the writer resorts to slang. Slang in heads, as well as in copy, lowers the tone of the paper and consequently lowers the readers' estimation of the paper. The headline, no less than the copy, should speak to the general reader, not to newsmen and other specialists.

Here is an object lesson from a San Diego newspaper. The second edition carried a six-column head in the society section: **Kids going to pot are aided.** Under the head was a three-column cut showing a girl sitting on a bed in a holding room at Juvenile Hall. The picture also revealed a toilet stool in one corner of the room. To the relief of the embarrassed society editor, the top line in the third edition was revised to **Teen narcotic users aided.**

Don't Repeat Words

Another restriction on headline writing is that major words in the headline cannot be repeated unless done so for effect in a feature head. The rule has little logic except to prevent obvious padding, such as **Campus will launch / campus chest drive** and **Wind-lashed blizzard / lashes plains states.**

If the main head contains a word like *fire,* the readout or banks could easily substitute a synonym. *Blaze* would be an acceptable one; *inferno* would not.

Repetition is sometimes used deliberately to heighten a feature: **Man leaves / nagging wife / for new nag; Thinkers failures, / professor thinks; New look? never! / old look's better; Pokey driving sends three back to pokey.**

Faced with the problem of making a statement in a nine-unit line, the writer has to grab the shortest nouns and verbs possible. He is tempted to use overworked words such as *hits, nabs, chief* or *set* because they help to make the headline fit. Or he may reach for short words with symbolic meanings, such as *flays, slaps, grills, hop* or *probe.* Nothing is "approved"; it is "okayed" (or "ok'd") or "given nod." All are headline clichés and have no place in today's paper. Yet even the trade papers continue to use them: **Miami Herald / grills Sinatra / in libel probe.**

The headline should not falsify the story. Many of the headlinese words do, at least by implication. If the story tells about the mayor mildly rebuking the council, the headline writer lies when he used verbs like *hits, slaps, scores, raps, rips* or *flays.* An *investigation* or a *questioning* is not necessarily a "grilling"; a *dispute* is not always a "row" or a "clash." *Cops* went out with prohibition. Today s word is *police.*

Others that should be shunned are "quiz" for *question,* "hop" for *voyage,* "talks" for *conference,* "aide" for *assistant,* "chief" for *president* or *chairman,* "solon" for *legislator* or *congressman,* "probe" for *inquiry,* "nabs" for *arrests,* "meet" for *meeting,* "bests" for *defeats,* "guts" for *destroys,* "snag" for *problem,* "stirs" for *incites* and "hike" for *increase.*

During America's involvement in Vietnam, millions of readers must have wondered what headlines were trying to say with the incessant use of "Viet" and its variations. The word was used indiscriminantly to refer to North Vietnam, South Vietnam, the Viet Cong, the North Vietnamese army, the South Vietnamese army and the Vietnamese people.

Down with Headlinese

Because of the strong impression a headline may make on a reader, courts have ruled that a headline may be actionable even though the story under the head is free from libel. Here are a few examples:

Don't Invite Libel or Contempt

Shuberts gouge $1,000 from Klein brothers

'You were right,' father tells cop who shot his son

McLane bares Old Hickory fraud charges

Doctor kills child

Gone to her drummer
A missing hotel maid being pursued by an irate parent

John R. Brinkley—quack

Creating the Headline

A wrong name in a headline over a crime story is a way to involve the paper in a libel action.

The headline writer, no less than the reporter, must understand that under our system a person is presumed innocent of any crime charged until he has been proved guilty by a jury. Heads that proclaim **Kidnaper caught, Blackmailers exposed, Robber arrested,** or **Spy caught** have the effect of convicting the suspects (even the innocent) before they have been tried.

If two masked gunmen hold up a liquor store owner and escape with $1,000 in cash, the head may refer to the two as "robbers" or "gunmen." Later, if two men are arrested in connection with the robbery as suspects or are actually charged with the crime, the head cannot refer to them as "robbers" but must use a qualifier: **Police question / robbery suspects.** For the story on the arrest the headline should say **Two arrested / in robbery,** not **Two arrested / for robbery.** The first is a shortened form of "in connection with"; the second makes them guilty. Even "in" may cause trouble. **Three women / arrested in / prostitution** should be changed to **Three women / charged with / prostitution.**

The lesson should be elementary to anyone in the publishing business, but even on the more carefully edited papers the heads are sometimes guilty of jumping to conclusions. This was illustrated in the stories concerning the assassination of President John F. Kennedy. Lee Harvey Oswald was branded the assassin even though, technically, he was merely arrested on a charge of murder. In a statement of apology, the managing editor of the New York *Times* said his paper should not have labeled Oswald an assassin.

In their worst days, newspapers encouraged headline words that defiled: **Fanged fiend, Sex maniac, Mad-dog killer.**

Even today some newspapers permit both reporter and copyeditor to use a label that will forever brand the victim. When a seventeen-year-old boy was convicted of rape and sentenced to twenty-five to forty years in the state penitentiary, one newspaper immediately branded him *Denver's daylight rapist.* Another paper glorified him as *The phantom rapist.* Suppose an appeal reverses the conviction? What erases the stigma put on the youth by a newspaper?

The copyeditor who put quotes around **Honest count** in an election story learned to his sorrow that he had committed a libel for his paper.

The following is a conviction head: **Residents glad / killer identified.**

Miscellaneous "Rules"

Emphasis in the headline should be on the positive rather than the negative. If the rodeo parade fails to come off as scheduled because of rain, the head makes a positive statement: **Rain cancels / rodeo parade,** not **No rodeo parade / because of rain.** The news value is lacking in the headline that says **No one hurt /**

as plane crashes. The positive statement would be **90 passengers escape injury / as plane crashes in mountain.** Here are three negating words in a headline: **Tax writers / veto lids on / oil write-off.** Better: **Tax writers / leave oil tax / as it stands.** Double negative: **President / bars ban on / Negro jobs.** Better: **President / orders jobs / for Negroes.**

The negative is illustrated in this headline from an English paper: **Only small earthquake; not many killed.**

The admonition does not apply to feature heads, where the negative helps make the feature: **No laws against drowning, but it's unhealthy; Not so gay nineties** (on weather story); **Laundry gives / no quarter until / suit is pressed.**

The question head, except on features, is suspect for two reasons: It tends to editorialize, and newspaper heads are supposed to supply answers, not ask questions. If the headline asks the reader a question, the answer, obviously, should be in the story. If the answer is buried deep in the story, the question headline should be shunned. A two-line, five-column, 48-point head asked, **Did Anastasia murder help kill barber shaves?** The lead repeated the same question, but the reader was compelled to look through a dozen paragraphs only to learn that the question referred to a frivolous remark that should have been used only to color the story.

On features, question heads have their place: **39-24-37 and that's topless?**

It's fun to write headlines because headline writing is a creative activity. Copyeditors have the satisfaction of knowing that their headlines will be read. They would like to think that the head is intriguing enough to invite the reader to read the story. When they write a head that capsules the story, they get a smile from the executive in the slot and, sometimes, some praise.

Enjoy the Game

Somerset Maugham said you cannot write well unless you write much. Similarly, you can't write good heads until you have written many. After they have been on the desk for a while, copyeditors begin to think in headline phrases. When they read a story they automatically reconstruct the headline the way they would have written it. A good headline inspires them to write good ones, too.

They may dash off a head in less time than it took them to edit the copy. Then on a peewee story they may get stuck. They may write a dozen versions, read and reread the story, and then try again. As a last resort, they may ask the desk chief for an angle The longer they are on the desk the more adept they become at shifting gears for headline ideas. They try not to admit that any head is impossible to write. If a synonym eludes them they search the dictionary or a thesaurus until they find the right one.

If they have a flair for rhyme, they apply it to a brightener: **Nudes in a pool / play it cool / as onlookers drool.**

Every story is a challenge. After the writer has refined the story it almost becomes the copyeditors' story. The enthusiasm they have for the story is reflected in the headline over the story. They seek to put all the drama, the pathos or the humor of the story into the headline. The clever ones, or the "heady heads," as one columnist calls them, may show up later in office critiques or in trade journals:

Council makes short work of long agenda

Hen's whopper / now a whooper

Stop the clock, / daylight time / is getting off

Lake carriers clear decks / for battle with railroads

'Dolly' says 'Golly' / after hellowful year

It's one giant leap for metkind (Baseball's world series winner)

Tickets cricket, / legislators told

Quints have a happy, happy, happy, happy, happy birthday (First birthday party for quintuplets of Catonsville, Md.)

6

Headline Requirements

Accuracy

The first requirement of a headline is that it be accurate. This comes mainly from close and careful reading of the story. Erroneous headlines result because the copyeditor doesn't understand the story, infers something that is not in the story, fails to give the full dimension of the story, or fails to shift gears before going from one story to another. Examples:

Family Weekly tied to Arab oil interests. The lead said the magazine had become a member of a corporate family that has close ties with the oil tycoons of Iran and Venezuela. Neither is an Arab nation. Iran is a Moslem country.

Proxmire in Qatar. But the story was about the ex-senator, William Fulbright.

Bench injures shin, / will be out indefinitely. The story said the Cincinnati catcher would be out of action several days.

Cowboys nip Jayhawks / 68-66 on buzzer shot. The lead said that Kansas (the Jayhawks) beat Oklahoma State (the Cowboys) by two points in a Big Eight conference basketball game.

Player shuns rain, wind and the course. If Golfer Gary Player had shunned them, he wouldn't have played. He conquered rain and wind to lick the course.

Paducah's / bonding law / enjoined. The city was enjoined from enforcing the law. A law can't be enjoined.

Rebozo details said hazy. The details weren't hazy; Rebozo was hazy about the details.

3 in family face / charges of fraud. They were arrested in a fraud investigation, but the charges were perjury.

United Brands / chairman falls / to his death. The story said the man jumped.

Black child's adopted mother fights on. The child didn't select the mother; it was the other way around. Make it "adoptive."

Do-nothing Congress / irks U.S. energy chief. The spokesman criticized Democrats, not Congress as a whole, and the "do-nothing" charge was limited to oil imports.

Iran would / fill Israeli oil needs. The story said that Iran seemed to assure Israel that it could count on additional oil supplies if it returned captured Egyptian oil fields. The story was qualified in two places, the head not at all.

Unite Michigan's parochial, / public schools, Romney says. Romney didn't ask for union; he flatly suggested closing of parochial schools and sending their pupils to public schools.

Four held / in robbery / of piggy bank. The bank was the loot; the robbery was at a girl's home.

White House / hints at ceiling / on oil spending. The subject of the story was oil imports.

Greek plebiscite set Dec. 8. The vote was set for Dec. 8. The setting didn't come on that date.

Patricia Neal well / after three strokes. The story said she wore a leg brace and heavy shoes and had a patch over one eye.

If that pooch bites / you can collect $200. The story said the animal had to have rabies and you may collect up to $200.

Didn't like her face / shoots TV announcer. A man fired a gun at her but missed.

Graham backs / sterilization view. Although he backed one viewpoint, he criticized the program generally.

Bishop says / segregation / is justified. The lead quoted the bishop as saying that Christians are not morally justified in aiding segregation.

Dixie Baptists lock doors to Negroes. The lead said they rejected an endorsement of church integration but referred the issue to member churches.

Schools help pay expenses / for Forsyth county's dogs. The story said the dog-tax money helps support the schools.

Civic ballet auditions / scheduled Saturday. One listens to auditions; one looks at tryouts or trials.

Youth, 19, breaks parole, / subject to whipping post. The story correctly said he had been on probation.

Circus clown's daughter / dies from high wire fall. Second paragraph of story: "The 19-year-old aerialist was reported in good condition at Paterson General Hospital with fractures of the pelvis, both wrists and collarbone."

India-China / relations / worsen. The story was datelined Jakarta and had nothing to do with India.

Chicago to see outstanding moon eclipse. The story wasn't about a moon eclipse; it was about an eclipse of the sun. And "outstanding" is hardly an appropriate way to describe an eclipse.

Brilliant modern study / of Holy Roman emperor. Story was a review of a book on Emperor Hadrian who was born A.D. 76 and died in 138. The Holy Roman Empire lasted from A.D. 800 to 1806.

Big three September sales / up 22,147 over year ago. The lead mentioned Chrysler, General Motors and American Motors. The latter is not one of the Big Three, but Ford is.

Israelis release Arabs / to regain heroes' bodies. Nowhere does the story call them heroes. The two were executed during World War II for assassinating a British official.

Akin to the inaccurate headline is one that goes beyond the story, that fails to give the qualifications contained in the story, that confuses facts with speculations. Examples:

Don't Overreach

West Louisville / students at UL / to get more aid. The lead said they may get it.

Integration may improve / learning, study indicates. But the lead was two-sided, indicating an improvement in one area and a loss in another. The headline should reflect divided results or views, especially in highly emotional news subjects.

Pakistan, U.S. discuss lifting / of embargo on lethal weapons. The story said, correctly, the embargo may be eased. And aren't all weapons lethal?

Arabs vote to support / PLO claim to West Bank. The story said that Arab foreign ministers voted to recommend such action to their heads of state. The head implies final action.

Schools get / 60% of local / property tax. This reflects fairly what the lead said but fails to reveal an explanation later in the story, that the schools get a proportion of the contributions of various levels of government—federal, state and local. Although the local property tax contributes 60 per cent, the amount is far less than 60 per cent of the total local property tax.

Here's what happens when a copyeditor gets carried away: **Bacon enlivens buttermilk muffins.** (The genius who thought of enlivening buttermilk muffins must be assumed to have done so with his tongue in his cheek and a piece of toast in his mouth.) **County heavens to explode with color.** (Perhaps a booster head for a fireworks display, but slightly exaggerated.)

A good headline tells the reader what the story says, not what the writer thinks the story implies. In the latter category are the imperative heads, the editorialized heads, heads that go beyond what the story says and heads that oversimplify.

A New York City newspaper splashed a 144-point headline over the story of the shooting of Medgar Evers, a civil rights advocate, in Alabama. The head: **Slay NAACP Leader!** The imperative head results when the writer starts the head with a verb: **Save eight / from fire; Buy another / school site; Arrest 50 pickets / in rubber strike; Find 2 bodies / nab suspect; Assassinate U.S. envoy.**

Gratuitous adjectives and loaded terms like *beatniks, peaceniks, thugs, cops, pinkos, yippies* and *hippies* may appear in

---

the story but should not be used in the headline unless they can be attributed. A quote mark around a word is not an attribution.

Every word in a headline should be justified by a specific statement within the story. Some stories are deliberately contrived to fetch a headline; that is, some are written in a fashion to mislead the headline writer. Was the sergeant who led a Marine platoon into a creek, drowning six recruits, drunk? Most headlines said he was, but the story carried the qualification "under the influence of alcohol to an unknown degree." Similarly, did Gov. Adlai Stevenson call Vice President Richard Nixon a national calamity or did Senator Joseph McCarthy actually call General George Marshall a traitor? The headlines said they did, but the quotations in both instances prove that the statements may be open to more than one interpretation.

Before writing a headline on a story quoting someone, the copyeditor should ask himself, "Is the quotation out of context?" Frequently, part of a quotation is used for the lead, only to be modified deeper in the story. A headline based on the unqualified statement can be a distortion.

The lead on a wire story read: "Dr. Timothy Leary, dismissed from Harvard for his experiments with hallucination drugs, told a Senate hearing Friday that use of LSD has gotten out of control, particularly among the nation's college students." The lead fetched this head: **LSD perils youth, / ex-prof tells senate.** The last two paragraphs softened the lead: "While unrestrained use of LSD by the nation's younger set has led to a crisis, Leary commented: 'This is not a crisis of peril but a crisis of challenge. There is nothing to fear from LSD. On the basis of statistics, there is more violence, more terror in a cocktail lounge of any big city on Saturday night than from 23 years of LSD.'"

Or take this common construction: **Author scores / federal misuse / of strip studies.** The head states as a fact that the federal government is misusing studies on strip mining. The story credited that view only to the author. In other words, the headline states an opinion as a fact.

Even though the headline reports in essence what the story says, one loaded term in the headline will distort the story. If Israel, for reasons that she can justify, turns down a compromise plan offered by the Unites States concerning the Gaza Strip and Gulf of Aqaba problem, the head creates a negative attitude among readers when it proclaims **Israel spurns US compromise.**

It is hard to put qualifications in heads because of the count limitations. But if the lack of qualification distorts the head, trouble arises. A story explained that a company that was expected to bid on a project to build a fair exhibit was bowing out of the project because the exhibit's design was not structurally sound. The headline, without qualification, went too far and brought a sharp protest from the construction firm's president: **Builder quits, calls / state world's fair / exhibit 'unsound.'**

Another temptation of the headline writer is to spot a minor, sensational element in the story and use that element in the head. A story had to do with the policy of banks in honoring outdated checks. It quoted a bank president as saying, "The bank will take the checks." In intervening paragraphs several persons were quoted as having had no trouble cashing their checks. Then in the eleventh paragraph was the statement "A Claymont teacher, who refused to give her name, said she had tried to cash her check last night and it had been refused." She was the only person mentioned in the story as having had any difficulty. Yet the headline writer grabbed this element and produced a head that did not reflect the story:

State paychecks dated 1974
Can't Cash It,
teacher says

The headline-writing process starts as soon as a copyreader starts reading the story. If the lead can't suggest a headline, chances are the lead is weak. If a stronger element appears later in the story, it should be moved closer to the lead. The point is so elementary that every reporter should be required to take a turn on the copydesk if for no other reason than to teach a reporter how to visualize the headline before beginning the story.

Get the News in the Head

Although the headline ideally emerges from the lead, and generally occupies the top line (with succeeding lines offering qualifications or other dimensions of the story), it frequently has to go beyond the lead to portray the full dimensions of the story. When that occurs, the qualifying paragraphs should be moved to a higher position in the story. Example: **U.S. firm to design / spying system for Iran.** The lead was qualified. Not until the fifteenth paragraph was the truth of the head supported. That paragraph should have been moved far up in the story.

The head usually avoids the exact words of the lead. Once is enough for most readers. Lead: "Despite record prices, Americans today are burning more gasoline than ever before and that casts some doubt on the administration's policy of using higher prices to deter use." Headline: **Despite record gasoline prices, / Americans are burning more fuel.** A paraphrase would avoid the repetition: **Drivers won't let record gas prices / stop them from burning up fuel.** Since the story tended to be interpretive, the head could reflect the mood: **Hang the high price of gasoline, / just fill 'er up and let 'er roar.**

A headline that gives no more information than the label on a vegetable can is aptly known as a label head. Generally these are the standing heads for columns that appear day by day or week by week, like **Social Notes** or **Niwot News.** They say nothing.

Headline Requirements

They defy the purpose of a display line, which is to lure the reader.

Almost as bad are the yawny, ho-hum heads that make the reader ask, "So what else is new?" The writer who grabs a generality rather than a specific for the head is more than likely to produce a say-nothing head. Such writers prefer **Many persons killed** to **1000 persons killed.** "Factors" is about the dullest headline word imaginable. **Factors slow / car input.** Something is responsible for either output or input. In this case, a parts shortage was the main cause.

Notice how little information is provided in the following samples:

Financial program explained

Development plans described

Class night to be today

Pan Am jet lands safely

Wadsworth derailment puts 13 cars off rails

Rotarians hear Korean bishop

Newark Rotary told of planning

Coroner seeks cause of why driver died

Autopsy scheduled for dead Akronite

Broyhill speaks at big picnic

Committee will study 2 problems

Readers read newspapers to get the news. If the headline tells them the obvious, they have been short-changed. Here are examples of the obvious statement:

Fall shirts / offer new / innovations (Not to be confused with those old innovations.)

Corn field selected as place for annual county husking bee

Warm house best in cold climate

Turkish ship sinks in water near Cyprus

Californian, 20, drowns in water of Lake Mohave

On some feature stories newspapers may permit a verbless head resembling those found on magazine pieces. Example: **A firing at The New Republic.** A secondary head or blurb gave details: **"What would appear to be / the end of Peretz's house- / cleaning follows the recent / resignation of another staffer, / Stanley Karnow, the former / foreign editor."**

Some stories, like announcements, offer little or no news to invite fresh headlines. Yet even if the second-day story offers nothing new, the headline cannot be a repetition of the first-day story head.

Suppose on Monday the story says that Coach Ralston will speak at the high school awards dinner. If Ralston is prominent, his name can be in the head: **Ralston to speak / at awards dinner.** On Thursday comes a follow-up story, again saying that Coach Ralston will be the awards dinner speaker. If the headline writer repeats the Monday headline readers will wonder if they are reading today's paper. The desk editor will wonder why copyeditors won't keep up with the news. The problem is to find a new element, even a minor one, like this: **Tickets available / for awards dinner.** So the dinner comes off on Friday, as scheduled. If the Saturday headline says **Ralston speaks / at awards dinner,** readers learn nothing new The action is what he said: **Ralston denounces / 'cry baby' athletes.** Or if the story lacks newsworthy quotes, another facet of the affair goes into the head: **30 athletes / get awards.**

A good lead, one packed with action verbs, cannot help but invite an action headline:

SAN BERARDINO—Two men were injured here Friday when their pickup truck careened off a roadway, snapped a utility pole in two and flipped onto its left side.

The head: **2 hurt as truck flips**

The headline must portray the story in context That is, the headline should not repeat what was said yesterday or the day before that or a week ago It may be a second-day story with a fresh angle. To judge the news fairly and accurately, the copyeditor must keep up with the news through daily reading of a newspaper. The headwriter must also know how the opposition displayed the story so that a different wording can be used.

There is no trick in writing a vague, generalized headline statement. The real art of headwriting comes in analyzing the story for the how, the why or the consequences. If the story has more than one dimension, the head should reflect the full story, not part of it. Take this horrible example: **D.J s company union (IAPE) / withdraws COLA provision.** That's three too many abbreviations (and D J's should be D J.'s). Worse, the head fails to capture the real meaning of the story, which was that the union (Independent Association of Publisher's Employes Inc.) reached an agreement with Dow Jones & Co. providing for across-the-board pay increases. In return, the union agreed to withdraw its

Get All the Dimensions

Headline Requirements 77

demand for a cost of living adjustment (COLA). And IAPE is an independent union, not a company union

Other examples:

Report says school 'integration' still not achieved. The report was already several days old. This was a columnist's view of the matter, calling for something more than a straight news head.

Carroll to use funds for coal-road repair. This was not the news. The governor had said previously that he might use general fund money. The head should have reflected the fact that the governor NOW plans to use road fund money.

Documents link / royal family / to sex scandal. Somehow the head should have told readers the story did not describe scandals in Britain's present royal family but concerned an unlordly lord in Queen Victoria's court almost a century ago

Cuspid clues: **Coroner says teeth aid in identifying dead.** That was news decades ago. The news, as explained in the story, was about the number of methods used in medical detective work.

Police chase, capture / 2 Alabama van thieves. Unless the item is for an Alabama paper, who cares about a run-of-the-mill crime? It turns out the thieves were 12 years old, a fact that should have been in the headline to justify the story.

If only one element emerges in the headline, the head fails to do justice to the story. This headline is weak: **Man injured / in accident.** At least one person in a community is injured in an accident nearly every day. The word *man* is a faraway word. *Driver* is closer. "Injured in accident" can be shortened to "Injured" if the word *Driver* replaces *Man*. Now the top line can read: **Driver injured.** A second element in the story shows that he was wearing a seat belt. Marrying the two ideas produces a head like this: **Injured driver / wore seat belt.** The original head is passable but weak. The revised head gives more information and is an attention-getter.

Notice how a good copyeditor can make a pedestrian head come alive and have more meaning:

Original	*Revised*
6 priests lose **duties after** **rap of bishop**	**Priests fired** **after calling** **bishop callous**
Man says robber returned **to house a second time**	**Intruder hits, robs man in home,** **returns later for lost jacket**
Gardening idea from Mexico **helps increase tomato output**	**Texan doubles tomato crop** **with Mexican water tip**
Four-car **accident** **Friday**	**6 injured** **as 4 cars** **pile up**

Gary project **funded by U.S.** **closes down**	**Soul Inc. runs** **out of money,** **closes in Gary**
Motorist, 59, dies **of apparent coronary**	**Motorist dies at wheel;** **car hits telephone pole**
4 air crashes, **radar system** **lack linked**	**Lack of radar** **guide blamed** **in 4 crashes**
Muskie urges Ford **to act on inflation**	**Muskie asks action** **on pay, price rises**
Vandals leave **$4,000 loss in** **N. side school**	**Vandals visit** **school for 3d** **time in week**
N.U. trustees o.k. **new hearing system**	**N.U. students get** **bigger judicial role**
Postman dies **in fall while** **washing walls**	**Wall washer** **killed in fall** **through window**
Children to host **fete for parents**	**Children to fete** **parents on 25th**
Senate amends bill to cut **pay increase for top judges**	**Senate amends bill to give** **top judges 15% pay boost**
Statistics **released** **on test**	**Here's that** **test, can** **you pass it?**
Report given on **teaching experiment**	**Geometry, phonics** **in kindergarten?**
Heart of glacier **Tunnel town** **inaugurated**	*Drama in Arctic* **25 imperiled** **by blizzard**
State approves **housing plan**	**State approves** **another dorm**
Colonel King **posts rules** **for drivers**	**Old decal** **or old tag** **means ticket**

Headline Requirements   79

	First stop: Egypt
News-Journal lists **travel forum dates**	**Yearn to travel?** **it's forum time**
10¢ fare is urged **for the elderly**	**10¢ fare is urged** **for those over 65**
Woman found **slain in home**	**Widow found** **slain in home**
Two persons killed, **6 wounded in attacks** **by Ulster terrorists**	**2 killed, 6 wounded** **by Ulster terrorists;** **6-year toll 1,238**

How to Muddle the Head

Because many words can be either verbs or nouns, the head-writer should make sure that such words can't be taken either way. The jackanapes reader will likely ascribe the wrong meaning:

Population growth: doom writers' field day. Cue: "doom" is intended as a noun. **Doom writers capitalize / on population growth.**

Study heralds cop selectivity profile. Cue: "heralds" is a verb, "cop" a noun. Better: **Study draws profile of an ideal cop.**

Flourish floors drabness. Cue: the second word is the verb.

Resort wear showing cues orchestra women's benefit. It's any-one's guess what this means with so many words that double as nouns or verbs.

Flexible can not dangerous. Can is a noun here, not a verb.

Grenades Viet police post. The writer intended the reader to read grenades as a verb.

Project job needs / with new method. "Project" is intended as a verb. Perhaps "foresee" would do the trick.

The lack of a verb may force the reader to reread the head:

4 children die / in fire while / mother away. If the count won't permit "mother is away," the head should be recast: **Mother away, / 4 children die / in home fire.**

Kidnaper / says mother / not good.

Physician says / President well. But "President" is the ob-jective case and the head literally says the physician is a capable elocutionist (unlike the kidnaper in the preceding head). By transposing the lines, President is in the nominative case and the verb is understood: **President well, / physician says.** The other might be revised: **Kidnaper / calls mother / 'no good'.**

Some desk chiefs have an aversion to using "to be" verbs in heads. Other insist that if the verb is needed to make the head clear it should be used or the head should be recast. Of-ten the lack of a vital auxiliary verb produces gibberish: **Rookie admits prisoners struck. Thai plea said / less important / than U.S. lives. East-west rail service said unfeasible**

---

80   *The Art of Editing*

Ex-convict / fatally shot / fleeing cop. Here is the copyeditor's thought: "Ex-convict (is) fatally shot (while) fleeing (from) cop." But many readers will follow the normal order of subject, then predicate, so they read "(An) ex-convict fatally shot (a) fleeing cop." Not good, but perhaps passable: **Ex-convict / killed while / fleeing police.**

Trooper kills man / who had slain wife. Does this mean the trooper killed the man who had slain his (the trooper's) wife? Or that the trooper killed a wife slayer? Or that he killed a man whose wife had been slain by someone else?

Official says CIA, FBI / may have 'destroyed' files. To most readers this means the two agencies possibly destroyed some secret files. The quote around "destroyed" suggests that perhaps they didn't destroy the files. The story, though, said that files previously reported as having been destroyed may still be in the hands of the CIA and FBI. A clearer head: **Official says CIA, FBI / may hold 'destroyed' files.**

An easy way to get tortured prose in headline is to clothe nouns in human garb. Like these:

Fear drives guardsmen to panic.

Tornadoes slice through Iowa.

Span crashes hurt four, none serious (Some writers apparently think a headline provides a license for changing an adverb to an adjective.)

Smoke brings firemen to Galt house (If smoke can impel action, it would "send" the firemen.)

Rains force roads to close, / few families to evacuate. (Rains can't force roads; they can force somebody to close the roads.)

Again, a cardinal rule in headline-writing is that the headline, standing alone, must be instantly clear to readers. If the headline puzzles them, they assume the story will also be puzzling and will turn to something they can understand. Examples:

Bob Walker in town: Street wrestler 'ads' to take. This is gibberish to readers. If they had taken time to read the story they would have learned that Bob Walker, a Marlboro Country man, had participated in the steer-wrestling contest at a stock show rodeo.

Scarcity sandwiches Jim / between signs of the times. This makes sense only if readers know that during an inauguration ceremony a student named Jim paraded through the audience wearing a sandwich board sign reading "I need a job."

Next surge / in food costs / to be mild. If it's mild, how can it be a surge?

Doctor urges / sex, abortion / rules shifts. What the good doctor said was that sex taboos are out of date.

Out-of-town / Busch strike / is felt here. Busch refers to a beer, specifically Budweiser.

Water falls; / calls build / to Niagara. Want to know what idea this head is trying to convey? The water pressure in Penns Grove had fallen and the water company had received many complaints.

---

5 from Mt. Pleasant win / handicapped essay prizes. What's a handicapped essay? Or was it the prizes that were handicapped?

Suit curbing shed, / fence sites loses. If readers take long enough, eventually they will understand that someone lost a law suit that would have restricted sites for sheds and fences.

Parked car collides with church. A church on wheels, perhaps?

Hatcher amasses huge edge in Gary primary. Change "edge" to "lead."

Elm disease is thriving throughout Longmont. Somehow, one doesn't normally think of a disease as thriving. Make it "spreading."

Shun the Pun

The rule is that a pun in a head must be a good one or the impulse to commit it to print should be suppressed. For the story on the end of the adventure strip "Terry and the Pirates" many papers could be expected to carry the line: **'Pirates' comic strip walks plank.** When they're bad they're awful:

**Unbreakable window solves
a big pane**

**Rod isn't Lavering / for
WCT 'big apple'**

Battle of Buicks Saturday

**You buffs 'auto' be told,
'Little Indy' revving up**

The following story and headlines well-illustrate puns and other problems.

The president of the American Foundrymen's Society told UPI in an interview that small, specialized foundries are shrinking in number because of problems concerned with scrap shortages, high material costs and the high price of conforming to anti-pollution laws and other requirements. Although the number of such small foundries is not great, the shrinkage is causing problems for the defense department, designers, manufacturers and investors. Overall, the statement said, the foundry business is flourishing as the nation's sixth largest industry in terms of value added.

Some headwriters could not resist the foundry-foundering pun and thus distorted the story's meaning:

**America's foundry business is foundering
Foundry business flounders**

(This proves that the writer couldn't distinguish between founders and flounders.)

Anyone for floundering foundries?

Other headwriters stressed only one dimension of the story:

The Art of Editing

Foundries dwindling

Foundry failures are accelerating

Foundry industry in big trouble

Foundry industry suffering shrinkage

A spot survey of papers using the story showed that slightly more than half (58 per cent) of the headlines were reasonably fair and accurate:

Small foundries are disappearing
Small foundries having big financial woes
Foundry firms hurt by material scarcity

A few headlines got both dimensions:

Industry, military hurt by foundry ills

A few were incredibly inept:

Foundry institute shrinkage eyed
Amateur boat builders face problems
Industry needs help, ferret out foundry

Taste in Headlines

Newspapers must, of necessity, reveal man's sorrows as well as his joys, his afflictions as well as his strengths. No story or headline should mock those who have misfortunes. The newspaper belongs in the parlor where good taste is observed.

A story related that a Johannesburg motorist, whose car stalled on railroad tracks, died under the wheels of a train when he was unable to release his jammed seat belt. The victim may have been unknown to readers in an American community but death is a common tragedy and should be treated with respect, something the copyeditor forgot: **Belted to death.**

A minor story told about a man digging his own grave, starving while lying in it for twenty-one days and dying two hours after being found. The headline: **Down ... and then out.**

Another story related how a woman survived a 200-foot leap from a bridge, suffering only apparent minor injuries. Investigators said the woman landed in about four feet of water near shore. The item was insensibly headed: **Higher bridge needed.**

Heads with Double Meaning

A headline is unclear if it can imply more than one meaning. Some readers may grasp the meaning intended; others won't. An ad writer for a coffee company created a double meaning in this slogan: "The reason so many people buy Red & White Coffee is that 'They Know No Better.'"

Wake up / on women, / court told. Imagine the disappointment of some readers when they learn the story was nothing more than someone urging the court to be more aware of women's rights.

Boy struck by auto / in better condition. Than if he had been hit by a truck?

Rector sees sex as gourmet meal. He said people would be healthier if they looked on sex as a gourmet meal rather than something distasteful.

U.S. to close / one Air Force / base in Spain / Moron facility will shut in December. The facility is in Moron, Spain.

Rape classes planned. Rape will be the subject of the classes.

YWCA opens / public series / with abortion. Abortions will be discussed at the first class meeting.

Catlett takes credit / for Cincinnati's loss. Then who took the blame?

Flint mother-in-law / wounded in argument. That's better than being shot in the head.

Place names like Virgin, Utah; Fertile, Minn., and Bloomer, Wis., inevitably invite a two-faced headline if the town is used in the headline:

Virgin woman	**Pastor to wed**
gives birth	**Marblehead girl**
to twins	

Other geographical terms:

Book in pocket	**Three Boston**
saves man shot	**waitresses shot**
in South End	**in North End**

Unusual family names of officials—Love, Fortune, Dies, Church, Oyster—also invite two-faced headlines:

Oyster probes	**Picks Fortune**
unknown jam	**for Indiana**
	revenue chief

Wallace attacks	
U.S. grant	

Billy Hooks	**Fink heads bridge**
patient in Durham	**charity unit**

Winchell defies	**Slaughter recreates**
Hoffman and Dies	**Constantine's Rome**

Presidents and presidential candidates have been victims of two-faced heads:

Ike to get girls' calf

**Goose given to
Eisenhower**

**LBJ giving bull
to Mexican people**

**Johnson putting rusty
on White House green**

**Robert Kennedy
stoned**

Case and *chest* produce these headlines:

**Ord Phillips gets
two years in
cigarette case**

**Chest plea issued for
mothers' milk bank**

**Brentwood man held
in stolen watch case**

Suit has double-meaning:

**Publisher freed
in New Orleans
mayor's suit**

**Coors drops
union suit**

Lost wife found in suit

**Solon sees backfire
in union suit**

The worst possible headline verb is *eyes:*

**Frear resting,
eyes return**

**Green eyes
major title**

**Sidewalks to be eyed
in Elsmere**

**Alleged Rhodes
perjury said
eyed**

More double-takes in headlines:

**Five nudes pinched
at stag show**

**Patients feel
doctors pinch**

**Suspect's counsel
says: Winsett
quizzed in nude**

**Governors' seats
held key to south**

**Swine housing
to be aired**

**Flies to attend
wedding of son**

**Police slay suspect
bound over for trial**

**Top swine prize
to county youth**

**Publisher says
bar endangers
press freedom**

**N.J. Assembly
passes drunk
driving test**

**Club to serve
world culture**

**Relatives served
at family dinner**

**Proud Optimists
fathers have sons
at banquet**

**Man with two
broken legs saves
one from drowning**

**Bed aflame, jumps
from fourth floor**

**Colonel's wife found by
body / holding knife in
hand**

**Wiley tours sewage plant /
gathers ammunition for
fight / against diversion
move**

**Burned-out pupils
use old high school**

**Local option fast time
offered to skirt problem**

**Thieu to ask LBJ
for newer arms**

**Boy chasing fox
found rabid**

**Franklin pair
is improved
after shooting**

**Wife charges husband
killed her for money**

**Andalusia girl
improved after
drinking poison**

**W. Side woman
dies of burns;
mate critical**

**Expectant mother, 23,
is anxious for facts**

**Sex educator says
kindergarten's the
time**

**Being a parent
can be a trial**

**President says women
responding adequately**

**Wedding held
before families**

**New restrooms
big asset
for shoppers**

**Telluride women
donate pots
for airplanes**

**Engineers to hear
ground water talk**

Illegitimacy talks

The Art of Editing

No water— **so firemen improvised**	**DuPont hits Talbot** **on billboards**
Two accused **of kidnaping** **slain man**	**Boy hurt; runs** **into bleachers**
Admiral likes **to make waves**	**Pennsauken's safety chief** **quits blaming politics**
Bradley school **getting new head**	**Youth hangs self in cell** **after uncle tries to help**
Brown eyes race **against Humphrey**	**Heroin busts up**
Glacier Lake still **up in the air**	**Handicapped** **hearing set**
Chef says U.S. **courts ulcers**	**Man who shot himself** **accidentally dies**
U.S. capital does well **in booming Venezuela**	**Stores on 4th** **between Walnut and** **Chestnut to dress up rears**
Turnpike bonds may bar **state aid for Sound span**	**State hunts teeth** **in swimming ban**
Pentagon requests **cut by committee**	**Rev. Branford** **funeral fixed**

Even the women's pages contain two-faced headlines:

Italian cookies easy to make	**Guide, don't push child**
Fresh dates are great	**Nurses awarded for poster art**
O'Brien peas in squash	**Strong attire right for bill's death**
Male underwear **will reveal new** **colorful sights**	**Carries on for husband** **Designer's death blow to theater**

Some feature stories are constructed so that the climax comes at the end, rather than at the beginning, of the story. Obviously, if the point of the story is revealed in the headline, the story loses its effectiveness. The following story calls for a teaser head or

**Don't Give
Away the
Punchline**

Headline Requirements   87

even a title. The point was dramatically made in Billy Rose's column, *Pitching Horseshoes* (used with permission):

One Saturday afternoon not long ago a night watchman named Stan Mikalowsky was window-shopping with his 5-year-old daughter, Wanda, and as they passed a toy shop the child pointed excitedly to a doll nearly as big as she was.

The price tag was only $1 less than the watchman's weekly pay check, and his first impulse was to walk away, but when the youngster refused to budge he shrugged and led her into the store.

When Stan got home and unwrapped the doll, his wife was furious.

"We owe the butcher for three weeks and we're $10 short on the room rent," she said. "So you got to blow in a week's pay for a toy."

"What's the difference?" said the night watchman. "Doll or no doll, we're always behind. For once let the kid have something she wants."

One word led to many others and finally Stan put on his hat and stomped out of the house.

Mrs. Mikalowsky fed the child and put her to bed with the doll next to her and then, worried about Stan, decided to go looking for him at the corner bar and make up with him. To keep his supper warm, she left the gas stove on, and in her haste threw her apron over the back of a chair in such a way that one of the strings landed close to a burner.

Fifteen minutes later when the Mikalowskys came rushing out of the bar, their frame house was in flames and firemen had to restrain the father from rushing in to save his daughter.

"You wouldn't be any use in there," a cop told him. "Don't worry, they'll get her out."

Fireman Joe Miller, himself a father, climbed a ladder to the bedroom window, and the crowd hushed as he disappeared into the smoke. A few minutes later, coughing and blinking, he climbed down, a blanket-wrapped bundle in his arms. . . .

The local newspaper headlined its story with the line which a De Maupassant would undoubtedly have saved for the finish:

**Fireman rescues life-size doll
as child dies in flames**

7

Writing and Editing

Journalism has always attracted or produced good writers. The better ones today rank with the stars of yesterday. As a class, however, reporters are at best mediocre as writers, partly because they must write under pressure and partly because they are restricted by the straitjacket of structured news style.

Narrative Writing

The mechanics of newspaper publishing have had something to do with the traditional style of news presentation. Advertising has had first priority in the page forms, with the remaining space accommodating editorial matter. Too often, makeup has controlled the length of the story, not the content of the story itself. Trimming has been from the bottom, thus forcing the inverted pyramid form, the "hugger-mugger" lead and details in descending importance.

Now that it is possible through computers to store both ads and editorial material until final makeup or to rearrange the makeup pattern, editorial material can have priority. Indiscriminate trims and plugs with inane fillers are no longer necessary. No story need be robbed of important and interesting details that may appear near the bottom of the story.

Stories need not be longer but they should give more serious treatment to a wider range of topics. Some executives see an increasing application of the narrative, magazine style to the newspaper story. There may be no news peg at all, but rather a wealth of new and interesting information that will make it news nevertheless.

Some of these concepts already have been tried successfully.

Some news events heavily covered by television have been presented in the narrative rather than in the traditional news style. An example of the narrative approach:

MADRID (UPI)—"You will write about me and my photo will be published on every front page," boasted 16-year-old Mariano Garcia two years ago. "I will be a great bull fighter one day."

This was his dream and the theme he returned to time and again during our 200-mile drive from Saragossa to Madrid.

It was on Feb. 23, 1964, in the outskirts of Saragossa that Mariano had asked me for a ride.

"I want to go to Madrid and start a career as a bull fighter," the boy said in the accents of his native Mancha.

Mariano's was a classic story of Spain: The eager youth deserting the misery of his sun-baked village with its white-washed walls for the danger and glory of the bull ring.

When he learned that I was a newsman, Mariano pulled a pencil stub and sort of calling card out of his pocket. The card bore an amateurish sketch of the Virgin Mary and Jesus. Across it he scrawled his name in bold letters.

"The Virgin and the Christ are my protectors," he said.

Then he talked with wide-eyed dreaminess of how the bull paws the ground with his left forefoot when excited, of his sudden charges, of the secrets of the matador's capework and of the "pata, rabo y orejas"—the hoofs, tail and ears of the bull—the highest honors the fickle Spanish crowd can pay a matador.

For two years, Mariano tried to get a start on the road to fame and fortune. It came not in Madrid, but at San Martin de Lavega.

The bull he met Thursday was six years old, fat, limping, and the sharp tips of his horns had been clipped. But the old bull could be dangerous. He had survived the ring once and remembered well how the matador evaded his charges and the hooking of his horns.

Mariano made three or four passes with his cape. But the bull was old and the boy was young and the fickle crowd was bored.

"Just a meletilla," some shouted, "just a beginner."

Another matador stepped in to divert the bull. But the animal had his eyes fixed on Mariano. Suddenly, he charged the boy and knocked him down.

Then the old bull drove his blunted left horn into Mariano's skull.

It was a quick kill, as the good matador's sword should be quick.

Mariano Garcia's mother and father carried his body in a blood-stained sheet to the local cemetery. And today I wrote the story Mariano promised I would write.

This type of storytelling has the quality once described by Earl J. Johnson of UPI: "to hold the reader's interest and stimulate some imaginaton to see, feel and understand the news."

Business and financial news may not be the most glamorous of subjects for most readers but *The Wall Street Journal* knows how to make such stories compelling. Here's an example of the Journal's personalized lead:

By William M. Bulkeley
Staff Reporter of *The Wall Street Journal*

GRAND RAPIDS, Mich.—The other morning Joachim Krassowski was inspecting an envelope of gray duck down when he spotted a lowly brown feather among the fluff. "It's a chicken feather," he declared with the disdain of a jeweler who has just discovered a rhinestone in a diamond tiara.

It's Mr. Krassowski's job to discover such aberrations. That's because he's a professional feather judger at North American Feather Co., one of the nation's largest independent feather brokers, which these days is doing a heavy business in the lightweight commodity . . . .

The page 1 feature carried this head: **Here's a Fluffy Story / About Joe Being Up / When All Is Down.**

Unfortunately, many news accounts are fact-recitals, not stories. "Most newspaper writing is, well, not writing at all," a veteran managing editor told the authors. "I spent 17 years as managing editor of a good Knight newspaper, the Charlotte *Observer*. During most of that time I looked at reporters through water-filmed eyes, begging them to boil it down, sharpen it, weed out redundancies, drop driblets of imagery in there. Finally I just up and left, roamed the country, trying to do it myself."

Edwin Newman, author of *Strictly Speaking*, deplores the degradation of the language and asks, "Will America be the death of English?" He argues that it may be too much to hope for the stilted and pompous phrase, the slogan and the cliché to be banished, but argues that they should not dominate the language.

The message was even more forcibly put by Wallace Carroll, editor and publisher of the Winston-Salem *Journal & Sentinel*.

The bastardization of our mother tongue is really a disaster for all of us in the news business. The English language is our bread and butter, but when ground glass is mixed with flour and grit with the butter, our customers are likely to lose their appetite for what we serve them.

Our job is to interpret—to translate. Yet our translators—that is our reporters and copyeditors—find it more and more difficult to do this basic job of translation. To begin with, they reach us from universities that are tending to become glorified jargon factories; and for four years or more they have been immured in a little cosmos where jargon is too often mistaken for knowledge or wisdom.[1]

No one can teach another how to develop a writing style. But writers can follow a few simple rules to make their writing clear and readable, if not literary. George Orwell listed six rules[2]:

1. Never use a metaphor, simile, or other figure of speech which you are used to seeing in print.
2. Never use a long word where a short one will do.

---

[1] *The Bulletin of the American Society of Newspaper Editors*, p. 2 (May 1970).
[2] *Shooting an Elephant and Other Essays* (London: Secker and Warburg, 1950), p. 100.

3. If it is possible to cut a word out, always cut it out.

4. Never use the passive where you can use the active.

5. Never use a foreign phrase, a scientific word, or a jargon word if you can think of an everyday English equivalent.

6. Break any of these rules sooner than say anything outright barbarous.

Other rules:

1. Use direct quotes for color, pace and emphasis.

2. When you use adjectives and adverbs, pinpoint them. It doesn't mean much to say an apple is round but it does when you describe it as being wormy.

3. Keep the paragraphs short.

4. Be human. Relate your writing to people.

Copyeditors have no business changing a writer's style. But copyeditors have every obligation to insist that the story be correct in spelling, grammar and syntax: It is their duty to make copy compact and readable.

Most copy can be tightened. Even if only a few words in a paragraph are removed, the total saving in space will be considerable. Some stories, notably material from the wires and syndicates, can be trimmed sharply. But the copyeditor should not overedit. If a story is so poorly organized it has to be rewritten, the story should be returned to the department editor. Rewriting is not a copyeditor's job. Nor should the copyeditor make picayunish changes. Indiscreet butchering of local copy is a sure way to damage morale in the newsroom.

Common Errors

A survey of several newspaper internal publications suggests that the following are among the most common errors that get by the copydesk:

Spelling Errors

Doubtless one reason so many misspelled words get by the desk is that copyeditors themselves can't recognize incorrect spelling, even of simple words. (See Appendix I for list of words frequently misspelled.) Here are but a few examples (correct spelling in parentheses):

accutely (acutely)
alledged (alleged)
alright (all right)

bellweather (bellwether)

brillant (brilliant)
chairmenships (chairman-
ships)
chieftans (chieftains)

committment (commitment)
compatable (compatible)
confidance (confidence)

controversey (controversy)
demagogery (demagoguery)

descendent (descendant)

disasterous (disastrous)

fiesty (feisty)

fugative (fugitive)
hyroglyph (hieroglyph)
intoxification (intoxication)

kibbutzers (kibitzers)

log-jamb (logjam)

paronoia (paranoia)

preemptory (peremptory)
prostrate surgery (prostate)

publically (publicly)

rappell (rappel)

After the Fact (Louisville [Ky.] *Courier-Journal*) lamented, **Disagreeables**
"Everybody knows that subjects and verbs should come in
matched pairs; singulars together and plurals together. But,
sadly, we let too many unmarriageables slip into the paper."
Examples:

There are two things that either Sloane or Hollenbach have... The
thought is: "...things that Sloane has or that Hollenbach has." Remember, when nouns are connected by either/or, neither/nor, ONLY
the noun closest to the verb should be considered in deciding whether
a singular or plural verb is required. If the second half of the noun is
singular, use a singular verb, and vice versa.
...the continuing lag in industrial production and the rise in unemployment is a result of inflation. (are)
An American Bar Association accreditation team six years ago, and
more recently a citizens' panel, have both recommended this. "Team"
is the subject; the verb must be "has." Parenthetical matter should be
ignored in selecting the number of the verb.
Ethington pulled a couple of hands from a basket and waved it...
(them)
It's moved to a point where the anxiety and the concern is unrealistic.
(are)
The monotony of the concrete walls painted in dull green and blue are
broken only... (is)
A two-thirds vote by both houses of Congress and ratification by three-
quarters of the states is necessary. (are)
...the Mormon church is like a huge tent, and each of the local units
are like the stakes that hold a tent in the ground. (is like stakes. When in
doubt, pick out the subject and predicate to make sure that they agree
in number. Don't let intervening words or phrases trip you up.)
The requests chairman said that only one letter was from someone
attributing their interest to... (his—or her)

"Since the investigation began," she said, "they (the FBI) has hit (questioned) all the lesbian feminists in town." Surely she didn't say "they has hit."

He said it is not necessary for the caller to give their number to police. (his—or her)

Strack contends that the activity of Boyer and his group and the accompanying bad publicity has cut down on the expansion of the park . . . (Reporters getting their numbers wrong often confuse the subject with a noun closer to the verb. Remembering that might help reporters to avoid such mistakes, but it would not explain why the mistakes get past copyeditors.)

The number of the verb to use with per cent or percentage is governed by the number of the noun that follows per cent or percentage, or is understood to follow them. "Forty per cent of his estate is in securities," "large percentage of the patients are children."

Word Clutter

Clutter words dirty a paper, waste space and get in the reader's way. Every day, stories die on the overhook because strings of clutter words didn't die at the typewriter or on the copydesk.

Reporters should be whacked when they write:

She was on the operating table from 8 *p.m.* last night until 5 *a.m.* this morning.

For mankind, *the biologists who study genetics* seem to offer . . . (geneticists).

He was a Democratic nominee for *U.S.* Congress from the 7th *Congressional* District in 1970 but lost in the *final* election to *incumbent* Rep. Donald W. Riegle Jr. (Not everyone can get four redundancies into one sentence.)

He said the USDA is *currently* spending . . .

Justice said Double Spring had been *in the process of* phasing out its operation . . .

Hayley has some 30 *different* (fish) tanks in his home.

Retired Adm. Jackson R. Tate slipped away to a secret retreat yesterday for his *first meeting* with the daughter *he has never met* . . . (Say it once and stop.)

Compression is one of the cardinal virtues in all writing. Compression means shortcuts to ideas. "It is always a baffling thing" becomes "It always baffles," thus saving some words and changing a weak verb into a strong one. "The field is 50 feet in length" should be "The field is 50 feet long." "He is said to be resentful" means simply "He is said to resent."

Pacing is gained by substituting short words for long words and single words for phrases: "big" for "enormous," "find" for "discover," "approving" for "applying its stamp of approval," "Smith's failure" for "the fact that Smith had not succeeded," "fieldwork" for "work in the field."

Compression eliminates the superfluous: "pledged *to secrecy* not to disclose," "wrote a formal letter of resignation" ("resigned"), "read from a *prepared* statement," "go into details" ("elaborate"). A few words may say a lot; a lot of words may say little.

Most copyeditors can add to the following list of circumlocutions.

A bolt of lightning (lightning)
A great number of times (often, frequently)
A greater number of (more)
A little less than (almost)
A small number of (few)
A large number of (many)
A period of several weeks (several weeks)
A sufficient number of (enough)
Absolute guarantee (guarantee)
Accidentally stumbled (stumbled)
Acres of land (acres)
Add an additional (add)
Added fillip (fillip)
Advance planning (planning)
Advance reservations (reservations)
All of a sudden (suddenly)
Already existing (existing)
Ample enough (ample)
Angry mob (mob)
Any one of the two (either)
Apartheid segregation (either, but not both)
Armed robbery (robbery)
Arrived here (arrived)
As a general rule (usually)
As for example (for example)
As in the case of (like)
Assessed a fine (fined)
At a later date (later)
At that time (then)
At the present time (now)
At which time (when)
At regular intervals of time (regularly)
At some future date (sometime, later)
At the hour of noon (at noon)
At 12 noon (at noon)
At 12 midnight (at midnight)
At the conclusion of (after)
At a meeting held here (at a meeting here)
At the corner of 16th and Elm (at 16th and Elm)
At the rear of (behind)
Auction sale (auction)

Baby boy was born (boy was born)
Bald-headed (bald)

Basic fundamentals (fundamentals)
Bitter quarrel (quarrel)
Bouquet of flowers (bouquet)
Brought to a sudden halt (halted)
Brown-colored cloth (brown cloth)

Called attention to the fact (reminded)
Came to a stop (stopped)
Canary bird (canary)
Cannot be possible (cannot be)
Climb up (climb)
Close scrutiny (scrutiny)
Collie dog (Collie)
Combine into one (combine)
Commute back and forth (commute)
Complete monopoly (monopoly)
Completely decapitated (decapitated)
Completely destroyed (destroyed)
Completely filled (filled)
Completely surrounded (surrounded)
Contain the blaze and keep it from spreading (keep the blaze from spreading)
Consensus of opinion (consensus)
Continue on (continue)
Controversial disputes (disputes)
Cost the sum of $5 (cost $5)
Current trend (trend)

Dead body (body)
Despite the fact that (although)
Detailed information (details)
Different kinds (kinds)
Disclosed for the first time (disclosed)
Draw to a close (end)
Due to the fact that (because, since)
During the predawn hours (before dawn)
During the time that (then, while, as)
During the winter months (during the winter)
Dwindled down (dwindled)

Easter Sunday (Easter)
Empty cavity (cavity)
End result (result)
Ended his talk (concluded)
Entered a bid of (bid)
Entire monopoly (monopoly)
Entirely destroyed (destroyed)
Equally as (equally)
Established precedent (precedent)
Estimated at about (estimated at)
Estimated roughly at
  (estimated at)
Exact replica (replica)
Exchanged wedding vows
  (married)
Expressed the belief (said)

Fellow classmates (classmates)
Few in number (few)
Filled to capacity (filled)
Final climax (climax)
Finally ended (ended)
First began (began)
First priority (priority)
First prototype (prototype)
Fishing trawler (trawler)
Flaming inferno (inferno)
Floor carpeting (carpeting)
For a period of 10 days (for
  10 days)
For a short space of time (for
  a short time)
For the purpose of advancing
  (to advance)
Foreign imports (imports)
Free gift (gift)
Free pass (pass)
Full-size replica (replica)
Fused back together (fused)
Future plans (plans)

General conclusion (conclusion)
General public (public)
Gemini twins (Gemini)
Golden wedding anniversary
  (golden wedding)
Grand total (total)
Guest speaker (speaker)

Heat up (heat)
Hidden pitfall (pitfall)
Hostile antagonist (antagonist)
Hot water heater (water heater)
Huge throng (throng)
Human being (human)

If that were the case (if so)
Important essentials (essentials)
Incumbent governor (governor)
In addition to (and, besides, also)

In back of (behind)
In case of (if, concerning)
In excess of (more)
In order to balance (to balance)
In respect to (about, on)
In the absence of (without)
In the near future (soon)
In the not too distant future
  (eventually)
In the event that (if)
In the immediate vicinity of (near)
In the neighborhood of (about)
In view of the fact that
  (considering)
Indicted on a charge (indicted)
Informed those attending the
  meeting (said)
Introduced a new (introduced)
Introduced for the first time
  (introduced)
Invited guests (guests)
Is going to (will)
Is a resident of Dover (lives
  in Dover)
Is in the process of making
  application (is applying)
Is of the opinion that (believes)
Is opposed to (opposes)

Jewish rabbi (rabbi)

Kept an eye on (watched)
Kept steady company (kept
  company)
Kept under surveillance
  (watched)
Killed outright (killed)

Large-sized man (large man)
Last of all (last)
Lift up (lift)
Long chronic illness (long
  illness, chronic illness)

Made an investigation of
  (investigated)
Made good his escape (escaped)
Major portion of (most of)
Married his wife (was married)
Massive size (massive)
Matinee performance (matinee)
Meet for the selection of (meet
  to select)
Mental telepathy (telepathy)
Merged together (merged)
Midway between (between)
Murals on the walls (murals)

New bride (bride)
New construction (construction)

New innovation (innovation)
New record (record)
New recruit (recruit)
Newly created (new)
None at all (none)
Noon luncheon (luncheon)
Not any one of the two (neither)
Not difficult (easy)
Null and void (void)

Off of (off)
Official business (business)
Officiated at the ceremony
(officiated)
Old adage (adage)
Old cliché (cliché)
Old pioneer (pioneer)
Old traditions of the past
(traditions)
On a stretch of road (on a road)
On account of (because)
On behalf of (for)
On two different occasions (twice)
Once in a great while
(seldom, rarely)
Opens its session Monday
(opens Monday)

Partially damaged (damaged)
Partially destroyed (damaged)
Past experience (experience)
Past history (history)
Past records (records)
Period of time (period)
Personal charm (charm)
Personal friendship (friendship)
Placed its seal of approval on
(approved)
Portable walkie-talkie
(walkie-talkie)
Possibly might (might)
Postponed until later (postponed)
Preprogrammed (programmed)
Prerecorded (recorded)
Present incumbent (incumbent)
Presently planned (planned)
Prior to (before)
Private business (business)
Private contractor (contractor)
Private industry (industry)
Probed into (probed)
Promoted to the rank of
(promoted)
Proposed project (project)
Put in an appearance (appeared)

Qualified expert (expert)

Receded back (receded)

Received his education at
(attended)
Recur again (recur)
Reduce down (reduce)
Refer back (refer)
Regular weekly meeting (meeting)
Rejected a proposal (refused)
Remand back (remand)
Repeat again (repeat)
Reported to the effect that
(reported)
Revise downward (lower)
Rio Grande River (Rio Grande)
Rise up (rise)
Rose to the defense of (defended)
Rough rule of thumb (rule
of thumb)
Rustic country (rustic or country)

Sahara Desert (Sahara)
Self-confessed (confessed)
Served as toastmaster (was
toastmaster)
Short space of time (short time)
Sierra Mountains (Sierras)
Since the time when (since)
Soaked to the skin (soaked)
Specific example (example)
Split in the middle (split)
Sprung a surprise (surprised)
Square-shaped (square)
Started off with (started with)
Still persists (persists)
Strangled to death (strangled)
Suddenly collapsed (collapsed)
Suddenly exploded (exploded)
Summer season (summer)
Surprising upset (upset)
Sworn affidavits (affidavits)

Taken to the hospital for treatment
(taken to the hospital)
Temporary recess (recess)
Tendered his resignation
(resigned)
Therapeutic treatment
(therapy or treatment)
There is no doubt that (doubtless)
Thorough investigation
(investigation)
Threatened walkout averted
(walkout averted)
Told his listeners that (said)
Total operating costs (operating
costs)
True facts (facts)
Two twins (twins)

Underground subway (subway)

United in holy matrimony (married)
Unsolved problem (problem)
Until and unless (unless)
Upward adjustment (increase)

Violent explosion (explosion)
Voiced objections (objected)

Well-known traditions (traditions)

Went on to say (continued, added)
Went up in flames (burned)
When and if (if)
Whether or not (whether)
Widow of the late (widow)
Widow woman (widow)
With the exception of (except)

Young juveniles (juveniles)

Wrong Words Good reporters are meticulous in presenting the facts for a story. Others are not so precise in their choice of words. By habit, they write "compose" when they mean "comprise," "affect" when they want "effect," "credible" for "creditable." They use "include," then list all the elements.

Each time a word is misused it loses some of its value as a precision tool. AP reported that "U.S. officials connived with ITT." There was no connivance, which means closing one's eyes to wrongdoing. The precise word should have been "conspired."

Note these examples that got by the copydesk:

Somehow Schnitzelburg never quite lost its dominating German influence. ("Dominating" is a verb; it can't do the work of an adjective. "Dominant" would do.)

He has been an "intricate part of the general community" ... (The writer meant "integral," meaning essential.)

The two officers are charged with dispersing corporate funds .... (The word is "disburse"—to pay out, to expend. Disperse means to scatter in various directions; distribute widely.")

An election challenger "kept raising a lot of cane," the story said. (It's Cain, with a capital "C," after the sibling-slayer.)

The head and lead said the shooting was Russian roulette. Body of story said police were holding a companion who allegedly held the gun against the victim's chest. (That is not the way you play Russian roulette.)

A story indicating that a man might not be qualified for his job says: "Miller refutes all that," and then he says why he is capable. ("Denies" would have been much better.)

A football pass pattern was referred to as a "flair out." ("Flair" means a natural talent or aptitude. The word is "flare" or expanding outward in shape or configuration.")

Sen. Wendell Ford was presiding officer of the Senate yesterday, a familiar roll for him. . . (The word is "role.")

". . . the Ontario provisional government. . ." as Geoff Vincent noted, "There has been a coup in Toronto." (It's "provincial.")

Mrs. Reece, a spritely woman . . . She may be a sprite—an elf or pixie—but what the writer probably meant was "sprightly"—full of life.)

His testimony about the night preceding the crime was collaborated, in part, by his mother. . . ("corroborated," perhaps?)

The MSD could be the biggest benefactor in Kentucky under a . . . reimbursement program. (It should be "beneficiary," one who receives; benefactor is the giver.)

The Art of Editing

The new hospital has spot lighting to give plenty of illumination to a late reader while letting his bed-neighbor go to sleep. (What he means is next-bed neighbor.)

The zoo is planning a program to propagate extinct animals.

Two of the nation's top automotive executives have criticized federal regulations as a way to improve highway safety. (The writer meant they would retard progress in automotive safety.)

Other terms frequently misused follow.

Absenteeism—"While pupil absenteeism in Cleveland public schools was not unusual, the survey showed that in some areas far more teachers than usual were out." Sometimes the word we use is technically correct but it gives the wrong connotation. By usage, the word *absenteeism* has come to mean deliberate, unnecessary absence. The word *absences* would have been better.

Adopted, passed—resolutions are adopted or approved; bills are passed. In legislative jargon, *passed* also can mean passed by for the day or for that meeting.

Aggravate, irritate—the first means to make worse. The second means to incite or provoke.

And, but—**State treasurer is Democrat but also servant of people,** the headline said. The implication here is that the official is a servant of the people despite the fact that he's a Democrat.

After, following—The first means next in time. The second means next in order.

Allude, refer—the first suggests without naming the thing specifically. The second names specifically.

Alternative, alternate—the first involves a choice. The second means in turns.

Amateur, novice—an *amateur* is a nonprofessional. A *novice* is a beginner.

Anesthesia—"Creighton had not even received anesthesia." The patient does not receive anesthesia. *Anesthesia* is the condition produced by an anesthetic.

Automated, mechanized—there is a tendency to write of things as automated where the thing is merely mechanized. *Automation* refers to the automatic control of machines.

Avenge, revenge—*avenge* for another. *Revenge* for self.

Bale, bail—a farmer's hay is *baled;* water is *bailed* out of a boat; a prisoner is released on *bail.* (*Bond* is cash or property given as a security for an appearance or for some performance.)

Belabor, labor—when one needlessly or tiresomely presses a point of argument or explanation he is laboring it. To *belabor* is to beat, hit or whip, primarily in the physical sense. A second meaning of *belabor* is to beat with words, perhaps repetitiously and perhaps even with considerable emphasis, but still by no means beating anyone with words.

Before, prior to—"Police said Trumbull's car went through a stop sign prior to the accident and that the investigation is continuing." *Before* is a thoroughly acceptable word.

Biannual, biennial—the first means twice a year. The second means every two years. The copyeditor could help the reader by substituting "every six months" for *biannual* and "every other year" for *biennial*.

Bills, legislation—"The President announced he will send Congress legislation aimed at liberalizing trade with Eastern Europe." *Legislation* is the laws enacted by a legislative power. The President, of course, is not such a power. What he sends to Congress is proposed legislation or bills.

Callus, callous—the first is the noun. The second is the adjective. Similarly: mucus, mucous; phosphorus, phosphorous.

Canvas, canvass—the first is a cloth. The second means to solicit.

Celebrant, celebrator—a *celebrant* presides over a religious rite. A *celebrator* celebrates.

Center around—something can be centered in, centered at or centered on, but it cannot be centered around.

Chafe, chaff—*chafe* means to irritate. The heating appliance is a chafing dish. *Chaff* means to ridicule good-naturedly. It also means husks or rubbish.

Coiffeur, coiffure—"It seems that a few females in this city want to be able to change coiffeurs, depending on the occasion, the same way women in general change clothes." No. What they want to change is their *coiffures*. A good coiffeur is too hard to find. A *coiffeur* is a hair-dresser. A *coiffure* is the style of hair dress.

Collision—"Cars driven by Robert F. Clagett and Mrs. Lois Trant were damaged yesterday when they collided on Denison Ave. Stonington police reported that Mrs. Trant stopped her car before making a turn into Isham St. and it was hit in the rear by the other vehicle." Two objects can *collide* only when both are in motion and going—usually but not always—in opposite directions. It is not a *collision* when one car is standing still.

Combine—"Maid o' Silk combined the spirit of old America in a modern dress for this year's holiday offering." When you combine you must put together at least two things. What Maid o' Silk did was to embody the spirit of old America in a modern dress—or convey it, or wrap it, or achieve it.

Compared to, compared with—the first uses specific similarities or differences: "He *compared* Johnson with Wilson." The second notes general or metaphysical resemblance: "You might *compare* him to a weasel."

Comprise, compose—*comprise* is not synonymous with *compose,* but actually almost its opposite. "The secretaries of State, Defense, Interior and other departments compose the cabinet." That is, they constitute it. "The cabinet comprises the secretaries of the State, Defense, Interior and other departments." That is, it includes, embraces, contains them.

Concert, recital—two or more performers give a *concert*. One performer gives a *recital*.

Conclude—arguments *conclude*. Speeches close or end.

Conscious, aware—we are *conscious* of what we feel, and *aware* of what we know.

Continuous, continual—if it rains steadily every day for a week it rains *continuously*. If it rains only part of every day for a week it rains *continually* or intermittently.

Cords, chords—the first refers to a string or small rope, an anatomical structure such as a spinal cord or vocal *cord*. Or it may be ribbed fabric or a unit of volume of wood. A *chord* is a string of a musical instrument or a combination of tones.

Couturier, couturiere—the first is a male. The second is a female.

Damage, damages—the first means loss or harm; the second is a legal word meaning money paid or ordered to be paid as compensation for loss or injury—the plural has no other meaning.

Dedication—"The dedication that Rev. Mr. Davis had for his mission was instilled early by his mother." *Dedication* means act or rite of dedication to a sacred use. What Mrs. Davis may have done was instill a sense of dedication in her young son's mind.

Deign—"How this case will eventually be decided we do not deign to say." *Deign* means to condescend, not dare or care.

Derelict—"'Lake Erie is so big,' Frank Kelly kept saying to his companion in their derelict 16-foot boat which had no power, no lights, no food." For a boat to be *derelict*, it has to be abandoned.

Details—"United States military spokesmen gave little details about the raids on the north." If you give little *details* you give much detail, but if you give few details you give little detail.

Disrobe—a haughty way of saying undress, unless done by royalty, priests and judges.

Ecology, environmental—ecology is concerned with the interrelationships of organisms and their environment. Environmental refers to conditions or forces that influence or modify surroundings.

Enormity—applies preferably to abnormal wickedness, but is often misused to mean enormousness.

Epitaph, epithet—the first is an inscription on a tombstone. *Epithet* is a descriptive adjective applied to someone—"old curmudgeon."

Escapees, escapers—the dictionary recognizes both. Why not settle for *fugitives*?

Farther, further—the distinction is between extension of space and expansion of thought.

Flaunt, flout—the first means to wave or flutter showily. The second means to mock or treat with contempt. "The students *flouted* the authority of the school board."

Flounder, founder—horses *flounder*—struggle, thrash about—in the mud. Ships *founder* or sink. Of course, horses can founder when they become disabled from overeating.

Fluoride, fluorine—stories have referred to water being fluoridated by the use of *fluoride*. The element is *fluorine* and the medium through which it is introduced into the water is one of a number of fluorides. Say, simply, "a fluoride is used."

Fulsome—fulsome praise is insincere praise, not copious. It means offensively excessive, insincere.

For example—"By eliminating the uncertainty of erratic weather the growers were able to develop stronger plants and better flowers. Jones' orchid seedlings, for example, are shipped to such distant points as Australia, Hawaii and South America." The distance to which they are shipped may be related to their strength and quality, but it isn't an *example* of that unless set forth in those terms, something like this: "Jones' orchid seedlings, for example, have successfully survived shipments and transplantings to points as distant as Australia."

Fortunate, fortuitous—the first means coming by good luck. The second means happening by chance.

Gantlet, gauntlet—you run a *gantlet,* a form of punishment. You put on a *gauntlet* or glove.

Gendarme—this is not the proper title for a Paris police officer. A city policeman is an *agent de police; gendarme* is reserved for the small-town officer.

Gibe, jibe—the first is to jeer, taunt or flout. The second means to shift sails, alter a course or, colloquially, to be in harmony.

Gorilla, guerrilla—the first is an ape. The second is a soldier or raider.

Grant, subsidy—a *grant* is money given to public companies. A *subsidy* is help to a private enterprise.

Grizzly, grisly—"Miss Karmel begins her work in a valley of shadows that deepen and darken as she heaps one grizzly happening upon the next." One *grizzly* heaped upon the next produces only two angry bears. The word the writer wants is *grisly*.

Half-mast, half-staff—masts are on ships. Flagstaffs are on buildings or on the ground.

Hardy, hearty—a story of four visiting policemen from Africa said they expressed appreciation for their hardy welcome. If that's what they said, they meant *hearty*.

Haul, hale—the first means to drag. The second means to take (haled into court).

Historic, historical—*historic* means famous in history; *historical* pertains to history, such as historic sites and historical novels. *Historic* is an overworked adjective used to describe an event that may or may not find a place in history.

Honor, celebrate—"The dinner was in honor of Brown's 50 years in the business." The dinner honored Brown, not his years in business. Use *celebrated* or *observed*.

Hopeful, hopefully—incorrect for "it is hoped" or "I hope." Literally, "in a hopeful manner."

Impassable, impassible—the first is that which cannot be passed. The second is that which can't suffer or be made to show signs of emotion.

Imply, infer—the speaker does the *implying,* and the listener the *inferring.*

In charge of—the person is in charge of the thing rather than vice versa.

Loath, loathe—the first means unwilling. The second means to hate.

Masterly, masterful—the first means skillful. The second means domineering.

Mean, median—in temperature, *mean* is the average of the extremes. If the high is 80 and the low is 50, the mean is 65. *Median* means that half are above a certain point, half below. *Average* is the sum of the units divided by the number of units. It also is now used to mean typical or ordinary.

Measles—a child has measles, not the measles. So, too, with mumps. Treat both as singular: *"Measles* is a virus disease."

Meticulous—"Attending physicians attribute the fact that she is still alive to the meticulous and devoted nursing she receives from her mother." As used here, *meticulous* is intended to mean careful, painstaking, watchful, vigilant, etc. It doesn't mean any of those things. On the contrary, it means being overcareful, finical or fussy about trivialities. In fact, a meticulous person really is a fuss-budget.

Negotiate—"He could not negotiate the hill in front of the hospital." You *negotiate* a loan or a treaty; you climb a hill.

Numbered—"Numbered among the pioneers of the industry is George Blandish." Can't tell the pioneers without a number?

Oral, verbal—all language is *verbal*—"of words." But only *oral* language is spoken. Verbal refers to the written form.

Peaceable, peaceful—the first is restricted to persons. The second is restricted to periods and countries.

People, persons—*person* is the human being. *People* are the body of persons—"American people." There is no rule saying a large number can't be referred to as *people*—"61 million people."

Plunge—"A dramatic cold front zipped through the city at 9 a.m. today plunging the thermometer 17 degrees in 25 minutes." Plunge the mercury or the temperature, but not the poor thermometer.

Podium, lectern—the first is a footstool or platform. The second is what speakers thump.

Populous, populated, populace—"Miss O'Brien's home is in a populated area in the center of town." Use *populous. Populace* means the common people of a community.

Predict—"Present and anticipated demand for goods indicates that last year should be another record-breaking year, officials of the firm predicted." You don't *predict* that something "already is."

Presently—this means after a little time or shortly. It does not mean at the present time. Try *currently* or *now*.

Prophecy, prophesy—the first is a noun. The second is a verb.

Quell, quench—uprisings, disorders, riots and the like are quelled. A fire—because water is the chief agency for putting it out—is *quenched,* doused, extinguished.

Raise, rear, raze—you raise animals and rear children. *Raze* means to destroy.

Ravage, ravish—the first means to damage or devastate. Armies may *ravage* a town. *Ravish* has several meanings—to fill with joy, to carry off by force, to rape. A ravishing blonde is enchanting.

Realtor—this is a registered trade name. It should be capitalized and used only to designate members of the National Association of Real Estate Boards.

Retire, resign, replace—*replace* for *retire* is a cold, curt and cruel word with which to publicly acknowledge years of faithful and interested service. Subtle differences in words can be important. To say that someone has quit a job when he resigned to accept another suggests that he left in a huff.

Roughshod, slipshod—"Mrs. Lawless told the *News* that traffic runs slipshod over her property." She meant *roughshod,* didn't she? *Slipshod* means slovenly.

Sewage, sewerage—*sewage* is human waste, sometimes called municipal or sanitary waste. *Sewerage* is the system to carry away sewage. They are sewerage (not sewage) plants. Industrial waste is the waste matter from factories. Some cities have storm sewers to carry away rain water and sanitary sewers for sewage.

Scheduled—"The meeting is scheduled next Saturday." When referring to an event in the future, the word *scheduled* must have a preposition after it, usually *for.*

Smith, smithy—*Smith* is the blacksmith. *Smithy* is the blacksmith shop.

Stanch, staunch—The first is a verb. The second is an adjective.

Sustenance, subsistence—"The two survived despite little besides melted snow for subsistence." No wonder they almost starved. The word is *sustenance.*

Tall, high—properly, a building, tree or man is *tall.* A plane, bird or cloud is *high.*

That, which—use *that* in a dependent clause: "This is the house that Jack built." In an independent clause, *which* is correct: "Jack's house, which has been in the same family for nearly a century, has been sold."

Total—may be either singular or plural as idiom dictates. When the word is itself the subject, treat it as singular when it has a definite article and as plural when it has an indefinite article. "The total of boxes found looted was eight." "A total of eight boxes were found looted." "A total of 239 Negroes have been jailed in Selma."

Little words can cause as much trouble as big ones. When a reporter can't decide which of two points is the more worthy of attention, he resorts to journalese by writing both into the lead, connecting them with *as*. "The school tax referendum was approved last night by a margin of nearly 18,000 votes as a strong campaign by anti-busing groups to defeat the increase failed." **Little Words**
Other examples:

Due to—incorrectly used at the beginning of a sentence or as a preposition. It must always modify a noun: His absence was due to illness. It should not be used in the sense of "because of." It is not a substitute for "owing to."

Feel—save the word *feel* for touching and feeling things and stop using it as a synonym for *think* or *believe*.

Held—o.k. if you can hold it in your hand. "The meeting will be at 7 p.m." (Not "will be held . . .")

In, into—if you're in the lake and feel like jumping, you jump in the lake. If you're in a boat on the lake and feel like jumping overboard, you jump into the lake.

Kin—relatives collectively, not as individuals.

Kudos—"The kudos in design . . . go to the creators of goods and services." *Kudos* is a singular noun and is generally considered humorous or colloquial.

Last, latest, past—last few days, in the past, his latest book.

Lay, lie—lay is transitive; it takes an object. "Watch as I *lay* the book on the table." Past tense is *laid;* present participle is *laying;* past participle is *laid. Lie* is intransitive; it takes no object. "The books *lie* on the table." Past tense is *lay;* present participle is *lying;* past participle is *lain.*

Less, fewer—*less* with amount; *fewer* with numbers. "Less sugar, fewer miles." *Fewer* means not so many. *Less* means not so much in quantity and not so very good in quality.

Like, as—reporters shouldn't use *like* as a conjunction as the Winston cigarette commercial does. Use *as*, a conjunction, to introduce a noun or pronoun of comparison; use *like*, a preposition, to introduce a clause or phrase of comparison. "You should heed his advice, as most of us do, like good boys and girls." "If you are like me you will do as I do." "Smells like a rose." "Looks as you would like to look."

None—often takes the singular verb, as do the following: *each, each one, everybody, everyone, nobody*. But if the distributive expression is followed by a plural noun, *none* should take a plural verb. "None of the volcanoes in Chile are active." When the meaning is "not one" it is better to use *not one* than *none* with a singular verb.

On, over—a person is hit *on* the head, not *over* it; or slapped *on* the face, not *about* the face.

Only—almost invariably this word is misplaced, thus altering the meaning of the sentence. Notice the changes in meaning by placing *only* in the following: "I hit him in the eye yesterday."

Prone—if a man is lying prone on the beach, nobody can step on his stomach. *Prone* means lying face down. *Supine* means lying face up.

Via—it means "by way of," not "by means of."

Would, could, should—a judge was quoted as saying a boy would remain in an institution until his eighteenth birthday. Actually, the judge sentenced the boy to an indefinite term and said he could remain there until his eighteenth birthday. To the boy's mother, there was a big difference. In reporting a speech concerning the problem of tobacco advertising as a hazard to children, the paper quoted the speaker as saying the broadcaster should make corrective moves on his own. In a follow-up story, the paper quoted him as saying the broadcaster would take corrective steps. One little word is involved here, but its connotation looms large to broadcasters.

Reader-stoppers An ear for language is as important as an eye for grammar. "This doesn't sound right," the copyeditor protests when he spots fuzzy passages. Careful reading of copy and application of his copy pencil will enable the copyeditor to ferret out unclear or nonsensical expressions.

As explained by one engineer to Mrs. Reed, one of the reasons for the high cost of repairing the streets is that the space between the concrete and the ground presents problems of pumping liquid concrete between.

(We can only hope that Mrs. Reed understands.)

Gangs of white rowdies roamed the area last night attacking cars bearing Negroes with baseball bats, bricks and stones.

(Who had the bats?)

The public launching ramps at Gordon Park are clogged full of the drifting debris and completely block off their possible use by early season trailer boaters.

(The writer should try to parse that sentence.)

A very nearly nude picture of actress Jayne Mansfield was flashed on the floor of the South Carolina Senate during discussion of a bill to ban obscene literature.

(Why were they flashing her picture on the floor?)

Three counties, Meigs, Pike and Vinton, get more than 85 per cent from the state. Morgan gets 90.3 per cent.

(Eh?)

Most of them are high school graduates averaging about 20 years old.

(Just how long do they stay in high school?)

Many of the 800 executives and clerical people will be transferred and some probably will be eliminated.

(That's rough on people.)

In Bedford Hospital with a bullet wound in his left chest is Salvatore Carcione.

(A person has but one chest. A woman has one bosom and two breasts.)

Victims in the other cars were not hurt.

(Then why were they victims?)

Monday will be the first day of a new way of delivering an expanded hot meal program to senior citizens in Genesee county.

(Would the "program" or the "meals" be delivered?)

But not long ago a truck backed up to the rear door of a suburban church, broke in and took an electric typewriter, a movie projector and other audiovisual equipment.

(Day of miracles.)

Roth ruled that Rupp's allegations that Total-Leonard had conspired to violate the antitrust laws by restricting production of gasoline to fix prices and that it had violated a contract with Rupp were not proved.

(That's putting too many words between subject and verb. Perhaps this: "Roth ruled that Rupp had failed to prove allegations that . . . ")

A story says that a woman can get an abortion in the second trimester if she has the money. It adds: But the poor are not so fortunate.

(Who says it's a matter of good fortune?)

One of the most spectacular swindles reported included a compound that, when mixed with gasoline, erupts in a puff of smoke.

(Swindles are not put together like a doctor's prescription. The swindle depended on use of a compound.)

An East Side homeowner shot and wounded a gun-toting robber who invaded his home early today, bound him and raped his wife.

(Yet the subject of the sentence is "homeowner.")

The delegation . . . was welcomed by 20,000 mostly black supporters.

(What color was the other part of each supporter?)

Writing and Editing   107

Many of the players hovered around 5 feet 2.

(They must have looked funny up in the air like that.)

Holland said he thought the entranceways . . . would eliminate much of the deer and other poaching.

(Or this way: " . . . would eliminate much of the poaching of deer and other animals.)

This is the first in an occasional series of stories . . .

(Or, "first in a series of stories that will appear occasionally.")

She had been billed previously as Roosevelt (Rosey) Grier's sister, the former pro football player . . .

(Women are succeeding all over the place.)

After his retirement, Thant had spoken wistfully of returning to India . . . but the political climate in Burma was not favorable to him, and the Thants moved instead to Harrison, N.Y.

(What would the political climate in Burma have to do with his moving to India? And why would the Burmese gentleman long for India?)

Some 16,000 bus drivers and other employes of Greyhound Bus Lines struck yesterday . . .

(Sixteen thousand bus drivers, plus an indeterminate number of other employes?)

A sweepstakes trophy will be awarded to the team with the most victories in each category.

(Most victories in all categories? Most "firsts"? Most "firsts," "seconds" and/or "thirds"?)

Indignant at being arrested after waiving extradition, Graham lashed out . . . .

(Was he indignant because of the facts leading to his extradition, or to his arrest?)

A misplaced time element leads to awkward construction:
Parents protesting the closing of Briensburg school yesterday tried to . . . .

(Did they protest yesterday only? Was the school closed yesterday? Or did they "try to" yesterday?)
Another:

Phillips, acting chairman yesterday of a parents steering committee, said, "All or none."

(Was he acting chairman yesterday only? If so, when did he deliver the quote?)

Dodson told police he had awakened and found his wife missing. **Omission**

(He didn't wake up and find her missing. He woke and found that his wife was missing.)

Robert Lowell, Pulitzer Prize-winning American poet who refused a White House invitation to express his disapproval of American policies in Vietnam, has been nominated. . . .

(The writer meant to say Lowell refused the invitation because of his disapproval.)

She was shot and killed through the throat. **Wrong Word Order**

An insufficient water supply problem for fire-fighting at Fitch Senior High school will be discussed next Thursday.

(Try this: "The problem of insufficient water supply for fire-fighting at Fitch. . .")

White segregationists waving Confederate flags and Negro integrationists marched past each other yesterday.

(Or did white segregationists waving flags march past Negro integrationists yesterday?)

Joseph H. Hughes Jr. of Los Angeles wrote to many of his late son's, Coast Guard Ensign Joseph H. Hughes III, friends.

(Translation: "wrote to many friends of his late son. . . .")

The students are mostly Negro.

(Are we saying they are half and half? Mulatto? Spell it out: "Most of the students are Negroes.")

The robbery weapon was an old children's cap pistol.

(Young children grow up to be old children, naturally.)

Fenton has been in trouble—jumping out a Detention Home window, **Confusing** trying to escape from County Jail, shot at by police in a stolen car, steal- **Antecedent** ing, sleeping in basements and hallways.

(We will not comment on the construction of the sentence, but simply suggest we should get those policemen out of that stolen car.)

The accidental ruling by the coroner last month removed the possibility of suicide in Miss McDonald's death.

(The coroner did not make an accidental ruling. He made an accidental-death ruling.)

The most intriguing new product of the year could be the atomic golf ball turned out by Goodrich, which can be found in the weeds by a small Geiger counter.

He caught one farm pond lunker on a plastic worm that weighed 6 pounds, 9 ounces.

(Some worm.)

Donald Vann, 22, was fined $25 yesterday on two charges after being accused of hitting a waitress during an argument with a crutch.

(Who won the argument, Donald or the crutch?)

His head shaved and drugged with sleeping pills, the youngster was dropped off on a residential street.

(Does this mean the victim's head was shaved with sleeping pills?)

Coach John Janosek will introduce his staff and team in an informal program to be followed by a short scrimmage.

A man is being held on charges of making obscene telephone calls to women which police say were filthy.

Miss Adele Hudlin agreed to give the dog a home, even though she already had two of her own.

(Does she have two homes or two dogs?)

They (the Smiths) have been married 24 years and have two children. Both are 53.

Exactness in Writing

Copyeditors, no less than reporters, should constantly seek to improve their knowledge of language. A dictionary may not be the best guide because some dictionaries are too permissive and frequently try to define one term with another as if the two were synonymous. Greater precision in usage can be found in works such as Bergen Evans and Cornelia Evans, *The Dictionary of Contemporary American Usage* (New York: Random House, 1957); Theodore Bernstein, *The Careful Writer* (New York: Atheneum, 1965) and *Reverse Dictionary* (New York: Quadrangle Books, 1975); Roy Copperud, *A Dictionary of Usage and Style* (New York: Hawthorn Books, 1964); Wilson Follett, *Modern American Usage: A Guide* (London: Longmans, 1966); Marjorie Skillin and Robert Gay, *Words Into Type*, rev. ed. (Englewood Cliffs, N.J.: Prentice-Hall, 1974); H. W. Fowler, *A Dictionary of Modern English Usage,* 2nd ed. (New York and Oxford: Oxford University Press, 1965); William Morris and Mary Morris, *Harper Dictionary of Contemporary Usage* (New York: Harper & Row, 1975); and Edwin Newman, *Strictly Speaking* (Indianapolis: Bobbs-Merrill, 1974).

8

Slips in Writing

Editors are leery of formulas for writing, but on one principle they are nearly unanimous: The lead of the story must be short. How short? A Hearst editor demanded short leads and finally got a one-word one. The Chicago *Tribune* applauded this three-word lead: "Money and race." Probably a better one: "Are nudes prudes?"

Honing the Lead

Some newspapers have set twenty words as the maximum. "If you can tell the story in fewer words, feel free to do so," they say. Ralph McGill, late editor of the Atlanta *Constitution,* liked what he called a flawless lead in the Bible: "There was a man in the land of Uz, whose name was Job."

Tom Fesperman, who writes a column for Enterprise Features Syndicate, uses short leads and short sentences to move his readers along:

There was a quail whose name was Hercules.
Don't ask me how he got that name. I have spotted a lot of quail in my time and I wouldn't call any of them Hercules.
Even so. Let us get on with the story.
It is not exactly accurate to say that Hercules was born in Arizona. It's more exact to say he was hatched. . . .

The copyeditor's eye brightens when he reads leads that rank with these classics:

Only in Russia could Peter and the Wolf die on the same night (Stalin's death).

Today the Japanese fleet submitted itself to the destinies of war—and lost.

They're burying a generation today. (Texas school explosion.)

The moon still shines on the moonshine stills in the hills of Pennsylvania.

Fifty thousand Irishmen—by birth, by adoption and by profession—marched up Fifth Avenue today.

Most lead problems arise when reporters try to see how much they can pack into the lead. Rather, they should try to see how much they can leave out of the lead:

Original	Edited
The former girlfriend of a man charged with killing a local bartender almost four years ago testified Monday that she has never seen another man who claims he killed the victim and that she was with him that night.	A man who says he actually committed the murder for which another man is on trial was contradicted in court Monday. —Roy H. Copperud
Columbia Gas Transmission Corp. has started discussions with its subsidiaries and major customers that could result in increasing the supply of natural gas to its Kentucky subsidiary—and thus to industrial users in the central and northeastern parts of the state who now face a total cutoff of supplies this winter.	Columbia Gas Transmission Corp. has started a search for ways to save industrial users in central and northeastern Kentucky from a threatened total cutoff of gas this winter. —Wallace Carroll

One way to avoid long, cluttered leads is to substitute simple sentences for compound ones:

LONDON, June 2—Ten years ago today, a 27-year-old princess was crowned Queen Elizabeth II, and Britain, in an outpouring of emotional fervor unmatched since, hailed her coronation as the beginning of a new Elizabethan era of splendor and achievement.	LONDON, June 2—Ten years ago today, a 27-year-old princess was crowned Queen Elizabeth II. Britain, in an outpouring of emotional fervor unmatched since, hailed her coronation as the beginning of a new Elizabethan era of splendor and achievement.

The lead should be pruned of minor details that could come later in the story if they are needed:

Donald E. Brodie, son of William Brodie, for more than three decades a member of the display advertising department of the News, and Mrs. Brodie, 106 W. 41st St., was graduated from Jefferson Medical College last week.	Donald E. Brodie, son of Mr. and Mrs. William Brodie, 106 W. 41st St., was graduated from Jefferson Medical College last week. For more than three decades, William Brodie was a member of the display advertising department of the News.

The lead need not be long to be cluttered:

First National is one of four American banks, and the American Express company, which issues travelers checks throughout the nation.	First National, three other American banks, and the American Express company issue travelers checks throughout the nation.

A good lead contains qualities other than brevity. It must inform and summarize. It must be straightforward; it cannot back into the action. It sets the mood, the pace and the flavor of the story. It accomplishes what the term implies: It guides, directs, points to and induces. If it is a suspended-interest lead, it must be so tantalizing and intriguing that the reader cannot help but continue. **Leads that Mislead**

The problems in achieving a good lead are many. The copyeditor will be especially alert for the following.

In his effort to get the maximum punch in his lead, the overzealous reporter may "needle" the opening. That is, he lets the lead overreach the story. The lead ignores some facts contained in the story. It stretches and therefore distorts. It is the type of lead that says, "All hell broke loose in city hall last night." Then the final sentence says, "When the dispute subsided the councilmen shook hands and the mayor adjourned the session."

"No matter how appealingly you wrap up the lead, it is no good if it gives a wrong impression or tells a lie," Joseph G. Herzberg told readers.[1] And again, "It is a plain fact that to some papers, the simple truth of the story is never enough. They dress it up and pump it up and they don't merely present it to the reader, they all but cram it down his throat."

The "souped-up" lead invites a sensational headline. If the copyeditor lets the overextended lead stand, then tries to top the lead with a calm headline, he is likely to have the headline tossed back with the suggestion he put more punch into it. Some copyeditors have been known to "doctor" the lead to justify a sensational headline.

Akin to the sensationalized lead is the opinion lead. This type of lead offers a judgment rather than fact. Often it fails to distinguish between mere puffery and news: "Construction features described as newer in concept than space travel will be part of the easy to operate and easy to shop in Almart store soon to open on the Kirkwood Highway."

John Smith returns home from a meeting and his wife asks, "What happened at the meeting?" "Well," replies John, "Jim Jones opened the meeting at 8 and Bill Prentice read the minutes of the previous meeting, and—" "Good night, John." **Don't Back into It**

Too many news leads read like secretarial reports, especially speech leads. Few care that a nursing consultant spoke to a group (when) (where) at the group's "regular monthly meeting," or the title of the talk. Readers want to know what she said.

[1] Joseph G. Herzberg, *Late City Edition* (New York: Holt, Rinehart and Winston, 1947, pp. 141, 143)

That's the news. They won't wade through three paragraphs to learn in the fourth paragraph that "the epileptic child should be treated as a normal person." The lead should get to the point of the story immediately. Like this:

Original	*Edited*
Dean David F. Snodgrass of the University of California's Hastings College of Law says the American Bar Association's longtime ban on news photographs in courtrooms is archaic and unrealistic.	The rule against news photographs in courtrooms is archaic and unrealistic, says a law school dean. —AP Writing Committee
The Brookside Club will consider a subcommittee proposal that calls for changes in representation on the Community Council at its meeting Wednesday noon in the Community Center.	Changes in representation on the Community Council will be considered Wednesday by the Brookside Club. —Roy H. Copperud

Indirect	*Direct*
An Atlanta businessman who joined two anti-Negro, anti-Jewish groups and turned over information to the FBI, today associated a man on trial for dynamiting the Jewish temple with race-hating John Kasper.	A man on trial for dynamiting the Jewish temple was linked today with race-hating John Kasper by an FBI undercover agent.

Inactive	*Active, Tight*
A top-ranking rocket AFD space weapons expert coupled a disclosure of his resignation from the Air Force today with a blast at the senior scientists upon whom the services rely for technological advice.	A top-level Air Force space weapons expert blasted civilian scientists today and said he has resigned.

Cliché Leads   Quick action by two alert policemen was credited with saving the life of....

Police and volunteers staged a massive manhunt today for a man who....

Say-Nothing Leads   If a say-nothing lead causes the copyeditor to ask, "So what else is new?" the chances are the readers will have the same reaction.

DETROIT—Somber was the word for the memorial services to American dead of the War of 1812 Sunday.

Fire so hot it burned the mud guards off and melted a small section of an aluminum trailer body damaged the trailer....

This is almost like writing, "Fire so hot that it burned the roof and walls and destroyed all the furnishings damaged the house of John Doe...."

Frequently, illogical leads occur when the writer presents the idea backwards or uses a non sequitur. **Illogical Leads**

State police attributed an auto collision and the alertness of witnesses to the rapid apprehension of Benjamin Petrucci. . . .

Either the apprehension was attributed to the collision and the alert witnesses or the collision and the witnesses were credited with the apprehension.

Hoping to encourage transient parking at its facilities, the city parking authority yesterday voted to increase rates at two lots.

Charging more for parking hardly seems the way to encourage more of it.

Three small brothers died last night in a fire that burned out two rooms of their home while their father was at work and their mother was visiting a neighbor.

Note how much clearer the revision is: "Left unattended, three small brothers perished in a fire last night that destroyed two rooms of their home. Their father was at work and their mother was visiting a neighbor."

Too much delay in identifying the central character: **Other Lead Problems**

An executive of the So-and-So League said today that . . .

A 15-year-old boy confessed . . .

A 19-year-old girl was injured . . .

A 73-year-old woman is alive . . .

A 55-year-old man ran berserk . . .

Such construction cannot help but bore the reader and is maddening to the copyeditor who is instructed to trim the story to one paragraph.

Another problem is overlong identification, sometimes even preceding the name:

Former Assistant Secretary of State for Latin American Affairs Lincoln Gordon said today . . .

At 7 p.m. yesterday 60 persons fled a three-story apartment building at 2523 E. 38th St. when a carelessly discarded cigaret sent smoke billowing through the building **Too Many Statistics**

Louis Ezzo, 29, of Plainville, a school bus driver, was charged by state police with speeding and violation of a statute limiting school bus speeds to 40 miles an hour at 3:30 p.m. yesterday on I-95 Groton.

A 14-year-old boy fired three shots into a third-floor apartment at 91 Monmouth St. yesterday to climax an argument with a 39-year-old mother who had defended her 9-year-old daughter against an attack by the boy.

Overattribution

Mimi La Belle, Blanktown exotic dancer, was arrested on a charge of indecent exposure last night, according to Officers George Smith and Henry Brown.

Underattribution

An Associated Press reference book comments, "Don't be afraid to begin a story by naming the source. It is awkward sometimes, but also sometimes is the best and most direct way to put the story in proper perspective and balance when the source must be established clearly in the reader's mind if he is properly to understand the story." An example:

All Delawareans over 45 should be vaccinated now against Asian flu.

The attribution should have been in the lead since this is opinion, the consensus of a number of health officials.

Second-Day Lead on a First-Day Story

Every veteran wire editor knows that frequently a wire story's first lead is better than its second, third or fourth. A lead telling the reader an airliner crashed today, killing fifty passengers, is better than a later lead saying an investigation is under way to determine the cause of an airline crash that killed fifty passengers. If the first lead tells the story adequately, why replace it with a second, and often weaker, lead?

First lead—"HOLYOKE, Mass.—At least six persons—four of them children—perished early today when a fire, reportedly set by an arsonist, swept a five-story tenement."

Second lead (with second-day angle)—"HOLYOKE, Mass.— The body of a little boy about two years old, was recovered today, raising the death toll in a tenement house fire to seven."

Third lead (back on the beam)—"HOLYOKE, Mass.—Seven persons—five of them children—perished when a general alarm midnight blaze, believed set, destroyed a five-story tenement."

Newspapers should be edited for their own readers, not for opposition newspapers or for radio and television stations. A new development may be the latest, but it is not necessarily the most important.

Adjectives Are Suspect

Effective adjectives strengthen nouns if they are informative rather than descriptive: "7-foot 1-inch Wilt Chamberlain" rather than "towering Wilt Chamberlain."

Many adjectives are redundant, "loaded," incorrect or misplaced.

Redundant—armed gunmen, chilly 30 degrees below zero, exact replica, foreign imports.

Editorial adjectives—blistering reply, cocky labor leader, so-called liberal, strong words.

Incorrect adjectives—"Whirring or grinding television cameras": Television cameras are electronic devices and do not whir or grind. "A Pole with an unpronounceable name": Every name is pronounceable by somebody. "An unnamed man": Every man has a name; the adjective should be *unidentified*.

Improperly placed adjectives—"Unfair labor practices strike": The practices, not the strike, are unfair. "The treacherous 26-mile Arkansas down-river race": The river, not the race, is treacherous. "The criminally insane building of Delaware State Hospital." "Juvenile Judge George Brown." "So their names have been removed from the barred from running for office for five years list": How's that again? "For area as well as migratory game bird hunters nationwide, the U.S. Fish and Wildlife Service has announced a most welcome change in migratory bird hunting regulations for the coming season." The reference is to hunters of migratory birds, obviously.

A reminder from a wire service sums up the adjective problem: "A statuesque Roman beauty" appeared as a witness in a trial. Ted Williams was said to be engaged to "a beauteous girl model." Dayton picked up "an attractive blonde." A New York girl arrested for possessing narcotics lived in "a lavish apartment" in the West Fifties. An actress killed herself in her "luxurious apartment." Most of these terms aren't really descriptive. How big is "statuesque," how pretty is "beauteous," what specific qualities make a woman "attractive" (and to whom?) and what is a "lavish" apartment? The arrested girl's abode turned out (the next day) to be an apartment of $2\frac{1}{2}$ small rooms.

Searching for the right word takes time. Editors urge copyeditors to omit an adjective rather than to rely on a shoddy term.

Clichés

A good writer uses a fresh and appropriate figure of speech to enhance his story. The copyeditor should distinguish between the fresh and the stale. This isn't always easy because some words and phrases are used repeatedly in the news report.

The Associated Press ran nearly 400,000 words of its copy through a computer to determine which of the tired words and phrases were used most frequently. The result: hailed, backlash, in the wake of, informed, violence flared, kickoff, death and destruction, riot-torn, tinder dry, racially troubled, voters marched to the polls, jam-packed, grinding crash, confrontation, oil-rich nation, no immediate comment, cautious (or guarded) optimism, limped into port.

Copyeditors can add to the list of tired expressions:

Acid test	Belt tightening
Affixed his name (signed)	Bitter (dispute)
Aide (health aide)	Blistering (accusation)
Alert policeman	Bloody riot
Alleged (police brutality, etc.)	Blueprint (for plan)
Area girl	Bold bandits
Average (reader, voter, etc.)	Bombshell (announcement, etc.)
Banquet (never a dinner)	Boost
Based (Dover-based)	Briefing

Brutal (murder, slaying)
Cardinal sin
Caught the eye of
Charisma
Charming lady
Circles (informed, that is)
Combed (for searched)
Confrontation
Controversial issue
Coveted trophy
Crack (troops, train, etc.)
Crippling amendment
Critical times
Crushing burdens
Cutback
Daring (holdup, etc.)
Deficit-ridden
Devastating (flood, fire)
Devout (Catholic, etc.)
Do your own thing
Down under (for Australia)
Dumped
—ees (trainees, escapees)
Experts
Eye (to see)
Eyeball to eyeball
Facility (power plant to privy)
Fashioned
Fiery (or bosomy) actress
Fiery holocaust
Fingered (pointed out)
Fire broke out, swept
Fire of undetermined origin
First and foremost
Flawed
Foot the bill
For real, for sure
Freak accident
Fuzz (for police)
Gap (generation, credibility, etc.)
Giant teamsters union
Go into a huddle
Guidelines
Hammer out
Hard-core, hard-nosed
Head to head
Heated exchange
Highlighted
High-powered cars
Hike
Hobbled by injury
Historical document
Hosted
Hurled
Identity crisis
Implementing
Initial (for first)
In case of
In nothing flat

In terms of
—ize (finalize, formalize)
Jaundiced eye
Junket
Keeled over
Know-how
Led to safety
Life style
Local girl
Lonely lovers lane
Long-smouldering
Luxurious (apartment, love nest, etc.)
Made off with
Meaningful
Miraculous (cure, escape, etc.)
Moderate smoker
Momentous occasion
Name of the game
Nitty-gritty
Normalcy
Operative (or inoperative)
Opt for
Overwhelming majority
Pad (for room)
Paddy wagon
Particular
Passing motorist
Phased in (or phased out)
Plush (hotel, apartment, etc.)
Police were summoned
Posh
Powerful (any Congressional committee)
Pressure (as a verb)
Pretty (usually with blonde and housewife)
Probe
Rampaging flood
Relocate (for move)
Reportedly, reputedly
Restless dragon (China)
Rhetoric (business, sports, etc.)
Seasoned (observers, etc.)
Senior citizen
Senseless murder
Shot in the arm
Simplistic
Snuffed out
Socialite
Sprawling plants
Staged a riot (or protest)
Standing ovation
Steaming jungle
Stems from
Stinging rebuke
Stomped
Structuring
Swank (hotel, etc.)

The Art of Editing

Sweeping changes	Unveiled
Swing into high gear	Upcoming
Task force	Upped
Teeny-boppers	Utilization (for use)
Tell it like it is	Value judgment
Tense (or uneasy) calm	Vast expanse
Terminate (for end)	Veep
Thorough (or all-out) investigation	Verbalize
Time (at that point in time)	Vicious tornado
Timely hit	Violence erupted
Top-level meeting	Violent explosion
Top priority	Well-known (citizen, lawyer)
Tragic accident	Whirlwind (tour, junket)
Triggered	Wreathed in smiles
Turn thumbs down	Yardstick
Two-way street	You better believe it
Ugly tempered mob	Young boys
Uneasy truce	

Careless use of the idiom (the grammatical structure peculiar to our language) occurs frequently in the news report. Usually the fault lies in the prepositions or conjunctions.

Know the Idiom

Three times as many Americans were killed than [as] in any similar period.

It remains uncertain as to when the deadline for the first payment will be made. (Omit *as to*.)

She had always been able to get through the performance on [of] this taxing role.

The economist accused him with [of] failing to make a decision. (You charge somebody with blundering but you accuse him of it.)

He said the guns are against the law except under [in] certain specified situations. (But, under conditions or circumstances.)

Dressen is no different than [from] other experts. (*Different* may be followed by *than* when introducing a clause: "The patient is no different than he was yesterday.")

Five men were pelted by [with] stones.

The reason for the new name is because the college's mission has been changed. (Is that the college's mission has been changed.)

He said he would not call on [for] assistance from police except as a last resort. (Call the police or call on the police for assistance.)

The council said that if open military force by Russia against Czechoslovakia is allowed to take place [to be exerted] without opposition, the "usefulness of the United Nations will be terminated." (Events, not force, take place.)

Costs have continued to rise but the brand still proudly refuses to knuckle down [under] the increasing economic pressure. (*Knuckle down* means to work energetically or apply oneself seriously. To *knuckle under* is to yield or give in.)

The students barricaded themselves inside the building in protest of [against] the University's policy. (Protests are directed to someone but against something.)

Several speakers paid credit [tribute] to former Gov. Stratton. (You pay tribute to but give credit.)

The proposals forbid lawyers, police and prosecutors from uttering [to utter] anything that might prejudice a future trial. (You forbid a person to do something but you prevent him from doing it.)

She presented the mayor a bouquet of roses. (She gave the mayor a bouquet; she presented the mayor with a bouquet.)

He was shot by [with] a .22 caliber bullet. (He was shot by a companion with a pistol. He was run over by an automobile.)

In other idiomatic expressions, the phrase should be correct.

These men and women could care less about Ford's legislative magic. (The correct phrase is "couldn't care less.")

Gerunds, but not past particles, require the possessive:

It was the first instance of a city [city's] losing its funds.

He said he didn't know anything about Hollenbach [Hollenbach's] interceding in his behalf.

Jargon   A university press release announcing a significant engineering meeting on the campus reported that one of the major papers would be on "The aerodynamic heating of blunt, axisymmetric, re-entry bodies with laminar boundary layer at zero and at large angles of yaw in supersonic and hypersonic air streams." To the consumer of news, that title is "Greek," or, as Maury Maverick would have termed it, *gobbledygook*. Translated, the topic suggested, "How hot does a space ship get when it swings back into the air around the earth?"

Doctors, lawyers, educators, engineers, government officials, scientists, sociologists, economists and others have their professional jargon or shoptalk peculiar to the profession. Sometimes this jargon is used to impress the uninitiated; sometimes it is a cover-up.

Here is how Daniel Melcher, president of the R. R. Bowker Company, translated three examples of gobbledygook.[2]

A mnemonic code of three, four or five characters was assigned to each primary source.
"Producers' and distributors' names are abbreviated."

---

[2] *The Library Journal*, September 1, 1964

beetle bailey by mort walker

© 1961, King Features Syndicate. Reproduced by permission.

Slips in Writing

121

Sources were provided with an effort-saving structured response form.

"Questionnaires were sent to producers and distributors."

The editorial work is paralleled by a machine processing effort that translates the worksheets into decks of punched cards.

"The entries are typed on cards which are then punched for ease of sorting."

A judge's ruling on a case involving an actress contained this sentence: "Such vanity doubtless is due to the adulation which the public showers on the denizens of the entertainment world in a profusion wholly disproportionate to the intrinsic contribution which they make to the scheme of things." That's pretentious verbosity. So, too, is this from an educator:

The educator will hold a practicum for disadvantaged children who are under-achieving in reading.

"Slow learners who can't read."

Translation is needed when a story on education contains "professional terms" such as *paraprofessionals, academically talented, disadvantaged* (culturally deprived, impoverished students), *ghetto* (inner-city or center-city) *schools* and *ungraded* and *nongraded classrooms*.

In a special study of state wire reporting, the Associated Press found that unintelligible jargon appeared in legislature stories ("resolves," "engrossment," "tucked in committee"), in alphabet soup references to agencies and organizations (SGA, the UCA, CRS, LTA and MMA), in Weather Service forecasts and in market reports. AP then noted, "Neither weather reports nor markets are sacrosanct to editorial pencils."

The copyeditor can help the reader by substituting laymen's words for technical terms and by killing on sight words like *implement* and the *-ize* words.

Following are translations of some technical terms that frequently appear in the news report:

Term	*Translation*
Motivated or motivationed	Moved
Object	Aim
Mentality	Mind
Percentage	Part
Ideology	Faith
Assignment	Task or job
Astronomical	Big

Nice-nelly expressions used as a cover-up are euphemisms:

Term	*Translation*
Audio-visual aids	Classroom movies
Container	Can
Continental breakfast	Juice, roll and coffee
Dialogue, conversation	Talk, discussion

Term	Translation
Planned parenthood	Birth control
Revised upward	Raised
Social disease	Syphilis
Underachiever	Loafer
Withdrawal	Retreat

Slang

Many editors will agree with this advice from the Associated Press: "Use of slang should be a rarity in the news report." Some editors might even dream that use of slang can be reduced in sports stories, in the signed columns, in comic strips and in ads.

Slang in direct quotations helps reveal the speaker's personality. The reader expects the gangster to use terms of the underworld. He does not expect the reporter to resort to slang such as "The Brinton household is a go-go preparing . . . for guests."

Some slang words should be avoided because they are offensive ("cops" for *policemen*, "gobs" for *sailors*, "wops" for *Italians*): others are avoided because they reveal a writer's carelessness ("got clobbered" for *defeated soundly*).

A few examples from a wire service show how a copyeditor can overcome the slang:

"The Supreme Court ruled today that a lower court goofed." What's wrong with the proper word *erred*?

A Los Angeles story spoke of a couple getting "a few belts in one of the local bars." What's wrong with *drinks* if that's what they got?

A Washington reporter wrote that "well-heeled admirers of the senator have shelled out $7,000." We suppose that *well-heeled* means wealthy and that *shelled out* means contributed.

Parallelism

Good usage insists that similar ideas or elements in a sentence be phrased in a similar structural or grammatical form. You would say, "I like gardening, fishing and hunting," not "I like gardening, fishing and to hunt." In the following, the word *requiring* makes a nonparallel construction: "Instead of requiring expensive cobalt drill bits, disposable brass pins are used."

Comparisons should compare similar things. Here is a sentence that compares an apple (the increase) with a pumpkin (the sales): "Consolidated sales of Cottontex Corp. for the first six months of this year were $490,000,000, an increase of $27,000,000 compared with the first half of last year." Use "an increase of $27,000,000 over the previous year's first half." "The soldier was ragged, unshaven, yet walked with a proud step." Make it read, "The soldier was ragged and unshaven, yet walked with a proud step."

Omission of *and* produces a nonparallel construction: "He worked on newspapers in Washington, New Jersey, New York, and on the Paris *Herald Tribune.*" Use "He worked on newspapers in Washington, New Jersey and New York, and on. . . ."

Slips in Writing 123

But *and* should not be used superfluously: "He was identified as John Delanor Smith, three times convicted on narcotic charges and who reportedly serves as an enforcer for Mafia drug bosses on the east coast."

Non Sequiturs

A non sequitur is an error in logic; the phrase means "it does not follow":

A guard at the Allied Kid Co., he died at 7:10 a.m., about five minutes after one of the youths implicated in the attack was taken into custody.

Guards die at 7:10 a.m., workers at 8:10 and executives at 9:10.

Worn on a chain with swivel and button, this model retails at $39.95.

How much if I just carry it loose in my pocket?

"Because breath is so vital to life," Burmeister explained, "the field of inhalation therapy and the development of breathing equipment has become increasingly important in medical science today."

It may be true that these things are increasingly important, but not because breath is vital to life. Breath was just as important to life 3,000 years ago as it is today.

Designed by the Caloric appliance people, this dispenser can be built into the wall or mounted on the surface.

Because the Caloric appliance people designed it?

Stored in an air-conditioned room in lower Manhattan, the tapes contain information on the reading habits of one million Americans.

The nature of the information on those tapes is not in any way related to the place of their storage, or the condition of the air there. An easy way to edit this sentence is to start with the subject: "The tapes, stored in an air-conditioned room in lower Manhattan, contain information. . . ."

Deferred Subject

Planned by Jones, Blake and Droza, Detroit architects, the new school has 18 classrooms in addition to such standard facilities as cafeteria and library.

This implies that it's a natural thing to expect a school planned by that particular firm to have 18 classrooms, etc.

Acclaimed as a collector's item, the new Early American decanter will make its appearance in stores in time for the holiday gift season.

Aside from the odd deferment of subject, how could any collector acclaim this new decanter before it even hit the market?

Completed three years ago, the plant is 301 feet by 339 feet and is a one-story structure containing. . . .

A plant of exactly that size could have been completed fifty years ago, or yesterday.

This particular error crops up most frequently in obituaries:

Unmarried, Jones is survived by his mother, Mrs. . .

Born in Iowa, he worked on two newspapers in Illinois before coming to St. Louis.

Watch for Danglers

The dangler is one of the most common errors committed by beginning writers and by all who write in a hurry. The writer knows what he means but he doesn't say exactly what he means, thus forcing the reader to rearrange the sentence so he can grasp its meaning. Examples:

If convicted of the assault and battery charge, a judge may impose any sentence he sees fit on the defendants.

"If convicted" applies to the defendants, not to the judge.

Utilizing two pipelines, 112 tons of carbon dioxide was pumped into the . . .

By mixing chemicals with the gas, the flame will change colors.

"Mixing chemicals with the gas causes the flame to change colors."

Besides being cut on the left cheek and bloodied in the nose, Zeck's purse was attached for $825.

Already hospitalized a month, doctors estimate it will be three or four months before he is out again.

An E-shaped building, the fire started in the southwest wing.

A "natural" fertilizer, he predicted that it would solve many problems.

After blowing out the candles atop his birthday cake in three puffs, a movie camera flashed old fight films on the screen near the bar.

The fluoroscopic system makes moving pictures and tape recordings of the mouth and throat while speaking, chewing and swallowing.

Short and readable, I finished it off in about 45 minutes.

Marines stationed atop the observation towers can watch the surrounding terrain for Viet Cong activity. Once spotted, marines are dispatched to chase the enemy.

Once spotted, marines probably had chicken pox or measles, or just spilled soup.

A man of many surprises, Johnson's announcement was his most stunning move.

Slips in Writing

Doctors told him he would eventually lose his sight after a chemical tank exploded in his face while serving in the European theater of World War II.

Married to an American girl, his food favorites still are Indian.

Munching idly on a salted cashew one day, a thought suddenly occurred to me.

Although spotted around MIG airbases in North Vietnam, yesterday's report was the first that the choppers were being used in combat.

Knowing that Peck was her favorite actor, he was invited to visit the girl in the hospital when he made a trip to Boston.

"Known to be her favorite actor, Peck was invited. . . ."

Mixed Metaphors　Legislative Hall here was swarming with lobbyists as the second session of the 121st General Assembly got under way yesterday.
With lawmakers treading water while awaiting Gov. Elbert N. Carvel's State and budget messages, due tomorrow, lobbyists had a field day.

In two paragraphs the story pictured Legislative Hall as a beehive, a swimming pool and an athletic field.

Breaking domestic ties with gold would make the nation's gold stock a real barometer of international fever for gold.

Do you shove that barometer under your tongue or what?

The TVCCA's board of trustees revealed last night that its own administrative funds are exhausted, thus adding fuel to the concern and consternation expressed by public and private agencies.

One way to repair that "mixaphor"—although not recommended—would have been to say, "adding fuel to the already blazing c. and c., etc."

They hope to unravel a sticky turn of events that was further complicated recently.

Did you ever try to unravel glue, molasses, maple syrup or other similar strings or yarns?

A former Texas rancher sank his spurs into one of the fondest dreams of Wilmington business and political leaders yesterday, then calmly stood and waited for the explosion.

A wire story lead from New York contained the phrase "a fire-drenched battleground." Copyeditors began wondering if the next flood story would refer to "water-scorched" lowlands.

Waldor plans to use the gathering to set the wheels in motion to launch himself as a mayoralty candidate.

A launching on wheels; the Navy might be able to use that.

Mock Ruralisms

Following is some advice from Leon Stolz of the Chicago *Tribune* in *English I* (June 1968): "If you hold your quota to one mock ruralism a century, your readers will not feel deprived." Expressions such as "seeing as how" or "allowed as how" are supposed to give a folksy touch. They don't. They merely make the writer sound stupid.

Foreign Words

When copyeditors come across foreign expressions in the news report they should be sure of the spelling, the use and the translation. Unless it is a commonly known expression, the copyeditor provides the translation if the reporter has not done so. Fowler's *Dictionary of Modern English Usage* (New York: Oxford University Press, 1965) says, "Those who use words or phrases belonging to languages with which they have little or no acquaintance do so at their peril." The headline writer who tried to add a flavor of French with "C'est La Killy" needed advice on proper usage of French articles. The number in Latin words can cause trouble. For instance, *data* is plural and *datum* is singular. But *datum* is rarely used and *data* can be either singular (as a synonym for information) or plural (as a synonym for facts). *Trivia* is always plural; *bona fides* is always singular. *Media, criteria, insignia* and *phenomena* are plural.

A foreign expression has its place in the report if it supplies a real need or flavor or has no precise native substitute (*blasé, chic, simpatico*).

Copyeditors frequently are confronted with problems of translation, not as a rule directly from a foreign language but from a foreign correspondent's translation. Translations made abroad are often hurried; many are the work of men and women more at home in a foreign language than in English, commented *English I* (October 1967). The translations may be accurate but not idiomatic. Following are examples cited in *English I:*

An AP dispatch telling of a factory explosion in Germany said, "Most of the victims were buried when the roof of a large factory hall came down following the explosion. . . . The blast . . . damaged five other halls. . . ." What is a factory hall? The copyeditor would have saved readers a puzzled moment if he had altered the dispatch to read, "Most of the victims were buried when the factory roof fell on them. The blast . . . damaged five other sections of the plant."

VATICAN CITY (AP)—The Vatican newspaper *l'Osservatore Romano*, commenting on the tragic soccer riot in Lima, Peru, said Monday that partisan zeal in sports must avoid "excesses that debase human conditions."

The Vatican daily carried a story from Lima on the Argentina-Peru soccer match incident in which hundreds were killed. A brief editorial comment printed at the end of the story expressed sorrow over the deaths.

"We do not refer to sports as a loyal and direct competition of wholesome energies," *l'Osservatore* said.

Slips in Writing 127

"Excesses that debase human conditions" is not idiomatic English. Humanity or the human condition may be what the Italian had in mind. We do *not* refer to sports as a loyal and direct competition of wholesome energies. The story as sent says the opposite of what was apparently meant.

The UPI Berlin bureau sent out a story quoting Chancellor Erhard: "We are ready also with the Soviet Union and the east European states to achieve good relations and an understanding that would make it possible for us to live together peacefully— as we have overcome a tragic past with our western neighbors." The words are English but the word order is Germanic. The translation in idiomatic English would have been as follows: "Just as we have overcome the tragic past in our relations with our western neighbors, so we are ready for an understanding with the Soviet Union and the east European states to establish good relations and enable us to live together peacefully."

Discretion must be used when the copyeditor undertakes revision of the translation. "We should not invite an international crisis by substituting a mistranslation for an unidiomatic one," cautioned an editor. Usually, the copyeditor, having called the matter to the attention of the head of the desk, can and should make the necessary repairs.

Newspapers display an affectation when they use foreign terms not readily understood by their readers. Examples:

Some (restaurants) have retained an authentic belle-epogue ambience. (What does it mean?)

When 13-year-old Pascale Le Tourze returns to her "lycee" in France . . . (What reader will use a dictionary to find out that Pascale will attend a French public secondary school?)

Grammar No one can say what the most common grammatical errors in news writing are, but near the top must be the misuse of the relative pronoun and punctuation. Punctuation is discussed in Appendix I.

Relative Pronoun Leon Stolz of the Chicago *Tribune* advised reporters and copyeditors, "If you have trouble deciding whether the relative pronoun should be who or whom, you can usually find the right answer by remembering that who is nominative, like the personal pronouns he, she and they. Whom is objective, like him, her and them. Turn the clause into an independent sentence and substitute a personal pronoun for the relative pronoun" [in *English I* (January 1968)].

Applying the Stolz formula:

After his decision to cancel the trip, he sent most of the officials who he had invited to attend.

He invited *they* to attend?

The repeal gives property owners absolute freedom in deciding who they will rent or sell to.

They will rent to *they*?

Miss Barbara Warren, who he met while they were medical students at Passavant hospital. . . .

He met *she*?

In his last eight games, covering $13\frac{2}{3}$ innings, the skinny Texan, who teammates call "Twiggy," has held opponents scoreless.

They call *he* Twiggy?

Mayor Daley will select the Democratic nominee to run against Dirksen, whom many feel is invincible as a candidate.

Many feel *him* is invincible?

The paper said two residents of the housing project were known to have seen a young man whom they said looked like the description of the sniper.

They said *him* looked like the description of the sniper?

Bachmann, who police quoted as saying he was inspired by Dr. Martin Luther King's assassination to shoot Dutschke, was recovering from wounds he received in a gun battle with police.

Police quoted *he* as saying?

He called on his listeners, whom he said represented the mainstream of the Democratic and Liberal parties, "to reject such a negative course, productive of nothing."

He said *them* represent?

The American was Leonard Levison, whom an air line official said was believed to be a merchant marine officer.

An air line official said *him* was believed to be a merchant marine officer?

Whomever you are and whatever your interests are, you would be entranced. . . .

You are *him*?

Summing Up

The following story illustrates some of the lessons in Chapters 7 and 8. The underscored words should get a copyeditor's attention:

---

two-level mountain residence four miles from Blankton m,
A ~~$30,000~~ home ~~four miles up~~ Sugarloaf Road was destroyed ~~that~~
Tuesday
~~this morning~~ in a fire ~~that~~ apparently ~~was~~ ignited by a propane
gas explosion, ~~sheriff's officers said.~~
dwelling
The ~~home~~, located in the Mountain Pines Subdivision, was
ablaze *when*
~~totally engulfed in flames~~ by ~~the time~~ Sugarloaf Volunteer
firefighters arrived ~~on the scene.~~
sheriff's officers
According to ~~Lt. Bill Kowalski of the Blankton~~ Sheriff's depart-
were
ment, the only injuries reported ~~at the scene was some~~ minor burns
m one *Mrs.* *t* *n*
to the leg of Margaret Zahner, one of two persons renting the
house for the summer. The owner ~~of the house,~~ Kenneth Ruth, is on
a three-month vacation.
Mrs. *n* *said*
S. Zahner, ~~who shares the house with Larry Sullivan~~, ~~told~~ officers
she was in the basement laundry room when ~~she heard~~ a small ex-
her *ing*
plosion, ~~which~~ ignited the ~~clothes she was wearing~~.
While *putting out* *she was burned*
~~The woman extinguished~~ the small fire, ~~receiving the burns during~~
she
~~the effort, and~~ ran from the house, ~~clutching her dog.~~ ~~As she was~~
Then
~~running from the house~~ to call authorities, she heard a second,
that caused *to insult*
~~more powerful~~ explosion ~~which sent~~ flames shooting ~~throughout~~
the structure.

(##)

The story has a lead problem. Who estimated the value if the owner was on vacation? (It turned out to be a bystander's guess. An accompanying picture showed it to be a two-level structure.)

The reporter has a problem with attribution, mentioning "sheriff's officers" then a specific officer. The story is loaded with clichés, redundancies and poor taste (the naming of the other occupant).

Even when edited, the story doesn't hang together. The age of the victim is not given. Further, the lead should emphasize the injuries to a person rather than damages to a building. A better version:

A 21-year-old Blankton County woman suffered minor leg burns Tuesday when a propane gas system exploded in her mountain residence four miles west of Blankton.

Margaret Zahner, who lives in the Mountain Pines subdivision on Sugarloaf Road, was taken to Blankton Community Hospital.

A sheriff's officer said Mrs. Zahner was doing laundry when a minor explosion ignited the building.

The structure was destroyed before members of the Sugarloaf Volunteer Fire Department arrived.

The building was owned by Kenneth Ruth of Blankton who is on vacation. A second occupant was away during the explosions and fire.

The Art of Editing

This chapter has tried to demonstrate some of the pitfalls in making the news readable and clear. It does not explain how to make stories interesting. But style is an individual thing and no one can tell another how to achieve it.

"Hard news" stories like accidents and disaster will continue to be written in the traditional inverted pyramid pattern even though that structure is dull, unimaginative and usually slow-moving. The urgency of the story is confined mostly to the head and the lead. Such accounts lack grace or style.

As newspapers start to pay more attention to ideas and changes, to cultural currents and people, fresh forms will appear. The trend is evident in the Style section of the Washington *Post.* What Style proposes, in the view of its advocates, is to mesh traditional reporting disciplines of research, accuracy, moral objectivity and clear thinking with a new freedom of literary expression.

In his introduction to *Writing in Style,* Thomas R. Kendrick said:

Style's writers demonstrate . . . a strong interest in sophisticated literary techniques: scene-by-scene story construction, extended dialogue, evocative detail and scores of other devices to achieve a mood and tone that may reveal far more about the quality and character of people and events than a chronicling of statements and actions.[3]

Even hard news has a human dimension, though it is most often neglected in the traditional mold. The sources, for example, are permitted to talk only in partial quotes. Somehow, the writer is reluctant to take the reader by the hand and help him see and hear and feel the story. The reader can't see where the action is taking place; there are no sounds and smells.

The characters talk a strange language. Walter Carroll put it this way at a seminar for the Louisville *Courier-Journal* staffers, "Can you imagine a friend's saying, 'Hey, did you know that John is going to be a gubernatorial candidate?'"

[3] Washington Post Writers Group (Eds.), *Writing in Style,* Washington: The Washington Post Co., p. iv, 1975. (Boston: Houghton Mifflin, distributors.)

Style Notes

Identifications Shakespeare knew the value of a name. In *Othello* he had Iago say, "But he that filches from me my good name / Robs me of that which not enriches him / And makes me poor indeed." A name misspelled is a person misidentified. Of all the errors a newspaper is capable of making, one of the most serious is a misspelled or a misused name. In radio and television it is the mispronounced name.

One of the important functions of the copyeditor is to make sure that all names in the copy are double-checked. The proper form is the form the person uses. He may be Alex rather than Alexander, Jim rather than James, Will rather than William. He may or may not have a middle initial, with or without a period (Harry S Truman). No one has yet explained why today's newspapers are so insistent on using middle names or initials of well-known men. After seeing Richard Nixon's name in the news hundreds of times, most readers didn't have to be reminded that the story concerned President Richard M. Nixon instead of plain Richard Nixon. Men's first names are seldom used alone, except in sports copy. The same should be true for first names of women.

Anyone resents an attempt at cleverness where his name is concerned. Such "cuteness" should be felled on sight:

Orange County will have a lemon as district attorney. Jack Lemon was elected to the job yesterday.

Of the five patrolmen on the staff, two are crooks.

The last name was Crook.

A title generally precedes a name unless it is a long title. It is Harley F. Taylor, principal of Philip C. Showell School, rather than Philip C. Showell School Principal Harley F. Taylor.

Nor should the story make the reader guess at the identification. Here is an example:

Albert A. Ballew took issue with Mayor Locher today for announcing in advance that the post of administrative assistant in the Safety Department will be filled by a black.

The president of the Collinwood Improvement Council commended the mayor for creating the post, but added. . . .

Now then, who is the president of the Collinwood Improvement Council? Will readers assume it is Ballew? The solution is so simple: "Ballew, president of the Collinwood Improvement Council, commended the mayor. . . ."

The first reference to any person is by full name and professional, scholastic or religious title, if appropriate. Titles may be used on second reference to aid the reader.

Newspapers traditionally have used Mrs. on first reference only with the husband's given name: *Mrs. John Smith* and *Mrs. Smith* thereafter; or, if it is her preference, *Gladys Smith* and *Mrs. Smith* thereafter.

Women on second reference are identified by Miss, Mrs. or Ms., according to the women's preference.[1] It is the responsibility of the reporter to determine which the woman prefers.

Editors may determine which women are sufficiently well-known in their professions to be referred to on second reference by last name only. Billie Jean King and Joan Sutherland, for example, could be identified as King and Sutherland, but the mother of a high school swimmer or the lead in a civic theater production probably could not be, unless that was their stated preference.

It may be Mrs. Richard Harris Jr., but not Mrs. Dorothy Harris Jr. Her husband may be Jr., but she is not.

Newspaper style may dictate that certain positions be neuterized (chairperson for chairman) but even this rule could lead to the absurd (*personkind* for *mankind*).

Editors can be fair to both sexes by eliminating purely sexist adjectives before women of accomplishment and by using plural forms when possible and substituting the relative pronouns *they* or *them* instead of *he* or *him*.

All males on second reference are identified by surname only although some newspapers use Mr. on second reference in obituaries of prominent persons.

[1] Some newspapers, e.g., The New York *Times,* use Ms. as an honorific only in quoted matter. in letters to the editor and. in news articles, in passages discussing the term itself. Generally, the given and last names are used in first reference and Mrs. or Miss (with the last name) on subsequent references. The honorifics may be dropped in subsequent references to women of pre-eminence who are no longer living.

Newspapers have no firm rule about when to identify a person as a girl or a woman, or as a boy, youth or man. Generally, a girl becomes a woman at 18; a male is a boy until he is 13, a youth from 13 to 18 and a man from 18 on.

Appropriateness should determine whether males and females 18 and older or even those under 18 should be referred to by the familiar given name.

A surname alone is used in half-column cutlines except when two or more half-column photographs of persons with the same last name are used with an article. In that case, first names or initials are needed.

Pupil describes a person attending grade school; *student* applies to those attending junior high school, high school, college or university.

A maiden name can cause trouble: "He married the former Constance Coleman in 1931." This is incorrect; Constance Coleman was Constance Coleman when he married her. He married Constance Coleman. His wife is the former Constance Coleman.

Woman is used as a general descriptive possessive—woman's rights. *Women's* is used as a specific—women's club (but Woman's Christian Temperance Union). It is women fliers, Young Women's Christian Association, women workers, but woman suffrage. It is never the Smith woman.

Foreign names are tricky. In Spanish-speaking countries, individuals usually have two last names, the father's and the mother's—Adolfo Lopez Mateos. On second reference, Lopez Mateos should be used. In headlines, Lopez Mateos is preferred, but Lopez will do.

A Chinese family name is usually given first, and the second part of the hyphenated name is given in lower case—Chiang Kai-shek, Lee Su-kun. On second reference, use Chiang, not Kai-shek.

In Arab names, *al* generally is hyphenated—al-Sabah, al-Azhar. Some Arabs drop the article—Mamoun Kuzbari, not al-Kuzbari. Compound names should be left intact—Abdullah, Abdel, Abdur. Pasha and Bey titles have been abolished. Royal titles are used with first names—Emir Faisel, Sheik Abdullah. *Haj* is used with the first name in both first and subsequent references—Haj Amin al-Hussein, Haj Amin.

The *U* in Burmese names means uncle, our equivalent of *Mr. Thakin* means master. *Daw* means Mrs. or Miss. Many Burmese have only one name—U Thant. If a Burmese has two names, both should be used—U Tin Maung, Tin Maung.

Some Koreans put the family name first—Park Chung Hee. The second reference should be Park, not Chung Hee, the given name.

Many Indonesians have only one name—Sukarno, not Achmed Sukarno.

Swedish surnames usually end in *-son,* and Danish names usually end in *-sen.*

Trade Names

Few editors have escaped letters that begin something like this: "Dear Sir: The attached clipping from your paper of July 14th contains a mention of our product and we very much appreciate this unsolicited publicity. However, the name of our product was used with a lower-case "c." As you know. . . ."

Makers of trade-name products want to protect their rights under the Lanham Trademark Act of 1947 and insist that in any reference to the product name the manufacturer's spelling and capitalization be used. This is to protect the trade name from becoming generic, as happened to aspirin, cellophane, escalator, milk of magnesia, zipper, linoleum and shredded wheat.

Much of the confusion and protest can be eliminated simply by using a generic term rather than the specific trade name—petroleum jelly for Vaseline, freezer for Deepfreeze, fiber glass for Fiberglass, tranquilizer for Miltown.

Where the product is trade-named and there is no substitute, the trade name should be used, especially if it is pertinent to the story. The withholding of such information on the ground of free publicity is niggardly.

Institutions should be labeled correctly—Bell Telephone System, not Bell Telephone Company; Lloyd's, not Lloyd's of London; D'Oyly Carte; J.C. Penney Co. (Penneys in ads, Penney's in other usages); American Geographical Society; National Geographic Society.

It is the Tomb of the Unknowns, not the Tomb of the Unknown Soldier.

Religion

Jewish congregations should be identified in news stories as Orthodox, Conservative or Reform, and the terminology of the congregation concerned should be followed in naming the place of worship as a temple or a synagogue. When grouping, the generic term is "Jewish houses of worship."

To help readers, the copyeditor should insert "branch of Judaism" or whatever other phrase might be necessary to convey the proper meaning.

Most Orthodox congregations use *synagogue.* Reform groups use *temple* and Conservative congregations use one word or the other, but *synagogue* is preferred. It is never *church,* which applies to Christian bodies.

Sect has a derogatory connotation. Generally it means a church group espousing Christianity without the traditional liturgical forms. *Religion* is an all-inclusive word for Judaism, Moslemism, Christianity and so on. *Faith* generally is associated with

Protestants. *Denomination* should be used only when referring to the church bodies within the Protestant community.

Religious labels can be misleading. *Jews* and *Judaism* are general terms. *Israelis* refer to nationals of the state of Israel and *Jews* to those who profess Judaism. The state of Israel is not the center of or the spokesman for Judaism. Some Jews are Zionists; some are not.

Not all denominations use *Church* in the organization's title. It is the First Baptist Church but the American Baptist Convention. It is the Church of Jesus Christ of Latter-day Saints (not Mormon Church); its units are Missions, Stakes and Wards. It is the Episcopal Church, not the Episcopalian Church. Its members are Episcopalians, but the adjective is *Episcopal:* Episcopal clergymen.

Mass may be *offered* or *celebrated*. High mass is *sung;* low mass is *said*. The rosary is *recited* or *said*. If mass is sung, the "high" should be omitted. The copyeditor can avoid confusion by letting the statement read something like this: "The mass (or rosary) will be at 7 p.m." An official presides at solemn high mass. Requiem mass is not necessarily high, but it usually is. It is *offered,* never "celebrated" or "sung." The Benediction of the Blessed Sacrament is neither "held" nor "given"; services close with it.

The order of the commandments varies depending on the version of the Bible used. Confusion can be spared if the commandment number is omitted. Also to be deleted are references to the burning of a church mortgage unless there actually is a burning ceremony. It is an elegant but ridiculous way of saying the mortgage has been paid off.

The usual style in identifying ministers is *the Rev.,* followed by his full name on first reference and *the Rev. Mr.* on second reference. If he holds a doctorate, the style is *the Rev. Dr.,* or simply *Dr.* on subsequent references. *Reverend* should not be used standing alone, nor should plural forms be used, such as the Revs. John Jones and Richard Smith. Churches of Christ do not use the term *reverend* in reference to ministers. They are called *brothers*.

Rabbis take *Rabbi* throughout.

Catholic priests who are members of orders take the initials of their order after their surnames: S.J., S.S., etc. Priests who are rectors, heads of religious houses or presidents of institutions and provinces of religious orders take *Very Rev.* and are addressed as *Father*. Priests who have doctorates in divinity or philosophy are identified as *the Rev. Dr.* and are addressed either as "Dr." or "Father."

The Church of Christ is not the same as the United Church of Christ. It is Seventh-day Adventists, but Seventh Day Baptists. When used as an adjective, Bahai is spelled Ba-hai.

The words *Catholic* and *parochial* are not synonymous. There are parochial schools other than Catholic schools. The writer should not assume that a person is a Roman Catholic simply because he is a priest or a bishop. Other religions also have priests and bishops.

Not all old churches merit the designation of *shrine.* Some are just old churches. *Shrine* denotes some special distinction, historic or ecclesiastical. Usually, shrines are structures or places that have religious connections or that are hallowed by their associations with events or persons of historic significance, such as Mt. Vernon.

Use *nun* when appropriate for women in religious orders. The word *sister* is confusing except with the person's name (Sister Mary Edward).

Death Stories

Persons die of heart *illness,* not "failure"; after a *long* illness, not an "extended" illness; *unexpectedly,* not "suddenly"; *outright,* not "instantly"; *following* or *after* an operation, not "as a result of" an operation; *apparently of a heart attack,* not of an "apparent heart attack." A person dies of a disease, not *from* a disease.

The age of the person who died is important to the reader. The copyeditor should check the age given with the year of birth. Generally, the person's profession or occupation, the extent of the illness and the cause of the death are recorded, but without details. The length of the story is dictated by the fame of the person. Winston Churchill's obit ran eighteen pages in the New York *Times.*

A person *leaves* an estate; he is *survived* by his family. Usage varies as to whether he is survived by his wife or his widow. He is survived by his children if they are children and by sons and daughters if they are adults.

If the family requests that the story include the statement that donations may be made to such-and-such organization, the statement should be used. Whether such a statement should contain the phrase "in lieu of flowers" is a matter of policy. Some papers, in deference to florists, do not carry the phrase.

A straightforward account of a death is better than one told euphemistically. The plain terms are *died,* not "passed away" or "succumbed"; *body,* not "remains" or "corpse"; *coffin,* not "casket"; *funeral* or *services,* not "obsequies"; *burial,* not "interment," unless interred in a tomb above the ground. Flowery expressions such as "two of whom reside in St. Louis" and "became associated with the blank company shortly after college" show no more respect for the dead than do the plain expressions "live in St. Louis" or "went to work for the blank company."

Few stories in a newspaper are more addicted to formula writing than the obituary. There isn't much the desk can do about the conventional style except to contrast it with those that take a fresh approach. Here is a lead from an Associated Press story:

New York—If you are a movie fan, you will remember Mary Boland as the fluttery matron, the foolishly fond mother, the ladylike scatterbrain.

The character actress who died yesterday at the age of 80 was none of these in real life.

The copyeditor should be on guard for the correct spelling of all names used in the death story and for slips such as "cemetary" for *cemetery* and "creamation" for *cremation*. Errors are inexcusable:

A postmorten failed to disclose the cause of death because the girl's body was too badly decomposed.

Thousands followed the cortege. The thousands must have been *in*, not "following," the cortege (the funeral procession). Even after death, a medal won by a serviceman is awarded to him. It may be presented to his widow, but it is not awarded to his widow.

If the service is at a funeral establishment, the name of the funeral establishment should be included for the convenience of mourners. It is not a "funeral home." A funeral service is *at* a place, not *from* it. A mass is *offered;* a funeral service is *held*. Even so, "held" usually is redundant. "The service will be at 2 p.m. Thursday..."

The passage should leave no doubt for whom the service was held. This one did leave doubt: "Services for 7-year-old Michael L--, son of a Genoa Intermediate School District official who was struck and killed by a car Monday in Bay City, will be held...."

People are *people,* not "assaults" or "traffic deaths" or "fatals" or "dead on arrivals":

A youth stabbed at a downtown intersection and a woman pedestrian run down by a car were among assaults on six persons reported to police during the night.

Hugo woman / among nine / traffic deaths

Dead on arrival at Hurley after the crash was Oscar W--, who was decapitated.

The events in a person's life that should be included in his obituary pose a problem for the desk. One story recited the death of a former school administrator who died at the age of 87. It said he had been the first principal of blank high school and had served in that capacity for seventeen years. Then the story recalled that he resigned two months before he was found guilty of taking $150 from the school yearbook fund and was fined $500. Should an account of a minor crime committed a quarter of a century ago be included in the obituary? To those who knew the former principal intimately the old theft was not news. Those who didn't know him so intimately could hardly care about the single flaw in an otherwise distinguished career.

The following death story illustrates several errors overlooked by the copyeditor:

Two Jefferson children[1] were killed when the automobile in which they were riding was struck[2] by another auto[3] Saturday night at the intersection of[4] Eastern Boulevard and Brooks Avenue in Clarksville.

They were killed instantly due to skull fractures[5] sustained in the accident,[6] according to Clark County Coroner Edwin M. Coots. Their father, George M. Gilbert Sr., 819 Morris Ave., was driving the car in which the children were riding.[7]

Three other Gilbert children were hospitalized. Lori and Brian are in satisfactory condition and Karen[8] is in intensive care at Clark County Memorial Hospital.

Michael was an eighth grade student at Parkview Junior High School and Christine attended Eastlawn Elementary School.[9]

In addition to their father, survivors include their mother, Mrs. George M. Gilbert Sr.;[10] a brother George M. Gilbert Jr.; and grandparents, Mrs. Emma Cannon, and Mr. and Mrs. Gobel Gilbert, all of Jeffersonville.

The funeral for Michael and Christine[11] will be at 2 p.m. tomorrow at Coots Funeral Home here,[12] with burial in Walnut Ridge Cemetery.

1. How old? 2. This implies blame. "Collided" is safe. 3. No mention made of the other car or its occupant(s). 4. Obviously it is an intersection. 5. The deaths were "attributed to," not "due to," Start the sentence with Clark County Coroner . . . 6. Redundant. 7. Say simply that the father was the driver of the Gilbert car. 8. What schools and grades did they attend? 9. What grade? 10. Redundant. 11. Victims' names have already been given. 12. Since this is an undated story, "here" refers to Louisville (place of publication). The mortuary is in Jeffersonville.

Reporters and copyeditors have no business playing doctor. If a child is injured in an accident, the seriousness of the injury should be determined by medical authorities. To say that a person who was not even admitted to the hospital was "seriously injured" is editorializing.

Medical News

Hospitals may report that a patient is in a "guarded condition," but the term has no meaning for the reader and should be spiked. The same goes for "he is resting comfortably."

No one can sustain a "fractured leg." He may suffer a *fracture of the leg* or a *leg fracture* or, better still, simply a *broken leg.* Injuries are *suffered,* not *received.*

A story described a murder suspect as "a diabetic of the worst type who must have 15 units of insulin daily." The quotes were attributed to the FBI. An editor commented, "In my book, that is a mild diabetic, unless the story means that the suspect is a diabetic who requires 15 units of regular insulin before each meal.

A wire service should not rely on the FBI for diagnosis of diabetes and the severity of the case."

The name of the doctor can be used in a medical news story under these circumstances:

1. If he is the attending physician to a prominent person, such as a governor.

2. If he is the officially designated spokesman for his medical society.

3. If his medical society has furnished his name as one from whom authoritative information may be obtained in his specialty and he has consented to the use of his name.

4. If he is an official, such as a state epidemiologist, the doctor is treated the same as any other individual in the news.

Doctor and *scientist* are vague words to many readers. *Doctor* may be a medical doctor, a dentist, a veterinarian, an osteopath, a minister or a professor. The story would be clearer if it named the doctor's specialty or the scientist's specific activity, whether biology, physics, electronics or astronautics.

Medical doctors diagnose the illness, not the patient. The proper term to use in determining the remedy or in forecasting the probable course and termination of a disease is *prognosis*.

Mothers are *delivered;* babies are *born*.

Everyone has a temperature. *Fever* describes above-normal temperature.

Everyone has a heart condition. It is news only if someone's heart is in bad condition.

"The wife of the governor underwent major surgery and physicians reported she apparently had been cured of a malignant tumor." It is unlikely that any doctor said she was *cured* of a malignant tumor. They avoid that word with malignant growths.

"A team of five surgeons performed a hysterectomy, appendectomy and complete abdominal exploration." Why the unnecessary details? It would have been enough to say, "Five surgeons performed the abdominal operation."

Unless they are essential to the story, trade names of narcotics or poisons should be avoided. If a person dies of an overdose of sleeping pills, the story should not specify the number of pills taken.

Also, use *Caesarean section* or *Caesarean operation*.

Usually, no sane person has his leg broken or his pockets picked. Use the passive tense: "His leg was broken"; "His pockets were picked."

Use the expression *physicians and dentists*, not *doctors and dentists*. The second suggests that dentists are not doctors.

A doctor who specializes in anesthesia is an anesthesiologist, not an anesthetist.

A person may wear a sling on his right arm. He doesn't wear his right arm in a sling.

"He suffered a severed tendon in his right Achilles' heel last winter." It was the Achilles' tendon in his right heel or his right Achilles' tendon.

"A jaundice epidemic also was spreading in Gaya, Indian health officials said The second disease claimed 30 lives." Jaundice is not a disease but a sign of the existence of one or another of a great many diseases.

Technical terms should be translated:

Term	Translation	Term	Translation
Abrasions	Scrapes	Suturing	Sewing
Contusions	Bruises	Hemorrhaging	Bleeding
Lacerations	Cuts	Obese	Fat
Fracture	Break	Respire	Breathe

An editor said, "Ever since the National Weather Service started naming hurricanes after females, reporters can't resist the temptation to be cute." He then cited the lead, "Hilda—never a lady and now no longer a hurricane—spent the weekend in Louisiana, leaving behind death, destruction and misery." That, the editor said, is giddy treatment for a disaster causing thirty-five deaths and millions in property damage.

Weather

Another editor noted that a story referred to "the turbulent eye of the giant storm." He remonstrated that the eye of the hurricane is the dead-calm center.

A story predicted that a hurricane was headed for Farmington and was expected to cause millions of dollars in damages. So the Farmington merchants boarded their windows, the tourists canceled their reservations—and the hurricane went around Farmington. This is the trouble when an editor lets a reporter expand a prediction into a warning.

The headline **Freeze tonight expected / to make driving hazardous** was based on this lead: "Freezing temperatures forecast for tonight may lead to a continuation of hazardous driving conditions as a result of last night's snow and freezing rain." The story made no mention of anyone's saying there would still be dampness on the ground when freezing temperatures arrived There wasn't and driving was unimpeded.

A lead said, "One word, 'miserable,' was the U.S. weatherman's description today of the first day of spring." The head was **Snow predicted / it's spring, miserable.** It was the weatherman's prediction, not his description. The sun stayed out all day, the clouds stayed away, and readers of the paper must have wondered where this U.S. weatherman was located.

Temperatures can become *higher* or *lower,* not "cooler" or "warmer."

On flood stories, the copy should tell where the flood water came from and where it will run off. The expression *flash flood* is either a special term for a rush of water let down a weir to permit

---

passage of a boat or a sudden destructive rush of water down a narrow gully or over a sloping surface in desert regions, caused by heavy rains in the mountains or foothills. It is often used loosely for any sudden gush of water.

Weather stories, more than most others, have an affinity for the cliché, the fuzzy image, overwriting, mixed metaphors, contrived similes and sundry other absurdities.

"A Houdini snow did some tricks yesterday that left most of the state shivering from a spine-tingling storm." Houdini gained fame as an escape artist, not as an ordinary magician. Did the snow escape, or was it just a tricky snow? After the lead, the twenty-two-inch story never mentioned the angle again. *Spine-tingling* means full of suspense or uncertainty or even terror. Sports writers are fond of using it to describe a close game, called a heart stopper by more ecstatic writers, often in conjunction with a gutsy performance. If a cliché must be used, a very cold storm is *spine-chilling,* not "spine-tingling."

"Old Man Winter yesterday stretched his icy fingers and dumped a blanket of snow on the state." How would reporters ever write about the weather without Old Man Winter, Jack Frost, Icy Fingers and Old Sol? Why do rain and snow never *fall*? They are always "dumped."

"At least two persons were killed in yesterday's snowstorm, marked at times by blizzard-like gales of wind." By Weather Service standards, this is an exaggeration and a contradiction. By any standard, it is a redundancy. A blizzard is one thing. Gales are something else. Gales of wind? What else, unless maybe it was gales of laughter from discerning readers.

An editor's moral: Good colorful writing is to be encouraged. But a simply written story with no gimmicks is better than circus writing that goes awry. To quote a champion image-maker, Shakespeare, in *Sonnet 94,* "Lilies that fester smell far worse than weeds." The writer who plants the festering lilies is only a little more guilty than the copyeditor who lets them grow. They have a way of reproducing.

Blizzards are hard to define because wind and temperatures may vary. The safe way is to avoid calling a snowstorm a *blizzard* unless the Weather Service describes it as such. Generally, a blizzard occurs when there are winds of 35 m.p.h. or more that whip falling snow or snow already on the ground and when the temperatures are 20 degrees above zero Fahrenheit, or lower.

A severe blizzard has winds that are 45 m.p.h. or more, temperatures 10 degrees above zero or lower and great density of snow either falling or whipped from the ground.

The Weather Service insists that ice storms are not sleet. Sleet is frozen raindrops. The service uses the terms *ice storm, freezing rain* and *freezing drizzle* to warn the public when a coating of ice is expected on the ground.

A cyclone is a storm with heavy rain and winds rotating about a moving center of low atmospheric pressure.

A *hurricane* has winds above 75 m.p.h.

A typhoon is a violent cyclonic storm or hurricane occurring in the China Seas and adjacent regions, chiefly from July to October.

Wind Table

Light	up to 7 m.p.h.	Strong	25 to 38 m.p.h.
Gentle	8 to 12 m.p.h.	Gale	39 to 54 m.p.h.
Moderate	13 to 18 m.p.h.	Whole gale	55 to 75 m.p.h.
Fresh	19 to 24 m.p.h.		

The word *chinook* should not be used unless so designated by the Weather Service.

Temperatures are measured by various scales. Zero degree centigrade is freezing, and 100 degrees centigrade is boiling. On the Fahrenheit scale, 32 degrees is freezing, and 212 degrees (at sea level) is boiling. On the Kelvin scale, 273 degrees is freezing, and 373 degrees is boiling. To convert degrees centigrade to Fahrenheit, multiply the centigrade measurement by nine fifths and add 32. To convert degrees Fahrenheit to centigrade, subtract 32 from the Fahrenheit measurement and multiply by five ninths. Thus, 10 degrees centigrade is 50 degrees Fahrenheit (See conversion scale in Appendix I.) To convert degrees Kelvin to centigrade degrees, subtract 273 from the Kelvin reading.

Weather Clichés

Fog rolled (crept or crawled) in	Mercury dropped
Jupiter Pluvius	(dipped, zoomed, plummeted)
Fog-shrouded city	Rain failed to dampen
Winds aloft	Hurricane howled
Biting (bitter) cold	Storm-tossed
Hail-splattered	

Disaster

Conjecturing about possible damage to settlements from forest fires is as needless as conjectures on weather damage. The story should concentrate on the definite loss. Stories of forest fires should give the specific area burned, the area threatened and the type of timber.

Most stories of earthquakes attempt to describe the magnitude of the tremor. One measurement is the Richter scale, which shows relative magnitude. It starts with magnitude 1 and progresses in units with each unit ten times stronger than the previous one. Thus, magnitude 3 is ten times stronger than magnitude 2, which, in turn, is ten times stronger than magnitude 1. On this scale the strongest earthquakes recorded were the South American earthquake of 1906 and the Japanese earthquake of 1933, both at a magnitude of 8.9. Intensity generally refers to the duration or to the damage caused by the shock.

In train and plane crashes the story should include train or flight number, the place of departure, the destination and times of departure and expected arrival. "Passenger train" is ad-

---

equate. "Crack passenger train" is a cliché. Airplanes may collide on the ground or in the air (not "midair"). Let investigators *search* the wreckage, not "comb" or "sift" it.

In fire stories, the sad truth is that in nine of ten cases where somebody is "led to safety," they're not. Except for an occasional small child, they simply have the common sense to beat it without waiting for a fireman to "lead them to safety."

In both fire and flood stories the residents of the area are rarely taken from their homes or asked to leave. Instead, they're always told to "evacuate" or they're "evacuated." What's wrong with *vacate*?

Eliminate terms such as *three-alarm fire* and *second-degree burns*.

"An estimated $40,000 worth of damage was done Jan. 29...." Damage isn't worth anything. Quite the contrary.

"The full tragedy of Hurricane Betsy unfolded today as the death toll rose past 50 and damages soared into many millions." *Damage* was the correct word here. You collect *damages* in court.

Disaster Clichés

Rampaging rivers	Tinder-dry forest
Weary firefighters	Raging brush fire
Fiery holocaust	Traffic fatals or triple fatals
Flames licked (leaped, swept)	(police station jargon)
Searing heat	

Labor Disputes Stories of labor controversies should give the reasons for the dispute, how long the strike has been in progress and the claims by both the union and the company.

Copyeditors should be on guard against wrong or loaded terms. Examples: In a closed shop the employer may hire only men already members of the union. In a union shop, the employer may select his employes but the workers are required to join the union within a specified time after starting work. A conciliator or mediator in a labor dispute merely recommends terms of a settlement. The decision of an arbitrator is binding. There is a tendency in labor stories to refer to management proposals as "offers" and to labor proposals as "demands." The correct word should be used for the correct connotation.

Strikebreaker and *scab* have no place in the report if used to describe men or women who act as individuals in accepting positions vacated by strikers. The expression "honored the picket line" frequently appears in the report even though a more accurate expression is "refused (or declined) to cross a picket line."

Union leader is usually preferred to *labor leader*. A longshoreman is a waterfront leader. A stevedore usually is considered an employe.

On estimates of wages or production lost, the story should have authoritative sources, not street-corner guesses. An individual, however voluble, does not speak for the majority unless he has been authorized to do so. Statements by workers or by minor officials should be played down until they are documented.

If a worker gets a 10-cent-an-hour increase effective immediately, an additional 10 cents a year hence and another 10 cents the third year, he does not receive a 30-cent-an-hour increase. His increase at the time of settlement is still 10 cents an hour. "The company has been on strike for the last 25 days." No. The employes are on strike. The company has been struck.

Criminal court terms should not be applied to labor findings unless the dispute has been taken to a criminal court. The National Labor Relations Board is not a court, and its findings or recommendations should not be expressed in criminal court terminology. In most settlements, neither side is "found guilty" or "fined." A finding or a determination may be made or a penalty may be assessed.

Financial News

A news release from a bank included the following: "The book value of each share outstanding will approximate $21.87 on Dec. 31, and if the current yield of 4.27 per cent continues to bear the same relationship to the market price it should rise to $32 or $33, according to . . ." The copyeditor changed the ambiguous *it* to *the book value*. Actually, the release intended *it* to refer to the market price, which shows what can happen when copyeditors change copy without knowing what they are doing.

Another story quoted an oil company official as saying that "the refinery would mean $7,000,000 in additional real estate taxes." It should have been obvious that this was a wholly unrealistic figure, but for good measure there was an ad in the same paper that placed the total tax figure at around $200,000 and said, "The initial installation will add about $7,000,000 a year to the economy of the state, not including taxes."

A story and headline said the interest on the state debt accounted for 21 per cent of the state government's spending. An accompanying graph showed, however, that the figure was for debt service, which includes both interest and amortization.

All who edit copy for financial pages should have at least some elementary knowledge of business terms. If they can't distinguish between a balance sheet and a profit and loss statement, between earnings and gross operating income, and between a net profit and net cash income, they have some homework to do.

This was brought home by a syndicated financial columnist who cautioned business news desks against using misleading headlines such as **Stocks plummet—Dow Jones average off 12 points.** It may be a loss, the columnist noted, but hardly a calamity. Dow Jones may indicate that the market is up, whereas it is actually sinking. Freak gains by a few of the thirty stocks in the Dow may have pushed up that particular indicator. Nor does a slight market drop call for a headline such as **Investors lose millions in market value of stocks.** They lost nothing of the sort. On that day, countless investors the nation over had substantial paper profits on their stocks. If they sold, they were gainers on the buying price in real terms; if they held, they had neither gains nor losses.

The Dow Jones Industrial Average is one of several indexes used to gauge the stock market. Each uses its own statistical technique to show market changes. The Dow Jones bases its index on thirty stocks. It is an index-number change, not a percentage change.

Reports of dividends should use the designation given by the firm (regular, special, extra, increases, interim) and show what was paid previously if there is no specified designation such as regular or quarterly.

The story should say if there is a special, or extra, dividend paid with the regular dividend and include the amount of previous added payments. When the usual dividend is passed, or reduced, some firms issue an explanatory statement, the gist of which should be included in the story.

Newswire stylebooks recommend that news of corporate activities and business and financial news should be stripped of technical terms. There should be some explanation of the firm's business (plastics, rubber, electronics) if there is no indication of the nature of the business in the firm's name. The location of the firm should be carried.

Savings and loan firms object to being called banks. Some commercial banks likewise object when savings and loan firms are called banks. There need be no confusion if the institution is identified by its proper name. In subsequent references the words *firm* or *institution* are used. Some newspapers permit *S&L Firm* in tight headlines. Actually a *firm* is a partnership or unincorporated group. It should not be used for an incorporated company. *Concern* is a better word for the latter.

Jargon has no place in the business story. "Near-term question marks in the national economy—either of which could put a damper on the business expansion—are residential housing and foreign trade, the Northern Trust company said in its December issue of *Business Comments*." Are near-term question marks economy questions marks? If so, can they put a damper on anything? Isn't all housing residential?

Major producers scrambled today to adjust steel prices to newly emerging industry-wide patterns. . . . The welter of price changes was in marked contrast with the old time industry practice of posting across-the-board hikes.

This approach apparently breathed its last in April, 1962, when it ran into a Kennedy administration buzzsaw, and a general price boost ini-

The Art of Editing

tiated then by United States Steel corporation, the industry giant, collapsed under White House fire.

Readers of financial pages read for information. False color is not needed to retain these readers. The following story should have been butchered on the desk:

Stock of the Communications Satellite Corporation went into an assigned orbit yesterday on three major stock exchanges, rocketing to an apogee of $46 a share and a perigee of $42 and closing at $42.37, unchanged.

It was the first day of listed trading on the exchanges. The stock previously was traded over-the-counter.

The countdown on the first transaction on the New York stock exchange was delayed 12 minutes by an initial jam of buy and sell orders. . . .

Two types of errors appear frequently in stories dealing with **Percentages** percentages. One is the failure to distinguish between percentage and percentage points; the other lies in comparing the change with the new figure rather than the original one. For example, when a tax rate is increased from $5 per $100 assessed valuation to $5.50, the increase is 10 per cent. New figure less old figure, divided by old figure:

$$\$5.50 - \$5 = .50; \frac{.50}{\$5} = .10 \text{ or } 10 \text{ per cent.}$$

"Jones pointed out that the retail markup for most other brands is approximately 33 per cent, whereas the markup on Brand J is 50 per cent, or 17 per cent higher." No. It is 17 percentage points higher but 51.5 per cent higher. Divide 17 by 33.

"Dover's metropolitan population jumped from 16,000 ten years ago to more than 23,000 last year, an increase of better than 70 per cent." Wrong again. It's a little less than 44 per cent.

Is the figure misleading or inaccurate? The story said, "A total of $6,274 was raised at each of the four downtown stations." This adds up to $25,096. What was meant was that "A total of $6,274 was raised at four stations." A not-so-sharp copyeditor let this one get by: "Almost 500,000 slaves were shipped in this interstate trade. When one considers the average price of $800, the trade accounted for almost $20 million."

Are terms representing figures vague? In inheritance stories, it is better to name the amount and let the reader decide whether the amount is a "fortune." One of the wire service editors noted, "Fifteen thousand might be a fortune to a bootblack, but $200,-000 would not be a fortune to a Rockefeller."

For some reason, many stories contain gambling odds, chances and probabilities. When a princess gave birth to a son, reporters quickly snatched on to the odds on his name. Anthony was 1:2, George was even money and Albert was 3:1. One headline

---

played up the third in the betting. The name chosen was David, an 18:1 shot. All of this shows the foolishness of newsmen who play into the hands of gamblers. If odds must be included in the story, they should be accurate. The story said that because weather records showed that in the last eighty-six years it had rained only nineteen times on May 27, the odds were 8:1 against rain for the big relay event. The odds mean nothing to readers except to those who like to point out that in the story just mentioned the odds actually were $3\frac{1}{2}:1$.

"Dr. Frank Rubovits said the children came from a single egg. He said the chance of this occurring 'probably is about 3 million to 1.'" He meant the odds against this occurring. The chance of this occurring is 1 in 3 million.

"The Tarapur plant will be the world's second largest atomic generator of electricity. The largest will be the 500-ton megawatt plant at Hinkley Point in Britain." A 500-ton megawatt plant makes no sense. What the writer meant was a 500-megawatt plant.

Some readers may rely on the idiom and insist that "five times as much as" means the same as "five times higher than" or "five times more than." If so, five times as much as $50 is $250 and five times higher than $50 is still $250. Others contend that the second should be $300. If earnings this year are $3\frac{1}{2}$ times as large as last year's, they are actually $2\frac{1}{2}$ times larger than last year's.

Insist on this style: 40,000 to 50,000 miles, not 40 to 50,000 miles; $3 million to $5 million, not $3 to $5 million.

"The committee recommended that a bid of $26,386.60 be accepted. After recommending the higher bid, the committee also had to recommend that an additional $326.60 be appropriated for the fire truck, since only $26,000 was included in the budget." The sum is still $60 short of the bid.

Equivalents should be included in stories that contain large sums. Most readers cannot visualize $20 billion, but they can understand it if there is an indication as to how much the amount would mean to each individual.

Here is an editor's advice to the staff:

We can do a service for those important people out there if we use terms they are most acquainted with. For example, to most of our readers a ton of corn is more easily visualized if it is reported as bushels, about 36 in this case. We normally report yields and prices in bushels and that is the measurement most readers know. The same goes for petroleum; barrels is probably more recognizable than tons. When the opportunity presents itself, translate the figures into the best-known measurement.

Nothing is duller or more unreadable than a numbers story. If figures are the important part of the story, they should be related to something—or at least presented as comparisons.

Two of the most common mathematical errors in news copy are the use of millions for billions and vice versa and a construction such as "Five were injured . . ." with only four persons listed.

Ships and Boats

Belay using nautical terms unless they're used properly. "Capt. Albert S. Kelly, the 75-year-old pilot who manned the Delta Queen's tiller yesterday . . ." What he manned was her *helm* or her *wheel*. Few vessels except sailboats are guided with a tiller.

A story referred to a 27-foot ship. Nothing as small as 27 feet is a *ship*. *Ship* refers to big seagoing vessels such as tankers, freighters and ocean liners. Sailors insist that if it can be hoisted onto another craft it is a boat and that if it is too large for that it is a ship. Specific terms such as *cabin cruiser, sloop, schooner, barge* and *dredge* are appropriate.

"A rescue fleet ranging from primitive bayou pirogues to helicopters prowled through the night." That should send the copyeditor to a dictionary so he can explain to readers that a pirogue is a canoe or a dugout.

"The youths got to the pier just before the gangplank was lowered." When a ship sails, the gangplank is *raised*.

Commercial ships are measured by volume, the measurement of all inclosed space on the ship being expressed in units of 100 cubic feet to the ton. Fuller description gives passenger capacity, length, age, and so on. Naval vessels are expressed in tonnage, the weight in long tons of a ship and all its contents (called displacement). A long ton is 2,240 pounds. All this is "Greek" to many readers. Copyeditors should translate into terms recognized by readers, who can visualize length, age and firing power more readily than tonnage: "The 615-foot Bradley, longer than two football fields, . . ."

A knot is a measure of speed, not distance (nautical miles an hour). A nautical mile is about $1\frac{1}{7}$ land miles. "Knots per hour" is redundant.

Some readers may understand when the story says, "The limestone carrier was en route home in ballast." All will understand if the story says simply that the ship was en route home empty.

Sports

Some of the best writing in American newspapers appears in the sports pages. So does some of the worst.

Many of the weaknesses could be minimized if sports copy were submitted to a universal desk for editing or if the sports copydesk were permitted to edit for all readers—the women, the teenagers and those with only a lukewarm interest in sports, as well as the sports experts. Too often, the sports copydesk permits the abuses of sports copy and magnifies the excesses.

Sports pages should be, and are, the liveliest in the paper. They have action photos, a melange of spectator and participant sports and an array of personalities. Sports writers have more

---

Style Notes 149

latitude than do other reporters. The good ones are among the best in the business; the undisciplined ones are among the worst.

Attractive pages and free expression mean little if the sports section is unintelligible to half the paper's readers. Too often, the editing reflects the attitude that if readers don't understand the lingo they should seek elsewhere in the paper for information and entertainment.

The potential for readers of the sports section is greater than ever because of the growing number of participants in golf, bowling, fishing, boating and tennis. The spectator sports, especially automobile racing, football, golf, basketball, baseball and hockey, attract great audiences, thanks to the vast number of television viewers. Thus the sports pages, if edited intelligently, can become the most appealing section in the paper. But first, writers and copyeditors must improve their manners.

A report of a contest or struggle should appeal to readers if it is composed in straightforward, clear English. The style can be vigorous without being forced, honest without being awesome. Sports fans do not need the fillips to keep their interest whetted. Those who are only mildly interested won't become sports page regulars if the stories are not understandable.

Know the Game One of the elementary rules in sports writing is to tell the reader the name of the game. Yet many stories talk about the Cubs and Pirates but never say specifically that the contest is a baseball game. Some writers assume that if the story refers to the contest as a "dribble derby" all sports page readers must understand that the story concerns a basketball game.

The story may contain references to parts of the game yet never mention the specific game. Here is an example:

Three Teams Tied in Sliceroo

Three teams tied for low at 59 in the sweepstakes division as the 11th annual Sliceroo got under way Thursday at Lakewood Country Club.

Deadlocked at 59 were the teams of . . .

In the driving contest, it was . . .

In the putting and chipping contest . . .

A best ball is set for Friday and a low net for Saturday, final day of the Sliceroo. A $5,000 hole-in-one competition on the 124-yard 11th hole is set for both final days.

Golfers will understand this story. But nongolfers, even many who enjoy watching golf matches on television, should be told outright that the story concerns a golf tournament. The added information would not offend the golfers. It might encourage a nongolfer to read on.

Some stories fail to state categorically who played whom. Again, the writer assumes that if he names the opponents' managers, all hard-core sports readers will recognize the contestants. Perhaps so, but the general reader might like to know, too. The legend under a two-column cut read, "They can't believe their eyes. Coach Andy S--, left, and Manager May S--, right, showed disbelief and disgruntlement as the Braves belt Pitcher Don C-- for five runs in the eighth inning of their exhibition baseball game Wednesday at Clearwater, Fla. The Braves won, 10–2." Now, whom did the Braves play?

Not ali readers understand the technical terms used to describe a sports contest. It might be necessary to explain that a seeded team gets a favored placement in the first round, and that if Smith beats Jones 2–1 in match play it means that golfer Smith is two holes ahead of golfer Jones with only one hole left to play and is, therefore, the winner. The name of the sport should be used in reference to the various cups. The Davis Cup is an international trophy for men tennis players. The Heisman Trophy is an award presented annually to the most outstanding college football player in the nation. America's Cup refers to yachting, and Americas Cup to golfing. Technically, it is *All-America,* not "All-American."

Answering more questions is one way to win more readers for the sports department. The key questions frequently overlooked are how and why. Why did the coach decide to punt on fourth down instead of trying to make one foot for a first down? How does a tournament get the funds to award $200,000 in prizes?

Unanswered Questions

"The shadow of tragedy drew a black edge around a golden day at Sportsman's Park yesterday, bringing home the danger of horse racing with an impact that cut through the $68,950 Illinois Derby like a spotlight in darkness." So, what happened?

The best training for copyeditors or the sports desk is a stint on the news copydesk. But before they go on the sports desk they should become familiar with the intricacies of all sports so they can catch the technical errors in sports copy. Here are examples:

"Center fielder Tony Cafar, whose fine relay after chasing the ball 'a country mile,' held Ripley to a triple." Unless Tony also made a throw of "a country mile," another player, the shortstop or second baseman, made the relay throw after taking a good throw from Tony.

When a writer covering a basketball game refers to a "foul shot," his reference should be nailed on the sports desk rim. The fouled player gets a free throw from the free-throw line, not the foul line or the charity lane.

The copyeditor also has to be alert for some of the wild flights of imagination used by sports writers. "The Tar Heels hurdled their last major obstacle on the way to an unbeaten season but still had a long row to hoe." Is this a track meet or a county fair?

The following passage is a sure way to discourage sports page readers:

Kanicki's troubles in yesterday's 27–6 victory over the Dallas Cowboys before 72,062, largest crowd ever to see the Texans, was the reason Gain was in the trenches to receive a shattering kick with 6:24 left in the game.

Style Notes 151

This example suggests another tendency in sports copy—turning the story into a numbers game. Box scores, league standings and records have a place in the sports story, but generally they should have a subordinate rather than a dominant role. It is questionable whether gambling odds or the role of gamblers should be used in either the story or the headline. Such intrusion often comes in races with their extra-special payoffs.

Abbreviated Sports

The addiction for abbreviation is strong in both sports copy and headlines. **Broncos get first AFL win over NFL** announces a headline. It means that Denver's professional football team scored the first victory of an American Football League team over a National Football League team.

The seventh paragraph of a story referred to the NPSA. The reader, if he was interested, had to reread the lead to know that the initials stand for National Professional Soccer League.

"Color" in Sports

An editor told his colleagues, "There is nothing more exciting than a good contest. There is nothing duller than reading about it the next day." Yet many spectators who watch a Saturday contest can't wait to read about it the next morning. What were the coaches' and players' reactions to the game? What was the turning point? How long was the pass that won the game? What's the reporter's comment on the crowd's behavior?

This should argue that if there is an audience for the report of a contest, the story needs no special flourishes. Loaded terms such as "wily mentor," "genial bossman," "vaunted running game," "dazzling run" and "astute field general" add little or nothing to the report. Adjectives lend false color. The Associated Press reported a "vise-tight race," "the red-hot Cardinals" and the "torrid 13–4 pace" as if these modifiers were needed to lure readers.

If all copyeditors were permitted to aim their pencils at copy submitted by the prima donnas of the sports world there would be no sentence structures like the following ones: "Benny (Kid) Paret showed 'very slight improvement' in his battle for life today while his embittered manager branded the New York State Athletic Commission's report absolving Referee Ruby Goldstein of blame for the boxer's condition as a whitewash."

"Maris, who has been bothered by a sore rib this spring, played eight innings yesterday, collected two singles and drove in a run." He didn't collect them; he hit them.

"Ortiz threw his first bomb in the second round when he nailed Laguna with a left and right to the jaw." How can you nail something with a bomb?

"Left-hander Norman, who started on the mound for Chicago, recovered from a shaky start and pitched six-hit ball for eight innings before a walk and a botched-up double play caused Manager Bob Kennedy to protect a 4 to 1 lead, as a result of a three-run homer by Ernie Banks in the seventh." The sentence is hard to understand because it is overstuffed and because the facts are not told in chronological order. Revised: "Left-hander

Norman started on the mound for Chicago. He recovered from a shaky start and pitched six-hit ball for eight innings. Then a walk and a missed double play caused Manager Bob Kennedy to bring in a new pitcher. Chicago was leading, 4 to 1, as a result of a three-run homer by Ernie Banks in the seventh."

Here is how to tell a story upside down: "Waldrop's 17-yard explosion for his eighth touchdown of the season punctuated a 65-yard march from Army's reception of the kickoff by a courageous Falcon team which had gone ahead for the second time in the game, 10 to 7, in the ninth minute of the final period."

An overstuffed sentence of any sort will be just as damaging, and harder to repair, than compound sentence leads. Note this one: "The heaviest betting non-holiday Monday crowd in the Balmoral Jockey club's eight years at Washington Park poured $1,066,919 into the machines yesterday on a nine-race program headed by the $7,500 Harvey purse, a six-furlong dash which drew six starters and was won by Mighty Fennec, piloted by Bill Hartack." Revised: "Horse-race fans put $1,066,919 into the Washington Park machines yesterday on a nine-race program. It was the heaviest betting non-holiday Monday crowd in the Balmoral Jockey club's eight years at the park. The $7,500 Harvey purse for the six-furlong race drew six starters. It was won by Mighty Fennec, ridden by Bill Hartack."

"'Statistics don't tell the story,' he explained, looking many straight in the eye." If he looked more than one person straight in the eyes while he said that, he must have been a long time between words.

It takes some editing to convert sports writers into Homers and Hemingways. At least, though, copyeditors can try to help writers improve their ways of telling a story.

Synonym Sickness

Copyeditors can excise clichés such as "pay dirt," "turned the tables," "hammered (or slammed) a homerun," "Big Eight hardwoods," "circuit clout," "gridder," "hoopster," "thin clads," "tanksters," "sweet revenge," "rocky road," "free loads" (foul shots), "droughts" (losing streaks), "standing-room-only crowds," "put a cap on the basket," "as the seconds ticked off the clock," "unblemished records," "paced the team," "outclassed but game," "roared from behind," "sea of mud," "vaunted defense," "coveted trophy" and "last-ditch effort."

They can insist on the correct word. Boxers may have *altercations* (oral) with their managers. They have *fights* with other boxers.

They can tone down exaggerated expressions like "mighty atom of the ring," "destiny's distance man" or "Northwestern comes off tremendous effort Monday" (Northwestern tried hard). They can cut out redundancy in phrases like "with 30,000 spectators looking on."

They can resist the temptation to use synonyms for the verbs *wins, beats* and *defeats:* annihilates, atomizes, batters, belts, bests, blanks, blasts, boots home, clips, clobbers, cops, crushes, downs, drops, dumps, edges, ekes out, gallops over, gangs up on, gouges, gets past, H-bombs, halts, humiliates, impales, laces, lashes, lassoes, licks, murders, outslugs, outscraps, orbits, overcomes, paces, pastes, pins, racks up, rallies, rolls over, romps over, routs, scores, sets back, shades, shaves, sinks, slows, snares, spanks, squeaks by, squeezes by, stampedes, stomps, stops, subdues, surges, sweeps, tops, topples, triggers, trips, trounces, tumbles, turns back, vanquishes, wallops, whips, whomps and wrecks.

They will let the ball be *hit,* not always banged, bashed, belted, blooped, bombed, boomed, bumped, chopped, clunked, clouted, conked, cracked, dribbled, drilled, dropped, driven, hacked, knifed, lashed, lined, plastered, plunked, poked, pooped, pumped, punched, pummeled, pushed, rapped, ripped, rocked, slapped, sliced, slugged, smashed, spilled, spanked, stubbed, swatted, tagged, tapped, tipped, topped, trickled, whipped, whistled, whomped and whooped.

They will let a ball be *thrown* and only occasionally tossed, twirled, fired and hurled.

They will let a ball be *kicked,* occasionally punted and never toed or booted.

They will resist the shopworn puns: Birds (Eagles, Orioles, Cardinals) soar or claw; Lions (Tigers, Bears, Cubs) roar, claw or lick; Braves (Tribesmen, Indians) scalp or tomahawk; Mustangs (Colts, Broncos) buck, gallop, throw or kick.

They will insist on neutrality in all sports copy, avoiding "home policy" slanting.

They will not make verbs out of nouns: "AP—Chicago manager Eddie Stanky nonchalanted the White Sox strike-breaker, saying, 'My food's going to taste the same. . . .'"

They will not string modifiers endlessly: "UPI—The Pistons won 29 and lost 40 under the guidance of the then only 24 years old DuBusschere."

Society One of the brighter changes in newspapers has been the transformation of the society pages, with their emphasis on club and cupid items, to the women's section or the family section, with a broader-based appeal. The philosophy of the new approach has been well expressed by two editors:

Pages of the Women's Section are edited not for the ladies who write the stories, not for the ladies who are the source of the stories and not for the gruff voice of the advertising department. They're edited for the people who buy the paper.

Women's pages were formerly edited for the few. Now the pages appeal to the woman as mother and working girl and as an intelligent human being involved in the total society.

The Art of Editing

Such sections still carry engagement announcements and wedding stories, but their added fare is foods, fashions, finance, health, education, books and other cultural affairs. They are edited for active women in all ranks, not solely for those in the top rank of society. They also are edited for the increasing number of men readers.

The better editors regard readers of the women's section as alert individuals who are concerned with problems such as prostitution, racism, civil disorders, women's prisons, alcoholism among housewives and educational reforms. Such editors strive to make their pages informative as well as entertaining.

Improvements are likely to continue. Some executives argue that newspapers should not segregate women, that material of special interest to the family should be scattered throughout the paper. Some maintain that club and social news should be held to a minimum because of low reader appeal. Others argue that the preoccupation with foods, fashions and furnishings squeezes out important items of women's activity. A quarter of a page devoted to a picture of a cherry pie might be trimmed a bit to accommodate a good story.

Some papers now handle engagements, weddings and births as court of record items. And a few charge for engagement and wedding stories and pictures unless the event is obviously news, such as the wedding of the President's daughter.

To add some spice to its pages devoted to wedding accounts, the Gannett Rochester Newspapers started a "Wedding Scrapbook" page to its Saturday section, "Brides Book for Greater Rochester."

Included are features on how the couple met, amusing incidents of the participants on the way to the ceremony, pictures of the couple in faraway places.

In many daily newspapers, especially the medium-sized and smaller ones, reports of engagements and weddings will perish slowly, if they will die at all. Still, some conventions may change —such as giving the bridegroom a break for a change. This point was delightfully argued by Paul Brookshire in his column in the South Dade (Homestead, Fla.) *New Leader,* and reprinted in *The Quill* (October 1967). Here are some excerpts:

In these days when the world is quaking in its boots and news of great significance is daily swept into newspaper trash cans for lack of space, it is sickening to read paragraph after paragraph about some little girl changing HER name to HIS.

The groom? He apparently wasn't dressed at all ... if he was even there. But Mother and Mother-in-Law? Yes. They were fashion plates in beige ensembles and matching accessories or something.

I ask you. Is it a wedding or a fashion show?

If it is a fashion show, why isn't it held in a hotel ballroom and why isn't the groom given a tiny bit of credit for the showing up with his clothes on?

The blackout of the bridegroom in wedding accounts is an unpardonable sin. If the groom is mentioned at all he is afforded as much space as an atheist gets on the church page.

And pictures. Did you ever see a photograph of a bridegroom? Maybe in the Post Office but not in the newspaper.

I'm going on record right now in favor of wedding announcements being run as legal notices—payable in advance by the father of the bride.

Better still, if the bride insists on giving a minute, detailed description of every inch of clothing she happens to have on her person, I suggest she take out a paid display advertisement.

In this manner, trade names may be used and shops that sold the girl all her glorious gear could get equal space on the same page.

Newspapers would reap untold profits from this arrangement and readers might be able to get some world news for a change instead of bouffant skirts highlighted with tiers of lace and aqua frocks with aqua tipped orchids and maize silk linen ensembles with . . . whatever you wear with maize silk linen ensembles.

Even though many newspapers have refined the society section, some retain a static style, especially on engagement and wedding stories. Wedding story leads usually read like these:

First Methodist Church in Littleton was the setting for the double-ring wedding rites of blank and blank.

Miss Blank has become the bride of Blank, it was announced by her parents, etc.

After a wedding trip to Las Vegas, Nevada, Mr. and Mrs. Blank will live in . . .

All Saints Roman Catholic Church was the setting for the single-ring rites . . .

Newspapers continue to use the following:

Stock words and phrases—holy matrimony, high noon, benedicts, exchanged nuptial vows.

Descriptive adjectives—attractive, pretty, beautiful, charming, lovely.

Non sequiturs—"Given in marriage by her parents, the bride wore a white silk organza gown with a sabrina neckline and short sleeves." "Wearing a gown of white lace cotton over taffeta with empire waistline, square neckline and short sleeves, the bride was given in marriage by her father."

Confusing collectives—"The couple is on a trip to northern Wisconsin and will live at blank Fairmount Ave., Whitefish Bay, when they return." Generally, a collective noun takes a singular verb when the noun indicates a group acting as a unit and a plural verb when it means individuals performing individual actions: "The Board of Park Commissioners gave its blessings. . . ." "The platoon fought its way up the hill. . . .""Their headquarters is in the Bennett building. . . ." "The crew have returned to their homes." Therefore, make it couple *are*, not *is*.

Details—gown and flower descriptions and social affiliations that reflect status.

Euphemistic headlines—**Betrothal told, Holy vows exchanged, Wedding ceremonies solemnized.**

Excerpts from an error-filled account of a wedding ($2\frac{1}{2}$ pages of copy) reveal the unbelievable triteness of such stories:

A petite white United Methodist Church nestled below the towering Rocky Mountains in Lyons, Colorado was the setting for the marriage of Shirley Ann M-- and Wesley William B-- on August 4. A happy sun brought warmth and color through the old-fashioned peaked stained-glass windows at precisely 3 p.m. when Gloria L. . . played The Wedding March, and guests stood from hand-carved oak seats, curved into an intimate half-circle to witness the double-ring ceremony.

. . . The Rev. D. L. N-- officiated at the afternoon ceremony amid arrangements of mint-green carnations, white gladiolas, and white daisies with giant white satin bows which adorned the alter. Pews were delightfully enhanced with waterfall baskets of fresh greenery and wild mountain flowers plucked early that morning from beside the St. Vrain River and tied with lime and powder blue satin ribbons.

. . . The Bride tossed her bouquet from the stairway and "went away" all dressed in white and yellow.

Copyeditors who handle news and features for the women's section will not allow writers to single out women's achievements by sex, such as housewife and woman doctor. They will delete phrases like "is affiliated with," "refreshments will be served," "featured speaker," "special guests," "noon luncheon," "dinner meeting." They will refuse to let a person "host (or hostess) a party," "gavel a meeting" or "chair a committee."

They will not let reporters go out of their way to use *female, feminine* and *ladies* in all manner of sentences where the word *women* would be proper and more appropriate.

They will catch slips such as "Mrs. Richard Roe, nee Jane Doe." *Nee* means "born" and people are born only with their surnames. The first (not Christian) name is given later.

They will remain on guard for awkward sentences:

Do you keep track of your weight and lose the first five or ten pounds too much?

Seniors realize the importance of proper dress more than younger students, but after a while they catch on.

All copy for this section, as well as for the other sections of the paper, should be edited for its news value. This should apply to the syndicated features as well as to the locally produced copy. The headlines should reflect as much care and thought as do those on page 1.

Style Notes   157

The copyeditors should not allow any story aimed at younger readers to contain anything that patronizes these readers. Even terms like *teen, teenager* and *youth* can be avoided, or at least can be held to a minimum. Copyeditors should make sure that both copy and headline talk up, not down to these readers.

10

The Copyeditor on Guard

Saying that something is the "first," "only," "biggest," "best" or "a record" seldom adds to a story. Often it backfires.

Perils of the Superlative

When President Johnson rode in a Canadian government plane, one wire service said he was the first American president to travel aboard an airplane of a foreign government. He wasn't. President Eisenhower flew in a Royal Air Force Comet from London to Scotland in 1959 to visit Queen Elizabeth.

Another wire service characterized Gouverneur Morris as "the penman of the Constitution" and Lewis Morris as the "only New York signer of the Declaration of Independence." The man who penned the Constitution was Jacob Shallus and there were four New York signers of the Declaration of Independence.

When President Johnson ordered the American flag to be flown at half-staff in mourning for Winston Churchill, the stories said, "This is the first time such an honor had been accorded to a foreigner." This is not so. President Kennedy ordered half-staffing after the death of Dag Hammarskjold.

A California obituary identified a woman as the "first postmistress" in the nation. A Missouri story reported the closing of America's "shortest commercial railroad." Both statements were disproved.

The Associated Press described Herbert Lehman of New York as "the first person of the Jewish faith ever to hold a Senate seat." The AP had to acknowledge that it was wrong by at least six men and more than 100 years. Jewish senators who preceded Lehman were David Levy Yulee of Florida, Judah P. Benjamin of Louisiana, Benjamin F. Jonas of Louisiana, Joseph Simon of

Oregon, Isidore Raynor of Maryland and Simon Guggenheim of Colorado.

When United Press International described the Flying Scotsman, a famous British locomotive, as the first steam locomotive to exceed 100 miles an hour, railroad buffs hurried to set the record straight. United States records show that on May 10, 1893, the New York Central No. 999 was timed unofficially at 112.5 m.p.h. on a one-mile stretch between Batavia and Buffalo, New York. On March 1, 1901, the Savannah, Florida and Western (later part of Atlantic Coast Line, later Seaboard Coast Line) No. 1901 was timed at 120 m.p.h. On June 12, 1905, the Pennsylvania Special traveled three miles near Elida, Ohio, in 85 seconds for an average of 127.1 m.p.h.

A story described New York's old 15-cent municipal transit fare as the lowest in the nation. San Francisco's also was 15 cents. Another story said Disneyland's 306-foot painting of the Grand Canyon would be "the longest painting in the world." The Battle of Atlanta painting in Atlanta's Cyclorama Building is 400 feet long.

A story from Louisville described a conviction as the first under a new law barring interstate shipment of gambling material. Two months earlier two men had been convicted under the same law. A Billy Graham rally was described as the largest for a single meeting. But a Rosary Crusade in San Francisco had been attended by 500,000, bigger than Graham's.

The story said, without attribution, that Mary Martin had been "seen by an astonishing 100 million persons in her two performances of Peter Pan." No one knows exactly how many persons watched the performances. At best, it was an estimate based on a projection of percentages of TV sets in use tuned to a certain program.

The foregoing are examples of the abused statistic that invades the news report. One story said that New York City has 8 million rats. Another quoted the American Medical Association as saying that only 5 per cent of Americans dream in color. How can anyone know such exact figures? Each year highway deaths become greater—because each year there are more vehicles on streets and highways. Highway deaths on holiday weekends are higher than normal because such weekends usually are longer. "The toll has dropped so that last year there were only 81 traffic deaths here, an all-time low." Since when? 1492? 1776? 1900? "The ships were built in record time." What was the previous record?

All superlatives should be checked. If they cannot be verified, at least they can be softened: "One of the most despicable crimes in the world . . ."; "One of the hardest-working actresses in Germany. . . ."

Most historical references also should be checked. A story said that Mrs. Helga Kraft, who was born in 1893, had been a former singer on the Chautauqua circuit and had appeared with Mme.

Schumann-Heink and Jenny Lind. Jenny Lind died in 1887, six years before Mrs. Kraft was born.

AP said the new defense budget calls for outlays "slightly below the record $79.9 billion by the Defense Department in 1945. (There was no Defense Department in 1945.)

Another AP story referred to the "turnover of jumbo C130 cargo planes." (But the C130 is not a jumbo type plane.)

Beware of the Hoax

Old stories have a way of appearing on the copydesk disguised as news. The following hoaxes are likely to show up occasionally:

—The story of a 16-year-old baby sitter who adhered to a freshly painted toilet seat for hours. A doctor administered to her, tripped and knocked himself out. Both were carried off in an ambulance for repairs and both sued the man who engaged the sitter.

—A woman driver flagged by a stalled motorist who asked her for a push. Told she would have to get up to 35 miles an hour to get the stalled car started, she backed off, gunned the motor and rammed his car at 35 miles an hour.

—The sheriff who was called to a farm to investigate the theft of 2,025 pigs discovered that only 2 sows and 25 pigs were missing. The farmer who reported the loss lisped.

—A farmer armed with a shotgun went to a chicken house to rout a suspected thief. The farmer stumbled, and the gun went off, killing all his hens.

—The story, usually from some obscure hill hamlet in the east of Europe or in Asia, of an eagle carrying off a three-year-old child.

—A Sunday driver who called police to report that someone stole the steering wheel and all the foot pedals from his car. A squad car was sent to the scene but before police arrived the man called back and said, "Everything is all right. I was looking in the back seat."

—Someone reports he has found a copy, in near perfect condition, of the Jan. 4, 1880, issue of the Ulster County *Gazette*. The paper is prized not only for its age but because it contains a statement made by the U.S. Senate to President John Adams following the death of George Washington twenty-one days earlier and refers to Washington as "Father of our country." Few copies of the original exist, but there are many reproductions.

—A story from Harrisburg, Pennsylvania, told about six students permanently blinded by looking at the sun after taking LSD. It was not until after the story had received wide play and had been the subject of editorials and columns that the hoax was discovered.

—Another story, this one in the form of a bulletin on the stationery of the Health Division of the Federal Housing Administration, warned that young women were in danger of developing fat legs by wearing miniskirts and exposing their legs to extremely cold weather. The story even went into clinical detail about how fatty tissue builds up as a protection against cold weather.

—A group of young stockbrokers got credit for plotting a hoax against New York newspapers during the depression days of the 1930s. They created a fictitious football team at a fictitious college and every Saturday during the fall they phoned in the results of the fictitious football game. The hoax was uncovered near the end of the football season when the fictitious college team began appearing in the ranks of the untied and undefeated teams.

—The bricklayer story makes the rounds periodically, usually with a change in locale. The story may have been reworked from a vaudeville gag of earlier days. It is recorded by a British accent comedian as a monologue under the title of "Hoffnung at the Oxford Club." Fred Allen used it as a skit on one of his radio shows in the 1930s. In 1945 the story was retold in an anthology of humor edited by H. Allen Smith. Three versions had their setting in Korea, Barbados and Vietnam. In World War II the "bricklayer" was a sailor on the USS Saratoga requesting a five-day leave extension. Here is the Barbados version, courtesy of UPI (1957):

LONDON, June 13—The Manchester Guardian today quoted as "an example of stoicism" the following unsigned letter—ostensibly from a bricklayer in the Barbados to his contracting firm:

"Respected Sir,

"When I got to the building, I found that the hurricane had knocked some bricks off the top. So I rigged up a beam with a pulley at the top of the building and hoisted up a couple of barrels full of bricks. When I had fixed the building, there was a lot of bricks left over.

"I hoisted the barrel back up again and secured the line at the bottom, and then went up and filled the barrel with the extra bricks. Then I went to the bottom and cast off the line.

"Unfortunately, the barrel of bricks was heavier than I was, and before I knew what was happening the barrel started down, jerking me off the ground. I decided to hang on and halfway up I met the barrel coming down and received a severe blow on the shoulder.

"I then continued to the top, banging my head against the beam and getting my fingers jammed in the pulley. When the barrel hit the ground it bursted its bottom, allowing all the bricks to spill out.

"I was now heavier than the barrel and so started down again at high speed. Halfway down, I met the barrel coming up and received severe injuries to my shins. When I hit the ground I landed on the bricks, got several painful cuts from the sharp edges.

"At this point I must have lost my presence of mind, because I let go the line. The barrel then came down, giving me another heavy blow on the head and putting me in the hospital.

"I respectfully request sick leave."

Perhaps, as one editor has suggested, the original version dealt with the building of the Cheops pyramid or the Parthenon. The story seems to appeal to the new generation of reporters and copyeditors.

Some others, though not hoaxes, are impossible or misleading:

—A man received a series of summonses to pay a tax bill. The notices said he owed $0.00 in taxes and $0.00 in penalties. He was warned that his personal belongings would be attached if he didn't pay. He sent the tax office a check for $0.00 and got a receipt for that amount Sometimes the yarn is applied to the nonpayment of a noncharge from an electric company and a threat to cut off service unless the bill is paid—or to a tuition demand on a student studying at a college on a tax-free scholarship.

—A fake obituary may be hard to catch but not this fraud that got by the desk of a New York newspaper: "The thallus or ruling monarch of the principality of Marchantia will arrive here today on a two-day visit as part of a State Department tour."

—Newspapers have worn out the gag about the man who answered "twice a week" opposite "sex" on a census questionnaire. Others that newspapers could do without include:

Undercover investigators yesterday said they ended a suburban sex ring where housewives worked as call girls to supplement the family income.

Smith will help to direct a volunteer effort embracing several thousand housewives, who will be calling on their neighbors for contributions.

In Germany yesterday, Mrs. R-- issued a statement to the German press agency in which she denied ever having improper relations with men other than her husband while in Washington.

Misquotations

Careful copyeditors would do well to keep a quotation reference at their elbows as they handle copy containing references to often-repeated quotations or attribution of such quotations.

They will stop reporters from attributing "Go west, young man" to Horace Greeley. The advice was given by John Babson Lane in 1851. Greeley used the expression in an editorial in The New York *Tribune* but amplified it: "Go west, young man, and grow up with the country."

Charles Dudley Warner, not Mark Twain, should get credit for "Everybody talks about the weather, but nobody does anything about it." Bill Nye, the humorist, originated the saying, "There are just two people entitled to refer to themselves as 'we'—one is the editor, and the other is the fellow with a tapeworm." Mark Twain later revised the statement: "Only Presidents, editors, and people with tapeworms have the right to use the editorial 'we.'"

Voltaire is wrongly credited with the quotation, "I may not agree with what you say, but I will defend to the death your right to say it." Most likely it is a paraphrase of Voltaire's "Think for

The Copyeditor on Guard 163

yourselves, and let others enjoy the privilege to do so too." General John J. Pershing did not exclaim, "Lafayette, we are here!" It was uttered by Charles E. Stanton, chief disbursing officer of the American Expeditionary Forces.

Careless writers attribute the "gilded lily" business to Shakespeare. But what Shakespeare wrote was, "To gild refined gold, to paint the lily." Similarly, the Bible does not say that money is the root of all evil. It says, "Love of money is the root of all evil." Music doesn't have charms to soothe the savage beast. Congreve said, "Music hath charms to soothe a savage breast." And Thomas Gray did not refer to "the maddening crowd," but to "the madding crowd."

Up to the time of his death, a South African dentist, Dr. Philip Blaiberg, had survived with an implanted heart. In an account of Dr. Blaiberg's death, a UPI reporter wrote that Dr. Blaiberg's last act was to scribble a quote from the Persian poet Omar Khayyám: ". . . for I shall not pass this way again." A Connecticut editor questioned the attribution, causing UPI to send out a correction. The probable author is Stephen Grellet and the usually accepted full quotation is, "I shall pass through this world but once. If, therefore, there be any kindness I can show or any good thing I can do, let me do it now. Let me not defer or neglect it, for I shall not pass this way again."

A sports column tribute concluded, "In the words of the late Grantland Rice: 'When the great scorer comes to write beside your name, / It's not whether you won or lost but how you played the game.'" What Rice really said was, "When the One Great Scorer comes to write against your name— / He marks—not that you won or lost—but how you played the game." Reporters should never quote poetry from memory. When poetry shows up in a piece of copy, the copyeditor should assume it's wrong and look it up.

The cutlines began, "Like Topsy, Baptist Hospital and Bowman Gray School of Medicine apparently just grew." The literary allusion is to Topsy's reply to Miss Ophelia's question, "Do you know who made you?" in *Uncle Tom's Cabin:* "'Nobody, as I knows on,' said the child with a short laugh . . . 'I 'spect I growed. Don't think nobody made me.'" It is a fine point, but it can be presumed that those familiar enough with the book to recognize the simile would wince at Topsy's newly acquired polish.

The story quoted a structural linguist's feelings about people who object to ending sentences with prepositions: "You remember what Winston Churchill said when an aide corrected a line in one of Churchill's speeches because it ended in a preposition? Churchill told the aide: 'This is an outrage up with which I will not put.'" Churchill was misquoted. What he said (and even this may be apocryphal) was, "This is the type of arrant pedantry up with which I shall not put."

A column criticizing the overuse of the word *gourmet* said, "I am reminded of the line of poetry which told of the moth flitting its wings signifying nothing." Was it perchance not a poem but a Shakespeare play, and not a moth flitting its wings but "a tale told by an idiot, full of sound and fury, signifying nothing?"

"We've come a long way since Commodore Vanderbilt said 'The public be damned.'" But the commodore never said it. It was William H. Vanderbilt, son of Cornelius, the so-called commodore, who made the remark.

"Robert Burns, the old Scotchman, said: 'Oh that we would see ourselves as others see us.'" Burns was a distinguished poet, hardly the "old Scotchman." Careful writers prefer *Scot* or *Scotsman* to *Scotchman,* as do the Scots themselves. The actual quotation: "Oh wad some power the giftie gie us / To see oursels as others see us!"

Copyeditors often have to decide whether to make corrections in direct quotations. Should they correct the syntax of the speaker? If the goof is within quote marks, should it remain? Did the speaker use poor English or did the reporter write poor English? Do the persons quoted get a friendly or an unfriendly pencil on the desk? Perhaps it was the writer rather than the speaker who used poor grammar. Usually the language is corrected in direct quotes unless, as one editor commented, it is done with malice aforethought when "we want to show someone ain't no good at talking," or the speaker is expected to abuse the language or a speaker, such as the President, makes a slip of the tongue.

Attributions

Copyeditors will save reporters from attribution log jams if they remember this question: Is it clear who is talking? If the reporter shifts to a second speaker, the story should identify the new speaker immediately, not at the end of the quotation. The reader assumes the first speaker is still talking.

Sometimes the source cannot be named, yet his statement is newsworthy. The editor assumes readers understand this when a story contains phrases like "a spokesman," "an usually reliable source," "a government official" and "it was learned." Many editors prefer not to use quotes around either fact or opinion ascribed to an unnamed source. Some observers understandably deplore the faceless source protection. These observers say, in effect, that if a government official with a special interest in Latin American affairs terms a resolution "worse than useless," why can't the fearless official be named? By withholding identity, papers shamelessly do other people's bidding.

Nonattribution denies the reader a very essential fact—often *the* essential fact—the source of the information, of the idea, of the speculation, of the proposal, of the supposition—even, sometimes, of the accusation. "Republican State Headquarters issued a statement today blasting. . . ." This is a statement of faceless political critics. Such statements should be attributed either to individuals or to official party organizations who are willing to stand behind them. There's no such organization as Republican State Headquarters.

SYNONYMS OF ATTRIBUTION. Is the synonym for *said* apt? Do "pointed out," "offered," "admitted," "disclosed," "noted," "revealed," "indicated," "conceded," "explained" or "cited the fact that" give the quotation an editorial tone?

Do the synonyms for *said* convey a hint of doubt as to the veracity of the credited source ("according to," "said he believes")? "According to" actually refers to the content, not to the speaker: "According to the mayor's letter . . . ," not "According to the mayor. . . ."

Does the writer use gestures for words?

"We're gonna put on a show, too," grinned Wags.

"Now I can invite my friends to play on the grass," Donna beamed.

"The bill will be paid," the official smiled.

"I heard something pop in my shoulder," he winced on his way to the dressing room.

No matter how good a grinner or wincer, how bright a beamer or how broad a smiler, you just can't grin, wince, beam or smile a quote. If it's a quip, that should be obvious from the context. If it isn't, saying so won't make it so. An exclamation mark may be used after a brief expletive but it looks silly after a long sentence.

Said is a simple verb that usually is preferable to others used in an effort to convey determination, skepticism, wit and so on. Most times the quoted matter can speak for itself. Many of the best writers use *said* almost exclusively. *Said* used repeatedly can give emphasis; it is not weakened by repetition.

Does the quoted word invite the reader to disbelieve the statement?

"Father Divine's blonde wife was at his bedside, along with his 18 'secretaries.'" By placing quotes around secretaries, the writer expressed an opinion, not a fact.

Do scattergun quotations bewilder the reader?

"The actress said she would wed Wilding 'at the end of the week.'"

"The blood-covered body of a 'brilliant' 19-year-old Williams College sophomore was found today—a rifle nearby—in a fraternity house room. Police Chief George A. Royal said it was 'apparently murder.'"

Is the source given immediately in a controversial quotation?

Where the information is disputable, the source should come at the beginning, not appended to the statement. "The administration budget has imposed a tremendous burden on consumers, it was contended by Senator John Doe in calling for revisions." Change it to read, "Senator John Doe called for revisions, contending that the administration budget has imposed a tremendous burden on consumers."

Does the quotation reveal precisely what the speaker said? "Stewart still maintains 'he called it as he saw it.'" You can't quote someone in the third person.

Does an awkwardly split quote interrupt the speaker? "'He,' said Jones, 'needs a wig.'"

Are the circumstances of the statement clear? Was the statement made in an interview, a report, a letter, a public speech? Was it in English or a translation? Was it prepared or extemporaneous? Was it made over a network or a single station? What network? What station?

Is the attribution overworked? In some crime or accident stories, phrases such as "police said" or "Patrolman Jones reported" are used in almost every sentence. A blanket attribution such as "police gave this account of the accident" would ease the monotony for the readers.

Added is not a good synonym for *said* unless it is used for an unimportant afterthought.

Tell Them, Don't Tease Them

News is regarded one way in the newspaper office and another way in the home, where, presumably, readers read newspapers. In the newsroom the reporter is constantly admonished to "keep 'em short." "How much do you have on that hotel death?" the city editor asks. "Enough for about four books," answers the reporter. "Hold it to two" orders the superior, "we're short on space today."

So the reporter prunes his story to two half sheets. The story lands on the copydesk and a copy pencil goes to work to get it even tighter.

All this, of course, is unknown to the reader who sits down to enjoy his newspaper. A headline catches his eye: **80-foot fall at hotel / ends actor's grim joke.** He begins the story: "'Watch me do a trick,' said the 26-year-old actor to his companion, and he stepped out the eighth-floor window of their downtown hotel early Sunday." Muses the reader, "I was downtown early Sunday morning. I wonder what hotel it was and what time." The story doesn't answer his questions. It did identify the victim. Also his companion. Near the end of the story was a brief description of the companion, Paul Lynde: "Lynde is a widely known actor, investigators said." "Funny I never heard of him," the reader again muses. "Wonder what he appeared in?" This was the story as sent by the Associated Press. For the morning papers the story failed to identify the hotel, did not give the time of the fall and identified Lynde only as a widely known actor. Readers of afternoon papers got some of the missing details. The hotel was the Sir Francis Drake, the time was "the wee hours Sunday morning" and Lynde was identified as a comedian who appeared in the Broadway and film versions of "Bye Bye Birdie" with Dick Van Dyke and in the movie "Under the Yum Yum Tree" as Imogene Coca's henpecked husband.

The ability to give details is the newspaper's great advantage over its competitors. Readers relate themselves to the news. The more involved they become in the events, the more avid readers they become. In short, they demand the whole story down to the last detail. If the story says, "Hastings Banda, the leader of Nyasaland, received his education in Ohio," the reader wants to know, "Where in Ohio?" "At what university?" "When?" He relates himself to the news. "I wonder if that's the same Banda I knew when I was at Ohio State in the fifties?"

A wire story on a plane crash in New York City said the 79 passengers included "two young opera singers en route to a South Carolina concert, prominent Southern businessmen, a former Virginia college beauty queen." The story as sent drew this protest from a client's managing editor: "Who the people are who die in these crashes is a point of equal or more interest than the circumstances of the crash. We all identify with them—where they are going, where they are coming from. I want to know what opera those opera singers were going to sing in." The details were in a side bar but the side bar did not go out on the single circuit.

A newspaper had a three-column photo and a six-inch story of the announcement that the Speakman Co. would move its general offices to new quarters. And what does the Speakman Co. do? The story didn't say.

A story related that a man had gone to court to fight for a seat in the legislature, but it did not tell which party he belonged to. Another told of a woman mugged while waiting for a bus at Delaware and Woodlawn Avenues, but did not give the time of this incident, which would be of interest to every woman who rides a bus.

When handling a story about an airplane crash, the cost of the plane is an important part of the piece and should be included well up toward the beginning.

In a wire story about a fighting policeman, the gist of the story was that the outcome of the bout would determine whether the policeman would try for the jackpot in the ring or give it up for his pay as a patrolman. Everything seemed to be in the story except the weight division, an important item to some boxing fans.

A story was about a drunk chimpanzee that supposedly escaped and created havoc around the countryside by trying to break into homes. But the story failed to tell who owned the chimp, what he was doing in the county, how he got anything to drink and what finally happened after a game warden arrived on the scene. These were basic questions the reporter forgot to answer. The copyeditor should have checked.

A paper had a three-column picture and story about consecration ceremonies at the Cherry Hill Methodist Church's new "Harlan House." The story told that Harlan House was named for "Miss Mollie" Harlan, that the Rev. Dr. Darcy Littleton took part in the ceremonies, that "Miss Mollie" is now buried in the Cherry Hill Cemetery, that Littleton is now with Goodwill Industries in Wilmington, that Dr. G. Harlan Wells spoke and the Rev. R. Jerris Cooke conducted the service. But when all this was said and the picture was examined, readers were still left to guess what Harlan House is or who Mollie Harlan was that the house should be named for her. Was she related to Dr. G. Harlan Wells?

A paper reported in detail the arrest of a minister on charges of operating a motor vehicle without a license, failure to carry a car registration card, disorderly conduct and disobeying a police officer. When three of the four charges were dismissed, the story failed to tell why. Answer: It is standard procedure to dismiss the license and registration charges when a driver has only forgotten to carry the documents with him.

A page-1 story told the fascinating details of a divorce decree upheld by the state supreme court but failed to mention the names of the parties in the case.

Another story gave an account of the senate's 78–8 approval of the President's trade bill but failed to tell who the eight opponents were and, even worse, how the senators from the paper's state voted on the measure. This was a revolutionary trade measure that had been in the news for months and was finally opposed by only eight men. Wasn't anyone who handled the story curious about their names?

A story under a March dateline said "the Bahais will celebrate New Year's eve at the Bahai center. There will be readings and music." The story continued, "New Year's Day tomorrow is known as Naw-Ruz." Couldn't the music and the refreshments be dropped and tell instead who or what are Bahais and what the heck New Year's is doing in the middle of March?

A skindiver stayed under water for thirty-one hours and spent much of his time reading a paperbacked book. No word to explain what kept the pages from disintegrating. (The paper was a glossy stock.)

A housewife won a fat prize in a magazine advertising contest. No hint what she did to win, a point made more important by the statement that the woman could neither read nor write.

Another story concerned a judge who reversed his own conviction of a union leader for breach of the peace. The reversal, said the story, was based on "new evidence" but failed to tell readers the nature of the new evidence.

A wire story from Los Angeles said that a legless man was ordered before his draft board to present documented evidence as to why he should not be registered 1-A. The story failed to tell how he lost his legs, a point that must have bothered several editors because a correction added the information that he had been without legs since birth.

The story said that the black students, 105 of the 120 Negroes enrolled at Northwestern, marched out of the building singing. It failed to mention the songs they sang, a detail that might have shed more light on their behavior.

If any part of the story is confusing, the copyeditor should supply explanations to make the story understandable. Obviously, the explanation should not be as hard to understand as the phrase itself. For instance:

Congress in 1946 waived government immunity to suits in tort (a civil wrong in which a legal action may lie) and permitted suits on tort claims against the United States.

The parenthetical explanation hardly aids most readers. If an explanation is required it should be one that really helps:

As a rule, a sovereign government may not be sued by its citizens unless the government consents. In 1946 Congress gave blanket permission to citizens to sue the United States government if they thought it was responsible for injuries to them or their property.

The story told of a boy who died, apparently of suffocation after he choked on a hot dog in his home. Police said the boy left the table after dinner and was found choking in his bathroom. His mother slapped him on the back in a vain attempt to dislodge the obstacle. Firemen took him to a hospital where he was pronounced dead. A few lines of first-aid instruction at the end of the story might have served to save other lives.

A woman who was hospitalized twice in a short time asked to be transferred from one hospital to another to be near her husband. What ailed hubby? It wasn't explained.

The Royal Navy dropped the unit *fathom* and started measuring depths in meters. The story told all about it. All, that is, except how long a fathom is.

A story contained the statement "where family income is below federal poverty levels" but neglected to tell the readers what the poverty level is by federal standards.

"There is little change in the pattern of news," an AP executive said. "The important difference is improvement in presentation, through explanation and interpretation."

"A bell captain in a midtown hotel was arrested for scalping World Series tickets." Why the reluctance to name the hotel? A directive reminded editors, "In these days, when GIs, businessmen, students, school teachers et al. are traveling throughout the world, such identification is often of interest to many readers. The part of town where a news event occurs is sometimes pertinent too in stories from the big cities that are frequented by travelers."

Here is a complete story as one newspaper printed it:

TALLAHASSEE, Aug 8—The simmering feud between Republican Gov. Claude Kirk of Florida and his Democratic cabinet erupted into a full-scale shouting battle today, and Kirk ordered an end to weekly cabinet meetings for the first time in state history.

Cabinet members immediately declared they would go on meeting anyway.

The stormy session began with the cabinet refusing to spend $35,000 on a federal state liaison office which Kirk wants to open in Washington.

Some readers must have wondered how a Republican governor came to have a Democratic cabinet, what officials belong to the cabinet, what can be accomplished by cabinet meetings not attended by the governor and whether the weekly meeting is required by law.

The first rule in writing or editing a story is to ask yourself: Who will read the item and what will they most want to know about the subject. Both the writer and the copyeditor should pare the story for word economy. They should not pare it for fact economy.

News presents the pertinent facts. That is, every story should answer all the questions the reader expects answered. If a big story returns after having been out of the news, it should contain a short background or reminder. Readers don't carry clips to check background.

Extraneous Facts

Robert J. Casey, Chicago *Daily News* reporter and author, once observed, "Too many facts can louse up a good story." If a fact isn't vital in telling the news, it should be omitted. It is an example of string saving. Stray bits have a way of bringing trouble. A buried reference to a thirty-year-old hanging "from an apple tree on Joe Smith's farm" brought a libel suit. Joe Smith was still living; the hanging wasn't on his farm. The reference added nothing to the story but taught the editor a lesson.

The following could be held to a short cutline; it is not worth five column inches of type:

Robert F. Kelly today was named chairman of this year's Democratic Jefferson-Jackson Day dinner.

The appointment was announced jointly by Democratic State Chairman John M. C-- and National Committeeman William S. P--.

Kelley, administrative assistant for 12 years to ex-Sen. J. Allen F-- Jr. in Washington, said he will name a dinner committee, site, date, and speaker in a "few days."

The Jefferson-Jackson Day dinner, traditionally held in late April or early May, is the largest meeting of its kind held by the Democrats each year.

Kelly said he already is trying to line up a "nationally known" speaker for the occasion.

Kelley, now associated with the legal department of the D-- Co., has been a member of the dinner committee for several years. This is his first assignment as chairman of the affair.

Kelly was a vice chairman of last year's Community Fund drive and has a wide background in party and civic affairs.

The Copyeditor on Guard

171

He is a past president of the Delaware State Society and the Administrative Assistants and Secretaries Club in the Nation's Capital.

More Precision

A school board (or board of education) is a group of individuals elected by the citizens to direct the operation of the school system. It is not a place, not an office, not a building, not the school system.

"He studied French under E. B. DeSauze, the retired supervisor of the School Board's language department." DeSauze was supervisor of foreign languages for the public schools. The School Board has no language department.

It is the American Museum of Natural History, not Museum of Natural History in New York City, the Smithsonian Institution, not the Smithsonian Institute.

The U.S. Supreme Court did not ban prayers in school. The court banned the requirement that children pray any particular prayer, or the writing by public authorities of a required prayer. The decision had to do with public schools. It did not interfere with required prayers in church-operated schools.

Gas and *gasoline* are not synonymous. Gas is either natural or manufactured. Some explosions are caused by gas, some by gasoline. The story and headline should contain the precise term. Similarly, in stories of food poisoning, the copy should specify whether the story is referring to canned or bottled foodstuffs.

Reporters and headline writers are fond of saying that taxes will "eat up" a will or a fortune or an estate. Taxes may deplete the check account but they can't eat up anything.

"A defective 20-millimeter cannon . . . suddenly fired and the shell killed one airman and injured another." The writer should have said *unexpectedly* rather than "suddenly," *a shell* rather than "the shell," *bullet, slug* or *projectile* rather than "shell."

Pistol is a general term for a small firearm. It can be single-loading, a revolver or an automatic. Clip-loading pistols are sometimes called automatics but they usually are semiautomatics or self-loaders. The barrel diameter of rifles and pistols is expressed in calibers (.22). A shotgun bore is expressed by its gauge (12-gauge) except for the .410.

"A 20-year-old robber was dead as the result of a gun battle in which 14 shots were fired at point blank range." "Point blank range" is an archaic expression based on the firing of cannon. Inasmuch as the expression is meaningless to today's readers, why use it?

Ethnic Groups

"It is perhaps the most cosmopolitan area in the city, stronghold of the Poles and densely populated with other ethnic groups including Czechs, Bohemians, Slovaks and some Italians."

Czechs and Bohemians are one and the same people. The Czech lands include Bohemia and Moravia. Some Bohemians prefer to be called Czechs. Slovaks are a separate people, although there is a strong language affinity. There is a difference between a Slovak and a Slovenian, as any editor will soon realize should he confuse the two.

Wire service copy sometimes fails to explain terms common in one section of the nation but not in another. For instance, readers may deduce that *bracero* is a Mexican laborer. If the word can't be explained, it should be eliminated so as not to puzzle readers who don't know Spanish.

An executive city editor gave the copy chief trouble for his failure to catch the idiocy of an "anti-Soviet" play written in the czarist days. Even though *Soviet* refers to, technically, an organizational system within the Communist structure, it is now generally accepted as a reference to the U.S.S.R. Russia, of course, is only one of the republics in the Soviet Union but is used as the equivalent of U.S.S.R. In headlines, *Russia* or *Soviet* means Soviet Union.

Britain or *Great Britain* refers to the largest of the British Isles and consists of England, Scotland and Wales. *United Kingdom* should be used when England, Scotland, Wales and Northern Ireland are meant. A Briton is a native or subject of Britain. Despite the fact that other nationals of the United Kingdom may be annoyed when *England* is used as the equivalent of *Britain* or the *United Kingdom,* the use of *England* in the wider sense is acceptable.

Edit to the Final Stop

"Tanglewood Barn Theater ended its regular season with a bang in its production of 'Wonderful Town' Wednesday night." Last paragraph: "The show will be repated at 8:15 p.m. through Sunday."

"His companion said Fennell dived from the boat, swam away, went under and never came up." Last paragraph: "Interment will be in Mt. Zion Cemetery." What was to be interred in lieu of the body that never came up?

"The largest single cost of the trial was jury expenses, which total $3,807." Later: "Another cost was $20,015 paid to extra guards and bailiffs."

A story concerned a robbery. Part of it went like this: "The suspect apparently hid in the store when it closed at 9 p.m. About 11 p.m. he confronted a security guard, Paul H. Hogue, 57, of 5625 Lowell Blvd., as he was turning off the lights in the budget store of the basement." Last paragraph: "According to parole officials, Hogue's parole was suspended June 6 for failure to report and he was being sought as a parole violator." A correction sufficed in this case, but a correction does no credit to the reporter or to the copyeditor.

Negated Negatives

The House voted 63 to 94 against overriding the committee's disapproval of a bill by Rep. Charles L. Hughes to repeal the women's eight-hour law.

The reader can't be sure at first or even on the third reading whether the vote favored or opposed the eight-hour law for women. He is obliged to take the time to spell it all out. The eight-hour day for women is on the books. Hughes introduced a bill to repeal it (negative 1). The committee disapproved (negative 2) the proposal, thus sustaining the existing law. If the House had voted to override (negative 3) the committee, it would have favored repealing the law. But the House voted against (negative 4) overriding, thus upholding the law as it stands. This is what the story should have said in the first place:

The House voted 94 to 63 to keep the women's eight-hour law.

How to put five negative ideas in one sentence: "Earlier the Senate refused to override its executive committee's disapproval of a bill to eliminate the non-communist oath required for state employes." The reader would have had less trouble understanding the sentence if it had been edited to read, "The Senate agreed with its executive committee that state employes should be required, as at present, to take a non-communist oath."

"There weren't many in the Turkey Day crowd of 11,554 who could doubt that Central lacked leadership in its 13–7 victory over Northern." Revised: "Few in the crowd of 11,554 could doubt that Central was well led in its 13–7 victory over Northern."

Taste

An editor of a morning newspaper said his newspaper likes to protect breakfast eaters against the incursions of unpalatable news. How then, he asked, did this sentence get to the breakfast table: "Plans to take still another sample were canceled when Hutchinson became ill and threw up." Actually, he *vomited*. Had the story said he became nauseated, anyone who is familiar with $10\frac{1}{2}$ beers—Hutchinson's load in less than $2\frac{1}{2}$ hours—would have gotten the point.

The Los Angeles *Times* and other metropolitan newspapers have adopted a screen code to control and avoid lewd advertising in entertainment copy. Marvin M. Reimer, one of the advertising executives of the *Times*, said, "It is not our intention to be either picayunish or prudish in our evaluation, but we are convinced that moral and social values have not decayed as frequently as portrayed, and we trust that together we can find a better standard of values in the area of good taste." Among subjects banned are bust measurements, compromising positions, double meaning, nude figures or silhouettes, nymphomania, perversion, and suggestive use of narcotics, instruments or alcohol. Words avoided include cuties, girlie, lesbian, lust, nymph, party girls, play girls, scanty panties, sexpot, strippers, third sex.

The caution should apply equally to amusement promotion copy and to all other copy. Both wire services direct their editors to downplay female anatomy. Copyeditors should apply heavy pencils to stories about the "ten best undressed women" and about an actress hired because of her uncommonly ample bosom.

There is no necessity to run everything turned in as news by the staff, the wire services or the syndicates. There is an obligation to print the news. There is also an obligation to edit it.

Some vulgarisms get into the report, usually when they are said by a public figure at a public gathering and in a justifiable news context. Most member papers used the following lead from London even though the AP headed the dispatch with a cautionary note: "'Gentlemen,' said Prince Philip, 'I think it is time we pulled our fingers out.'"

But the editor of a Dayton, Ohio, newspaper was forced to resign when management panicked because fifty callers protested after the editor had approved the inclusion of dialog, including words connoting sexual intercourse, in a page-1 murder story. The fact that the dialog was from a direct transcript of testimony during the hearing had no effect on management's decision. Nor did the fact that 110,000 or so other readers didn't complain.

Is *s.o.b.* milder than the full expression? If the President of the United States refers to a syndicated columnist an an "s.o.b.," that's news. The columnist in question passed off the slur by saying the President obviously meant "sons of brotherhood." Another President used the phrase "sons of business."

When Jack Ruby shot Lee Harvey Oswald, accused of assassinating President John F. Kennedy, he is purported to have exclaimed, "I hope I killed the son of a bitch." The quote appeared in the news dispatches from Dallas. There was a day when editors would have substituted dashes or asterisks for the words. Some bannered the quote, but with initials: **Jack Ruby—"I hope I killed the s.o.b."**

Frankness used in good taste is preferable to yesterday's euphemisms, such as "social disease" for *syphilis,* "intimate relationship" for *sexual intercourse,* "assault" for *rape.* Why refer to washrooms and toilets in public buildings, such as schools, as "bathrooms?" Ever try to take a bath in one?

The following story was published in a daily under a two-column headline: **Coed Reports Rape**

An 18-year-old university student claimed she was raped early Sunday morning by a man she met in a local nightclub, sheriff's officers said.

The woman said she was drinking and dancing with the man at the Sweet Lass lounge before accepting a ride to the man's apartment. The man invited her to his apartment for some drugs, she told officers.

When the couple arrived at the apartment, the man invited the woman into the bedroom and the woman accepted. The man then partially undressed the woman (she completed the undressing) and attempted to have sexual relations with her, she said.

The woman told police she said no to the man but did not resist his advances.

After a brief period, the woman said the man "gave up, rolled over and went to sleep."

While the man slept, the student said she got dressed and went to her dormitory. Because of her intoxicated condition, the woman said she was unsure whether the sexual act was completed.

The reporter should never have submitted this nonstory, except possibly as an FYI (for your information) for the amusement of the newsroom. The story should never have passed the city desk and certainly should have been challenged on the copydesk. No one was arrested or charged, so there was no news value. It is, at best, but idle chatter and has no place in a family newspaper.

11

Legal Limitations on the Press

The editor who lives in constant fear of a damage suit, the copyeditor who sniffs libel in every story and thereby tries to make the safe safer and the reporter who thinks it is cute to refer to an inept councilman as a simian have no place on a newspaper. The first procrastinates and vacillates, the second makes the copy vapid and the third lands the publisher in court.

Neither the reporter nor the copyeditor need be a lawyer, but both should know enough about the legal aspects of journalism to know when to consult a lawyer. Some of these trouble spots are discussed in this chapter.

The press can use its immense freedom vigorously. It is only when it abuses its freedom that it faces punishment.

We need no license to establish a press and start publishing. Nor must we submit copy to any censor before or after publication. We can criticize the government and its officials severely and have no fear that the doors to the newspaper will be padlocked. In our system, no government—federal, state, county or municipal—can be libeled. The newspaper is not a public utility. It can reject or accept any story, advertisement, picture or letter it wishes.

We do not have to beg or bribe officials to get a quota of newsprint. The newspaper is not dependent on the government for government advertising (except for the possible exception of legal advertising). We do not face the threat of withdrawal of the government's privileges should we disagree with its policies.

Courts generally cannot enjoin a publication, although it was done in the *Pentagon Papers* case. Punishment, if any, comes after publication. Long ago we rejected the notion that the greater the truth, the worse the libel. We can report, portray or comment upon anyone who becomes newsworthy. Even the President is not immune from publicity either in his public or in his private life. Criminal libel is almost nonexistent. Most libel is considered a civil wrong.

References to a half-dozen United States Supreme Court decisions will indicate the scope of the freedom the press enjoys. Our earliest cases helped to establish the principles that truth is a defense in libel, that the jury may determine both the law and the fact. The Court has held that there can be no previous restraint on a newspaper, even on one judged to be a nuisance. The Court has affirmed that it is not libelous to comment adversely upon the government itself. The Court has prohibited a discriminatory tax on the press. The Court has told judges that neither an inherent nor a reasonable tendency are sufficient to justify restriction of free expression, that contempt of court is to be used only where there is a clear and present danger of interfering with the orderly administration of justice. The Court has held that comment on or about public officials is privileged, even if false, provided there is no malice. The Court did not license reckless disregard of the truth but accepted belief in the truth of facts stated. The privilege is now generally recognized in regard to comment on the public acts of public figures as well as of public officials.

This brief review is intended to remind editors of the unusual liberties we enjoy. It should not deter editors and publishers from maintaining a constant vigil to preserve and extend these freedoms. We still have the problems of news management at all levels of government. We still have some judges and attorneys who would dry up most news of crime until after the trial. We still cannot use cameras in the courtroom. We still have judges who prohibit use of names of trial jurors. We still have those who would like to censor what we read, hear or view. We still wrestle with the problem of what constitutes obscenity and who is to decide what is obscene. Worst of all, we have many in our society who care little about press freedom. If these people could have their way they would return to sixteenth-century England and the Court of Star Chamber where any criticism of the realm was promptly punished. What some people don't realize is that the freedom to read, to listen and to view is their right, not the special privilege of any commercial enterprise.

The Libel Hazard

Publishers and broadcasters face risks far greater than do most other professional or business executives. More than a century ago a London editor, John T. Delane of the *Times,* said, "The Press lives by disclosures." All disclosures are hazardous. If

The Art of Editing

errors occur, they are public and may subject the error maker to liability.

The day is rare when any publisher or broadcaster doesn't commit errors—wrong facts, wrong names and identifications, wrong addresses, wrong dates, wrong spelling or pronunciation, wrong grammar, wrong headlines. Fortunately, only a handful of such errors are serious enough to cause or threaten a lawsuit.

Few libels are deliberate. Nearly all result from erroneous reporting, misunderstanding of the law or careless editing.

1. The common assumption that if a person involved in a story appears to be one who cannot prove damages as a result of the publication, it is safe enough to go ahead and use the story. Wrong, because under the law, if the article is libelous per se, damages are presumed. The amount is left up to the jury. ***Misunderstanding the Law***

2. The common assumption that if a statement originated from an outside source, it is safe. Wrong, because a newspaper is responsible for whatever it publishes from whatever source— advertisements, letters, feature stories.

3. Feeling that if a person is not named, he may not sue. Wrong, because a plaintiff sometimes can be identified by means other than name.

4. The feeling that if the harmful statement concerns a group, individual members cannot sue. Wrong, because some groups are small enough (juries, team members, councilmen) so that each can be identified and therefore each may have a case.

5. Misjudging the extent of the defense of privilege to report truly and fairly a judicial proceeding.

6. Misjudging the extent of privilege in an arrest. Statements by the police as to the guilt of the prisoner or that the prisoner "has a record a mile long" are not privileged. All persons are presumed innocent until they are proved guilty.

7. The assumption that if a court case has a bizarre aspect it can be embellished to the point of falsifying it. *Time* magazine once used this "Dutch" lead on a story detailing the suicide of Enzo de Bonze, son-in-law of the then Prime Minister of France, Gaston Doumergue, in the presence of the minister's wife:

Yesterday Curtis B. Dall, son-in-law of President Roosevelt, shot himself in the White House in the presence of his estranged wife and Mrs. Roosevelt. He died later in the day.

If such event were so briefly reported in the U.S. Press, neither readers nor publishers would be satisfied. Yet almost an exact parallel of that tragedy occurred in the Hotel Continental apartment of Premier Gaston Doumergue. . . .

Time's defense that the lead was purely fictitious proved to no avail.

Carelessness in Reporting and Editing

The following categories may prove to be dangerous.

1. Crime stories where there has been no arrest or charge of crime.

2. Mistaken identity. Similarity of names doesn't necessarily mean similarity of identity. Persons in trouble often give fictitious names. Identification should be qualified by phrases such as "who gave his name as. . . ," "listed by police as . . ." or "identified by a card in her purse as. . . ." In listing addresses in crime and police court stories, some papers use the block instead of a specific number. Several families might live at the same address.

3. Stories where the defense of truth is hard to prove or cannot be accepted into evidence.

4. Clothing the damaging statement with *alleged* or *allegedly*.

5. "Needled" headlines. Qualifications are difficult in a headline because of the limited character count. The assumption is wrong that as long as the story is safe the head can take liberties. Many readers read only the headline. A cutline also may be libelous. Within the story itself, statements cannot be taken out of context to create a libel. The story must be taken in its entirety. If a story has been written as a series, all the stories must be considered together.

6. The assumption that a person with an unsavory reputation can't be libeled. Wrong. He may be a notorious drunk but that doesn't necessarily make him a thief. Further, juries may take pity on "the unfortunate" and award him nominal damages. Jurors sometimes reason peculiarly. A Fond du Lac paper said a certain man was arrested for stealing a diamond pin. It was not a pin but a brooch. The error should have been immaterial because the gist of the report was true. But the jury felt it had to find for the plaintiff because the report was not literally true. It awarded only $1.25 in damages and permitted the plaintiff to tax only $1.25 of his costs against the defendant.

7. Confession stories pose dangers until the confession has been admitted in evidence in court. In pretrial stages, it is safer to say merely that the prisoner has made a statement.

8. The assumption that any statement made by one person to another about another is privileged if the reporter can prove that the first person actually made the statement about the second. Wrong in most states. If A tells a group that B is a liar, the reporter must be prepared to prove, not that A made the statement, but that B is, in fact, a liar.

Libelous Statements

Anything in a newspaper is libelous if it is false and if it damages a living person's reputation or has an adverse effect on his means of earning a living. The same applies to businesses and to institutions.

A story is defamatory if it accuses a living person of a crime or immorality or imputes a crime or immorality to him; if it states or insinuates that a person is insane or has a loathsome or contagious disease; if it tends in any way to subject the victim to public hatred, contempt or ridicule or causes others to shun him or refuse to do business with him; if it asserts a want of capacity to conduct one's business, occupation or profession.

Wrong assumptions sometimes can make a statement defamatory. A man who sets fire to a dwelling is not necessarily an arsonist. A man who kills another is not necessarily a murderer.

Some items in a newspaper are false but not necessarily defamatory. A false report that a man has died usually is not libelous. But if the person is a professional man and he can prove that because of the false statement his business has suffered to the extent of a provable amount, he may be able to collect that amount. To say of a mother that she has given birth to a daughter is not necessarily libelous. If she has been married only two months, she has a cause for legal action, provided she has not given birth, or there is no valid proof that she has.

Praising a doctor for his fine work in treating certain patients may be neither false nor defamatory, but it could injure him in his profession because of his ethical code prohibiting puffery.

Libel can be avoided or at least reduced if everyone on the staff exercises responsibility in accuracy, exactness and judgment. But even when libel does occur it need not terrify the staff. Some cases are not serious enough to entice a lawyer to take the case to court. Some lawyers hesitate to get involved in libel cases, especially if they are politically ambitious and covet the newspaper's support.

A statement may cause a reader pain and anguish, but mere vituperation does not make a libel; it must be substantial. It is not enough that the statement may disturb him personally. It must damage him in the estimation of his community or of those with whom he does business.

Only the man libeled has cause for action. His relatives, even though they may have suffered because of the false and defamatory statements, have no recourse in libel. The offended person must bring his suit within the statutory period (ranging from one to six years depending on the jurisdiction). If he should die before or during the trial, there is no continuation of the case by survivors.

If he has been libeled, he may ask the publication to print a correction. This could satisfy him because it tends to set the record straight. In states having retraction laws, the plaintiff can collect only provable damages if the retraction is made on request and within a certain time limit. A correction provides evidence of lack of malice.

Some newspapers may offer to run a correction, possibly offer a nominal payment, then get a release from further liability. This procedure saves the costs and hazards of a trial.

Suppose the plaintiff insists on taking the rascal editor into court. The plaintiff must hire a lawyer and pay the filing fee. He should be advised of the defenses available to the newspaper—constitutional defense, truth, privilege, fair comment, right of reply. Because libel concerns reputation, the plaintiff's character, good name and esteem can be put at issue. If he has a skeleton in the closet, he may hesitate to have his past revealed in court. If he is a public figure, he will have the burden of proving the material was published maliciously.

Suppose the plaintiff should win in lower court. He may get damages of hundreds of thousands of dollars—or only a few cents. If the defending publisher loses, he doubtless will appeal, even to the U.S. Supreme Court if the question involves a constitutional violation. Is the plaintiff able to pay appeal court costs if he should lose? Finally, publishers can get libel insurance at nonprohibitive costs, especially if there is a deductible clause. The protection is primarily for excessive judgments, usually of the punitive type.

Most of the larger dailies have their own lawyers to advise them on sensitive stories. Some lawyers urge, "When in doubt leave it out." But the publisher's attitude is, "This is something that should be published. How can it be published safely?" On these extrasensitive stories, where the precise wording has been dictated by an attorney, the desk should make no changes. The headline must be as carefully phrased.

Libel may involve business corporations as well as individuals. A corporation, partnership or trust or other business may be damaged if untrue statements tend to prejudice the entity in the conduct of its trade or business or deter others from dealing with it. Nonprofit organizations likewise may collect damages resulting from a publication that tends to prejudice them in the public estimation and thereby interferes with the conduct of their activities.

Libel Defenses

Constitutional

In a landmark decision in 1964, the United States Supreme Court ruled that the Constitutional provisions of the First and Fourteenth Amendments could be used as a defense against libel if the defamatory words were used to describe the public acts of public officials and were published without actual malice. (Times Co. v. Sullivan, 376 U.S. 254, 1964).

The court argued that debate on public issues should be uninhibited, robust and wide-open, and that the debate could well include vehement, caustic and sometimes unpleasantly sharp attacks on government and public officials.

The *Times* decision defined malice specifically and placed the burden of proving actual malice upon the plaintiff. The court said that actual malice consists of knowledge that a statement is false or shows a reckless disregard as to whether it is false.

The ruling was later extended to include public figures who thrust themselves into the vortex of public debate. (AP v. Walker, 383 U.S. 130, 1967)

It was used to permit robust discussion in criminal libel cases (Garrison v. Louisiana, 379 U.S. 64, 1964) and in privacy cases where the issue is in the public interest (Hill v. Time, 385 U.S. 374, 1967).

Finally, the *Times* rule was extended to include private persons involved in public interest issues (Rosenbloom v. Metromedia, 403 U.S. 29, 1971).

In 1974 the Court rejected the Rosenbloom plurality decision and ruled that the Constitution does not require that private persons involved in public issues prove actual malice in suits for defamation (Gertz v. Welch, 418 U.S. 323, 1974).

Private individuals may recover actual damages for injury such as impairment of reputation and standing in the community, personal humiliation and mental anguish and suffering, without proof of a dollar loss. Punitive damages were to be confined to a showing of actual malice.

One effect of the Gertz decision was to permit the states to make their own interpretation of libel and damages. One state supreme court upheld compensatory damages based on "a reckless disregard as to whether the published statements were true," and allowed exemplary damages because of "a wanton or reckless disregard of the rights and feelings of the plaintiffs." Thus, in this case the common law on libel retains its fictions— the assumed reputation of the plaintiff and the assumption of damages as a result of an assault on the plaintiff's reputation.

Truth is an absolute defense to libel in some states. In other *Truth* states, truth must be accompanied by good motives and justifiable ends. When truth is offered in evidence, it must be substantial, not hearsay or secondary proof. Mere repetition of what someone else said is not admissible evidence of truth. The truth must be as broad and as complete as the publication upon which the charge was made. Truth offered in evidence need not mean the literal accuracy of the published charge but rather the substance or gist of the charge.

If the defending publisher relies on a document as evidence to show truth, he must be sure the document can be produced at the trial and be admitted in evidence. If he relies on a witness to give testimony as to truth, he must be assured the witness is qualified to testify. To take an extreme example, a publisher could not rely on the testimony of a doctor who is prohibited from violating doctor-patient relationships. In questionable cases of provable evidence, evidentiary matter such as notes, references and pictures should be kept in the paper's files at least during the statutory period, or time when the case can be pursued. Any republication of a story will start a new statutory period.

Privilege   Reports of official, judicial, legislative, executive or administrative proceedings—federal, state or municipal—may be published and successfully defended as qualified privilege.

The qualifications are that the report be fair and substantially accurate and complete, without comment, on matters constituting or relevant to official action or performance of such public bodies or officers.

For example, a food inspector may make an official report to a board of health describing conditions he found at a certain establishment. His information, even though false, may be reported safely as long as the newspaper observes the qualifications just mentioned. If truth is required in the newspaper account, then privilege would be worthless as a defense. What a food inspector may say about Sunday school teachers at a meeting of a service club is not privileged. It is only the official conduct of an officer, acting in his official capacity, that can be defended as privileged. If the police say something not within the scope of their duty to make public, no privilege attaches. It is not made legally safe by prefacing the report with the phrase "police say" or "police reported."

Statements of attorneys or civic organization officials usually are not privileged, nor are press releases from all government bureaus.

Not even all acts of public officials or all actions before official groups are necessarily privileged. Pretrial and grand jury proceedings, for instance, are held to determine the extent of evidence available to warrant a trial or prosecution and are frequently one-sided. The fact that a pretrial hearing was held or that the grand jury is in session and for what purpose may be reported. Results of the hearing and the returns of the grand jury, of course, may be reported.

In many states the mere filing of a complaint, petition, affidavit or other document is not privileged. Anyone can go to the court clerk and file a complaint containing false, scandalous and damaging statements about another merely upon payment of a docket fee. Proof of the fact that libelous statements are contained in the document is not a basis for privilege. The gist of the complaint, without the specifically damaging parts, may be reported, along with an answer by the defendant. Even if the defendant is not available or prepared to answer, the fact that the paper tried to give both sides evidences lack of malice. Federal filings are normally privileged.

Sealed records usually are not privileged.

Some states hold that the agenda of a city council is not privileged because it may contain complaints and criticisms that may never come before the meeting. Of course, the open meeting of the council is privileged.

Confessions usually have no legal standing until they are introduced as evidence and accepted by the court. Reporting a pretrial confession is dangerous, particularly if the defendant later is acquitted, if the court refuses to allow the confession or if the confession implicates others. The usual practice today is to state simply that the prisoner made a statement to the police or to the prosecuting attorney. Also, the fact that the police are questioning a man about a crime does not mean, necessarily, that the man is a suspect.

In detailing charges, the reporter should give specific, not generalized, accusations. Some terms used in newspaper reports, such as "black market operations," are not even statutory offenses.

Some quasi-official proceedings, such as ecclesiastical hearings or those involving labor disputes, may be reported as privileged provided the report observes the qualifications already mentioned.

Some public meetings afford no privilege in themselves, but a report of such meetings is justified when there is general public interest. Certainly the public has an interest in the discussion of taxes, public funds, health and welfare and community morals. When subjects of public interest are discussed at conventions, caucuses, community clubs, stockholders' meetings and the like, they are reported, even though the meetings are not privileged occasions. Again, even when the occasion is not strictly privileged, every attempt should be made to give both sides of the controversy.

Newspapers are free to discuss public affairs and to comment upon the conduct of public officials. This defense has three qualifications: (1) The comment is founded upon facts or what the publisher had reasonable grounds to believe are facts. (2) The comment is not made maliciously. Here, the burden of proof is on the plaintiff. (3) The comment does not involve the private life or moral character of a person except where such has a direct bearing upon his qualifications or work.

Fair Comment and Criticism

Anyone who puts himself or his work before the public is subject to public assessment of his performance, however strong the terms of censure may be. Decisions of the U.S. Supreme Court suggest that, short of malice and reckless disregard of their truths, all debates on public issues should be uninhibited, robust and wide-open, and that it may well include vehement, caustic and sometimes unpleasantly sharp attacks on government and public officials. The same freedom could very well apply to comments on anyone in the public eye.

This should not be construed as license. Character and public reputation are priceless possessions and are not good hunting grounds simply because a person holds public office, aspires to public office or in any manner offers himself or his talents to the public. There is a difference between assessing the fitness of a candidate or commenting upon the products of a public performer and a reckless attack on his character and reputation.

Corrections

The publication of a correction technically admits the libel and therefore negates truth as a defense. But when the defense of truth is not clearly evident, the publisher should willingly correct. The correction operates to refute the plaintiff's claim of malice. A refusal to correct may be used to show malice.

When made, the correction should be full and frank and used as conspicuously as the article complained of.

A reporter obtained her story over the phone from the judge's secretary. She took her notes in shorthand. When she transcribed her notes, she mistook DWS (driving while under suspension) for DWI (driving while intoxicated) and thus wrote falsely that a certain person had pleaded guilty to driving while intoxicated. Even if this story had been edited by another it is unlikely the copyeditor would have caught the error. The paper should have printed a correction to indicate lack of malice and to escape punitive damages should the injured person sue for libel.

But a second story was not a clear correction and this should have been corrected by a copyeditor. The headline read **Ex-sheriff's / patrolman / admits count.** The lead: "A man who five months ago was suspended from the Franklin County Sheriff's Patrol was arraigned in municipal court here yesterday, pleading guilty to driving for the past nine years on a suspended license." Later, the story said that the patrolman had been dropped from the force for "misuse of authority" and later qualified that statement with another to the effect the patrolman had to resign on order of the Office of Strategic Information, USAF, Ft. Ethan Allen, Vermont.

The patrolman sued for libel. The defense tried to argue that the crime of driving while the license was suspended was as serious as the crime of driving while intoxicated and therefore the newspaper should not be held accountable for a minor error. The jury disagreed and returned a judgment of $3,500 for the former patrolman.

Reply and Consent

An individual may ask to reply in a newspaper to another's attack upon him in a newspaper. Even though the reply is defamatory, it will be privileged for the individual and the newspaper, provided the defamatory matter is essential to support a contention that the original attack was false and the reply is not substantially stronger than the original.

If the disputants in a public controversy insist on arguing their cases in the newspapers—in stories, letters or advertisements—the publisher may ask the contenders to contract to assume all liabilities in the event of a suit. The device inevitably forces the arguments to be more temperate.

If an individual volunteers a comment to a newspaper in reply to a statement made against him by another, it is assumed he has consented to the publication of his comment and he would have no recourse for damages.

In all issues fraught with libel the newspaper can reduce its hazards by carefully attempting to show both sides of a controversy. If the reply can be used along with the original story, the better. By giving both sides equal prominence—in headlines or in text—the newspaper at least demonstrates a lack of malice.

Contempt of Court

The copyeditor has little if any concern with direct contempt of court—wilful disobedience in the presence of the court, such as taking photographs in the courtroom without the court's consent. The copyeditor is concerned mainly with constructive or indirect criminal contempt—accounts, headlines or cutlines that disregard the dignity and authority of the court or which tend to impede the administration of justice.

The copyeditor who handles a court story may find it almost impossible to verify every fact contained in the account. If the story concerns a running trial, the copyeditor can obtain the clippings of previous stories and at least double-check the names of the principals, the precise action and the correct legal terms.

Here are examples of reporting errors as given by one district judge to the authors: "By way of example, probation was confused with parole, the defendant was reported to have been sent to the penitentiary when such was not the case, the wrong defendant was named in one story, two cases were reported consolidated for trial which was not the case, and in another story the reporter had the action taking place in the wrong court. These are not particularly serious errors but are indicative of the inaccuracy that is common in this type of reporting."

Such errors do not reflect to the credit of a newspaper that prides itself on accurate reporting and editing of all the news it prints. Even though most errors in reporting legal proceedings are not serious enough to bring citations against the reporter or the newspaper, they have deserved the contempt expressed by many judges concerning inaccuracies in the court report. Justice Wiley B. Rutledge commented in the Pennekamp v. Florida decision (328 U.S. 331, 1946), "There is perhaps no area of news more inaccurately reported factually, on the whole, though with some notable exceptions, than legal news." And Justice William O. Douglas in the Craig v. Harney case (331 U.S. 367, 1947), said, "Inaccuracies in reporting (legal news) are commonplace."

Such comments should put the copyeditor on guard on all legal copy.

Right of Privacy

A libel action is brought to protect a person's reputation against defamation. Privacy is an action to protect personality rights. The distinction between the two is not as clear as it once was because privacy is now being used as an alternative to libel or in conjunction with libel.

Privacy is an expanding legal doctrine with so much vagueness and ill-defined limits that the press has difficulty in knowing where it stands legally.

Privacy encompasses four torts:

1. Intrusion upon the plaintiff's seclusion or solitude, or into his private affairs.
2. Public disclosure of embarrassing private facts about the plaintiff.
3. Publicity which places the plaintiff in a false light in the public eye.
4. Appropriation, for the defendant's advantage, of the plaintiff's name or likeness.

Newspaper accounts generally concern newsworthy subjects who have forfeited, voluntarily or involuntarily, their rights of privacy. Privacy does not protect a person or his actions if they are a matter of legitimate public interest. Newsworthiness is based on three basic components: public interest, public figures and public records.

One of the shady areas in privacy is the duration of "legitimate public interest." In one case, the court held, in effect, that there was legitimate public interest in an infant child prodigy and in a follow-up article twenty-seven years later under the heading "Where Are They Now?" But identification of persons in connection with stories of long-past crimes is legally dangerous unless, again, there is legitimate public interest in the retold story.

In 1968 a bridge over the Ohio River collapsed and forty-four persons lost their lives, including Melvin Aaron Cantrell. About five months later a reporter and a photographer for the Cleveland *Plain Dealer* went to Point Pleasant, W. Va., and did a follow-up feature on the Cantrell family. The story contained some inaccuracies and implied that Mrs. Cantrell was present in her home when the journalists were there. Five photographs were printed, depicting the home as dirty and run down and the children poorly clothed and untidy.

The Cantrells then sought a $1 million libel-invasion of privacy judgment against the *Plain Dealer*. The U.S. Court of Appeals in Cincinnati reversed the judgment but said there was no evidence of any activity related to the bridge disaster which would naturally have rekindled public interest in the event. "Nevertheless," the court continued, "we believe the journalistic judgment of a newspaper publisher...cannot be circumscribed by linking newsworthiness solely to the passage of time." On December 18, 1974, the U.S. Supreme Court in effect upheld the jury's award of $60,000 in actual damages against the publisher and the article writer. Justice Stewart warned against inferring that states henceforth could apply a more relaxed standard of liability in false-light cases.[1]

Generally, a person who voluntarily participates in a public event abandons his or her privacy. Thus, a newspaper may legitimately display the types of persons who join the Easter parade. But a newspaper in Alabama had to pay damages to a woman photographed while her skirts were blown above her head by an air jet in a fun house at a county fair.

Some risk is involved in printing photographs taken of people without their consent in their home or in a hospital bed. Pictures showing ways to beat the summer heat may be humorous to readers but not to the hefty lady fanning herself under a tree in her own backyard.

Truth may not always be accepted as a defense in a privacy invasion case, but truth, combined with privilege, is a defense. That is, the defense is adequate if the information is truthful, comes from an open, public trial or comes from court documents that are open for public inspection. The Supreme Court has ruled that even in states where identification of a rape victim is forbidden, civil damages cannot be collected for privacy invasion provided the report is true and privileged.

Knowing or reckless falsehoods or even falsehoods "plainly implied" invite damages for invasion of privacy even if the incidents or those involved are newsworthy, i.e., in the public interest.

The copyeditor's responsibility is to make sure the story can have but one interpretation. Loosely written stories that invite reading "between the lines" to determine what the reporter intended to say are unsafe.

The increasing number of damage suits claiming invasion of privacy could suggest that eventually privacy intrusion will concern editors as much as libel actions. Again, the defenses, truth or public figure, may have to be weighed against needless harmful details that intrude on privacy. When the essential facts of a story have been reported, that should suffice. But some papers overkill by piling on endless intimate details of the subject's personal life. An example was the story of the ex-marine who deflected a pistol aimed at the President of the United States. Subsequent stories, printed in some papers, that leaders in a gay community had identified the ex-marine as a homosexual added little, if anything, to the dimension of the original account.

States recognize privacy in statutes such as those prohibiting identification of rape victims and juvenile delinquents. Utah gives corporations a right of privacy. And both Utah and Virginia

---

[1] William E. Francois, *Mass Media Law and Regulation*, pp. 131, 132 (Columbus, Ohio: Grid, 1975).

permit surviving relatives to bring privacy actions against the exploitation of the names or likenesses of deceased relatives. The federal courts recognize an action for an invasion of privacy.

Some authorities see the Privacy Act of 1974 in conflict with the Freedom of Information law. The privacy act, together with actions of state legislature, are designed to prevent the use of government-held information about private individuals outside of government, or abuse of that information inside government. Of particular concern to news-gatherers is the drive to destroy or seal arrest records and even conviction records.

Juvenile Delinquents

Some states permit the publication of news or pictures of juvenile delinquents—defined as anyone under the age of eighteen. Many officials insist that names of juvenile offenders be withheld on the theory that there is greater opportunity for rehabilitation if the youth is not stigmatized by publicity that may affect him for the rest of his life.

In some states the children's code gives exclusive jurisdiction to the juvenile court over offenders under fourteen, regardless of the acts committed, and gives concurrent jurisdiction to the district court over youngsters between sixteen and eighteen, unless the crime involved is punishable by either death or life imprisonment if committed by an adult. In murder cases involving youths fourteen and over, the district court has original jurisdiction. These states make it a misdemeanor to publish the names, pictures or identity of youths under eighteen or that of the parents, guardians or places of residence of children involved in any crime or in dependency cases within the state's jurisdiction.

Publicity may be given under the following circumstances:

1. Public hearings. A U.S. Supreme Court decision extends to juveniles the same due process of law guarantees provided adults in criminal proceedings. The juvenile has the same rights against self-incrimination, to representation and even to a jury trial. Even in juvenile court, the youngster has a right to a public trial if he requests it. But after the finding of the jury at a public trial, the juvenile could still be placed before a juvenile court for disposition—out of sight of the press and the public.

2. Permission of the court. If the code permits it, the judge may, at his discretion, allow publicity concerning the hearing on a juvenile. Frequently, the judge of a juvenile court allows reporters to attend juvenile court sessions but does not permit identification of the youthful offender. There may be publication of news of such cases that may serve as a warning to violators of laws for the protection of children, provided that any reference to any child involved be so disguised as to prevent identification.

3. Traffic cases. Names of persons of any age may be used in traffic cases.

Copyeditors should be alert to the distinction between a juvenile and a minor, the latter being defined as anyone under the age of twenty-one.

A new federal law on juvenile justice provides for the first time a uniform federal policy against disclosure of case records to the media, but not to police or other courts.

Probate

The value of an estate contained in a will filed for probate or proving is a newsworthy item and invariably is included in the reporter's story, usually in the lead. Because the lawyer who files the will for probate is required to estimate the total value of the estate, his figure invariably is low. The exact amount will not become known until several months later when an inventory is filed.

The proportions of the bequests and to whom they are to be made are factual items. Both the story and the headline should make clear that the dollar value of the estate is only an estimate.

Plagiarism and Copyright Infringement

Plagiarism and copyright infringement are still other fringe areas concerning the copyeditor. Only the expression of news, not the news itself, can be copyrighted. Even if a newspaper does not protect itself by copyrighting the entire paper or individual stories, it still has a property right in its news and can prevent others from "lifting" the material.

It is assumed that copyeditors will be so thoroughly familiar with the contents of opposition papers and exchanges that they will be able to spot material that copies or paraphrases too closely the work of others.

If a wire service sends out a story based on the story of another member or client, copyeditors should not delete the wire service credit to the originator of the story. Nor should they delete any credit on stories or pictures. They may, if directed, compile stories from various sources into one comprehensive story, adding the sources from which the story was compiled.

If their own paper publishes a story to be copyrighted, copyeditors should insure that the notice is complete—the notice of copyright, the date and by whom.

In editing book review copy, copyeditors should have some notion of the limits of fair use of the author's quotes. The problem is relatively minor because few copyright owners would object to the publishing of extracts in a review, especially if the review were favorable. If the review has to be trimmed, the trimming probably would come in the quoted extracts.

Other Restrictions

The states as well as the federal government have regulations dealing with matters such as false reports on the condition of financial institutions, advocacy of a violent overthrow of the government and misleading advertising or promotion of stocks and securities.

Postal regulations cover a substantial range of prohibitions— libel, threatening matter, counterfeit forecasts, matter tending to aid or abet a mail fraud, photographs of money and stamps, pornography and promotion of lotteries.

A lottery is any scheme containing three elements—consideration paid, a prize or award and determination of the winner by chance. This includes all drawings for prizes and raffles, and games such as bingo and keno. It is immaterial who sponsors the scheme. Pictures and advertising matter referring to lotteries and similar gift enterprises are barred from the mail.

Newspapers are not permitted to announce them or to announce results. Federal law now exempts newspapers in states with legal lotteries as long as they confine themselves to reporting state lotteries. Stories may also be used in cases where something of news value happened as a result of the lottery. An example would be a story concerning a laborer who became wealthy overnight by having a winning ticket on the Irish Sweepstakes. This would probably be considered a legitimate human interest story rather than a promotion for horse races and lotteries.

Newspapers may use illustrations of paper money provided the illustration is in black and white, less than $\frac{3}{4}$ or more than $1\frac{1}{2}$ times the actual size and is used as nonadvertising. No individual facsimiles are permitted. In advertising, there can be no illustrations of paper money, checks or bonds, except that money may be used in numismatic advertising and savings bonds may be used in connection with Treasury Department sales campaigns. The rules apply to paper money, checks, bonds and securities.

Illustrations in black and white, but not individual facsimiles or individual photographs, are permitted for any purpose including advertising for both U.S. and foreign coins.

Color illustrations of U.S. stamps are prohibited regardless of whether they are canceled or demonetized. Color illustrations of foreign stamps are permitted provided they have official cancellation marks. Uncanceled stamps may not be shown in color.

Crime and Courts

No longer do American editors play crime by the standards of past generations. They print crime news but they no longer regularly rely on a crime story, even a sex-triangle murder, to boost street sales. Topics such as space and ocean exploration compete with crime for the attention and interest of today's more sophisticated readers.

Crime is a part of the news record, however, and has to be

carried if newspapers are to fulfill their obligations to the readers. Minor crimes, unless they have unusual angles, generally are merely listed. When it is presented in detail, the crime story should be done with the same thoroughness and sensitivity that experts give other subjects. Some observers argue that newspapers should offer more news of criminal activities—but with the constructive purpose of showing the community the origins and anatomy of crime.

Copyeditors who handle a crime story should make sure that the report contains no prejudicial statements that could deprive the defendant of a fair trial. Their headline should avoid labels.

One editor admonished his staff, "We should be sensitive about assumption of guilt, not only to avoid libel but to avoid criticism and a bad impression on readers." The caution was occasioned by this lead: "With the dealer who sold a 32-caliber pistol to Mrs. Mariann C-- apparently located, Shaker Heights police today were using handwriting expert Joseph Tholl to link the accused slayer of Cremer Y--, 8, to the weapon purchase." The whole tone of this lead is an assumption of guilt and the effort of police to pin the crime on somebody. It should have said the police were seeing whether Mrs. C-- was linked to the gun purchase—not trying to link her.

Here is a conviction lead:

FAYETTEVILLE, N.C. (AP)—Two Negro marines are being held without bond after terrorizing a family, stealing a car, and trading shots with officers.

They were identified as etc.

They told officers after their Saturday night capture they were members of the National Abolitionist Forces, which they described as a militant Negro group.

In reference to this story, the general news editor said in part, "We do not have a formal set of guidelines for handling crime news, but this story certainly does not conform to regular AP practice. It makes us authority for that statement that the two men held had terrorized a family, stolen a car and traded shots with officers. All we should have said was that they were charged with doing all those things, and who had made the charge."

Correct Terminology

Newsworthy trials are covered in detail so that essential information may be conveyed to the public at a time when it will not interfere with the judicial process. Newspapers have an obligation to expose wrongful acts of public officials and to deal with crisis conditions in ways intended to restore and to maintain public order.

Copyeditors have to have some knowledge of legal terms and the legal process if they are to make the story and headline technically correct yet meaningful to the layman. *Arrested* is a simple verb understood by all readers. It is better than *apprehended* or *taken into custody*. It is equal to *captured*. A person who is cited, summoned or given a ticket is not arrested.

An *arraignment* is a formal proceeding where a defendant steps forward to give the court his plea of guilty or not guilty. It should not be used interchangeably with *preliminary hearing*, which is held in a magistrate's court and is a device to show probable cause that a crime has been committed and that there is a likely suspect.

Bail is the security given for the release of a prisoner. The reporter reveals his ignorance when he writes, "The woman is now in jail under $5,000 bail." She can't be in jail under bail. She can be free on bail or she can be held in lieu of bail.

A *parole* is a conditional release of a prisoner with an indeterminate or unexpired sentence. *Probation* allows a person convicted of some minor offense to go at large, under suspension of sentence during good behavior, and generally under the supervision or guardianship of a probation officer.

The word *alleged* is a trap. Used in reference to a specific person (Jones, the alleged gambler), it offers no immunity from libel. Jones may be charged with gambling or indicted for gambling. In both instances, *alleged* is redundant. The charge is an allegation or an assertion without proof but carries an indication of an ability to produce proof.

The same can be said for other qualifiers, particularly *accused*. Calling a man an "accused murderer" or an "accused abductor" in a sense convicts him of murder or abduction. If a man is first called an "accused assassin," then is freed of the charge, would he be referred to as the "exonerated assassin"? Such qualifiers are unjustified, damaging and perhaps actionable. Headline writers resort to "alleged slayer" to save space and to avoid possible action. "Slaying" is not usually listed as a statutory crime. "Shot and killed" suggests two actions; "shot to death" is better.

A jail sentence does not mean, necessarily, that a man has been jailed. He may be free on bond or free pending an appeal.

Listing the wrong name in a crime story is the surest route to libel action. Thorough verification of first, middle and last names, of addresses and of relationships is a "must" in editing the crime story.

Normally, names of suspects who are being held for questioning or investigation should not be included in the report. A person branded a suspect, then later released for lack of evidence, remains branded. There is time to list names after a formal charge has been filed. The federal government, unlike many state agencies, first gets the evidence, then files the charges.

Names of women or children in rape cases or attempted rape cases should not be used. Nor should the story give any clue to their addresses in a way by which they can be identified. An exception is when the rape victim is murdered.

Sentences may be consecutive or concurrent. If a man is sentenced to consecutive three-year terms, he faces six years of imprisonment. If his sentences are concurrent, he faces three years. But why use these terms? The total sentence is what counts with the readers and the prisoner.

If a man has been sentenced to five years but the sentence is suspended, he gets a suspended five-year sentence, not a five-year suspended sentence.

Juries are of two kinds—investigative (grand) and trial (petit). If a grand jury finds evidence sufficient to warrant a trial, it issues a *true bill*. If sufficient evidence is lacking, the return is a *no-bill*. "Jones indicted" means as much as "the grand jury indicted Jones." To say "the grand jury failed to indict Jones" implies it shirked its duty.

A *verdict* is the finding of a jury. A judge renders decisions, judgments, rulings and opinions, but not verdicts. Although verdicts are returned in both criminal and civil actions by juries, a guilty verdict is found only in criminal actions. Judges declare, not order, mistrials. Attorneys general or similar officials give opinions, not rulings.

Corpus delicti refers to the evidence necessary to establish that a crime has been committed. It is not restricted to the body of a murder victim; it can apply as well to the charred remains of a burned house.

Nolo contendere is a legalistic way of saying that a defendant, although not admitting his guilt, will not fight a criminal prosecution. *Nolle prosequi* means the prosecutor or plaintiff will proceed no further in his action or suit. The reader will understand the translation more readily than the Latin expression.

The Fifth Amendment guarantees the due process of law protection for all citizens. The report should not suggest that the use of this protection is a cover-up for guilt. Phrases such as "hiding behind the fifth" should be eliminated.

The story should distinguish between an act itself and an action. Replevin, for example, is an action to recover property wrongfully taken or detained. Trouble will arise if the copyeditor lets the reporter translate the action too freely: "Mrs. Marsh filed the replevin action to recover furniture stolen from her home by her estranged husband." So, too, with the tort of conversion. "Wrongful conversion" may imply theft, but neither the copy nor the head should convey such implication.

Keeping track of the plaintiff and the defendant should pose no problem except in appellate proceedings where the original defendant may become the plaintiff and vice versa. The confusion is not lessened by substituting *appellee* and *appellant*. The best way is to repeat the names of the principals.

In some civil suits the main news peg is the enormous sum sought by the plaintiff. Whether the same angle should be included in the headline is questionable. In some damage claims the relief sought is far greater than the plaintiff expects to collect. The judgment actually awarded is the news and the head-line.

Misused Terms Copyeditors can "tidy up" the crime and court report by watching for the following:

All narcotics are drugs but many drugs are not narcotics.

A defendant may plead guilty or not guilty to a charge or of a crime. Technically, there is no such plea as innocent. A defendant may be judged not guilty by reason of insanity. He is not innocent by reason of insanity. An acquittal means he has been found not guilty. The danger of dropping the *not* has caused some editors to insist on using *innocent* rather than *not guilty*.

All law suits are tried in courts. *Court litigation,* therefore, is redundant.

Statements are either written or oral (not verbal).

"Would-be robber" has no more validity than a "would-be ballplayer."

The word *bandit* is suspect because it has the flavor of hero-ism and tends to glorify the hoodlum.

The word *lawman* has no place in the report. It can mean too many things—a village constable, a sheriff's deputy or the sheriff himself, a prosecutor, a bailiff, a judge, an F.B.I. agent, a revenue agent and so on. *Lawman* in contemporary America is a "hillbilly" word. Its merit is that it suggests a social setting. Almost always a more precise word will be found more suitable in a newspaper.

Use *sheriff's deputies* rather than *deputy sheriffs*.

Divorces are granted or obtained. Medals are won or awarded.

"Hit-and-run," "ax-murder," "torture-murder" and the like are newspaper clichés. They should be changed to "hit by an automobile that failed to stop," "killed with an ax," "tortured and murdered."

There's no such thing as an *attempted holdup*. A holdup is a holdup even if the bad guy got nothing from the victim.

Misplacement of words makes the reporter and the copy-editor look ridiculous:

"An 80-year-old man . . . pleaded guilty yesterday to reduced charges of attempted indecent and immoral practices in Jefferson Criminal Court."

"Seven persons have been fined . . . for impaired driving in Fenton District Court."

Legal Jargon Example of legal jargon: "The case was continued for disposition because the attorney requested no probation report be made on the boy before adjudication."

W. J. Brier and J. B. Rollins of Montana State University in 1963 studied some Missoula, Montana, adults as to their understanding of legal terms. [Bush, *News Research for Better Newspaper,* Vol. I (1966).] Following are the terms incorrectly defined by more than half the respondents:

Accessories before the fact—those charged with helping another who committed the felony.

Extradition—surrendered the prisoner to officials of another state.

Arraigned—brought to court to answer to a criminal charge.

Bound over—held on bail for trial.

Indicted—accused or charged by a grand jury.

Civil action—pertaining to private rights of individuals and to legal proceedings against these individuals.

Extortion—oppressive or illegal obtaining of money or other things of value.

Remanded—sent the case back to a lower court for review.

Continuance—adjournment of the case until later.

Felony—a crime of a graver nature than a misdemeanor, usually an offense punishable by imprisonment or death.

Writ of habeas corpus—an order to bring the prisoner to court so the court may determine if he has been denied his legal rights.

Administratrix—administrator; always a female.

Stay order—stop the action or suspend the legal proceeding.

An information—an accusation or a charge.

Venire—those summoned to serve as jurors.

Demurrer—a pleading admitting the facts in a complaint or answer but contending they are legally insufficient.

Other misunderstood terms include:

"Released on her personal recognizance"—released on her word of honor to do a particular act.

". . . make a determination on the voluntariness of the man's confession"—decide whether his confession is voluntary.

". . . the plaintiff is . . ."—". . . the suit was filed by . . ."

Terms that should be translated include: *ambulatory* (movable), *bequest* (gift), *debenture* (obligation), *domicile* (home), *in camera* (in the judge's office), *liquidate* (settle), *litigant* (participant), *paralegals* (legal assistants), *plat* (map), *res judicata* (matter already decided).

If a man loses his voting right, he is *disfranchised,* not disenfranchised.

Lawyers are fond of word-doubling: *last will and testament, null and void, on or about, written instrument.* Another is *and/or.* "The maximum sentence . . . is a $20,000 fine and-or 15 years imprisonment." The maximum would be the fine and 15 years.

Few readers understand the meaning of the word *writ* (a judge's order or a court order). "In a petition for a writ of mandamus, the new bank's incorporators asked the court. . . ." The copyeditor should have changed that to "The new bank's incorporators asked the court to. . . ." or if the term mandamus

---

Legal Limitations on the Press   197

was essential, it should have been explained (a court order telling a public official to do something).

Euphemisms   Euphemisms include "attorney" for *lawyer,* "sexually assaulted" or "sexually attacked" for *raped.* Not all jurists, who profess to be or are versed in the law, are judges, and certainly not all judges are jurists.

Threadbare Phrases   Following are some threadbare phrases: stern warning, brilliant defense, gin mill, shattered body, police speculated, on the lam, Portia, soberly pronounced sentence, robed justices, curfew clamped.

Be Exact   A *robber* steals by force. A *thief* steals without resorting to force. Theft suggests stealth. A *burglar* steals by entering or breaking into a building. If a burglar is caught in the act, pulls a gun on the homeowner and makes off with the family silverware, he is a robber. It is redundant to call him an armed robber.

Theft and *larceny* both mean the taking of what belongs to another. *Larceny* is the more specific term and can be proved only when the thief has the stolen property on him. Pickpockets and shoplifters are thieves.

"Statutory grounds for divorce" is redundant. All grounds for divorce are statutory in the state where the divorce is granted.

Charge has many shades of meaning and if often misused. "The psychologist charged last night that Negro high school students generally do not think of the university as a friendly place." The statement was more an observation than a charge.

Members of the Supreme Court are judges or justices, but not supreme judges. The title of the U.S. Supreme Court's chief justice is Chief Justice of the United States.

Words such as *looted, robbed* and *swindled* should be used properly: "Two men were fined and given suspended sentences yesterday in Municipal Court for stealing newsracks and looting money from them." "Thieves broke into 26 automobiles parked near the plant and looted some small items." Money is not looted. That from which it is taken is looted. Nor is money robbed. A bank is robbed; the money is stolen. "A man in uniform swindled $1,759 from a war widow." No, the person is swindled, not the money.

Some papers object to saying that fines and sentences are *given,* on the ground that they are not gifts.

Some police reporters like to say a guy went berserk and barricaded himself in the house with a gun. Rarely does a man do that.

A felony is a crime of a graver nature than a misdemeanor. Generally, a felony is punishable by death or by imprisonment in a penitentiary.

12

Picture Editing

Rewriting often can turn a poorly written news story into an acceptable one. Little can be done to change the subject matter of a cliché photo, such as tree plantings, ribbon cuttings, proclamation signings and the passing of checks, certificates or awards from one person to another. Yet many of these talk situations are used simply because of the tradition that "chicken dinner" stuff must be photographed.

It would be a rare occasion when a city editor would permit his reporters to share their time with sports, society, Sunday supplement or with the advertising department. Yet, that is what happens on some papers with a small staff of photographers.

One consequence is that often good local news and feature stories miss the additional information that accompanying pictures could provide. Another is that too often mediocre, space-wasting pictures from the wire services or syndicates get more attention than they deserve.

A picture editor is almost as essential to a newspaper as a city editor. Some executive should be responsible for assigning photographers to news and feature events. Someone in authority should insist that most pictures, including those from news agencies, be edited and that cutlines be intelligently written.

If it is a good picture, it should get a good play, just as a top story gets a big headline. If pictures are a vital part of the story, editors should be willing to cut back on words, if necessary, to provide space for pictures. Some events can be told better in words than in pictures. Conversely, other events are essentially graphic and need little or no text to get the message across.

Pictures can "dress up" a page. But if their only purpose is to break up the type, they are poorly used. The large number of pictures used—even on front pages—without an accompanying story suggests that the pictures are being used for their graphic value rather than for their story-telling value. Ideally, the pictures should be a marriage with stories.

Still pictures, even action shots, may not be able to compete with television but still photography—the print media's tool—can add color to words and can capture moods. Originality starts with the picture. Its values are interest, composition and quality of reproduction.

A small poor-quality picture should be rejected because the flaws will be magnified in the enlargement. Facsimile prints may be retouched but the quality is seldom as good as pictures made from glossy prints. Generally, pictures reproduce better if they are reduced rather than enlarged.

Reproduction Processes

Pictures arrive at a newspaper in several forms:

1. Papier-maché mats. A mat is an impression made from a screened halftone upon a cardboard-weight paper. It is cast into a type-high metal block and placed in a form in letterpress printing. In offset, a print from which the mat was made is pasted on the page layout. A mat cast cannot be cropped, enlarged of reduced. Its shape, however, can be altered by sawing the cast.

2. Boilerplate. This is a thin metal plate made from a screened halftone and attached to a metal or wood base for letterpress printing. Boilerplate cannot be edited.

3. Glossy or photographic print. The picture is transferred through a screen to a plate which is then engraved to produce a halftone. The plate is mounted on a patent base for letterpress printing. In offset, the glossy is rephotographed and the negative stripped on the negative of the page layout.

4. Plastic plate or photoelectric engraver. A lathelike machine contains two cylinders. Copy is attached to one cylinder and as the cylinder rotates it is scanned by an optical device. A plastic sheet is mounted on the second cylinder. An engraving stylus, activated by the optical unit, cuts or burns a depression on the plate. The plate is then mounted on a patent base for letterpress printing.

Direct Transmission

AP's Wirephoto and UPI's Telephoto pictures are transmitted over a leased telephone wire from one bureau to another or directly to newspapers. The transmitter consists of a revolving drum on which a picture is placed. A light focused on the print is reflected into a photoelectric cell and converted into electrical impulses and transmitted over a telephone line. The re-

The Art of Editing

ceiver unit also contains a drum on which heat-sensitive paper is attached. As the drum revolves the paper is exposed to a beam, then proceeds to a processor to produce wet positive prints. Portable units enable a photographer to send pictures from any place where there is a telephone outlet.

Facsimile Prints

This process has been widely used by the wire services to deliver black and white still pictures to newspapers and broadcast stations. Reproduction of the original copy is made on tissue-thin paper by an electrolytic process. Charges of electrical energy are recorded on paper, made visible by a metallic toner. Pictures emerge in a continuous roll and are then cut and handled in the same manner as glossies. Facsimile prints have poor definition and frequently show scan lines. Because they fade or turn yellow when stored, they lack archival quality.

UNIFAX II. This method, developed for UPI, uses an improved electrostatic process (similar to that in a copier machine), and produces glossy prints rather than facsimile prints. A specially treated paper gives sharp definitions and a range of 32 to 64 gray tones. The receiving unit delivers 8-by-10 pictures, sheared and stacked.

AP LASERPHOTO. Here, a helium-neon laser beam scans a picture at the transmitter. The reflected laser light is converted into electrical signals for transmission over telephone lines. A newsroom receiver picks up the signals and uses them to modulate a laser beam which, in turn, exposes a sensitive dry silver paper to form an image on glossy paper. The paper is then cut, heat processed and stacked (Figure 12–1).

Figure 12–1. AP Laserphoto receiving unit. [*Photo courtesy of Boulder (Colo.) Daily Camera.*]

Since Laserphoto is a dry process, no processing chemicals are required, continuous tone is maintained and scan lines are eliminated.

Digital Signals Pictures, like words, can be placed in a computer. The editor then returns the picture to a VDT screen to be sized and edited by keyboard operation. Or, the editor may superimpose a rectangle of arbitrary size and shape on the display. When he has specified the portion of the picture to be retained, he commands the computer to scale the cropped picture to any specified size.

The key to this process is digitizing, or the conversion of gray levels to a binary code, the language of the computer. Text matter is digitized by keyboarding, each letter or character being represented by a binary code, or number combination. A two-dimensional image consists of small unit areas of constant brightness or picture elements known as pixels. In transforming the picture to numbers the dark and light values of each pixel are measured and assigned a numeric value. For color prints, the pixels define color tones which similarly are represented by a binary code.

Output from the computer reverses the process. The binary code in the computer is converted from digital to analog data to produce an electrical signal. The signal is then put through a laser conductor to expose the image either on sensitized paper, on film or on a film negative page.

Pictures may be sent on digital telephone wires to regional hubs and stored under computer control. The picture editor views the pictures on a screen and selects those he desires. The pictures are then delivered either in digital form for computer storage or in analog (or data to activate a laserphoto).

Picture Editing

Whatever the subject and the composition, many pictures can be improved by some editing. The pictures may need no more than a slight retouching to sharpen profiles or to eliminate static background. Retouching can be accomplished with an airbrush, an instrument that applies a liquid pigment to a surface by means of compressed air (Figures 12–2a and 12–2b). Retouching also can be done by brushing on a retouching liquid or paste (Figures 12–3a and 12–3b) or by using retouching pencils of varying colors.

When time permits, some of the more prosaic shots can be dramatized by judicious cropping to sharpen the point of interest.

Even retouching and cropping may not be sufficient to achieve the maximum impact in news and feature photos. Here are some things that might be done:

Figures 12–2a and 12–2b. Editing a picture. The original picture (upper) was retouched slightly with an air brush to highlight the faces, thus preparing the lower picture for publication. [*Photograph courtesy of the Denver Post.*]

Figure 12–3a. The weekly *Range Leader* of Cheyenne Wells, Colo., teased its readers with this shot of three mule deer caught in a fog. A cutline is necessary to tell readers why their eyes deceive them. [*Photo by Bob Scales, courtesy of the Range Leader.*]

1. Changing the standard sizes of photos. Some picture editors automatically accept a standard proportion, say two columns wide and five inches deep, for the majority of pictures. Tests have indicated, however, that a picture of three or four columns will get greater reader response than a two-column picture. Even the cutline of a four-column picture gets more readership than the cutline of a two-column picture.

A good news photo, like a superb news story, deserves a smash play, big enough to bring out all the dramatic impact of the photo. It might call for a picture five columns wide and twelve to sixteen inches deep. The nearly square rectangle might be more effective in a long vertical cut or a shallow horizontal cut (See Figures 12–11a and 11b).

2. Changing the shapes of photos. Newspaper pictures need not adhere to the standard rectangular shapes. Advertising and magazine illustrations demonstrate the effectiveness of silhouettes or of round and oval shapes or perspective or mood shapes. Tilting can suggest more action. Some pictures can be

Figure 12–3b. A photographer can get a silhouette effect by brushing on white retouch liquid. The copy print was made on RC (resin-coated) paper to keep the paper base from absorbing solutions during processing.

mortised, others split and still others arranged into a montage or a collage. A mortise is a notch cut into a picture to accommodate text or display lines.

3. Selecting the number of photos. The picture editor generally has enough pictures available. His problem is to find enough good ones in the bundle to add interest and variety to the pages. Too many pictures resemble those that have been used before. Too many are used simply because they go with stories but add little or nothing to the stories. Too many are single shots that give the readers only part of the story. Picture sequences—two or more shots of the same (or similar) scene—afford one solution. Picture sequences help give the reader a sense of continuity of action, provide feeling of movement or contrast. They say to readers, in effect, "Here is the way it is now and here is the way it was before," or "Here's the way it looked from one vantage point and here's the way it looked from another" or "This is the way it looked from the outside and here is the way it looks from the inside."

Picture Editing

Pictures As Copy

When the picture has been processed, someone—reporter or photographer—supplies the information for the cutline. The picture and cutline information then go to the appropriate department whose editor decides whether to use the picture and, if so, how to display it.

Before submitting a picture to the art or engraving department, the editor supplies enough information to get the correct picture in the correct place with the correct cutline. A picture, like a story, generally carries an identifying slug. To assure that the picture will match the engraving, the cutline, and, if need be, the story, the editor uses a slugline.

A slip of paper clipped on the picture normally contains information such as:

Slug or picture identification.
Size of the desired engraving.
Engraving instructions.
Department, edition and page.
Date wanted.
Date and time picture sent to engraving.
Whether the picture is with or without a story.

The picture is then routed either directly to the engravers or indirectly through the art department to the engraving department. In offset the picture goes to the photography department. The cutline goes to the composing room. Cutline copy contains, in addition to the cutlines, essential directions to match cutline and picture.

Some photo editors use a style like the one shown in Figure 12–4.

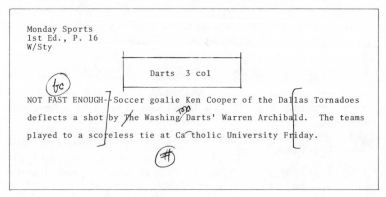

Figure 12–4. Photo cutline style.

When a picture has been edited and sent to the art department or the photography department and the cutline has been written and sent to the composing room, the editor records the picture on a slugsheet. This shows the picture slug; the size of the cut;

the department getting the picture; the time, date and edition; the space occupied by the cut and the cutline; and whether the picture accompanies a story.

If the picture is to go with a story, the information is carried on both the cutline and the story copy. The reason is obvious. Unless properly slugged, the story may turn up on page 3 and the photo on page 16.

Sometimes the photo may be separated from the story deliberately. A teaser picture may be used on page 1 to entice readers to read the story on another page. If a long story has two illustrations, one illustration often is used on the page where the story begins and the other on the jump page. On major events such as the death of a president, pictures may be scattered on several pages. In that event, readers are directed to these pages by a guideline such as "More pictures on pages 5, 7 and 16."

The plate returned from the engraving department contains the slug printed in crayon or grease pencil on the reverse side of the plate. The proofs accompanying the plate likewise carry the slug. In offset, the original photo and instructions are attached to the negative before being sent to pasteup. Even with these precautions, the danger remains that the printed picture will carry the wrong identification.

Sometimes the plate or negative inadvertently is made in reverse. The result can be ludicrous, particularly if the picture shows a sign, if the principals are wearing uniforms containing letters or numerals or if, as in the instance of Senator Robert Kennedy during his campaign for the presidential nomination and after his assassination, pictures showed him with his hair parted on the left rather than on the right.

The person responsible for checking page proofs makes sure the correct headline is over the correct story and that the cutlines under pictures of a local politician and a jackass are not reversed.

Unless the picture is to be cropped, the cut will be enlarged or reduced in proportion to the width and depth of the photograph. A simple method of determining this proportion is to draw a diagonal line from the upper-left to the lower-right corner on the back of the picture, measure the desired width of the cut along the top of the picture and make a vertical line. The point where it intersects the diagonal indicates the depth of the cut. Or, the diagonal may be drawn from the upper-right to the lower-left corner of the back of the picture. The desired width of the cut is then indicated along the bottom of the picture.

If the picture margins are uneven, the editor may place a sheet of tissue paper over the picture and draw the diagonal and connecting lines on the tissue to determine depth of the cut. Or, he may measure the picture area and use a mathematical propor-

The Enlarging, Reducing Formula

Picture Editing

$48:34::60:X$

$34 \times 60 \div 48 = X$

tion to determine cut depth. Suppose the picture is 48 picas wide and 60 picas deep and the desired width of the cut is 34 picas. Then, 48:34::60:X. The answer is $42\frac{1}{2}$ picas in depth.

If the editor decides to have the cut 34 picas wide and 45 picas deep, then X will be substituted for one of the picture measurements to determine the extent of the crop to produce the 34 by 45 proportion. If X is substituted for the width of the picture, then X:34::60:45. 45X equals 2040, and X equals 45.3. Subtracting 45.3 from 48 shows a crop of 2.7 picas on the width of the picture.

A plastic or paper proportion wheel works out the proportion quickly and accurately (Figure 12–5).

Some picture editors place a plastic sheet over the picture. Column widths and inches are drawn on the sheet and a string

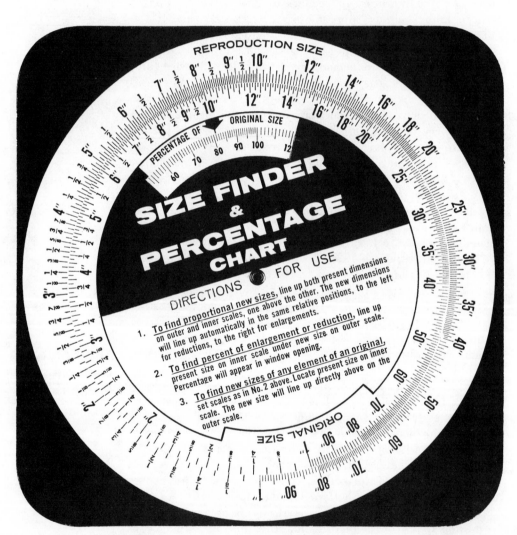

Figure 12–5. Example of disc showing enlargement and reduction ratios. The finder is set at dimensions in Figure 12–8 with $4\frac{1}{8}''$ on the inner circle matching $3\frac{3}{8}''$ on the outer circle. The figure $6\frac{5}{16}''$ is opposite the inner figure of $7\frac{3}{4}''$, or $\frac{1}{5}$ reduction.

Figure 12–6. A clear plastic sheet placed over a photograph enables a picture editor to size a picture quickly. A string attached to the plastic sheet is extended from the upper-left to the lower-right corner of the picture to show the depth of the picture in five columns or less.

is attached to the sheet in the upper-left corner. By positioning the string from the upper-left to the lower-right corners of the picture, the editor can determine the depth of the enlargement or reduction (Figure 12–6).

Pictures may be reduced in any proportion, but generally newspapers adhere fairly closely to standard reductions such as one fifth, one third and one half. A typical scaling (widths in inches) for 16-pica columns is:

1 column—$2\frac{1}{4}$ inches
2 columns—$4\frac{3}{4}$ inches
3 columns—$7\frac{1}{4}$ inches

4 columns—$9\frac{3}{4}$ inches
5 columns—$12\frac{5}{16}$ inches
6 columns—15 inches

Figure 12–7 shows picture cropping to achieve one fifth, one third, and one half reductions in 11-pica columns.

The cut usually is a bit narrower than the column or columns it is expected to occupy, especially in papers that sink the column rules. Some editors like to make pictures in outside columns flush to the outside.

PICTURE PICA SIZE	PICTURE COL. SIZE	SIZE	$\frac{1}{5}$ RED.	$\frac{1}{3}$ RED.	$\frac{1}{2}$ RED.	TYPE COL. SIZE
10.4	1 col.	$1\frac{11}{16}$ INCHES	$2\frac{1}{8}$	$2\frac{1}{2}$	$3\frac{3}{8}$	11. PICAS
21.8	2 col.	$3\frac{9}{16}$	$4\frac{1}{2}$	$5\frac{3}{8}$	$7\frac{1}{8}$	22.4
33.	3 col.	$5\frac{1}{2}$	$6\frac{7}{8}$	$8\frac{1}{4}$	11	33.8
44.4	4 col.	$7\frac{3}{8}$	$9\frac{1}{4}$	11	$14\frac{3}{4}$	45.
55.8	5 col.	$9\frac{1}{4}$	$11\frac{9}{16}$	$13\frac{3}{8}$	$18\frac{1}{2}$	56.4
67.	6 col.	$11\frac{1}{8}$	$13\frac{7}{8}$	$16\frac{3}{4}$	$22\frac{1}{4}$	67.8
78.4	7 col.	13	$16\frac{1}{4}$	$19\frac{1}{2}$	26	79.
89.8	8 col.	$14\frac{7}{8}$	$18\frac{5}{8}$	$22\frac{1}{4}$	$29\frac{3}{4}$	90.4

Figure 12-7. Reduction table for illustrations [*Courtesy of the Denver Post.*]

Some Tips on Cropping

A photograph is a composition. The composition should help the reader grasp the picture's message clearly and immediately. If the picture is too cluttered, the reader's eyes scan the picture looking for a place to rest. But if the picture contains a strong focal point, the reader at least has a place to start. A prime job of a picture editor, therefore, is to help the photographer take out some unnecessary details to strengthen the overall view.

It could be that some elements within the picture are stronger than the full picture. Some picture editors try to find these interest points and patterns by moving two L-shaped pieces of cardboard over the picture. This helps to guide him in his cropping. He looks for a focal point, or chief spot of interest. If other points of interest are present, he tries to retain them (see Figures 12-9a and 9b). He searches for patterns that can be strengthened by cropping. The pattern helps give the picture harmonious and balanced composition. Among these patterns are various letter shapes—L, U, S, Z, T, O and geometric patterns such as a star, a circle, a cross or a combination of these.

Because most news and feature pictures contain people, the picture editor strives to help the photographer depict them as dramatically as possible, whether or not the finished product is pleasing to the subjects in the picture. He must decide how many persons to include in the picture, how much of a person to include and what background is essential. He lets the picture breathe by allowing some white space.

Unless the picture editor is also an artist, he uses a grease pencil to make crop marks on the margin of the photo (Figure 12-8). Or he may place a sheet of tissue paper over the picture and make the crop marks on the tissue. Instead of using scissors to effect a silhouette, a swash cut or even a mortise, he lets the artist outline with china white and airbrush retouching. If he

Figure 12–8. Crop marks applied to a print on facsimile paper. The original picture was $5\frac{3}{4}''$ wide and $7\frac{3}{4}''$ deep, then cropped to $4\frac{1}{8}''$ wide. Desired width is $3\frac{3}{8}''$. The proportional depth is $6\frac{5}{16}''$. See Figure 12–5.

wants a tilted photo, he suggests that the engraver remount and retake the picture. Generally an artist is the best judge of how much retouching and cropping are needed (see Figures 12–9a and 9b).

A mortise normally should be made in a nonvital spot in the picture. For newspapers, an outside mortise or notch (cut on the edge of a picture) is easier and less expensive to handle than an inside mortise (cut inside the picture).

Figure 12–9a. Footprint on the lunar soil. An example of how cropping (b) can bring out an interesting detail in a photograph (a). The close-up view was photographed with a lunar surface camera during the Apollo 11 lunar surface extravehicular activity. [*Photographs courtesy of the National Aeronautics and Space Administration.*]

Figure 12–9b.

The Art of Editing

The picture editor makes the same kind of editorial judgment about a picture that the city editor and the wire editor make about a local story and a wire story. Does the picture tell the whole story or only part of it? Does it distort, editorialize, mislead? Does it omit important details or include details that create an erroneous impression? In other words, is the picture loaded?

The point was raised by James Russell Wiggins, former editor of the Washington *Post,* during a lecture at the University of North Dakota (reported in *Editor & Publisher,* February 22, 1969). "The camera," he said, "can be a notorious, compulsive, unashamed and mischievous liar."

To illustrate, he said he once declined to print a photograph of President Harry Truman walking across the platform of Union Station before a backdrop formed by a row of caskets just shipped in from the Korean War. "What that camera said was that the Korean War was 'Truman's War,' just what thousands of the President's critics were saying."

He also commented on the distorted portrait of policemen during civil disorders. The pictures may have been representative of the action but they failed to tell what really happened in perspective and why.

"The camera does not tell the truth," said Wiggins, "and because what it tells is not the whole truth, skepticism about the media rises in the minds of readers who know that policemen, whatever their undoubted faults, are not always wrong."

A picture may be striking and it may be narrative. But if it conveys a false or distorted impression it would be better left unpublished.

Picture editors often can show subjective judgment in the selection of pictures. Suppose an editor has four or five pictures of a public figure. Some editors will select the picture showing the figure more favorably; others will pick one depicting him less favorably. Many of the pictures used of former President Nixon, even before his resignation, were editorialized. Pictures of two labor leaders, John L. Lewis and George Meany, invariably showed them glowering.

The cocktail glass is another picture syndrome. If the President is toasting a visiting dignitary at a state dinner the picture doubtless will show the President holding a cocktail glass. Whether the glass has to be included in a candid shot of the First Lady is a judgment call, unless the cocktail is relevant.

It was a tragic fire in a metropolitan area. A woman and a child took refuge from the fire on an ironwork balcony. As firemen tried to rescue the woman and child, the balcony collapsed, plunging the woman to her death and the child to a miraculous survival. Photographers took sequence shots of the action (Figure 12–10a and 12–10b). Should a picture editor use the gruesome pictures?

Pictures Can Lie

Gruesome Pictures

Figure 12–10a. Two of the controversial sequence shots of a fire tragedy in a Boston apartment. Scores of readers protested the use of these widely distributed photos. Most editors defended the use of the pictures. [*Photos by Stanley Foreman of the Boston* Herald-American, *distributed by UPI.*]

Figure 12–10b.

Some readers will be incensed, accusing the papers of sensationalism, poor taste, invasion of privacy, insensitivity and a tasteless display of human tragedy to sell newspapers.

Picture editors could reply that their duty is to present the news, whether of good things or bad, of the pleasant or the unpleasant. Defending the judgment to use the pictures on page 1, Watson Sims, editor of the Battle Creek (Mich.) *Enquirer and News,* said "The essential purpose of journalism is to help the reader understand what is happening in this world and thereby help him to appreciate those things he finds good and to try to correct those things he finds bad" (*Editor & Publisher,* August 30, 1975.)

Of the flood of pictures depicting the war in Vietnam, surely among the most memorable were the Saigon chief of police executing a prisoner, terrified children fleeing a napalm attack, the flaming suicide of a Buddhist monk. Such scenes were part of the war record and deserved to be shown.

Photos of fire deaths may tell more than the tragedy depicted in the burned and mangled bodies. Implicit could be the lessons of inadequate inspection, faulty construction, carelessness with matches, arson, antiquated fire-fighting equipment or the like.

Picture editors have few criteria to guide them. Their news judgment and their own conscience tell them whether to order a picture for page 1 showing a man in Australia mauled to death by polar bears after he fell or dived into a pool in the bears' enclosure in a zoo. Of the hundreds of pictures available that day, surely a better one could have been found for page 1. If the scene is such as to cause an editor to turn away and say "Here I don't belong," chances are the readers will have the same reaction. Not all of life's tragedies have to be depicted. The gauge is importance and newsworthiness.

Picture Pages   Some newspapers devote an entire page to pictures with no text. Some use part of the page for pictures, the rest for text matter. (Figures 12–11a, 12–11b, 12–12). Some pages are made up with unrelated photos; some are devoted to related pictures. Some use part of the page for sequence pictures, leaving the remainder for unrelated pictures or text matter. Probably the majority of papers use the back page of a section for pictures, although some use the front page of a section. More and more picture pages now appear in color.

A few pointers on picture pages:

1. Three or four large pictures make a more appealing picture page than eight or ten smaller ones.

2. Let one picture, the best available, dominate the page.

3. Emphasize the upper-left portion of the page either with a dominant picture or a large headline, say 72 points.

4. Crop some of the pictures severely to achieve either wide, shallow, horizontal ones or narrow, long, vertical ones. On a page made up of unrelated pictures, some should be in standard sizes (three, four or five columns) in the event the editor has to replate with new pictures.

5. In a picture series or sequence, place a big picture in the bottom-right corner of the page. It is the logical stopping point.

6. Let the page breathe. White space makes both the pictures and the text stand out. One editor figures an eight-column page as seven columns to assure adequate white space.

7. Don't align pictures with a T square. An off-alignment often provides extra white space or leaves room for a cutline.

8. If a picture page has to be made up in a hurry, pick the best picture, rough-sketch it on a dummy, slug and schedule the picture and get it to the engraver or photo department. Then go on with the other pictures. The cutlines can be written last.

9. On the completed dummy, give the printer some leeway. Indicate on which sides the cuts may be trimmed to fit the layout.

10. Vary picture page patterns. Don't make today's picture page look like last Saturday's.

11. Cutlines need not be as wide as the pictures. In fact, a narrow cutline may be easier to read than a wider one and a narrow cutline is yet another device to allow more white space. On bottom-of-the-page pictures the cutline for the left-of-page picture might be set flush left and the cutline for the right-of-page picture flush right.

12. In sequence or series pictures, don't repeat in one cutline what was said in another.

13. If all the pictures were taken by one photographer or provided by one wire service, a single credit line on the page will suffice. Too many credits give the page a bulletin board effect.

14. In a photo-essay page, keep the cutlines as brief as possible. Usually, the pictures tell most of the story, especially if the headline has established the theme.

15. Headlines generally are more effective at the left or right of the page or under the main pictures. Sometimes the head may be overprinted on the main picture if the type does not rob the picture of important details.

Cutline Guidelines

Picture texts are known by many names—cutlines, captions, underlines (or overlines), legends. A caption suggests a heading over a picture, but many editors use the term to refer to the lines under the picture. *Legend* may refer either to the text or to the heading. If a heading is used, it should be under, not over, the picture. A *leader* means the capitalized or italicized group of words, usually no more than one third to one half the line starting the cutline.

Figure 12–11a. Cropping pictures to fit the story. These pictures, two in a series of four, were severely cropped to emphasize the long narrow stairs. The effectiveness of the picture shapes can be seen in the photo story (Figure 12–12). Instructions on the back of each picture carried the slug (stairs 1, stairs 2, stairs 3, stairs 4), the size ($5\frac{1}{2}$ by 11 inches for one and $2\frac{1}{2}$ by $9\frac{1}{2}$ inches the other), the edition (City), page (Pic Page) and the time and date that each picture was sent to the engraving department.

Figure 12–11b.

UPS and DOWNS
IN LEAD, S.D.

By ROBERT W. (RED) FENWICK

Denver Post Staff Writer

This is one of Lead, S.D.'s most scenic stairways—with curving handrail, covered by one hanging foliage. Town has become tourist mecca.

They say there are probably more sensible climbers in picturesque Lead, S.D., than anywhere else in the West. Life in Lead (pronounce it "Leed") is one continual round of ups and downs—up one stairway and down another.

Much depends, of course, upon where one lives with respect to his place of employment. But if he walks, the average citizen there can be fairly certain of being somewhat out of breath either when he gets to work in the morning or when he gets home at night.

Like any other good municipality, Lead builds and maintains its streets, sidewalks and alleys. But unlike most other cities, Lead also has built and maintains a highly picturesque system of stairways to connect upper and lower streets.

In all, Lead's mountainsides are decorated with 1,336 feet of stairways. Of these, 1,172 are built of wood, and 162 of concrete.

The longest stairway rises 372 feet from Ridge Road to Railroad Ave. The next longest is 90 feet.

Mile-high and mile-deep Lead, now a bustling city of perhaps 4,500, was born in 1876 when gold was discovered there at the head of Gold Run Gulch. Neighboring Deadwood had ridden its gold crest a year earlier and, when Lead sprang into being, there were 25,000 wealth seekers in Deadwood Gulch.

According to the South Dakota Guide Book, Lead was the largest city in the state at one time. In March 1900, it was all but destroyed by fire. Another fire once almost burned down the upper workings of the world famous Homestake Mine there.

And during World War II, Lead almost be-

came a ghost town when the federal government shut down gold production. When facilities eased, the Homestake fired up and pushed to mile-deep mine shafts beneath the city in a network of more than 200 miles.

Lead once again became one of the most popular tourist attractions in South Dakota's exquisitely-beautiful Black Hills.

Pictured on this page are some of Lead's many stairways. And if these pictures lead you to Lead—it will be a (stair)-step in the right direction.

Two young residents of Lead, Jody Harland, left, and Sandra Bierer, are going down, down, down, heading other way means puff, puff, puff.

The copyeditor "sells" the reporter's story by means of a compelling headline. By the same token, the picture editor can help control the photographic image with a cutline message. The primary purpose of the cutline message is to get the reader to respond to the photo in the manner intended by the photographer and the picture editor.

Readers first concentrate on the focal point of the picture, then glance at the other parts. Then, presumably, most turn to the cutline to confirm what they have seen in the picture. The cutline provides the answers to questions of who, what, where, when, why and how, unless some of these are apparent in the picture.

The cutline interprets and expands upon what the picture says to the reader. It may point out the inconspicuous but significant. It may comment on the revealing or amusing parts of the picture if these are not self-evident. The cutline helps explain ambiguities, comments on what is not made clear in the picture and mentions what the picture fails to show if that is necessary.

The ideal cutline is direct, brief and sometimes bright. It is a concise statement, not a newsstory. It gets to the point immediately, avoiding the "go back to the beginning" of the background situation.

If the picture accompanies a story, the cutline doesn't duplicate the details readers can find in the story. It should, however, contain enough information to satisfy the readers who will not read the story. Ideally, the picture and the cutline will induce readers to read the story. Normally the cutline of a picture with story is limited to two or three type lines.

Even when the picture relates to the story, the cutline should not go beyond what the picture reveals. Nor should the facts in the cutline differ from those in the story. Example: In a train wreck story: "None was believed seriously injured." Accompanying cutline: "Most of the seriously injured were in the diner."

Cutlines stand out in the newspaper's sea of words and strike the reader with peculiar force. Every word should be weighed, especially for impact, emotional tone, impartiality and adherence to rules of grammar and the accepted language.

Anyone who tries to write or rewrite a cutline without seeing the picture risks errors. The writer should examine the cropped picture, not the original one. The cutline has to confine itself to the portion of the picture the reader will see. If the cutline says a woman is waving a handkerchief, the handkerchief must be in the picture. In a layout containing two or more pictures with a single cutline, the cutline-writer should study the layout to make sure that left or right or top or bottom directions are correct.

Figure 12–12. Picture page emphasizing vertical shapes in pictures and a stair-stepped caption. [*Courtesy of the Denver Post.*]

Although no one should try to write a cutline without first looking at the picture, it frequently happens that pictures have to move to the engraver (or to the photography department in offset) quickly. The editor removes the cutlines (from wire service and syndicated pictures) and jots down the slug and size of the pictures and any revealing elements in the pictures that might be added to the cutlines. Time permitting, a proofsheet showing pictures and their cutlines should be given to the picture editor.

When the cutline has been composed, the writer should compare the message with the picture. The number of people in the picture should be checked against the number of names in the cutline. Everyone appearing prominently in the picture should be identified. If a person is so obscured in the crowd that he is not easily identifiable, that fact need not be brought to the reader's attention.

If the writer composes a cutline from a negative or engraving, he will do well to remember that the plate or negative is a reverse of the picture. The person on the left will appear on the right in the printed picture.

Writing the Cutline

1. Don't tell the obvious. If the girl in the picture is pretty or attractive, that fact will be obvious from the picture. The picture will tell whether or not a man is smiling. It may be necessary, however, to tell why he is smiling. An explanation need not go as far as it did in the following: "Two girls and a man stroll down the newly completed section of Rehoboth's boardwalk. They are (from left) Nancy Jackson, Dianne Johnson and Richard Bramble, all of West Chester." An editor remarked, "Even if some of the slower readers couldn't have figured out the sexes from the picture, the names are a dead giveaway."

2. Don't editorialize. A writer doesn't know whether someone is happy, glum or troubled. The cutline that described the judge as "weary but ready" when he arrived at court on the opening day of the trial must have made readers wonder how the writer knew the judge was weary.

3. Use specifics rather than generalities. "A 10-pound book" is better than "a huge book." "A man, 70," is more descriptive than "an old man."

4. Because the readers know you are referring to the photograph, omit phrases such as "is pictured," "is shown" and "the picture above shows."

5. Use "from left" rather than "from left to right." The first means as much as the second and is shorter. Neither *left* nor *right* should be overworked. If one of two boys in a picture is wearing a white jersey, use that fact to identify him. If the President is in a golf cart with a professional golfer, readers shouldn't have to be told which one is the President.

6. One of the worst things you can say about a person in a photo is that he is "looking on." If that is all he is doing, he is superfluous. Perhaps something like this will help: "William McGoo, background, is campaign treasurer."

7. Don't kid the readers. They will know whether this is a "recent photo." Give the date the photo was taken. Also, let readers know where the picture was taken—but not how. Most readers don't care about all the sleet and snow the photographer had to go through to get the picture. Also, readers aren't stupid. If the cutline says three persons in a Girl Scout picture are looking over a drawing of a new camp, readers aren't fooled if the picture shows two of the girls behind the drawing; they obviously can't be looking it over. If a special lens was used, resulting in a distortion of distance or size, the reader should be told what happened.

8. The present tense enhances the immediacy of pictures. The past tense is used if the sentence contains the date or if it gives additional facts not described in the action in the picture. The cutline may use both present and past tenses, but the past time-element should not be used in the same sentence with a present-tense verb describing the action.

9. Make sure the cutline is accurate. If a commercial photographer supplies the picture and the identification, double-check the names. The paper, not the photographer, gets the blame for inaccuracies. Cutline errors occur because someone, the photographer or the reporter accompanying the photographer, failed to give the picture desk enough, or accurate, information from which to construct a cutline. Apparently assuming that any big horn is a tuba, a cutline writer talked about a horn player with half his tuba missing. His editor was quick to reprimand, "Umpteen million high school kids, ex-bandsmen and musicians in general know better."

10. Double-check the photo with the cutline identification. The wrong person pictured as "the most-wanted fugitive" is a sure way to invite libel. It is usually safer to say *held* or *arrested* than "murder suspect."

11. Writing a cutline requires as much care and skill as writing a story or a headline. The reader should not have to puzzle out the meaning of the description. Notice these jarring examples: "Fearing new outbreaks of violence, the results of Sunday's election have been withheld." "Also killed in the accident was the father of five children driving the other vehicle." "Yum! Yum! A corn dog satisfies that ravishing Fair appetite." The word, obviously, was *ravenous,* not *ravishing.* Don't hit the reader over the head with the obvious. If the photo shows a fireman dousing hot timbers after a warehouse fire and a fireman already has been mentioned in the text, it is ridiculous to add that "firemen were called" in the cutline.

Other reader-stoppers:

In a cutline under a photo of Patty Hearst: "Her clothes were

---

Picture Editing 223

those in which she was arrested Thursday with four other persons." Must have been crowded in there.

"Bernard Breeck, left, a diver, and Forrest Perry, a member of the crew of the work barge in background, discuss the day's work after coming ashore after efforts were continued to raise a sunken barge in the Ohio River just downstream from the foot of Third Street in Louisville." Generally short sentences are easier to read, easier to set and easier to correct.

12. Avoid last-line widows or hangers. The cutline should be written so that the final line is a full line, or nearly so. If the writer knows the number of characters per pica in the type used for the cutline, he can set the typewriter stops so that each typewritten line corresponds with the type line. When the lines are doubled (two 2-columns for a four-column cut), the writer should write an even number of lines. If the cutline is to be placed in the space left by a mortise, it is essential that the writer determine the maximum characters the space will accommodate. Most pictures are indented at least 1 pica on each side. A usual practice is to make a corresponding indention or more in the cutlines. Some newspapers use this count.

11-Pica Column		*14-Pica Column*	
One two-column line—57 typewriter units		35 units for each column	
Three-column line	—$1\frac{1}{2}$ typewriter lines	Two-column	—set 29 picas
Four-column line	—2 typewriter lines	Three-column—set 44 picas	
Five-column line	—$2\frac{1}{2}$ typewriter lines	Four-column	—set 59 picas

Count just under the maximum line or circle a word that could be dropped by the compositor. To correct a cutline with a widow, make the correction near the end of the cutline to eliminate unnecessary resetting. In a layout of two or more pictures, running side by side, each picture should have the same number of lines beneath it, regardless of the width of the pictures.

13. Cutlines should be bright if warranted by the picture. Biting humor and sarcasm have no place in cutlines.

14. The cutline should describe the event as shown in the picture, not the event itself. Viewers will be puzzled if the cutline describes action they do not see. Sometimes, however, an explanation of what is not shown is justified. The picture shows a football player leaping high to catch a pass for a touchdown. Viewers might like to know who threw the pass.

A wire service delivered a combination of three pictures showing the Vice President as he played in a celebrity golf tournament. He missed a putt, then buried his head in his hands. But golfers looking closely saw the third picture obviously was not taken on the green, and that while the Veep had a putter in two pictures he held a wood in the third. The cutline should have explained that after he missed the putt he grabbed another club, walked off the green and then showed his displeasure at the miss.

15. Because a lapse occurs between the time a picture of an

event is taken and the time a viewer sees the picture in the newspaper, care should be taken to update the information in the cutline. The first report said that three bodies were found in the wreckage. Subsequently two more bodies were found. The cutline should contain the latest figure.

Or, for a picture taken in one season but presented in another, the cutline should reflect the time difference. Example: "Big band singer Helen O'Connor (left) reminisces with Pat and Art Modell backstage at Blossom Music Center this summer...." Reading that on December 1, it is difficult to decide when it happened, especially with a present tense verb and frost in the air.

16. In local pictures, the addresses of the persons shown may be helpful. If youngsters appear in the picture they should be identified by names, ages, names of parents and addresses.

17. If the picture is exceptional, credit may be given to the photographer in the cutline, perhaps with a brief description of how he achieved his creation. On picture pages containing text matter, the photographer's credit should be displayed as prominently as the writer's. Photo credit lines seldom are used on one-column or half-column head shots.

18. Although pictures normally carry cutlines, mood, or special occasion pictures sometimes appear without cutlines if the message is obvious from the picture itself. Not all who look at pictures will also read the cutlines. In fact, the drop-off is severe enough to suggest that many readers satisfy their curiosity merely by looking at the picture.

19. In writing a series of cutlines for related shots, use only one picture slug, followed by a number—moon 1, moon 2 and so on.

20. Some papers use one style for cutlines with a story and another style for cutlines on pictures without a story (called *stand-alones* or *no-story*). A picture with a story might call for one, two or three words in boldface caps to start the cutline. In stand-alones a small head might be placed over the cutline (Figure 12–13).

21. The heading over the cutline should clue the reader as to the event shown in the picture. It helps him see at a glance the meaning of the picture. When possible, the heading should give the picture's locale to help the reader gauge his interest in the picture. Some studies have indicated that readers get less erroneous interpretations of the subject matter of the picture when the cutline is topped by a properly written heading.

If the dateline is knocked out in the cutline, make sure that somewhere in the cutline the location is included. Example: "GUARDING GOATS—Joe Fair, a 70-year-old pensioner, looks over his goats Rosebud and Tagalong, the subject of much furor in this northeastern Missouri community, boyhood home of

NEWS PHOTO BY DAVID L. CORNWELL

Potential pies

Although it's more than a month until jack-o'-lanterns will be needed for the festivities of Allhallows eve, the seasonal harvest of pumpkins has begun in the fields of Valley View Farms in Adams County.

Onion harvest

Onions previously dug from the ground were being topped and boxed by a six-man crew working at the Yosh Nigo farm on U.S. 50, near Uranium Downs this morning. Onions are among the last of the season's crops which farmers are hastening to gather while the weather is still good.

Sentinel photo by Dennis Hogan

All weld and good

Sparks fly as Larry Page welds a latch on the door of a boxcar. He was working yesterday in the Penn-Central Railroad yards outside of Jeffersonville, Ind.

Staff Photo
by Bud Kamenish

HIGH-RISE EXCITEMENT—Fans on balconies watch first lap of qualifying race for the Long Beach Grand Prix. Brian Redman won main event in a Lola before an estimated 75,000 spectators.

DETAILS IN SPORTS SECTION

Times photo by Joe Kennedy

The way it was, then...

No, this wasn't taken from last night's bout in Manila when champion Muhammad Ali faced Joe Frazier for the third time. This shot was taken during the 15th round of their first meeting in March, 1971, when Frazier floored Ali in the final round to win a decision and the heavyweight title. During their second encounter, in January 1974, there were no knockdowns and very little else. Ali was a 2-1 favorite around the world to win, but in Manila the odds dropped to 6-5 for Ali. (Defender photo)

Sargent Shriver

Figure 12–13. Cutline styles. Edmund Arnold, an authority on typography, argues that when display type is added to the cutline, readership increases as much as 25 per cent.

Mark Twain...." The Missouri community was Hannibal, but the cutline didn't say so.

The same pictures from news agencies and syndicates appear in smaller dailies as well as in metropolitan dailies. Some papers merely reset the cutline supplied with the pictures. Most, if not all, such cutlines should be rewritten to add to the story told in the picture and to indicate some originality on the paper's part.

The mood of the cutline should match the mood of the picture. The cutline for a feature photo may stress light writing. Restraint is observed for pictures showing tragedy or dealing with a serious subject.

13

An Introduction to Type

An editor who wants to help his audience read faster and easier should understand how to use type. Type ranks in importance with pictures and page makeup as attention-getting devices on a newspaper page. If incorrectly used, type may become an impediment to reading.

Using type correctly, however, is difficult because it involves understanding at least seven different dimensions, each of which affects readership in some way. For example, suppose an editor must decide how to set a headline. Not only must he choose a particular family of headline *typeface*[1] from among hundreds of alternatives, but he must also decide, at the same time, the specific size, weight, width of letter, length of line, spacing between lines and style in which to set the headline. These seven decisions usually must be made quickly because there isn't much time to give to it each day. The readability of these headlines is thus affected every day, depending on how all seven decisions relate to each other, and whether they represent the best of all alternatives.

If an editor does not understand type, he may order a headline in a typeface that is virtually unreadable, or one so unusual that it calls attention to the shape of the letters rather than to the meaning of the words. Although the words may be well-written, their meaning is obscured because readers begin to notice how unusual the typeface looks. Their attention is thus distracted from the meaning of the words. It is important, therefore, to understand that type is a vehicle by which words may be

[1] *Typeface* refers to that portion of type printed on paper. Types, like human beings, are recognized by their faces.

printed on many copies of paper quickly. The vehicle is never a substitute for communication, only an aid to the process. Type, therefore, should be unobtrusive. One of the most important rules for using type correctly deals with its unobtrusive character. This rule holds that:

Any typeface that calls attention to itself rather than to the message represents a poor choice. Type calls attention to itself when it is very large (in proportion to other type on the page), when it has an unusual design or when it is set in an unusual arrangement. In such cases, type distracts the readers' attention from the message.

Learning How Types Differ

To use type effectively, the beginner should start by studying how typefaces differ. Thousands of typefaces exist and every year new faces are added to the list. The beginner should learn to dissect the characteristics of typefaces so that their differences become larger and more noticeable. Eventually, through experience, the beginner will see the differences that seemed so difficult to discern at first.

To learn how type differs, it is important to know the various classifications of differences. Types differ by size, design characteristics, style, families, widths, weights, and methods of mechanical production. The following pages summarize the most significant classifications by which types are differentiated.

Classification of Typefaces by Point Sizes

Most typefaces are measured in units called *points*. A point is a unit of printer's measurement of about $\frac{1}{72}$ inch. Twelve points equal 1 pica, and 6 picas equal 1 inch. Although type could be classified by picas or inches (for example, 72-point type could be called 6-pica type or 1-inch type), it is common practice to limit classification to point-size identification.

Types come in a limited range of sizes in most print shops or newspapers, and within this range are carefully spaced intervals. For example, metal type usually is manufactured from 4 point (the smallest-sized type) to 96 point. Larger sizes of type may be in the form of wood (for letterpress printing) or photographs (for offset printing). There are some exceptions to this range; but not many in common use. The sizes of type most often available in newspapers and print shops, and considered to be standard sizes are as follows:

6, 8, 10, 12, 14, 18, 24, 30, 36, 42, 48, 60 and 72 point

In phototypesetting, 28- and 56-point type sizes are often used.

At the lower end of the range, the intervals vary by only 2 points, whereas at the upper end, the intervals vary by 12 points. The reason for this variance is that smaller sizes are used to fill a given amount of space and small variances are needed, but larger sizes are used mostly for headlines and small differences would be unnoticeable.

In some of the larger newspaper plants the smaller intervals vary by only 1 point so that the editor may be able to designate 5½-, 6-, 7-, 8-, 9-, 10-, 11-, and 12-point type if he needs it.

Occasionally, an editor may want a type size that does not exist, such as a 40-point type. In such a case he may compromise by selecting a 36- or 42-point type size instead, or he can take a 36-point type print and have it enlarged photostatically. Because so little time is available in the production of a newspaper, editors find it more convenient to use standard-sized type.

In Figure 13–1 are examples of the various sizes of typefaces.

SIZE IN POINTS	
6	abcdefghijklmnopqrstuvwxyzabcdefghijklmnopqrstuvwxyzabcdefghijklmnopqrstuvwx
7	abcdefghijklmnopqrstuvwxyzabcdefghijklmnopqrstuvwxyzabcdefghijklmnopqr
8	abcdefghijklmnopqrstuvwxyzabcdefghijklmnopqrstuvwxyzabcdefghijkl
9	abcdefghijklmnopqrstuvwxyzabcdefghijklmnopqrstuvwxyzabcdefg
10	abcdefghijklmnopqrstuvwxyzabcdefghijklmnopqrstuvwxyzabcd
11	abcdefghijklmnopqrstuvwxyzabcdefghijklmnopqrstuvwxyza
12	abcdefghijklmnopqrstuvwxyzabcdefghijklmnopqrstuvw
14	abcdefghijklmnopqrstuvwxyzabcdefghijklmnopqr
18	abcdefghijklmnopqrstuvwxyzabcdefg
24	abcdefghijklmnopqrstuvwxyz
30	abcdefghijklmnopqrstu
36	abcdefghijklmnopqr
42	abcdefghijklmno
48	abcdefghijklmn
60	abcdefghijkl
72	abcdefghij

Figure 13–1. Most frequently used type sizes. [From *A Typographic Quest, Number Three, New York: Westvaco, 1965, p. 4.*]

Classification of Type by Families

Just as members of the same human family tend to have similar facial characteristics, so do members of a type family. A type family includes all variations of a given type having common characteristics. Some type families have many variations; others have few. Figure 13–2 shows one of the large families of typefaces.

Helvetica Hairline

Helvetica Light

Helvetica Regular

Helvetica Medium

Helvetica Demi-Bold

Helvetica Bold

Helvetica X-Bold

Helvetica Bold Condensed

Helvetica X-Bold Condensed

Helvetica Bold Condensed

Helvetica X-Bold Condensed

Helvetica Medium

Helvetica Bold

Figure 13–2. Some members of the Helvetica family.

Typefaces may be classified as either oldstyle or modern. Care must be taken not to be confused by these terms, however, because they do *not* refer to periods of time. The term *oldstyle,* for example, does not mean that this type is "old" in terms of time even though it was first created about 1470. It is still being designed today. Modern type, on the other hand, was first created around 1800 and also is being designed today. Therefore, the style elements are important and the time elements are not. Today there are many versions of both oldstyle and modern typefaces. Each designer, although keeping the main characteristics, creates slight differences in his typefaces to make them unique.

Oldstyle type is considered a warm and friendly face and is often employed where large masses of type must be used, such as in books or newspapers. The following characteristics help to identify oldstyle types:

1. It has the appearance of being drawn with a broad-nibbed pen. The effect of using such a pen is the creation of variations in the widths of most letters. Therefore, letters have both thick and thin elements. But the identifying device differentiating oldstyle from modern is a gradual transition from the thin to thick elements of each letter. These gradual transitions can be created by drawing with the broad-nibbed pen. Figure 13–3 shows these transitions and how they were created.

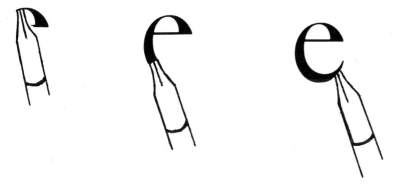

Figure 13–3. Thick and thin elements of a letter are caused by drawing with a broad-nibbed pen held at a certain angle. Type designers simply retain the thick and thin characteristics in their versions of oldstyle typefaces.

2. A serif is a horizontal line that appears at the top and bottom of most letters. Exceptions are a, c, e, g, o, t and capitals O and Q. All serifs on oldstyle types have brackets, a small curve connecting the serif to the main portion of a letter. Again the reason for such brackets is to make the transition gradual from one element to the other. Arrows point to brackets in Figure 13–4.

Oldstyle and Modern Type Classifications

Oldstyle Types

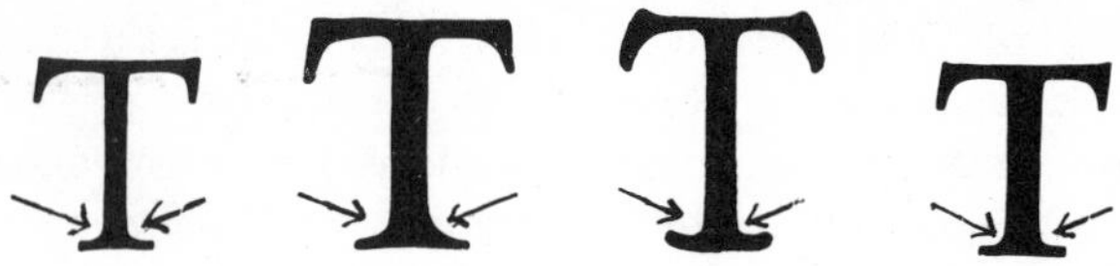

Figure 13–4. Various serifs on oldstyle type faces. Arrows point to brackets.

3. The weights of letters usually are distributed unevenly so they are not in the center. The thickest portion of each letter is near the bottom rather than the center. There are some exceptions to this principle but not many. The dotted lines in Figure 13–5 represent the thickest portion of the curves.

Figure 13–5. Curved letters showing uneven distribution of weights in oldstyle types.

4. Slanting serifs precede letters such as d, h, i, n, p, q and r. The slants occur at the top only. They are indicated by dotted lines in Figure 13–6.

Figure 13–6. Slanting serifs.

5. When oldstyle types are printed en masse, such as on book pages, they have a rich, mellow appearance. No single characteristic makes one letter stand out from the others. Although any

Simplicity is a very important feature in typography, because it produces the direct appeal. It is this element of simplicity, which makes for easier reading as well as better comprehension, that the intelligent businessman seldom fails to praise, and the absence of which he seldom fails to notice and condemn. And, moreover, it is the kind of printing that is more profitable to produce from a mechanical standpoint. On the general run of work there

Figure 13–7. Sample of oldstyle type.

one letter may have irregular contours, when printed en masse the irregularities tend to disappear. Oldstyle type, therefore, is easy to read because it is not fatiguing. Sharp, noticeable contours, such as on modern type, often bring about reader fatigue. Note the appearance of the mass of oldstyle letters in Figure 13–7.

Modern type, first designed near the end of the eighteenth century, is identified by the following characteristics: *Modern Type*

1. The thin parts of letters are very thin and there is great contrast between thick and thin elements (see Figure 13–8).

A B C

Figure 13–8. Modern type showing contrast between thick and thin elements.

2. The serifs are unbracketed (or have no curves at the bottom). Thus the thick element of the letter abruptly joins the thin serifs (see Figure 13–9).

Figure 13–9. There are no brackets on serifs of modern type.

3. The top serifs of letters such as r, n, h, i, b, d, j, k, l, m, n, q, v, u, w and x are horizontal and very thin (see Figure 13–10).

hiiklmn

Figure 13–10. Top serifs of modern type tend to be flat.

4. The widest portion of curved letters is vertical in modern types and it is not slanted as in oldstyle (see Figure 13–11).

Figure 13–11. Verticalness of wide portion of letters in modern typefaces.

5. There is an abrupt transition from the thick to thin elements in modern typefaces in contrast to the more gradual transition in oldstyle types (see Figure 13–12).

An Introduction to Type 233

Education

Figure 13–12. Abrupt transition from thick to thin elements of letters in modern type.

6. Modern types tend to have a business-like, cold, precise connotation. They are best printed on coated paper such as enamel and usually require more space between lines than do oldstyle types. At times, modern typefaces may be fatiguing to read because of their precise appearance. Figure 13–13 shows a paragraph of modern type.

> Simplicity is a very important feature in typography, because it produces the direct appeal. It is this element of simplicity, which makes for easier reading as well as better comprehension, that the intelligent businessman seldom fails to praise, and the absence of which he seldom fails to notice and condemn. And, moreover, it is the kind of printing that is more profitable to produce from a mechanical standpoint. On the gen-

Figure 13–13. A sample of modern typeface: Bodoni light. Contrast this sample with the oldstyle type shown in Figure 13–7.

Transitional Typefaces Are Usually Called Modern

In the world of type design one may occasionally find faces having both oldstyle and modern characteristics. Sometimes these typefaces are labeled as *traditional,* but most often they are simply called modern. Transitional typefaces were created between the eras of oldstyle and modern. Because the characteristics of transitional faces tend to be a combination of both oldstyle and modern, and because there are so few faces that fall into this classification, there is no need to identify type by the term *transitional* (see Figure 13–14).

Classification of Type by More Definitive Style Characteristics

Although it helps to know the differences between oldstyle and modern typefaces, these differences are not enough to identify and/or specify type for printers. A more discriminating classification divides type into broad classifications termed roman, italic, text, sans serif, script, cursive and square serif. This method of classification has sometimes been called the *race* of a type. Thus roman types might have been created in Rome and italic types created in Italy. But it is better to think of these classifications as simply style characteristics that help in differentiating and identifying typefaces. Roman type is best

Roman Type

ABCDEFGHIJKLMNOPQRS
abcdefghijklmnopqrstuvwxyz

Figure 13–14. Baskerville type, a traditional face.

identified by other characteristics. It has a vertical shape; it has serifs; it usually has combinations of thick and thin elements in each letter (called stem and hairlines, respectively) (see Figure 13–15). Some type experts consider all vertically shaped letters to be roman, even those without serifs or with no variations in the widths of letter elements (stem and hairline).

A B C D E F G H I J
Q R S T U V W X Y

Figure 13–15. Roman typeface.

This form of classification, therefore, may be confusing to the beginner because a roman type will have two purposes: one to distinguish it from sans serifs and the other to distinguish it from italics. For simplicity's sake, it is best to use the classification as first described.

Italic Type

Italic types are characterized by their slanted letter shapes. Although italic types were originally designed to make it possible to print many letters in relatively little space, their use today is limited to citations or words that must be emphasized. They also are used in headlines and body types. Today, italic types are designed to accompany roman types, so that there is consistency in the family of design. Figure 13–16 shows a roman and an italic type of the same family.

ABCDEFGHIJKLMNO pqrstu
ABCDEFGHIJKLMNO pqrstu

Figure 13–16. Roman and italic faces of the Bodoni Bold family.

Sans Serifs (or Gothic) Types

In America, printers use two terms to identify typefaces having no serifs. One is *sans serif;* the other is *Gothic.* The term *sans serif* comes from the French word *sans,* meaning "without," or *without* serifs. The other term, *Gothic,* is a misnomer. Originally Gothic type meant the churchy-looking types Americans often called "Old English." But today printers use the term *Gothic* also to refer to serifless type.

An Introduction to Type

235

Sans serif typefaces are made in many variations, some of whose differences are hardly discernible except to the trained eye. Figure 13–17 shows a small sample of these sans serif variations available to the editor for body type or headline purposes.

Grotesque Bold

LINING GOTHIC CONDENSED NO. 3*

News Gothic

POSTER GOTHIC

RAILROAD GOTHIC

Figure 13–17. A small sample of sans serif variations.

Text Type   Text type is often incorrectly called Gothic because it looks like Gothic architecture of the middle ages. But printers call it text because it appears to have a texture, like cloth, when printed in large masses. These letters were originally drawn with a broad-nibbed pen and were created to show a minimum of curves. Today the type is used for church printing or where a conservative headline is needed. Students should never have text set in all-capital letters for two reasons: (1) It was never drawn that way originally, having always utilized capital and lower case letters; (2) it is difficult to read when set in all-capital letters (see Figures 13–18 and 13–19).

ḪARD ꚋꙮ ꞍEAꝹ

Figure 13–18. Cloister Text set in all-capital letters.

Easier to read

Figure 13–19. Cloister text set in capital and lower case letters.

Script Type   Script-style letters resemble handwriting. Although the type designers have tried to make it appear as if all the letters are joined, small spaces can be seen between each letter. Some script letters appear to have been written with a brush, whereas others look as if they were drawn with a calligraphic pen. Script type, too, should never be prepared in all-capital letters because it is hard to read in that form (see Figures 13–20 and 13–21).

Cursive Types   Cursive type styles are characterized by their ornateness. Although they look much like script typefaces, they are easily differentiated from script because of the amount of space be-

HARD TO READ

Figure 13-20. Brush script type set in all capitals.

Easier to read

Figure 13-21. Brush script set in capital and lower case letters.

tween letters. Script typefaces have little space between letters. Cursives are used mostly in advertising but occasionally are used for compartmentalized headlines on the women's page (see Figure 13-22).

Raleigh Cursive

ABCDEFGHIJKLMNOPQ
abcdefghijklmnopqrstuvwxyzabcdefghi 12345

Lydian Cursive

ABCDEFGHIJKLMNOPQRST
abcdefghijklmnopqrstuvwxyz 12345

Mayfair Cursive

ABCDEFGHIJKLMNOPST
abcdefghijklmnopqrstuvwxyzabcdefg 12345

Figure 13-22. Three different kinds of cursives.

Square serif type is similar to sans serif except that it has square serifs, and no brackets. Occasionally it may be called slab-serifs. There are no thick and thin elements to any parts of letters. It is a bold-looking typeface and is limited to occasional headline use. Very few newspapers use square serif types for regular headlines; it is most often used in advertising. Some varieties of square serifs are shown in Figure 13-23.

Square Serif Types

Most typefaces are manufactured in normal (or regular) widths. Regular widths comprise the greatest amount of reading matter. But wide and narrow type also is available. Type manufacturers have created extracondensed, condensed, expanded and extended typefaces in addition to regular. These extra widths, however, are not manufactured in all type sizes or families. Therefore, it is necessary to check with the printer to

Type May Be Classified by Letter Widths

Karnak Medium
ABCDEFGHIJKLMNOPQR
abcdefghijklmnopqr 12345

Girder Heavy
ABCDEFGHIJKLMNOPTW
abcdefghijklmnopqrs 12345

Stymie Bold
ABCDEFGHIJKLMNOW
abcdefghijklmnop 12345

Figure 13–23. Three varieties of square serif types.

see whether he carries the width desired or whether it is manufactured (see Figure 13–24).

Figure 13–24. Variations in letter widths.

Type Classification by Weights

Type may be classified by the weight of the letter. Most typefaces are manufactured in lightface and boldface. Some faces are manufactured in medium, demibold heavy, and ultrabold as well. The terminology here tends to be confusing. One manufacturer titles his medium-weight type demibold, whereas another calls his medium. The terms *heavy, bold,* or *black* also may mean the same thing. Figure 13–25 shows common examples of type weights.

Type Differentiated by Method of Production

Type may also be differentiated on the basis of the mechanical method by which it is composed or by the manufacturer. Occasionally, a manufacturer designs a typeface that, although it uses a common family name, is different from all others. For example, Caslon is a typeface designed by many manufacturers. The Caslon manufactured by the American Type Founders may be different from that manufactured by the Ludlow Company, the Bauer Type Founders, or the Merganthaler Company. If the user wants such a special typeface, he must specify which kind of Caslon he wants and identify the manufacturer. Newspaper editors usually do not require such precise choices of

Bauer Beton Light

Bauer Beton Medium

Futura Demibold

Bauer Beton Bold

BERNHARD GOTHIC HEAVY

Bernhard Gothic Extra Heavy

Bauer Beton Extra Bold

Futura Ultrabold

Figure 13–25. Various weights of typefaces.

typefaces and therefore do not need to specify the company or method of production.

Other Ways To Differentiate Type

The following discussion concerns other facts about typefaces that should be known by persons who want to use type intelligently. These facts serve as means of further differentiating type.

A *font* is a printer's term for an assembly of metal letters of the alphabet purchased from the type manufacturer. The font specifically refers to type of one family and one size. It includes enough capital and lower case letters to enable the printer to set sentences.

Small Capitals

Occasionally an editor may want a special-sized capital letter included in a subhead or in the text that is smaller than normal capital letters. These smaller letters are called *small capitals* and their unique characteristic, other than being small, is that they can be composed on typesetting machines without elaborate preparations. Small capitals are often used when special emphasis is needed, usually for a man's name or the titles of books. Many kinds of typesetting machines used for newspaper work are able to set small capitals with almost no special effort (see Figure 13–26).

FOURTEEN POINT WEISS ROMAN

Figure 13–26. Capitals and small capitals.

Ligatures

Ligatures are two or three letters manufactured on one piece of type. This practice started in the early days of printing and has been continued to this day, but for a different reason. In certain

---

fonts of metal type, the letter "f" overhangs the letters "i," "l," or "f" and interferes with the way they print on paper. The overhang is called the *kern* of a letter (see Figure 13–27).

Figure 13–27. The kern of a letter "f" interferes with the "i".

When the kern of an "f" was forced together with the dot of an "i" or an "l" or another "f," the overhang would break. For that reason type manufacturers created ligatures, or single pieces of type on which two or three of the letter combinations were cast (see Figure 13–28).

fi ff ffi fl ffl

Figure 13–28. The five ligatures are usually available in type.

When the manufacturers of high-speed line-casting machines faced this problem, they created a special letter "f" having no overhang. Nevertheless, the ligatures were still available to be used in the setting of newspaper and book reading material, and so to this day they may be used, depending on the whims of the operator. They are unnecessary except in type being set by hand. Figure 13–29 shows a word using the ligature "ff."

Effective

Figure 13–29. Use of a ligature in a word.

How To Measure Type from the Printed Page

When type is measured by laying a ruler on a letter cast in metal, there is no problem in discerning its size. Because most users of type do not have easy access to metal type, they must be able to measure type as it is printed on a type page or type specimen book. Although most such books indicate the sizes of all types shown, it is still important to know how type is measured.

A difficulty arises in measuring printed letters because it is difficult to determine where the bottom of each letter is located. Underneath each letter on a metal piece of type is a space called the *shoulder*. Shoulder space is created to allow room for the descenders of letters, such as g, p, q and y. Specifically, the problem is to estimate correctly how much space should be allowed for the shoulder when there are no descending letters in a line of printed type (see Figure 13–30).

PROFITS

Figure 13–30. This word is difficult to measure because there is no way to estimate the depth of the shoulder precisely.

To dramatize and explain this problem, Figure 13–31 shows imaginary lines by which letters are created on type. These lines are called (1) base line, on which all letters other than g, p, q and y rest; (2) cap line, to which most capital letters and tall letters rise; (3) lower case line, where small letters align (called the "x" height of letters); and (4) descender line. Each line helps in aligning letters.

Figure 13–31. Drawing of a piece of type and imaginary lines that serve to align letters.

In measuring the letter "h" it is necessary to allow room for the shoulder underneath the letter. The ascenders rise above the lower case line and the descenders appear below the base line. Thus, when one wants to measure type from a printed page, he must allow space for the descenders. He can accurately determine ascender space by looking for a capital letter or one with an ascender. If it were necessary to measure the point size of a line of capital letters it would be necessary to take the space normally used for descenders into consideration in order to have an accurate measurement (see Figures 13–32 and 13–33).

Figure 13–32. This word can be measured accurately by drawing a line across the ascender (the "d") and another line across the descenders ("q" and "p") and measuring the distance between the two lines.

An Introduction to Type   **241**

E E E E E E E

Figure 13-33. Why type is so difficult to measure. All of these capital "E's" are 48 points in height, but each has a different size shoulder.

How To Select and Use Type Effectively

One of the best ways to learn how to select and use type effectively is to develop a sense of what looks right. The first step in developing this sense is to learn to differentiate typefaces easily. Once this differentiation has been learned, some simple fundamentals of type-use plus artistic principles will help the beginner use discrimination in selection.

For many years printers learned rules for selecting and using type. Now many of these rules have been rejected in favor of a common sense approach to what looks right in print.

For example, the old rule was never to mix oldstyle and modern typefaces. But today they may be mixed if the contrast between them is not too strong and if an unequal amount of each is used.

If a headline is set in Futura Bold (a modern typeface) and the paragraphs of an editorial are set in Caslon (an oldstyle face) the result may be pleasant. The decision to combine the two depends, however, on the knowledge that contrast in print is desirable, but it can be neither too weak nor too strong. The following principles of typography and artistic design are presented as guideposts for developing a sense of what looks right.

The Objectives of Good Typography

The foremost objective of good typography is to select legible typefaces. They are easy to read and enable a person to read faster than he could with less legible faces. Furthermore, legible faces encourage the reader to read more of what has been printed simply because they present fewer obstacles to reading.

Which typefaces are the most legible? The answer is that almost all faces manufactured exclusively for use as body type in books, magazines and newspapers are legible. But display types (18 point and larger) may or may not be legible, especially when set in long lines. In advertising, some unusual typeface may be used in a headline of one or two words. Because there may be much white space around the headline, it may not seem illegible. But if that same typeface were to be used in a newspaper headline, it might be difficult to read. The amount of white space surrounding type affects legibility.

But the most significant difference between types that are legible and illegible has more to do with whether readers are familiar with them. Familiar typefaces, or those in most common use, tend to be read the easiest. When unusual typefaces that are ornate or grotesque are used, readers stop to look at the uniqueness of the letter shapes and this process slows reading.

Figures 13–34 and 13–35 show examples of illegible and legible typefaces.

EDUCATION

Figure 13–34. Illegible, especially if set in lines, because it calls attention to its odd shape. It is an uncommon face.

Education

Figure 13–35. Legible, because it contains gentle transitions from thick to thin elements, because it does not call attention to its design, and because it is used so often that readers are familiar with it.

White Space and Legibility

To achieve legibility through selection and use of typefaces, one ought to choose types most familiar to readers. If there is a need to select a typeface that readers may not find familiar, then it should be surrounded with extra white space. White space has the effect of giving the reader more time to absorb the details of unusually shaped letters. If space is limited, however, it is always better to select the more common typefaces so that additional white space need not be used.

The principle of using white space to increase legibility of type accounts for the fact that type appearing in all-capital letters is read about 12 per cent slower than the same words appearing in capitals and lower case letters. There is simply more white space surrounding a line of lower case letters than a line of capitals. Another reason lower case letters are read faster than all-capitals is that it is easier to determine the shape of words.

In addition to the general use of white space, however, legibility is also controlled by the arrangement of letters, spacing between words, spacing between lines and widths of lines. Each manner of control should be considered separately, and afterwards they should be considered in total. Here are some guidelines for each:

ARRANGEMENT OF LETTERS AND WORDS. Any style of arrangement that calls attention to itself and not the message is poor. Therefore, common arrangements are best. Flush left headlines are in common use and are interesting, yet easy to read. (see Figure 13–36).

All Plans Complete
For Victory Meeting

Figure 13–36. A flush-left headline. It is easy to read because it is one style often seen in newspapers.

If, however, letters should be set in a vertical arrangement, they would be very difficult to read easily and quickly as Figure 13–37 demonstrates.

Figure 13–37. Difficult to read. Type set like this is rarely seen. The arrangement calls attention to itself; not to the message. Also, each letter must be read separately, and then combined into words.

WORD SPACING. Narrow word spacing is always to be preferred to wide word spacing because readers do not read one word at a time; but groups of words. Narrow word spacing makes it possible to glance at a group of words at one time, quickly.

LINE SPACING. The research on line spacing is indeterminate. Yet there is a feeling that lines with generous space between them are easier to read than those tightly spaced. Obviously, there is a point where too much space between lines becomes unsightly. Figures 13–38 and 13–39 show examples of various kinds of line spacing. Therefore, too much space between lines of a headline is undesirable. One must judge whether there is too much space by deciding whether all lines can be read as a single entity, (desirable) or as a collection of individual lines (undesirable).

Heat Wave Hits Cities Near Coast

Figure 13–38. It is obvious that more spacing between lines is needed.

WIDTH OF LINE. Although various formulas can be used to determine how long a line of type can become before it appears difficult to read, the width can also be determined in other ways. One of the best ways is to examine a line of type as it appears

Heat Wave Hits Cities Near Coast

Figure 13–39. Words are easier to read with generous spacing between the lines. However there is a point where too much line space deters reading.

in a catalog of typefaces. Judgment based on experience can be used to determine the point at which the typeface begins to be difficult to read. It is also apparent that longer widths can be used if more space is placed between the lines. The extra white space between the lines helps the reader keep his place and move to each succeeding line easily. Any extremes in width, however, should be avoided. Extremely short or wide lines are difficult to read.

READER FATIGUE. A final dimension of legibility is the degree to which a typeface tires the reader's eyes. Unfortunately, this is an area where there is no research and a great deal of opinion. Common sense, however, indicates that boring typefaces (because they have no thick or thin variations in letters) tend to be fatiguing. Therefore, all sans serif typefaces tend to be fatiguing. In addition, unusually light or very bold typefaces also tend to be tiring if printed in large quantities.

A second objective of good type selection and use is to seek aesthetically pleasing typefaces. Of the thousands of existing typefaces, some are more beautiful than others. The most beautiful ones are those in prominent use. Occasionally new faces are introduced that do not find wide acceptance immediately, and these should be sought for and used despite their seeming unpopularity.

An important objective of good typography is that of selecting typefaces that harmonize with the message content. Some faces are more appropriate than others for general headlines, editorials, captions under cartoons or advertising. The connotation of typefaces, therefore, is important. Connotation of type represents the feeling that it engenders. For example, type with a very black look connotes strength, as does large type. A lightface italic, on the other hand, connotes daintiness (see Figure 13–40).

WIDTH OF LETTERS. In a previous discussion, attention was directed to the variations in the shoulder space of different typefaces. Figures 13–33 showed that, although each of the letters was a 48-point typeface, there were significant and observable differences in the space underneath each letter. Now attention is called to the variations in the widths of letters.

Other Considerations in Selecting and Using Type

Elegance
Clearcut Initial—French Script

MODERNISM
Kabel Light

DIGNITY
Forum

UNUSUALNESS
Newfangle

Antiquity
Satanick

NATURE
Sylvan

Sincerity
Baskerville

STRENGTH
John Hancock

Distinctiveness
Civilité

CHEAPNESS
Mid-Gothic

Figure 13–40. Connotations of various typefaces. [*Courtesy International Typographical Union.*]

Figure 13–41 shows different 36-point typefaces. Although each is 36-point size, there are differences in widths. The only way to know and appreciate these differences is to study type catalogs, where samples of different faces are printed. If the reader is aware of the differences in the widths of letters, he can choose the typeface that best meets his needs.

AEMNPQRSWT adegiory
Caslon Bold

AEMNPQRSWT adegiory
Stymie Bold

AEMNPQRSWT adegiory
Bodoni Bold

Figure 13–41. A comparison of various 36-point typefaces. Note variations in widths of letters.

SELECTION OF "BODY" TYPES. Body types are used for the major part of the reading matter in newspapers. They are usually composed in sizes ranging from 7 point to 14 point. The selection of body types requires an additional consideration beyond those already mentioned: the appearance of the type in large masses. Some typographers call this appearance the

BASKERVILLE, 12 pt.   2 pt. leaded. .2.3 characters to 1 pica

Simplicity is a very important feature in typography, because it produces the direct appeal. It is this element of simplicity, which makes for easier reading as well as better comprehension, that the intelligent businessman seldom fails to praise, and the absence of which he seldom fails to notice and condemn. And, moreover, it is the

BODONI LIGHT, 12 pt.   2 pt. leaded. .2.2 characters to 1 pica

Simplicity is a very important feature in typography, because it produces the direct appeal. It is this element of simplicity, which makes for easier reading as well as better comprehension, that the intelligent businessman seldom fails to praise, and the absence of which he seldom fails to notice and condemn. And, moreover, it is the

BOOKMAN, 12 pt.   2 pt. leaded. .2.2 characters to 1 pica

Simplicity is a very important feature in typography, because it produces the direct appeal. It is this element of simplicity, which makes for easier reading as well as better comprehension, that the intelligent businessman seldom fails to praise, and the absence of which he seldom fails to notice and condemn. And, more-

CENTURY SCHOOLBOOK, 12 pt. 2 pt. leaded. .2.1 characters to 1 pica

Simplicity is a very important feature in typography, because it produces the direct appeal. It is this element of simplicity, which makes for easier reading as well as better comprehension, that the intelligent businessman seldom fails to praise, and the absence of which he seldom fails to notice and con-

GARAMONT, 12 pt.   2 pt. leaded. .2.2 characters to 1 pica

Simplicity is a very important feature in typography, because it produces the direct appeal. It is this element of simplicity, which makes for easier reading as well as better comprehension, that the intelligent businessman seldom fails to praise, and the absence of which he seldom fails to notice and condemn. And,

KENNERLY, 12 pt.   2 pt. leaded. .2.4 characters to 1 pica

Simplicity is a very important feature in typography, because it produces the direct appeal. It is this element of simplicity, which makes for easier reading as well as better comprehension, that the intelligent businessman seldom fails to praise, and the absence of which he seldom fails to notice and condemn. And, moreover, it is the kind of printing

SANS SERIF LIGHT, 12 pt.   2 pt. leaded. .2.5 characters to 1 pica

Simplicity is a very important feature in typography, because it produces the direct appeal. It is this element of simplicity, which makes for easier reading as well as better comprehension, that the intelligent businessman seldom fails to praise, and the absence of which he seldom fails to notice and condemn. And, moreover, it is the kind of printing

STYMIE MEDIUM, 12 pt.   2 pt. leaded. .2.2 characters to 1 pica

Simplicity is a very important feature in typography, because it produces the direct appeal. It is this element of simplicity, which makes for easier reading as well as better comprehension, that the intelligent businessman seldom fails to praise, and the absence of which he seldom fails to notice and con-

TIMES NEW ROMAN, 12 pt.   2 pt. leaded. .2.3 characters to 1 pica

Simplicity is a very important feature in typography, because it produces the direct appeal. It is this element of simplicity, which makes for easier reading as well as better comprehension, that the intelligent businessman seldom fails to praise, and the absence of which he seldom fails to notice and condemn. And, moreover, it

20th CENTURY MEDIUM, 12 pt. 2 pt. leaded. .2.4 characters to 1 pica

Simplicity is a very important feature in typography, because it produces the direct appeal. It is this element of simplicity, which makes for easier reading as well as better comprehension, that the intelligent businessman seldom fails to praise, and the absence of which he seldom fails to notice and condemn. And, moreover, it is the

Figure 13–42. Twelve point typeface samples (reduced in size). Note mass appearance of variations in weights and widths of letters.

"coloring" of a printed page, even though the page is printed in black print on white paper. Some types have a distinctly black appearance when they appear in large masses, whereas others have a very gray appearance. Others have what might be called a pleasant tone. Although ten different samples of body type are shown in Figure 13–42, there are obvious differences in the

An Introduction to Type

mass appearance of these types. One reason for the differences is the weight of the letters themselves, and the other is the amount of white space between lines. The beginner should notice that the amount of space between the lines appears to vary between samples even though standard 2-point leading has been used in each. The significance of the line space variations is that different typefaces have shoulder spaces of different sizes, which accounts for the differences in spaces between lines. It is almost impossible to know how a given typeface will appear en masse unless a sample is examined first.

Tips on Using Type

1. Roman, italics, and boldface type faces should not be set in the same line because there will be too much contrast. Too much contrast makes reading difficult. Most often good typography is limited to either roman and italic or roman and boldface type faces in the same line.

2. Type should not be set in very short or very long measures. Both are difficult to read. A rule of thumb that will help determine the maximum line length is to use the width of $1\frac{1}{2}$ alphabet lengths as a guide. This requires that the user first either have alphabets (lower case) set to the required width or find a sample in a type book and then measure the width. Slight variations in this measured width will not matter.

A line of type should rarely be set less than four picas wide because it is difficult to fit many words in such a small space. Even a four-pica width should be limited to very small type such as 6- or no more than 7-point type. On the other hand, type should rarely be set longer than 30 picas wide. Exceptions to this rule are situations where the type being set is 18 points or larger in height.

3. For headlines, too many different sizes or faces should be avoided on the same page. The best technique is to use monotypographic harmony, meaning harmony based on the use of a single type family. But, when many different sizes or variations of the same family are used, the effect is unharmonious. However, if an editor requires more than one type family on a single page, then the number should be limited to two, with one being used predominately, and the other sparingly.

4. Agate ($5\frac{1}{2}$-point) type is used exclusively for box scores of athletic games and long lists of names (such as in a graduating class). But this type size should never be used for the main text of a story. Because of its size, it is compact and saves space, but it is always a supplement to the main body of reading matter.

5. The beginner should watch for unusual and unsightly spacing between letters of a word set in large type. This usually occurs when setting combinations of any of the following capital letters: A, L, P, T, V and W. For example, A and V have more white space between them (AV) than do N and I (NI), or other

similar combinations. When any of the above letters is used in combination in large headline, the printer should be asked to cut the type in such a way as to eliminate the unsightly space. He may be willing to do so if time is available. However, in phototypesetting, it is easy and therefore advisable to overlap capital letters to avoid unsightly letter spacing.

6. A change of pace in typefaces for headlines is attractive if it is not overdone. This means that an italic or an ultraboldface headline may be used on a page that has predominantly roman typeface headlines. When more than one such variation is used, the contrasting effect is lost.

7. Contrast is a key to beautiful typography. But the contrast should be relatively strong. When headline typefaces are used that are different, but not radically so, the mixture on a page will appear to be "a wrong font," rather than a contrasting headline.

8. Narrow word-spacing is easier to read than wide word-spacing. Both "hot" and "cold" typesetting machines often produce wide word-spacing. If not controlled, wide word-spacing calls attention to itself and not the meaning of the words.

The competent editor should know and understand how to select and use type, though the opportunity to use this knowledge may be limited, especially in smaller newspapers. Yet even within the limited number of typefaces or sizes available in any plant, there are often many alternative types that could be used. Under any circumstances, if the editor makes a poor choice of type, he may detract from the appearance of a page and make it hard to read. Therefore, he should be able to translate words into type forms to maximize communication on a page, other things being equal. It is obvious that "the other things being equal" refers to well-written and edited copy. Good type selection is no substitute for poor writing and editing, because type is the vehicle for words, not the message.

The best way to understand type is to be able to differentiate the many kinds of existing type. Unless the slight variations in letters shapes are known, one typeface may appear as good as another. Once the differences in typefaces have been learned, however, the editor can develop an aesthetic sense, or taste, of what looks attractive in print, based on some elementary artistic principles.

Developing a sense of artistic judgment in type is best done by studying type in print, no matter where it appears. For example, beautifully set type often appears in a magazine, a book, or a financial report. If the editor works at developing a sensitivity for what looks good in print, he will be alert to such printing. Then he will make a mental note of the way type was set or why it looks so good and eventually will use this idea, by adjusting it to the newspaper environment, if it is at all possible. In this manner the editor uses type to aid communication.

An Introduction to Type

How Type Is Set: The New Technology of Typesetting

Setting (or composing) type, essentially consists of assembling letters into lines and sentences in a form whereby they may be printed. For many years, the only kind of typesetting was that done by hand, an unbelievably slow process when compared to present methods. The production of newspapers was therefore necessarily slow. The invention and adoption of line-casting typesetting machines, more popularly known as "Linotypes," enabled publishers to greatly speed up the production of their newspapers. The effect of using Linotypes was that more pages could be produced more quickly than could possibly have been done by older methods. The Linotype continued to be the most widely used technique of setting type until about 1966, when the announcement of some exciting new developments in typesetting methods offered newspaper publishers opportunities for drastic change.

At that time, a number of typesetting inventions began to be accepted and adopted by many newspapers throughout the country. At first, adoptions were made mostly by smaller newspapers, but gradually, in succeeding years, larger newspapers began to either change to the new methods, or make plans to change in the near future. The rapid spread of these new inventions might best be called revolutionary, because they resulted not only in radically new methods of setting type, but in radically new ways of producing the entire newspaper. Almost every facet of newspaper production was changed.

What was so unusual about these changes? The answer was that type was now being set photographically, and with the aid of computers. Furthermore still other inventions resulted in new kinds of equipment that was to be used in conjunction with the photosetter to optimize newspaper production speed. Two such machines that were revolutionary were the video display terminal (VDT) and the optical character reader (OCR). The VDT allowed the reporter to not only type his original story and have the words show up on a video display screen, but now he could correct and edit that story without touching a piece of paper. The VDT could then operate the phototypesetter after the reporter was satisfied with his story. The OCR method enabled the reporter to type his story on a special electric typewriter, edit it on the same machine, and then feed his written story to the OCR to "read" the words on the paper and operate the phototypesetter subsequently.

It is important to note that in many newspaper plants, the product of phototypesetting machines have found greatest use with the offset printing process. In most situations, such newspapers *had* been printed by the letterpress printing process. In fact, hand-set and machine-set type were best adapted to letterpress printing. Letterpress consists of printing from raised letters directly on paper. But in the offset method, printing is indirect because after the printing plate is coated with ink and water it first prints on a rubber sheet (called a blanket) and then from the blanket onto paper.

The phototypesetting machines work very well with offset printing presses, although it could be used, with more difficulty, in the letterpress process. When used with offset, however, the photoprints are pasted directly on a page format, along with screened pictures (so that halftones will reproduce the pictures). Then the entire page is photographed as a single entity, converted into a negative, and finally into a printing plate (Figure 13–43 and 13–44).

In order to gain a better perspective of the revolutionary changes in typesetting and newspaper production, one must realize that after the original inventions began to be adopted, subsequent improvements resulted rather quickly, as many companies competed with each other to get on the market with a better product. Each major improvement has been called a "generation" of typesetters. In a period of less than ten years the newspaper industry has adopted a third generation of machines, with the fourth generation having been perfected to such an extent, that it is ready to come onto the market at this time.

The basic phototypesetting technique consists of placing a film negative of each letter in a sentence in front of a light source, and then shining light through the negative onto light-sensitive photographic paper. The result is a picture of letters assembled into lines (see Figure 13–45). In phototypesetting, letters are photographed at very high speeds. The output of the machine may be a photographic positive or negative paper (or film). Once enough lines have been set photographically, they can be pasted onto a page form, photographed, and converted into a printing plate.

The first generation of phototypesetters were really a modification of hot typesetting machines (where each letter of the alphabet was first made in the form of a mold (called a "mat" for short). Hot lead was forced into the molds, thereby producing a line of metal type. These mats were modified by replacing the molds with a film negative of each letter. Type was set by having an operator press a key that would release a mold for each letter, from a storage compartment, and then assemble them into a line of mats. Then each mat was placed in front of a light source; light was projected through the negatives one at a time, until the entire line was photographed. After the first line was set, the photographic paper would be advanced ready to receive a new line of letters.

First generation phototypesetters were really photo-mechanical in nature, and therefore relatively slow. Perhaps the fastest that it could set type was about 20 lines a minute, depending, of course, on the versatility of the operator.

The second generation of phototypesetters were different from their predecessors. Not only could they set type faster, but

An Introduction to Type   **251**

Friedman denies plan board power cut

By JULIE BENNETT
Lerner Newspapers
Correspondent

NORTHBROOK—Village President Gerald Friedman has denied charges that initial meetings between developers and village board members have foreclosed the decision-making powers of the village plan commission.

The charges were made by Howard Wolfman during a plan commission hearing last week. Wolfman, vice president of the Concerned Citizens and a candidate for the village board, noted that the developer present, Norman Rudenberg, mentioned having discussed his plan previously with the village board's real estate and zoning committee.

WOLFMAN CHARGED THAT such a discussion, "implies a foregone conclusion at the village board level before a decision is reached, whatever that might be, by the plan commission."

"We view this as an inherent weakness in our vil-

lage's rezoning procedure," he said.

Friedman, however, feels that the pre-hearing meeting practice strengthens the village's zoning stand. "By looking at a developer's plan before the hearing process begins, we save a lot of time and effort. If there's no way a proposal can succeed, then the developer knows he would be wasting his time, and ours, in filing it."

He added that the committee which usually meets with developers includes plan commission chairman John Reinert and members Robert Mason, Norman

Jacobs and Manny Minoff, plus the board's real estate and zoning committee chairman Howard Hoaglund and members Robert Patterson and Barry Nekritz.

"This group does not make up the majority of either board," Friedman continued. "The meetings are announced publicly and anyone can attend."

ACCORDING TO FRIEDMAN, plans which vary greatly from village zoning ordinances rarely get beyond the initial meeting. "Ninety per cent of them die right there." One exception, he added, was Dunbrook

shopping center developer Bruce Pillman's plan expand his row of stores to the east. Although m bers of the review committee told him there was chance they could approve his plan, Pillman w through the hearing process anyway. He was tur down, and now has a lawsuit pending against the lage, asking the courts to rezone the land instead.

Plan commission chairman Reinert told Wolf during the Nov. 19 Hearing that, "This commissic not being foreclosed. We are a recommending bo and the village board tends to follow our recomme tions in zoning matters."

HOWEVER, COMMISSION MEMBER Anth Buckun said he agreed with Wolfman. "Why sh such plans go to the village board first? I don't war waste my time if the board has made a foregone clusion."

In reference to the particular re-zoning matte request from Rudenberg for an annexation of 13 a on Dundee Road and re-zoning of the front 4½ acres a commercial complex, Friedman said that the c mittee had met three or four times. "But at no did we indicate our approval of the plan."

Under village ordinances, a re-zoning or anne tion is subject to a public hearing before the member plan commission, which then recommends tion to the village board. The recommendation is binding on board members, who make the final d sion in such matters.

Inflation hits village budget

NORTHBROOK—Inflation has hit the village budget.

A six-month budget update, prepared by finance director Robert Sutton, shows that building permit revenue is expected to run $100,000 below budget estimates by the end of the 1975 fiscal year.

The sag in the construction industry is blamed for the revenue loss. When Sutton prepared the 1975 budget last summer, he had estimated $400,000 in revenue from building permit fees. Last week he revised that figure to $300,000.

THE LOWER FIGURE anticipates a sharp drop in the rate of residential and commercial and industrial construction during the rest of the fiscal year, which ends April 30, 1975.

The drop in other construction means that the village will realize more than half of its building permit revenue this year from the Northbrook Court shopping center complex on Lake-Cook Road. That development, now under construction by Homart, a Sears Roebuck-owned subsidiary, is expected to pay $155,000 in permit fees before the end of April.

Under village policy, building permit fees are assessed, not for profit, but to cover the cost of inspection while a construction project is under way.

SUTTON'S BUDGET UPDATE presented to village board members during their informal work session Monday night, Nov. 25, contained one pleasant surprise. Sales tax rebates are up 7 per cent over expectations for the first half of the fiscal year, he said.

In most other budget matters, the village government seems to be "on target," Sutton reported.

Expenses in some areas also have been lower than estimates. The village had planned to spend almost $50,000 on major street repairs last summer. However, the cement driver strike postponed most of that work, which will be rescheduled for next year.

Camera equipment, drugs taken in break-in

NORTHBROOK—Burglars used a shopping cart to break into the Walgreen drug store, 1975 Cherry, early Sunday morning. They escaped with a large quantity of drugs and camera equipment.

The break-in was discovered by men working on a newspaper delivery truck, who arrived at the store early Sunday, Nov. 24.

According to police, someone had used a shopping cart to break through a window of the store. Quantities of about 45 different drugs, including tranquilizers and amphetamines, were missing.

HAIL TO THE CONQUERING heroes! The Glenbrook North band and a gymnasium full of happy residents await the arrival of the victorious Glenbrook North Spartans Saturday night from Normal, Ill. The Spartans won the first state high school football championship in a 19-13 overtime win against East St. Louis. (Photo by Robert Ramsay Jr.)

Seniors' housing needs surveyed

NORTHBROOK—This week the Northbrook man Relations Commission with the cooperation of the members of the Northbrook Clergy Assoc. distribute a survey of the housing needs and pre ences to residents over age 62.

The purpose of this survey is to determine housing needs of the elderly because the present h ing facilities in Northbrook may not meet the range of seniors' housing needs.

The results of this survey will be reported by Human Relations Commission to the village boa early 1975 with its overall report of the housing n of Northbrook.

The North Shore Senior Center and the Northb Park District Senior Citizens Group will also be s ing out surveys to its Northbrook members. Those idents 62 and over not belonging to any of the ab groups may pick up a survey questionnaire at the lage hall, 1225 Cedar Lane, or call the village ha 272-5050 and have a survey forwarded to them.

$1.8 million District 30 expansion plan okayed

By JOANNE KANTER
Lerner-Life Newspapers
Correspondent

A PLAN designed to add 27,000 square feet to Northbrook-Glenview District 30 schools at an estimated cost to residents of approximately $1.8 million was approved by the school board Nov. 21.

The decision came after a year of turmoil and inflation had wrecked the board's plans to build a fourth school. The original plan was to build a new junior high school and convert the present three schools into K-5 facilities. However, cost estimates of plans for the new junior high school exceeded the bonding power of the district and the board was forced to reconsider its decision.

The latest decision, and the one the board hopes will be implemented speedily, is to make Maple School into a sixth, seventh, eighth grade junior high school and to renovate Wescott and Willowbrook to accomodate K-5.

JOHN SCHLOSSMAN of Loebl, Schlossman, Ben-

nett and Dart, architects for the school district, brought three plans to the school board meeting but the board quickly rejected two of them as too costly. The board voted on the minimum building plan because it said that is all it can afford at this time.

The plan calls for the addition of four classrooms at Wescott, expansion of the present multi-purpose room at Willowbrook into a gymnasium and the addition of the following at Maple: four science rooms, two learning disability rooms, one special education/reading room, one art room, one home economics room, one industrial arts room, an addition to the library media center and locker rooms, showers and gym storage.

SCHLOSSMAN SAID the plan implies the continued use of mobile classrooms at Wescott.

"Each month I come hoping something will change, but it never does," said board president John Parker. "Instead of having a Cadillac we may have to be satisfied with a Chevrolet." However, Schlossman said the district never had plans for "a Cadillac."

Board members again harped on the amount of $42 per square foot for building costs estimated by the architect's firm.

Schlossman said he was "shocked" by the cost estimates but he "would be reluctant to say costs could be cut per square foot." He said the estimates were based on experience and checked with two independent cost estimators.

Before voting for the new plan, board member ome Baer, who has been the strongest proponent fourth school, tried once more to put across the ide building a junior high school for only seventh eighth grades at the present time. However, non the other board members concurred with his opi and the matter was dropped.

SUPT. THEODORE KAMATOS said the buil program will enable the district to maintain its ed tional program plan but may have to trim some vices such as more lunch periods and less gym.

One side issue which was brought up by a resi was the fact that when Maple School, which is loc north of Willow Road, becomes the junior high sc it will draw students from both south of Willow, G view, and north of Willow, Northbrook.

The resident said she feels it is an emotionally setting experience for the students to be realigne sixth grade and then split up again at the high se level.

Glenview students attend Glenbrook South School while Northbrook students attend Glenb North High School. Both high schools are a part o trict 225.

Parker said the board has requested from Dis 225 that all children from District 30 attend one school but has received no encouragement for plan.

Schlossman said he should be able to have a formal plan for the board for the Dec. 16 meetin

Fire victim's identity found

NORTHBROOK — A 16-year old youth burned to death in a fire near Northbrook early Sunday morning.

Late Tuesday afternoon, police and Cook County morgue officials made positive identification of the youth. He was Peter Reisner, of 1825 Beechnut, Northbrook, the son of Peter and Ursula Reisner.

According to Deputy Fire Marshal Ed Mathein, firefighters discovered the body at about 4:30 a.m. Sunday when they went to a field behind 1835 Oakwood to put out what had been reported as a rubbish fire.

Mathein said that the body was found in the charred remains of a shed, which had been built by youths in the Countryside area. The shed was about 200 feet from the nearest house and 300 feet away from the Illinois tollway, Mathein said.

Although the cause of the fire was still under in-

vestigation, Mathein said Monday that "it looks accidental."

A spokesman for the Cook County Sheriff's police, the agency investigating the death, said "It doesn't look like foul play."

Since the fire occurred in the unincorporated area, Northbrook police are not investigating the death. However, a police officer said he understood that at least one teenager had been living in the shed.

Mathein reported that firemen had seen a small stove, a Coleman lantern and several charred cans at the scene.

A memorial service will be held for Reisner at 1:30 p.m. Saturday, Nov. 30 at Lutheran Church of the Ascension, 460 Sunset Ridge Road, Northfield.

He is survived by five brothers and a sister.

THE AFTERMATH OF A tragedy. Only a few charred sticks remained of a shack in the Glenbrook Countryside area where a young boy burned to death early Sunday morning.

Figure 13-44. An offset negative film.

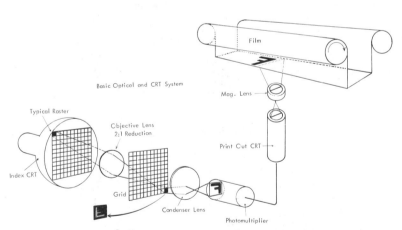

Figure 13-45. An oversimplified drawing of the phototypesetting concept using cathode ray tubes. Light from CRT shines through lens, then through film negative, and eventually onto photographic film paper. [*Courtesy Mergenthaler Company.*]

Figure 13-43. [*opposite*] A full page pasteup. This page is now ready to be converted into an offset printing plate. [*Courtesy Lerner Newspapers.*]

the method of photographing the letters were also different. At least four different modes of negatives were developed by various competitors. All letters of the alphabet, numbers and punctuation marks were prepared on a single film negative surface such as a disc, a rectangular grid, a drum, or a film strip (see Figure 13–46). With all the letters now being in such close proximity to each other, it was now possible to move them, more quickly than older machines, into position to be photographed. But again, light was projected through the negative for each letter, onto a light sensitive photographic paper to achieve a printed image. The newer generation machines resulted in a typesetting speed of about 150 lines a minute.

The third generation machines, now achieving wide distribution, are almost totally electronic. They use a cathode ray tube (CRT) as a scanning device. The scanning device throws a light through a lens, and then through each of the letters in a sentence on the negative surface. Behind the negative is a photoelectric cell that picks up the light and delivers it to another cathode ray tube, which in turn eventually prints the letter originally scanned on photographic paper (Figure 13–47).

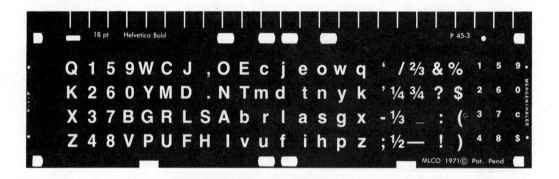

Figure 13–46. Film strip used on the V-I-P Phototypesetter, and the strip on a drum. [*Courtesy Mergenthaler Company.*]

Figure 13–47. Mergenthaler's Linotron Phototypesetter Model 505TC-100. This machine can set over 400 lines of type a minute. [*Courtesy Mergenthaler Company.*]

In reality this scanning device builds a letter, not in one piece as earlier machines had done, but by the addition of lines (and/or dots) until the entire letter is formed (see Figure 13–48). While this may seem to be a slower process of photographing letters onto light-sensitive paper, it is not. In fact, third generation typesetters can set as fast as 500 lines a minute, or about a 230 per cent increase in speed from second generation machines.

Figure 13–48. How a letter is built by the CRT phototypesetters (enlarged). The human eye cannot see the lines without the use of a magnifying glass. To the naked eye, the letter is solid and not composed of lines.

In the near future, a fourth generation of typesetter may be widely accepted. The distinguishing feature of this typesetter will be that it uses a laser beam in the setting process. Furthermore, unlike the first three generations, this machine will have no photographic negative to shine light through. Instead a laser beam will generate letters from a memory control, electronically, through a series of strokes, and build letters somewhat like that of CRT machines, but without a master negative. Fonts of type will be stored in the memory unit of this machine, and can be called forth by pressing a button. This machine can set 1,000 lines a minute.

In addition, the laser typesetter will be able to generate line art and halftones and therefore enable the user to makeup all of the elements of a page on a video display tube. When the page is made up, it may be printed on photographic paper, ready for conversion to an offset printing plate.

Phototypesetters As Part of a Total System

In theory a phototypesetter could be operated with only a keyboard and a computer. After the copy is typed on a keyboard, a computer determines both hyphenation and line justification. (Justification means aligning letters so that they are even with all other lines on the left- and right-hand sides of columns). However, most phototypesetters being installed in newspaper plants are operated in conjunction with either a VDT or an OCR, in addition to a computer. The assembly of these various operating machines wired to each other is called a "system." The objective of a system is to save time and effort by avoiding needless repetition, and by arranging work so as to be done in a minimum amount of time.

To explain how these various machines might operate in a system, the following is a brief description of what happens to a news story, from the time it is brought into the newspaper by a reporter to the time it is set in type (Figure 13–49).

The preceding description is only one kind of system that a newspaper could use. There are many others that could be used with different machines connected in different arrangements.

Figure 13–49a–l.

a. Reporter first fills out slip of paper telling that he has a story.

b. Slip is routed to various editors so they will know that the story exhits.

c. Reporter types copy on VDT keyboard. He then corrects and edits it, watching the video screen as he types changes. Story is thus proofread for the first time.

d. When reporter is satisfied, he sends story to computer for storage. Other stories written by other reporters are also in storage.

e. City editor who assigned story now retrieves it from storage for checking. If it needs editing, he does it using the VDT. This is also the second proofreading.

f. City editor sends story back to computer for storage, after he is satisfied with it.

g. News editor (who received report slip earlier), calls it up, writes headlines. He also specifies kind of type, size, and width of line. He returns story to computer for storage.

h. But, if the story needs further editing, he may have it printed out on paper at 360 lines a minute speed. Then he can edit on paper, and later, edit on VDT.

i. When he is finished, news editor sends story back to computer.

j. When news editor is ready to dummy page, he can ask computer to print all sluglines on VDT. Or he can check over report slips to find stories he wants.

k. When ready, news editor calls up each story on VDT, determines its length (printed out in inches at top) and begins to dummy page.

l. After dummying, he presses a button that sends body copy and headlines to be set on a phototypesetter, which delivers a photoprint. Story now goes to a printer for pasteup.

A

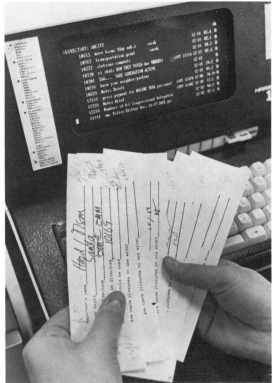

B

C

D

Figure 13–49a–d. [*Legend opposite.*]
[*Photographs courtesy Davenport, Iowa, Quad City Times.*]

E

F

G

H

The Art of Editing

I

J

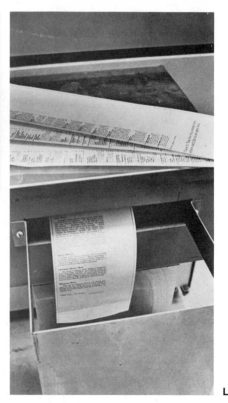

```
◊     106400 church pg. 17 groundbreaking        ◊          12-19  19.5 ◊⌐
<uf36><cc22>+
Ground-Breaking+
For Elderly Ho+
<uf1>⊟
     Port Byron Mayor Joe Johnson and representatives of Churches United of
Upper Rock Island County were on hand Thursday at groundbreaking ceremonies for
a $1.5 million elderly housing project designed to serve low-income elderly in
upper Rock Island County.⊟
     Construction for the 24-unit high-rise apartment complex in Port Byron is
being made possible by a $650,000 loan from the Farmers Home Administration and
```

K

L

Figure 13–49e–l. [*Legend on page 256.*]

An Introduction to Type   259

Pagination Machines

One of the ideas conceived in the new technology is a machine that can—with the aid of a computer, a video display terminal and a phototypesetter—produce a complete page of type and pictures, properly positioned as an editor desires, ready to be converted into a plate. In fact, the idea has been conceived of even going one step further: producing a plate ready for offset printing, directly from the video display terminal. At present it is possible to type stories, edit and proofread them, and in the case of advertisements, position elements of an ad. However, the page must still be dummied on a sheet of paper, or on a video display terminal. Halftone pictures cannot be handled very well on present machines, and technology has not advanced to the point where an entire page can be converted directly into a printed plate. On those machines where advertisements can be made up, using a VDT, the pictures in the ad can be positioned only in outline form. The pictures will have to be converted to screened prints and later pasted into position on the phototypeset ad. There is a great deal of optimism in the industry that a pagination machine will be developed, although it may be a number of years before it is ready for mass production.

Hot Versus Cold Type

Phototypesetting is classified as a form of "cold type," meaning that no hot metal is used in setting type. There are other forms of cold type, however, that are occasionally used in newspaper production. One is called "strike-on", consisting of a typewriter with letters that appear as printed letters. Therefore, when one types words and lines, the printed sheet can be used for offset printing, in the same manner as phototypesetting. Other forms of cold type are paste-down and transfer letters.

Hot type, on the other hand, is set with the use of hot metal. Such type comes from the line-casting machines where the metal is heated to about 550 degrees so that it can flow freely enough to fit into letter molds, and then cool down quickly enough to be used almost immediately. Hand-set type doesn't quite fit into either the hot or cold category, but since the letters were originally cast from hot metal, it is often called a hot-type method.

Although cold-type methods are sweeping the country, hot-type methods have not disappeared entirely. In fact, newspaper publishers usually have such a large investment in Linotype machines that it is unlikely that they will completely replace them with cold-type machines in the near future. Eventually, however, most hot-type machines will be replaced by cold type. This may take many years.

The following discussion covers the most widely used hot-type machines to be found in newspaper plants throughout the country.

Hot-Type Methods of Typesetting

The most widely used methods of setting hot type are known as Linotype, Monotype, and Ludlow. Linotype, Ludlow and Monotype are trade names as well as generic product names.

LINOTYPE. Two companies manufacture automatic line-casting machines—Merganthaler Linotype Company and Intertype Company. The operating principles of both machines are identical. A line-casting machine is really three machines combined into one operation: (1) an assembling machine for gathering molds (called matrices) into lines of type; (2) a casting machine for pouring hot metal into the molds and forming the line of type; and (3) a distribution machine for distributing the matrices of each letter back into their proper storage places.

For each letter of the alphabet there are matrices stored in a metal container called a *magazine*. When the operator presses a letter key, the matrix drops into a gathering device and is kept there until a line of matrices has been assembled. When the operator presses a lever, the entire line of matrices is moved into casting position, where hot metal is forced into the crevices in the matrices forming the line of letters (Figure 13–50).

The hot line is then pushed out to cool, while the matrices of letters are carried back to the magazine to be used for other lines of type. The line of type is typically called a *slug* or *linotype slug* (Figure 13–51).

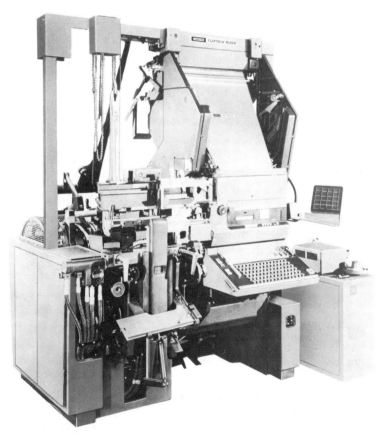

Figure 13–50. Elektron Mixer Linotype Machine. [*Photograph courtesy Mergenthaler Linotype Company.*]

An Introduction to Type 261

Figure 13–51. Linotype slugs. [*Photograph courtesy Mergenthaler Linotype Company.*]

LINE-CASTING MACHINES WITH TELETYPESETTER SYSTEM. Many newspapers have installed high-speed auxiliary machines in their plants to be operated in conjunction with a line-casting machine. The technique consists of two machines, which when used with a line-casting machine enables the operator to set as many as 13 to 14 lines a minute compared to the 6 or 7 lines a minute an efficient operator can set. Though the technique consists of two separate steps, it is still faster than manually set operations.

Essentially, the TTS system consists of an operator pressing keys on a perforator unit in which holes representing each letter are punched in a tape. When the tape is finished, it is placed in an operating unit attached to the side of a line-casting machine. The holes activate the keys of the line-caster and operate it at high speeds. The operation of the line-caster is the same as it would be if the machine were operated manually.

MONOTYPE. The Monotype machine also consists of two units: a tape puncher and a casting unit. But there are significant differences between the Monotype and the TTS system. The first difference is that Monotype is used primarily for setting large headlines or display type in advertisements, while teletypesetters are used mostly for setting body types. Relatively few newspapers have monotype equipment, although some large magazines not only have the equipment to set headlines, but body type as well.

The second difference is the manner in which each produces

type. The Monotype caster produces individual letters cast from molds of each letter, while the Teletypesetter system, working in conjunction with a line-casting machine, produces single lines of type, one at a time.

The technique of setting type on the Monotype starts, however, in the same manner as that of setting type with a Teletypesetter. In both techniques, a tape is punched on a perforating keyboard, but the tape is about three inches wide compared to the TTS's one-inch-wide tape. The caster is specially made for the tape of a Monotype and will not accept any other. Because Monotype casters produce individual letters, much greater skill is required to handle them than Linotype slugs (Figure 13–52). For that reason, Monotype is used mostly for printed material where speed is not as urgent as it is in newspaper work. Newspapers rarely use Monotypes. On the other hand, books, magazines and advertising material are often set on this machine.

LUDLOW MACHINE. The Ludlow machine is a means of casting type from matrices that have been set by hand. The operator first assembles a line of matrices and then places them into a casting device that produces a slug. Ludlows are often used for setting large headline type because the Linotype machine will not set type larger than 36 point. Ludlow can produce type as large as 144 points. Ludlow slugs are often recognized by the fact that they have an overhang on each side of the base (see Figures 13–53 and 13–54).

Figure 13–52. Monotype, showing that each letter is a separate piece of type. [*Photograph courtesy Lanston Monotype Company.*]

Figure 13–53. The Ludlow caster between two racks containing various kinds of typefaces in matrice form. [*Photograph courtesy Ludlow Typograph Company.*]

Figure 13–54. Ludlow slugs (top) cast from matrices assembled by a Ludlow composing stick (bottom). [*Photograph courtesy Ludlow Typograph Company.*]

14

Fundamentals of Newspaper Design

When a newspaper editor arranges news, pictures and other stories on a page, he is, in effect, packaging his product. In fact, there is great similarity between editors' and manufacturers' packages. Both use the package as a convenient means of shipping contents to consumers and both use the package as a means of helping consumers use the product.

An editor aids the reader when he arranges news content in an orderly and easy-to-read manner. Occasionally, news stories are so unusual or interesting that a reader will disregard poor design and suffer his way through the newspaper. But that doesn't occur every day. More often, most readers drop off after the front page until they encounter the next interesting section. An editor's goal in packaging is to help the reader read faster and read more of what has been written on all pages.

Packaging the News

The package has another, less obvious, function than making the contents easy to read. When a manufacturer plans his package front he places information about the contents in the form of a pattern that communicates through the appearance of the entire design as well as the words. This kind of communication may be thought of as the connotation of the news. Editors also may arrange the news so that the design resulting from his arrangement connotes something beyond the meaning of the words. Such connotations may range from a design telling the reader that a story is significant and serious to another design emphasizing a light-hearted, tongue-in-cheek approach (see Figures 14–1, 14–2, and 14–3). Connotations of the newspaper's

The Pensacola News-Journal FOCUS
Section B

Editorials 2B
Bob Duke 2B
Paul Jasper 2B
Max Rafferty 2B
Voice of the People 3B
Business 5B

Drunk Again . . .

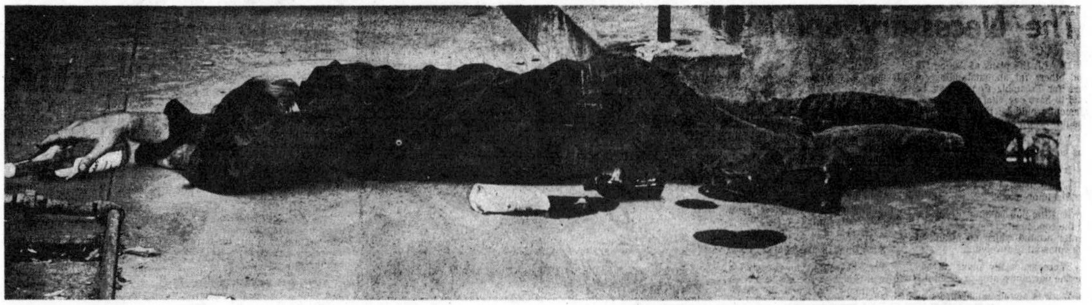

(Pensacola News-Journal photo by Ken Ross)

. . . for the 183rd Time

By PAUL JASPER
News-Journal Editorial Associate

RUDOLPH JONES likes the accommodations at the Escambia County Jail.

So much so that over the past eight years or so he's given them his custom on 51 separate occasions, for periods ranging from overnight to upwards of 90 days.

He says he doesn't like the City Jail so well.

Yet he's been there 132 times over roughly the same period of years.

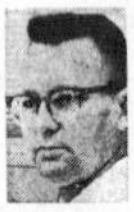

JASPER

In short, within less than a decade, Rudolph Jones (a pseudonym) has been jailed a total of 183 times, each time for drunkenness or some related offense.

He's spent more of his time in jail during this period than out, so much so that he considers his brief excursions into the outside world in the light of "vacations."

Jones is one of that legion of men throughout the nation who are known as habitual drunkards; men whose life is a never-ending cycle of a drunk, jail, another drunk, and another jail.

But as of July 1, 1973, Jones' life-style is scheduled to change, along with the lives of his fellows around the state.

For on that date drunkenness, per se, ceases to be a criminal offense and becomes instead a community health problem, as established by law passed during the 1971 session of the Florida Legislature.

The legislation is generally hailed as a forward step, though there are some public officials and others who view it with varying degrees of misgiving.

There are reasons for both views.

Look at it statistically from the standpoint of Escambia County alone:

From January to August, 1971, the Escambia Sheriff's Department arrested a total of 8,022 persons — 899 of them, or better than 10 per cent, on drunkenness charges.

During the first six months of 1971, the Pensacola Police Department made 2,804 adult arrests, including 1,030 for drunkenness, or more than 35 per cent.

★

THAT'S A lot of time and public money: Time spent in making the arrest, in booking the prisoner, in court action; money in policeman's salaries, judge's salaries, food and lodging for the prisoner.

And most of it is a waste. For such arrests have no deterrent effect, no basis for a cure. They serve one purpose only: to get the drunk off the street before he harms himself or someone else.

And there are many like Rudolph Jones in the files of the police and sheriff's department here.

Inspector James Davis, of the city police department, cites these examples based on consolidated files dating back to 1963:

—A man who in the five years between 1963 and 1968, when he died, was arrested 159 times by the city police alone. (Individual charge sheets, by the dozen, ranged back to 1949.)

—A man and wife who seem to be racing each other for the arrest record. Since 1963, he's been arrested by the city police 103 times; she's been arrested 106 times.

—During the first six months of 1971, one individual was arrested 15 times by the police department, and another 14 times; neither of them referred to above.

For these reasons, Davis, for one, welcomes the idea of treating drunkenness as a disease rather than a crime. Listen to him:

"Alcoholism appears to manifest certain characteristics that are similar in many ways to sickness. There is apparently a very strong pressure or the element of compulsion present — physical, mental or emotion — which transcends mere desire or appetite, and which the afflicted person cannot control without some kind of medical or psychological help.

"The theory of rehabilitation for the alcoholic is based on the premise that the alcoholism is symptomatic of some kind of maladjustment which is often unknown to the victim or not recognized by his or her family.

"The alcoholic needs help. The alcoholic problems of most of these unfortunate people who frequent our jails are aggravated by chronic physical, mental, emotional and social disabilities which no jail is properly equipped to handle."

And one reason Rudolph Jones probably likes the County Jail better than the City Jail (although he's more often downtown than in the county) is because of these secondary problems.

The City Jail, for instance, has no jail uniforms and some drunks have no extra clothes. So while they are the city's guests they are often forced to wear dirty, sometimes vomit-stained, clothing for days at a time, unless somebody voluntarily helps them, Davis said.

★

DRUNKS fall down and need hospital care; they don't eat regularly or properly, so they have a high susceptibility to diseases of all sorts. And as they grow older they are able to work less and less, so that jail in a sense becomes their home.

Davis cites the case of a man who never was arrested until his wife died when he was 52 years old, leaving him alone, and emotionally or psychologically unfit to look after his own affairs. That was in 1955. He was arrested 71 times before he died in 1967.

So in response to this, and problems relating to drug abuse, came the Florida Comprehensive Alcoholism Prevention, Control and Treatment Act of 1971; said by some to represent "the most progressive step toward a viable plan to deal with alcohol-related problems in our state's history."

The catch:

The program is unfunded and no one knows exactly how

(CONTINUED ON PAGE 4B)

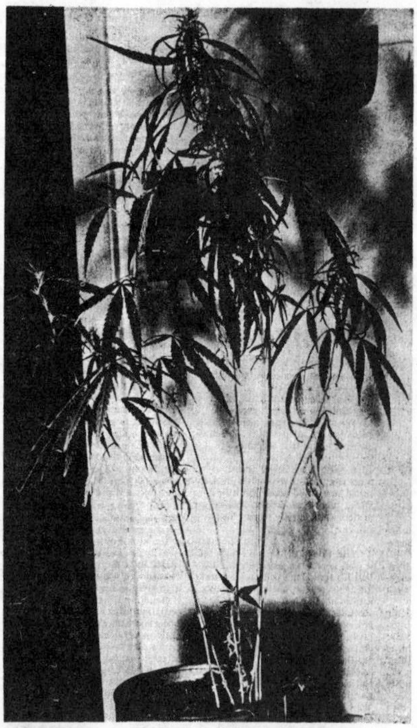

The villain of the piece? Marijuana, raw material for hallucinations.

The Alarming Increase

Youth and Drug Abuse: Why?

By TOM BELL
News-Journal Editorial Associate

"**THERE IS** no drug problem."

"But there are problems of youth that lead to drug abuse."

This is the opinion of West Florida professionals who daily counsel drug abusers.

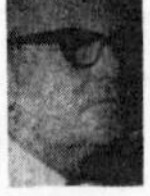

BELL

What are these problems that lead youths to drugs as an alternative to facing the problems and realities of life?

Are they different, more difficult problems than those of the youths of other generations?

Most professionals involved with the drug "scene" do not believe they are. They believe the problems are the same, but manifest in a different way, because of a basic erosion in the character of our society.

And they all agree — the misuse of drugs, the sniffing of glue and thinner and metallic paints and the drift to narcotics is spreading in West Florida with unexpected speed.

"Spreading with alarming rapidity," said Curtis Golden, 1st District state attorney.

"The most frightening thing is glue sniffing among the very young." — Ronald Yarbrough, psychologist and director of the Drug Abuse and Treatment Program of the Escambia County Mental Health Center.

"A frightening prospect for the future." — Dr. W. Reed Bell, former president of the Escambia County Medical Society.

Yarbrough said he sees the drug abuse problem from a special perspective, as a psychologist counseling those who have defined a problem and come to him for help.

"And the use of narcotics, especially heroin, is on the increase in Escambia County," he said, "just in the last six months.

"Six months ago most of the youths hooked on heroin were referred to us by the juvenile courts, after arrests. Now family doctors, school counselors and parents are bringing heroin addicts to us."

★

DO THE professionals, these men who daily deal with the results of drug abuse, believe there is a bridge between the smoking of marijuana and narcotic addiction?

"There are two categories of marijuana smokers," said the Rev. Taylor Hill, director of Escambia County's Head Stop, which includes the Agape House.

"There is the defeated adolescent and the sophisticate of grass," he said.

"The sophisticates are the young executives and the college crowd — the advocates of the legalization of marijuana."

The sophisticate is typified by a quote from a young premedical student:

"A surge of Eastern mysticism is connected with marijuana," he said. "There is a breaking loose, looking at things in a new way. Pot is peaceful, booze isn't. It (marijuana) encourages communication, understanding and love, and ties together with the desire for peace. Everyone knows it's not really harmful. Because alcohol is socially accepted, we show our contempt for society by rejecting it and smoking pot."

"Then there is the defeated adolscent," Hill said. "One boy told Father Daniel Egan, New York anti-drug abuse leader, 'Pot fools you. When I smoked marijuana I felt I was the best mechanic in the world. But I made a lot of mistakes. I hurt my hands. In reality, it doesn't expand your mind at all.'

"A California girl said, 'I didn't get along with my parents. I started messing around at 13 . . . I met a girl who put me on pot.'

"And another adolescent said, 'I didn't like myself. My parents didn't admire me. I drank for a while, and then I tried marijuana.' "

In Hill's opinion, substantiated by other West Florida professionals, it is the defeated adolescent who is in danger of graduating from marijuana to the more dangerous drugs and the narcotics... One girl said, "Marijuana is something to turn to. It brings people together, and it fits in with love and peace."

This, then, is the society of marijuana — the coterie of pot:

— The sophisticates of grass, who believe the only thing wrong with marijuana is that it is not legal.

— The defeated adolescent, whose future, and perhaps his life, is in danger.

★

HILL summarizes the case against legalization of marijuana—against a licit bridge to heroin:

"You won't find anyone hooked on the hard drugs advocating the legalization of marijuana," he said. "It represents a way of life to them. To them it (marijuana) is drug oriented at best."

Is society responsible for youths turning to drugs rather than reality?

"We are living in a chemically oriented culture," Yarbrough said. "Television tells us chemistry can change our lives. If you can't sleep, take this pill. If you have trouble getting started in the morning, take this one.

"When the kids see their parents depending on pills to get them through the day, drugs become a way of life to them. This pills-for-parents philosophy certainly influences them.

"This chemical orientation is an important manifestation of society that may lead many youths to the misuse of drugs."

But he emphasizes caution must be used. The drug abuse problem is complex, and must be examined in the broad spectrum.

The authorities agree, the

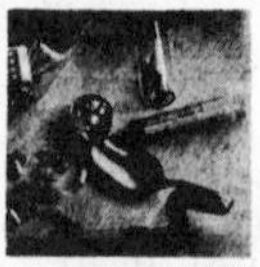

Paraphernalia

habitual users have three common characteristics:

— The lack of a sense of responsibility

— They have no concept of time, gratification must be now, they cannot project themselves into tomorrow.

— They cannot identify with the adult society, nor with their families.

"It adds up to lack of maturity," Dr. Bell said. "For the first two years of life the infant is self-centered. This narcissism is carried over in the immature adult.

"This characteristic is evident in these kids who are habitual users. They are introspective, completely self-involved and worried only about what is going to happen to them."

★

WHY?

What has caused this immaturity — this willingness to lose oneself in drugs rather than live in reality?

The authorities agree. It is not solely the availability of drugs.

"If drugs were not available, it would be alcohol," they say.

"The habitual drug abuser has no real interest," said John Krasowski, University of West Florida graduate student and Head Stop counselor. "He can't project himself into the future, and he has no goal, immediate or future. I've never run across a drug abuser who was successful at anything, maybe because he never has been given the opportunity."

Yarbrough believes adolescence (12-20), the age of experimentation with drugs, is the most important formative time of life.

"This is when life really is beginning," he said. There are important psychological changes. Adolescents feel more intensely than adults, because they still have part of the innocent child in them.

"Adults work at making reason more important than feeling. Adolescents don't do this. They believe that if you don't take advantage of this thing right now, this feeling will go away forever.

"There never will be another friend like this one; there never will be another love affair.

"This makes communications with adolescents difficult. They find it hard to meet a situation half way. Ev-

(CONTINUED ON PAGE 4B)

Figure 14–1. Design of this page emphasizes story at top. [*Courtesy Pensacola Florida, News-Journal.*]

Figure 14–2 [OPPOSITE]. Design emphasizes human interest story in box. [*Courtesy Dayton Ohio Journal Herald.*]

THE JOURNAL HERALD

VALLEY

168th Year · No. 301 · Dayton, Ohio · 15 Cents

Friday

December 19, 1975

Weather

Today's high in mid 30s
Overnight low in low 20s
Partly cloudy and cold
Probability of precipitation 20 percent
Details on Page 2

QUOTE OF THE DAY: "My God, this is a black university. How can we be discriminating against blacks? — Paul Raeder, a spokesman for Wilberforce University, responding to a charge that the university habitually discriminates against blacks who work there. Page 48.

U.S. quits UNESCO meeting

The United States, Israel and 11 Western nations yesterday pulled out of a UNESCO meeting after Arab and Communist nations voted to inject the United Nations General Assembly's "Zionism equals racism" resolution into proposed guidelines for mass media. Page 6.

Taft urges ouster of Callaway

Sen. Robert Taft Jr. has joined the growing chorus of Republicans who think President Ford should find a new campaign manager."I think it might be wise to look for somebody else," the Ohio senator said yesterday in Washington. Page 11.

Justice to take oath today

John Paul Stevens will be sworn in today as a Supreme Court justice, and President Ford has announced he will attend the ceremony. Stevens is Mr. Ford's first Supreme Court nominee. Page 15.

Humphrey tops Ford in poll

If they had to choose a President now, the American people would elect Democratic Sen. Hubert Humphrey over Gerald Ford by a 52 to 41 percent margin, according to a recent Harris poll.If Ronald Reagan were the Republican candidate, he would also lose to Humphrey, but by a smaller margin of 50 to 43 percent, the poll indicates. Page 39.

Ohio cities may need aid

The Ohio legislature should be prepared to provide financial assistance to cities unable to cope with the unfavorable bond market, a Cleveland banker testified to a joint committee studying the state's economy. "As New York City found out late, the cities are creatures of the states," he said. Page 7.

KSU bankruptcy fear disputed

Whether Kent State University is indeed on the brink of bankruptcy as stated by trustees at their meeting last month is being disputed by the KSU faculty senate, which asserts that the $15 tuition increase per quarter authorized by trustees last month to balance the university budget eliminates the problem. Page 37.

FORUM

Whalen and aid to Angola

American assistance for one of the factions involved in the Angolan civil war can never return benefits commensurate with the risks and the costs involved, in the opinion of U.S.Rep. Charles W. Whalen, who gives his views in a piece on page 5.

MODERN LIVING

Over the hill at three

There's a 16-month period in a child's life — between eight months and two years — that is the most significant period in his development, says a Harvard research scientist, and if a youngster doesn't have it together intellectually or socially by age three, to an extent it could limit his ability to achieve. p. 33.

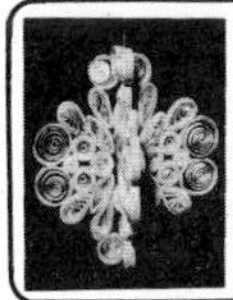

Christmas ornaments: back to basics

Page 35

62 Pages

Index

	Page		Page
Aces on Bridge	60	Medical column	35
Action Line	49	Modern Living	33-36
Amusements	40-44	Obituaries	
Erma Bombeck	33	Classified	52
Business	28-32	Deaths	51
Classified	52-59	Sports	17-23
Comics	60	Today's events	40
Daily Record	46	TV-radio	61
Horoscope	60	Weather	2
Ann Landers	34	Roz Young	33

Telephone 223-1111
Customer service toll free
1-800-762-2357

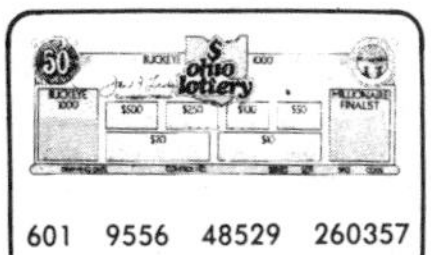

601 9556 48529 260357

Super Santa: 11 28 37 21

6715 78774 760337

Page 3

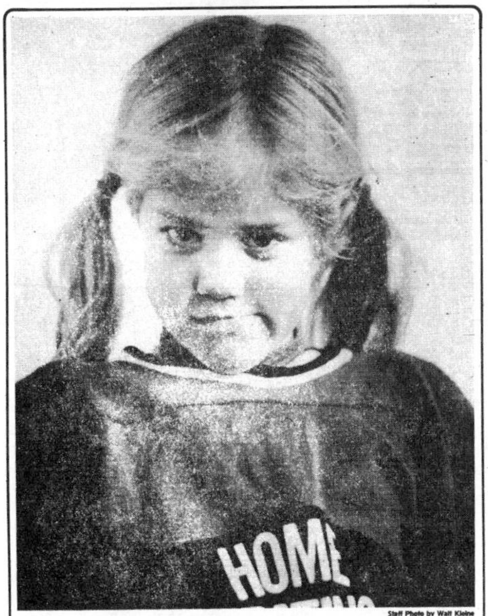

Staff Photo by Walt Kleine

Cari in her hockey duds

Mommy said OK to Cari's hockey

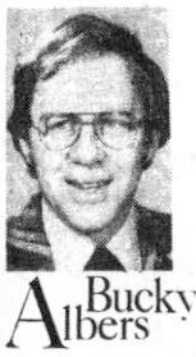

Bucky Albers

It was fully one hour after her team had played its game at the Kettering Ice House, but Cari Timura still wore her hockey skates. Too restless to sit along the rink and watch her older brother's game, she was engaged in another game.

Six-year-old Cari, not yet acquainted with precautions necessary to preserve a good edge on her skates, was clopping around on the tile floor in the lobby, playing a 'one-on-one' game against one of her teammates. Her pigtails flipped from side to side as she swung her stick at a paper cup disguised as a hockey puck.

It was evident the only girl player in the Dayton Amateur Hockey Association's South Division is not a little sissy who would fit in better at a tea party.

WHEN HER FATHER, former University of Dayton football star Andy Timura, first heard Cari wanted to play hockey, he reacted the way most fathers would. "Over my dead body," he said.

Then, reacting in what is not necessarily the way most mothers would, Mary Timura told her daughter she could play if she wanted to.

This was last season when Cari, still in kindergarten, was taking figure skating lessons and watching with envy as her two brothers (Drew, 11, and Westy, 9) played hockey.

"She talked about it all summer long," Mrs. Timura said. "Right before registration we asked her if this was really what she wanted, because we were going to make her stick with it. She said yes.

"I didn't have any objections. They're all well protected, and I don't feel you can differentiate at this age. She's just as capable as some of the boys."

DAHA's Mite Division is open to youngsters 5 to 8, but because there is sometimes quite a disparity of abilities among 5- to 8-year-olds, it was decided this year the 5- and 6-year-olds could play in a separate subdivision which would concentrate on teaching hockey.

Cari didn't want any part of that. She wanted to play like her brothers. Nobody has regretted permitting her to, although there might have been some reservations if they'd seen her preparing for the first practice.

"Andy didn't know the first thing about hockey equipment," Mary Timura recalled with a smile. "He didn't know how to put all of the paraphernalia on. Her brothers had to dress her."

MALE CHAUVANIST pigs apparently are cultivated young, because some of Cari's teammates on the Home Heating & Cooling squad reacted unfavorably to her.

"During one of our first practices," coach Bob Hart said "a couple of the boys came up to me and said, 'I don't want to play if there's a girl on the team.' I told them to forget about it."

The boys didn't completely forget about it. Cari got angry at times during the workouts, because she felt some boys were pushing and tripping her unnecessarily.

"I was so nervous when she played her first game . . . and I'm not when the boys are playing," Mrs. Timura admitted. "But I wasn't worried about her getting hurt or anything. In fact, I think she's more apt to hurt someone else. She has good athletic ability."

COACH HART agrees. "Those two brothers of hers must really work her over, because she's aggressive on the ice. She has come on strong. She's really a hustler. I consider her part of my first line defense. When I want my horses on the ice, I put her out there.

"Really, at that age you don't notice. With the long hair the boys are wearing, you're used to seeing hair sticking out from under the helmet anyway. She's one of the guys. I get the biggest kick out of her."

Hart's team has played three games, losing 5-0, tying 5-5 and suffering a 3-2 defeat in its most recent game Monday night when a player accidentally scored for the opposite team.

After the game, Cari was proud she "knocked Chris Anderson down." In addition, she reported that she "almost got a goal, but the referee blew his whistle" before she could shoot.

ASKED HOW HER teammates were treating her, she reported, "One of them said, 'You're not good.' But that was Ronnie. He's the one who scored in our goalie net. I'm better than him."

The next project for the first grader from Normandy Elementary School is to score a goal. "If I play center, I will," she predicted, noting that Coach Hart uses the players in more than one position. "He's a nice coach, because he doesn't yell or anything like the others do," she said.

Cari is not the first girl to play hockey in DAHA. Two years ago an 11-year-old girl named Lisa Hanauer played in the North Division, and this year there's another girl active in the North. Last year 12-year-old Dinah Denmark played in the South, but she didn't return for a second season either.

And Cari already senses her new career won't be a lifelong thing. "I won't play anymore when I'm a lady," she said.

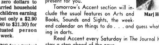

Tax will hurt lowest paid

Los Angeles Times/
Washington Post Service

WASHINGTON — The federal government's withholding bite from a worker's paycheck will rise Jan. 1 and the reduction in take-home pay will be proportionately higher for the lowest paid workers, who will lose the benefit of special tax credit on their first $4,000 in income.

Because Congress upheld President Ford's veto of a bill which would have extended through June 30 temporary tax reductions that otherwise run out Dec. 31, former, and bigger, withholding rates take effect again with the new year.

Neither Congress nor the President wanted to raise taxes in an election year — precisely the effect a return to last April's withholding will have — but Mr. Ford said he would not countenance a continued tax reduction without a similarly sized cut in federal spending.

WHEN CONGRESS sent him the tax cut — which would total $14.2 billion if continued for all of 1976 — without a spending ceiling, Mr. Ford vetoed the bill. He had proposed a tax cut and a spending ceiling totaling $28 billion.

David Bradford, deputy assistant secretary of the treasury for tax policy and tax analysis, said the government has "no option" but to put the old withholding rates into effect Jan. 1, even if a compromise between the President and Congress appeared likely.

According to figures provided by the Internal Revenue Service, that would mean an increase from zero dollars to $4.90 for a married household head with two children earning $100 a week, but only a $2.90 rise (from $18.40 to $21.30) for a similarly-situated person earning $200 a week.

WITHHOLDING for a typical single person earning $100 a week would rise from $10.90 to $13.40 a week, or $2.50, while a single person earning $200 a week would face only a $1.50 increase, from $33.50 to $35.00.

This happens because the temporary tax reductions — as well as the vetoed measure — contained a special provision for poor taxpayers which permitted them a tax credit of 10 percent of their earned income up to a maximum of $400, decreasing to nothing as their incomes rise from $4,000 to $8,000.

Tax credits are subtracted directly from taxes owed, and a married person with two children earning $100 a week would have no income tax liability after deducting the credit, so this person would face no withholding.

House fails to override Ford's tax veto, Page 3

Federal withholding rates are not actual tax rates, but are devised to reflect what a person's tax bill will be at the end of the year.

UNLESS THE President and Congress reach a compromise before Jan. 1, which appears unlikely, the minimum standard deduction which is now $1,600 for individuals and $1,900 for joint returns will fall to $1,300 across-the-board. The vetoed bill would have raised the flat deduction to $1,700 for individuals and $2,100 for joint returns.

The $30 tax credit per person will disappear. The vetoed bill would have contained a $35 tax credit.

Christmas past is Accent focus

The Accent will be on Christmas past in tomorrow's Journal Herald.

And for those who read The Journal Herald before 1969, it will be a delightful piece of nostalgia. That's because we're going to feature a Marj Heyduck Christmas story.

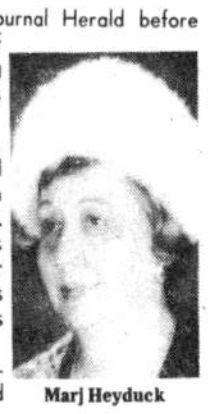

Marj Heyduck

Marj's "Third and Main" column probably was this area's best read and most quoted newspaper column from 1943 until her death in 1969. Marj found out who Santa Claus really was when she was seven — or at least she thought she did. This 1963 column is an early Christmas present for you.

Tomorrow's Accent section will include the usual features on Arts and Books, Sounds and Sights, the weekend calendar on things to do . . . and guess what's happening in darts.

Read Accent every Saturday in The Journal Herald and stay a step ahead of the news.

Christmas nightmares

Vietnam leaves mark

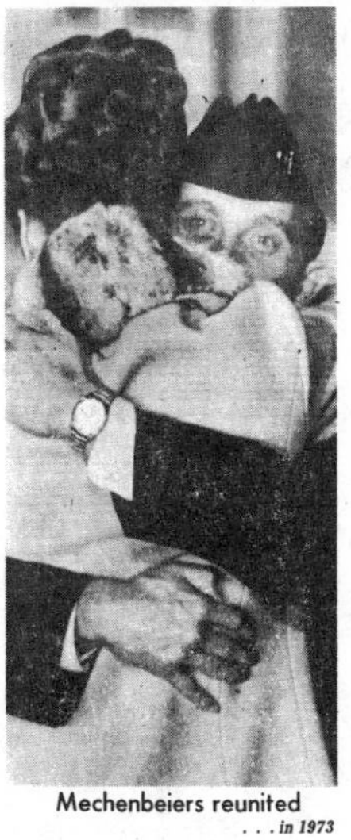

Mechenbeiers reunited
. . . *in 1973*

By George Esper
Associated Press Writer

The war is over, and Vietnam is perhaps forgotten by many, but the playbacks come more frequently at Christmas time for those it touched. This is a story about three of them in Ohio — Ed Mechengier, former prisoner of war, who lives with his wife Jerri near Springfield; a Vietnamese refugee who lives in Cambridge and a 73-year-old Greek immigrant who lives in Canton.

"He's flying with the guard this afternoon," said Jerri Mechenbier.

She paused to count on her fingers.

"This is the third Christmas we'll be together. "He was gone seven Christmases. I had to stop to count on my fingers. We were talking about this the other day. It really brings to light how long he was gone."

Ed Mechenbier, 33, who lives with his wife, Jerri, in farm country near Springfield, was a prisoner of war in North Vietnam until 1973 when he was released. His F4 Phantom fighter was shot down in 1967 during a mission 40 miles northeast of Hanoi.

Mechenbier got out of the Air Force last June after more than 11 years and now works as a civilian at Wright-Patterson Air Force Base. But he is still flying with the Air National Guard in Springfield.

"When he was gone at first," recalls Jerri, "I realized that not all people are happy at Christmas. Many people are troubled, sad, but it just doesn't show on the outside. I was naive. I thought till then that everyone was happy all the time at Christmas. I had a happy-go-lucky life up until then.

"I'm going to enjoy every minute of Christmas, just stay at home and we're fortunate that we both can be with our families."

(Continued on Page 3)

'Tango' raises furor in Oakwood

By Fred Lawson
Journal Herald Staff Writer

Bob Mills, owner and operator of Cinema South in Oakwood, has been charged with showing an allegedly obscene movie, *Last Tango In Paris*, in a complaint filed by an Oakwood resident.

Mills is scheduled to appear in Oakwood Municipal Court this morning to enter a plea.

He said last night he will enter an innocent plea and then "pursue a court suit involving at least $1 million against the ones bringing the suit, including some members of the police department and city officials."

HE ALSO SAID, as a result of the complaint, he will consider changing the theater's fare from showing family to X-rated films.

The charge was filed by Richard W. Ulbrich, of 126 W. Dixon Ave. He said last night he complained Sunday night to police after viewing the 4:30 p.m. showing of the film.

Oakwood police confiscated the film Wednesday night with a warrant following Ulbrich's complaint, according to Gould.

Confiscation came a day after the movie completed its run at the Oakwood theater.

The charge is a first-degree misdemeanor, and the maximum penalty upon conviction is six months in jail or a $1,000 fine.

The movie also has been showing at the Salem Mall Cinema, but was not shown Wednesday night nor last night "because of technical difficulties," according to a theater spokesman.

IF A TRIAL IS necessary, it will be set "as soon as possible," Oakwood Municipal Judge Irvin H. Harlamert Jr. said.

Harlamert said he issued the warrant.

Ulbrich said:

". . . To stop obscenity and pornography, (citizens) have to sign a complaint with their local police, and then insist their prosecutor and judge take action — or else elect those who will.

"In Oakwood, we are fortunate in having police, a prosecutor and judge who are willing to take action."

He said he went to the movie Sunday afternoon to determine for himself if it is obscene, "and it is."

Mills denied the charge and said several court rulings have found it not obscene, the most recent by a court in Hamilton County.

"We are not garbage peddlers, we try to give people the best of movies."

267

whole design may give the reader the feeling he is reading a conservative paper or one that is liberal or old-fashioned, or progressive. The editor, therefore, is concerned with the orderly arrangement of the news as well as with creating a page design with connotations that are appropriate to his philosophy of news presentation.

Makeup Versus Design

The term *design* may be used in three different ways in newspaper operations. *Design* may refer to the basic format of the entire newspaper. Since such a format is rarely changed, newsroom personnel are not allowed to tamper with it. It is not within the province of this book to discuss overall newspaper design, although some of the material within the next three chapters cover various aspects of it.

A second use of the term *design* refers to the structure or arrangement of news on an individual page. After a page has been made up, the arrangement represents a page design. Obviously the makeup man will try to keep each page's design consistent with the overall design of the entire newspaper.

A third use of the term is as a substitute and slightly different form of the term *makeup*. To design a page is to plan for, or conceive of, its total structure. To design a page differs from making up a page only in that there is more preplanning involved than there is in makeup.

In the following three chapters, discussion involves the latter two uses of the term.

At least two basic methods can be used to create a newspaper page design. One is a building technique of makeup. The other is building, but with concern for the appearance of the entire page. Makeup consists of building a page, element by element, until all the space is used. Each page is sketched on a sheet of paper called a dummy by placing the most important elements at the top of the page, then placing less important stories next to or underneath the main story or picture, downward, until the space is filled. As the editor sketches the dummy, he can change the position of stories by simply erasing notations in one place and repositioning them in another place. When he has finished, the editor gives the dummy to the printer, who assembles the type for body copy, headlines and pictures (and advertisements, if any) using the dummy as a blueprint. When all the type has been assembled on a page, it is ready to be processed for the final printing of the newspaper.

A page dummy, when completed, represents a design. The concept of makeup, then, is that the sum of the parts equals a design. The term *design* means form, or structure, and the structure is not complete until the last bit of space on a page has been used. In many instances, the makeup editor has only a vague idea of how the design will eventually look. Because he is under the pressure of a deadline, he often assigns heads to stories and orders pictures without giving much thought to the final appearance of the page. Even if he has some idea of how the page should look after completing the dummy, the result may look quite different from what he planned, simply because, after placing the top stories on the page, he could not find stories of the correct length to fit on the page in the way he wanted them to fit. In fact, the fitting of news on a page dummy is somewhat like assembling a jigsaw puzzle, except that the result of a puzzle is predictable. Page layout may be quite unpredictable. Therefore, the page often takes shapes that are neither orderly nor attractive. Although the makeup editor may be able to emphasize the most important stories, the page design may be unattractive.

Made-up pages often are cluttered because the editor lacked control once the top stories were dummied. Sometimes, only the top half of the page is interesting, whereas the bottom half fades away. Other times makeup results in story placement where the reader may find it difficult to locate the remainder of a story continued in adjacent columns. Such problems do not occur when the entire page is planned as a total design. It would seem that the total design concept would be preferred to the technique of makeup.

Most editors, however, make up rather than design pages. But more interest is shown in preplanned pages than those built piece by piece. Designing a page represents a different approach to newspaper packaging because the designer is better able to control the final appearance of the entire page. The makeup editor can control only the placement of important stories. A designer can control not only the placement of important stories but also the appearance of the entire page, because either he has a mental picture of the page he wants or he experiments with alternative page designs by first drawing a number of rough sketches; he then selects the best design.

In the latter technique, the makeup editor gets an idea of what the entire page might look like after he has examined the stories available and attempts to visualize them in a contemporary format.

Yet page makeup also has some advantages that must be weighed against totally designed pages. Makeup is easier and achieved more quickly than designed pages. Because time is extremely important in meeting press deadlines, makeup is often preferred. Furthermore, makeup is much easier on inside pages, where the advertising department controls page design to a great extent.

Therefore, the question of makeup versus design is not one that can be decided totally in favor of one or the other. The total design concept is best for pages where there are no advertisements. Makeup is best for all other pages and where little time is available. The goals of both are the same, to create pages that are easy to read in a contemporary format.

The Objectives of Newspaper Makeup and Design

Design exists primarily to facilitate readership. A newspaper is a collection of many stories, pictures, features and advertisements. When they are haphazardly placed within the newspaper or on any given page, they become a deterrent to reading because the effect is confusing. Foremost in planning a page is the goal of making every page easy to read. Newspaper pages should be designed so that as a result of being easy to read more people will read faster than they have before and read more of what has been written.

Newspapers are in competition with dynamic media such as television and radio. But even print media such as magazines and books are much easier to read than newspapers because they are more attractively designed. Obviously, it is easier to design magazines because more time is available for the arrangement of stories. But readers are not likely to be sympathetic with the problems of newspaper makeup editors. Readers know which media are the easiest and most pleasant to read. Therefore every effort should be made to overcome any inertia readers may have when they read a newspaper page. With this general objective in mind, it is then possible to state the specific objectives as follows:

First, the editor should arrange the news in an orderly and convenient-to-read manner. When news is so arranged, the reader will be faced with a minimum of obstacles to overcome. He will know where every story starts and, if it is necessary to carry the story into another column, where the story ends. It should be easy for him to know which stories are important and which are not. It should also be easy for him to find any special news or feature of interest with a minimum of effort and confusion. Orderly arrangement is a significant criterion of good design.

Second, news should be packaged in a format whose design is consistent with the nature of contemporary design found outside the newspaper. Furniture, automobiles and the architecture of buildings all reflect contemporary design. The format of a newspaper is the frame of reference in which the news is read. Contemporary news should therefore be packaged in a contemporary format. Modern design is symbolic and tells the reader that the newspaper is attuned to the times and is perceptive of what is going on in today's world. The design should communicate nonverbal symbols such as liberalism, conservatism, strength of character, or even concern for social welfare. These qualities represent the image of the newspaper. Images are only feelings, attitudes and opinions, but they are important in making the newspaper's efforts appreciated. In the field of consumer product categories—Cadillacs, for example—convey an image of high social status and affluence, whereas Volkswagens convey an image of economy and convenience. Each manufacturer plans the design of his product so that it is consistent with what he wants consumers to believe about his product.

Third, and perhaps most important, the design should be more exciting to readers than ever before. The best way for newspapers to compete with other more exciting media is to upgrade the drama of design. Census data estimates show that the proportion of young persons in this country is steadily growing. If these estimates become a reality, newspapers will have to appeal more to young persons in the culture. Young persons are most appreciative of new, exciting and dramatic designs. Every effort should be made to get these persons to read newspapers more and to make it a habit.

Finally, the newspaper is a visual arts medium and is often evaluated in the same light as other visual arts. A newspaper should be attractive both as a visual arts medium and as a modern package because beauty for its own sake is one of the broader values in an affluent society. Newspaper design should reflect this value when presenting the news.

The means of achieving the objectives of design are through application of artistic principles of design. The newspaper is a graphic art form, using words, pictures, color, lines and masses subject to the same principles of artistic design as other graphic art forms. Some graphic design principles suggest underlying bases for news page designs. The principles most applicable to newspapers are known as balance, contrast, proportion and unity.

Principles of Artistic Design Applied to Newspapers

Balance means equilibrium. It means that a page should not be overwhelmingly heavy in one section or extremely light in another. The consequence of designing an unbalanced page is that readers may have a vague feeling of uneasiness because of the concentration of weight in only one or two sections of the page. Most readers do not know whether a page is balanced or unbalanced. They are not artists and do not know the principles of artistic design. Yet they often know that a certain page "feels" better to read than do other pages. The goal of good designing is to bring about a feeling of equilibrium on each page. In newspaper design, the most frequent means of bringing about imbalance is to make the page top-heavy by placing large and bold headlines at the top while using almost insignificantly light headlines at the bottom. Another cause of imbalance is the practice of placing a large, dark picture at the top without having one of similar size or weight at the bottom. As a result of imbalance, readers' eyes tend to gravitate toward the bolder sections of the page and away from the lighter portions. Assuming that every element on a page has value, an unbalanced page, theoretically, is more difficult to read than a balanced page.

Balance: A Means of Making the Page Appear Restful

Balance in newspaper design is achieved by visually weighing one element on a page with another on the opposite side of the page, using the optical center as a fulcrum. The optical center is a point where most persons think the true mathematical center is located. It is a little above and to the left of the mathematical center. The practice of visually weighing one element on a page against another does not lead to precise balancing, but there is no need for that degree of precision. All that is required is a feeling of equilibrium on a page, not precise mathematical weighing.

Which elements need balancing? Any element on a page that has visual weight should be balanced. To determine which elements have visual weight one need only squint at a page and notice that much of the printed material disappears. What remains are pictures, headlines and black type rules of any kind. Although it is true that even body type has some weight, it isn't significant enough for consideration in visual weighing. The goal is to distribute prominently weighted objects pleasantly on the page.

Balance is most often done by weighing elements at the top of a page with those at the bottom, rather than doing so from side to side. The principle of balance is the same as that of balancing a heavy person with a light person on a seesaw. The heavy person must move close to the fulcrum, whereas the lighter person must move farther away on the opposite side of the fulcrum.

To implement the principle of balance, the most outstanding elements, such as bold or large headlines at the top of a page, should be weighed against similar headlines at the bottom. If the bottom of the page has no bold or large headline, the page is likely to be top-heavy. Plans should be made to include such headlines at the bottom. The same procedure should be followed in placing pictures on a page. A headline or picture at the bottom need not be as large or as bold as those at the top because it is farther away from the fulcrum (see Figure 14–3).

Page balance may be formal or informal. Formal balance is achieved by placing headlines and pictures of the same size on either side of a page. It is sometimes called symmetrical rather than formal balance because one side of the page tends to mirror the other. In that sense there is balance. But symmetrical design may be unbalanced from top to bottom. Most newspapers employ an informal balance from top to bottom. The feeling of equilibrium is there even though it is not obvious.

Contrast   Contrast is the principle of using at least two or more elements on a page, each of which is dramatically different from the other. One may be a light headline contrasting with a bold headline. Another might be a small picture contrasting with a larger one.

Figure 14–3 [OPPOSITE]. Page is balanced diagonally by pictures. [*Courtesy Rockford, Illinois, Register-Star.*]

Good morning

Register-Star

Partly sunny

Partly sunny and much colder, high around 38. Tonight, fair and cold, low around 20.

(Details on Page A7)

Vol. 16, No. 105—A GANNETT NEWSPAPER | ROCKFORD, ILLINOIS, SATURDAY, DECEMBER 6, 1975 | METRO | 20 CENTS

Inside

Basketball scores

Auburn 68
Jefferson 44

Harlem 64
Belvidere 56

Boylan 67
Guilford 62

East 61
Freeport 46

West 60
DeKalb 53

Details in Sports Section

Ford faces tough talks

President Ford arrives today in the Philippines for brief talks with President Ferdinand Marcos, and there are indications the United States faces tough going in its effort to retain control of important military bases in that area. Complete details on A2.

New role for Floberg

Children with developmental disabilities will be housed in the Floberg Center for Children, Rockton, as the center ends its role as a home for neglected and dependent children. Center director Dan J. Pennell said the center had sought the new role since the Division of Children and Family Services began placing children in foster homes rather than institutions. Complete details on Page A3.

Market drops sharply

The stock market posted another sharp decline Friday to finish off its worst week of the year. The Dow Jones industrial average fell 10.31 to 818.80, leaving it with a net loss of 41.87 points for the week — its worst weekly showing since September, 1974. Complete details on B6.

Studying the Bible

Mrs. Ivory Hughes organized an interracial Bible study for women that meets in various homes. Through their frequent meetings the women have become friends and find that although they are from different backgrounds their lives run along parallel lines. Complete story on Page A5.

Editorially speaking

Bodyguard was a surprise to Mary Lee Leahy. Tom Reay's Saturday Notebook . . . Page A6

We salute junior tackle football coach Glenn Carlson . . . Page A6

Columns

Nuclear wastes transportation dangers are outlined by Jack Anderson . . . Page A6

British ambassador evidently doesn't understand the United Nations, says William F. Buckley Jr. . . . Page A6

Index

Church news . . . A5
Columns
Dr. Blasingame . . . B5
Ann Landers . . . B5
Bridge . . . Magazine
Comics . . . Magazine
Crossword . . . B5
Editorials . . . A6
Heartline-Help! . . . A4
Horoscope . . . B5
Markets . . . B6, 7
Movies, TV . . . Magazine
Obituaries . . . B8
Sports . . . B1-4
Want Ads . . . B9-15
Weather . . . A7

This is a 3-section, 36-page newspaper

Notice to Subscribers

To start newspaper home delivery or to report a service problem, phone: 962-4433 ask for the Circulation Department.

AP wirephoto

Florence County, S.C., sheriff William Barnes, wearing tie, talks with newsmen
Six bodies found in shallow graves in remote area near Florence, S.C.

Shallow graves yield 6 bodies

LAKE CITY, S.C. (AP) — Police found three bodies Friday in a shallow burial site where three other bodies had been unearthed the day before.

Officers indicated there may be yet another body buried in the remote area of northeastern South Carolina.

Florence County Sheriff William Barnes said the bodies of four men and two women were discovered in three graves located about 25 yards apart in a wooded area near a soybean field.

He said five bodies appeared to be those of adults and one was believed to be that of a 15-year-old boy.

Barnes said none of the victims had been positively identified but tentative identification had been made from clothing. All were believed to have been from the North Charleston area, he said.

He declined to speculate on the cause of death pending forensic examinations at the Medical University of South Carolina in Charleston.

But Barnes said he believes the burials did not take place at the same time. He said all the bodies were badly decomposed.

Barnes said a suspect was in custody on an unrelated charge. However, he declined to identify him or to reveal the name of an informant being held as a material witness.

Neither Barnes nor spokesmen for the State Law Enforcement Division (SLED) would comment on what led to the grisly discovery. However, one source indicated the informant had led officers to the site.

A SLED source said the investigation began in North Charleston two months ago, moved to nearby Williamsburg County and then centered in on the Lake City section of Florence County.

One police source who asked that his name not be used said a car theft ring was believed to be connected in some way with the case.

3 Walker aides tell committee that Goff is liar

By LEE HICKLING
Gannett News Service

WASHINGTON — Maverick Democrat Donald Page Moore demanded Friday that the Senate subcomittee on longterm care of the aging clear his name of charges that he ordered a halt to investigations of contributors to his 1974 campaign for Cook County state's attorney.

Moore said former Illinois Department of Public Aid official John Goff lied outright when he claimed that Moore had done so, while acting as director of special investigations for Gov. Daniel Walker.

Two other Walker administration figures branded Goff's Nov. 15 testimony — to the effect that they hid information about welfare scandals from federal investigators — as lies.

"Mr. Goff's testimony was totally false and totally without merit," said DPA Director James L. Trainor.

John B. Simon, who was special counsel to the DPA director during investigations of welfare and Medicaid irregularities in 1974 and 1975, said Goff's statements about him were "totally false."

Moore, who is running as an independent Democratic candidate for the Cook County state's attorney nomination next March, demanded that the subcommittee clear his name by issuing a statement "promptly and clearly . . . that there's either evidence of wrongdoing on my part or there isn't."

Goff said, under oath, that a Moore subordinate, Laura Staples, had ordered him to lay off investigation of Medicaid fraud on the part of contributors to Moore's campaign.

Moore denied this categorically. He said he had never told Goff anything of the kind, didn't believe any of his subordinates had done so, and that the individuals named as contributors had never — according to his records — given a cent to his campaigns.

Sen. Charles Percy, R-Ill., the ranking minority member of the subcommittee, said he would have a statement drawn up to the effect that there is no evidence to corroborate Goff's charges. Newspapers, he said, had misinterpreted Goff's testimony — the former IDPA official, he said, had said specifically that it wasn't Moore who told him to lay off.

Percy said he would ask subcommittee chairman Frank Moss, D-Utah, to join him in signing the statement.

Sen. Lawton Chiles, D-Fla., said he thinks the subcommittee has been used to play a political "game of gotcha," springing damaging charges against high elected officials — it was clear he meant Gov. Walker — without giving them adequate warning and a chance to reply.

Moore, calling Goff's charges "ludicrous," said he had never been accused of a serious unethical act in 19 years as a lawyer and public figure. "Joe McCarthy used to do this," he said. "I didn't like it then, when I was working for the American Civil Liberties Union, and I don't like it now."

Joel Edelman, Trainor's predecessor as state director of public aid, was the only one of the day's four witnesses who didn't label Goff's charges as lies. But Edelman said Goff was wrong in his interpretation of an incident earlier this year in which Goff was ordered to hold up cancellation of welfare checks to some 3,000 ineligible persons on Chicago's South Side.

A computer crosscheck with Department of Labor records had turned up the names of the 3,000 as being employed and thus ineligible. Goff said he was ordered to delay striking them off the rolls until after a primary campaign and said Edelman told him the order came from Walker.

Edelman said Walker never told him any such thing. He said the impending primary was not the reason he ordered a delay in the cancellations.

The reason was, he said, that a number of persons — including South Side priest George H. Clements of Holy Angels Church — had voiced concern that welfare checks were going to be unjustly canceled. A delay was decided on, Edelman said, in order to conduct field checks and verify the computer's indication that the welfare recipients involved were actually working and so ineligible for aid.

Goff disagreed strongly and consented to go ahead with the cancellations only after being threatened with dismissal, Edelman said.

But the former DPA director, who is now working as executive director of the legislative advisory committee on public aid, didn't disagree with Goff's estimate that hundreds of millions of dollars in public assistance is being wasted in Illinois because of inefficiency and fraud.

Edelman said the DPA could be doing much more than it is to root out abuses in welfare and Mediciad.

Public Aid Director Trainor, the first witness at a subcommittee hearing Friday, said it was completely untrue that — as Goff said — he or anyone else ordered information withheld from auditors or investigators for the Department of Health, Education and Welfare, the Department of Agriculture or the General Accounting Office.

Federal inspectors and auditors, he said, have had "full access" to DPA files and records. "They got all the information they needed, and that was relevant," Trainor said.

Trainor described Goff as an "unsettled and confused individual" who had neglected his duties in developing computer programs for the governor's task force, in order to pursue unauthorized investigations on his own.

Nevertheless, Trainor said, he turned over the results of some of Goff's "unauthorized surveillance activities" to the U.S. attorney in Chicago for investigation. This contradicted testimony by Goff that the results of his investigations had not been turned over to the proper authorities for possible prosecution.

Police pay can't be cut—attorney

Work hours can be reduced for Rockford policemen but the amount of annual pay they receive must remain the same, a police association attorney said Friday.

Proposed reductions in city police wages would violate the city's contract with the Policeman's Benovelent and Protective Association (PBPA), the association's attorney wrote in a letter Friday to Rockford Mayor Robert McGaw.

McGaw has proposed a reduction in the number of work hours of city employes, including policemen, and proposed a reduction to their pay. Bernard P. Reese Jr., PBPA attorney, said the wage reduction would be a violation of the city's two-year contract with PBPA.

Police wages are based on an annual rate, Reese said, so if hours are cut the police should not receive a reduction in pay.

The contract expires Dec. 31, 1976. The contract was bargained in "good faith," Reese said in the letter to McGaw, and "any effort to cut their (police) pay would be a deliberate violation of the city's contractual liability."

Mayor McGaw could not be reached for comment Friday night.

Members of the American Federation of State, County and Municipal Employes (AFSCME) also have a "binding agreement" with the city and will not bear the entire burden of the proposed cutback, AFSCME local president Richard Lemke said.

"We're still holding that we have a binding agreement with the city," Lemke said.

Joanne White, chairman of the Rockford City Municipal Employes Council, said non-union city employes are being urged to protest enmasse the proposed pay cuts at Monday's city council meeting.

McGaw, it was learned earlier this week, is planning to cut 12 paid holidays and change to a 37.5-hour week instead of a 40-hour week to save the city $300,000 during 1976.

Dale Gulbrantson, PBPA local president, has said the association would seek a court order against the proposal even before it goes into effect. McGaw has said the hour and wage cuts are an alternative to layoffs.

Among Christmas shoppers--

Fire truck kills three

SAN FRANCISCO (AP) — A hook-and-ladder fire truck hurtled into pedestrians at a crowded downtown intersection Friday, killing three persons and critically injuring three others, police said.

The victims "looked like puppets" as they flew threw the air, a witness said.

The intersection of 6th and Market streets was puddled with blood and strewn with shoes, eyeglasses, handbags and a smashed pair of crutches.

An unidentified man was dead on arrival at San Francisco General Hospital, and hospital authorities identified the other two fatally injured persons as William Moore, 65, and Angelina Moreno, 77, addresses unknown.

The injured were Marty Sanderson, 34, of Oakland, Calif.; Ronald Lambert, 45, of San Francisco and Jimmy Fitzpatrick, 23, a college student from Union, N.J., the hospital said. They suffered head and internal injuries, a spokesman said.

Police initially had reported seven injured, but later revised the figure.

The accident victims were standing on a bus and trolley car boarding island near a number of large stores packed with Christmas shoppers.

Fire officials said the hook and ladder was responding to a fire report from a florist shop three blocks away.

Auto-truck crash kills Rockford man

BYRON — An unidentified Rockford man was killed in a car-truck collision Friday night on Illinois 2, about one mile north of Byron.

A semitrailer truck loaded with corn, driven by Charles Praum, Davis, was southbound on Illinois 2 en route to Hennepin. He collided headon with the northbound car.

After the collision, the truck went into a ditch on the other side of the road. Maurice Brauer, Pecatonica, said the loss of the tractor, trailer and the corn was estimated at $26,000.

Authorities withheld indentification of the dead victim pending notification of next of kin. They were not expected to release the name until later this morning. Praum was taken to a doctor's office where he was treated and released.

Photo by Tom Cliff

Bicentennial pinwheel. . .

Mary Alice Heely studies this pinwheel with a Bicentennial theme made by Growth Enterprises and which will be among items on display at the Holly Daze Art Faire today and Sunday at 315 W. State St., in the Downtown Mall. The event, which is being sponsored by the Rockford Park District, Rockford Art Association, The Collection, and A Step Up, will include singing by area high schools, movies for the children, and baked goods.

Hoffa's body sought

DETROIT (AP) — Authorities believe the body of ex-Teamsters President James R. Hoffa may be buried in a Jersey City, N.J., landfill closed for the past six years, two sources have confirmed.

One of the sources, a law enforcement official, said Friday: "It's Hoffa's body they believe is buried at Moscato's Dump."

A search warrant was issued Tuesday by U.S. Magistrate William Hunt of Newark, indicating the FBI wanted to search the trash dump for the body of Armand Faugno, a reputed underworld soldier who has been missing for about a year.

"The Faugno angle was a smokescreen," said the second source, a non-law enforcement source who is intimately familiar with activities of the Teamsters Union. "Law enforcement officials think there's a good possibility Hoffa is there in the dump. It's logical. It makes sense."

The law enforcement source said the U.S. Organized Crime Strike Force in Newark sought the search warrant for Faugno because "They had a better chance of obtaining a search warrant for Faugno than for Hoffa. Faugno is from the East Coast." According to sources, Faugno was known to frequent night spots in the area around the Jersey City landfill.

The source close to the Teamsters Union said that "the government has turned someone (into an informant) who is close to the killing."

The source said authorities are operating on the theory that Hoffa got into a car voluntarily outside the Machus Red Fox Restaurant on July 30, was killed and his body then hauled out to the East Coast, where it was buried in the dump.

The closed-down landfill reportedly is owned by Philip Moscato, 41. New Jersey sources say Moscato includes among his close associates a number of known underworld figures but is not a known member of a mob family. Moscato does not have any convictions, the sources said.

Meanwhile, government prosecutors planned a lineup today to show three New Jersey Teamsters officials to a secret witness who says he saw the abduction of Hoffa.

The Teamsters will appear before the witness in a police lineup at the Oakland County Jail. Robert Ozer, head of the U.S. Organized Crime Task Force in Detroit, disclosed in open court earlier this week the lineup was sought to corroborate grand jury testimony from yet another secret informant.

Ozer said that man appeared before the grand jury and named three men alleged to have abducted the former Teamsters boss.

Ozer's disclosure that a grand jury witness named names and that an individual who witnessed Hoffa's abduction had been found are the most startling developments in the more than four-month-old case.

Because one element is different from the other, the page is made to appear lively and interesting.

Contrast, therefore, is a means of preventing artistic pieces from becoming dull. Almost all art forms are created with some contrast in them—especially musical compositions, plays and printed material. A symphony, for example, contrasts a fast and loud first movement with a soft and slow second movement. A play has a relatively quiet scene contrasting with a lively scene. A book or magazine may have most pages printed in black and white contrasting with full-color illustrations.

In page makeup and design, contrast prevents a page from appearing too gray, a problem that occurs when there is too much body copy and too many light headlines. Gray pages appear uninviting and forbidding.

Sometimes the makeup man finds that he has a similar problem on pages where he deliberately tries to balance a page at the expense of achieving contrast. His balanced page may appear too restful and dull. He can change one or two elements on that page such as a headline or picture and thereby brighten the page considerably. A bolder headline or picture, carefully placed, may provide the contrast he needs.

Indiscriminate use of contrast, however, is undesirable. If a page has too much contrast it may overpower the reader because the contrasting elements call attention to themselves and not to the page as a whole. The goal is to provide pleasant, not overpowering, contrast. To achieve this goal the makeup man will have to develop a sense of good taste.

Contrast may be achieved in four general ways: by shape, size, weight and direction. Shape contrast may consist of a story set flush on both sides in opposition to another story set flush left, ragged right. Or an outline picture may be used with a rectangular-shaped picture.

Size contrast may be shown by using a large illustration on the same page with a smaller one, or large type contrasted with smaller type.

Weight contrast may employ a picture that appears very black with a lighter picture, or a story set in boldface type contrasted with one set in lighter typefaces.

Direction contrast could show vertically shaped stories contrasted with horizontally shaped stories.

These contrast alternatives are but a few of many that are possible on any given page. An objective of designing a page, however, is to achieve pleasant, rather than harsh or extreme, contrast. Too many contrasting elements on a single page may be artistically unsound and unattractive.

Proportion Proportion is the principle of comparative relationships. In newspaper design the length of one line may be compared with the length of another, or the shape of one story with shapes of others, or the width of a photograph with its depth. The goal of designers is to create pages in which the proportions of elements are pleasing to the eye. Certain proportions in this culture tend to look more pleasing than others. The Greeks were largely responsible for working out the proportions of many of their temples in classical dimensions. Artists and designers try to use pleasing proportions in their works because the public has come to appreciate such relationships. For example, artists rarely use a square shape in preparing their work because a square appears dull and uninteresting. More pleasing is a rectangle in which the length is greater than the width. Unequal proportions usually are more attractive than equal proportions. For that reason, newspapers, magazines and books have pages that are designed with the width being less than the depth.

In newspaper design, pleasing proportions should be considered in planning the sizes of pictures, headlines and even divisions of pages. Unfortunately, the design of newspaper pages often does not reflect the principle of good proportions even though the size of paper pages does. The problem is that makeup men tend to think in terms of fitting news into columns, each of which is poorly proportioned. They can't be sure that the shape of the main story on a page is pleasantly related to other story shapes on that page. Persons using the total design concept are better able to control relationships and proportions than are makeup men.

The beginner with little or no artistic training will have to develop a sense of proportion by following certain basic principles:

1. The best proportions are unequal and thereby not obvious. Therefore, an element on a given page should not have square dimensions, whether it is a picture, story shape, box or division of a page.

2. There are many pleasing proportions that can be used, but one of the easiest and most pleasing is a 3:5 relationship. It is easy to remember and easy to use. To determine the shape of a story, for example, the makeup man needs only to decide arbitrarily one dimension (either the width or the length). Then by multiplying (or dividing) that dimension by 1.62,[1] the other dimension may be found using the 3:5 proportion.

3. While the beginner can easily learn to calculate the unknown dimensions to arrive at a 3:5 proportion, he will find it more convenient to guess at the proportions. Of course, such guesswork should be done only after he has studied what pleasing proportions look like. Then he is in a position to guess, because he has developed a sense of what is attractive. But it is simply impractical for a makeup editor to size every story and picture by mathematical calculations. In fact, mathematical

[1] 1.62 is a factor of a 3 to 4:85 relationship (Most often called 3:5 for the sake of convenience). The 3 to 4:85 relationship is also sometimes called a golden oblong shape.

precision is not a desirable goal in deciding on proportions because it limits artistic imagination.

Also, most persons are not perceptive of precise mathematical proportions. But it should be obvious that a single-column story 11 picas wide and 64 picas long is not proportionately pleasing (Figure 14–4). For that reason, the page designer might divide that column into two equal-depth columns where the new dimensions would be 22.5 by 32 picas. If these dimensions were checked by the formula above, it would be found that the 32-pica dimension should really be 36.450 picas (22.5×1.62). But few persons will object or complain about the difference.

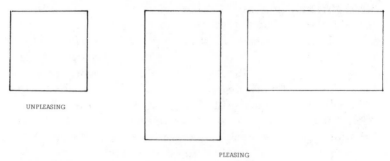

UNPLEASING

PLEASING

Figure 14–4. Unpleasing and pleasing proportions.

4. In dividing a page, some unequal proportions should be used for determining the relationship of one area to another. For convenience, a 3:5 relationship might again be used. But any proportion that is obvious should be avoided. Therefore, it would not do to divide a page in half either vertically or horizontally. The areas employed in the total design concept are those whose proportions are critical to the aesthetic appearance of the entire page. But in traditional page makeup, it is very difficult to divide a page in pleasing proportions unless the columnar approach to placement is abandoned.

In determining the relationships of parts to wholes, the goal is to avoid exaggerated proportions as well. As attempts are made to have unequal dimensions, there is the danger that they will become exaggerated. That is why the 3:5 proportion is suitable for most page design problems. When pleasing proportions are used on a page, the result may not only be interesting but attractive.

Unity The principle of unity concerns the effect of a page design that creates a single impression rather than multiple impressions. Stories on a page that has unity appear as if each contributes a significant share to the total page design. A page that does not have unity appears as a collection of stories, each of which may be fighting for the reader's attention to the detriment of a unified page appearance.

Lack of unity often results when stories are dummied from the top of the page downward. The makeup editor is building a page piece by piece and cannot be sure how each story will contribute to the total page design until he has completed his dummy. At that point, however, he may find that he does not have enough time to shift stories around to achieve unity. The result is that readers may find it difficult to concentrate on any one part of a page because of too many centers of interest. A unified page, on the other hand, appears as if everything is in its correct position, and the page is therefore interesting.

How does one plan for a unified page? Through keeping the design of the entire page in mind at all times while working on any part of it. Each story, therefore, must be visually weighed against all other stories in terms of the probable appearance of the entire page. In page makeup, the editor may have to shift some stories around on the dummy until a satisfactory arrangement has been found. As with the other principles of artistic design, an appreciation of this one will have to be developed by makeup editors through a sensitivity to good design.

Although the objectives of newspaper design may be clear enough, the beginner may have difficulty implementing them because he cannot visualize the structure of a page before it has been completely dummied. Sometimes, even after a page has appeared in print, the beginner may not be able to see the design easily. To overcome this difficulty, he should resort to the process of drawing heavy black lines around each story on a printed page. Now the design will emerge. The editor can now critically examine his total page design (see Figures 14–5, 14-6, and 14–7).

Visualizing Total Page Structure

If a page is studied in the above manner occasionally, the beginner may be able to develop a feeling for page structure that should improve his ability to create effective page designs.

A preliminary step to page makeup is the decision about how many pages an issue will have. An executive may start by considering the ratio of news to advertising. In the past a popular ratio was 40 per cent news to 60 per cent advertising. Today the ratio of news to advertising may be much smaller for many newspapers (30 per cent news, 70 per cent advertising). Although the smaller percentage of news may be used, it does not necessarily mean that less news than before is appearing in the newspaper. Because volume of advertising may be greater than before, a larger amount of news may be used in a 30:70 ratio than in a 40:60 one.

How the Number of Pages in an Issue is Determined

Press capacity, however, is another consideration in determining the number of pages in an issue. Some presses will print only in multiples of 8. None will print an odd number of pages without wasting space. Even for those presses that will print even numbers, there may be some objection by executives for printing an issue of, for example, 14 pages because a single loose sheet

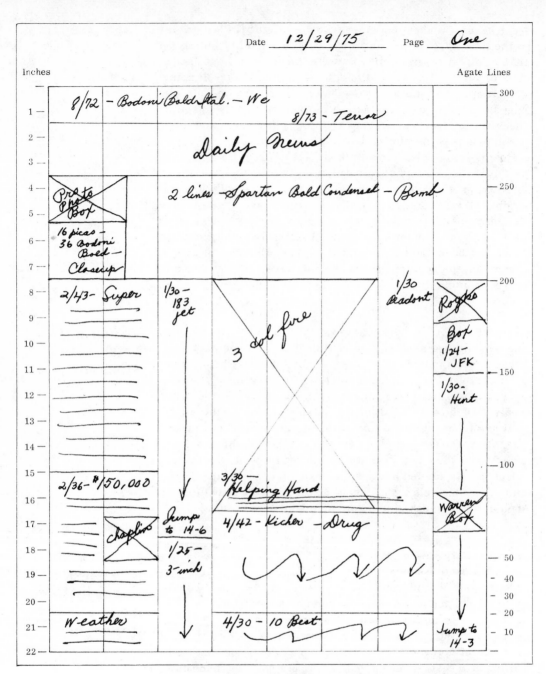

Figure 14–5. Page dummy. (See how this dummy is translated into type in Figure 14–6, and the page design in Figure 14–7.) [*Courtesy Chicago Daily News.*]

containing 2 pages must be inserted into a paper where three sheets are folded to print 12 pages. It is easier to increase the number of pages to 16, where four sheets of paper are folded.

When press capacity, or any other reason, requires that the volume of news or advertising be decreased, news is usually cut.

Occasionally, however, an advertisement may be moved to another day in order to make the columns fit the number of pages required.

Once the editor has a schedule of stories, their lengths and the page numbers that they have been temporarily assigned, he is ready to make up each page that has space remaining on it. In essence, he will position stories on each page dummy until most of the space has been filled. The remaining space is filled by the printer with leading or briefs. Some editors dummy only the most important stories and allow the printer to fill the remainder of the page. Others dummy the entire page. A better-looking page can be achieved if 90 per cent or more of a page has been dummied because there is better control over the entire page design than in partial-page dummying.

Principles of Page Makeup

Page makeup consists of preparing a dummy, which serves the same purpose as a blueprint—it tells the printer where to place each story, how long it will be and how it should be shaped. A goal of the makeup editor should be to make the dummy as clear, accurate and concise as possible. Many dummies turn out to be a mass of scribbling rather than a neatly prepared blueprint that enables the printer to assemble type for a page with a minimum of confusion. The pressure of time is often blamed for hard-to-read dummies. But the consequence of poor preparation may mean that time is wasted in the composing room when the printer tries to decipher the dummy. Therefore, every effort should be taken to make the dummy neat, accurate and concise.

The Mechanics of Dummying

Some guidelines for preparing a dummy are as follows:

1. A front page dummy is started by indicating the amount of space that the nameplate will take. Some newspapers have specially prepared dummies with space already allocated for the nameplate. Where this is not available a line should be drawn across the dummy indicating that the nameplate will occupy a certain depth.

2. Because most headlines have been assigned a number or some other designation in a headline schedule, this number and the slug for the story should be written wherever the story is to be placed on the dummy.

3. When a story with a one-column headline is noted on the dummy, the headline and slug word are indicated at the top of the story and a horizontal line is drawn across the column at the end. No arrows are needed to indicate that the story is to read in a downward direction. But when a story is continued to an adjacent column, then arrows should be used to show where the story is continued. The arrows warn the printer that the story has not been completed in the column where the headline appeared. Whenever there is some doubt about where a story is continued, arrows should be used. But if they can be avoided,

Figure 14–6. How the dummy in Figure 14–5 appears in type. [*Courtesy Chicago Daily News.*]

Figure 14-7. The design of the page shown in Figure 14-6. [*Courtesy Chicago Daily News.*]

they should be, because they tend to clutter the dummy. When a single-column story is ended at the very bottom of the page, an endmark should be used.

4. Two-column lead paragraphs, cutlines and odd-measured stories (such as a $1\frac{1}{2}$-column width) should be indicated on the layout by drawing wavy lines the width of the type. Straight lines should not be drawn as they may be confused with finish or "30" lines.

5. Pictures or cartoons should be labeled appropriately with the slug word and an indication that it is either a picture or cartoon. Some newspapers use a large X drawn to the corners of the picture to make it clear that the space is to be used for a picture and not a story.

6. Boxes are indicated by drawing a rectangle to the dimensions required and labeling the drawing with the word *box*.

7. Jumps should be indicated by the word *jump* (or RO for runover) and the page number to which the story is to be continued.

8. If a story of two or more columns reads into a single column, then a cutoff rule will probably be used to separate the material that appears under the headline from nonrelated material. Also, an arrow should be drawn from the headline into the appropriate column where the story is to be continued. If a banner headline reads out into a deck, this too should be indicated by an arrow.

9. Any makeup arrangement that is radically different from what has been used before should be indicated with notations if there is doubt that it will be clear to the printer. Sometimes only an arrow is needed; sometimes a few words will explain the situation.

Positioning The most important stories are assigned those places on the dummy that tend to be centers of interest. A center of interest is any position that because of its location tends to draw the reader's eyes. The upper-left and upper-right positions on a page are major centers of interest. The two lower corners also are centers of interest but not to the extent that the upper corners are.

Readers tend to enter a page by looking at the upper-left corner first. This is natural because most pages of books are read by starting in the upper-left corner and then proceeding in a right-hand direction until the end of the line has been reached. There is, therefore, a left to right direction in reading. Because readers start at the top of the page, both the left and right corners are major centers of interest.

Newspaper pages, however, can be arranged so that readers follow lines of directional force. A line of directional force may be a large headline, a cutoff rule, a picture, or even a column of type. Such lines are simply devices that lead the reader's eyes from one part of the page to another. A banner headline, for example, is so powerful that it moves the reader from the left to the right direction until he reaches the last column. But then, instead of returning to the left as one usually does when reading lines in a book, the editor can introduce a two-column readout headline at the extreme right, literally forcing the reader to remain at the right and thereby leading him downward into the column of body type. In the same manner, a single-column story with a large one-column headline can serve as a line of directional force urging the reader to move downward in the column.

A basic principle of positioning, therefore, is to lead the reader in an orderly manner through the strategic placement of stories. Obviously, a reader will often assert his own independence by selecting stories of interest to him regardless of the makeup editor's efforts to lead him through the page. But if stories are placed so that directions are not confusing, the reader may be encouraged to read more of the page. Perhaps the simplest way of starting to make up a page, then, is to place the most important stories in the centers of interest first and the other stories in remaining positions until the entire page is filled.

An alternative procedure is to place the most important story in the upper right or upper left positions and then balance that story diagonally across the page at the bottom. The other two diagonally facing corners might then receive the next two stories.

Beginners should remember that the most important part of the page is the upper left rather than the upper right corner. Only when a banner headline is used does the upper right corner assume the most important position.

There are few restrictions in the positioning of pictures. Traditionally, pictures have been placed somewhere at the top of newspapers. But there is little reason for placing them there. Pictures may be placed anywhere on the page with powerful effect. *The Continuing Studies of Newspaper Readership* (cited previously) showed that readers will search for pictures no matter where they are on a page. In fact, even relatively unimportant positions such as the bottom or lower center will receive high readership. As a consequence, pictures ought to be placed on the page in positions that enhance the total design.

If it is necessary to position a picture at the top because it accompanies an important story, then attempts should be made to balance it with another picture at the bottom, diagonally. Many front pages suffer from top-heaviness because a picture is used only at the top and nothing is used to balance it at the bottom. By their nature, pictures become centers of interest and draw attention away from stories of modest weight.

Another consideration in positioning is story shape. In past **Vertical and** years, story shape has not been a major consideration of makeup **Horizontal makeup** editors. But within recent years, when makeup editors have sought ways of making pages more attractive, story shapes have become important. The selection of the most appropriate shapes involves a number of considerations. The first one has to do with preventing a page from becoming one-directional. If there are

---

Fundamentals of Newspaper Design 283

too many vertically shaped stories all leading the reader's eyes downward, then the page looks old-fashioned and unattractive. Newspapers circa 1850 were all vertical in shape, and vertical makeup is distinctly old-fashioned. To avoid verticalness, an attempt should be made to achieve horizontal makeup. Horizontal makeup is distinguished by the fact that stories are continued into three or more adjacent columns and the shape of such stories is horizontal. Although a story may be continued into the next adjacent column, this does not necessarily produce horizontal makeup because the shape of the story may be vertical. Another distinguishing feature of horizontal makeup is that stories are squared off at the bottom. This means that the depth of each column where the story is continued is the same (Figure 14–8). However, a page using horizontally shaped stories exclusively may be as monotonous as one where all stories are vertically shaped. The best looking pages have a mixture of shapes (Figure 14–9).

'Famous' on Way, Says Adams

Fabulous Beltline Development Seen

By ART THOMASON
Telegraph Staff Writer
A gigantic Christmas package was opened Wednesday at a Pride, Inc., meeting and it contained millions of dollars in future development along the Beltline Highway, including a Famous-Barr store in an enclosed mall shopping center.

Alton developer Homer Adams told the Pride board "unequivocally" that Famour - Barr will build a department store and mall containing 600,000 square feet under roof.

The announcement by

Adams was the first official confirmation that Famous-Barr would build on the site located on the southeast corner of the Beltline and Seminary Road.

Famous-Barr, the parent store of the May Co., is one of the nation's largest retailers.

The May Co., is currently building one of its Venture Department discount stores on the northwest corner of Seminary and the beltline. Adams, too, developed the Venture project.

Adams said a separate development from Seminary west to Washington Avenue

along the Beltline also is planned. The tract includes 14 sites designed for small businesses and not connected with the shopping center.

The shopping center will be the largest in the Alton area with enough parking for 5,000 cars, he said.

Adams also forecast that Beltline development should boost the immediate Alton area population to 100,000 by the 1970's.

The developer outlined other future development for the Beltline, some of it already under construction, including the Belscot

Shopping Center, an amalgamation of the Bell Scott department stores; a Tri-City Grocery Co. store in the same shopping center complex which is under construction on the south side of the beltline near Buckmaster Lane. They were:

(1) A gigantic motor city — an elaborately designed outlay of businesses that sell anything with a motor;

(2) A 10-acre recreational center that will hopefully feature the Cinerama design, with inside recreational facilities and a

large civic center;

(3) Conversion of the old brickyard at Alby Street Road into a 200-acre light industrial park, called the North Port Industrial Park;

(4) The Veterans of Foreign Wars Legion Post home, just north of the Beltline on Alby Street Road;

(5) A MacDonald's hamburger restaurant, now nearing completion near Washington Ave.;

(6) A Taco's restaurant that will feature Mexican dishes;

(7) A new Christian

Science edifice near the Temple Israel, between Pierce and Levis lanes.

Adams promised that the development connected with his firm would use sophisticated landscaping techniques to protect residential areas and enhance the natural beauty.

For example, the developer pointed out that the Central Hardware Store, Bettendorfs and the Venture Store will be virtually screened from the view of residential areas behind it by using a landscaping plan that will beautify the area.

Figure 14–8. Horizontally shaped story. [*Courtesy Alton, Ill., Evening Telegraph.*]

Avoiding Odd-
Shaped Stories
A second consideration in makeup should be that of avoiding odd-shaped stories. In traditional makeup many stories are not squared off and take odd shapes. One such shape looks like an "inverted L" (Figure 14–10). It is caused by using a two- or three-column headline over a one-column story. The effect is like an upside-down "L." When more than one inverted L-shaped story is used on a page, they tend to destroy the simplicity of the design. Because an inverted L may be used at the upper right-hand side and another one in the upper left-hand side, the design becomes complex. Other stories and pictures must fit around these shapes and it is not an easy task. For example, the space underneath an inverted L-shaped story in the right-hand

Figure 14–9 [OPPOSITE]. Mixture of vertical and horizontal makeup on same page. [*Courtesy Boston Globe.*]

The Art of Editing

Urban renewal, budgets are issues

6 Massachusetts cities go to polls tomorrow

By Paul Langner
Globe Staff

Urban renewal, city planning, budgets, schools, police protection and crime are among the issues that, with varying degrees of intensity, concern voters in six Massachusetts cities who will vote tomorrow in preliminary elections for mayor, alderman or councilman, and school committeeman.

Mayoral races are being held in Beverly, Newburyport, Salem, and Somerville. In Peabody, Mayor Nicholas Mavroules is unopposed in his bid for a fifth consecutive two-year term.

In Newton, Mayor Theodore Mann is in the middle of a four-year term to which he was elected in 1973. At that time, Newton broke with the two-year term tradition and is now the second city in the commonwealth (Boston is the other one) to have four-year mayoral terms.

Turnout is expected to be light in the preliminary elections that will nominate candidates for the final elections on Nov. 4.

Newton voters, for example, will nominate four candidates for alderman-at-large from Ward 4 out of six contestants. Two will be elected in November. While voting for aldermen-at-large is citywide, they must live in specific wards and be elected as ward aldermen-at-large.

Similarly, in Ward 3, three candidates are seeking two nominations for election to school committeeman-at-large. Ward 7 in Newton has a ward alderman race with three candidates vying for two nominations and Ward 8 has four candidates for two nominations.

Among the issues in Newton are the question of permitting the Perini Corp. to build an apartment complex on land it owns on Commonwealth avenue, opposite the Marriott Hotel and near Norumbega Park; 100 percent revaluation of real property; and returning some control over the school budget to the board of aldermen.

Candidates in Newton are generally opposed to full valuation because, as one puts it, "revaluation puts the burden on the homeowner."

Full valuation was ordered by the Supreme Judicial Court in January, as a result of a suit by the town of Sudbury. Most cities and towns assess property at rates far below market value, sometimes as low as 20 percent.

This practice keeps many homeowners' taxes down even though tax rates are high. Full valuation could multiply the annual tax bill as much as four to five times in some cities.

Newton property is now assessed at 40 to 60 percent and the tax rate is $159 per $1000 of assessed valuation.

In Somerville the issues among six candidates for mayor are money, flight of business, vandalism, car theft, and a tax rate that has risen by $59.40 in five years. It is now $199.70.

Mayor S. Lester Ralph, seeking his fourth consecutive two-year term, is opposed by James F. Brennan, a real estate and insurance broker whom he unseated six years ago: Francis Leo McCarthy; Thomas F. August; William M. Rafferty and and Mary Sogliero.

Miss Sogliero says she knows how to bring $50 million into Somerville. "With my talent, ability and determination I will do it," she says, declining to outline specific plans, except that she would remove concrete street islands to facilitate snow removal. She is not considered a serious candidate.

More serious charges are being brought by McCarthy who says that the mayor used Federal funds badly by building parks.

Voting hours

Voting hours in tomorrow's preliminary elections in Massachusetts are: Beverly, 10 a.m. to 8 p.m.; Newburyport, 8 a.m. to 8 p.m.; Newton, 7 a.m. to 8 p.m.; Peabody, 8 a.m. to 8 p.m.; Salem, 8 a.m. to 8 p.m.; Somerville, 8 a.m. to 8 p.m.

On Oct. 7, preliminary elections will be held in Attleboro, Brockton, Chicopee, Fitchburg, Gardner, Gloucester, Haverhill, Holyoke, Lawrence, Lowell, Lynn, Marlboro, New Bedford, Pittsfield, Springfield, Taunton, Westfield and Woburn.

On Oct. 14, a preliminary election will be held in North Adams.

Final elections in all 39 Massachusetts cities are Nov. 4.

Ralph dismisses such charges, and those by Brennan that police protection is inadequate, as "typical election year rhetoric."

He says that police protection is not necessarily a matter of the numbers of patrolmen but depends on "the quality of the police force."

On the charge by both Brennan and McCarthy that Somerville's bonded indebtedness has increased from $5.5 million in 1970 to $34.6 million this year, the mayor says that from 40 to 65 percent of that is reimbursable by the state and he claims that Somerville's municipal bond rating is AAA.

He admits that auto thefts are a problem, but says that the city has taken steps that have decreased them by a third. A special police squad has been organized to combat auto thefts and the courts have refrained from sending young offenders to jail, making them work for the city instead at $2 an hour until such damage as they have done is paid off.

For August, who is finishing his first term as an alderman and who was Ralph's first city solicitor, the No. 1 issue in the city is crime.

"Before I was an alderman I thought the thing people were most concerned about was the tax rate," August, an attorney, said. "But the thing I hear the most about from the people of the city is the need for better police protection. That's the critical question. We need more and better trained men on the force."

An attempt to reach Rafferty, at the Somerville address he gave the Election Commission, failed. A woman, identifying herself as his daughter-in-law, said that Rafferty did not live at the address.

Besides the mayoral race, there are races for city assessor, aldermen, and school committeemen, 49 candidates in all.

In Newburyport, three candidates are seeking nomination for the mayoral election on Nov. 4, and 31 are vying for councilman-at-large, school committeeman, and ward councilmen tomorrow.

Mayor Byron J. Matthews is seeking his fifth consecutive term and is opposed by Raymond H. Abbott, a social worker for the commonwealth, and James F. Ronan, a retired Coast Guard officer.

In Beverly, one of the challengers to Mayor James A. Vitale is not impressed with experience in government. Philip Dunkelbarger, a 27-year-old professional planner and current executive secretary of the Southern Essex Solid Waste Council, says the present city government plans poorly, budgets unrealistically, and has inadequate industrial development programs.

The tax rate rose $3.90 last year and is now $67.50. This, Dunkelbarger says, is based on unrealistic budgeting for such items as snow removal, street lighting, health insurance premiums for city employees, fuel, and capital improvements.

He says that city government lives "in a fool's paradise in its budgeting," and that industrial development has "been stymied by the establishment."

A man who rattles off sums down to the dollar, Dunkelbarger has written a 120-page program outlining what needs to be done. He says that he has been campaigning since November and that his chances have gone from "hopeless" to "even."

Vitale termed Dunkelbarger's accusations "groundless" and said Beverly's tax rate is "the lowest in Essex County for a city or town of our size." Dunkelbarger, he said, "has never prepared a municipal budget and has never been elected to public office."

Vitale said his accomplishments are "obvious and visible" and cited as an example the completion of Tozier road under Rte. 128, extending from the center of town to North Beverly. "The road has brought in more tax revenues than anything else that's happened here in years," he said.

The third candidate, Peter F. Fortunato, is campaigning on his 14-year experience in city government. He is now president of the board of aldermen.

In Salem, Albert D. Kopiecki, an electrical worker, is attacking the administration of Mayor Jean A. Levesque for alleged mishandling of the construction of a 1000-car parking garage and a five-story city hall annex.

The garage, says Kopiecki, is "a white elephant," and unnecessary. Moreover, it costs to park there after the garage was built with tax money, he says.

The five-story annex, Kopiecki says, will benefit the builder, Mondev, a Canadian developer, and will cost Salem taxpayers $2 million over the 20-year contract.

The city has leased two floors in the building and the Mondev concern will lease out the rest. Levesque says that he and the city council preferred this arrangement to building a city-owned annex to city hall because it would produce tax income for the city.

The mayor also disagrees that the garage is a white elephant. "We are in the midst of an urban renewal program, and when the downtown is revitalized, there will most certainly be a need for the garage."

Levesque is seeking his second full term. He was elected mayor by the city council two and a half years ago when Mayor Samuel Zoll was named a judge. He won his first full term in the following election.

The third candidate for mayor of Salem is Carl E. Petersen, a 34-year-old school teacher and vice chairman of the school committee.

Petersen, who is a college teacher, said he is a candidate because Salem needs leadership and direction, and the present administration has failed to provide it. He said the city is not "moving ahead."

Salem voters will also nominate candidates for election of four councilmen-at-large, and for the three wards.

In Peabody, there is neither a mayor's race nor a race for councilman-at-large in the preliminary election.

Mavroules is unopposed in his bid for a fifth consecutive term, and there are only 10 candidates for the five councilman-at-large positions. Five will be elected in November.

Wards 1, 4, and 6 have preliminary races with a total of 10 candidates.

Nine candidates are running for six nominations for school committeeman. Three will be elected on Nov. 4.

The Ortiz apartment in Lowell, or what is left of it, is being torn down today. (Bill Curtis photo)

All lost, Lowell victim says; chief says blast no accident

By Nick King
Globe Staff

LOWELL — Two free nights in a Holiday Inn and Carmen Cruz wants to go home.

She cannot go home, though, because her rented apartment, or what's left of it, will be torn down today.

The two-story frame building nearly collapsed from the force of the violent explosion in Lowell's Centerville section early Saturday.

One building was leveled and several other apartments and businesses were damaged extensively by the blast, which injured 23 persons, including Mrs. Cruz, and left her family and 75 other persons temporarily homeless. Windows in buildings for a half-mile radius were shattered.

"We lost everything," the 27-year-old mother of two young children said in an interview yesterday. "The house will be torn down and we won't get anyting out of it. Everything was wrecked."

Mrs. Cruz said she thought a bomb had gone off when she was shocked out of her sleep shortly after 3 a.m. Saturday by the ceiling caving in on her bed. According to investigators poking through two blocks of rubble yesterday, she might not be far from the truth.

Lowell Fire Chief Paul V. Beauregard said the explosion was "not accidental" and that "foul play was definitely involved."

Investigators have discovered that the cap to a gas main in the basement of Jake's Cafe had been removed. But the chief and officials of the Lowell Gas Co. also believe that more than gas exploded, reducing Jake's Cafe to a pile of wooden splinters and twisted steel.

Yesterday, two gas company explosives experts, one from New York and the other from Tennessee, began going through the rubble to determine if dynamite or another explosive was set off.

Meanwhile, Mrs. Cruz, whose apartment was adjacent to Jake's Cafe, said: "Right now I'm thinking that we're all alive." As she spoke, she held her children with her common law husband Raymond Ortiz at her side.

Under other circumstances Mrs. Cruz might have welcomed a few nights in a motel, courtesy of the Red Cross. She is on welfare and pregnant with her third child. But like many of the whites, blacks and Puerto Ricans living in the low income Centerville section, Mrs. Cruz can ill afford the kind of near-disaster that struck Saturday.

She must make regular visits to the hospital, where doctors watch her leukemia and her pregnancy. Mrs. Cruz fears she may lose her child because of the blast.

"I hit my stomach trying to find my way out of the house," she said. "Everything was coming down on top of me. Everything I touched kept coming apart."

On reflection, Mrs. Cruz realizes she has even more reason to feel lucky to be alive than the others displaced by the explosion. Four months ago she was renting the apartment above Jake's, a building which does not exist any more.

And Mrs. Cruz said her mother almost decided to visit her Friday night to help take care of the children. If she had, she would have slept in the guest bed which was covered by wooden timbers shaken loose by the explosion.

Jules Choate, 20, one of the few persons awake at the time of the blast, was playing cards in the kitchen of his family's wooden two-story apartment a block from Jake's.

"I was sitting at the kitchen table and all I caught a glimpse of was the back door going by me, this close," he said, his slender hands measuring out no more than 12 inches. "I thought it was a hurricane so I hit the floor. But it was all over like that," he said, snapping his fingers.

Choate, his brother, his three sisters and their parents all lived in the $40-a-week four bedroom apartment. The Red Cross has found them new quarters but Jules said there is a lot more to be done.

"We lost most of our clothes and furniture. It's hard to get those pieces back together nowadays," said Jules, who dropped out of school in the 10th grade and currently is unemployed.

The Ortiz family, homeless after the early Saturday explosion in the Centerville section of Lowell, are Carmen, her husband Raymond and their two children Freedom, 1, and Carmen, 2. (Bill Curtis photo)

House tackles budget today; welfare restorations doubtful

By Jonathan Fuerbringer
Globe Staff

The Massachusetts House of Representatives today will begin debate of a proposed $2.79 billion state budget, and the Dukakis administration and advocacy groups are not hopeful of restoring of much of the $400 million slashed from human services programs' budget by the House Ways and Means Committee.

Welfare Comr. Jerald L. Stevens said Friday that he is looking to the Senate for restoration of most of the $367.5 million the Ways and Means Committee cut from the $1.4 billion welfare budget submitted by Gov. Michael S. Dukakis.

"I am fairly confident of restoration in the Senate," Stevens said. "I am hopeful for fighting it out in the House . . . not winning . . . but laying a base in the House.

"What I am looking for in the House is not so much the votes to overturn (the cuts) so much as informing the leadership and the members of what the cuts mean," Stevens said. "I want to make clear the impact in human terms."

Laying this base, Stevens said, will give the administration and other advocates for restoration some support when and if the Senate restores the cuts and the budget goes to a House-Senate conference committee to iron out the differences.

Hubert Jones, a spokesman for a coalition of human services advocacy groups, also said that they are aiming their lobbying at the Senate, where they think they have the best chance of winning restoration of the cuts.

James A. Kelly Jr. (D-Oxford) chairman of the Senate Ways and Means Committee held out some hope for the administration and advocacy groups when, after the unveiling of the House budget cuts, he said he would move to restore about $100 million to the human services budget.

Dukakis, last Wednesday called for the restoration of about $20 million in mental health, public health, correction, and children's services. These cuts, he said would endanger Federal funds for mental retardation, threaten the closing of preschool programs for handicapped children and deprive 2800 prison inmates of basic medical care.

Then on Thursday, the governor called for restoration of the proposed welfare cuts in the House Ways and Means budget. These cuts, Duakis said would deprive more than 100,0000 working poor and 28,-0000 unemployable general relief recipients of all medical care. In addition, the cuts would eliminate optional medical services, including prescription drugs, adult dental care, eyeglasses for adults under 65, and clinic coverage, for hundreds of thousands of recipients on welfare.

The welfare Department said the cuts would also leave with inadequate funds children's service, mandated by law and would mean a reduction of at least $48-a-month in Aid to Families with Dependent children.

Debate on the budget had been scheduled to begin last Thursday, but was delayed to 1 p.m. today because John J. Finnegan (D-Dorchester), House Ways and Means chairman, was ill. He is expected to return today, but could not be reached for comment yesterday.

Also delayed by Finnegan's illness were efforts to agree on the size of the deficit the budget would produce. Ways and Means set the deficit at $230 million, down from the $687 million in the $3.28 billion budget Dukakis sent to the Legislature in June.

But the administration challenged the committee's calculations, and estimated the deficit, even with all the committee's cuts, at $460 million. The restorations the administration is seeking would bring the deficit to over $500 million.

Despite the dispute, the House has moved along with preparation of proposals tax to cover just the $230 million deficit. Those taxes, which on an annual basis (one quarter of the fiscal year is already over) would raise $333 million, depend mostly on a hike of the sales tax from 3 percent to 5 percent. The taxes also expected to come up for debate in the House this week. Any restorations or changes in the deficit, however, would force changes in the tax package.

According to the administration, the main reason for the difference in the deficit figures is that the committee overestimated savings from its cuts. For example, the committee funded the state's Medicaid account at $306 million. the administration said that even with all the cuts the committee proposed — including elimination of all medical care for the working poor and ending optional medical care for hundreds of thousand of other recipients — the Medicaid account should be $468 million — $162 million more than the committee's estimate. The Medicaid budget would be between $500 million and $520 million if the cuts were restored.

Stevens said he has talked with Ways and Means about the underfunded accounts. The dispute is still unresolved and may not be resolved today according to Tim Taylor, press aide to Thomas McGee (D-Lynn), House speaker.

Negro Clergyman Defeated

Council of Churches Picks Woman Leader

From Our Wire Services

DETROIT, Dec. 4. — Dr. Cynthia Wedel, an Episcopalian and ardent advocate of women's rights, won overwhelmingly over a Negro clergyman Thursday to become the first woman president of the National Council of Churches.

Mrs. Wedel, of Washington, defeated the Rev. Albert B. Cleage Jr. of Detroit 387-93 in secret balloting at the NCC's triennial general assembly.

When the vote was announced, Mr. Cleage, the first Negro candidate for the presi-

Profile and Picture On Page 3

dency, went to a microphone on the assembly floor and castigated what he called the "White racist establishment of the NCC."

"This organization is anti-Christ and until young people or oppressed people take over, you'll remain anti-Christ" Mr. Cleage declared. "Time is

Continued on Page 3, Col. 8

Korean Report Raps Operation of Center By Buck Foundation

By EDWARD N. EISEN
Of The Inquirer Staff

The State Commission on Charitable Organizations made the Pearl S. Buck Foundation produce a letter Thursday from Korea's embassy highly critical of the foundation's work in that country.

The letter, by Sung Kwoo Kim, counsel and consul general at the embassy in Washington, said a 10-day inspection in August at the foundation's Sosa Opportunities Center, west of Seoul, showed unsanitary conditions, overcrowding, misuse of funds and other shortcomings.

REASONS DIVULGED

The letter was produced at a commission hearing on the foundation's appeal for a license to solicit funds in Pennsylvania. The foundation was to have presented new evidence, as demanded by Joseph J. Kelley Jr., Secretary of the Commonwealth.

Figure 14–10. Two inverted L-shaped stories. [*Courtesy Philadelphia Inquirer.*]

column usually requires a picture to fill the space underneath the headline. If another headline is placed underneath the upper headline, the result may be confusing (Figure 14–11). To avoid inverted L-shaped stories, the makeup editor should either use a single-column headline over a one-column story or wrap a story to the number of columns that the headline covers. A three-column headline then would have a story wrapped underneath for three columns, presumably, squared off. It is easier to design an attractive page by manipulating squared-off (or rectangularly shaped) stories than by using odd shapes such as the inverted L.

Another kind of odd shape is one in which a story is continued to adjacent columns but each column depth containing the story is a different length (Figure 14–12). Such shapes also tend to make the page look unattractive.

Wraps A major consideration in makeup is the problem of what to do with stories that must be continued into adjacent columns. Should they be jumped or wrapped into the next right-hand column? Jumps are undesirable for reasons given earlier. The best procedure is to wrap (or turn[2]) a story underneath a headline. It is very poor makeup procedure to wrap a story underneath another story because the reader may have difficulty locating the continuation. If it is necessary to wrap a story under-

[2] A *turn* is another name for a *wrap*.

Reservoir Is Rejected As School Site; Land Pledged to Developer

The City Planning Commission on Tuesday rejected suggestions to place a high school over the Belmont Reservoir because of a commitment to a group seeking to erect an office building there. Instead, the commission said, the Board of Education ought to consider using air rights over the reservoir's filter beds, just east of the reservoir.

The reservoir was one of four sites given tenative approval Monday at a meeting of the commission, the board and the Fairmount Park Commission. It was the only one involving city land.

TRADE HINTED

Two of the other sites comprise park land and the fourth a tract of "five points," Monument rd. and Conshohocken ave., owned by builder John McShain, who said he wanted to construct an apartment complex there.

The two park sites are at Edgley st. and Belmont ave. and at 53d st. and Parkside ave.

In a related development, City Council Majority Leader George X. Schwartz said he and Mayor James H. J. Tate agreed that the city might be willing to transfer city land to the Fairmount Park Commission if the commission will surrender park land for a school site.

OFFICES PLANNED

There is ample precedent for such a transfer, he said. Schwartz, chairman of the council's finance committee, said he favored the Edgley st. and Belmont ave. site for the new school.

Charles Ingersoll, vice chairman of the Planning Commis-

Tate Is Considering Ousting Mrs. Bennett From School Board

Mayor James H. J. Tate has grave doubts about whether to reappoint Mrs. Ruth Bennett to the Board of Education, he said Tuesday. Tate, reached by telephone in San Diego, Calif., where he is attending a convention, responded to searing criticism for his failure to fill three vacancies on the board from the Citizens Committee on Public Education.

The committee said it is "appalled" by Tate's failure to fill the vacant seats on the nine - member board. The mayor, the committee said, is in violation of the Home Rule Charter in leaving the seats vacant.

Tate said he is "not satisfied" with the two lists of candidates submitted to him by the educational nominating committee, which must submit from three to six names for each vacant seat. Under the charter, the mayor is required to choose from among these names.

Tate said he would reappoint board member William Ross, a leader of the Interna-

Teachers Held In Drug Raid Are Suspended

Three young Philadelphia schoolteachers were suspended from their duties Tuesday following their arrests for illegal possession of narcotics.

The three were released on $1 bail each and slated for a Dec. 19 hearing at the 19th Police District, 61st and Thompson sts. after three members of the narcotics squad raided their West Philadelphia apartments Monday night and allegedly found what laboratory tests showed to be hashish and a pipe with residues of marijuana.

All three lived in an apart-

Figure 14–11. Headlines placed underneath two inverted L-shaped stories. The effect may be confusing. [*Courtesy Philadelphia Inquirer.*]

neath another story, then a cutoff rule is used to separate the story on top from that underneath (Figure 14–13). When a story is wrapped underneath another story set in a different kind of type or a longer column width, there is less danger of confusing the reader than when it is wrapped underneath a story set in the same kind of type and same column width. Obviously, stories wrapped underneath pictures, where the cutlines are set in different kinds of type, are not apt to be confusing (Figures 14–14 and 14–15).

Fundamentals of Newspaper Design 287

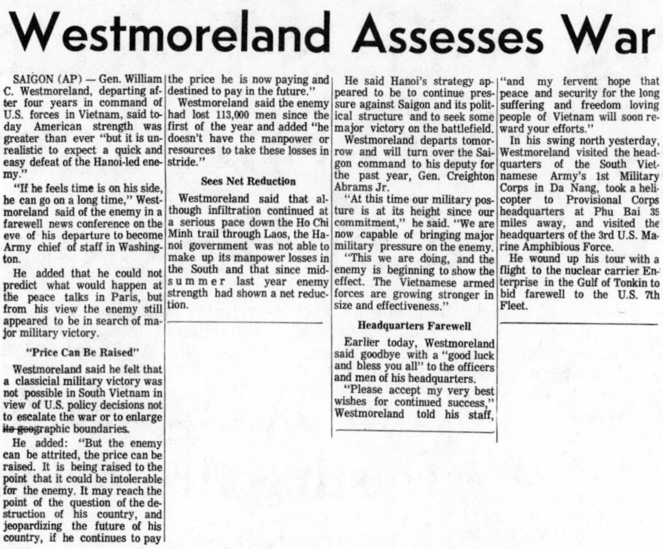

Westmoreland Assesses War

SAIGON (AP) — Gen. William C. Westmoreland, departing after four years in command of U.S. forces in Vietnam, said today American strength was greater than ever "but it is unrealistic to expect a quick and easy defeat of the Hanoi-led enemy."

"If he feels time is on his side, he can go on a long time," Westmoreland said of the enemy in a farewell news conference on the eve of his departure to become Army chief of staff in Washington.

He added that he could not predict what would happen at the peace talks in Paris, but from his view the enemy still appeared to be in search of major military victory.

"Price Can Be Raised"

Westmoreland said he felt that a classicial military victory was not possible in South Vietnam in view of U.S. policy decisions not to escalate the war or to enlarge ~~its geog~~raphic boundaries.

He added: "But the enemy can be attrited, the price can be raised. It is being raised to the point that it could be intolerable for the enemy. It may reach the point of the question of the destruction of his country, and jeopardizing the future of his country, if he continues to pay the price he is now paying and destined to pay in the future."

Westmoreland said the enemy had lost 113,000 men since the first of the year and added "he doesn't have the manpower or resources to take these losses in stride."

Sees Net Reduction

Westmoreland said that although infiltration continued at a serious pace down the Ho Chi Minh trail through Laos, the Hanoi government was not able to make up its manpower losses in the South and that since midsummer last year enemy strength had shown a net reduction.

He said Hanoi's strategy appeared to be to continue pressure against Saigon and its political structure and to seek some major victory on the battlefield.

Westmoreland departs tomorrow and will turn over the Saigon command to his deputy for the past year, Gen. Creighton Abrams Jr.

"At this time our military posture is at its height since our commitment," he said. "We are now capable of bringing major military pressure on the enemy.

"This we are doing, and the enemy is beginning to show the effect. The Vietnamese armed forces are growing stronger in size and effectiveness."

Headquarters Farewell

Earlier today, Westmoreland said goodbye with a "good luck and bless you all" to the officers and men of his headquarters.

"Please accept my very best wishes for continued success," Westmoreland told his staff, "and my fervent hope that peace and security for the long suffering and freedom loving people of Vietnam will soon reward your efforts."

In his swing north yesterday, Westmoreland visited the headquarters of the South Vietnamese Army's 1st Military Corps in Da Nang, took a helicopter to Provisional Corps headquarters at Phu Bai 35 miles away, and visited the headquarters of the 3rd U.S. Marine Amphibious Force.

He wound up his tour with a flight to the nuclear carrier Enterprise in the Gulf of Tonkin to bid farewell to the U.S. 7th Fleet.

Figure 14–12. Odd-shaped story. [*Courtesy Cedar Falls, Iowa, Record.*]

When a story is wrapped into an adjacent column at the top of a page without a covering headline it is called a raw wrap. In many instances raw wraps are undesirable and are forbidden at all times by some newspapers. The makeup editor faced with a raw wrap should ask that a headline be written to cover the wrap and make it clear that the wrap belongs to the headline above it. But occasionally it is permissible to use a raw wrap at the top of

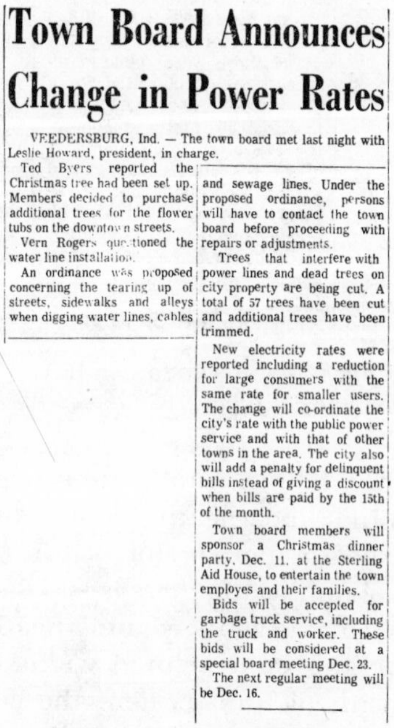

Town Board Announces Change in Power Rates

VEEDERSBURG, Ind. — The town board met last night with Leslie Howard, president, in charge.

Ted Byers reported the Christmas tree had been set up. Members decided to purchase additional trees for the flower tubs on the downtown streets.

Vern Rogers questioned the water line installation.

An ordinance was proposed concerning the tearing up of streets, sidewalks and alleys when digging water lines, cables and sewage lines. Under the proposed ordinance, persons will have to contact the town board before proceeding with repairs or adjustments.

Trees that interfere with power lines and dead trees on city property are being cut. A total of 57 trees have been cut and additional trees have been trimmed.

New electricity rates were reported including a reduction for large consumers with the same rate for smaller users. The change will co-ordinate the city's rate with the public power service and with that of other towns in the area. The city also will add a penalty for delinquent bills instead of giving a discount when bills are paid by the 15th of the month.

Town board members will sponsor a Christmas dinner party, Dec. 11, at the Sterling Aid House, to entertain the town employes and their families.

Bids will be accepted for garbage truck service, including the truck and worker. These bids will be considered at a special board meeting Dec. 23.

The next regular meeting will be Dec. 16.

Figure 14–13. Wrap underneath a cutoff rule.

PAMPERED, SANTA

Conyers Offered Replacement Tree

By RON TAYLOR

A Conyers housewife has offered a cedar she nurtured from a seedling to replace a giant artificial Christmas tree which mysteriously vanished from a Rockdale County shopping center.

Mrs. Kelly S t o c k t o n said Wednesday her tree has been fertilized "just like my flowers" and is now taller than her house.

She offered the cedar to merchants at the Rockdale Shopping Center after county residents went there Monday for tree-lighting ceremonies only to find that the 17-foot gold tree had disappeared.

It apparently had been hauled away by burglars. Merchants discovered it missing last Saturday as they prepared for Monday's celebration.

Mrs. Stockton said she nourished her mammoth tree with Vigoro after extracting it from woods when it was only 12 inches high and planting it in her front yard.

She says she has no qualms agout sacrificing her tree for the Yule season.

"IT'S BLOCKING my view from my picture window," she said, adding that she no longer has enough lights to continue her own annual Christmas decoration of the tree.

Mrs. Stockton said the tree she is offering without charge is the second cedar she has pampered to adulthood in her front yard. The merchants are weighing the offer. Another tree planted when Mrs. Stockton and her husband moved into their Flat Shoals Road home subsequently was chopped down and decorated for Christmas use in the Stocktons' living room.

Mrs. Stockston said she plans to go to the woods for another seedling after the present cedar is cut down.

Dr. Roland Reagan, president of the shopping center's merchants association, said the association would gladly accept Mrs. Stockton's gift but that he is not certain workmen will be able to get it up in time for Christmas display.

IT WAS REAGAN and several other merchants who discovered the disappearance of the big artificial tree.

It had been stored atop a store in the middle of the shopping center, but when merchants went up on the store roof Saturday they found no trace of the tree or its protective plastic covering.

Businessmen speculate burglars stole it and sold it to some other city in 'need of a tree.

Figure 14–14. Wrap underneath a two-column lead paragraph without a cutoff rule.

an advertisement where there is no doubt in the reader's mind that the wrap belongs to the headline on the left (Figure 14–16).

When there is not enough time to reset a headline to a wider column measure, another makeup procedure is to avoid having to make wraps by filling the remaining space with stories of shorter length. Or, perhaps, a longer story can be shortened by cutting off some of the longer stories and combining them with fillers.

In dummying a page care should be taken to avoid the kind of wrap shown in Figure 14–17 where the reader is asked to jump from the bottom of a page to the very top above the ad. The size of the ad makes it appear as if the story has ended at the bottom. The makeup man should either cut the story and end it at the bottom (placing a new story above the ad) or find a shorter story to place at the left of the ad.

When most of the page has been dummied, the makeup procedure is complete. Small spaces may remain because all stories did not fit precisely. The page dummy is sent to the composing room where a printer begins to assemble type and pictures into a page form. The remaining space may be filled in two ways:

Filling Remaining Space

Senate approves $700 exemption on '70 wage tax

By Tom Littlewood
Sun-Times Bureau

WASHINGTON — The Senate disregarded President Nixon, its Finance Committee and the House Wednesday and voted to raise the personal income tax exemption from $600 to $700 next year and $800 in 1971.

This is the amount a taxpayer can subtract from his taxable income for himself and each dependent in the family. The amendment, by Sen. Albert Gore (D-Tenn.), carried 58 to 37.

If it survives the Senate-House conference committee and is part of the tax bill finally signed into law by the President, the exemption would redistribute some $9 billion in contemplated tax cuts. It would not affect income tax due in April.

Relief for big families

By increasing exemptions instead of cutting rates by at least 5 per cent and raising the standard deduction available for non-itemizers, the measure would give more relief to large families, especially in the middle-income group who are paying off mortgages, and less to those who make $20,000 or more.

The version reported by the Senate Finance Committee would have provided about $4.5 billion in general rate cuts. A similar rate schedule cleared the House last summer.

Mr. Nixon has warned that he might veto a tax bill that drains off too many tax dollars while inflation is still a problem.

The President wrote Senate leaders on Tuesday, saying an $800 exemption would reduce income taxes too early and by too much, about $4.8 billion. Gore disputed the short-run revenue effects of his plan.

Worried about the political risk in the easily understood exemption issue, the Republicans tried to outmaneuver Gore, but wound up more shattered and distraught than before.

First, moderates tried to put over a compromise by Sen. Charles H. Percy (R-Ill.) that would have spread smaller increases over a longer period, cushioning the inflationary impact.

But the White House and the Treasury Department refused to accept Percy's proposal of 2 $50-a-year increases until $750 was reached in 1972. Only half of the 42 voting Republicans supported Percy, and his amendment failed 72 to 23.

Scott flays administration

After Gore's amendment won, Minority Leader Hugh Scott (R-Pa.) engaged in an unusual public chastisement of the Republican administration.

He said the Treasury had "gone down to a resounding and glorious defeat" because it refused t listen to his advice and settle for the

North Shore salutes Crane

Representing planeloads of North Shore residents who flew to Washington Wednesday to honor their new 13th District congressman, Bernard E. Pederson (right) of Palatine presents Congressional Seal to Rep. Philip M. Crane. House minority leader Gerald Ford and the Illinois Republicans in the House later met the group at a reception. (Sun-Times Photo)

Percy compromise.

"I do hope," he told the Senate sarcastically, "that responsible officials in the Treasury of my own administration will realize we understand more about Senate strategy than they do."

A Treasury official later said the tax cuts in Percy's proposal, combining a higher exemption and some rate reductions, were excessive over the long run.

Percy and Sen. Ralph T. Smith (R-Ill.) both

Turn to Page 26

Figure 14–15. Wrap underneath a picture. [*Courtesy Chicago Sun-Times.*]

(1) If the space is large enough, fillers may be used. Editors assign someone the responsibility for seeing that there are a sufficient number of fillers available each day. (2) If the space is relatively small, then it is filled by leading. Leading is first

---

2— Section 5   Thursday, November 13, 1975   THE HERALD

Diabetes and blood pressure

About a year and a half ago my doctor said I had high blood pressure and put me on medicine. In a short time my tests showed I was low on potassium, and he put me on potassium medicine and gradually increased it because my level was so low.

Then he did a glucose test and said I'm a borderline diabetic. If I understand what I read, sometimes when there is no diabetes in the family and it shows up, it can be caused by high blood pressure medicine. Is this so?

If my blood pressure is causing the problem why can't they just give me other medicines? I know there are

The doctor says
by Lawrence E. Lamb, M.D.

other medicines they can use.

Also, I'm 52 and going through the menopause. I'm somewhat overweight and trying to lose, as I need surgery for a bladder repair. I have a fibroid

tumor, so the doctor won't give me hormones for my hot flashes. He says it will cause me to bleed badly. Is it true that fibroid tumors sometimes dry up after the change in life? I have been to two doctors, and one says surgery now, the other to wait until I get my weight down.

I see you are really having a time. First, please make every effort to lose weight as it may help relieve your blood pressure and high blood sugar problems. Why don't you try my weight losing diet? It has helped a lot of people to lose weight. Send 50 cents for The Health Letter number 4-7, Weight Losing Diet. Address your letter to me in care of Paddock Publications, Radio City Station, New York, N. Y. 10019.

You are right, some high blood pressure medicines will cause the blood sugar to be high. It is often stated, though, that they merely unmask an underlying diabetic, but you are beginning to get on theoretical ground there. The same types of

medicine can and will cause the loss of potassium. And I would tend to agree that there are other medicines that could be used. The medicine used to eliminate salt and water that causes these problems, though, is very useful in combination with other medicines. The combination usually makes it possible to handle a patient's problem without so much risk of complications from the medicines.

Another problem with glucose toler-

ance tests is that they will give a result similar to that in diabetic if the person has not been eating any carbohydrates recently. Unless the patient is properly prepared for the test, it is of limited usefulness.

Estrogen hormones do enable fibroids to grow. If they are just under the lining of the uterus, hormones may cause you to bleed. And, some fibroids do shrink after the menopause. In general people do better

during and after surgery if they have no weight problems. Nevertheless when it needs to be done surgery can be done in really quite heavy people. I suspect your surgeon thinks he will get a better result if he is able to operate after you have lost weight.

Meanwhile I would suggest making every effort you can to lose weight to try to get out of this combined mess you are confronted with.

(Newspaper Enterprise Assn.)

An offer guaranteed to make you feel warm all over. *FREE*

Figure 14-16. An example of a raw wrap.

The Art of Editing

Weekend garden show attracts 500 visitors

If this masked message at the intersection of Broad and Spring streets in Mankato looks suspiciously like a one-way sign, that's because it is a one-way sign. The sign will remain covered with a bag until noon Sunday, when this bag — and all others along Broad between May and Hickory streets — will be removed and Broad will become a one-way street. Also at noon Sunday, the,

DUBLIN (AP) — The Irish government tonight assumed sweeping powers to intern any citizen because of what it called "a secret armed conspiracy" against the state.

Prime Minister Jack Lynch said in a ,statement that Ireland's police forces had uncovered a plot to kidnap prominent personalities, carry out raids on banks and even attempt murder of leading officials.

He said he was taking Ireland out of the European Human Rights Convention in order to intern suspected citizens without trial.

The prime minister said the government has already ordered establishment, of "places of detention" for the internees.;

"Police authorities have informed the government," the prime minister's state ment said, "that reliable information has come into their possession to the effect that a secret armed conspiracy exists in the country to kidnap one or more prominent persons. Connected with this conspiracy are plans to carry out armed bank previous tries could muster no more than 23 votes to stop the project he has called an environmental monster, an economic ship of fools, and a flying white elephant.

And it was a personal defeat for the President who had mustered his personal, since in common parlance a monument is a testimonial to something, and usually to something good or endearing. A marker, however, is simply just that — calling attention to an event or a site of some historical significance without necessarily judging any philosophical overtones.

THE HANGING of 38 Sioux Indians in Mankato in 1862 remains the greatest single mass execution in U.S. history.

It was an irrefutable happening. It cannot be, should not be, erased from history books even as some persons see positive value for at least eliminating it from both sight and mind.

PLANS ARE TO rotate groups of 25 students who live there for three weeks at a time. The first group has just finished up its stint there in the midst of final repairs to get the formerly vacant house restored to liveable condition.

Mankato State students go to Marshall Junior High as teacher aides under the professional education block arrangement which groups all education courses into one quarter so students can use the time in a variety of field experiences as well as classroom work. This consists primarily of sophomores and juniors going into teaching but does not include student teachers who go out separately.

The arrangement ties in with the MSC School of Education's goal to give students preparing to be teachers experience with a variety of school situations. During the quarter the students also visit other types of schools in southern Minnesota.

Both Marshall Junior High School and Mankato State College benefit through the venture. It gives Marshall teachers some assistance in the classroom while giving Mankato State a convenient way to provide students with inner city school experience, increasingly important in present day education.

AT THE SAME time it gives Marshall Junior High an art gallery. Marshall art teacher Pat Morley had felt students should have a place off the school grounds where they could exhibit and even sell the art works they develop in school. Now the first floor of the three-story house is used for an art gallery while the upper two floors house the Mankato State students.

cerned with the environment than appeals to technological progress, the Senate has dealt a stunning and perhaps fatal setback to the supersonic transport, - the plane President Nixon wants as the flagship of the nation's global jet fleet.

Backers of the SST project, trying to rally from the shock of Thursday's 52-41 vote to kill $290 million in federal SST subsidy money, said they would try to salvage at least part of the program in a House-Senate conference.

The victors, savoring the taste of their 11-vote triumph, say there is little chance the Senate or even the House would now approve a conference report containing any of the $290 million appropriation originally earmarked to continue work on two SST prototypes.

It was a personal victory for Sen. William Proxmire, D-Wis., who in two

sential to the future of the American aviation industry.

The loss was particularly bitter for two powerful Democratic senators—Warren G. Magnuson and Henry M. Jackson—whose home state of Washington is the headquarters of the economically depressed Boeing aircraft company, prime SST contractor.

The vote drew 18 Republicans and a number of Southern conservatives into the anti-SST camp and most observers found only one basic explanation:

An overriding concern with protecting the environment in an atmosphere in which the SST had become, rightly or wrongly, a symbol of unplanned progress and misplaced national priorities.

The debate that preceded the vote was a catalogue of potential environmental, economic and political criticism.

I can speak for most Mankatoans in saying that we are not particular friend or foe of the "Here were hanged 38 Sioux Indians" marker that has stood for decades at Front and Main.

And regularly we are called upon to explain it, if not defend it — like today as the result of a letter from Bob and Marjorie Olson, 1206 S. Elizabeth St., Mount Pleasant, Mich.

THEY WRITE on stationery bearing the emblem of a Madison, Wis. motel:

"Dear Editor:

"Yesterday while traveling through Mankato, we were appalled to see that old monument '38 Indians were hanged here' still stands. At the present time when we are endeavoring to rebuild America, monuments like these are a detriment.

"In our home town, we have 100 Chippewa Indian boys and girls in the public schools. And we are still confronted with reminders of past transgressions as we seek to assimilate and educate this minority group.

"These youth are our friends. We hope they never have the occasion to travel Highway 14 past that stone in Mankato, Minnesota.

"PERHAPS the people who live in the area have become so accustomed to this monument that the inscription says nothing to them. Perhaps a group of citizens or the local government would consider razing the monument.

"As former Minnesotans and fellow Americans, we appeal to you to remove this ignominious reminder of our early history."

Not a 'monument'

I appreciate the Olsons' viewpoint. It is understandable from a passerby, and it is imperative that it is commented on in return since every year our town is observed by a new army of travelers and populated by a large number of new residents.

You will notice, back in the first paragraph, that I revealed myself as something of a semanticist.

I do not know the thinking of those who authorized the marker and placed it. It could very well be, considering the survival mentality of those frontier times, that there was a note of "revenge fulfilled" and "justice served" by our forebears who, incidentally, did not have as we have the perspective of history's hindsights to guide their judgements.

Yes, it might have been regarded as a monument in those days and the decades immediately following just as our generation only 20 years ago believed the Nuremberg trials to be the epitome of justice arrived at in conscience.

I first came to Mankato in 1926.

I'VE NEVER regarded the stone as anything but a marker, even though as a boy I was intrigued by the fact that Indians once habited the vale of tears we call home but was not truly aware how cruelly they were rousted out.

I insist that most other Mankatoans, too, see it not as a monument of boast but as an enigmatic marker to the past.

And we are supported by the opinions of full-blooded Indians of today, who also recognize it as a marker of inglorious but unerasable history that should be permitted to stand. And no splashes of red paint or the cutting edge of a bulldozer, please.

The well-intentioned but uptight, bleeding-heart liberals could make a far better and more persuasive contribution.

They should criticize us instead for having failed miserably to erect suitable monuments of pride — monuments not

The old house is also becoming a community center of sorts. Youngsters from the neighborhood and the school pitched in with Mankato State students to clean up and paint up during the fall quarter. They seem to enjoy coming in to "rap" with the college students. Neighborhood mothers provide cookies for the special events there. Last week an art show and open house officially opened Awareness House. This week Mankato State education professors had a meeting there with Marshall parents to get the parents' view on how teaching could be improved.

Basic repairs such as replacing broken windows were financed by the St. Paul Housing Authority, but the interior of the building was bare at the beginning of the quarter. Neighbors and the Cordoza Furniture store took care of that with the donation of furniture and dishes.

Marshall students are involved in a variety of ways. The industrial arts class has done minor repairs and is going to care for interior maintenance. Home economics girls are planning to make drapes and science class students are going to take care of the yard.

THIS IS ALL part of the original intent that the center be a joint college-school-community cooperative venture.

The experience for Mankato State students is not restricted to the school

Figure 14–17. A wrap from the bottom to the top of a page may confuse the reader.

Fundamentals of Newspaper Design   291

applied to the lead paragraph downward until the column is filled. However, leading is easy to do only when using hot type. Cold type leading is difficult after a paragraph has been set.

Flexibility in Makeup

In planning the makeup of large newspapers, some attention should be given to flexibility of design to accommodate late-breaking news. There are two considerations in planning for a flexible design. The first one is a mechanical consideration. Can one or two stories be replaced without too much effort? Re-making a page is a task that should be accomplished in the shortest amount of time to meet a press deadline. It may be necessary to rejustify as many as six columns of news in order to accommodate a late story. When the story to be replaced is odd-shaped, involving complex wraps, it will take more time to remake than it might if it were simply shaped. The new story may not be as long as the one it replaces, or it may be longer. Therefore, planning must be geared to making the design simple and flexible enough for any contingency.

A second consideration is the effect that a major story change will have on total page design. Although it is impossible to know how a late-breaking story will be shaped, it may be possible to anticipate how various-shaped stories will affect the design. If the original design is simple, chances are that any changes can be adapted easily to the old design without destroying the original appearance.

Traditional Makeup Concepts

Some kinds of newspaper makeup reflect many years of practice. For convenience of identifying these papers they may be called "traditional;" meaning they look the same as newspapers have always looked. Although it is hard to describe traditional makeup specifically because varying designs are used, a number of identifying characteristics can help one know that it is, indeed, a traditional makeup. Following are the main characteristics of traditional makeup:

1. Nameplates are almost always at the very top of the front page. Occasionally, a single story may be placed on top.

2. All important stories also are placed at the top of the front page.

3. Headlines are graded with larger ones tending to be placed at the top.

4. The most important story is usually placed in the upper right corner of the front page. Occasionally, it will be placed in the upper left corner.

5. Datelines almost always have a type rule above and below them on the front page. Sometimes, these are parallel rules, other times they are single line rules.

6. Stories are usually wrapped from the left to the right. Often wraps appear under two- or three-column headlines. However,

The Art of Editing

one of the columns wrapped is usually of unequal length when compared to others. (Stories are rarely squared-off)

7. Most often a large illustration is used alone at the top of the page. When more than one illustration is used, it is often also placed at the top of the page. (Illustrations tend to be neither strongly vertical nor horizontal in shape.)

8. Inside pages often have a picture in the upper left or right corners. Rarely are they buried down in the page.

9. Cut-off rules are often used to separate stories. Column rules are also often used.

10. The entire bottom of the front page tends to be gray in appearance.

11. Formal balance is often used on the front page and the left side often is designed to resemble the right side.

In general then, traditional makeup, consisting of a number of different designs, is recognizable. It does not resemble, in any way, magazine design and makeup, something that more contemporary newspaper designs tend to do.

In recent years, a growing number of editors have actively sought ways of making newspaper page formats more contemporary in appearance. At first there was some resistance to changing makeup designs. After all, readers rarely complained about a newspaper's appearance, and traditional makeup had served newspapers well for many years. Larger newspapers offered the most resistance.

Three Contemporary Makeup Concepts

But the world around newspapers began to change. Architecture, design of cars, tools, clothing and many other articles began to reflect a distinctly contemporary appearance. But by contrast, newspapers appeared old-fashioned. As a result, the number of editors seeking more contemporary designs grew. Furthermore, the new technology of newspaper production also was a motivating factor. As publishers began to adopt many of the new machines, it appeared to be a natural time for them to also make changes in makeup and design.

The pressure for new forms of makeup resulted in at least three new concepts being adopted by many newspapers throughout the country. Interestingly, the first attempts at change were simply modifications of traditional formats. The three concepts are called: Modular, Grid and Total Design.

The oldest of the three ideas is called the modular concept. In this approach stories are arranged in modules. A *module* is a unit or component of a whole (or a page), in which each unit has a specific function. In modular makeup, a single story (or sometimes a group of stories) is placed into a unified group, separate from all other modules or groups on a page (see Figure 14–18). Often the module is enclosed in a boxed rule

Modular Makeup

See page 298.

See page 299.

See page 300.

(Figure 14–19). Sometimes, it may simply be set off from other modules by the generous use of white space on all four sides (Figure 14–20).

There are two major objectives in using modules. The first is that a module clearly separates and features a story inside it. As a result the story cannot easily be missed by the reader. Although a single story may be placed in a module, the technique may be used with a number of stories, say two in one module; or, the entire page may be arranged in modules.

The second major objective of modular makeup is that it is relatively easy to change stories inside it, should a late-breaking story occur, or should there be any reason for replacing a story.

See page 301.

It is relatively easy to implement the modular concept because it can be used with almost any style of makeup. On a page designed in traditional makeup, any story that is boxed with a rule on all four sides is a module (Figure 14–21). These boxes may be placed wherever they look best on a page. Such boxes look best with lighter rules such as hairline, one-, two- or three-point thicknesses, or with a Ben Day rule. One of the principles of making modules look attractive is that of using a generous amount of white space inside boxed rules. A minimum of 12 points should be used, and for even greater attractiveness, 14 to 16 points would be preferable, on all four sides.

One of the requirements for the best use of this technique is that all stories ought to be squared off. By squaring off, a story exists simply as a rectangle that is relatively easy to replace if necessary. When stories are squared off they need not be placed in boxes, and such stories can be positioned almost anywhere on a page. When they are not boxed, they can be set apart from other stories by generous amounts of white space above and below them.

When designing an entire page in modular form, either type rules or white space may be used to separate stories. Column rules, coupled with cut-off rules can be the separating devices

See page 302.

(Figure 14–22). If a newspaper does not use column rules, then white space in columns and above and below stories may be used to separate stories.

The Grid Concept

The grid concept carries the modular idea one step further. Although the modular concept is flexible and can be used with almost any kind of makeup, the grid concept has to stand alone as a single unit. A grid consists of an entire page of modules of varying sizes designed in a distinctly contemporary style. The concept gets its name from the meaning of the term *grid*. A *grid* may be defined as a pattern of intersecting lines forming rectangles of various sizes and shapes. From this definition one can understand why a football field is often called a gridiron. In newspaper design, the grid lines are usually column spaces and/or spaces separating stories.

The intersecting lines of grid makeup are not accidentally designed, in fact, they are highly structured. They are carefully placed to divide a newspaper page into very clean-cut and simple-appearing modules whose whole total effect is contemporary. Stories are usually squared off and designed into either vertical or horizontal shapes. Furthermore, the division of space on a page is usually unequal—never mathematically equal (Figure 14–23). One can never conceive of a grid makeup with *See page 303.* three-column stories on the left, and three-column stories directly opposite on the right-hand side of a page. Most often the page would be divided (from left to right) into two and four columns or one and five columns, but never three and three (Figures 14–24 and 14–25). In the same manner, pages are *See pages 304 and 305.* never divided equally from top to bottom.

The objective of grid makeup is to design pages that take advantage of contemporary artistic principles to give it a "now" look, found in magazines, books, and other printed material, and at the same time, make the entire page more interesting. The makeup man has complete control of how the page will look when he is using grid makeup—his pages never look as if they were accidentally designed. The top of the page is never top heavy as is found in traditional makeup. But story placement is still based on the importance of each story; more important ones get more featured treatment. The main difference, however, between grid and traditional makeup is that although important stories get featured treatment, in grid makeup all other stories also have a good chance of being seen and are not buried or lost to the reader.

Obviously, the grid concept has limitations in that the grid design tends to be somewhat restrictive. Although there are many alternative grid approaches, the makeup man usually has to decide early when dummying a page, in favor of one particular grid pattern to the exclusion of all others (Figure 14–26).

The total design concept is almost identical to the grid concept ***The Total Design*** with one exception: Total design is created specially to dra- ***Concept*** matize the news so that print pages are exciting to look at. On the other hand, a grid design may possibly be not only dull to look at, but even confusing. Dramatization in the total design

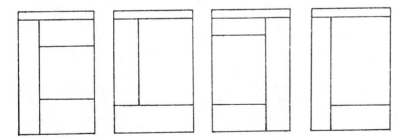

Figure 14-26. Examples of various grid space divisions.

See page 306. concept occurs because the total design of a page must be thought out ahead of time (Figure 14–27).

To implement this concept several principles may serve as guides:

1. A general approach is to create a basic format that serves as a rough model for the entire page. One then attempts to fit the news into that model. To save time, the designer may have prepared a number of different models to serve as guides that fit the day's news (see Figure 14–26). It is obvious that the nature of the news should determine the nature of the format. More spectacular formats are more appropriate for spectacular news. By having an idea book comprising many different basic formats, the designer can study the news and then find one or more that possibly, with some revision, can fit the news.

2. The nature of a basic format is a page divided into broad areas, each of which is pleasingly proportional and the sum of which adds up to an exciting design. The basis for division is the rectangle. There is no need for an odd-shaped story to appear anywhere on the page. Rectangles of different shapes, directions and weights provide the differentiation needed for an attractive total design.

3. No matter which alternative format is used as a guide, it must be simple, dramatic and contemporary. There should be no frills, no artificial devices, no clutter. Like modern architecture, there should be a great deal of open space that allows each story to breathe without severely competing for attention with a story next to it.

4. Any basic format may be changed in any way that best accommodates the news. *In other words, this approach does not ask that the designer simply try to force news into a pre-arranged format.* But the basic format, because it has been well thought out, should be kept in mind at all times while the adjustments are being made.

5. One of the most important features of this approach is a reduction in the usual number of stories that must appear on a page. There are relatively few stories on this kind of page, and because there are so few, more white space is available between the columns, between headlines and pictures and between the lines of type. The generous use of white space, carefully placed, is essential. The white space should not appear in one part of a page when other parts appear black and crowded. It is the white space that helps make the page appear dramatic. The space between columns, for example, should never be less than 14 points wide and perhaps as much as 2 picas wide.

Because fewer stories can be used on such pages, a summary of the news is desirable. Many readers may not be inclined to search the paper for news that formerly appeared on the front page. The summary of news is a convenient way to help the reader know what is going on. Page references for additional details will enable him to read more if he wants to.

6. Another way to achieve a dramatic design is to use large stories and pictures in bold shapes that dominate the page. In addition, the use of large hairline boxes may enhance the stories and pictures inside.

7. Most of the news matter may be set to the paper's standard column widths. However, headlines may have to be written after the designer decides how a given story fits on a page. In other words, he is conscious of the total design as he decides where and how any story will appear on the page.

Obviously not every editor is willing or able to use one of the three preceding concepts. In many newspapers the publisher or editor does not want to lose the recognition value of a format that has been used for twenty or more years. On the other hand, they are willing to allow some "tinkering" with a basic design (along contemporary lines, of course.)

The Mixed Concept

The following two chapters discuss contemporary ideas that could be mixed with traditional elements to modernize page makeup. Perhaps it would be more logical for the editor to adopt completely contemporary makeup using modular, grid or total design approaches. But when some improvement in page makeup is required, the recommendations to be found in the following chapters represent techniques that are usually better than the status quo.

An under-the-weather Shea visits the animal hospital in Evanston with owner Noreen Kainov. It's a costly proposition, but Shea seems appreciative.

Tribune Photos by Guy Bane

The cost of Fido's care

Is pet insurance the best policy?

By Christine Winter

YOUR PET MAY be your best friend when it's bright-eyed and bushy-tailed. But what about when it's literally as sick as a dog and the medical bills start climbing beyond the limits of your budget?

Could you handle an unexpected $300 in veterinary bills—not covered by insurance and not deductible from your income tax—or would you do the merciful thing, as far as your finances are concerned, and put your pet to sleep rather than put out the cash?

Based on studies conducted by his and other insurance firms, the president of a pet health insurance company, which is no longer in operation, estimates that 1 out of 12 pets undergoes surgery in its lifetime and 1 out of 5, hospitalization.

THOUGH VETERINARY fees have not climbed at the same breakneck pace as those in the human health fields, they still have risen high enough for many to consider veterinarians, who are riding the crest of a pet craze and are unencumbered by high malpractice insurance rates, as the medical world's nouveau riche.

Here are some estimates of what you may have to pay should your dog or cat come down with a disease —and they are as susceptible to many of the same diseases as humans—or meet with an accident. Prices vary greatly with the size of the animal and frequently with the neighborhood in which the vet's office is located.

THE NATIONAL average for hospitalization is about $3 a night. It can be as low as $3 or $4 in outlying areas and as high as $12 to $15 in affluent suburbs. Most inoculations in the Chicago area cost between $5 and $10, and spaying a dog can range from $50 to $100 and a cat, from $35 to $40. A routine office visit is often $10 for a general practitioner, $20 for specialist. The cost of suturing usually starts at $10, and X-rays can range from $10 to $12 for a small animal to $20 to $25 for a large one that must be tranquilized.

Surgery without major complications, according to one former insurer, may average $40 to $50, but easily could exceed $100 for a large animal.

And emergency surgery, especially if it involves using pins and plates to set shattered bones [one local vet recalls putting $41 worth of "hardware" into

...Koscialek, shaking his head over two years with Muffin, is confident his dog will beat premium vs. medical expenses insurance odds.

...Grace Davidson's beagle, Andrew, has cost her $100 a year for the last six years in vet expenses due to an allergy.

Pet insurance isn't in Lorraine Bosacki's budget. Still, with Max's allergies and eye problems, she has had to spend about $50 beyond the cost of normal shots.

a large dog] easily can reach several hundred dollars.

Veterinarians explain they must pay the same as regular doctors for lab tests, drugs, and anesthetics.

IS THERE AN alternative for loving but financially strapped pet owners when Rover develops a tumor or Fluff steps under a passing car? Other than the Anti-Cruelty Society's one charity clinic in the city, which must limit its services to those most in need, it seems not.

At first glance, it would appear that some form of pet health insurance may be the answer. However, past attempts have always failed, even though most veterinary associations describe the concept as "basically sound." But most also add that they are skeptical of the workability of any such program.

As many as 30 companies or plans have come and gone in past years, and nobody seems to know why the programs "just don't take off."

PART OF THE problem seems to be the difficulty in predicting mortality rates and coming up with actuarial tables for animals, especially mixed breeds.

Dr. Ronald Horning of the Chicago Veterinary Medical Association pinpointed the compressed or short lifespan of dogs and cats as being one of the major problems.

"You just aren't paying premiums over a 70-year life-span the way you do for-humans," he said. "As a result, most of the programs that have come along have simply been too costly for the average person."

"SUPPOSE YOU HAD a dog for 11 years, and it had one serious bout with illness and ran up a $250 veterinary bill," said one local veterinarian. "At the time, of course, you'd wish you had insurance. But most of the policies I've seen run about $25 to $35 a year, and at that rate, you would be better off taking your chances over the 11-year span and paying the one bill."

"But even when plans with fairly low premiums have come along, the indication has been that the public is simply not interested," said Don Mahan, executive director of the Southern California Veterinary Medical Association. "Pet health insurance just hasn't found a market.

"One plan that was tested in California and is very similar to a program that is successful in England sold less than $1,000 worth of policies in the first year,

though it had the cooperation of the state veterinary association," he said.

ON THE WHOLE, local pet owners, interviewed at an animal hospital in Evanston and whose experiences and expenses with their animals have varied widely, don't look on pet health insurance as a panacea, though a few see possibilities in the concept.

Lorraine Bosacki, owner of two large dogs, admits she has run into only about $50 worth of expenses beyond the cost of normal shots with her animals, mostly on allergies and eye problems.

"I'd really have to think about any type of pet insurance program. Over the years I haven't had that much trouble, although a neighbor spent $200 when her dog fractured its leg. But I think it's a chance you take."

Noreen Kainov also sees it as pretty much of a gamble; her young dog has needed only routine shots and spaying, procedures that wouldn't be covered under most policies.

CANDY WILLHITE, the owner of four dogs, has experienced some of the expense of sick animals, having financed two hip operations, the most recent of which cost between $150 and $200. But she still sees insurance as too expensive over the long run, especially for a number of animals.

"If the premiums were minimal, I might think about it; but I'm just not enthused," she said.

S. W. Koscielak agreed, because he feels that Muffin, his dog, would probably beat the insurance odds. In two years, he was making his first trip to a vet for his dog's minor illness.

"That would have been two years of paying, and I'd rather just take my chances," he said.

But there are those who think the idea might have merit if it could be worked out by a reliable insurance company they could trust.

GRACE DAVIDSON'S beagle, Andrew, has cost her at least $100 a year for the last six years because of an allergy.

"I think that an insurance policy would have been worthwhile for us over the years," she said, but added she would never consider putting Andrew to sleep.

Continued on following page

Continued on following page

Furs will go far with the proper treatment

By Marylin Stitz

LIKE A BABY, a fur needs tender loving care. Whether you own a mink coat, silver fox chubbie, or a mouton jacket, you must take care of it. And if you baby it properly, you can lengthen a fur's life several years.

Max Alper, owner of Alper-Richman Furs, Ltd., offers a few fur-saving pointers.

WEARING A FUR:
● Wear it gently; avoid stress and strain on seams and edges. When sitting, relax the fur around your shoulders and body. Try not to sit on it any longer than necessary.
● Don't carry packages or handbags under your arm; this will break the hairs and wear out one section prematurely.
● Always wear a neck scarf to protect against friction and prevent damage from oil and makeup.

DAILY STORAGE:
● Keep your garment on a long-necked, padded hanger with the collar standing up, cuffs rolled down. Also, make certain the closet is away from the incinerator or hot water pipes. Heat dries out the natural fats and oils.
● Allow plenty of room for the fur; don't crush it against other garments. Never, never cover a fur, even in a garment bag; it needs to breathe.

EXPOSURE TO WEATHER:
● Rain and snow can be damaging. When you get home, shake off excess water and brush lightly along the grain. Then let it dry, naturally, in a cool, dry room. Don't hang it near a fire or radiator.
● If water has soaked through to the leather underneath, take the garment immediately to your furrier for treatment.

CLEANING AND LONG-TERM STORAGE:
● Never use fabric spot removers. Always take a fur to your furrier for cleaning or repairs. Most repairs can be made at minimal cost.
● Dust, dirt, and grime are a menace. Furs should be cleaned and glazed at least once a season. Some women think air-conditioning or cedar closets provide adequate

Continued on following page

Continued on following page

Only a rare woman would object to pampering a Natural Canadian Fisher coat, for $10,500. York Furriers.

Tribune Photos by David Nystrom

Care will bring long wear from this Norwegian blue fox jacket. From Traeger-Bolon Furs.

PEANUTS — I JUST CALLED THE OLYMPIC COMMITTEE. / YOU CAN'T COMPETE IN THE OLYMPICS BECAUSE YOU HAVE NONE OF THE NECESSARY QUALIFICATIONS. / I'M CUTE!!

Monday in Tempo

Joanne Alter, the first woman Democrat ever elected to serve as a commissioner of the Metropolitan Sanitary District, lost Mayor Daley's blessing when she decided to try for the party's nomination as lieutenant governor of Illinois. Still, she plans to win, she says in a conversation with Margaret Carroll in Monday's Tempo.

Smile

It's amazing how they can squeeze a 200-pound tuna into one of those little cans.

298

Figure 14–18. (Pet insurance story) An example of a module not boxed. [*Courtesy Chicago Tribune.*]

Sports

Bengals reserving judgment on latest NFL owners' offer

BY BOB QUEENAN

Most of the Cincinnati Bengals players reserved judgment yesterday on the latest proposal by the National Football League Management Council.

But you get the feeling from talking to veteran members of the team that they generally approve of this latest offer.

Here's a sampling of what the Bengals think of the proposal made public on Monday and distributed to the players by offensive captain Bob Johnson yesterday.

RON CARPENTER — "I want to study the full proposal, but if they've made the economic and pension benefits I've heard about, I'd be in favor of it. I'm not too hung up on the freedom issues and I just hope to get it settled. I had a speaking engagement last night and that was the No. 1 topic. The fans all talk about the money we're making and the high ticket prices."

AL BEAUCHAMP — "They've got some good things in there. I'm anxious to get it settled so it relieves speculation what might happen or what won't."

JOHN REAVES—"It gets my vote of approval. It looks good to me. I thought it was a very generous offer. I'd like to get it cleared up so we concentrate on winning football games. Then too, I think the fans are tired of it. If it keeps up, they'll stop showing up at ball games." There were more than 2000 "no shows" last Sunday.

KEN ANDERSON — "I've only read about it in the paper, and I want to wait and read it in detail. I did have a favorable first impression from what I've read and I'd like to get it out of the way."

JIM LECLAIR—"It sounds pretty good from what little I've seen."

RUFUS MAYES — "At least they've made some other offer and the Players Assn. came off its stance and is listening. "I'm sorry it had to come a year-and-a-half late. I'd have to tear (break) it down and study it, but on the surface it looks okay. I try to put it out of my mind, but it comes back and haunts. There's too much at stake. But I feel good about this."

RON PRITCHARD — "I think it's good, fine and what I see, I'd approve of."

BOB JOHNSON—"I don't want to comment now. I'd prefer to wait and see what everybody says after they've seen the proposal. And from what I understand, the offer is still negotiable to a point and they're (NFL Management Council and Players Assn. representatives) still talking about it. It definitely shortens training camp by a week."

CHIP MYERS — "I'm really indifferent to it. I've almost given up on the players trying to use logic. It's so irrational. I see what Boston did in trying to bring people together. But some of the leaders don't want logic. We've voiced our opinion and it wasn't even considered. I want to forget about it and just get ready for the next football game. Making the playoffs is more important than the freedom issues. I don't believe the freedom issues have helped or hurt two per cent either way. We don't want this to be like basketball. We've got to restore the confidence of the people."

PAUL BROWN—"It's a costly thing to management, but if it will solve this impasse I'm for it. We've taken our best shot. This goes beyond what a lot of people can handle (financially). I was just hoping it would involve the exhibition season and the scheduling, but it didn't."

Players to vote Monday

CHICAGO (UPI)—National Football League players will vote on a contract proposal it was announced yesterday after negotiations between management and player representatives collapsed in an amicable stalemate.

Player representatives, charging that management changed its position "very little" in two days of negotiations, decided to submit the contract proposal Monday for a vote of the membership.

KERMIT ALEXANDER, president of the association, said the negotiating committee "has a position, but we're going to wait to allow our members to understand what's going on."

"I thought if we could not reach an agreement, we could agree to submit the offer to binding arbitration," said Ed Garvey, executive director of the players association. "It (arbitration) was rejected. We offered to submit it to impartial fact fining and it was rejected. We finally offered to let (Commissioner Pete) Rozelle make recommendations which both sides would consider and that was rejected. We found we could not reach agreement."

SARGE KARCH, the chief management negotiator, said "we believe that the proposal is a very attractive one, particularly economically. It offers a great deal of money and we don't see how the players could turn it down.

"We told the players that this was our best shot, and if we could add one thing, what we called plus one, that would get the approval of this group, to tell us what it was. Give us a plus one.

"They came back with the same seven points that have kept us apart for the last 18 months."

If the contract is rejected, Karch said, "We're right back where we were, back to bargaining. They have the right to take collective action. They have the right to strike, and we have the right to go about our business. We have every hope that it will be approved."

ALEXANDER SAID that any chance of a strike would depend, too, upon "what the players decide."

"We're making proposals," one of the player negotiators, Dick Anderson of the Miami Dolphins, said during a break, "and they go out and then come back in a little while and say no."

"It's my gut feeling that it will be rejected," Chicago Bears' player rep Bobby Douglass said.

Anderson pointed out that while the owners claimed there was considerable improvement in the pension proposal, there was no provision for cost of living increase and that the players could not get a pension until the age of 55 or 65. "We have to wait 25 or 30 years for it," he said.

Lawrenceburg track schedules awards night

Lawrenceburg Speedway will hold its 1975 Awards Banquet Nov. 15 at Scarlato's, 9th and Plum streets, Cincinnati.

The dinner will be limited to the first 100 couples buying tickets in advance. No tickets will be sold at the door. Contact Carroll or JoAnne Hamilton, 11459 Gravenhurst drive, Cincinnati.

Bearcats sign 6-8 Aussie cager

BY BARRY COBB

The University of Cincinnati already is reaping benefits from its basketball trip to Australia last summer.

UC announced today that Jerry Doyle, a 6-8 lefthanded shooter from Melbourne, Australia, has signed a basketball grant-in-aid with the Bearcats.

Doyle, who will be 22 years old Nov. 17, arrived in Cincinnati on Monday and will start classes as a freshman at UC next week.

THE BEARCATS met Doyle during their summer trip but didn't play any games against his AAU-style team.

"A friend of mine had written to me about him and we saw him when we were there," explained UC assistant basketball coach Jim Mitchell, who watched Doyle work out.

"He's got enough size at 6-8 and we feel his potential is very great. The training facilities are very limited over there and he thought he'd improve a great deal if he came over here.

"He has a lot of natural quickness," Mitchell added. "He weighs about 200 now but we feel he can go to 220 or 225. His size made us very interested in him plus the Olympic coach over there was very high on him."

DOYLE IS NO stranger to American basketball. As a teenager he played with an Australian team which made a basketball tour of the United States for 18-and-under-age players.

"A lot of people who knew his background were very high on him," said Mitchell. "He's a mechanical type player now and it will take a while for him to get adjusted to our terminology. It's not going to be an overnight miracle. But we felt his size was something we were willing to take a chance on."

Last January Doyle helped Australia win the New Zealand Games Tournament, averaging 11.2 points a game.

ACCORDING TO Mitchell, persuading Doyle to come to Cincinnati to play basketball with the Bearcats was an easy matter.

"He was really interested in getting an American education," Mitchell said, "plus a chance to play on an American team."

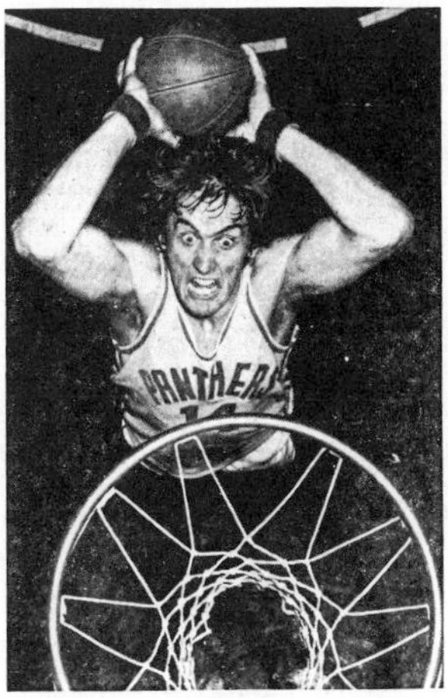

JERRY DOYLE

Gale Catlett, the Bearcats' head coach, has yet to see what Doyle can do on the hardwood.

"I've never seen him play," Catlett said, "but it's a chance to help a young man get an education. Ask me Dec. 1 and I'll tell you how good he is after we've had him six weeks."

The Bearcats open practice Oct. 15 and play their first game Nov. 20 with Athletes in Action.

NCAA RULES prevent schools from providing transportation costs for athletes to and from school so Doyle was forced to pay his own way to Cincinnati.

Two-way air fare between Cincinnati and Australia is $1771.68. Before arriving here Doyle stopped to visit friends on the West Coast.

Doyle, who is single, will live in a campus dormitory. He will be enrolled in a basic freshman course, Mitchell said, with possible emphasis on architecture or art courses.

In Australia, Doyle had been playing AAU-style basketball. His scholarship was a regular NCAA approved grant-in-aid and required a 2.0 high school grade average for enrollment at UC.

Norman hurls 4-hitter as Reds top Astros 5-3

BY EARL LAWSON

HOUSTON—A guy never likes to see his own team lose. Still, Roger Craig had to experience a touch of self-satisfaction last night as he watched Fredie Norman pitch the Reds to a 5-3 victory over the Houston Astros.

Craig, pitching coach for the Astros these days, was Norman's manager when Fredie was pitching for the Los Angeles Dodgers' Albuquerque, N.M., farm club back in 1968.

Norman was recuperating from a sore arm in those days. And, it was Craig, by Fredie's self admission, who taught him to be a pitcher instead of a thrower.

THE FACT THAT Norman pitching for the Dodgers' Spokane, Wash., farm club the following year, complied a 13-6 won-and-lost mark, accompanied by a 2.62 earned run average, tells you just how good a teacher Craig was.

So does the four-hitter Norman pitched last night as he won his 10th victory in his last 11 decisions and his 12th of the season against only four defeats.

Home runs by Cliff Johnson and Larry Milbourne, the latter's coming with a runner aboard in the third inning, accounted for the Astros' three runs off Norman.

The home run by Johnson is excusable. He's a big, strong free swinger who's capable of hitting good pitches out of the park.

NOT EXCUSABLE, though, was the homer by Milbourne, his first of the season. Because, as Red manager Sparky Anderson undoubtedly told Norman there's no way Milbourne should have gotten a fast ball to hit in that particular situation.

The home run pitch to Milbourne was the only bad one made by Norman, whose control was practically flawless.

Usually Norman does a little too much nibbling at the plate. He takes hitters to the full count enough times to make Red manager Sparky Anderson more than a little jittery.

Such, though, wasn't the case last night. In fact, Norman didn't walk a batter and struck out four before giving way to Rawly Eastwick in the ninth inning.

FREDIE DIDN'T depart because he was tiring. It's just that Anderson saw a chance to give Eastwick another save and didn't want to pass up the opportunity.

That's Sparky. He wants to see his players win as many titles as possible. And Eastwick, who now has 21 saves, has a chance to beat out the Cardinals' ace relief hurler Al Hrabosky for the league lead.

The Reds, in racking up their 104th victory of the season, putting them 50 games over the .500 mark, tagged lefty Mike Cosgrove with the loss.

Three of the Reds' runs came in the second inning. Singles by Plummer, Cesar Geronimo and Ken Griffey accounted for the first run. Pete Rose singled home the other two.

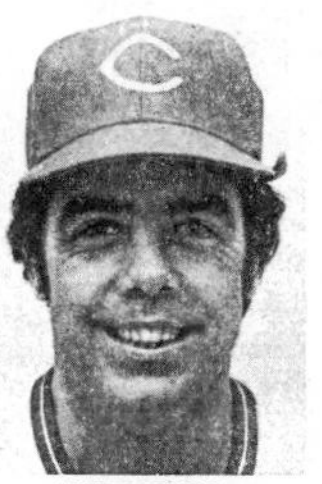

FREDIE NORMAN

JOE MORGAN'S infield hit and Tony Perez's double to right center gave the Reds a fourth run in the third inning. The fifth and final run came in the eighth when Griffey doubled for his third hit, stole third and scored on Geronimo's infield out.

Norman will have one more tuneup before he goes against the Pirates in the second game of the playoffs. That'll come Sunday when the Reds wind up the regular season against the Atlanta Braves at Riverfront Stadium.

Norman readily admits that he's flattered that Anderson has selected him to start one of the three playoff games.

After all there aren't many pitchers Norman's size—5-8 and 170-pounds—in the majors.

ONCE NORMAN thought his size was a detriment. Too many managers thought he didn't have the stamina to pitch in a regular starting rotation.

In fact, Fredie can remember only twice when he opened a season in the regular starting rotation of a major league club.

The first time was 1972 at San Diego. But then as Norman will admit, the competition that season wasn't the greatest since the Padres were an expansion club only four-years-old.

Even after Norman notched a 12-6 record after his mid-season acquisition from the Padres in 1973, Anderson still was not convinced Fredie was for real. It's why Norman opened the 1974 season in the bullpen.

NOW, THOUGH, Anderson will tell you he's convinced the Reds would have beaten out the Dodgers for the division title last year if Norman had opened the season as a starter.

Sparky has a point. Because once Norman was thrown into the rotation last year he won eight of 10 decisions and compiled a 1.91 earned run average before he pulled a muscle in his rib cage.

Right now opposing batters are seeing the same Norman they faced before his injury of last year. And, it's the reason the Pirates will be seeing Fredie in that second game of the playoffs.

Coach 'no part' of Issel trade

LOUISVILLE, KY. (UPI)—Coach Hubie Brown said yesterday he wanted to make it clear he had nothing to do with the Kentucky Colonels' trade of Dan Issel to the Baltimore Claws, a transaction of the veteran forward still refuses to accept.

"I'd like to make it clear that none of us on the coaching staff had anything to do with the trade of Dan Issel," the Kentucky coach said in an interview at the opening of the ABA championship team's fall training camp. "The trade was completely done by John Y. Brown (husband of the club's majority owner)."

Issel was dealt Friday to Baltimore's new ABA club for center-forward Tom Owens, a reported $700,000, and undisclosed "future considerations."

Issel so far has refused to report to Baltimore, claiming he had a no-trade clause in his contract. Owens also has not reported.

OWENS PLAYED LAST year for the Memphis Sounds, whose franchise was moved to Baltimore. Owens and his attorney, Art Morse of Chicago, claim Memphis has breached his contract, leaving him free to make his own deal. He has made a deal to play with Houston at a high salary.

Hubie Brown said he has known Owens since Owens was a sophomore in high school. But, said Hubie, "I would not ask a player to come here just on a friendship basis, especially a fellow who would get $75,000 less than he can make in Houston."

Figure 14–19. (Bearcats) Module in a box. [*Courtesy Cincinnati Post.*]

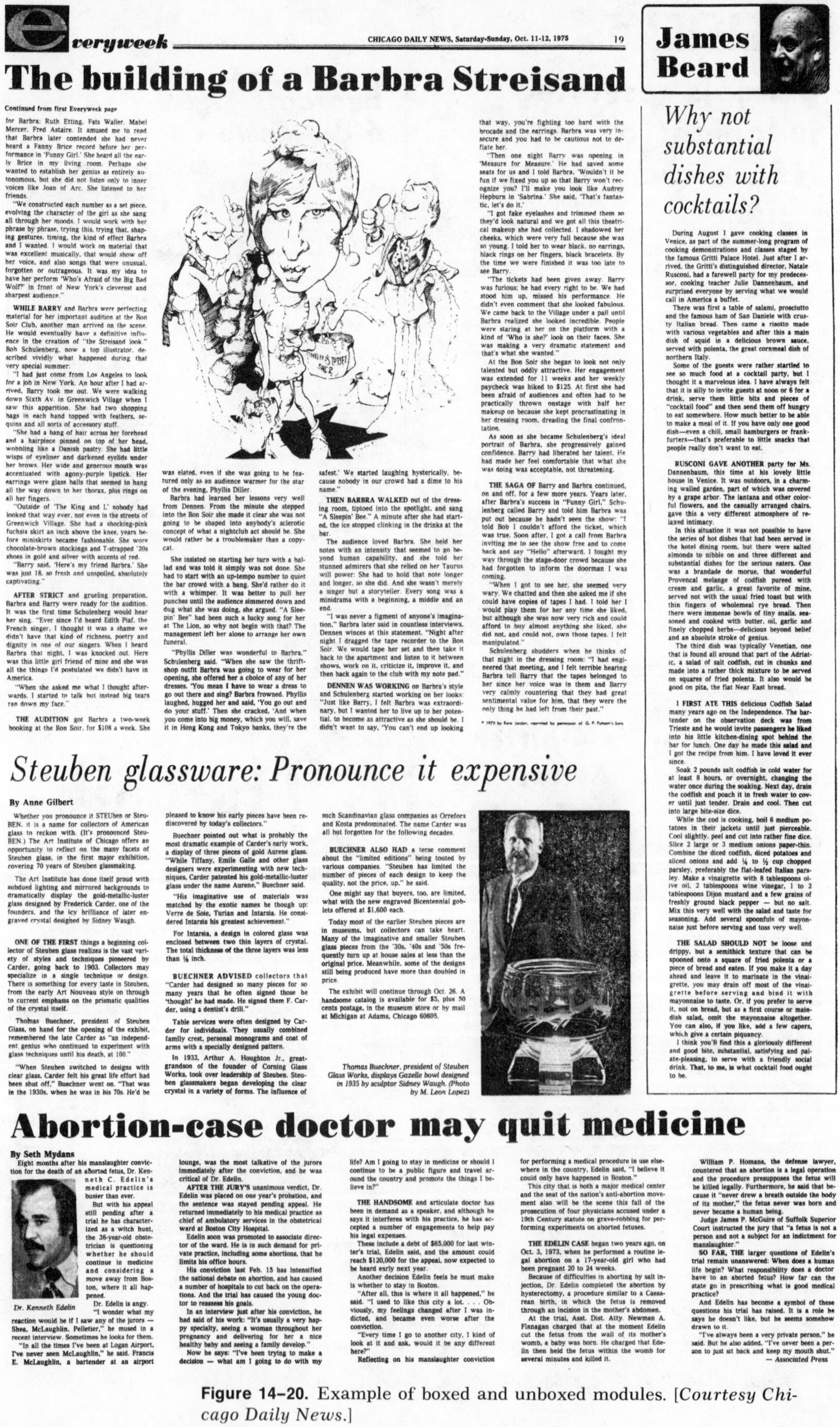

everyweek — CHICAGO DAILY NEWS, Saturday-Sunday, Oct. 11-12, 1975 — 19

The building of a Barbra Streisand

Continued from first Everyweek page

for Barbra: Ruth Etting, Fats Waller, Mabel Mercer, Fred Astaire. It amused me to read that Barbra later contended she had never heard a Fanny Brice record before her performance in 'Funny Girl.' She heard all the early Brice in my living room. Perhaps she wanted to establish her genius as entirely autonomous, but she did not listen only to inner voices like Joan of Arc. She listened to her friends.

"We constructed each number as a set piece, evolving the character of the girl as she sang all through her moods. I would work with her phrase by phrase, trying this, trying that, shaping gestures, timing, the kind of effect Barbra and I wanted. I would work on material that was excellent musically, that would show off her voice, and also songs that were unusual, forgotten or outrageous. It was my idea to have her perform 'Who's Afraid of the Big Bad Wolf?' in front of New York's cleverest and sharpest audience."

WHILE BARRY and Barbra were perfecting material for her important audition at the Bon Soir Club, another man arrived on the scene. He would eventually have a definitive influence in the creation of "the Streisand look." Bob Schulenberg, now a top illustrator, described vividly what happened during that very special summer:

"I had just come from Los Angeles to look for a job in New York. An hour after I had arrived, Barry took me out. We were walking down Sixth Av. in Greenwich Village when I saw this apparition. She had two shopping bags in each hand topped with feathers, sequins and all sorts of accessory stuff.

"She had a bang of hair across her forehead and a hairpiece pinned on top of her head, wobbling like a Danish pastry. She had little wisps of eyeliner and darkened eyelids under her brows. Her wide and generous mouth was accentuated with agony-purple lipstick. Her earrings were glass balls that seemed to hang all the way down to her thorax, plus rings on all her fingers.

"Outside of 'The King and I,' nobody had looked that way ever, not even in the streets of Greenwich Village. She had a shocking-pink fuchsia skirt an inch above the knee, years before miniskirts became fashionable. She wore chocolate-brown stockings and T-strapped '20s shoes in gold and silver with accents of red.

"Barry said, 'Here's my friend Barbra.' She was just 18, so fresh and unspoiled, absolutely captivating."

AFTER STRICT and grueling preparation, Barbra and Barry were ready for the audition. It was the first time Schulenberg would hear her sing. "Ever since I'd heard Edith Piaf, the French singer, I thought it was a shame we didn't have that kind of richness, poetry and dignity in one of our singers. When I heard Barbra that night, I was knocked out. Here was this little girl friend of mine and she was all the things I'd postulated we didn't have in America.

"When she asked me what I thought afterwards, I started to talk but instead big tears ran down my face."

THE AUDITION got Barbra a two-week booking at the Bon Soir, for $108 a week. She was elated, even if she was going to be featured only as an audience warmer for the star of the evening, Phyllis Diller.

Barbra had learned her lessons very well from Dennen. From the minute she stepped into the Bon Soir she made it clear she was not going to be shaped into anybody's sclerotic concept of what a nightclub act should be. She would rather be a troublemaker than a copycat.

She insisted on starting her turn with a ballad and was told it simply was not done. She had to start with an up-tempo number to quiet the bar crowd with a bang. She'd rather do it with a whimper. It was better to pull her punches until the audience simmered down and dug what she was doing, she argued. "A Sleepin' Bee" had been such a lucky song for her at The Lion, so why not begin with that? The management left her alone to arrange her own funeral.

"Phyllis Diller was wonderful to Barbra," Schulenberg said. "When she saw the thrift-shop outfit Barbra was going to wear for her opening, she offered her a choice of any of her dresses. 'You mean I have to wear a dress to go out there and sing? Barbra frowned. Phyllis laughed, hugged her and said, 'You go out and do your stuff.' Then she cracked, 'And when you come into big money, which you will, save it in Hong Kong and Tokyo banks, they're the safest.' We started laughing hysterically, because nobody in our crowd had a dime to his name."

THEN BARBRA WALKED out of the dressing room, tiptoed into the spotlight, and sang "A Sleepin' Bee." A minute after she had started, the ice stopped clinking in the drinks at the bar.

The audience loved Barbra. She held her notes with an intensity that seemed to go beyond human capability, and she told her stunned admirers that she relied on her Taurus will power: She had to hold that note longer and longer, so she did. And she wasn't merely a singer but a storyteller. Every song was a minidrama with a beginning, a middle and an end.

"I was never a figment of anyone's imagination," Barbra later said in countless interviews. Dennen winces at this statement. "Night after night I dragged the tape recorder to the Bon Soir. We would tape her set and then take it back to the apartment and listen to it between shows, work on it, criticize it, improve it, and then back again to the club with my note pad."

DENNEN WAS WORKING on Barbra's style and Schulenberg started working on her looks: "Just like Barry, I felt Barbra was extraordinary, but I wanted her to live up to her potential, to become as attractive as she should be. I didn't want to say, 'You can't end up looking that way, you're fighting too hard with the brocade and the earrings. Barbra was very insecure and you had to be cautious not to deflate her.

"Then one night Barry was opening in 'Measure for Measure.' He had saved some seats for us and I told Barbra, 'Wouldn't it be fun if we fixed you up so that Barry won't recognize you? I'll make you look like Audrey Hepburn in 'Sabrina.' She said, 'That's fantastic, let's do it.'

"I got fake eyelashes and trimmed them so they'd look natural and we got all this theatrical makeup she had collected. I shadowed her cheeks, which were very full because she was so young. I told her to wear black, no earrings, black rings on her fingers, black bracelets. By the time we were finished it was too late to see Barry.

"The tickets had been given away. Barry was furious; he had every right to be. We had stood him up, missed his performance. He didn't even comment that she looked fabulous. We came back to the Village under a pall until Barbra realized she looked incredible. People were staring at her on the platform with a kind of 'Who is she?' look on their faces. She was making a very dramatic statement and that's what she wanted."

At the Bon Soir she began to look not only talented but oddly attractive. Her engagement was extended for 11 weeks and her weekly paycheck was hiked to $125. At first she had been afraid of audiences and often had to be practically thrown onstage with half her makeup on because she kept procrastinating in her dressing room, dreading the final confrontation.

As soon as she became Schulenberg's ideal portrait of Barbra, she progressively gained confidence. Barry had liberated her talent. He had made her feel comfortable that what she was doing was acceptable, not threatening.

THE SAGA OF Barry and Barbra continued, on and off, for a few more years. Years later, after Barbra's success in "Funny Girl," Schulenberg called Barry and told him Barbra was put out because he hadn't seen the show: "I told Bob I couldn't afford the ticket, which was true. Soon after, I got a call from Barbra inviting me to see the show free and to come back and say "Hello" afterward. I fought my way through the stage-door crowd because she had forgotten to inform the doorman I was coming.

"When I got to see her, she seemed very wary. We chatted and then she asked me if she could have copies of tapes I had. I told her I would play them for her any time she liked, but although she was now very rich and could afford to buy almost anything she liked, she did not, and could not, own those tapes. I felt manipulated."

Schulenberg shudders when he thinks of that night in the dressing room: "I had engineered that meeting, and I felt terrible hearing Barbra tell Barry that the tapes belonged to her since her voice was in them and Barry very calmly countering that they had great sentimental value for him, that they were the only thing he had left from their past."

© 1975 by Rene Jordan, reprinted by permission of G. P. Putnam's Sons

James Beard

Why not substantial dishes with cocktails?

During August I gave cooking classes in Venice, as part of the summer-long program of cooking demonstrations and classes staged by the famous Gritti Palace Hotel. Just after I arrived, the Gritti's distinguished director, Natale Rusconi, had a farewell party for my predecessor, cooking teacher Julie Dannenbaum, and surprised everyone by serving what we would call in America a buffet.

There was first a table of salami, prosciutto and the famous ham of San Daniele with crusty Italian bread. Then came a risotto made with various vegetables and after this a main dish of squid in a delicious brown sauce, served with polenta, the great cornmeal dish of northern Italy.

Some of the guests were rather startled to see so much food at a cocktail party, but I thought it a marvelous idea. I have always felt that it is silly to invite guests at noon or 6 for a drink, serve them little bits and pieces of "cocktail food" and then send them off hungry to eat somewhere. How much better to be able to make a meal of it. If you have only one good dish—even a chili, small hamburgers or frankfurters—that's preferable to little snacks that people really don't want to eat.

RUSCONI GAVE ANOTHER party for Ms. Dannenbaum, this time at his lovely little house in Venice. It was outdoors, in a charming walled garden, part of which was covered by a grape arbor. The lantana and other colorful flowers, and the casually arranged chairs, gave this a very different atmosphere of relaxed intimacy.

In this situation it was not possible to have the series of hot dishes that had been served in the hotel dining room, but there were salted almonds to nibble on and three different and substantial dishes for the serious eaters. One was a brandade de morue, that wonderful Provencal melange of codfish pureed with cream and garlic, a great favorite of mine, served not with the usual fried toast but with thin fingers of wholemeal rye bread. Then there were immense bowls of tiny snails, seasoned and cooked with butter, oil, garlic and finely chopped herbs—delicious beyond belief and an absolute stroke of genius.

The third dish was typically Venetian, one that is found all around that part of the Adriatic, a salad of salt codfish, cut in chunks and made into a rather thick mixture to be served on squares of fried polenta. It also would be good on pita, the flat Near East bread.

I FIRST ATE THIS delicious Codfish Salad many years ago on the Independence. The bartender on the observation deck was from Trieste and he would invite passengers he liked into his little kitchen-dining spot behind the bar for lunch. One day he made this salad and I got the recipe from him. I have loved it ever since.

Soak 2 pounds salt codfish in cold water for at least 8 hours, or overnight, changing the water once during the soaking. Next day, drain the codfish and poach it in fresh water to cover until just tender. Drain and cool. Then cut into large bite-size dice.

While the cod is cooking, boil 6 medium potatoes in their jackets until just pierceable. Cool slightly, peel and cut into rather fine dice. Slice 2 large or 3 medium onions paper-thin. Combine the diced codfish, diced potatoes and sliced onions and add ¼ to ½ cup chopped parsley, preferably the flat-leafed Italian parsley. Make a vinaigrette with 8 tablespoons olive oil, 2 tablespoons wine vinegar, 1 to 2 tablespoons Dijon mustard and a few grains of freshly ground black pepper — but no salt. Mix this very well with the salad and taste for seasoning. Add several spoonfuls of mayonnaise just before serving and toss very well.

THE SALAD SHOULD NOT be loose and drippy, but a semithick texture that can be spooned onto a square of fried polenta or a piece of bread and eaten. If you make it a day ahead and leave it to marinate in the vinaigrette, you may drain off most of the vinaigrette before serving and bind it with mayonnaise to taste. Or, if you prefer to serve it, not on bread, but as a first course or main-dish salad, omit the mayonnaise altogether. You can also, if you like, add a few capers, which give a certain piquancy.

I think you'll find this a gloriously different and good bite, substantial, satisfying and palate-pleasing, to serve with a friendly social drink. That, to me, is what cocktail food ought to be.

Steuben glassware: Pronounce it expensive

By Anne Gilbert

Whether you pronounce it STEUben or SteuBEN, it is a name for collectors of American glass to reckon with. (It's pronounced SteuBEN.) The Art Institute of Chicago offers an opportunity to reflect on the many facets of Steuben glass, in the first major exhibition, covering 70 years of Steuben glassmaking.

The Art Institute has done itself proud with subdued lighting and mirrored backgrounds to dramatically display the gold-metallic-luster glass designed by Frederick Carder, one of the founders, and the icy brilliance of later engraved crystal designed by Sidney Waugh.

ONE OF THE FIRST things a beginning collector of Steuben glass realizes is the vast variety of styles and techniques pioneered by Carder, going back to 1903. Collectors may specialize in a single technique or design. There is something for every taste in Steuben, from the early Art Nouveau style on through to current emphasis on the prismatic qualities of the crystal itself.

Thomas Buechner, president of Steuben Glass, on hand for the opening of the exhibit, remembered the late Carder as "an independent genius who continued to experiment with glass techniques until his death, at 100."

"When Steuben switched to designs with clear glass, Carder felt his great life effort had been shut off," Buechner went on. "That was in the 1930s, when he was in his 70s. He'd be pleased to know his early pieces have been rediscovered by today's collectors."

Buechner pointed out what is probably the most dramatic example of Carder's early work, a display of three pieces of gold Aurene glass. "While Tiffany, Emile Galle and other glass designers were experimenting with new techniques, Carder patented his gold-metallic-luster glass under the name Aurene," Buechner said.

"His imaginative use of materials was matched by the exotic names he though up: Verre de Soie, Turian and Intarsia. He considered Intarsia his greatest achievement."

For Intarsia, a design in colored glass was enclosed between two thin layers of crystal. The total thickness of the three layers was less than ⅛ inch.

BUECHNER ADVISED collectors that "Carder had designed so many pieces for so many years that he often signed those he 'thought' he had made. He signed them F. Carder, using a dentist's drill."

Table services were often designed by Carder for individuals. They usually combined family crest, personal monograms and coat of arms with a specially designed pattern.

In 1933, Arthur A. Houghton Jr., great-grandson of the founder of Corning Glass Works, took over leadership of Steuben. Steuben glassmakers began developing the clear crystal in a variety of forms. The influence of such Scandinavian glass companies as Orrefors and Kosta predominated. The name Carder was all but forgotten for the following decades.

BUECHNER ALSO HAD a terse comment about the "limited editions" being touted by various companies. "Steuben has limited the number of pieces of each design to keep the quality, not the price, up," he said.

One might say that buyers, too, are limited, what with the new engraved Bicentennial goblets offered at $1,600 each.

Today most of the earlier Steuben pieces are in museums, but collectors can take heart. Many of the imaginative and smaller Steuben glass pieces from the '30s, '40s and '50s frequently turn up at house sales at less than the original price. Meanwhile, some of the designs still being produced have more than doubled in price.

The exhibit will continue through Oct. 26. A handsome catalog is available for $5, plus 50 cents postage, in the museum store or by mail at Michigan at Adams, Chicago 60605.

Thomas Buechner, president of Steuben Glass Works, displays Gazelle bowl designed in 1935 by sculptor Sidney Waugh. (Photo by M. Leon Lopez)

Abortion-case doctor may quit medicine

By Seth Mydans

Eight months after his manslaughter conviction for the death of an aborted fetus, Dr. Kenneth C. Edelin's medical practice is busier than ever.

Dr. Kenneth Edelin

But with his appeal still pending after a trial he has characterized as a witch hunt, the 36-year-old obstetrician is questioning whether he should continue in medicine and considering a move away from Boston, where it all happened.

Dr. Edelin is angy.

"I wonder what my reaction would be if I saw any of the jurors — Shea, McLaughlin, Pelletier," he mused in a recent interview. Sometimes he looks for them.

"In all the times I've been at Logan Airport, I've never seen McLaughlin," he said. Francis E. McLaughlin, a bartender at an airport lounge, was the most talkative of the jurors immediately after the conviction, and he was critical of Dr. Edelin.

AFTER THE JURY'S unanimous verdict, Dr. Edelin was placed on one year's probation, and the sentence was stayed pending appeal. He returned immediately to his medical practice as chief of ambulatory services in the obstetrical ward at Boston City Hospital.

Edelin soon was promoted to associate director of the ward. He is in such demand for private practice, including some abortions, that he limits his office hours.

His conviction last Feb. 15 has intensified the national debate on abortion, and has caused a number of hospitals to cut back on the operations. And the trial has caused the young doctor to reassess his goals.

In an interview just after his conviction, he had said of his work: "It's usually a very happy specialty, seeing a woman throughout her pregnancy and delivering for her a nice healthy baby and seeing a family develop."

Now he says: "I've been trying to make a decision — what am I going to do with my life? Am I going to stay in medicine or should I continue to be a public figure and travel around the country and promote the things I believe in?"

THE HANDSOME and articulate doctor has been in demand as a speaker, and although he says it interferes with his practice, he has accepted a number of engagements to help pay his legal expenses.

These include a debt of $65,000 for last winter's trial, Edelin said, and the amount could reach $120,000 for the appeal, now expected to be heard early next year.

Another decision Edelin feels he must make is whether to stay in Boston.

"After all, this is where it all happened," he said. "I used to like this city a lot. . . . Obviously, my feelings changed after I was indicted, and became even worse after the conviction.

"Every time I go to another city, I kind of look at it and ask, would it be any different here?"

Reflecting on his manslaughter conviction for performing a medical procedure in use elsewhere in the country, Edelin said, "I believe it could only have happened in Boston."

This city that is both a major medical center and the seat of the nation's anti-abortion movement also will be the scene this fall of the prosecution of four physicians accused under a 19th Century statute on grave-robbing for performing experiments on aborted fetuses.

THE EDELIN CASE began two years ago, on Oct. 3, 1973, when he performed a routine legal abortion on a 17-year-old girl who had been pregnant 20 to 24 weeks.

Because of difficulties in aborting by salt injection, Dr. Edelin completed the abortion by hysterectomy, a procedure similar to a Caesarean birth, in which the fetus is removed through an incision in the mother's abdomen.

At the trial, Asst. Dist. Atty. Newman A. Flanagan charged that at the moment Edelin cut the fetus from the wall of its mother's womb, a baby was born. He charged that Edelin then held the fetus within the womb for several minutes and killed it.

William P. Homans, the defense lawyer, countered that an abortion is a legal operation and the procedure presupposes the fetus will be killed legally. Furthermore, he said that because it "never drew a breath outside the body of its mother," the fetus never was born and never became a human being.

Judge James P. McGuire of Suffolk Superior Court instructed the jury that "a fetus is not a person and not a subject for an indictment for manslaughter."

SO FAR, THE larger questions of Edelin's trial remain unanswered: When does a human life begin? What responsibility does a doctor have to an aborted fetus? How far can the state go in prescribing what is good medical practice?

And Edelin has become a symbol of these questions his trial has raised. It is a role he says he doesn't like, but he seems somehow drawn to it.

"I've always been a very private person," he said. But he also added, "I've never been a person to just sit back and keep my mouth shut."

— *Associated Press*

Figure 14–20. Example of boxed and unboxed modules. [*Courtesy Chicago Daily News.*]

Dolphins Block Eagles
Game Coverage — Page 1-C

Reds Even Series
Complete Coverage — Page 1-C

The Philadelphia Inquirer

Historic Philadelphia's Oldest Daily—The Bicentennial Newspaper

Vol. 293, No. 105 © 1975 The Philadelphia Inquirer Monday, October 13, 1975 15 CENTS

Super Sunday

'Interacting,' 325,000 Jam the Parkway

By CHARLES LAYTON
Inquirer Staff Writer

The idea behind Super Swap, a feature of this year's Super Sunday extravaganza, was that you could bring your lest favorite possession down to Benjamin Franklin Parkway and trade it off for somebody else's least favorite possession.

"This is a flower that I got from my ex-boyfriend. It has no more meaning for me," Carol Kuczynski, 20, said of the greenish, bluish, unpleasant-looking plastic plant she had been hauling around for the past two hours.

Try as she might, Carol couldn't unload the thing. She had offered to swap it to various people for a ring, a necklace, a flower pot, a silk bouquet, a macrame set and a teddy bear, but it was just no deal.

It was the same with Carol's cousin, Barbara Kuczynski. "No one wants an incense burner. I even polished it," she said.

And Maxine Wilson, a woman in her 50s, tried in vain to palm off a wooden serving dish cut in the shape of a pig. A present from a sister-in-law.

Even though, as they say on Wall Street, trading was slow, there was much laughter and joking and intermingling, and that was the whole point, anyway.

"The main purpose is to have people interact rather than shuffle along in a daze," one of this years Super Sunday promoters had said.

Interact they did. Two young Philadelphians named Ron Baxter and Tony Griffin broke out a banjo and a guitar at the intersection of 22nd Street and the Parkway. Before long,

(See SUPER on 4-A)

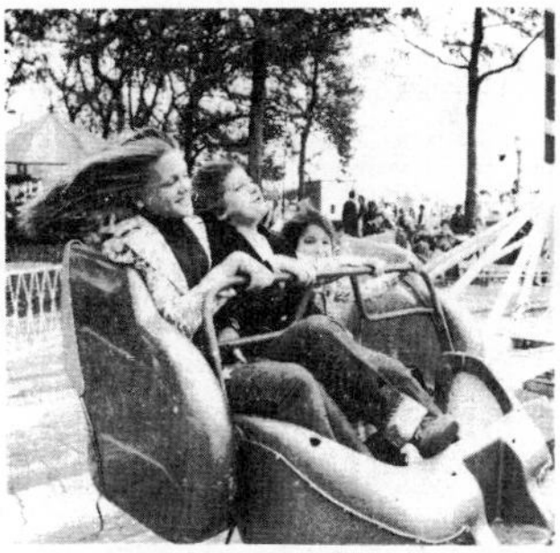

Philadelphia Inquirer / EDWARD J. FREEMAN

A hair-straiightening spin on a whirling ride on the Parkway

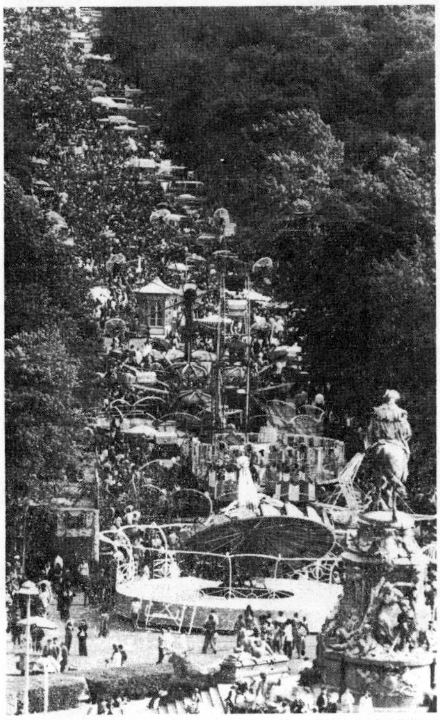

Philadelphia Inquirer / RUSSELL F. SALMON

A super view from the roof of the Art Museum of the crowd jamming the Parkway

Soviet Oil Deal Delayed

Grain Agreement Close: Kissinger

From Inquirer Wire Services

WASHINGTON — Secretary of State Henry A. Kissinger said yesterday that the United States was close to concluding a grain deal with the Soviet Union but that further negotiations were still required before an oil-purchase agreement could be reached.

Kissinger said both issues were being discussed "in a parallel framework," leaving the impression that the Soviet Union would have to make concessions on the sale of oil if it hoped to wrap up a substantial U.S. commitment to sell grain during the next five years.

The original U.S. intention was to conclude the negotiations on the two agreements at the same time. Whether that will be done now, given that the grain talks have moved more rapidly, is not certain. U.S. officials made it clear that the two issues were still inextricably linked.

The United States is trying to get the Soviet Union to sell oil at a discount. One official said that the United States could already buy oil anywhere on the international market.

"American companies are not going to find it particularly attractive to go to a new source, one that is virtually untried, unless there is an incentive," he said. That incentive would be price.

For the United States, a discount would serve to show the major oil exporters that they cannot unilaterally determine price.

On the other hand, the Soviet Union does not want to appear to be undercutting Arab oil producers. However, one official said, price can be calculated in a variety of ways.

Kissinger, appearing on the NBC's

(See KISSINGER on 2-A)

6-Alarm Fire Breaks Out At Refinery

A six-alarm fire broke out last night at the Atlantic-Richfield Refineries at 26th Street and Passyunk Avenues.

The first alarm was sounded at 6:39 p. m. and the others followed by 7:15 p. m.

First reports said that there was heavy smoke coming from the refinery, and that three or four gasoline-storage tanks were involved. No injuries were reported.

Three fireboats were dispatched immediately on the Schuylkill to assist land-based equipment, and firemen on the scene were requesting additional help. Units reporting the fire apparently were having difficulty reaching the scene because of traffic tie-ups in the area.

Traffic was diverted from the 26th Street exit of the Schuylkill Expressway. Penrose and Passyunk avenues were closed to traffic in the area, creating a large traffic jam as crowds headed home from Super Sunday.

'So-So' in Chicago; Father Has No Job

A Refugee Family: Life in America

Another in a Series

By WENDELL RAWLS JR.
Inquirer Staff Writer

CHICAGO — It was 10:30 on a misty morning, and almost everyone in Hoang Trong Bieu's family was busy.

His 5-year-old daughter, Hoang Thi Mong-Ha, was guiding a blue crayon carefully within the lines of a train engine in a coloring book as part of a kindergarten assignment in Room 8 in the basement of Ravenswood School.

Hoang Trong Tuan, 6, Bieu's elder son, was learning to say the word "this" in June Campbell's first-grade class one floor above in Room 15.

Bieu's sister-in-law, Dao Thi Lien, 18, was in class at nearby Amundsen High School. And Bieu's nephew, Hoang Trong Tung, 20, was at work at a glass company, making $3.00 an hour.

Bieu's wife, Duong Thi Mong-Oanh, 30, was in a North Shore suburban Chicago home baby-sitting for $20 a day plus transportation expenses.

Bieu was baby-sitting, too—for his 2-year-old son, Hoang Trong Hai. A month after leaving the Vietnamese refugee camp at Fort Indiantown Gap, Pa., and settling here, Bieu still has not found a job in this city, where the unemployment rate is 10.2 percent.

"My family must make sacrifices because I have no job," Bieu said, his eyes slowly glazing in a rare display of emotion. "If I had a job, everyone in my family would be very happy in Chicago. But right now they are so-so."

Even without an income from Bieu, the family is not forced to struggle economically. The combined wages of Bieu's wife and nephew are almost $200 a week after income taxes, and the family already is able to pay their own rent and utilities and buy food without the aid of their sponsor, Diane and Shevlin Ciral.

"Actually, the family is adjusting to life in Chicago quite well," Mrs. Ciral said. "The children seem to be doing beautifully in school, and Tung and Mong-Oanh are very popular with their employers. We could find a low-paying job for Bieu, but we are trying for a job that pays well."

The Cirals and Bieu thought he had

(See REFUGEES on 2-A)

Priest's Plea Brings Guns to Collection Box

Associated Press

COLUMBUS, Ohio — Parishioners at a suburban church turned in 18 handguns yesterday as the priest appealed during special weekend services for a ban on cheap handguns.

"Please listen to me," the Rev. Richard Engle told parishioners at St. Philip the Apostle Church in suburban Whitehall yesterday morning. "I am not a nut, I am not a radical, I am not a Communist. I am just a concerned person.

Father Engle, 50, who served in Word War II as an infantryman, started off the donations with his own target pistol, which he had owned for 17 years.

A spokesman for St. Philip's said that 18 handguns and as many toy pistols had been brought to the church during the six Masses yesterday. He added that more that 2,000 attended the services, 40 percent more than usual.

As Father Engle, dressed in green vestments, greeted parishioners in the brilliant sunshine, six uniformed Columbus policemen checked each weapon to make sure that it was empty. The guns are to be melted down into small crosses and distributed to the donors.

After Father Engle's sermon, the box of guns was carried to the altar, where it remained until the end of Mass.

The priest recounted an incident involving a parishioner and a 15-year-old boy who broke into his home and stole five dollars. The parishoner told Father Engle he was afraid that if he had a gun he would have shot the young intruder.

"What value is a 15-year-old boy?" Father Engle asked. "No thing is worth more than a person's life."

Parishoners were invited to sign petitions calling for a ban on the possession and sale of the cheap handguns known as Saturday-night specials, a 15-day cooling-off period between sale and possession of handguns and mandatory licensing of all gun owners.

Father Engle said his protest against "the flooding of America with handguns" was conceived after the two apparent assassination attempts against President Ford and a report by the National Catholic Conference on World Peace.

"Today's liturgy says to "walk in the light of the Lord," Father Engle said. "But we are walking in the darkness of fear. Our homes have been turned into fortified castles, even arsenals."

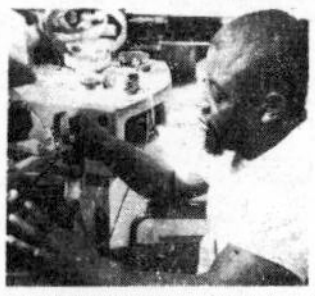

A 'CHARITY CASE'? Not Jerry Owens, 38, who is confiined to a wheelchair but really "making it" as an engraver, thanks in part to a vocational program sponsored by the United Fund. Page 1-B.

Weather & Index

SUNNY AND PLEASANT today. Highs around 70. Fair tonight. Lows in the mid 40s. Precipitation probability zero percent. Full weather report, Page 13-D.

THE FIRST DAY as a househusband finds Mike McCready short on breakfast supplies and long on time waiting at the dentist's office. Diary of a Male Housewife, [illegible] Page 1-D.

Action Line	15-D	[illegible]	14-D
The Arts	4-B	[illegible]	15-D
Business	8-C	Living	1-D
Classified	2-D	Obituaries	16-D
Comics	14-D	Puzzles	13-D
Crossword	13-D	Sports	1-C
Editorials	6-A	Television	2-D
Features	15-D	Weather	13-D

Bowser

The Pragmatic Challenger

By LAURA FOREMAN
Inquirer Political Writer

Charlie Bowser careens through the late night streets of Northeast Philadelphia at the wheel of his little Pacer, trying to make up time en route to his last campaign stop of the night.

"A frantic race to an empty place," he quips. He's late — not the half hour to 45 minutes late that he ordinarily runs, but two full hours late — and he expects that by the time he gets to Temple Judea on North Broad Street for the Cardoza Lodge's candidates forum night, there'll be nobody there but the cleanup crew.

He's almost right. When he pulls into the parking lot at 11 p.m., other cars are headed out. But inside, some 50 [illegible] men who've just digested three hours of political [illegible] are still milling around. Somewhat [illegible] they take their seats as the Philadelphia Party candidate for mayor approaches the rostrum.

Then something odd happens.

As Bowser speaks, the restless crowd grows quiet, then attentive, then rapt.

When he asks for questions from the floor — the standard signal for a speech-weary crowd to let proceedings grind to a halt — nobody moves for the door. They stay and ask questions. The answers bring more questions. And when it's all over, the hour is approaching midnight and a sizable number of those in the audience seem wide awake. They shake hands with the candidate and assure him that he has their vote.

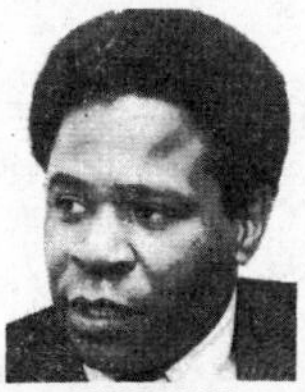

CHARLES BOWSER
. . . doesn't waste words

Charlie Bowser is good with crowds, possibly because his speeches are an interesting reflection of the man himself — part evangelist, part maverick, part philosopher, part shrewd pragmatist.

It's arguable that his pragmatism failed him when he decided on his long-shot bid to unseat incumbent Mayor Frank L. Rizzo. But Bowser bases his campaign on two premises that he espouses with the zeal of the true believer: First, Frank Rizzo can be beaten. Second, he, Charles W. Bowser, is the man fated to do it.

His reasoning goes like this:

- In last May's primary, Rizzo beat State Sen. Louis G. Hill, who had Democratic organization backing, by about 32,000 votes — the lowest margin of any Democratic primary winner in years. Moreover, Bowser argues, upwards of 20,000 of the 32,000 were switchover votes from Republicans who changed their registration to vote for the mayor.
- By contrast, when Mayor James H. J. Tate bucked the Democratic machine in 1967 in a primary similar to this year's, Tate defeated Alexander Hemphill by about 68,000 votes.
- In the May primary, Rizzo garnered only 29.5 percent of the city's registered Democratic vote. This shows that "an overwhelming number of Democrats were opposed to Rizzo

(See CANDIDATE on 2-A)

Figure 14–21. Boxed module that calls attention to story in box. [*Courtesy Philadelphia Inquirer.*]

Carnivals Highlight Chicago Summers

Photos by June Hielscher

By Darlene Napody

As soon as the ferris wheel creaks into motion and the calliope notes sound, Chicagoans abandon their front stoops and television sets to crowd the summer fairs and carnivals.

The biggest is the widely-promoted Free Fair, which annually nets $75,000 to $100,000 for the Back of the Yards Council, a group of West Side community organizations. Sprawling over an athletic field at 4700 S. Damen Ave., the fair opens July 6 for a 28-day run. Free parking is a lure that partially makes up for the honky-tonk booths and rides.

The carnival at St. Benedict's Church, 2215 W. Irving Park Road, is more compact, more friendly, and adds the bonus of a good fireworks display. This year it will be held June 15 to June 19.

For some unusual and good food during the same week, there is the carnival at Our Lady of Vilna Church, 2327 W. 23rd Place. The featured items are bundukis (a Lithuanian sandwich of chopped ham in a bun) and kugelis (potatoes in sour cream). The dates are June 13 to June 17.

Food is also more important than games at the August 21st picnic at St. Andrews Greek Orthodox Church, 5649 N. Sheridan Road. Visitors can join in the Greek folk dancing,

have a reasonably priced shiskebab dinner and finish it off with loukoumadis, the traditional fried pastry dipped in honey.

Back to the south side for one of the more intimate and pleasant fairs, St. Michael's Church, 2325 W. 24th Place, puts on its annual Music and Pizza Fair July 16 through July 26. Somebody is always performing, and clams, Italian sausage and watermelon are available.

An Italian atmosphere also infuses the two festivals that mark the July 16 feast day of St. Mary of Mt. Carmel.

An evening candlelight procession through the street highlights the miniature county fair at St. Mary of Mt. Carmel Church, 6722 S. Hermitage Ave.

The bigger event on this feast day is in suburban Melrose Park. Up to 20,000 people pack the streets for the festivities at Our Lady of Mt. Carmel Church. The celebration is climaxed by a procession in which a statue of the Virgin Mary, brought from Italy around the turn of the century, is carried through the streets. A full panoply of concessions, rides, and gaiety surrounds the procession

The fairs are promoted for money, and they make it. But the lure is not charity; it is fun for young and old alike.

Street Gospel Swings

By Dave Sullivan

If the sun's out and the weather's warm, Jim Brewer hauls his electric guitar and amplifier to the corner of Maxwell and Peoria streets Sunday morning.

Against the background of a flaking, red brick wall Jim and five other "Brothers and Sisters" sing, play, shout, dance and pray hard-driving gospel music. The guitar and the gospels he spins out of it are Jim Brewer's life. He had little choice, as he explained.

"I lost my eyes after I was born. My mother took me to a white doctor in Noo Orleans, Loosiana. An' by me bein' a kid, he put some medicine that wuz too strong in my eyes."

Jim's parents knew that he wouldn't ever be able to work regularly since his sight was almost totally destroyed. So his father went into Brookhaven, Miss., where the family lived, and bought a guitar from a lady named Miss Lindsay.

"And he brought the guitar there one night. He made him a fire in the fireplace,

it wuz kinda de fall of de year. He took de guitar outa de case. I begin to hear him playin'. That's the first I know a guitar big enough to remember.

"I wanted to learn because I believed some day it might benefit me somethin'!" From his father, his grandfather, his friends Jim began to pick up knowledge of music, even though he couldn't tune the guitar right when he first got it.

"I had it tuned in the open chords, and I was just chordin' here and there, here and there."

He learned not only from friends and relatives, but also from wandering singers who came through Brookhaven. "There was this blind fellow named Johnny Williams. Whenever he come to town I could tell. I wouldn't make nothin'.

"But I didn't git angry with him. I found this out—if you git angry with a person 'cause he knows more'n you, you never will learn nothin'. That's the way it goes."

Today, others learn from Jim Brewer.

To Keep His Creativity Intact

J.D. Salinger Seeks Seclusion

By Jill Kasle

To his neighbors in tiny Cornish, N.H., J. D. Salinger is a name on a mailbox. To the New Hampshire Bell Telephone Company, J. D. Salinger is an unlisted number.

To his mailman, Salinger is a nuisance. The mailman was forced to equip his car with special brakes to get over the unpaved country road leading to Salinger's remote home.

Along the cocktail circuit in Connecticut, where he lived before fleeing to New Hampshire, Salinger was known as an amusing fellow with an enthusiasm for Zen Buddhism and yoga. As one cocktailer remarked: "There was a time when he would go home and stand on his head."

To Ernest Hemingway, he was Staff Sergeant Salinger during World War II when the two men served together in Europe. Whenever their area was under attack, Salinger would dive into a foxhole to peck out casually-worded stories. Upon reading them, Hemingway commented succinctly: "Jesus, he has a helluva talent."

And to millions of people — the ones who were 16 years old in 1951 or the ones who will be 16 tomorrow or the ones who are always endlessly 16—Salinger is a demigod. His book, The Catcher in the Rye, is Bible to countless 16-year-olds, and Holden Caulfield, the book's math character, is part of many teenagers' alter egos.

Salinger's ability to speak to young people more effectively than any of his contemporaries is a natural talent for a man who has an unconcealed affection for children. "Some—in fact, all—of my best friends are children," he once remarked.

Salinger's appeal to college students equals Ernest Hemingway's popularity during the 1920's, although their styles differ. Hemingway was the author of cold detachment, whereas Salinger insists on bringing himself frankly, obtrusively, and lovingly into the picture.

An interesting paradox exists between Salinger the author and Salinger the man. The author Salinger has refined the technique of encounter instead of escape as an

answer to the futility of life. The other Salinger seems to be running away from the world, seeking privacy the way other men seek pleasure.

Salinger's home is set far back from the road in Cornish. It is a typical New England cabin surrounded by a typical six-foot-high redwood fence. Salinger lives the life of a recluse because he feels isolation keeps his creativity intact. He seems to have hung up a sign addressed to the world: "Do not disturb during working years."

Undisturbed, the man of isolation becomes the author of encounter. Because he is as much a part of his characters, he has to be explained through their eyes. Some

J. D. Salinger

of his characters—skillful combinations of imagination and autobiography—are more plausible than Salinger.

There are fascinating glimpses of the author in his classic character, Holden Caulfield. Holden yearns to do the unconventional; so does Salinger. Holden, a modern-day Huckleberry Finn, wants to retreat to an innocent nature; Salinger fled the horrors of suburbia for rustic New Hampshire. And for both Holden and his creater, the ultimate condemnation is the word "phony."

This sensitive, intense man is the product of a middle-class Jewish-Irish family. Jerome David Salinger was born in New York City in 1919. A solemn, polite child, he

liked to take long walks by himself. At 15, because of poor grades, his parents banished him to Valley Forge Military Academy, the model for Pency Prep, Holden Caulfield's alma mater.

Salinger, following the classic story of the aspiring young writer, spent his days struggling with mathematics and his nights writing feverishly, his blankets over his head to hide the beam of his flashlight from the duty officer.

After military school, Salinger drifted among universities, attending three but being graduated from none. After a two-year hitch with the army in Europe, he holed in Greenwich Village to write.

His best work during this period was a group of short stories published in various magazines about the Gladwaller and Caulfield families. Holden, the younger son of the Caulfield clan, became Salinger's main interest in 1948. In 1951 The Catcher in the Rye appeared. It is Holden Caulfield's—and possibly J. D. Salinger's—autobiography.

Holden Caulfield, who became saint and savior for millions of teenagers, stumbled into the literary world through the back door. He wore a dirty trench coat and a red hunting cap placed backwards on his head, its peak pulled down snugly over the base of his skull. He was defiant and rebellious, refusing to accept conventional society and yet aching to find his place in it.

In the mid-1950s, Salinger created the gaudy and eccentric Glass saga. His whole life has since become wrapped up in Sid and Bessie Glass and their seven weird children. The youngest child, Franny, is the heroine of the first half of Franny and Zooey. Like Holden Caulfield, she suffers intensely from overexposure to all that is phony.

Salinger's intimate, almost self-conscious style and the small volumes of work which he has produced have caused critics to conclude that writing is difficult for him. Yet writing is the only way of life for this complex, highly introverted man, who encounters public life vicariously through his characters while remaining in his own private world of creativity and genius.

Figure 14–22. An entire page divided into boxed modules.

The Morning News

Wilmington, Delaware, Thursday, June 5, 1975 • • Volume 187, Number 133, Fifteen Cents

weather
Cloudy today and tonight with a chance of showers. High today near 80, low tonight in the 60s. Cloudy tomorrow.

Ford is upheld on jobs-bill veto

By Richard L. Lyons
Washington Post Service

WASHINGTON — The House failed by 5 votes yesterday to override President Ford's veto of the $5.8 billion jobs bill, and that should bury the notion that the 2-to-1 Democratic majority in the House produced a veto-proof Congress.

"If you can't win this one, you can't win any of them," Minority Whip Robert Michel, R-Ill., told Democrats just before the vote.

It had been widely assumed that if the House were ever to be able to override the veto of a controversial bill it would be this one, which provided money for 900,000 jobs when 9 million are out of work, and which was drafted by Rep. George H. Mahon, D-Tex., the conservative chairman of the House Appropriations Committee, with the all-out backing of Speaker Carl Albert, D-Okla.

But when it cme to the vote yesterday, it was 277 to 145 to override, five short of the two-thirds vote required by the Constitution to force a bill into law over the president's opposition.

(Rep. Pierre S. du Pont IV, R-Del., was recorded as not voting on the override issue.)

This was a big win for the president, just back from his trip to Europe, and another frustrating loss for House Democrats who can't seem to get organized despite their huge majority. Of course, a presidential veto is worth a lot of votes, and Democrats have their chronic problem of a shrinking but still significant group of Southern conservatives who vote with Republicans against big spending.

See JOBS BILL—P. 2, Col. 1

Senate missile backers score hit

WASHINGTON (UPI) — The Senate yesterday defeated efforts by liberals to put a $23.8-billion ceiling on spending for new weapons and to reject a program to increase the accuracy of the nation's nuclear-warhead missiles.

By a vote of 52 to 42, the senators rejected arguments that a bill authorizing $110 million for research on improved accuracy and power of five weapons systems might bring a destructive war closer.

Earlier, the Senate easily defeated an attempt to out $1.2 billion from the $25-billion weapons and research procurement bill.

Sen. J. Strom Thurmond, R-S.C., advocating the program for improved missile accuracy, summed up for its supporters in a simple analogy: "If a man buys a rifle to go out there and shoot game, he wants the most accurate gun he can get. If the United States goes out and buys missiles, they ought to have the same thing."

Sen. Thomas J. McIntyre, D-N.H., opposing the program, said "these programs run counter to our national security because they put a hair trigger on nuclear war and will draw Soviet fire by giving them an incentive to strike first in a period of crisis."

The debate, after a long closed-session discussion of top secret Pentagon strategies, indicated the new accuracy program was designed to perfect a guidance system to enable a missile to fly from the United States to within 300 feet of its target. Current accuracy apparently is within 900 feet.

"It doesn't make any difference," said Sen. John O. Pastore, D-R.I., an opponent of counterforce. "If you drop a two-megaton bomb on this capitol plaza, you won't be able to find the White House."

Sen. Henry M. Jackson, D-Wash., said the United States could not afford to give Russia the opportunity to have greater accuracy.

The senators voted down opposition to the accuracy program after liberals attempted to push through the cut in funds for weapons procurement.

The Senate defeated the effort on a roll call vote of 59 to 36 after a spirited debate during which 34-year-old Sen. Sam Nunn, D-GA., vigorously challenged 73-year-old Sen. Stuart Symington, D-Mo., a former Air Force secretary, who had proposed the across-the-board cut.

The Symington amendment, co-sponsored by Sen. Edward M. Kennedy, D-Mass., Sen. Alan Cranston, D-Calif., and others, had also been attacked by pentagon and White House officials in calls to senators.

Sen. Joseph R. Biden Jr., D-Del., supported the effort to trim military spending.

"This was a modest proposal," said Biden. "It would have cut the fat from military weapons procurement without damaging the

See SENATE—P. 4, Col. 4

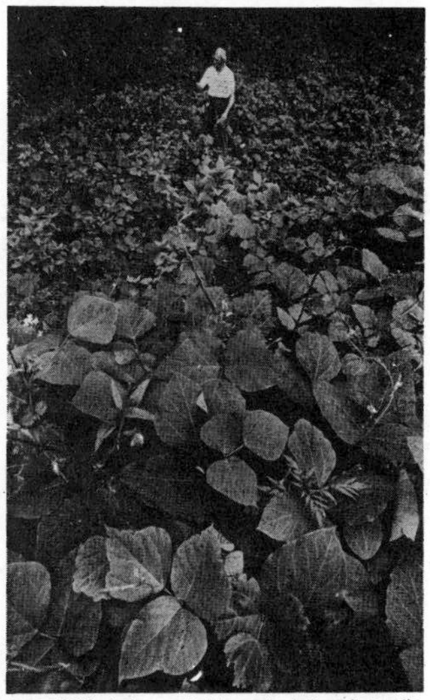

Clayton Hoff is about as engulfed by creeping kudzu as he says the Rockford Park Condominium apartments could be if they're not careful. (Staff photo by Donaghey Brown)

No malpractice crisis in Del., lawyers told

By Virginia Delavan

A malpractice bill backed by the Medical Society of Delaware was introduced in an atmosphere of national "hysteria" and doesn't square with the Delaware situation, a prominent lawyer said yesterday.

Edmund N. Carpenter II said the General Assembly is being misled by claims that patients here are collecting huge sums from doctors and thus driving malpractice insurance premiums through the ceiling.

Speaking to about 300 lawyers and judges at the annual Bench and Bar Conference, Carpenter declared: "We need to take action . . . to see this bill is not rammed through in the hysteria of the moment . . ."

Carpenter is a past president of the state bar association and 2 weeks ago was named to head a special association committee on medical malpractice. He said Delaware has the time to wait and weigh the success of proposed solutions in New York, California and other states where the problem admittedly has reached the crisis stage.

A bill introduced last week in the House of Representatives, but not expected to pass this session, would take malpractice claims out of the courts and have them decided by a special panel appointed by the governor.

The legislation would set a $100,000 limit on the amount a patient could recover from a doctor's insurance company in most cases. If the panel deemed the patient's injury "catastrophic," he or she could get up to $200,000 more from a special state fund.

According to his information, Carpenter said, only one malpractice suit has gone against a Delaware doctor since 1971 — and that verdict was later reversed.

He referred to the case of a New Castle couple who sued two surgeons over an unsuccessful vasectomy performed on the husband. They won $5,000 from a jury, and the trial judge subsequently nullified the award.

Although not all out-of-court settlements in malpractice cases are made public, those he knows about haven't been "excessive," Carpenter said.

Elsewhere, some patients have

See NO—P. 4, Col. 1

Cursed kudzu gnaws at state

By John D. Gates

"Don't worry," John H. Prest said the other day. "It won't get to Wilmington for a few years."

Prest, who works for the Du Pont Co. and lives on a farm near Bear, was joking about the kudzu vine he has down on the farm.

In the South, kudzu is not something you joke about. The vine, imported sometime late in the last century from China or Japan, is considered a menace akin to bubonic plague.

It chokes trees, telephone poles buildings and most anything else in its way. Used sometimes for erosion control because of its dense root system and rapid growth, the kudzu vine has proved somwhat uncontrollable, creeping up over the rodside banks it was supposed to protect from erosion and engulfing the neighborhood.

Around Wilmington, kudzu is taken less seriously. Says a spokesman for the county extension service of the University of Delaware's agriculture department: "There's very little up

See CREEPING—P. 2, Col. 4

Price of sugar plunging

NEW YORK (AP) — Sugar prices, which reached unprecedented heights 7 months ago, have declined so sharply this year there is now talk of reimposing price supports.

The price for raw sugar, which is used to make the finished product, is about 15 cents a pound — less than one-fourth the record high of 65.5 cents a pound last November.

The retail price for refined sugar has dropped less sharply as refiners seek to sell the sugar made from raw sugar bought before the price dropped.

The national average for refined sugar in April, according to the Bureau of Labor Statistics, was $2.09 a 5-pound bag, compared with $3.14 in December and 85 cents in January 1974.

Although the current price for raw sugar is still twice the historic averages, commodity analysts foresee further drops ahead and note that domestic growers fear further declines could wipe out their investments.

"There's talk among growers of going to Congress wtih a united front," said one high-ranking official in the Department of Agriculture, who emphasized the government had no present plans to support prices.

"If spot prices get down to the 10-cent level, the growers will descend on Washington like locusts," said a Wall Street commodities analyst who asked to remain anonymous. Such a level was a "definite possibility," he said.

At the Department of Agriculture, the Economic Research Service has begun a study of the relationship of price and production over the next 5 years. "We're looking at alternatives ranging from free trade to reimposition of target prices," said Robert Bohall, who heads the study.

Bohall said the House Agriculture Committee plans hearings this summer to see what should be done.

Last year Congress ended the Sugar Act, which for 40 years had protected domestic growers by adjusting imports to meet a target price. Critics of the act said it was unnecessary in a shortage situation with prices far above the 11.45 cent-a-pound target.

Any attempt to revive the act to help growers would probably run into fire from consumers, who like the declining prices.

Panic and a worldwide shortage drove sugar prices to last year's record level. Refiners, worried about supplies, bought 3 to 6 months ahead as late as last December, some observers say.

Ford to announce candidacy soon

WASHINGTON (NYT) — President Ford will announce his 1976 candidacy this month, the White House press secretary, Ron Nessen, said yesterday. Other Republican sources said the formal declaration would probably come within 2 weeks.

The president's return from Europe, according to his intimates, signals the beginning of a 90-day period during which the elements of a campaign structure will be assembled so he can begin an intense political effort this fall.

In the past, incumbent Presidents have raised money and put together organizations without making formal announcements until their efforts were well under way.

But Ford is in no position to follow their example.

For one thing, unlike them, he has never before faced a national or even a statewide electorate. For another, he is eager to dispose completely of the belief that he does not intend to run.

Most important, the president's flexibility is limited by the new federal campaign financing statute. Under the law, any money raised and any money spent, whether in the form of cash or services, must be reported promptly.

By announcing more than a year before the Republican National Convention, Ford will cause himself some problems, the shape of which is not entirely clear. There may, for instance, be difficulty in deciding which of his trips and which of his television appearances are political. Should opponents get equal broadcast time? Should his campaign committee pay for his transportation?

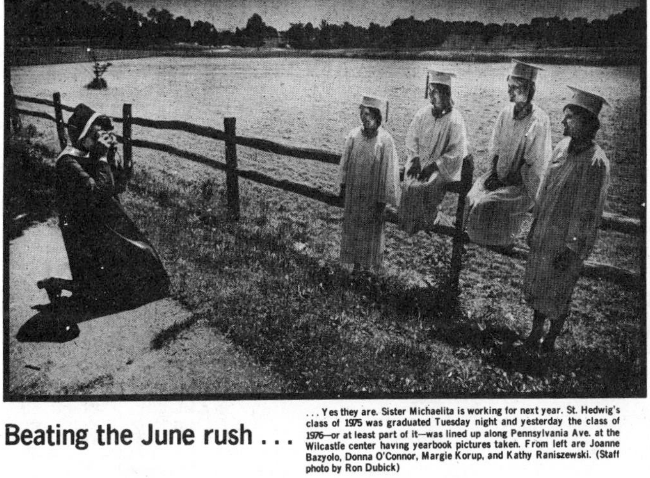

Beating the June rush . . . . . . Yes they are. Sister Michaelita is working for next year. St. Hedwig's class of 1975 was graduated Tuesday night and yesterday the class of 1976—or at least part of it—was lined up along Pennsylvania Ave. at the Wilcastle center having yearbook pictures taken. From left are Joanne Bazyolo, Donna O'Connor, Margie Korup, and Kathy Raniszewski. (Staff photo by Ron Dubick)

inside the news

A judge permits a hospital to amputate a sick man's leg despite the objections of the patient and his family. Page 45.

Checking back on last year's fire which burned newspapers collected for a Meadowood School fund drive, the school's mothers club has rallied for the project's completion. Page 20.

Australian authorities wonder what would happen if a box of taipan snakes would break open in a U.S. post office. Page 7.

17-year-old Caroline Kennedy, the late president's first born and only daughter, graduates today from Concord Academy. Page 10.

New-car sales in May are the best for Detroit since October, suggesting a possible summer upturn for the depressed industry. Page 23.

The Public Service Commission delays action on approval of stock and bond offerings by DP&L, creating possible financial bind for the utility if the situation is not resolved promptly. Page 23.

The Texas Rangers trade absent Willie Davis to the St. Louis Cardinals. Page 29.

The state baseball tournament resumes today. Monte Martin reports. Page 29.

Arts	38	Editorials	8
Astrology	44	Events	22
Bridge	44	Living	41
Business	23	Obituaries	43
Coins	22	Record	43
Comics	44	Sports	29
Crossword	44	Television	37

Figure 14–23. Grid makeup with white space serving as unobtrusive grid separations. [*Courtesy The Morning News, Wilmington Delaware.*]

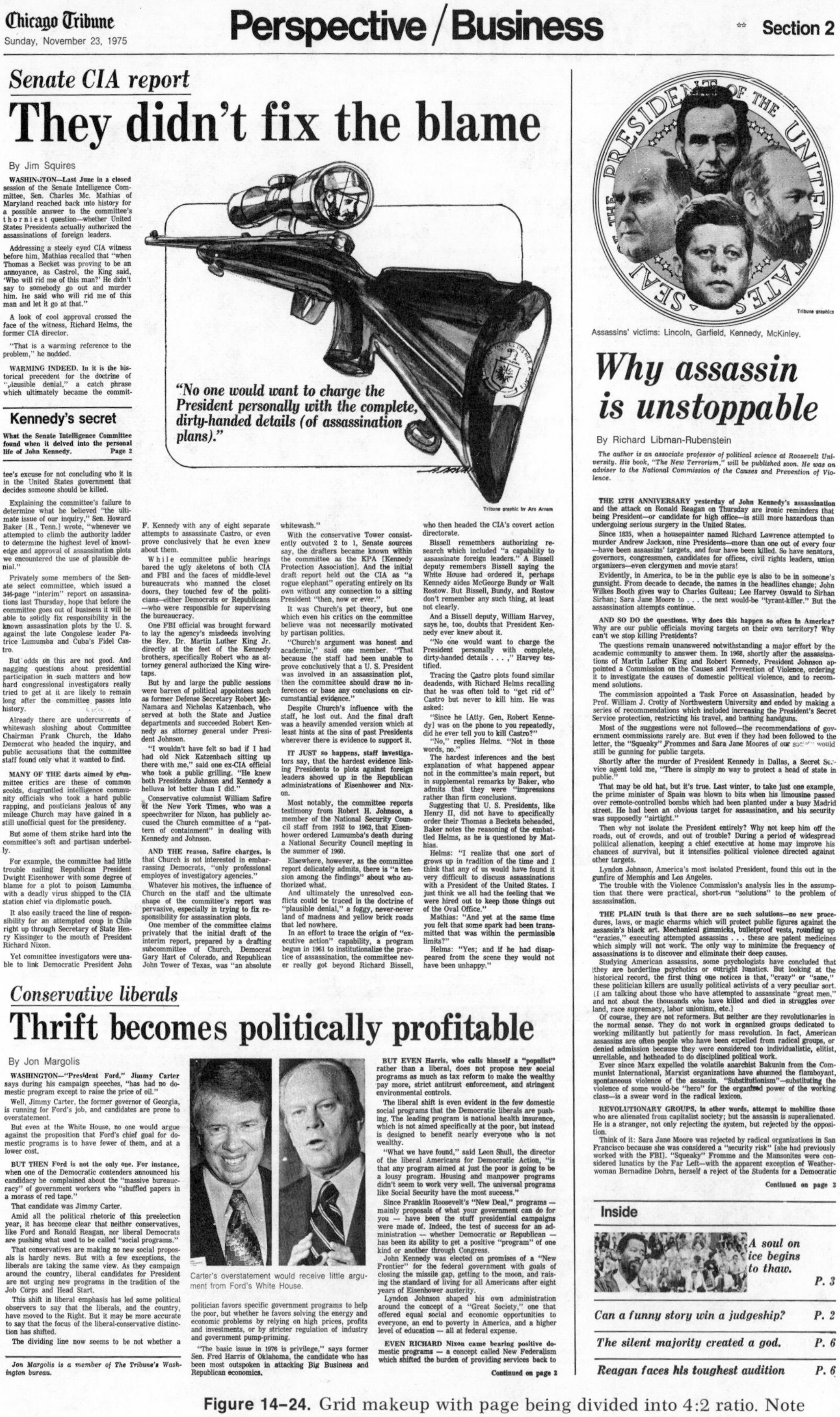

Chicago Tribune
Sunday, November 23, 1975

Perspective / Business

Section 2

Senate CIA report

They didn't fix the blame

By Jim Squires

WASHINGTON—Last June in a closed session of the Senate Intelligence Committee, Sen. Charles Mc. Mathias of Maryland reached back into history for a possible answer to the committee's thorniest question—whether United States Presidents actually authorized the assassinations of foreign leaders.

Addressing a steely eyed CIA witness before him, Mathias recalled that "when Thomas a Becket was proving to be an annoyance, as Castro, the King said, 'Who will rid me of this man?' He didn't say to somebody go out and murder him. He said who will rid me of this man and let it go at that."

A look of cool approval crossed the face of the witness, Richard Helms, the former CIA director.

"That is a warming reference to the problem," he nodded.

WARMING INDEED. In it is the historical precedent for the doctrine of "plausible denial," a catch phrase which ultimately became the committee's excuse for not concluding who it is in the United States government that decides someone should be killed.

Explaining the committee's failure to determine what he believed "the ultimate issue of our inquiry," Sen. Howard Baker [R., Tenn.] wrote, "whenever we attempted to climb the authority ladder to determine the highest level of knowledge and approval of assassination plots we encountered the use of plausible denial."

Privately some members of the Senate select committee, which issued a 346-page "interim" report on assassinations last Thursday, hope that before the committee goes out of business it will be able to solidly fix responsibility in the known assassination plots by the U. S. against the late Congolese leader Patrice Lumumba and Cuba's Fidel Castro.

But odds on this are not good. And nagging questions about presidential participation in such matters and how hard congressional investigators really tried to get at it are likely to remain long after the committee passes into history.

Already there are undercurrents of whitewash sloshing about Committee Chairman Frank Church, the Idaho Democrat who headed the inquiry, and public accusations that the committee staff found only what it wanted to find.

MANY OF THE darts aimed by committee critics are these of common scolds, disgruntled intelligence community officials who took a hard public rapping, and politicians jealous of any mileage Church may have gained in a still unofficial quest for the presidency.

But some of them strike hard into the committee's soft and partisan underbelly.

For example, the committee had little trouble nailing Republican President Dwight Eisenhower with some degree of blame for a plot to poison Lumumba with a deadly virus shipped to the CIA station chief via diplomatic pouch.

It also easily traced the line of responsibility for an attempted coup in Chile right up through Secretary of State Henry Kissinger to the mouth of President Richard Nixon.

Yet committee investigators were unable to link Democratic President John F. Kennedy with any of eight separate attempts to assassinate Castro, or even prove conclusively that he even knew about them.

While committee public hearings bared the ugly skeletons of both CIA and FBI and the faces of middle-level bureaucrats who manned the closet doors, they touched few of the politicians—either Democrats or Republicans—who were responsible for supervising the bureaucracy.

One FBI official was brought forward to lay the agency's misdeeds involving the Rev. Dr. Martin Luther King Jr. directly at the feet of the Kennedy brothers, specifically Robert who as attorney general authorized the King wiretaps.

But by and large the public sessions were barren of political appointees such as former Defense Secretary Robert McNamara and Nicholas Katzenbach, who served at both the State and Justice departments and succeeded Robert Kennedy as attorney general under President Johnson.

"I wouldn't have felt so bad if I had had old Nick Katzenbach sitting up there with me," said one ex-CIA official who took a public grilling. "He knew both Presidents Johnson and Kennedy a helluva lot better than I did."

Conservative columnist William Safire of the New York Times, who was a speechwriter for Nixon, has publicly accused the Church committee of a "pattern of containment" in dealing with Kennedy and Johnson.

AND THE reason, Safire charges, is that Church is not interested in embarrassing Democrats, "only professional employes of investigatory agencies."

Whatever his motives, the influence of Church on the staff and the ultimate shape of the committee's report was pervasive, especially in trying to fix responsibility for assassination plots.

One member of the committee claims privately that the initial draft of the interim report, prepared by a drafting subcommittee of Church, Democrat Gary Hart of Colorado, and Republican John Tower of Texas, was "an absolute whitewash."

With the conservative Tower consistently outvoted 2 to 1, Senate sources say, the drafters became known within the committee as the KPA [Kennedy Protection Association]. And the initial draft report held out the CIA as "a rogue elephant" operating entirely on its own without any connection to a sitting President "then, now or ever."

It was Church's pet theory, but one which even his critics on the committee believe was not necessarily motivated by partisan politics.

"Church's argument was honest and academic," said one member. "That because the staff had been unable to prove conclusively that a U. S. President was involved in an assassination plot, then the committee should draw no inferences or base any conclusions on circumstantial evidence."

Despite Church's influence with the staff, he lost out. And the final draft was a heavily amended version which at least hints at the sins of past Presidents wherever there is evidence to support it.

IT JUST so happens, staff investigators say, that the hardest evidence linking Presidents to plots against foreign leaders showed up in the Republican administrations of Eisenhower and Nixon.

Most notably, the committee reports testimony from Robert H. Johnson, a member of the National Security Council staff from 1952 to 1962, that Eisenhower ordered Lumumba's death during a National Security Council meeting in the summer of 1960.

Elsewhere, however, as the committee report delicately admits, there is "a tension among the findings" about who authorized what.

And ultimately the unresolved conflicts could be traced in the doctrine of "plausible denial," a foggy, never-never land of madness and yellow brick roads that led nowhere.

In an effort to trace the origin of "executive action" capability, a program begun in 1961 to institutionalize the practice of assassination, the committee never really got beyond Richard Bissell, who then headed the CIA's covert action directorate.

Bissell remembers authorizing research which included "a capability to assassinate foreign leaders." A Bissell deputy remembers Bissell saying the White House had ordered it, perhaps Kennedy aides McGeorge Bundy or Walt Rostow. But Bissell, Bundy, and Rostow don't remember any such thing, at least not clearly.

And a Bissell deputy, William Harvey, says he, too, doubts that President Kennedy ever knew about it.

"No one would want to charge the President personally with complete, dirty-handed details . . . ," Harvey testified.

Tracing the Castro plots found similar deadends, with Richard Helms recalling that he was often told to "get rid of" Castro but never to kill him. He was asked:

"Since he [Atty. Gen. Robert Kennedy] was on the phone to you repeatedly, did he ever tell you to kill Castro?"

"No," replies Helms. "Not in those words, no."

The hardest inferences and the best explanation of what happened appear not in the committee's main report, but in supplemental remarks by Baker, who admits that they were "impressions rather than firm conclusions.

Suggesting that U. S. Presidents, like Henry II, did not have to specifically order their Thomas a Beckets beheaded, Baker notes the reasoning of the embattled Helms, as he is questioned by Mathias.

Helms: "I realize that one sort of grows up in tradition of the time and I think that any of us would have found it very difficult to discuss assassinations with a President of the United States. I just think we all had the feeling that we were hired out to keep those things out of the Oval Office."

Mathias: "And yet at the same time you felt that some spark had been transmitted that was within the permissible limits?"

Helms: "Yes; and if he had disappeared from the scene they would not have been unhappy."

"No one would want to charge the President personally with the complete, dirty-handed details (of assassination plans)."

Tribune graphic by Arn Arnam

Kennedy's secret

What the Senate Intelligence Committee found when it delved into the personal life of John Kennedy. Page 2

Assassins' victims: Lincoln, Garfield, Kennedy, McKinley.

Tribune graphics

Why assassin is unstoppable

By Richard Libman-Rubenstein

The author is an associate professor of political science at Roosevelt University. His book, "The New Terrorism," will be published soon. He was an adviser to the National Commission of the Causes and Prevention of Violence.

THE 12TH ANNIVERSARY yesterday of John Kennedy's assassination and the attack on Ronald Reagan on Thursday are ironic reminders that being President—or candidate for high office—is still more hazardous than undergoing serious surgery in the United States.

Since 1835, when a housepainter named Richard Lawrence attempted to murder Andrew Jackson, nine Presidents—more than one out of every four—have been assassins' targets, and four have been killed. So have senators, governors, congressmen, candidates for offices, civil rights leaders, union organizers—even clergymen and movie stars!

Evidently, in America, to be in the public eye is also to be in someone's gunsight. From decade to decade, the names in the headlines change; John Wilkes Booth gives way to Charles Guiteau; Lee Harvey Oswald to Sirhan Sirhan; Sara Jane Moore to . . . the next would-be "tyrant-killer." But the assassination attempts continue.

AND SO DO the questions. Why does this happen so often in America? Why are our public officials moving targets on their own territory? Why can't we stop killing Presidents?

The questions remain unanswered notwithstanding a major effort by the academic community to answer them. In 1968, shortly after the assassinations of Martin Luther King and Robert Kennedy, President Johnson appointed a Commission on the Causes and Prevention of Violence, ordering it to investigate the causes of domestic political violence, and to recommend solutions.

The commission appointed a Task Force on Assassination, headed by Prof. William J. Crotty of Northwestern University and ended by making a series of recommendations which included increasing the President's Secret Service protection, restricting his travel, and banning handguns.

Most of the suggestions were not followed—the recommendations of government commissions rarely are. But even if they had been followed to the letter, the "Squeaky" Frommes and Sara Jane Moores of our society would still be gunning for public targets.

Shortly after the murder of President Kennedy in Dallas, a Secret Service agent told me, "There is simply no way to protect a head of state in public."

That may be old hat, but it's true. Last winter, to take just one example, the prime minister of Spain was blown to bits when his limousine passed over remote-controlled bombs which had been planted under a busy Madrid street. He had been an obvious target for assassination, and his security was supposedly "airtight."

Then why not isolate the President entirely? Why not keep him off the roads, out of crowds, and out of trouble? During a period of widespread political alienation, keeping a chief executive at home may improve his chances of survival, but it intensifies political violence directed against other targets.

Lyndon Johnson, America's most isolated President, found this out in the gunfire of Memphis and Los Angeles.

The trouble with the Violence Commission's analysis lies in the assumption that there were practical, short-run "solutions" to the problem of assassination.

THE PLAIN truth is that there are no such solutions—no new procedures, laws, or magic charms which will protect public figures against the assassin's black art. Mechanical gimmicks, bulletproof vests, rounding up "crazies," executing attempted assassins . . . these are patent medicines which simply will not work. The only way to minimize the frequency of assassinations is to discover and eliminate their deep causes.

Studying American assassins, some psychologists have concluded that they are borderline psychotics or outright lunatics. But looking at the historical record, the first thing one notices is that, "crazy" or "sane," these politician killers are usually political activists of a very peculiar sort. [I am talking about those who have attempted to assassinate "great men," and not about the thousands who have killed and died in struggles over land, race supremacy, labor unionism, etc.]

Of course, they are not reformers. But neither are they revolutionaries in the normal sense. They do not work in organized groups dedicated to working militantly but patiently for mass revolution. In fact, American assassins are often people who have been expelled from radical groups, or denied admission because they were considered too individualistic, elitist, unreliable, and hotheaded to do disciplined political work.

Ever since Marx expelled the volatile anarchist Bakunin from the Communist International, Marxist organizations have shunned the flamboyant, spontaneous violence of the assassin. "Substitutionism"—substituting the violence of some would-be "hero" for the organized power of the working class—is a swear word in the radical lexicon.

REVOLUTIONARY GROUPS, in other words, attempt to mobilize those who are alienated from capitalist society; but the assassin is superalienated. He is a stranger, not only rejecting the system, but rejected by the opposition.

Think of it: Sara Jane Moore was rejected by radical organizations in San Francisco because she was considered a "security risk" [she had previously worked with the FBI]. "Squeaky" Fromme and the Mansonites were considered lunatics by the Far Left—with the apparent exception of Weatherwoman Bernadine Dohrn, herself a reject of the Students for a Democratic

Continued on page 3

Inside

A soul on ice begins to thaw. P. 3

Can a funny story win a judgeship? P. 2

The silent majority created a god. P. 6

Reagan faces his toughest audition P. 6

Conservative liberals

Thrift becomes politically profitable

By Jon Margolis

WASHINGTON—"President Ford," Jimmy Carter says during his campaign speeches, "has had no domestic program except to raise the price of oil."

Well, Jimmy Carter, the former governor of Georgia, is running for Ford's job, and candidates are prone to overstatement.

But even at the White House, no one would argue against the proposition that Ford's chief goal for domestic programs is to have fewer of them, and at a lower cost.

BUT THEN Ford is not the only one. For instance, when one of the Democratic contenders announced his candidacy he complained about the "massive bureaucracy" of government workers who "shuffled papers in a morass of red tape."

That candidate was Jimmy Carter.

Amid all the political rhetoric of this preelection year, it has become clear that neither conservatives, like Ford and Ronald Reagan, nor liberal Democrats are pushing what used to be called "social programs."

That conservatives are making no new social proposals is hardly news. But with a few exceptions, the liberals are taking the same view. As they campaign around the country, liberal candidates for President are not urging new programs in the tradition of the Job Corps and Head Start.

This shift in liberal emphasis has led some political observers to say that the liberals, and the country, have moved to the Right. But it may be more accurate to say that the focus of the liberal-conservative distinction has shifted.

The dividing line now seems to be not whether a politician favors specific government programs to help the poor, but whether he favors solving the energy and economic problems by relying on high prices, profits and investments, or by stricter regulation of industry and government pump-priming.

"The basic issue in 1976 is privilege," says former Sen. Fred Harris of Oklahoma, the candidate who has been most outspoken in attacking Big Business and Republican economics.

BUT EVEN Harris, who calls himself a "populist" rather than a liberal, does not propose new social programs as much as tax reform to make the wealthy pay more, strict antitrust enforcement, and stringent environmental controls.

The liberal shift is even evident in the few domestic social programs that the Democratic liberals are pushing. The leading program is national health insurance, which is not aimed specifically at the poor, but instead is designed to benefit nearly everyone who is not wealthy.

"What we have found," said Leon Shull, the director of the liberal Americans for Democratic Action, "is that any program aimed at just the poor is going to be a lousy program. Housing and manpower programs didn't seem to work very well. The universal programs like Social Security have the most success."

Since Franklin Roosevelt's "New Deal," programs — mainly proposals of what your government can do for you — have been the stuff presidential campaigns were made of. Indeed, the test of success for an administration — whether Democratic or Republican — has been its ability to get a positive "program" of one kind or another through Congress.

John Kennedy was elected on promises of a "New Frontier" for the federal government with goals of closing the missile gap, getting to the moon, and raising the standard of living for all Americans after eight years of Eisenhower austerity.

Lyndon Johnson shaped his own administration around the concept of a "Great Society," one that offered equal social and economic opportunities to everyone, an end to poverty in America, and a higher level of education — all at federal expense.

EVEN RICHARD Nixon came bearing positive domestic programs — a concept called New Federalism which shifted the burden of providing services back to

Continued on page 2

Carter's overstatement would receive little argument from Ford's White House.

Jon Margolis is a member of The Tribune's Washington bureau.

Figure 14–24. Grid makeup with page being divided into 4:2 ratio. Note that this page could also be called modular. [*Courtesy Chicago Tribune.*]

peninsula

Morning News, Wilmington, Del., Thursday, June 5, 1975 • • 13

Cicione levels new blast at Wier

By Ron Williams
Dover Bureau Chief

DOVER - Sen. Anthony J. Cicione, D-Elsmere, took the Senate floor yesterday for his latest blast at Atty. Gen. Richard R. Wier Jr., whom Cicione called a "dangerous man."

After apologizing for using the Senate as a forum for his criticism, Cicione launched into a 5-minute tirade against Wier and his office. It wasn't the first time. Cicione called Wier "incompetent" to hold office Monday when Wier appeared before Cicione's Joint Finance Committee to plead for more money and staff members than the committee was willing to give him.

Cicione yesterday said newspaper reports quoting Wier as saying it was typical of Cicione not to return the attorney general's telephone calls were typical of Wier. "He needn't call me ever again," Cicione told the Senate. "From now on I will not talk to that gentleman unless it's in my office with a witness . . . he's a dangerous man."

Cicione began his criticism of Wier after he discovered that two bills had been drafted by members of Wier's staff. Among other things, Wier has told the Joint Finance Committee — which refused to give the attorney general his present staff of 34 deputies for 1976 and instead proposed that it be cut to 27 — that bill-drafting for legislators would be abolished if the staff was not kept at its present level.

One of the bills that set Cicione off was sponsored by Sen. Herman M. Holloway Sr., D-Wilmington, a member of the Joint Finance Committee. That bill would appropriate about $133,000 for five more deputies next fiscal year, bringing the staff to 32. Wier, however, has said he couldn't perform his job without at least his present 34. Holloway's bill, introduced and assigned to the Senate Finance Committee, chaired by Cicione, would retain four federally-funded attorneys and one regular state-paid deputy.

Holloway said he feels the people of the state favor keeping the attorney general's staff intact and he hopes Cicione will report the bill out of committee.

The telephone question came about when Wier said he had made several calls to Cicione at home concerning the mysterious green sedan Cicione claims had been following him over a 6-week period.

Cicione has hinted that Wier ordered the tailing, but Wier has emphatically denied this. Cicione has refused to release the license number of the car although he claims to know the owner is a state employe.

A deputy in Wier's office said it is unusual that someone who was followed for several weeks never bothered to call the police.

Speaker of the House Casimir S. Jonkiert, D-Wilmington, has said he also was followed by the same green car.

Cicione and Jonkiert made the claims about the car after Wier told the Joint Finance Committee his office was investigaitng reports that legislators had threatened to cut Wier's budget unless the attorney general dropped political investigations.

Not news, DP&L says of contracts to build N-plant

By Eleanor Shaw
Dover Bureau

DOVER — Delmarva Power & Light Co. already has awarded the construction contract for its proposed nuclear power plant near Summit, the General Assembly learned yesterday.

DP&L confirmed last night that parts of the contract — worth an estimated $1.1 billion — were awarded in 1972 and last year to United Engineers and Constructors Inc., of Philadelphia. A spokesman said no announcements were made because "we didn't think it was news."

The news reached the floor of the House after Gov. Sherman W. Tribbitt told a meeting of legislative leaders he had learned that the general contract had been awarded and was unhappy because none of the subcontractors were from Delaware.

While not disputing that last night, a DP&L spokesman said the company is "making a real effort to utilize local firms who submit the lowest bid." He said he didn't know whether any Delaware firms had yet been selected as subcontractors for the massive project.

Tribbitt's private announcement became public as Rep. Joseph P. (Jody) Ambrosino Jr., R-Edgemoor Terrace, took the House floor to criticize DP&L for advancing to this stage without all the required government permits. In response, DP&L said the contract was awarded early because it takes awhile to do all the preliminary work necessary before construction can begin.

But Ambrosino said he would introduce a bill today that would impose a 2-year moratorium on construction. He said questions about the plant's safety, efficiency, cost and disposal of radioactive waste materials haven't been answered adequately.

The Federal Nuclear Regulatory Commission approved the construction of this power plant in February, although it said more information would be necessary before construction permits were issued. The two 766-megawatt nuclear generators will be built on the Chesapeake & Delaware Canal, just north of Summit, and are scheduled for completion in 1984. A spokesman said the company hopes to begin construction late this year.

There have been several public hearings, and there is strong opposition to the project on the grounds that safety standards are inadequate both for construction and operation.

DP&L says the plant is needed to meet the rising demand for electricity. It also says the project would boost Delaware's economy by providing hundreds of construction jobs.

The objections raised yesterday focused on this point since it would seem that out-of-state contractors would not hire as many Delawareans as expected. Tribbitt was said to be especially upset at the lack of in-state subcontractors.

But Rep. John Matushefske, D-Wilmington Manor, a former ironworker, said workers in Delaware unions will have first crack at all the construction jobs since the contractors must work through local union halls for all their hiring. He estimated that as many as 2,500 people will be working on the project at its peak.

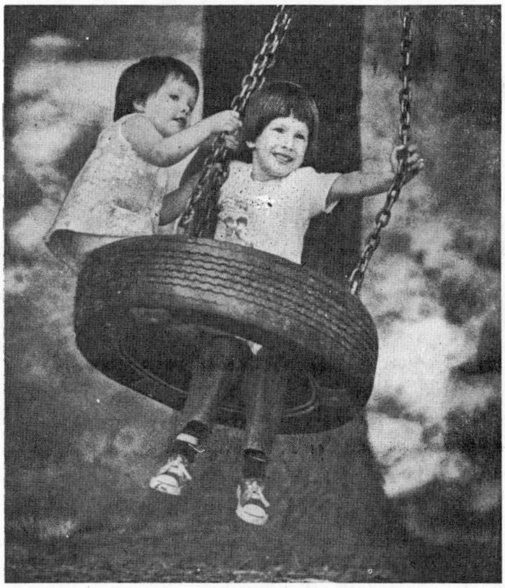

Kids never tire Believe it or not, their names are Jack and Jill—Jack and Jill Watkins, ages 5 and 2—but they seem to have very little interest in buckets of water. They prefer the swing at Brandywine Springs Park, off Newport Gap Pike and Faulkland Rd. (Staff photo by Fred Comegys)

Ex-principal gets social services job

By Wendy Fox

Delaware's newly named social services director is a retired high school principal with a reputation as a strict disciplinarian.

Charles E. Smith was named yesterday to succeed Miklos T. Lazar as director of the state's division of social services, effective July 1. Lazar agreed to resign Tuesday when Earl McGinnes, secretary of the Department of Health and Social Services, asked him to.

McGinnes wouldn't comment on the reasons for Lazar's dismissal, other than to say, "I think Mr. Smith will do a better job in running the division."

Lazar and McGinnes have been at odds for some time, and Lazar said Tuesday he had been expecting his dismissal for 2 months.

The dismissal came the same day as the release of a report by a House committee recommending several changes in the management of the state's welfare system, handled by the division. McGinnes had supported a December audit which said the state's welfare program was in a "state of utter, chaotic shambles."

Smith, 67, retired in 1972 after being with the New Castle public schools for 44 years, the last 26 of those as principal of William Penn High School. He was educated in Churchill, Md., public schools, receiving his undergraduate degree from Washington College, Chestertown, Md. He got his master's from Duke University in 1940.

A Democrat, Smith lost to Rep. Robert T. Connor, R-New Castle, in the race for the state House of Representatives last November. He lives at 14 Crippin Dr., Penn Acres.

Smith couldn't be reached yesterday, but McGinnes said he thinks Smith's educational background will serve him well in running the division.

"I think public education is probably the major social service in this country," McGinnes said.

He added that when Smith signs on in his new $27,050-a-year job, he will be forfeiting the $12,000 yearly pension he received when he retired from the school system and $3,000 a year in Social Security benefits.

"He says he's only going to net about $5,000" by joining the division, McGinnes said.

Lazar is now earning $26,000 a year as division director, but the new state budget includes money to raise that to $27,050 as of July 1.

McGinnes would not comment on any of the changes he said he was planning for the division, saying he wanted to wait until Smith had been in the job for about a month.

As William Penn principal, Smith suspended 250 students in 1971 for demonstrating for a more lenient dress code. He was noted for being a strict moralist, and there was the time in 1969 when he removed the cover from a Newsweek magazine before letting his students see it. The cover showed a half nude man and woman embracing.

Schoolmen face puzzle of the shrinking dollar

By Larry Nagengast

Delaware educators are asking each other a dismaying riddle this week: When is a dollar worth only 98 cents?

The answer: When state education dollars are distributed on a formula basis and the Joint Finance Committee decrees a 2 percent budget cut.

The tough thing about the situation, as far as public school officials are concerned, is that the committee's budget slash, approved Monday, is but a small part of the financial woes facing local school districts.

The combination of recession and inflation that has been staggering Delaware residents for more than a year will hit school systems in full force. The hope that declining enrollments will help ease the pain is becoming illusory.

Yes, there will be fewer students in the public schools this fall, but the things schools must provide cost much more than the money that might be saved by having fewer kids in the classroom.

Whether there are 25 or 35 students in a room, it has to be heated and lit. Fewer meals might be served in cafeterias, but food costs more. The cost of operating a bus doesn't change when it carries 50 students instead of 55.

The best example of how rising costs are overtaking declining enrollments is in the Conrad Area School District, which should have about 350 fewer students in September. That ought to mean a reduction of about 20 teaching posts, a savings of at least $200,000. But the school board has approved a $6.5 million budget, $700,000 more than was needed for the current year, a 12 percent increase.

The killing element in the school-spending equation is nonsalary costs, an area often ignored as salaries for educators have risen steadily in the last decade.

State Department of Public Instruction officials have developed a "cost of education" index, which shows rises in nonsalary costs. The figures used to prepare 1975-76 budgets are a year out of date, since they cover June 1973 and June 1974 costs. But the increase in that period was a whopping 29.2 percent.

The two key components in the index, utilities and teaching supplies (paper, pencils and the like) each rose by 55 percent in the period, and are continuing to rise.

The hikes are forcing new pressures on school officials to handle local tax revenues with care, but the problem is that tax revenues aren't increasing.

Most school districts are now levying operating taxes at the maximum rate permissible without a referendum. Three districts— De La Warr, Laurel and affluent Alexis I. du Pont — have failed to win voter approval for tax hikes. A fourth, Newark, succeeded last fall, and a fifth, Marshallton-McKean, is trying Saturday.

School officials in other districts would dearly love to have voters approve higher taxes, but their crystal balls tell them the effort won't succeed.

Taxpayers, hurting enough from recession and inflation, aren't willing to increase their taxes voluntarily, school officials say. Moreover, they note the public believes fewer students mean reduced costs and voters show occasional dissatisfaction with school performance.

Further, New Castle County school officials note voters are unwilling to consider further tax hikes when they feel a metropolitan remedy to the Wilmington school desegregation suit would require higher school taxes, without a referendum.

"We will pare wherever we can, but each year we have to pare more," says Laurence Hopp, the superintendent in De La Warr, where austerity is a way of life. In Alexis I. du Pont, considered the gem of Delaware's school systems, Supt. James B. Pugh is talking of a De La Warr-style program next year, with all sorts of programs reduced or eliminated and about 30 fewer teachers on the payroll.

School officials are hoping to concentrate their budget cuts in areas that won't have a direct impact on instruction, but the enrollment drops are making teachers the big losers in the situation. 95 teachers lost jobs in Wilmington, 50 (including 22 part-timers) in Alfred I. du Pont, 29 in Alexis I. du Pont, 20 in Conrad, 17 in De La Warr, and so on. If enrollment projections improve, many will return to their jobs, but a good number will be looking for other work.

For school officials no relief is in sight. Consider the following points:

■ Local school boards generally have no more room to raise taxes without a referendum, and boards don't think voters would approve.

A request for a $2.3 million appropriation to cover increases in already-incurred utility bills is bottled up in a House committee. A similar bill passed last year. If it doesn't happen again, school offi-

See SCHOOLMEN—P 43,

Del. counties welcome Md. plan to build tire reefs

By Nancy Kesler
Sussex Bureau

A recent request by Ocean City, Md. for old tires to build artificial fishing reefs has come as good news to two Delaware counties.

Ocean City hopes to establish three reefs this year with 100,000 ties in each. Almost 40,000 have already been baled and are ready to barge to the sites off the Ocean City beach.

Mayor Harry Kelly said it could be the beginning of a series of reefs which are designed to provide protection and spawning areas for fish, and give recreational fishermen a good place to drop their lines. A similar reef system was established off the North Carolina coast.

William C. Henry, Sussex County engineer, said if Ocean City took tires ordinarily disposed of at county landfills, it would be a big help to the county landfill program.

Henry H. Gunther, sanitary engineer for Kent County, echoed Henry's comments, saying Kent officials have already visited Ocean City to discuss the project.

Kent County charges residents to dispose of the tires, which Gunther says don't stay buried well. The tires also take up a lot of space. Gunther estimates the county may be collecting as many as two tires per person each year. If so, then between Kent and Sussex there are enough tires thrown away to completely satisfy Ocean City's needs.

Gunther said Kent was looking at the economics of the situation, hoping the tires could be transported to Ocean City for about what Kent now charges to dispose of them.

Fishing enthusiasts along the Delaware Coast have been trying to establish a similar reef near sunken ships about 6 miles off the Indian River Inlet. Howard Symour of the Delmarva Artificial Reef Association said the group ran out of money last fall after sinking about 4,500 tires over a period of several years.

He said his group would like to sink another 10,000 tires. The cost, he said, would be about $1,500 in barge fees and cement to weight the tires.

State sends bulk of tax refunds

From the Dover Bureau

DOVER — A major check-writing effort last weekend completed the bulk of the Delaware income tax refunds due the state's taxpayers.

3,610 checks totaling $405,000 were mailed, bringing to 155,600 refunds totaling $17.5 million for the year, according to Department of Finance Secretary John Malarkey.

Malarkey said refunds averaged $112, about $15 more than last year's average. "The only remaining returns to be processed are a few very troublesome ones we have been working on," Malarkey said. "We expect those claims to be straightened out in the next couple weeks."

Malarkey said this would be the first year in recent history that all returns would be processed and refunds mailed by June 30.

Kent firemen win battle of the callboard

By Sam Waltz
Dover Bureau

DOVER — Kent County volunteer firemen and the levy court made peace this week.

Levy court commissioners voted to remove the switchboard telephone from the emergency callboard room used to dispatch firemen and ambulances throughout the county.

The telephone had been installed for a 30-day trial the last week of April without the knowledge or consent of the firemen. The county maintained the hookup was necessary to provide an answering service for the switchboard after other county offices closed about 4:30 or 5 p.m. The callboard is operated 24 hours a day by two-man shifts.

About 50 firemen appeared before levy court last week as representatives for the county's approximately 2,000 volunteer firemen. In a strongly emotional argument that had political overtones too, the firemen demanded that the telephone hookup to the switchboard be removed.

By a 4-2 vote, the levy court complied on Tuesday. Commissioners John T. McKenna, D-Dover, and Samuel G. Thomas, D-Camden, dissented.

lottery

Maryland weekly winners:
159438, 03559, 722-54.
New Jersey Wednesday winner:
31384.
Pennsylvania Double Dollars:
267918, 90596,
1169, 268, 6.

Figure 14–25. Grid makeup with page being divided into 5:1 ratio. [*Courtesy The Morning News, Wilmington Delaware.*]

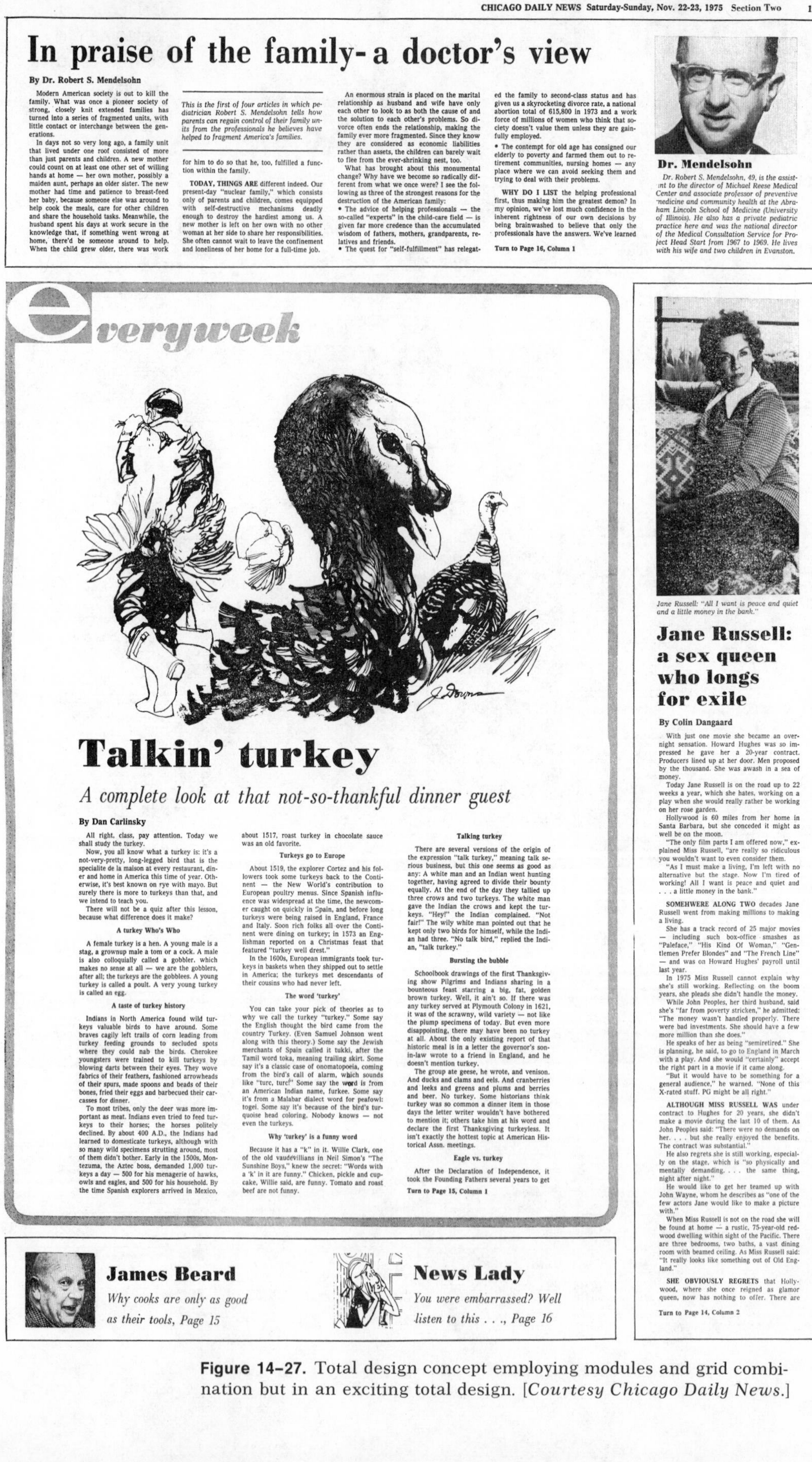

CHICAGO DAILY NEWS Saturday-Sunday, Nov. 22-23, 1975 Section Two 13

In praise of the family- a doctor's view

By Dr. Robert S. Mendelsohn

Modern American society is out to kill the family. What was once a pioneer society of strong, closely knit extended families has turned into a series of fragmented units, with little contact or interchange between the generations.

In days not so very long ago, a family unit that lived under one roof consisted of more than just parents and children. A new mother could count on at least one other set of willing hands at home — her own mother, possibly a maiden aunt, perhaps an older sister. The new mother had time and patience to breast-feed her baby, because someone else was around to help cook the meals, care for other children and share the household tasks. Meanwhile, the husband spent his days at work secure in the knowledge that, if something went wrong at home, there'd be someone around to help. When the child grew older, there was work for him to do so that he, too, fulfilled a function within the family.

This is the first of four articles in which pediatrician Robert S. Mendelsohn tells how parents can regain control of their family units from the professionals he believes have helped to fragment America's families.

TODAY, THINGS ARE different indeed. Our present-day "nuclear family," which consists only of parents and children, comes equipped with self-destructive mechanisms deadly enough to destroy the hardiest among us. A new mother is left on her own with no other woman at her side to share her responsibilities. She often cannot wait to leave the confinement and loneliness of her home for a full-time job.

An enormous strain is placed on the marital relationship as husband and wife have only each other to look to as both the cause of and the solution to each other's problems. So divorce often ends the relationship, making the family ever more fragmented. Since they know they are considered as economic liabilities rather than assets, the children can barely wait to flee from the ever-shrinking nest, too.

What has brought about this monumental change? Why have we become so radically different from what we once were? I see the following as three of the strongest reasons for the destruction of the American family:

• The advice of helping professionals — the so-called "experts" in the child-care field — is given far more credence than the accumulated wisdom of fathers, mothers, grandparents, relatives and friends.

• The quest for "self-fulfillment" has relegated the family to second-class status and has given us a skyrocketing divorce rate, a national abortion total of 615,800 in 1973 and a work force of millions of women who think that society doesn't value them unless they are gainfully employed.

• The contempt for old age has consigned our elderly to poverty and farmed them out to retirement communities, nursing homes — any place where we can avoid seeking them and trying to deal with their problems.

WHY DO I LIST the helping professional first, thus making him the greatest demon? In my opinion, we've lost much confidence in the inherent rightness of our own decisions by being brainwashed to believe that only the professionals have the answers. We've learned

Turn to Page 16, Column 1

Dr. Mendelsohn

Dr. Robert S. Mendelsohn, 49, is the assistant to the director of Michael Reese Medical Center and associate professor of preventive medicine and community health at the Abraham Lincoln School of Medicine (University of Illinois). He also has a private pediatric practice here and was the national director of the Medical Consultation Service for Project Head Start from 1967 to 1969. He lives with his wife and two children in Evanston.

everyweek

Talkin' turkey

A complete look at that not-so-thankful dinner guest

By Dan Carlinsky

All right, class, pay attention. Today we shall study the turkey.

Now, you all know what a turkey is: it's a not-very-pretty, long-legged bird that is the specialite de la maison at every restaurant, diner and home in America this time of year. Otherwise, it's best known on rye with mayo. But surely there is more to turkeys than that, and we intend to teach you.

There will not be a quiz after this lesson, because what difference does it make?

A turkey Who's Who

A female turkey is a hen. A young male is a stag, a grownup male a tom or a cock. A male is also colloquially called a gobbler, which makes no sense at all — we are the gobblers, after all; the turkeys are the gobblees. A young turkey is called a poult. A very young turkey is called an egg.

A taste of turkey history

Indians in North America found wild turkeys valuable birds to have around. Some braves cagily left trails of corn leading from turkey feeding grounds to secluded spots where they could nab the birds. Cherokee youngsters were trained to kill turkeys by blowing darts between their eyes. They wove fabrics of their feathers, fashioned arrowheads of their spurs, made spoons and beads of their bones, fried their eggs and barbecued their carcasses for dinner.

To most tribes, only the deer was more important as meat. Indians even tried to feed turkeys to their horses; the horses politely declined. By about 400 A.D., the Indians had learned to domesticate turkeys, although with so many wild specimens strutting around, most of them didn't bother. Early in the 1500s, Montezuma, the Aztec boss, demanded 1,000 turkeys a day — 500 for his menagerie of hawks, owls and eagles, and 500 for his household. By the time Spanish explorers arrived in Mexico, about 1517, roast turkey in chocolate sauce was an old favorite.

Turkeys go to Europe

About 1519, the explorer Cortez and his followers took some turkeys back to the Continent — the New World's contribution to European poultry menus. Since Spanish influence was widespread at the time, the newcomer caught on quickly in Spain, and before long turkeys were being raised in England, France and Italy. Soon rich folks all over the Continent were dining on turkey; in 1573 an Englishman reported on a Christmas feast that featured "turkey well drest."

In the 1600s, European immigrants took turkeys in baskets when they shipped out to settle in America; the turkeys met descendants of their cousins who had never left.

The word 'turkey'

You can take your pick of theories as to why we call the turkey "turkey." Some say the English thought the bird came from the country Turkey. (Even Samuel Johnson went along with this theory.) Some say the Jewish merchants of Spain called it tukki, after the Tamil word toka, meaning trailing skirt. Some say it's a classic case of onomatopoeia, coming from the bird's call of alarm, which sounds like "turc, turc!" Some say the word is from an American Indian name, furkee. Some say it's from a Malabar dialect word for peafowl: togei. Some say it's because of the bird's turquoise head coloring. Nobody knows — not even the turkeys.

Why 'turkey' is a funny word

Because it has a "k" in it. Willie Clark, one of the old vaudevillians in Neil Simon's "The Sunshine Boys," knew the secret: "Words with a 'k' in it are funny." Chicken, pickle and cupcake, Willie said, are funny. Tomato and roast beef are not funny.

Talking turkey

There are several versions of the origin of the expression "talk turkey," meaning talk serious business, but this one seems as good as any: A white man and an Indian went hunting together, having agreed to divide their bounty equally. At the end of the day they tallied up three crows and two turkeys. The white man gave the Indian the crows and kept the turkeys. "Hey!" the Indian complained. "Not fair!" The wily white man pointed out that he kept only two birds for himself, while the Indian had three. "No talk bird," replied the Indian, "talk turkey."

Bursting the bubble

Schoolbook drawings of the first Thanksgiving show Pilgrims and Indians sharing in a bounteous feast starring a big, fat, golden brown turkey. Well, it ain't so. If there was any turkey served at Plymouth Colony in 1621, it was of the scrawny, wild variety — not like the plump specimens of today. But even more disappointing, there may have been no turkey at all. About the only existing report of that historic meal is in a letter the governor's son-in-law wrote to a friend in England, and he doesn't mention turkey.

The group ate geese, he wrote, and venison. And ducks and clams and eels. And cranberries and leeks and greens and plums and berries and beer. No turkey. Some historians think turkey was so common a dinner item in those days the letter writer wouldn't have bothered to mention it; others take him at his word and declare the first Thanksgiving turkeyless. It isn't exactly the hottest topic at American Historical Assn. meetings.

Eagle vs. turkey

After the Declaration of Independence, it took the Founding Fathers several years to get

Turn to Page 15, Column 1

Jane Russell: "All I want is peace and quiet and a little money in the bank."

Jane Russell: a sex queen who longs for exile

By Colin Dangaard

With just one movie she became an overnight sensation. Howard Hughes was so impressed he gave her a 20-year contract. Producers lined up at her door. Men proposed by the thousand. She was awash in a sea of money.

Today Jane Russell is on the road up to 22 weeks a year, which she hates, working on a play when she would really rather be working on her rose garden.

Hollywood is 60 miles from her home in Santa Barbara, but she conceded it might as well be on the moon.

"The only film parts I am offered now," explained Miss Russell, "are really so ridiculous you wouldn't want to even consider them.

"As I must make a living, I'm left with no alternative but the stage. Now I'm tired of working! All I want is peace and quiet and . . . a little money in the bank."

SOMEHWERE ALONG TWO decades Jane Russell went from making millions to making a living.

She has a track record of 25 major movies — including such box-office smashes as "Paleface," "His Kind Of Woman," "Gentlemen Prefer Blondes" and "The French Line" — and was on Howard Hughes' payroll until last year.

In 1975 Miss Russell cannot explain why she's still working. Reflecting on the boom years, she pleads she didn't handle the money.

While John Peoples, her third husband, said she's "far from poverty stricken," he admitted: "The money wasn't handled properly. There were bad investments. She should have a few more million than she does."

He speaks of her as being "semiretired." She is planning, he said, to go to England in March with a play. And she would "certainly" accept the right part in a movie if it came along.

"But it would have to be something for a general audience," he warned. "None of this X-rated stuff. PG might be all right."

ALTHOUGH MISS RUSSELL WAS under contract to Hughes for 20 years, she didn't make a movie during the last 10 of them. As John Peoples said: "There were no demands on her. . . . but she really enjoyed the benefits. The contract was substantial."

He also regrets she is still working, especially on the stage, which is "so physically and mentally demanding. . . . the same thing, night after night."

He would like to get her teamed up with John Wayne, whom he describes as "one of the few actors Jane would like to make a picture with."

When Miss Russell is not on the road she will be found at home — a rustic, 75-year-old redwood dwelling within sight of the Pacific. There are three bedrooms, two baths, a vast dining room with beamed ceiling. As Miss Russell said: "It really looks like something out of Old England."

SHE OBVIOUSLY REGRETS that Hollywood, where she once reigned as glamor queen, now has nothing to offer. There are

Turn to Page 14, Column 2

James Beard

Why cooks are only as good as their tools, Page 15

News Lady

You were embarrassed? Well listen to this . . ., Page 16

Figure 14–27. Total design concept employing modules and grid combination but in an exciting total design. [*Courtesy Chicago Daily News.*]

15

Contemporary Makeup and Design Practices

Almost every newspaper editorial office has a set of rules, written or unwritten, to be followed by those engaged in makeup. These rules may have been handed down from one generation to another so that over the years they may have become inflexible. Even when the rules do not have a long history, they tend to be inflexible. Young makeup editors, especially, are not expected to challenge or change them. The assumption is that because they are founded on traditional makeup practices, they must be good. Consequently, there have been few radical changes in makeup and design within the last fifty years.

Evaluating Makeup Rules

Recently, however, makeup editors have been making changes, some of which appear radical when compared with traditional makeup. These editors have been evaluating all the older makeup rules and have found many to be logically indefensible. Therefore, they have substituted new and more logical makeup techniques for older ones. In some cases, they have used research to show an older makeup rule invalid.

Anyone who wants to create contemporary design ought to examine the rules of makeup to see whether they should be continued or replaced with something better. One example, perhaps, will suffice to illustrate the need for evaluation.

In its makeup manual a large metropolitan newspaper still maintains that headlines placed underneath pictures must be set in all-capital letters. The reason given is that when type is set in all caps it forms an imaginary straight line next to the picture. If a headline is to be placed above a picture, then it should also be set in all caps so that there will be no ascenders of letters next to the picture.

The assumption underlying the rule is that lower-case letters are harder to read when placed next to pictures because the ascenders or descenders form a ragged imaginary line next to the straight line of the photograph. Capital letters, on the other hand, form a straight imaginary line and are therefore easier to read.

The assumption, of course, is wrong, Research on the readability of type has shown that individuals read by recognizing the shapes of words rather than by visually sighting each letter and forming a word (Figure 15–1).[1] Only when faced with unfamiliar words might a reader sight each letter. Therefore, lines set in lower-case type are really easier to read than lines set in all caps. The same research also showed that all cap lines are read about 12 per cent slower than those set in caps and lower case.[2] The rule, therefore, is invalid. Yet no one has taken the trouble to question it and even today it is still used.

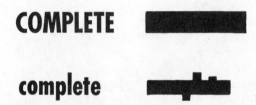

Figure 15–1. Lower case word shapes are easier to recognize and read than all-capital word shapes.

Although there is not enough research on which to base all makeup rules, some research is available. Where there is no research, rules will have to be evaluated on the basis of reason and logic. Even then, care must be taken not to confuse the needs of contemporary readers with those of the past. In a less sophisticated age, where graphic design was not considered as important as it is now, many makeup rules were appropriate. Today, such rules are not valid. The use of "30" dashes to separate the end of one story and the beginning of another is an example. Years ago it was thought to be logical to separate stories with a short line such as a 30 dash. But many such dashes on a page proved to be unsightly. Today they have been replaced with white space. Therefore, when young persons weigh makeup rules they ought to consider the age in which they live as well as each rule's potential effectiveness versus its limitations, using the standards of good makeup and design as a basis.

The following discussion suggests details that distinguish contemporary makeup from more traditional forms.

[1] Miles A. Tinker, *Legibility of Print* (Ames: Iowa State University Press, 1963), pp. 57–61.
[2] *Ibid.*

The nameplate of a newspaper (often incorrectly called the masthead) is the name usually appearing at the top of page 1. Editors sometimes want to move the nameplate to other positions on the page because they assume that everyone knows the name of the newspaper he is reading and the space occupied by the nameplate might be better used for other purposes. Once a decision has been made to move the nameplate, then a question arises: Where on the page would the nameplate be most appropriate? Editors sometimes want to move it indiscriminately, considering the significance of news the most important criterion for positioning stories. Such editors feel that the nameplate is much less significant and therefore may be moved anywhere at almost any time. At other times, the nameplate seems to be moved around on page 1 without any apparent reason.

On one hand, the logic of moving it from day to day seems reasonable. After all, most readers know the name of the newspaper without looking at the nameplate. But on the other hand, there are a number of reasons for keeping it in the top position most of the time. In debating the reasonableness of moving it around on the front page, one must consider all the purposes a nameplate serves.

Other than for simple identification purposes, a nameplate communicates the philosophical position of the publisher. The typefaces chosen for nameplates usually are distinguished-looking and have strong connotations. The best position for communicating these connotations is at the top of the page because the top position itself communicates a feeling of authority. Any object standing foremost among other objects is judged to be more significant. When an object is buried, its importance is diminished.

But another consideration has to do with the importance of the top position in serving as an anchoring device that provides readers with a feeling of stability as they read the paper. The nameplate usually represents the starting point for examining the contents of page 1. If it is not in its traditional position, the reader may sometimes have a sense of uneasiness and a slight loss of familiarity with the paper. Whereas he knows the news may change, the nameplate position will not, and he is thereby given a page whose stability tends to make reading comfortable.

Furthermore, postal regulations require that a newspaper indicate that it is second-class material somewhere within the first five pages of the paper. In the past, this material might be placed in the editorial page masthead, or it might be buried in a box on page 2. But it is also placed in small type near the nameplate, perhaps within the dateline rules that appear underneath it. If the nameplate serves this purpose, then it should remain at the top.

A final reason for keeping the nameplate at the top relates to its function in the total page design. A nameplate floated down in the page becomes a component of the page's design and there-

Positioning of Nameplates

by complicates the process of makeup and design. It is usually easier to make up a front page when the nameplate is at the top, with some exceptions of course.

Yet there is some logic to defend the decision to move it if the move is not radical and if it is not done often. There are times when an eight-column, horizontally arranged story might well be placed above the nameplate. This story may be of such significance that the editors want to be sure that everyone sees it. The very top position should provide such assurance. But if this practice becomes regular, the importance of the nameplate is thereby diminished (Figure 15–2).

There is also some logic to support the idea that a nameplate may be moved from side to side, but always at the top of the page. One of the most unsightly makeup devices of newspapers are the ears. When the editor wishes to eliminate them, he may do so by moving the nameplate to either side of the page and moving a one- or two-column story to the top. Another reason for moving the nameplate to the side may be to make room for more news than would be possible otherwise (Figure 15–3). Perhaps the editors who are most likely to experiment with moving the nameplate are those involved with publishing college newspapers. Their decisions to move it sometimes is based on the need to be creative. What is creative, however, may not be easy to read.

There are other uses for nameplates throughout the newspaper, but these do not involve moving the front page nameplate. For example, some newspapers have identical nameplates on pages 1 and 3. The effect of this arrangement is to present a second front page to readers so that different kinds of news may be featured on each front page. Although national news might be used exclusively on page 1, local news might be featured on page 3.

Finally, there are modified nameplates that may be used in various sections of the newspaper. Women's pages, sports, or financial pages also might have special nameplates. In reality, however, these are standing headlines rather than nameplates, and although they are designed to resemble the front page nameplate, their function is to introduce special sections of the newspaper.

Contemporary Headline Placement

When the traditional-minded makeup editor thinks of headlines, he tends to think of large display typefaces placed at the top of stories. This treatment is logical for pages designed to be strongly vertical in appearance. But when makeup is conceived of as being horizontal through the use of rectangularly shaped stories, headlines may be set in many different ways. These ways not only serve the purpose of summarizing the news but of making the page appear modern.

When horizontally shaped stories are used on a page, the headline may be placed in at least three places, and possibly a fourth. It may be placed at the left- or right-hand side, the center, or the bottom of the story. The last-named position is not as desirable as the others, but all are different from the traditional top position (Figures 15–4, 15–5 and 15–6).

If the headline is placed at the side of a story, it looks best if it aligns with the top line of body type. But the headline may be set flush left or flush right, both being contemporary treatments. The best position is at the left side of stories because readers proceed from the left to the right. Occasionally, the headline may look attractive when placed at the right.

When a story is given horizontal treatment, and it is long, the headline may be embedded in the center with type on all sides. There is some danger that a reader could be confused by this arrangement if he starts reading directly underneath the headline instead of starting at the top of the left-hand column. To avoid that, the makeup man must not start a sentence directly underneath the headline. This arrangement also requires the typesetter to plan his work carefully so that he can set type around the headline. Because such treatment takes extra time, it is used primarily for feature stories.

Finally, a headline may be placed at the bottom of a story when the story is clearly set off from the remainder of the page, such as in a large box. When the headline is at the bottom of the box, it will be apparent that it belongs to the story above. If not set inside a box, there is a possibility the readers may assume it belongs to some other story.

Treatment of Lead Paragraphs

Lead paragraphs of most stories consist of placing the first paragraph at the top of a story, set in type sizes that are larger than body type and, sometimes, leaded. The widths of most lead paragraphs are the same as body type, although occasionally they are set one or even two columns wider than the body type. Lead paragraphs are often made to stand out not only from the headlines above them, but from the body type below.

In contemporary newspaper design, however, lead paragraphs are often given more prominence than they would receive in traditional design. The feeling is that because lead paragraphs have replaced the old headline decks, they deserve more prominence. Decks were formerly used to summarize a story, with each deck featuring one outstanding aspect of that story. The lead paragraph, by employing more words set in smaller-sized type than decks, did a better job of summarizing the essential details. But as lead paragraphs came into common use, they were often accorded no better type treatment than body type. In contemporary design, they have been made more dramatic

Area teen-age pregnancies jump 33%

by LUISA GINNETTI

The number of reported teen-age pregnancies in the Northwest suburbs has increased by almost 33 per cent this year, according to records at Crossroads Clinic, Palatine.

Barbara Michelin, program director at the clinic, said the number of pregnancies thus far this year, in girls ages 12 to 18, is 736. Officials predict the total will reach 800 by the end of the year.

The number of teen-age pregnancies

in 1974 totaled about 600, Mrs. Michelin said.

MRS. MICHELIN SAID she is alarmed about the dramatic increase in teen-age pregnancies in the Northwest suburbs and said much of the problem is rooted in the home where parents fail to "treat their children as children."

"Parents want their children to be mature adults at a tender age but yet remain children," she said. "We are seeing the results of a generation that married too young, had their children

too young and are now pressuring their children to marry young."

Mrs. Michelin said the factors cited by teen-agers for becoming pregnant are excuses rather than reasons.

"We find a distinct pattern of alcoholism among one or both parents and the young people feel they are not being noticed," Mrs. Michelin said. "They want affection they are not receiving at home. This is the most stated reason."

PARENTS ALSO FAIL to recognize that children are young people with

their own identity and opinions, she said, and they fail to let their children state their views at home.

Mrs. Michelin said the factors also say their parents have a double standard telling children to "do as I say, not as I do."

"We find 14-and 15 year-old girls planning their pregnancies so they can get married and have a baby to love. They fantasize a better life than what they have."

More than 74 per cent of the pregnant teen-agers counseled at Cross-

roads this year are from Catholic homes. Mrs. Michelin said these girls admit they have had little or no sex education in the home, including discussion on emotions and morals.

"PARENTS ARE QUICK to blame others, like the school, but parents are the ones who dictate to educators what should be done in schools," she said. "Parents should take a stricter look at themselves."

"It's unfortunate that a problem like this has to be brought to a person's doorstep in order for it to be

realized," Mrs. Michelin said. "It's a tragic way to face reality."

A majority of the girls who visit the clinic are seeking information about abortions, she said. Mrs. Michelin said Crossroads does not tell a girl whether she should have an abortion but instead counsels her about the factors she should consider in making a decision.

The clinic emphasizes, however, that the decision on abortion should be up to the girl and not her parents,
(Continued on Page 2)

GOOD MORNING!

The HERALD
PADDOCK PUBLICATIONS
Elk Grove Village

19th Year—161   Elk Grove Village, Illinois 60007   Monday, November 24, 1975   4 Sections, 28 Pages   Single Copy — 15c each

Snow

TODAY: Cloudy, snow flurries accumulating 1 to 2 inches. High 30, low 20.

TUESDAY: Cloudy, snow flurries ending. High in the 20s.

Map on Page 2.

Vandals damage 29 cars in lot at condominium

Vandals damaged 29 cars in the parking lot of Village-on-the-Lake condominiums in Elk Grove Village, police said Sunday.

Roof tops and tires were slashed, and motor oil was poured on a Jeep, police said. Windshield wipers were torn from the cars and apparently scraped along the car bodies.

Hub caps were stolen, and most of the vehicles were entered and rummaged through. Police were investigating thefts from the cars, but no information was available Sunday.

POLICE SAID a patrolman discovered hub caps missing from several vehicles Sunday morning, and when he stopped to investigate, he

found other vehicles had been vandalized.

The complex is located at the 800 block of Wellington Avenue. The vandalism had occurred sometime Saturday night or early Sunday, police reported. Total damage estimates were not available.

Residents were out inspecting their cars late Sunday morning, and police were dusting the damaged cars for fingerprints.

Eric Jannasch of the complex reported to investigating patrolman Stephen Schmidt that the convertible top to his auto was slashed and ripped by the vandals. Jannasch also reported that the seats to his auto were slashed open during the vandalism spree.

Gazebo proposed for Disney Park

Disney Park has been proposed as the site of a gazebo planned by the Elk Grove Park Board for community concerts and other events.

Park Comr. James L. Cashman said his committee looked at five different park sites before determining Disney Park would be the best. He said the gazebo, if approved, would be located south of Biesterfield Road and just east of the tennis courts.

The location of the gazebo will be discussed at today's 8 p.m. meeting of the park board at the park office, 499 Biesterfield Rd. Also to be discussed is locating the historical society museum on park property.

CASHMAN SAID the Disney Park site would be best for the gazebo because it is convenient for population centers, including senior citizen apartments; is not adjacent to residences; has parking, can easily be guarded against vandals and is aesthetically pleasing.

Roosevelt Park and Lions Park also
(Continued on Page 5)

The inside story		
	Sect.	Page
Bridge	2	6
Classifieds	4	1
Comics	2	5
Crossword	2	6
Dr. Lamb	3	4
Editorials	1	6
Horoscope	2	6
Movies	2	6
Obituaries	1	8
School Lunches	1	4
School Notebook	1	5
Sports	2	1
Suburban Living	3	1
Today on TV	2	6

A reminder . . .

The home delivery rate for The Herald will be increased to 80 cents per week effective Nov. 24. The rate adjustment was made necessary by sharply rising costs of distribution, newsprint and manufacturing.

ERIC JANNASCH, of Village-on-the-Lake condominiums in the 800 block of Wellington Avenue, Elk Grove Village, shows Patrolman Stephen Schmidt the damage to his auto caused by vandals during the weekend. Police said 28 other autos in the complex were vandalized.

Mental center weighs extra cash

The Elk Grove-Schaumburg Townships Mental Health Center could receive an additional $160,000 in federal funds for its proposed center if it can successfully appeal to the state for a change in its funding classification.

Anne Fraser, the center's development coordinator, said Friday the mental health center could qualify for two-thirds federal aid rather than 40 per cent if the reclassification can be obtained. As it stands now, the center is eligible for $240,000.

Ms. Fraser said the state classified municipalities in 1973 on a basis of need for federal funding programs,

and Elk Grove Village came in very low.

"WE WILL APPEAL this ranking," she said. "We're going to write to state officials and ask them to reconsider."

Ms. Fraser said hope for reclassification exists because the original rankings were based on poverty, not mental health needs, and the rankings were meant as a plan and not a legal guideline.

She said the center can only qualify for the 40 per cent federal funding because of the low ranking, although the full federal program permits the two-

thirds funding.

Based on the current $600,000 cost projection for the new facility to be built west of Ill. Rte. 53, the center could receive $400,000 if the two-thirds funding were approved.

IF THE BUILDING were built today, Ms. Fraser said it would cost $530,000. Because the building won't be constructed for two years, building costs are expected to rise to $600,000.

The mental health center board Thursday approved $6,000 for architect fees, with the facilities planning committee to choose either O. Kleb and Associates, Oak Brook, or FGM

Inc., Aurora, for the work. Kleb will only be considered if it lowers its proposed fee which is 1 per cent higher than the other firm's low estimate, Ms. Fraser said.

The mental health center board also has decided to call its fundraising association the Friends of the Elk Grove-Schaumburg Townships Mental Health Center, and an attempt will be made to incorporate the group as a not-for-profit organization.

Tentatively proposed membership fees are $5, $10, $25, $50 and $100. There will also be business memberships.

Chicago invasion unlikely: scientist

'Killer bee' fears exaggerated

by JILL BETTNER

An invasion — sometime in the 1990s — by so-called South American killer bees is about as likely as an army of Martians eating Chicago, according to some entomologists.

In fact experts are surprised at the amount of publicity the little buzzers are getting. Many say the publicity is spreading science fiction scare stories, but the bees, supposedly on their way here from South and Central America at the rate of between 200 and 300 miles a year, continue to get a lot of attention in the media.

One Chicago entomologist, Stanley Rachesky, of the University of Illinois cooperative extension service, said

the stories about deadly swarms of bees launching a massive attack on the U.S. "make interesting reading," but he makes light of them.

"I'VE HEARD SO many different stories. Everybody is hypothesizing," he said. "I, myself, have absolutely no concern about these bees at this point. They're so far away and the chances of them coming here are so remote that it's like worrying whether a plague is going to hit next year."

Rachesky said the bees, who reportedly could cross into Texas sometime between 1988 and 1994, have been studied seriously by scientists for the past two years. Most of the discussion, even among many experts,

however, is still "cocktail party talk."

"Right now, this thing is still in the raised eyebrows stage," Rachesky said. "According to talk I just heard, the population of bees has stabilized and the terrain of that area of the world has confined them to just certain parts of South America. People tend toward sensationalism, but by the time they get here, they'll be so cross-bred I doubt they'll be dangerous."

Other entomologists are less convinced. Orley R. Taylor, of the University of Kansas, recently told a conference of science writers that while he deplores reports the bees could cause a wave of death to humans and

animals, he believes the creatures should not be lightly dismissed.

"THERE'S NOTHING to suggest they are a serious threat to public health or safety, but they are aggressive and they certainly will be aggressive when they enter the United States," Taylor said.

Taylor, who heads one of two U.S. Dept. of Agriculture teams of scientists doing research on the bees, said though Brazilian authorities have reported the bees have killed between 100 and 300 persons in that area since 1957, there is no cause for panic in this country.

Officials here are more concerned
(Continued on Page 2)

INVASION PLAN—B

312

The Skokie Life

A Lerner Newspaper serving the people of Skokie

The paper with the want ads

Vol. 24—No. 19 | Four Sections, 72 Pages | THURSDAY, JANUARY 8, 1970 | 10 Cents Per Copy | Want Ads, Section Three, Pages 6-17

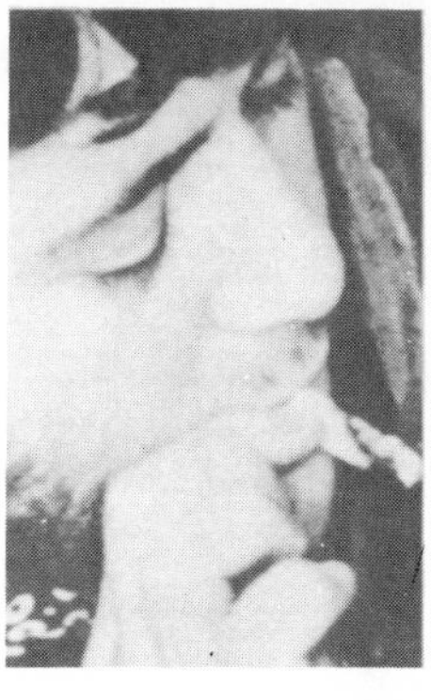

Drugs: is there an answer? See Focus on LIFE-land. Section 1-A, page one.

2,000 residents ask tax repeal

By CHARLENE LOUIS
Lerner Newspapers Correspondent

SKOKIE—Skokie Board of Trustees was presented Monday night with some 2,000 signed cards requesting the repeal of the five per cent municipal utility tax adopted by the board last summer.

Reinforcing the citizen demand was a delegation of some 40 persons, representing both homeowners and industry.

WHILE THE people did not get what they most hoped for—an immediate board vote to repeal the tax—they did get something definite—the promise of several trustees that the board will look at the tax again, when the picture regarding monies accruing to the village from the new sales tax and state income tax is fact rather than guesstimate.

The village finance officer will probably not be able to establish a pattern from these figures until about April or May. Currently, the village has received only $64,784 as its pro-rata share of the income tax.

As confrontations go, the skirmish this night in Village hall was rather short, with the people making their presentations, and most of the trustees offering a statement in return.

PRINCIPAL spokesman for the gallery was village merchant Norman Schack. He talked about how burdensome the tax has become, and about how a group of people have banned together to ask for its review, as occurred in Morton Grove. The drive was led by Mrs. Fred Nemeroff, 8119 Kilbourn.

Schack noted that the new tax had won approval by a 4-3 vote, and suggested that perhaps some of the "ayes" might consider becoming "nays," "especially in view of the additional sales tax and state income tax monies coming to the village," he said.

However, the key point of his argument was that the utility tax monies would no longer be needed since the village won't be using some $500,000 in the budget for a capital investment this fiscal year."

SCHACK WAS obviously referring to the fact that $350,000 budgeted for new incinerator grates will not be spent in the current fiscal year. (A new method of garbage disposal is being considered).

As long as the village does not need this, let's repeal it." he said. "If you prove need, that's another thing."

The idea of "a floating $500,000 in the budget" was reputed vehemently by Trustee Edward Fleischman. A succession of business people and residents came before the podium to give their reasons for protesting this new tax.

Edwin Stone of a Skokie firm, Metal Treating and Engineering, chided that the tax imposes a great burden on the small businessman. "The amount of this tax on me will exceed what I will pay for the state income tax."

WILLIAM NIGUT, 8232 Karlov, who ran for Con-Con, charged that responsibility for the defeat of one of the Skokie library referenda could be laid on the shoulders of the four village officials who voted for the utility tax."

When it was Fleischman's turn, his remarks developed into something of a speech. He was trying to get several points across. First, that it was "wonderful" that the people come up here to express their feelings and their interest.

However, he said, "It shows that we need to amplify our reasons for needing this tax and our attitudes toward it."

THE BUDGET study, he said, pointed out that we needed more money.

"But the question was how to get it. Nobody wanted the utility tax; but we thought it was more equitable."

"We also made it part and parcel of the tax ordinance that we would have to review the tax on or before Aug. 30, 1970, because then we would know how much money these new taxes would be bringing in."

"Today, by chance," he continued, "we went over the budget income and outgo to date. We found out that as far as revenue goes, we are close to $400,000 short.

"With $350,000 unspent, if we come out with a bal-

(Continued on page 3)

NORMAN SCHACK

What's happening

CELEBRATION . . . Mr. and Mrs. Ben Wasken, 8027 Kilpatrick, Skokie, celebrated their 40th anniversary, Dec. 28, with a dinner at Pyrenees restaurant for relatives and close friends.

INSTALLATION . . . Andy Nickols of Lincolnwood is a co-chairman of the Variety Club of Illinois' installation luncheon to be held Monday, Jan. 12 at 12:30 p.m. in the Windsor room of the Pick-Congress Hotel. Henry Markbreit, 9517 Keeler, Skokie, will be installed as second assistant barker and Harry Balaban, 420 Brierhill, Deerfield, will be installed as dough guy.

ON DEAN'S LIST . . . Jean Dalicandro, daughter of Mr. and Mrs. Robert Dalicandro, 8631 Karlov, Skokie, is eligible to become a candidate for the honors program as a result of the 3.6 average earned during the Fall Quarter at Ohio State university in Columbus.

Jeanie, a Freshman in the Humanities college, is a graduate of Regina Dominican high school in Wilmette. She is listed in the 1969 Edition of Merit's Who's Who Among American High School Students, which features the top 3 per cent of the nation's graduating seniors.

VOTER REGISTRATION . . . Skokie Village Clerk William Siegel has announced that the village will conduct a voter registration drive through Jan. 20.

New residents, recently naturalized citizens, and young adults who have just turned 21 must register in order to vote in this important election year, Siegel said.

Village hall, 5127 Oakton, is open from 8:30 a.m. to 5 p.m. weekdays and from 8:30 a.m. to noon Saturdays. Call OR 3-0500 for further information.

VEEP . . . Robert Shonfeld, 6951 Knox, Lincolnwood, has been elected a vice-president of Clinton E. Frank, Inc., Advertising. Shonfeld joined the agency in 1957 as an account executive.

INSTALLATION . . . Henry Markbeit, 9517 Skokie, will be installed as second assistant chief barker of Tent 26, Variety Club of Illinois, at the installation luncheon to be held on Monday, Jan. 12, at 12:30 p.m. in the Pick-Congress hotel. Andy Nickols, 4066 Touhy, Lincolnwood, is a co-chairman for the affair.

TO SPEAK . . . Keigler E. Flake, consultant for subscription television at Zenith Radio Corp., 1900 N. Austin, Chicago, will be guest speaker Jan. 19 at the Lincolnwood Men's club.

His subject, "Subscription Television: what is it?" will include the development of STV, what it will mean to the public and action by federal authorities to control STV.

Flake, a retired U.S. Marine Corps colonel, managed Zenith's Hartford, Conn., STV experiment and was named vice-president-general manager of RKO General's WHCT-TV in 1966.

The Men's Club meeting will be held at the Kenilworth Inn, 7100 Lincoln, Lincolnwood.

Brotman resigns post in District 74

By JUDITH HEYMAN
Lerner Newspapers Correspondent

LINCOLNWOOD—The Lincolnwood School Board Tuesday accepted a letter of resignation from Board Member Robert Brotman and formulated plans to appoint a successor.

The board will entertain applications from those people who have appeared before the nominating caucus or any other residents of the community.

INTERESTED persons should contact Dr. Marvin Garlich, superintendent of Dist. 74, to file an application by Thursday, Jan. 15.

Candidates will be interviewed and a selection made at the next school board meeting, Jan. 20, which will be held at 7 p.m. rather than 8 p.m., the regular scheduled hour.

The new board member will then stand for election April 11, to fulfill the remaining one year of Brotman's term.

LEGALLY, the board must fill the position by Feb. 3, 1970, or the County Superintendent of Schools can call a special election.

Brotman resigned in order to take a position in Palo Alto, Calif. He is an accountant and in the words of Board President, Shirley Garland, "has been a valuable asset to this board, and we greatly regret his leaving."

There will be three additional vacancies to be filled on April 11. The three-year terms of Mrs. Garland, Dr. Theodore Balsam and Eric Moch expire. According to nominating caucus standards (one person can serve only two successive terms) only Moch and Dr. Balsam are eligible. Mrs. Garland is completing her sixth year on the board.

NOMINATING petitions for school board membership must be filed between Feb. 25 and March 20, between 8 a.m. and 4 p.m. on any school day with Eugene Moody at the school district's administration building.

In other business the board delayed approval of a restaffing plan for Todd Hall presented by Dr. Garlich.

Since enrollment will be down, the plan called for replacing one homeroom with an art room and using the funds allotted for a section teacher to provide a full-time physical education teacher. This plan would not increase the budget.

"**THE ART ROOM** would facilitate the duties of the art teacher," according to Dr. Garlich.

He explained that dropping a section would not increase the 2nd grade-class size, which would decrease from an average of 27 or 28 pupils to about 26 per class. However, it would increase the first grade class size by about 2 pupils per room.

Board members questioned whether they should not use the decreased enrollment as an opportunity to commit themselves to smaller class size. They also wanted time to consider other possible uses for the additional space, such as a remedial reading class. A decision will be made at the next board meeting.

DR. GARLICH stated his position to a remedial reading teacher for primary grades, saying that "if the primary teacher has any expertise, it is in the field of teaching reading.

"I have never seen a successful remedial reading program for that age level, because some children will never be good readers no matter what the instruction. This kind of program simply gives the classroom teacher an excuse to evade her duties."

He added that he does believe in reading diagnosis for those grades.

Dr. Garlich defended his re-staffing program for Todd Hall stating, "We are in an enviable position in terms of enrollment. Within the next few years I also see a decrease in the enrollment at Rutledge, which may free some space there for other programs."

Employes get preview of village diabetes test project

DR. SAMUEL L. ANDELMAN, Skokie health director, supervises as Nurse Florence Lazerson, draws blood sample from William Macdougall, village animal control officer during a preview of the village's diabetes detection program. Appointments for the program which begins Jan. 11. can be made by calling the Health Department, OR 3-0500.

SKOKIE—Samuel L. Andelman, health director, Skokie Health department announced that Skokie employes had a "sneak preview" of the public screening tests for diabetes detection to begin Sunday morning, Jan. 11.

Wednesday, Dec. 24, was a private day at the Skokie Health department.

Employees from Village Hall had been instructed to partake heavily of carbohydrates (sugars and starches) for the few days preceding the test and to fast from midnight the night before, with no food or water.

IN THE MORNING they drank an orange-flavored glucose solution and exactly one hour later a blood sample was drawn and sent to the laboratory to be tested for the amount of glucose in the blood.

Those who participated agreed that it was a smooth, simple procedure and were glad to find out whether or not they were suspected diabetics. The health department does not make diagnoses, what they hope to do is uncover the so-called 'hidden' diabetics.

Results of the tests are confidential and reported only to the person's private physician, with permission, if it is felt that further testing is advisable.

Dr. Matthew M. Steiner, chairman of the preventable Disease committee, and his committee, Dr. Herbert Lipschultz, chairman of the Skokie Board of Health, Dr. Melvin Chertack, Dr. Frank DiGilio, Dr. Lawrence L. Golden, Dr. John Gruhn, Bernard Kramer and Martin Lebedun, say there may be 2,500 people from 30 through 59 years of age in Skokie who unknowingly have diabetes.

If you are in this age group and live in Area 1, call Florence Hack, coordinator for the Diabetes detection program, OR 3-0500, and make an appointment.

JAN. 11, at 9 a.m. marks the beginning of this community program, brought to the public without charge. Area 1 is bounded on the north by Dempster, on the east by Skokie boulevard, and on the west and south by Skokie's natural boundaries. Testing in the other areas will be made known at a later time.

Many technicians and volunteer workers will be needed to aid this effort. Please call Mrs. Hack, OR 3-0500 and offer your services.

Auto-bargain section introduced by LIFE

A NEW SERVICE offered by The LIFE, beginning Jan. 8, will be our Super-Auto Mart section, which will feature a choice of automobile bargains, both new and used.

Dealers serving the entire LIFE-land areas, from Skokie, Morton Grove, Niles, Lincolnwood, Glenview, Des Plaines, Highland Park, Highwood, Deerfield, Fort Sheridan, Northbrook and Lake county, will advertise in this regular two-page section.

Edward Berliant, general manager of White and Cronen Ford, 9401 Milwaukee, Niles, said "Since most of our customers are from this area, we want to take care of the people in our vicinity through this service, where it has a more personal touch."

Mel Waldorf, president of Public Pontiac, 7501 N. Lincoln, Skokie, said "I think it will be advantageous for local people particularly at this time of the year. Like any other business, after January we have heavy inventories, and this is a good time for people to buy."

Red Weiss, used car manager at Walton Motors, 5050 Dempster, Skokie, said "We feel it will be advantageous for local people to buy locally, for the best service."

Super-Auto Mart will be advertised on WLFD TV, Channel 32, on WEEF and WSDM am-fm radio and on bus cards in Skokie.

Figure 15–2 [OPPOSITE]. Story above nameplate. [*Courtesy Elk Grove Ill., Herald.*]

Figure 15–3 [ABOVE]. Nameplate moved to the side. [*Courtesy Lerner Newspapers, Chicago, Illinois.*]

First of two sewer survey reports given city Monday

The first of two sewer survey reports was presented to the city council Monday at its regular meeting. The report concerned the sanitary system and was compiled by city engineers, Casler and Associates of Jacksonville.

The city council two months back voted $3500 for the survey, then later voted another $3500 for a storm sewer survey. The latter will be presented at a later date.

The Casler report is based on the idea of repairing the present system, adding relief or bypass sewers where necessary, the building of a new treatment plant to handle the western half of the city and the rehabilitation and additions to the present sewerage disposal plant east of the city.

The engineer's report gave the city several alternate plans but all are based on the idea of repairing the present system and treatment plant plus the new plant. The city sewer committee, Citizen's Sewer committee and mayor will meet in the next 60 days to study the report.

It is expected that the complete repair of the system and relief mains would not exceed $243,000 including all extra fees such as legal and engineering. The two treatment plants, old work and construction of a new one, would

cost approximately $410,000. The city could apply and probably receive a Federal grant of $120,000 for the latter work, leaving a balance of $290,000. The city would have to sell bonds to pay for the bulk of the cost with some work payable by reserve funds in the three city utility departments which presently total over $100,-000.

Presently the city is debt free, owning its own water, gas and sewerage departments.

The main part of the repair work of the present system would consist of a televised survey of the system which would tell exactly where all leaks and breaks were located. The breaks would have to be repaired by excavation and with new materials to the lines. Leaks would be filled with a plastic grout which would seal them. A machine, with the grout, is sent through the line and automatically fills the leaky spots. The work done by the tv method is guaranteed and it is estimated that repairs along this line would

last 20 or more years.

City workmen would be used to excavate and repair the major breaks in the line.

The new treatment plant would be constructed north of the city and would take some of the load off the present treatment plant which is not adequate for the number of residents presently served by it. New state laws also require some changes at the plant which would be incorporated with the repairs.

The new treatment plant would have pumping station and an influent sewer while the present plant would be repaired. Present plant would be repaired to meet state requirements and would provide for a tertiary treatment, flood protection and chlorination.

The report also shows that projecting the present population trends of the city that the present system and the treatment plant would not be able to handle the load. Auburn's population was 2441 in 1965 and is expected to be close to 2800 by 1970 with a projected population of 3500 by 1975.

Figure 15–4. Headline at the left of the story. [*Courtesy Cedar Falls Iowa Record.*]

By Tillman Durdin

HONG KONG—China-watchers are inclined to believe the Mao Tse-Tung-inspired Great Proletarian Cultural Revolution on the Communist mainland is at long last becoming a spent force.

Recent developments represent a decided gain for right-wing forces and a sharp setback for the radical aims and the most ardent partisans of the revolution as it was originally conceived.

Directives from Peking in the last two months widen still further the authority and the latitude of the military of conservative, bureaucratic elements allied to the military in a common desire to bring order and stability out of the chaos generated by the revolution.

The Red Guards and other "rebel" revolutionaries have been the instrument and power base of the so-called Cultural Revolution group in Peking, a directorate headed by Chen Po-Tan, an intimate of Communist party Chairman Mao Tse-Tung, with Mao's wife, Chiang Ching, its deputy director.

In late 1966 and early 1967 the Red Guards and other radicals were on effective force.

They rampaged about the country spreading and mercilessly enforcing the tenets of the new Maoism, disrupting the

China-watchers see shift from Mao revolution

old power structure at all levels, 'dragging out" the old power-holders for denunciation and dismissal, staging massive demonstrations and fomenting a profound revolutionary climate.

Early in the game, however, these vanguard elements revealed what eventually became their greatest weakness and the cause of their downfall. They developed factions that began to fight each other in struggles and disputes over what was and who genuinely represented the Cultural Revolution and the Maoist philosophy.

In many cases officials threatened by the Cultural Revolution formed protective Red Guards of their own. These were set against guard groups seeking their ouster.

Since all groups, as well as the officals backing them, professed boundless

loyalty to the revolution and Mao, it became difficult, indeed, often impossible, for officials and army men not directly involved to tell if any one Red Guard group was more genuinely Maoist than another and which to favor.

The faction fighting added chaos to turmoil.

Last fall the Peking leadership, under pressure from the army and moderates, authorized the military to move in and restore order. There was relative stability over the winter, but the Cultural Revolution's left-wing reasserted itself again this summer and the predictable faction-fighting flared up again on a national scale.

The regime now has authorized another crackdown, once more presumably because of arguments from military lead-

ers and the Maoist right wing that to let the mounting strife go on would risk national disintegration.

This time the measures taken to subordinate the Red Guards and other revolutionaries of the left may mean the coup de grace for this sector of the Cultural Revolution.

Even Mao-Tse-Tung, whose concept of the revolution is "leftist and radical," has had to admit disillusionment with the Red Guards. Reliable Peking sources report here that he broke down and wept in a session with five Red Guard leaders in Peking in late July during which he bitterly condemned them for their disunity and failure to carry through effectively revolutionary objectives.

Mao has, reluctantly, it can be assumed, given his signature to directives which have authorized military units to suppress faction-fighting with arms, if necessary, normalize railway traffic, particularly along the Vietnam supply route through Kwangsi, and push through the formation of new power organs, or revolutionary committees, in provinces where they had not been organized at the end of July.

Closely related to these measures was a directive from Mao which proclaimed workers and peasants, backed by the army, as the leading force in the Cultural Revolution. Student Red Guards along with older intellectuals have been told they must integrate with the workers and peasants in a subordinate status.

Figure 15–5. Headline in the center. [*Courtesy Cedar Falls Iowa Record.*]

in appearance and placed in more obvious positions relative to the remainder of the story.

When headlines are moved to the sides, center or bottom of a story, the lead paragraphs may be placed underneath the headline. However, in such cases, they should be set in a typeface and size that clearly contrasts with the remainder of the body type. Because the goal is to give them display treatment, the difference between lead paragraph appearance and body type appearance should be marked (Figure 15–7). The typeface should be one or two points larger than body type, set in sans serif, boldface or italic. Leading is necessary to make the lead stand out and yet be readable. One final treatment may be to set the lead paragraph flush left with ragged right, a distinctly contemporary appearance.

by dennis wheeler

[Newspaper story columns — "Thanksgiving" teaser text]

With Thanksgiving approaching, it is that time again to pause and consider the historical background for one of our most beloved holidays.

The Thanksgiving story, known to most of us from our earliest grade school days, is one of bravery in the face of giant adversity; one of achievement in the hour of supreme testing. It inspires reverence and hope in all of us. It is one of the true roots of our well-known American stick-to-itness.

You all remember, of course, how it happened back there in 1621. The Pilgrims had arrived at Plymouth Rock and had established their tiny foothold on the wild North American continent. Their lives beset by disease and tribulation, they managed to survive for some months. And then came winter, and near starvation. And the first Thanksgiving, at which the noble Pilgrims raised their eyes heavenward to thank the Almighty for providing them with enough food to make it through the long night of winter.

THOSE, OF COURSE, are the bare facts of the Thanksgiving tale. But people sometimes lose sight of how the Plymouth Rock adventure fit into the larger fabric of history. They overlook what was going on in the rest of the world; they forget against what historical backdrop the Pilgrim landscape was painted.

Well, I can help. A history buff of sorts, I can supply some of this additional information, the better to illuminate our heritage.

First of all, remember that the Pilgrims landed in North America at about the same time that old Will Shakespeare was writing his stuff back in England. In fact, some historians surmise that when Shakespeare wrote the famous line "Out, out, brief candle!" in MacBeth, he was referring to Candle Mather, the famous Bible-thumping leader of the Pilgrims, who was expelled from England by the King for complicity in burning Joan of Arc at the stake.

IT IS ALSO noteworthy that the landing of the Pilgrims took place shortly after the English defeated the Spanish in the famous sea battle of 1588, that's the one in which Sir Francis Tarkenton defeated the Spanish Armadillo mainly because the captains of the Armadillo's ships lost the toss and had to fight into the wind.

That's important because if the Armadillo had won, we might all be speaking Spanish today instead of English. But then on the other hand it is questionable whether the Spanish could have colonized North America as successfully as the English did. The Spanish are, after all, warm weather people, so they probably would have taken one look at cold Plymouth Rock and said, "No way, señors."

Besides, everybody knows you can't raise tacos in New England.

And don't forget the French.

AT THIS TIME, the French, led by Father University of Marquette and Louis XVI Joliet were selling booze to the Indians and canoeing down the Cal-Sag canal. One wonders what would have happened if communications in those days had been what they are today. If they were, the French would have heard on the 6 o'clock news that the Pilgrims had landed in Massachusetts, and (knowing them) they would have built the Erie canal across the Appalachian mountains and invaded Massachusetts from the west. Who knows? The battle of Bunker Hill could have happened 150 years early. I ask you: if that had occurred, where would Boston be today? In Montreal, that's where.

Not only that, we'd be speaking French today instead of English. Which means the entertainment center of New Orleans would be called be the German Quarter.

Why the German Quarter? Well, it's obvious. Because at about the same time the Pilgrims landed, the 73rd battle for Alsace-Lorraine was being waged between the French and the Germans in the Black Forest. The Germans won that one, and in the subsequent Peace of Westphalia, Adolph Hitler was able to wrest huge territorial concessions from the losing Frenchmen. And among these would have been a piece of New Orleans, which had just been explored by University of Marquette and Louis XIV Joliet and claimed for France.

AND IT would have stuck, because you can grow sauerkraut in a bayou.

But let's not jump so lightly over the Indians in this analysis. Remember, the Vikings, who under the leadership of Eric the Weird invaded the continent in the 11th Century, tried unsuccessfully to turn New York harbor into a fiord, and left in disgust two days later.

Most historians agree the Indians could have easily held on to North America against all European intruders if they had done just three things:

— Dumped the tea into Boston harbor themselves instead of letting revolutionaires dressed up as Indians do it. Everybody knows the economy of the colonies would have buckled under without tea.

— LISTENED, WHEN Sitting Bull solemnly warned, "You can't trust no white men" instead of retorting, "Sitting, that's a lot of Bull."

— Let Custer go instead of massacring him. Custer was such a lousy general he would have lost the West without any help from anybody.

But no. The Indians chose instead to attack trains and observe treaties. It was the latter act, of course, that spelled their downfall.

But what does all this have to do with Thanksgiving?

Well, it's simple. It all shows how differently the loose end of the sweater of history might have unraveled. It shows that almost any combination of events, had they occurred even a little differently, could have resulted in there being no Thanksgiving at all.

AND THAT would have been a terrible shame.

Because one thing is crystal clear: you can readily grow thankfulness for our many blessings anywhere in the North American continent.

. . . Thanksgiving's Place in History?

Figure 15–6. Headline at the bottom of a story. [*Courtesy Tinley Park Ill., Star Tribune.*]

The traditional way of identifying photographs is to place cutlines underneath them. Overlines and underlines may be used alone or with cutlines. If the photograph is less than three columns wide, the cutlines are set full width, but if the photograph is wider, the cutlines may be wrapped in two columns underneath. When overlines and underlines are used, they are usually centered.

In contemporary makeup, cutlines may be set flush left, with ragged right or flush right with ragged left (Figure 15–8). When it is necessary to wrap cutlines into two adjacent columns, the flush left or flush right approach does not look pleasing. If, however, two pictures of the same size are placed next to each other

New Approaches to Cutlines, Overlines, and Underlines

[Newspaper interview clipping — "U.S. policy in Viet Nam" teach-in]

Figure 15–7. Lead paragraph in center.

Contemporary Makeup and Design Practices 315

Boat delivery
in Britian

Policemen deliver a bottle of milk to Arthur Philpott. 70, by rubber raft yesterday in Yalding, England. Philpott has refused to leave his house since Sunday when torrential rains caused flooding throughout much of southeast England. Having submerged the basement of the Philpott's home, the raging flood waters began to seep into the upper story of the house, but Philpott refused to leave. See story page 16. (UPI Telephoto).

Figure 15–8. Cutlines set flush right, ragged left. [*Courtesy Cedar Falls Iowa Record.*]

(because they are related), it may be possible to set the left cutlines flush left and the right cutlines flush right.

A particularly modern style of cutline treatment, borrowed from magazine makeup, is to place them at the lower side of photographs. In such positions, they may be set in very narrow measures (from 6 to 9 picas in width), flush on both sides. But they also may be given the flush left or flush right treatment. In the latter instance the cutlines are set differently, depending on which side of the photograph they are to be placed. When placed on the right side, they should be flush left, and when placed on the left side, they should be set flush right (Figures 15–9 and 15–10) because the type nearest the photograph is aligned and looks more attractive.

Overlines may be repositioned above cutlines placed at the sides of cuts. They, too, may receive the same flush left or flush right treatment as the cutlines. When positioned that way, there probably will be a large amount of white space above the overline (or above the cutlines when there is no overline). But this white space will enhance the appearance of the treatment and should not be considered wasted space.

Getting ready for inaugural

Although the next president has not yet been elected, work has already begun on erecting a presidential inaugural platform and a television tower on the east front of the Capitol. Here Ignatius A. Jones of Waldorf, Md. unloads lumber. (UPI Telephoto)

Figure 15-9. Cutlines at the left, flush both sides. [*Courtesy Cedar Falls Iowa Record.*]

Freaks, Refers, and Other Inserts and Their Effects on Page Design

In traditional makeup practices, editors often inserted freaks, refers or other material into the main body of a story. The ostensible purpose of breaking into a story was to provide information that would help the reader better understand the news. But, no matter what the purpose was, the effect of any break in the news was a break in the reader's continuity.

What are the most likely alternative actions a reader may take when he is confronted by an insert? He may notice the insert, ignore it temporarily and, upon finishing the article, return and read it. Another alternative is that the reader may ignore it entirely. Or, he may stop and read it and then try to pick up the thread of thought in the remainder. But no matter which he does, the insert must break the flow of reading, if only for an instant, and because it impedes readership, it is undesirable.

Inserts also may be undesirable because they interrupt the rhythm of reading. Even if the reader stops to read the insert, he may not read much more of the story.

Editors often tend to make inserts a continuing practice, perhaps at least one in every edition. Too many inserts on one day may make the page appear to be full of spots that are unattractive and uninviting. Even when one insert is used, it stands out as a spot on the page. The makeup editor interrupts the reader, with rules and even a small headline within the insert. That one spot, then, may hamper the efforts of the editor to design a pleasing page because inserts tend to call attention to themselves.

The question then arises about what to do with the material that may have been used in inserts? One answer might be to place that material at either the beginning or the end of the story, set in italics or boldface and indented. Perhaps it can be incorporated into the body of the story and not be obtrusive.

Oil spire plumbs ocean

Soaring 340 feet into the air like a spire, this crane is part of a new derrick for a pipe-laying vessel used to service offshore oil and gas fields. Owned by Standard Oil Co. (Ind.) and DeGroot Offshore Ltd., the vessel, Ocean Builder I, has the capacity to lift 2,000 tons.

Figure 15–10. Cutlines at left; set flush right, ragged left. [*Courtesy Chicago Daily News.*]

Finally, by careful analysis of the news, the editor may treat additional editorial material as another story and place it adjacent to the story in question. If there is reference to a picture, then this may be incorporated into the story, set in lightface italics.

Boxed Stories The use of boxed stories in contemporary modular makeup is radically different from that in traditional makeup. In traditional makeup, a short, human interest story or an insert might have been placed in a box. Rarely was a long story boxed.

In contemporary makeup, there is a need to dramatize a story or there is a need to dramatize the makeup on a given page, and a large boxed story is used. There is, of course, a danger in using too many such stories on a page. If only one is used per page, it may liven that page considerably.

When boxing a story, the editor assumes it is significant. Perhaps it is not as significant as the top two stories on the page, but it is still of major importance. The procedure, then, is to place the entire story in a hairline box. The story must, of course, be squared off so that it fits neatly into the box. A photograph may accompany the story. But the keys to making this box look attractive are the use of hairline rules and more than an ordinary amount of white space inside the box. The only function of the hairline rule is to set the story apart from all other stories on the page. It usually will not look well if any heavier-weight rules are used. If a fancy border of any kind is used it will call attention to itself and not to the contents of the box. The white spaces, especially between the rules and the body type, are the framing devices that, with the hairline rules, make the story stand out and easy to read. Headlines within a box also may be set smaller and in lighter-faced types than those normally used because the rules and white space framing the box make a larger-sized type unnecessary. There is little competition from headlines outside the box.

Boxes, therefore, should be no less than two columns wide, and preferably-larger so that they may have dramatic impact. Some editors place at least one such box on every page where possible as a means of adding dramatic impact to the pages. The position of such boxes on a page depends on the sizes and weights of other elements. When other headlines on the page are large and bold, a boxed story should be placed at the opposite side to bring about page balance. Often, they look well at the bottom of the page. In some cases, they might well be used in place of the number-one story (upper-right side).

There is enough evidence available through research studies to prove that stories that have been jumped or continued to other pages lose a great deal of readership (see Chapter 2). Nevertheless, the practice of jumping stories sometimes cannot be avoided. Consequently, there should be a policy regarding the design of such heads.

There are two related problems that arise in the design of jump heads: (1) how to make them easy to find on a page; and (2) how to keep their design consistent with both the page and overall newspaper design. The first problem may seem to be easily resolved by setting the headlines in larger and bolder typefaces than other headlines. But if the type is too large or too bold, then it will call attention to itself and tend to make the page look unattractive. If it is too light, readers may not be able to

Policy for Design of Jump Heads

find the heads. Both problems may be resolved if the following guidelines are observed.

1. The typefaces and style of arrangement should be consistent with the headline schedule used for other headlines.

2. The number of lines and sizes of type used for jump heads should be the same as if the jumped portion were a separate story. In such a case, the story length and importance would be considered.

3. A contrasting typeface may be used to help the head stand out. If Tempo has been used for most other headlines, a Bodoni Bold italic may provide the necessary contrast.

4. Stars, bullets, or asterisks, if they are not too obtrusive, may precede the first letter of the jump head to serve as attention-getting devices.

5. Ben Day screens may be used in the background for such heads. This is done easily for a newspaper printed by the offset technique. Where letterpress is being used, perhaps the page number from which the story originally started may be placed in a screened background. If a number of such page numbers could be screened and kept in logo form on the stone, they could be inserted easily under jump heads.

Tombstoning in Contemporary Design

Almost every editor, be he from the largest metropolitan newspaper or the smallest high school paper, knows that tombstoning should be avoided. But tombstoning was considered a poor make-up practice in an age where only 6-point hairline rules were used between columns. Because some newspapers have used hairline rules of even less than 6 points (2- or 3-point rules), there was more of a danger that a reader might read across the column into the adjacent headline and be confused (Figure 15–11).

But in contemporary design, where the space between columns is at least 9 points and as much as 2 picas, tombstoning may not be objectionable. There may be so much white space between the columns that the reader can't be confused into reading a headline in the adjacent column. Then the only objection to tombstoning may be that there is not enough variety shown when two headlines of the same size, weight and number of lines are placed next to each other. This is a design consideration and one of the heads may be changed to provide more type variety on the page.

Banner Headlines and Readout Problems

The use of daily across-the-page banners has been abandoned by many modern newspapers and often replaced by spread heads without readouts. But when a story is assigned a banner headline, it is assumed that the body copy will be placed in the extreme right-hand column. Even though the first, or left-hand,

ISRAEL

From Page 1

before the council convenes in which "circumstances may change."

He said the intention to boycott was "not a matter of principle. I see it as a form of political warfare."

The foreign minister is known to take a more conciliatory attitude toward the Palestinians than Prime Minister Yitzhak Rabin.

A few hours earlier, Rabin told newsmen that Israelis who called for recognizing a Palestinian state are "posing question marks . . . which both our enemies and our friends will interpret as weakness."

But Rabin also sidestepped questions on whether Israel would boycott all future talks that included the PLO, saying it "depends on what the government

LEBANON

From Page 1

850 soldiers were involved in the operation.

Ambulances recovered 70 bodies and 90 wounded persons from several combat zones during the day, but scores of other victims were lying in streets where rescuers couldn't enter because of the shooting.

The Phalangists claimed Christian victories on a broad front, saying they forced the Moslem militiamen to retreat 500 to 800 yards from positions overrun Monday.

Ibrahim Kuleilat, leader of the Nasserite militia that had occupied the Jewish quarter, conceded his men had pulled back under Christian assaults "to re group." But he said that in other areas the Moslem advance "is still continuing."

Figure 15–11. Tombstoning jumped heads.

column is the most important position on the page, the right-hand column is the one which enables the reader to continue reading the story without returning to the left side of the page (Figure 15–12). In contemporary design, a number of questions arise affecting the reader's ability to continue reading the story smoothly. The answers to these questions lead to principles of handling banner headlines and readouts.

Can the story be continued in any other column? The reason for wanting to place the story elsewhere is to provide a change of pace and variety in makeup. The answer to the question is that there are few occasions when the story can be continued elsewhere. Least effective is to continue the story to an inside column. The reason it should not be placed anywhere but in the extreme right-hand column (with exceptions that will be noted) is that the reader will have to search for it if placed elsewhere (Figures 15–13 and 15–14). Although one may argue that the reader will not have to search very long, any time—even a fraction of a second—is too long. That fraction of a second may be just the timing that is necessary for the reader to search for some other interesting story. After all, he already knows the material in the banner headline and perhaps he isn't interested enough to continue when there are any impediments to his read-

Howlett backs Dixon for secretary

Column 1

'Tac' cops stalk crime in disguise

Special police teams wage war on pushers

By Patricia Leeds

IT WAS ONE of those hot, muggy days in July. To make matters worse, he was crammed in the back seat of the car under a blanket to conceal him from the narcotics peddler.

The wait seemed interminable. He was bathed in perspiration. Suddenly he heard the informant making the deal with the pusher . . .

He threw back the blanket and for a moment he was paralyzed. His hands and feet were so cramped he could hardly hold the gun or stand up—somehow he made it.

"Police officer! Hold it!" he shouted.

The pusher just looked at him—not knowing whether to believe him or not.

"My hair was plastered down from the sweat, my shirt was soaked, my hand wobbled," policeman William Frapolly recalled.

"I think he was wondering whether to run or not. And I don't know if I could have chased him the way my legs felt numb."

LUCKILY HIS partners converged on

Seeks end to rivalry on ticket

By Neil Mehler
Political editor

MICHAEL HOWLETT has thrown his support to State Treasurer Alan Dixon for the Democratic nomination for secretary of state, believing Dixon to be the strongest potential candidate for the post, persons close to Howlett said Thursday.

Dixon and Howlett are both seeking party backing to run for governor in the primary against Gov. Walker, but Dixon says he will step aside if Howlett will back him for Howlett's present post of secretary of state.

Party sources said Howlett, who is vacationing in Florida, hopes to resolve the conflict between Dixon and Lt. Gov. Neil Hartigan for the secretary of state

Atty. Gen. William Scott says he'll back any Democrat who opposes Dan Walker for governor. But he hasn't backed Republican candidate James Thompson. Story in Sec. 2, p. 1

nomination by the time slatemaking begins Monday at 9:30 a.m. in the La Salle Hotel.

THE SOURCES SAID Hartigan "may have misread Mayor Daley — a lot of

Figure 15–12. Readout into right hand column. [*Courtesy Chicago Tribune.*]

FIRE HITS W. SIDE HOSPITAL

FORAN TELLS PROBE PLANS OF SLAYINGS

U. S. Grand Jury Inquiry Set

60 Patients Carried from Their Rooms

BY DAVID GILBERT

Fire and smoke spread thru the Franklin Boulevard Community hospital last night, forcing 60 of the 104 patients in the hospital to be evacuated from their rooms.

The fire started shortly before

Tax Reform Bill Is Approved by Committee Vote

BY PHILIP WARDEN
(Chicago Tribune Press Service)

Washington, Dec. 19—Agreement was reached on a tax bill today which raises the personal exemption to $750 by 1973, boosts social security checks

Figure 15–13. Readout into inside column. [*Courtesy Chicago Tribune.*]

ing. This is the problem of all makeup devices. None should slow the reader more than a fraction of a second. If they are considered individually, each makeup device may seem to be effective. But when there are many such devices on a page, the even rhythm of reading may be broken and reading becomes a troublesome rather than a pleasant experience.

When stories are continued from a banner headline to any column other than the extreme right, a cutoff rule is used to separate the banner from nonrelated stories. The assumption is that because the only column not carrying a cutoff rule must be the one where the story is continued, it will be obvious at a glance. Indeed, it is obvious at the right-hand side, less obvious

Figure 15–14. Readout into left hand column. [*Courtesy Chicago Tribune.*]

when placed at the left-hand side (first column) and almost obscure when placed inside. Cutoff rules help, but not much. It is hard to find the column where the story is continued.

Another question arises when using a banner headline. Can more than one story relating to the banner headline be arranged so that the banner reads into each story successfully? Such an occasion might be when an election story breaks and one political party wins both gubernatorial and mayoral races. The banner headline may therefore refer to both stories. When the readout headlines are only one column wide, they are often hard to find. But when they are two or more columns wide, they are relatively easy to find.

A final question concerns whether a banner headline should lead into a multiple- or single-column headline? One of the older makeup rules was that when a large-sized type was used in a top headline, the reader's eyes would have difficulty in adjusting to smaller types in the decks or lead paragraphs. Therefore, the reduction in size was supposed to be at least 50 per cent. If a 120-point headline was used for the banner, then it should read into a headline of no less than 60-point type. The 60-point type would then read into a 30-point deck, which in turn might read into an 18-point deck and from there into a 10-point lead paragraph. There was never any valid evidence that readers had difficulty in adjusting their eyes to the changes in type sizes. Therefore, the only reason for reading from a banner into a multiple-column headline is simply to provide more details in the headline than could have been included in the banner. The only trouble with multiple-column headlines is that they usually lead into a single-column story, leaving the space underneath to be filled in the best way possible. If a headline for a nonrelated story is placed underneath a multiple-column headline, the effect might be to confuse the reader. At times a picture is placed underneath. But neither of these solutions looks attractive.

In contemporary makeup, banner headlines often lead into a single-column headline, a simple device. Or, if a banner is used, it may lead into a three-column headline and a story may be

---

Contemporary Makeup and Design Practices   323

wrapped for three columns underneath, through the process of squaring off the bottom. A final alternative is to limit the use of banner headlines to rare occasions. When it is used with a multiple-column readout it won't look awkward because the news is so sensational. Too many multiple-column headlines on a page, however, make the page spotty because these headlines appear dark (being set in bold typefaces and relatively large-sized types). They become centers of interest because of their weight and may be difficult to balance.

Other Contemporary Treatments

Other practices differentiate the traditional from the contemporary made-up newspaper. Some practices are the result of major editorial policy and can be changed only by those in top authority, such as a publisher or an editor. Others, however, are within the province of the makeup editor, who daily has the option of using traditional or contemporary treatments of editorial material.

Elimination of Column Rules

One of the distinguishing features of contemporary design is the elimination of column rules from the newspaper. The purpose is to bring more light (or white space) into the page and to bring about a cleaner looking page. When column rules are used, they simply add blackness to the page even though they separate the columns. But the additional white space not only separates the columns, but makes the page more inviting to the reader because it is less black-appearing.

In eliminating column rules, editors did not simply replace a 6-point hairline rule with 6 points of white space. They added more white space so that the columns were more clearly separated. The minimum amount of white space between columns seems to be 9 points, but more is preferred. The better-designed newspapers use no less than 12 points of white space and many use more.

Reduction in the Number of Columns to a Page

To gain more white space on a page, editors who use contemporary makeup have reduced the number of columns to a page from eight to as few as five (Figure 15–15), which releases more space to be used between columns than was formerly possible. In contemporary makeup it is not unusual to find some pages with 14 to 18 points of space between columns.

Another benefit of reducing the number of columns to the page is that the body type is made more readable because the line widths are increased. From a standard 11-pica width, some newspapers have increased the column widths to more than 14 picas. (The *National Observer* uses a $15\frac{1}{2}$-pica width.)

On the inside pages, the reduction in number of columns has proved to be harder to work with because advertising often is sold on a basis of a narrower column width. Some newspapers

Figure 15–15 [OPPOSITE]. Four column page. [*Courtesy Life Newspapers Chicago, Illinois.*]

The Sunday Life

A Lerner Newspaper serving Skokie, Morton Grove, Niles, Lincolnwood, Des Plaines, East Maine, Golf and Glenview

Vol. 55—No. 8 | Two Sections, 22 Pages | SUNDAY, NOVEMBER 23, 1975 | 20 Cents Per Copy | Want Ads, Section 2, Pages 3-11

Dist. 65 reorganization

College Hill may close

By AL BERNSTEIN
Lerner-Life Newspapers
News Editor

THE FIRST OF FOUR planned public sessions on the proposed reorganization of District 65 schools will be held at 8 p.m. Monday, Dec. 1, at Nichols school, 800 Greenleaf, Evanston.

Among the highlights of the district's 19-page reorganization report is a proposal to convert College Hill school, 9000 Forest View, Skokie, into a teacher service center. Both Noyes school, 927 Noyes, Evanston, and Miller school, 425 Dempster, Evanston, would be converted into specialized centers, according to the proposal.

The proposed conversion of College Hill did not bring strong protests at the Monday, Nov. 17, school board meeting, as a similar proposal of school closing had brought in 1974. That earlier recommendation by former Supt. Joseph Porter was criticized sharply by parents in the College Hill area, and led to several stormy confrontations at school board meetings.

MONDAY'S RECOMMENDATIONS by Supt. Joseph Hill were greeted calmly by College Hill representatives in attendance. Several residents said they understood the economic woes that have made a reorganization necessary.

If the plan were adopted, College Hill students would have the option of attending either Timber Ridge school, 3701 Davis, Skokie, a "non-graded" type school, or Walker school, 3601 Church, Evanston, a "graded" school.

The proposed boundary, which is based partially on a recent survey of parents and teachers, would return black student enrollment in all schools to a 20 to 37 per cent level.

The overall plan will be discussed at three more meetings after the Dec. 1 session. The meetings, all starting at 8 p.m., will be: Dec. 15 at Chute school, 1400 Oakton, Evanston; Jan. 5 at Haven school, 2417 Prairie, Evanston; and Jan. 12 at Skiles school, 2424 Lake, Evanston.

THE SCHOOL BOARD is expected to vote on the plan at its Jan. 25 meeting.

The plan was formed as a result of a growing financial deficit, declining enrollment and an apparent trend toward racial segregation in the district.

In addition to boundary changes, the plan calls for sale of the district's administration building, 1314 Ridge, Evanston. Administrative offices would be moved to Skiles school.

The reductions of staff, maintenance savings and moving of the administrative offices is estimated to save the district about $523,458 a year.

The plan calls for the elimination of two administrative positions: assistant superintendent and the superintendent of buildings and grounds. That will save the district $85,000 annually.

A district spokesman said all school administrators, including Hill, will be available to answer questions of individuals as well as groups. Hill will be available personally at 8 p.m. on four different occasions: Dec. 2 at Chute, Dec. 4 at Haven; Dec. 9 at Nichols, and Dec. 11 at Skiles.

Special ed director now to get $37,200

By ROBERT FEDER
Lerner Newspapers
Correspondent

VERNON FRAZEE, executive director of the Niles Township department of special education (NTDSE), was granted a $2,400 raise Nov. 12, increasing his total salary to $37,200 for 1975-1976.

A 10-member committee comprised of one representative from each of Niles Township's nine elementary and one high school boards approved Frazee's increase along with those of two other NTDSE administrators, Gary Hahn and Margaret Estes.

Hahn, director of the department's secondary school programs, received a $1,200 increase to $22,700, and Estes, director of elementary programs, received a $1,250 increase to $21,950.

NTDSE is jointly operated by all ten school districts and provides special education services at elementary and high schools as well as at the Molloy center, 8701 Menard, Morton Grove.

THE VOTE TO APPROVE Frazee's raise was 7-3 and to approve the other administrators' 6-4, with some committee members expressing concern about the size of the increases.

Committee member Mary Helen Archibald, who is also board president of District 74, which administers NTDSE funds, objected strongly to the raises.

"A $2,400 raise for Frazee is excessive in this day and age where rate referendums for schools are losing all over the place," she said.

While noting that she was satisfied with the administrators' performance, Archibald said she opposed the idea of "automatic raises every year for administrators. There's no reason we should feel locked in, especially when money is so tight," she said.

Frazee told The LIFE he was not disturbed by the sentiments of Archibald and other committee members about his raise.

"I SEE THIS AS a totally across-the-board problem universally in the north suburban area. The days when an administrator's feelings get hurt because he didn't get a pay raise are over," Frazee said.

"Most administrators have the intelligence and maturity to realize that (raises) no longer reflect an evaluation of their performance; that's a reflection of a problem of money. If they had given me less money (this year), I would not have been angry or hostile and I certainly would not have resigned," he said.

District 74 Supt. Marvin Garlich defended the raises and said, "We believe he (Frazee) is the top man in special education in the state and his salary should reflect that. The questions that have been raised are nothing new and our only answer is that it's a matter of judgment."

Garlich, District 68 Supt. Paul Rodgers and District 219 (Nilehi) Supt. Wesley Gibbs comprise the committee that recommended Frazee's increase to the 10-member NTDSE board.

Frazee recommended the raises for the other two administrators in his department.

INSTRUCTOR BARBARA PEDERSEN LED these two youngsters through an exercise during skating instruction at the Skatium, 9300 Bronx, Skokie. Five year olds Staci Deitch and Aaron Joffe are among the many youngsters taking skating lessons at the Skatium. Registration is now open Monday through Friday 10 a.m. to 7 p.m. and Sundays 1 to 3 p.m. at the Skatium. The next session will start on Dec. 5.

Delay plan to end CTA No. 13 bus

By GREG HINZ
Lerner Newspapers
Staff Writer

THE PLA TO DROP CTA's No. 13 bus route from downtown Skokie to Jefferson Park when a new North Suburban Mass Transit District (Nortran) line starts Dec. 1 has been blocked, at least for the time being.

The new Nortran line, along Oakton from Des Plaines to Skokie and then south to Jefferson Park, is still expected to begin service Dec. 1. But even though its southern leg will be almost identical to the existing CTA route, the Regional Transit Authority (RTA) wants to continue CTA service until completion of a review of suburban bus fare structures.

Dick Brazda, an RTA planner, said RTA made the decision to prevent riders from having to pay extra fares.

CURRENTLY, HE POINTED OUT, No. 13 riders can transfer to other CTA service in Jefferson Park for only a dime. But since Nortran and CTA generally do not honor each other's transfers—and will not, at least until after the fare review is completed—if the CTA line were dropped patrons of the new Nortran line would have to pay both a Nortran and a CTA fare if they wanted to continue their trip from Jefferson Park.

Brazda also pointed out that the two lines follow different routes in one area. The CTA line jogs east through the LeClaire avenue section of Skokie, while the new Nortran line would go down Central.

The RTA board is expected to consider the suburban fare review within the next two months. When it is finished, Brazda said he expects the CTA line will be dropped and the Nortran line shifted to serve the LeClaire area.

IN THE MEANTIME, though, Skokie, which pays about $3,300 a month for the No. 13 line, will have to keep doing so at least until next spring. Skokie promised to do so when it accepted RTA funds to make up part of the deficit on the line, but had asked RTA to allow it to end the service.

Village transportation task force chairman Walter Flintrup was sharply critical of the RTA decision.

"I can't understand why they would be objecting to it (dropping the No. 13)," he said. "The two lines are duplicating . . . If it was a business there would be no reason to continue it."

SKOKIE LIBRARY BOARD PRESIDENT Rabbi Karl Weiner (left) and Italian artist Tito Salomoni display one of Salomoni's surrealistic paintings. Salomoni, making his first visit to the United States, donated two lithographs to the library at a luncheon Wednesday, Nov. 19. Looking on is Bernard Schutz, owner of Prestige gallery, 3909 Howard, Skokie, which is holding a showing of Salomoni's paintings at restige through Nov. 30.

Police warn drivers of holiday hazards

LOCAL POLICE departments are warning area drivers to be more careful on motor trips during the holiday season.

Police advise:

- Plan a sensible schedule. Know your route and get enough rest before departing.
- Keep a check on weather reports. Adjust your driving schedule to give you more time to reach your destination.
- Be prepared for the worst that winter may have to offer. Carry reinforced tire chains for severe snow and ice conditions that might be encountered.
- If you get caught in a storm, keep alert to announcements of emergency locations and alternate routes.
- Slow down on slippery roads. Allow considerably more distance between cars.
- Stay alert for icy spots. Ice lasts longer on bridges, overpasses and shaded areas.
- Drive ahead of your car—plan every maneuver well in advance. Accelerate and steer smoothly. Pump brakes when stopping to maintain both steering and stopping control.

Holiday party Dec. 2 for Skokie seniors

IT WILL BE A time for greetings between friends and songs of both Chanukah and Christmas at the second annual holiday party for older Skokie residents from 1-4 p.m. Tuesday, Dec. 2, at the Skokie American Legion hall, Lincoln and Cleveland.

The party will be hosted by the senior council of Skokie.

Mayor Albert Smith will be guest of honor and volunteers who have donated hours to teach driver examination classes, worked on service projects, assisted with mailings, handled clerical work, made telephone calls and have done friendly visiting, etc., will be recognized.

The Cho:alaires, a Skokie choral group, will offer songs of both holidays.

Sol Lazerson and Birdie Grote will each present a musical number.

Mr. and Mrs. Mario Finamore and Mr. and Mrs. John Kauparek will dance two ballroom numbers.

All Skokie seniors are invited to the Skokie senior council holiday party. There is no fee. Call 673-0500, ext. 208, for more information.

Panelists to discuss sexism in Judaism

IS THERE EQUALITY for women in Judaism?

This question will be discussed by four Jewish women at 8 p.m. Tuesday, Dec. 9, at Skokie Valley Traditional synagog, 8824 East Prairie, Skokie.

The panelists include Lottie Rosenson, past president of the Religious Zionists of Chicago; Mildred Hurwitz, past chairman of Israel bonds, women's division, Youth Aliyah vice president of Chicago Hadassah and board member of the Women's Committee of the Zionist Organization of Chicago (ZOC); Suzanne Basinger, past national vice president of the National Federation of Temple Sisterhoods; and Ruth Rothstein, vice president and executive director of Mt. Sinai hospital medical center, the only woman administrator of a major hospital in the country.

More than 1,200 women are expected to attend.

J. I. Fishbein, editor and publisher of the Sentinel, a co-sponsor of the forum with ZOC, said there is considerable controversy regarding the status of women in the Jewish religion.

Mikva reelection bid to be told Monday

CONG. ABNER MIKVA (D-10th) is expected to announce at a press conference Monday, Nov. 24, that he will seek reelection to his second term.

Mikva has called a press conference in Evanston to "discuss his plans for the 1976 election," and most observers expect him to run in the March Democratic primary.

He was elected by about 2,000 votes in 1974 over former congressman Samuel Young. He had lost a close election to Young in 1972.

Young is also a candidate for the 1976 election. He is facing a challenge in the GOP primary from Daniel Hales, a Winnetka attorney.

Blood draw Tuesday at LW legion hall

THE LINCOLNWOOD blood drive will hold a drawing from 4:30 to 7:45 p.m. Tuesday, Nov. 25, at American Legion Hall, Lincoln and Keeler, Lincolnwood.

Blood chairman Leni Gordon said O-positive blood is especially needed at the drawing.

An appointment can be made by calling 673-1540.

use the wider column widths for news and narrower column widths for advertisements. Makeup of such pages may be difficult because of the differences in measures.

Limited Use of Cutoff Rules

The cutoff rule is used sparingly in contemporary makeup. Wherever white space can be substituted for a cutoff rule, it should be used. When white space is substituted, a bit more space is used so that the reader will clearly understand that two stories near each other are not related in any way. But there are certain times, especially when the page is crowded, that a cutoff rule is necessary. In such a case, the makeup editor should not hesitate to use it.

Headline Styles in Contemporary Makeup

The flush-left headline style is used almost exclusively in contemporary makeup. Droplines, inverted pyramids and hanging indentions are styles of the past. Flush left is preferred because it is free-form in appearance, a style that is distinctly modern and because it is so easy to set on the Linotype machine, especially on machines with automatic quadding devices. On the other hand, each of the other three styles of headlines mentioned are difficult to set and they call attention to themselves because of their unusual shapes.

Three other headlines styles are sometimes considered contemporary. Each may serve a special purpose, so they are rarely used extensively. They are kickers, hammerheads and wickets.

In using a kicker, hammerhead, or wicket, the disadvantages may outweigh the advantages. The danger is that these devices may call too much attention to themselves, primarily because they are attention-getting devices. If more than one of these are used on a page, the effect may be a series of white spaces that tend to destroy the harmony of page unity. As an alternative to these headline treatments, makeup men could use a boxed story or have headlines set to the right or in the center of a story. The latter are contemporary treatments that accomplish the same task but do not call too much attention to themselves.

Use of Body Copy Set Flush Left, Ragged Right

One of the most dramatic design treatments is a column of body type set flush left, ragged right (Figure 15–16). Like the flush left headline, its free-form gives a page a contemporary appearance found in modern furniture, swimming pools and architecture. The use of one such column to a page also provides pleasant contrast to the remainder of the type, which is justified on both sides. Finally, such type allows more white space into the page than the flush left and flush right columns and this results in a cleaner looking page. In planning pages, care should be taken not to overdo the use of the flush left, ragged right style of column. When the entire page is set this way, the charm and elegance of the style is lost because there is too much of it. Another suggestion for its use is that more leading may be required to make the lines easier to read. When they are set solid, they seem to be crowded. With the addition of even a 1-point lead per line, they appear to be easier to read.

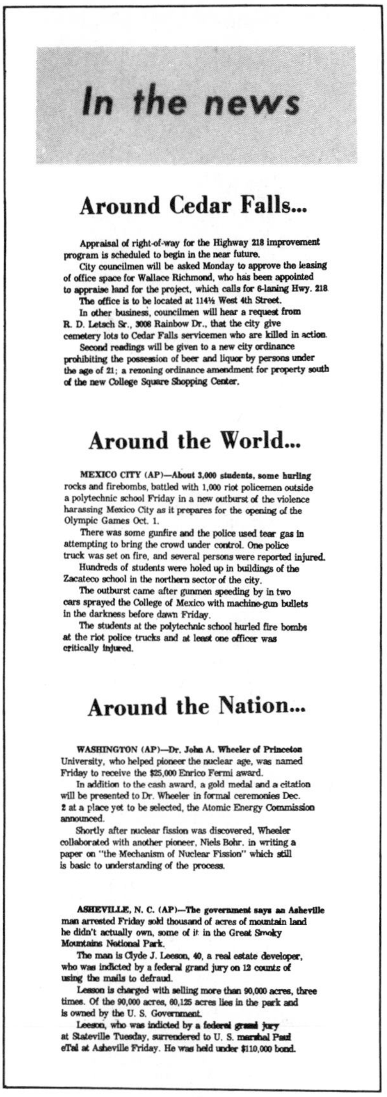

In the news

Around Cedar Falls...

Appraisal of right-of-way for the Highway 218 improvement program is scheduled to begin in the near future.

City councilmen will be asked Monday to approve the leasing of office space for Wallace Richmond, who has been appointed to appraise land for the project, which calls for 6-laning Hwy. 218

The office is to be located at 114½ West 4th Street.

In other business, councilmen will hear a request from R. D. Letsch Sr., 3008 Rainbow Dr., that the city give cemetery lots to Cedar Falls servicemen who are killed in action.

Second readings will be given to a new city ordinance prohibiting the possession of beer and liquor by persons under the age of 21; a rezoning ordinance amendment for property south of the new College Square Shopping Center.

Around the World...

MEXICO CITY (AP)—About 3,000 students, some hurling rocks and firebombs, battled with 1,000 riot policemen outside a polytechnic school Friday in a new outburst of the violence harassing Mexico City as it prepares for the opening of the Olympic Games Oct. 1.

There was some gunfire and the police used tear gas in attempting to bring the crowd under control. One police truck was set on fire, and several persons were reported injured.

Hundreds of students were holed up in buildings of the Zacateco school in the northern sector of the city.

The outburst came after gunmen speeding by in two cars sprayed the College of Mexico with machine-gun bullets in the darkness before dawn Friday.

The students at the polytechnic school hurled fire bombs at the riot police trucks and at least one officer was critically injured.

Around the Nation...

WASHINGTON (AP)—Dr. John A. Wheeler of Princeton University, who helped pioneer the nuclear age, was named Friday to receive the $25,000 Enrico Fermi award.

In addition to the cash award, a gold medal and a citation will be presented to Dr. Wheeler in formal ceremonies Dec. 2 at a place yet to be selected, the Atomic Energy Commission announced.

Shortly after nuclear fission was discovered, Wheeler collaborated with another pioneer, Niels Bohr, in writing a paper on "the Mechanism of Nuclear Fission" which still is basic to understanding of the process.

ASHEVILLE, N. C. (AP)—The government says an Asheville man arrested Friday sold thousand of acres of mountain land he didn't actually own, some of it in the Great Smoky Mountains National Park.

The man is Clyde J. Leeson, 40, a real estate developer, who was indicted by a federal grand jury on 12 counts of using the mails to defraud.

Lesson is charged with selling more than 90,000 acres, three times. Of the 90,000 acres, 60,125 acres lies in the park and is owned by the U. S. Government.

Leeson, who was indicted by a federal grand jury at Stateville Tuesday, surrendered to U. S. marshal Paul eTal at Asheville Friday. He was held under $110,000 bond.

Figure 15–16. An example of news set flush left, ragged right.

Subheads in Makeup

In traditional forms of makeup, long gray columns were often broken by the use of boldface paragraphs. Perhaps every fourth or fifth paragraph might be set boldface and indented one en on each side to minimize the effect of the boldness. It is true that pages never became masses of dull grayness through the use of intermittent boldface paragraphs. On the other hand, the page did become full of spots that distracted the reader somewhat and also made the page look too bold.

Subheads are usually three or four word summaries of an important fact in a paragraph immediately below it. The paragraphs selected should be about every fourth or fifth one after the lead. However, there is no rule requiring them to be at any precise places in a story. They should be placed wherever they look best in breaking up a long gray mass of reading matter.

The practice of using subheads, however, in place of boldface paragraphs is contemporary in style. The best way to use subheads is to set them flush left, keeping them consistent with the main headline styles. Then, too, they should be set in boldface italic, boldface sans serif, or any distinctly contrasting typeface. Because these lines will be so short and infrequent, they will not glare at the reader as the boldface does. In some newspapers, editors have tried subheads set flush right rather than flush left with apparent success. Centered subheads tend to look old-fashioned, however.

Another acceptable form of subhead is a boldface read-in of the first two or three words in selected paragraphs. This form of head looks fairly attractive, but not as much as a free standing head, that might require 2 points of space above and below it.

Some editors have tried using various-sized dots or bullets at the beginning of a paragraph as a means of breaking up large gray masses of type. Instead of allowing the usual one-em paragraph indention, the dot is placed in the indented space. The effect, however, is to call attention to the dot. In fact, dots are sometimes used to help the reader find paragraphs that are more significant than others. So the makeup editor might place a dot before key paragraphs. But neither technique is as adequate as the use of subheads (Figure 15–17).

A further consideration in the proper use of subheads is the amount of space above and below them. Generally, the best technique is to use about 4 points above and 2 points below as a means of clearly breaking up the mass of grayness and as a means of nullifying a bit the effect of a contrasting typeface (Figure 15–18).

What To Do with Ears In the discussion of nameplates, it was suggested that the ears be eliminated by moving the nameplate either to the left or right side of the page and bringing a column of news up to the top. But when the newspaper's policy is to keep the nameplate in the center, then there is the likelihood that ears will be used to fill the gaps of white space on either side.

In contemporary design, ears have been eliminated because they have become distracting devices that call attention to themselves rather than to the news columns. Most often ears are set within a boxed rule of some kind and no matter how light these rules, they set the ears off from everything else on the page. They not only distract from the news but they distract from the nameplate itself. Therefore, white space is preferable to ears. Only when the rules have been eliminated and the typeface used is unobtrusive (small and lightface types) should ears be used. In such cases, the ears will not tend to distract.

Picture Size and Placement In the scheme of contemporary makeup, pictures are given dramatic treatment. They are sized larger, but that is not the main consideration. Now they are sized to be strongly vertical

**By ELLEN SCHMITZ
and BILL FURLOW**

Two firms that later became the city's first and second choices as preferred developers for the block across Fifth Street from Fountain Square helped make a decision that limited the competition they would face on the project.

This fact emerged yesterday in a series of interviews with City Manager William V. Donaldson, City Urban Development Director Winston E. Folkers and others.

Donaldson said this key decision was that the project must include three elements—a luxury hotel, office tower and retail-entertainment enterprises.

"I'm surprised we got anyone who said that he would build all three," Donaldson added.

DONALDSON became Cincinnati city manager on June 15, replacing Henry Sandman, who had been acting city manager since the resignation of E. Robert Turner became effective March 1.

(Turner is now a vice president for public affairs of the Cincinnati-based Federated Department Stores.)

Donaldson said the decision that the project must include all three ele-

ments—a luxury hotel, office tower and retail-entertainment enterprises — "had already been made" when he arrived in Cincinnati.

Donaldson said yesterday he did not know how the decision was made or who participated in making it.

WINSTON E. Folkers, the city's urban development director, said later that the decision "came out of discussions" which involved members of his staff, officials of the Greater Cincinnati Chamber of Commerce and two proposed developers.

The two developers participating in these discussions were the John W. Galbreath Co. of Columbus and the Gerald D. Hines Interests of Houston, which have since become the city's first and second choices as recommended developers for the block, Folkers said.

"Somewhere along in April or May," Folkers said, "it was decided that the multi-use project be developed in toto" because one element "helps the other."

THAT DECISION, Donaldson acknowledged in an interview yesterday, was, in effect, to let the office tower and retail-entertainment facilities subsidize what the hotel might lose.

This decision also severely

Figure 15–17. Bold face indentations help relieve grayness of page.

Dets. Joseph McSorley, Bernard Joseph and Howard Baynard.

The three teachers were arraigned before Municipal Judge Ralph Dennis.

Police said they presented a search and seizure warrant to Miss Pincus at 6:30 P. M. Monday at her second floor apartment. They said they found a package wrapped in foil allegedly containing hashish lying on a table.

WAITED FOR SECOND

Miss Pincus attended the University of Wisconsin.

The officers said they then spent several hours in Stetzer's third floor apartment w   g his ret 1.

It was estimated that as much as 20 acres might be needed for such facilities.

OPPOSITION VOICED

Any use of park land for school purposes, however, would have to be approved by the park commission, which has demonstrated strong opposition to the plan.

The only site among the four suggested which the Board of Education could purchase through condemnation is the Five Points tract.

Tate opposes use of this land, however, because its private use could mean attractive ratables for the city.

The Board of Education is

Figure 15–18. Improper and proper line spacing of subheads.

Contemporary Makeup and Design Practices   **329**

or strongly horizontal. The effect of such boldly shaped pictures is a dramatic change in page appearance, a change that makes a page look exciting. The reader can't help but look at the main picture, nor can he help notice the difference in the entire page. Not every picture lends itself to such treatment, but when one is available and is significant, it should be handled in a contemporary manner. The makeup editor must have the imagination to look at a smaller-sized picture and be able to visualize it in a larger size (Figures 15–19 and 15–20).

See pages 332 and 333.

When such boldly shaped pictures are used, an increase in the amount of white space in the total page design should be made. Otherwise the picture alone may be too strong for all other material on the page and readers may have difficulty reading the news. White space should be increased between columns, headlines, and stories as compensatory devices.

At times, questions arise about the use of pictures in outside columns and the directions in which individuals are facing. In the former situation, pictures may be used anywhere, even in outside columns if the page is designed with adequate white space between columns. When the page appearance is tight because of 2- or 3-point column rules used throughout the paper, a picture in an outside column may not look attractive. In the latter situation, it has been the traditional practice to have individuals looking into the paper rather than out of it. The assumption is that when a person shown in the picture is looking away from the page, the reader, too, will tend to look in the same direction and perhaps turn to some other page. Research is not available to prove the truth of this assumption and it is doubtful that it is true. But occasionally a reader may find it distracting and for that reason pictures ought to be faced inwardly. Most readers have been brought up on pages designed with pictures facing into a page.

Finally, there is a question about the traditional makeup practice of not placing pictures on the folds. Contemporary makeup ignores this practice because it started in the days when newspapers were sold folded, primarily from newsstands. Readers might make a decision to buy or not buy a newspaper on the basis of which newspaper looked best. Because only the top half of the paper was visible on the stand, it was prepared in such a way as to make it attractive. Any picture printed across the fold could not be seen in its entirety. Perhaps a sale might have been lost if only half a picture were seen. Therefore, pictures were never positioned across the folds. Now the practice seems unreasonable. Although papers are still delivered folded, they are read unfolded and the entire picture is thereby visible. The only drawback is possible damage to a picture caused by printing on cheap newsprint. The picture may be unsightly because it is on the fold.

Another objection to placing pictures on the fold was that because the picture was a piece of art, it should not be ruined by the fold. Here, the reasoning is questionable. Readers ordinarily do not perceive pictures as art forms and are not upset because it appears on the fold. If the details of a picture should be obliterated because of a fold, then there might be some objection to the practice. But this rarely, if ever, happens. The main and only consideration about picture placement is to find the position where it best harmonizes with every other element on the page.

Elimination of Type Rules

Contemporary design is recognized easily because it is so simple. One of the ways that makeup editors have used to simplify pages was to remove as many type rules from the page as possible. For that reason, column rules were the first to be eliminated, and the effect was attractive. Once these rules were eliminated, more white space appeared on the page and it began to be easier to read than when rules had been used.

Next to go were jim dashes and finish dashes. Jim dashes were used to separate decks of a headline or to separate headlines from body type. But they were not needed. Finish or 30 dashes are still used in some newspapers but they too have been eliminated by many other editors. The white space at the end of a story did not confuse the reader as it was feared. In fact, the white space made the page easy to read because it eliminated one more black line that cluttered the page.

Now two more rules should be eliminated if possible. The first is the cutoff rule, which should be used sparingly. White space, too, should be substituted wherever possible. Finally, the dateline rules at the top of page 1 and inside pages should be removed. These also add to the clutter.

Features of Contemporary Makeup

The preceding discussion concerned major elements of contemporary makeup practices. If all were used, and with discretion, the results would be a newspaper that looked as follows:

It would be simply designed. It would be functional. It would be dramatic and exciting. It would be clean-looking. It would be slower-paced than traditionally designed papers. Older designs often looked hectic and bewildering. Newer designs would show the effect of planning and sophistication. Thus a modern newspaper would be inviting and easy to read.

Contemporary Makeup Checklist

The checklist that follows is a convenient means of evaluating the design and makeup of any given page, according to the principles of contemporary makeup. The values given for each criterion are those used by many editors who use contemporary makeup and design. But it should be noted that there are sometimes exceptions to each criterion. In such cases, allowances can be made as explained. A perfect score is 125.

Problems in Achieving Contemporary Makeup and Design

The authors have examined, personally, hundreds of newspaper pages submitted to the Inland Daily Press Association Makeup and Design Contests over a period of 16 years and found the following significant problem areas in achieving contemporary makeup.

1. *Cluttered pages.* Clutter means that the arrangement of

Deerfield wins 5A title 14-7

Continued from page 1

day," said Adams. "So we went to an inside belly series in which either Percak or Wise read the blocks of the tackles and then take off."

Yet that run by Percak would never have occurred had not Carlson's screen pass to Percak gone for 15 yards and a first down on the Warriors' 36 earlier in the climactic drive.

"We were worried about the screen," said Boylan coach Ben Murray. "We tried to defend it, but Carlson is a good passer and we were trying to stop his rollouts and bootlegs. You can't stop everything." But Boylan's defensive ends, John Aramovich and Kevin Fahey, controlled Carlson most of the game.

THEN DEERFIELD found itself against the wall as Boylan quarterback Mike LaLoggia whipsawed the Titans downfield with some sharp passing in the final minutes of play. LaLoggia missed on a couple of bombs, but his pass to Joe Stellern took the ball 16 yards to the Deerfield 24. Stellern tried to run wide and out of bounds on the next play. He gained four yards but failed to stop the clock, forcing Boylan to call its last time out with 16 seconds left.

LaLoggia then rolled right and was dropped for a three-yard loss by Pete Herman's shoe-string tackle. LaLoggia never got another chance. The Warriors had climaxed a perfect season with a tense finish and followed in the footsteps of another Central Suburban League team, Glenbrook North, which won last year's title.

Yet it could have been Boylan's turn. The Titans [11-2] capitalized on one interception, turning it into a third period score and might have had another on an interception by Aramovich, after Carlson's toss was tipped in the air by an oncharging lineman.

Had not Carlson stopped Aramovich with a face mask grab, the 195-pound senior might have gone all the way. As it was Boylan had a first down on the Warriors 40.

"THAT WAS A TURNING point for us," said Murray. "We couldn't take the ball in. Our defense was tiring and we needed some momentum." Deerfield had recovered the football for 13 plays and had driven to the Rockford 24 before the theft.

Instead, Boylan got three yards on two runs and an incomplete pass. A punt in the end zone gave Deerfield the ball on its 20 and 16 plays later the Warriors scored.

Carlson's first interception, in the third quarter, was returned by Stellern 12 yards to the Deerfield 41. With fullback Bill Roy punishing the defense for 15 yards in four carries, the Titans rolled to the Deerfield 16. There, on third-and-five, LaLoggia hit end Dan Voellinger over the middle deep in the end zone for the touchdown. Stellern's kick with 5:05 left in the third period tied the game 7-7.

CARLSON'S BEST series came in the first quarter when he found Don Chester down the sideline on a perfectly-timed fly pattern. Chester, well-defended by Steve Anderson, still made a marvelous catch on the Boylan 12 for a 47-yard gain. Three plays later the 190-pound Carlson bootlegged around his left end and scored from the 8, and kicked his first of two extra points.

Actually, Deerfield succeeded on fourth down plays three times during the game. The Warriors also drove 74 yards to the Rockford 16 in the second quarter but Carlson's 29-year field goal attempt was wide right.

Although the statistics favored the Warriors [321 to 205 yards total offense] and although Wise and Percak picked up 96 and 96 yards rushing, the title was in jeopardy until the final second. It was the only way to play for a championship.

Deerfield fans pour onto field at Normal, Ill., Saturday celebrating Warriors' Illinois 5A high school football title as final gun sounds. Rockford Boylan was the 14-7 victim.

Scoreboard

[Scoreboard tables: College football, NHL standings, Golf, Auto racing, NBA standings, Prep football, Prep events, Boxing, AP cage poll, College events, WHA scores, ABA scores, Prep basketball, College cage, Gymnastics, Track and field, Bowling, High school football summaries]

Deerfield's Don Chester intercepting Rockford Boylan pass during first quarter. Theft set Warriors' 4-play, 59-yard scoring drive in motion in first quarter.

Figure 15–19. Boldly shaped vertical and horizontal pictures. [*Courtesy Chicago Tribune.*]

Week that was--wild!

By Jack Wilkinson
Staff Writer

ANN ARBOR, Mich. — There are certain subversives who are suggesting it's different this year. That the buildup to Ohio State-Michigan just isn't the same. For those skeptics, a daily chronicle of the week of THE GAME, complete with a bumper-sticker, banner or T-shirt thought for each day:

SUNDAY: "Woody has a big mouth, but Bo has jaws" — Tom Slade, Michigan quarterback, has returned from the Illinois game, but is still uptight about THE GAME. So he announces he'll skip his classes this week, except for his labs. That's pressure: Tom Slade, Michigan's quarterback, class of '74, is now in Michigan's dental school.

MONDAY: "OHOWIHATE OHIO STATE" — That bumper sticker is posted on the antlers of a stuffed deer's head. The deer is propped up in a barber's chair and covered with a white towel. Bo Schembechler meets with the press and doesn't kick anyone out. Michigan athletic director Don Canham gives his last two tickets to former track great Jesse Owens, an Ohio State alumnus. Reportedly, Canham doesn't scalp them.

TUESDAY: "You can always tell a Buckeye, but you can't tell him much" — The pace is definitely picking up. So are ticket prices, because everyone isn't Don Canham. Slade swears he saw a scalper exchange four good seats together for a $1,000 check. People are getting between $25 and $75 on most of the $7 tickets.

The "Retaliation Bowl News" out of Bucyrus, Ohio, predicts a 23-9 Michigan victory. Afterwards, the story continues, Woody Hayes is unemployed as OSU drops football. The game ended with Ohio State playing the Michigan girls' softball team. Reportedly: "Neither team got up for at least 20 minutes after the final gun." And the Mafia is controlling Ohio State.

There is a Frank Zappa concert in Crisler Arena tonight. A 14-year-old paper vendor will be missing Wednesday morning. His mother thinks he's hiding inside Michigan Stadium until the kickoff Saturday.

WEDNESDAY: "Bleep the Bucks" — Bo explodes in practice. A free-lance photographer working for UPI is spotted shooting sequence films from an apartment balcony overlooking Michigan's practice field. The photographer has his film confiscated by the Washtenaw County prosecutor's office. And Bo says the press is making too much of this game.

The first prediction on THE GAME comes from a self-proclaimed sports nut who charts bio-rhythms of various sports figures. He says

Michigan will win: Bo's emotional and intellectual bio-rhythms are clearly superior to Woody's.

Michigan ticket manager Al Renfrow predicts a record crowd "because the Ohio State band is bigger this year and we'll have more protection and security people." Everyone counts here, but not in a socialist sense.

THURSDAY: "Woody' is a four-letter word" — Schembechler refuses to hold a press conference with UPI in attendance. He moves it to his office and freezes everyone in personality. It's only a good, clean, hard-hitting game. Bo resigns from the UPI college coaches' board.

"If they'll (UPI) do that for a football game," Bo says, "can you imagine the phones that have been tapped, the rooms that have been bugged, with all the things going on in this country more important than a football game?"

At a pep rally in the Mud Bowl, Bo seethes while announcing that a camera crew from Channel 10 TV in Columbus did a short film on him — and later secretly took pictures of the Wolverines practicing and showed them back in Ohio. Channel 10 is the station that airs The Woody Hayes Show.

FRIDAY: For Jimi Hendrix freaks, "Blue and

Turn to Page 32, Column 1

Field Gen. Woody Hayes barks instructions, encouragement and a few warnings to his troops prior to Saturday's battle. (AP)

Bull news isn't ALL bad (really)

Ohio's thug exports

--Page 32

Hands off!

Easy Leyden's 6-7 John Hendler (right) leaps high to steal the ball away from Hinsdale South's 6-3 Brian DeYoung during Friday night's Des Plaines Valley League game in Franklin Park. DeYoung was attempting to shoot on the play before Hendler so rudely interrupted. Hendler scored 17 points in East Leyden's 87-57 victory. Story on Page 34. (Daily News Photo/Don Bierman)

Special to The Daily News

OMAHA—The Bulls lost their eighth straight game Friday night and heaved a collective sigh of relief.

An unlikely development. But the way coach Dick Motta's men have been going lately, they'll take the slightest ray of sunshine and bask in it.

And they got more than a slight ray Friday. While they were falling before the Kansas City Kings 107-98, Jerry Sloan was back in Chicago, in the Passavant Pavilion of Northwestern Memorial Hospital, undergoing an arthroscopy of his sore right knee.

The verdict: No surgery will be needed.

SLOAN HAS been plagued by water on the knee and it was feared there might have been cartilage damage. But the test showed no evidence of it and the hustling guard is expected to return to action in about two weeks.

Of course, if the Bulls aren't able to win a game without him, that might even be too late. They'll be playing five times in that span, beginning with Tuesday's meeting of the Cleveland Cavaliers in Chicago.

Their 3-10 record, worst in the NBA, already has them five games behind first-place Detroit in the Midwest Division. And a loss in their next outing would equal the club losing-streak mark of nine.

"This is the longest losing streak I've ever had in my life, but we can laugh at it," said Bob Love. "Nobody is tight. We can talk about it.

"It'd be a mistake to write us off. Each game we try to eliminate what we did wrong the last time. Tonight the forwards all played a good game—except me."

Love scored 15 points but insisted, "I know I didn't do what I'm capable of doing."

FOR A WHILE Friday, it appeared the Bulls might snap out of it. After surrendering a 13-4 advantage to the Kings, they roared back to take the lead at 16-15 and held a 26-23 edge at the quarter break. It was 46-46 at halftime.

But the Kings shot a blistering 65 per cent in the third

NBA standings

EASTERN CONFERENCE
ATLANTIC DIVISION

	W	L	Pct	G.B.
Philadelphia	11	6	.647	—
Buffalo	9	5	.643	½
Boston	7	5	.583	1½
New York	6	10	.375	4½

CENTRAL DIVISION

	W	L	Pct	G.B.
Washington	7	4	.636	—
Atlanta	8	5	.615	—
New Orleans	5	7	.417	2½
Houston	5	7	.417	2½
Cleveland	4	9	.308	4

WESTERN CONFERENCE
MIDWEST DIVISION

	W	L	Pct	G.B.
Detroit	8	5	.615	—
Milwaukee	6	6	.500	1½
Kansas City	6	7	.462	2
BULLS	3	10	.231	5

PACIFIC DIVISION

	W	L	Pct	G.B.
Golden State	9	5	.643	—
Los Angeles	7	6	.538	1½
Seattle	7	8	.467	2½
Phoenix	5	6	.455	2½
Portland	5	10	.357	4½

FRIDAY'S RESULTS
Boston 118, New York 101
Philadelphia 131, Portland 111
Detroit 104, Buffalo 94
Kansas City 107, BULLS 98
Phoenix 107, Houston 91
Los Angeles 116, Milwaukee 104

SATURDAY'S GAMES
Cleveland at New York
New Orleans at Atlanta
Golden State at Washington
Portland at Buffalo

SUNDAY'S GAMES
Philadelphia at Atlanta
Boston at Cleveland
Houston at Los Angeles
Milwaukee at Seattle

quarter. once hitting seven shots in a row, and only an 11-point barrage by Norm Van Lier kept the Bulls alive. The Kings broke a 67-67 tie and took an 81-75 lead into the fourth period.

They held it, but not without a struggle. The Bulls began the quarter with baskets by Love and Van Lier to close the gap to two.

After Ollie Johnson scored for Kansas City and Love answered, the Kings ran off eight successive points to build a 91-81 bulge. With the count 95-85, though, the Bulls outscored the Kings 8-2, Mickey Johnson contributing seven of the points, and suddenly it was 97-93.

TOM BOERWINKLE'S layup brought the Bulls to within 101-97 with about a minute left, but Sam Lacey responded with a layup for the Kings, and that was the crusher.

Hawks' road finale 4-pointer

By George Vass

This isn't exactly "showdown" time because the Black Hawks are eight points ahead of the second place Vancouver Canucks (tied with St. Louis) but it's a vital game all the same.

"It's a four-pointer and those are all big ones," said Hawk coach Billy Reay, whose team takes on the Canucks Saturday night at Vancouver. "First place is very important to us and winning this one would be another stride toward it.

"I've been very pleased with the way the team has been going on this roadtrip. I've had teams before that hustled and gave the effort this team has, but not many that gave more."

A VICTORY Saturday not only would extend the Hawks' unbeaten streak to 11 (W6, T4), but make this one of their most successful road trips ever. With three ties and a victory so far on this trip they've got five points in four games. Getting seven would exceed Reay's hopes.

Reay called up a reinforcement for the defense Friday from Dallas, farming out little-used center Rob Palmer. He added defenseman Dave Logan, 21, who is 5-10 and 190 pounds. Logan had one goal and three assists at Dallas this season.

"With Phil Russell and Bill White both out I didn't want to

go any longer with only four defensemen," said Reay. "I didn't want to have to move John Marks back on defense because he has been playing so well at left wing."

Russell may be back sooner than first expected. It turns out he suffered only a slight crack in his right kneecap on Nov. 6 and may be out only two more weeks rather than the four to six predicted earlier

BY THE time Russell gets back, White should also be healthy again. He underwent surgery to reattach a pelvic

muscle two weeks ago and may be able to start working out by week after next.

After the five-game road trip is concluded at Vancouver, the Hawks will have the schedule swing their way. Their next four games, starting with Wednesday's against the Toronto Maple Leafs, will be at home.

One feature of this road trip has been the steady hammering of the Hawks' offense. They've scored at least four goals in each of the four games and during the 10-game streak have outscored the opposition 44-27.

Lanier to Knicks?

By United Press International

Is Bob Lanier the next big man the New York Knicks' money can buy?

A radio station in Olean, N.Y., scene of the 6-11 Lanier's collegiate days at St. Bonaventure, says the once-great Detroit Pistons' mainstay center will be traded to the Knicks for forwards John Gianelli, Phil Jackson and a barrelful of cash.

The Knicks refused to comment.

Lanier didn't play for the Pistons in their 104-94 victory over the Buffalo Braves Friday night but it wasn't because he was en route to New York. He

was on the bench nursing his always-pained high-priced knees.

Judging by Friday night's games, however, the Pistons didn't need Lanier's services while the Knicks most certainly could have used him.

Pistons' backup center Lindsay Hairston held Buffalo's high-scoring Bob McAdoo to 29 points. In his last three games, McAdoo had averaged 41 points.

The Knicks earlier this month hoped to have "bought" their way into the post-season playoffs by purchasing 6-9 Spencer Haywood from the Seattle SuperSonics for $1.3 million.

Complete prep coverage on Page 34

20 left feet tangle in LaGrange cage victory

It certainly didn't remind anyone of a ballet, as La Grange coach Ron Nikcevich later admitted. In fact, it could have been compared to watching Marjorie Main dancing with Rudolph Nureyev. Finesse, it wasn't.

"We've been spotty in practice and we have a lot of uncertainties," said Nikcevich. "I like stability, a set lineup. But things still are up for grabs."

"Every kid saw areas of his game to concentrate on in practice," concluded Niles West coach Bill Schurr. "Maybe we've been too loose in practice, especially with our free-throw shooting. That certainly hurt us tonight. No, it wasn't a ballet out there."

But Nikcevich and Schurr, two of the most successful high school coaches in the Chicago

area, are wise enough to know that a single basketball game in November isn't reason to slash your wrists. Wait until March.

FOR THE RECORD, La Grange slipped past Niles West 61-59 on reserve forward Tom Mueller's 10-footer with only one second left in the overtime period.

The victory was costly for the Lions, however, because 6-3 forward Bill Folkerts limped off the floor at the end of the first quarter and never returned. The injury later was diagnosed as a likely fracture in his left foot and he will be sidelined indefinitely.

La Grange blew a 12-point lead in the first half and frittered away a seven-point lead in the last 3½ minutes of the fourth period.

Niles' Marty Fabian sank three long jumpers down the stretch to narrow La Grange's lead to 52-51 with 38 seconds remaining. Jim Ekenberg intercepted a pass and the Indians got three shots before Kline was fouled with no time left.

BRUNER CONVERTED his first free throw but missed the second attempt to force an overtime period. "We had our opportunities to win," Schurr said. "But they made their free throws down the stretch and we didn't."

In the overtime, La Grange grabbed a 59-55 edge with only 33 seconds left on a basket by Mueller, two free throws by Joe Reetz and Konrad Kaltenbach's free throw.

But Niles West evened matters with 17 seconds left on Bruner's two free throws and

Tommy Arns' basket, setting the stage for Mueller's last-second shot.

Both coaches saw some encouraging signs amid the rubble. Nikcevich singled out the consistent play of Reetz, a senior guard who didn't letter a year ago. Joe contributed 14 points to lead the Lions. Jeff Wolf, La Grange's 6-8½ center, netted 13 before fouling out with 2:10 left in the overtime.

ALSO ENCOURAGING was the off-the-bench play of Mueller (nine points, five rebounds), guard Jamie McMillin and 6-6 junior Bruce Bykowski (10 points, eight of them in the fourth quarter).

"We made a lot of mistakes," said Nikcevich. "Our kids are inexperienced and they got too anxious at times, especially when we were

trying to run out the clock. But even though we were looking bad, the kids held up under pressure. They didn't crack."

"I was pleased by the way our kids came back," said Schurr. "And there were some other pluses—the good scoring we got from our three guards (Fabian, Arns and John Anastos), Bob Zyburt's fine defensive effort and the way we played after Zyburt fouled out."

Zyburt, a 6-6 senior, had 10 points and seven rebounds when he left with 2:57 left in the fourth period and his team trailing by seven. Bruner finished with 15 points, Arns 13 and Anastos 11.

"But we need more scoring from our big kids (Zyburt and Bruner)," concluded Schurr. "And those free throws . . ."

Figure 15–20. Boldly shaped vertical pictures. [*Courtesy Chicago Daily News.*]

CONTEMPORARY MAKEUP AND DESIGN CHECKLIST

Evaluate your page on a scale from 0 to 10 points on each criterion. If your page fulfills the criterion perfectly, give it 10. If less than perfect, give it any number from 0 to 10. Note: there are occasionally some exceptions to each criterion. If your page qualifies for an exception to any criterion, then give the criterion any number between 0 and 10 that you think is applicable.

Score: 0 - 10

1. Page should be balanced from top to bottom and side to side. If page is top heavy it is not balanced. Deduct points for formal balance. ....

2. Avoid extreme vertical or horizontal makeup. Each used to an extreme is unsightly. Good design uses both horizontal and vertical—but in unequal amounts without becoming extreme. ....

3. Is there enough openness, cleanliness, or white space on the page? White space should be fairly well distributed, not concentrated on one part of the page. ....

4. Is there enough white space between columns? Usually 12 points are the minimum, but 16 to 18 points are better. On the other hand, more than 18 points between columns may be unsightly. ....

5. Is there good contrast in the size of pictures? Poor design consists of small-sized pictures, or pictures whose dimensions are almost square. The larger and more dramatic the picture, the more likely the page will be attractive. Large pictures should be strongly vertical or horizontal. ....

6. Is the nameplate modern and contemporary? Old-fashioned nameplates detract from the appearance of the entire page. ....

7. Is the pattern of the entire page simple and uncluttered? Generally simple patterns are uncluttered. To get a feeling about the totality of design half close your eyes in order to make the type and words less obvious. ....

8. Is the page exciting and/or dramatic in totality (aside from the news)? ....

9. Have you avoided large masses of gray type matter (that tends to be boring)? ....

10. Are headline sizes and weights appropriate for the body type? Many times headlines are either too large or too bold, or both, and tend to spot the page. ....

Score: 0 - 5

The following are worth only five points totally (or 0 to 5)

11. Have you avoided too many different sizes and kinds of type faces? ....

12. Are there few type rules on the page? (Avoid as many rules as possible) ....

13. Is there no more than one "inverted L-shaped story" on the page? ....

14. Is there at least one dominating story on the page (but not much more)? ....

15. Have you avoided anything that might call attention to itself and not the news? ...

334 TOTAL SCORE

stories on pages looks unplanned. Why would an editor deliberately make up a page without planning? The answer is that he probably did not intend for it to appear that way—but it did. Clutter is found when part of a page is overcrowded with stories and pictures and the other part is clean. Clutter also is found when an important story is buried among a group of unimportant stories. Finally clutter is found when a page has too many centers of interest so that a reader cannot easily focus his eyes on any one story because of the competition of other stories.

2. *Jig-saw puzzle makeup.* When stories are wrapped to nearby columns and are of varying column lengths, the page tends to look like a jig-saw puzzle. Not only is such a page difficult for a makeup man to plan, but it is sometimes difficult for a reader to find the continuation of stories in adjacent columns. Such pages are confusing and unattractive to readers.

3. *Pages that are too dark in appearance.* Sometimes a page will appear dark and foreboding to the reader. This may happen because all the elements of a page are heavy in appearance. If a large, bold headline is used along with dark illustrations, and headline typefaces that are too large for the body copy, the entire page may appear much to dark. Obviously such a page will be uninviting to some readers. No page should ever appear like that.

4. *Pages that are too gray.* Occasionally, the opposite occurs; a page is gray and consequently dull. Headline typefaces are medium to light. Pictures are small and not dark. There may not be much white space between columns or between stories. Such pages are also uninviting to many readers.

5. *A device calls too much attention to itself.* One of the most unattractive kind of pages is that where a single element calls too much attention to itself. This element may be a nameplate that is too bold. Or it may be a cartoon, a four-color picture, a single story with too much emphasis on it or too much white space in only one section of the paper.

6. *Top-heavy pages.* Top-heavy pages tend to call too much attention to the upper stories, suggesting that those at the bottom are unimportant. (See Chapter 16 for a further discussion on this subject).

7. *Pictures are too small.* Small pictures tend to look like spots on a page rather than important communication in visual form. They detract rather than enhance a page.

8. *Pictures are square rather than being horizontal or vertical.* Square pictures tend to be uninteresting, while a mixture of horizontal and vertical pictures tend to bring about pleasant space contrast.

9. *Two or more pictures are about the same size.* When two or more pictures are about the same size, they tend to look unattractive. One of these pictures should be dominating, while the others should be subordinating. Such contrast-sized pictures help make the entire page interesting.

10. *White space is unevenly distributed.* When one part of a page has much white space and other parts do not have such abundance of space, the imbalance not only calls attention to itself, but the entire page looks unattractive.

If the principles of contemporary makeup are practiced, as explained in this chapter, all of these just-named problems can be solved. The solutions are relatively simple to make. But they do require a sensitivity to the makeup of the entire page. Practice in designing pages whose total makeup is interesting and readable is an important goal for any editor.

16

Makeup of Special Pages

Older textbooks on the subject of makeup usually included a section on front page design patterns. These patterns were recognizable styles of arranging news articles on the front page and were given descriptive names that helped identify them: brace, focused, symmetrical, quadrant, vertical or circus makeup. In this text, however, a discussion of older front page patterns has been omitted because they are not relevant to contemporary makeup practices. These patterns were old-fashioned, artificial, unattractive and inflexible and were not necessarily based on the best principles of artistic design.

The Front Page

Contemporary makeup, on the other hand, is modern, functional, attractive and very flexible. It is also based on the principles of artistic design. Contemporary makeup patterns, especially those of front pages, may be continually changing, just as the design of objects outside the newspaper changes. Therefore, any pattern that is contemporary today may not be after a period of time. Designer Gyorgy Kepes noted that:

> The laws of visual perception are conditioned by the visual habits of time. Visual communication can be efficient only if it adapts itself to the new landscape and the new psychology of contemporary man. . . . design, to be efficient must make significant adaptations to the contemporary scene.[1]

Kepes argued that communication is optimized when it is placed in the framework of the world as contemporary man per-

[1] Gyorgy Kepes, "Function in Modern Design," in *Graphic Forms* (Cambridge Mass.; Harvard University Press, 1949), p. 10.

ceives it. It is the front page, more than any other, that can and should reflect changing formats to keep up with changing man. Contemporary design is never static. Its beauty is based on the excitement of design that surrounds each individual reader.

Also to be found in some older makeup textbooks was the admonition that makeup must be used to design newspapers that looked like newspapers. This was necessary because readers might be disturbed if newspapers should take on new and unfamiliar designs. Contemporary man, however, often likes and appreciates new and unfamiliar designs—not at first, perhaps, but in the long run. New designs eventually will be appreciated the most. Makeup of newspapers, therefore, should not be limited to techniques and practices editors always have used. Editors should borrow from whatever graphic communication has been shown to be successful, such as magazines, books and possibly even advertisements.

It should be noted again, however, that newsroom personnel are not allowed to change the design of the entire paper. This is not their prerogative; it is the management's. They do have many opportunities from day to day, working within the overall design framework, of creating attractive and readable new page designs. They have more such opportunities on special pages than they do anywhere else within the newspaper.

Concept of Front Page Makeup   One carryover from the older makeup textbooks, however, still makes sense, namely that the front page ought to be a showcase of the newspaper. Because the front page does not carry advertising, its makeup is free from restrictions, so that it may reflect whatever the editor wishes it to reflect. Editors, however, although agreeing on the showcase concept, have not agreed on what should be displayed in the showcase. If one looks at the makeup of most front pages in this country, one will not find anything particularly exciting unless it happens to be the news. If the news is not exciting, then the front page showcase may have little to show.

There is an urgent need for editors to use the front page showcase to reflect a more sincere interest in the legibility of the page. It is suggested, therefore, that of all possible alternatives that might be featured in the showcase the most significant one is that the editor of the newspaper show that he cares a great deal about individuals' reading problems. The front pages of many newspapers do not reflect this interest. Front pages are not always easy to read, especially when they are compared with other printed communication such as books or magazines. They are designed, instead, on the basis of a traditional format that represents the easiest and quickest way to get the newspaper on the street in order to meet its deadlines.

Underlying the showcase concept, therefore, should be the following bases for front page makeup.

1. The makeup should reflect the editor's concern for the

reader so that the page is not only easy to read but attractive and inviting. The front page should be easier to read than any other page in the newspaper. Any device that impedes reading should be eliminated or replaced, no matter how important it may be for editorial purposes. The use of freaks, refers, insert and kickers have worthwhile editorial purposes, but they often mar the appearance of the page design.

2. The front page should also reflect the contemporary scene more than any other page in the newspaper. There is more opportunity on the front page than any other page to achieve this goal. It is not reasonable to place news in an old-fashioned setting, and the front page should not look like front pages of bygone days.

3. The front page should be orderly. But the order need not be graded from the most important stories placed at the top of the page to less important stories at the bottom. Other kinds of order can accomplish the same goal.

4. In addition to reflecting contemporary design, the front page should be distinctive, with a personality of its own. Although it should serve to set the tone of the entire paper, the front page personality should be one that readers like and respect because the news on that page is the most significant in the paper.

5. Readers should be offered alternative designs rather than one that is used every day with little change. Although it is true that readers may learn to like a format with no differences from day to day, such formats are not reasonable because the news changes, and designs should reflect these changes. The design itself, therefore, as well as the words, helps to communicate.

One of the most important ways of achieving a well-designed page 1 is to use the principle of artistic dominance. Front pages are often busy and cluttered because there are too many stories competing for the reader's attention. As a result, the reader often doesn't know where to look. He may direct his attention somewhere at the top because the largest and blackest headlines are located there. Even when a few strong headlines are located elsewhere on the page, the reader can't focus his attention easily without some distraction from other headlines. In other words, the competition for attention is often too great. Another problem with front page structure is that the shape of the main story, aside from its headline, is often not dominant. A single- or double-column story, no matter how long, does not necessarily dominate a page. As a result, many front pages lack unity. Graphic designer Maitland Graves stated the problem as follows: "Equality of opposing forces produces incoherence.... Without dominance, a design disintegrates."[2]

Structure of Page 1

[2] Maitland Graves, *The Art of Color and Design,* (New York: McGraw-Hill, 1941), p. 53, 54.

To overcome the pull of competing headlines and stories lacking any visual power at all, the structure of the front page should employ the principle of dominance.

The makeup man can employ this principle by first selecting one element to dominate the page. This element will undoubtedly be the story with the greatest news significance. Then, by careful placement, arrangement in columns, spacing and headline treatment, he can achieve his goal of page dominance. The one element, however, need not be a story alone. It may consist of a story and a related picture, a number of related stories, or a large picture alone (Figure 16–1 and 16–2). A hairline box around the element, including generous amounts of white space, may help achieve dominance. But the traditional banner headline, with accompanying multiple-column deck, reading into a single-column story is not an example of page dominance.

When one element dominates a page, all other elements will clearly be subordinate. But this relationship is very subtle. An element may overdominate a page to such an extent that the reader has trouble reading shorter stories. On the other hand, the dominant element may not be dominating enough to keep it from competing with secondary elements. Here, the makeup man simply has to develop a sense of good design. The situation demands a sensitivity that tells the editor when an element is either too strong or too weak, neither of which may be correct.

Furthermore, a major factor in creating a pleasing page structure involves shaping the main element so that it is pleasing as well as dominating. The makeup man will have to use his sense of pleasing proportions to determine the shapes that add the most to page structure. Rectangular shapes are best. Odd shapes such as the inverted L are poorest.

Finally, the placement of the dominating element is related to its size. When a story with a bold headline is crammed into a small corner of the page, the remainder of the page may be hard to make up in a pleasing arrangement. The dominating element, therefore, should be relatively large and placed in positions close to the optical center of the page. To have stories long enough to be a center of dominant interest, the editor may have to create a policy that makes longer stories possible. Many newspapers have no such policy, and as a result it is hard to create front page dominance with relatively short stories.

New Ordering on Front Page

The order of traditional makeup on page 1 was always to place the most important story in the upper-right corner. Other important stories may have been placed in the upper left, and less important stories were placed underneath. This is a logical way of ordering the placement of stories but it isn't the only way. In fact, it isn't suited to contemporary design because it tends to produce top-heavy pages and pages that never seem to vary in appearance.

A new ordering is based on the rotation of reading from the largest story to the smallest one, where the largest story is the

The Art of Editing

most dominant one. But now the most dominant story may be placed anywhere on the page, and because it is so dominant, it will be read first (assuming that the reader is interested in the news content). The reader easily sees where the most dominant story is located and proceeds from there to less dominant stories until he has finished reading the page. Because the dominant story may be moved from day to day, there should be no fixed pattern of front page makeup that becomes prosaic. Each day should bring about an exciting design showing that the makeup editor is attuned to placing the news of the day in a format unique for that day.

When reading a particular story, the reader's order is from the top down. When the story is continued to adjacent columns, however, the order is back up again to the top of the next column in which the story is continued. The best way to inform the reader where the story is continued is to wrap it at the top of the next column, underneath a headline. The squared-off design should immediately tell the reader the order of procedure without the loss of even a second.

Listed below are some recurring problems contributing to poor makeup and design on the front page. If the reader's best interest serves as the underlying basis for makeup, these problems will not occur. But because they have occurred so often, they are mentioned here.

Problems To Avoid in Front Page Makeup

1. Use of a daily banner headline. Readers either resent newspapers that use a large banner headline daily or they learn to discount the effect of large type used in such headlines. They assume that what is printed is not necessarily most important. In some newspaper offices, banners are used each day because it has become traditional since the days when newspapers were sold on newsstands. Editorial policy should be changed so that banners are used only when the news warrants them. If not, then the entire page structure is forced into a page makeup where the readout almost always occurs at the top right, or, perhaps, somewhere at the top. It is difficult to create a contemporary design when a banner headline is used each day.

2. Breaking a page into two distinct sections. When the makeup editor attempts to use contemporary design through the use of page domination, there is the possibility he may divide the page into two distinct parts. This has the effect of asking the reader to read either one or the other part but not both. One part does not naturally lead into the other. Therefore, attempts should be made to prevent such a dichotomy from occurring. The makeup editor will have to be alert to the division of space into two parts. When he finds a line of white space that extends for eight columns across the page, he is apt to be dividing the page horizontally. When he uses a rule eight columns wide to separate elements on the page, the same thing may occur (Figure 16–3). In other words, the makeup man isn't deliberately dividing the

---

Makeup of Special Pages 341

Illness, no jobs mean no Christmas for many

Why do the more than 500 families for whom Friend-In-Deed Fund help has been requested this Christmas need a hand?

Illness, desertion, unemployment—just plain hard luck—are outlined in the letters asking consideration:

"The father has been out of work for some time. They have five children. The father has had four heart attacks and has to go back in the hospital . . ."

"There are two little girls. The father deserted them and the mother is not able to work . . ."

"The older children understand that their mother can't get the things that they want. But the youngest won't understand why Santa doesn't come this year . . ."

"Her husband has been in a nursing home for years. She gets by on very little money . . ."

"He recently lost his job and they are expecting another child in a few months . . ."

"Two children were just returned to her from a foster home where they had been placed because she was sick and could not care for them. When the children were returned, their stepfather decided he couldn't cope . . . so he split, taking what little money she had . . ."

"Her check every month goes on rent and bills . . ."

"The 18-year-old son was badly burned and will be in the hospital about a year. The father has had back surgery . . ."

"She has three small kids . . . She had a fire not long ago . . . She was trying to work part time to make ends meet, but got sick and had to quit. Her house was broken into . . ."

Friend-In-Deed contributions

A Friend	$2.00
Lynn Schroeder, Taylorville	1.00
In Memory of loved ones, by John P. Kreppert	3.00
A Friend	20.00
Jackson Club of Sangamon County	25.00
A Friend	10.00
Charlie & Dorothy Warren, in lieu of Christmas Cards	15.00
A Friend	1.00
Jan, Doug, & Jill Anderson	6.00
A Friend	5.00

Turn to page 2, col. 2

The above are examples that come from a few of the hundreds of letters received.

The goal of the Friend-In-Deed Fund is to relieve the sadness for a moment at Christmas with a gift of food or clothing or toys, perhaps all three, from the people of the Springfield area.

You can help this cause by sending your contribution today to:

Friend-In-Deed
State Journal-Register
313 S. 6th St.
Springfield, Ill. 62701

Or bring it to the first floor offices of the newspaper between 8 a.m. and 5 p.m.

Every cent donated will be used to help the needy. All operational expenses of the fund will be borne by the State Journal-Register and its employes.

How many of the needy can be helped and to what extent depends on the amount of money donated.

Receipts through Tuesday totaled $10,889. Last year $24,500 was contributed and help was given to 420 families.

The State Journal-Register

Good AFTERNOON! On Wednesday, Dec. 17, 1975

Springfield, Illinois, a Bicentennial community — 15 Cents

AMERICAN REVOLUTION BICENTENNIAL 1776-1976

Find 260 pounds of gold hidden on plane

CHARLESTON, S.C. (UPI) — A worker found 260 pounds of gold valued at $550,000 hidden in the cargo hold of a plane chartered by the Air Force Tuesday.

Patrick T. O'Brien, special agent in charge of investigations for the U.S. Customs Office here, said the gold was brought into this country illegally on the DC8 owned by Overseas National Airlines Co. of New York. The company said it knew nothing about the gold.

O'Brien said officers believe the gold might have been stolen from a Saudi Arabian resident. An invoice found in one of the boxes of gold indicated the gold was supposed to have been moveo from Zurich, Switzerland via Frankfurt, Germany to Saudi Arabia.

"The gold was actually seized because it was smuggled into the United States, O'Brien said.

The gold was found around midday Tuesday by a civilian employe of the Charleston Air Force Base who was removing spare seats from the plane's cargo compartment. The worker found boxes containing 118 bars of gold; each bar weighing 2.2 pounds.

"The price of gold is $132 an ounce so that means the shipment was worth just over $550,000," O'Brien said.

An Air Force official said the plane was chartered from Overseas National Airlines to fly military personnel from Charleston to Frankfurt. The plane was flown by a seven member crew employed by Overseas National.

"We have no evidence that anyone from the crew was involved," O'Brien said. "The crew denies all knowledge of the gold."

The plane was allowed to leave the Charleston Air Force Base Tuesday afternoon after about a two hour delay.

O'Brien said flight logs for the plane showed it was in Frankfurt two weeks ago, then went to Saudia Arabia, Miami, Oakland, Calif., Los Angeles, Las Vegas, Miami and then Charleston. The seven member crew was not changed during any of the flight.

"The gold was destined from Zurich via Frankfurt to Jeddah, Saudia Arabia and it was supposed to be left there but wasn't," O'Brien said. "We don't know why it wasn't left and there was no report of theft.

"This makes us wonder what was going on, for someone to forget 260 pounds of gold. We find that hard to believe.

First reports said the gold was estimated to be worth at least $1 million but O'Brien said that estimate was made during the confusion surrounding the seizure of the gold and later turned out to be excessive.

The gold is being held by Customs officials in Charleston.

Proud tower last to go

The camera caught the tower of the First United Methodist Church a[s] it toppled at 1:45 a.m. today from its position as one of the olde[st] landmarks in downtown Springfield. Soon the last vestige of th[e] church will disappear and the building will be remembered only i[n] historical papers. The tower had occupied a prominent corner of th[e] business district for more than a century. Photo by Bill Hagen.

Iran says West is to blame for the world economic crisis

PARIS (UPI) — Iran said today that the world economic crisis was caused not by higher oil prices but by the West's own bad economic policies.

Secretary of State Henry A. Kissinger, in an opening speech Tuesday to the international conference on energy and raw materials, blamed both the world recession and the impoverishment of Third World nations on the quadrupling of oil prices over the past two years.

But Iranian Interior Minister Jamshid Amouzegar, in his speech to the 27-nation conference, disputed this.

According to Iranian officials, Amouzegar said the West's recession was caused by the fiscal and monetary policies of some Western nations — an apparent reference to U.S. policies. As for the developing countries, he said, their trouble stems from their inability to get good prices for their raw materials on Western markets and from inflation and the low level of Western aid.

Amouzegar rejected Kissinger's proposal for a floor price lower than the present world oil price of $11.51 per barrel.

"To blame the world's problems on OPEC (Organization of Petroleum Exporting Countries) decisions is not only unconvincing but has negative influence on the dialogue which, if it is to be a success, must open in the spirit of good will and mutual respect," Amouzegar said.

Dunlop may resign if Ford vetoes labor bill

WASHINGTON (UPI) — Labor Secretary John Dunlop will be forced to consider quitting his Cabinet post if President Ford vetoes a controversial bill dealing with the rights striking union members, sources close to Dunlop say.

The sources said a veto would seriously damage the secretary's credibility. Dunlop fashioned the compromise measure earlier this year and assured labor leaders that Ford would sign it.

Ford has been under heavy pressure recently from Republican conservatives to veto the bill to placate supporters of Republican presidential challenger Ronald Reagan, who opposes it. White House officials predict he will veto it.

The bill, which the AFL-CIO has been seeking for 25 years, would allow picketing union members to shut down an entire construction site in a dispute with a single subcontractor. It passed the Senate 52 to 43 and the House 222 to 189 — both margins short of the two-thirds required to override a Ford veto.

Sources said Dunlop, a longtime friend of construction industry leaders, has been working grimly on behalf of the measure in recent days.

The sources agreed with opponents and proponents of the bill that Ford had not decided finally whether to sign or veto the bill.

If Ford vetoes it, sources said, Dunlop certainly will be forced to consider submitting his resignation. But they emphasized that Dunlop has never told them he would quit or consider quitting.

Robert A. Georgine, head of the AFL-CIO's Building Trades Department, told a news conference Tuesday he has discussed the situation daily with Dunlop. "As far as I know he thinks the President is going to sign the bill," Georgine said.

John Dunlop

"I have no doubt whatsoever the President is going to sign this bill," Georgine said. "He is an honest man. He has a great deal of integrity."

Senate Democratic leader Mike Mansfield meanwhile indicated Congress may delay sending Ford the bill to avoid a possible pocket veto while Congress is in recess.

Dunlop himself drafted a portion of the bill that would overhaul collective bargaining in the construction industry. He also won the approval of labor and some management officials for it.

City man found dead after apartment fire

A 20-year-old Springfield man was found dead on some bed covers and clothing in a closet when city firemen responded to a fire alarm at his apartment about 5:45 a.m. today.

Sangamon County Coroner Norman Richter identified him as Perry Jay Snapp, 20, of 2619½ S. 6th St., an employe of the Mosler Safe Co., 2619 S. 6th St., the past six months.

Fire officials said a burning cigarette probably started the blaze, which caused $1,250 damage, including $850 damage to the building and $400 damage to the apartment contents.

Richter said the Snapp body had been blistered and charred somewhat by the fire, which seriously damaged a sofa Snapp may have been lying on when the blaze started.

The sofa was positioned so that it faced a television set, which reportedly was on when officials arrived at the residence.

Richter said Snapp was known to be a smoker.

The fire is being investigated by the Springfield department's Fire Safety Division.

Richter said it appeared Snapp h[ad] been "confused" when he tried to [get] out of the apartment and made a wr[ong] turn into a closet in a corner of the re[si]dence bedroom.

A spokesman at the city fire depa[rt]ment said firemen who were dispatch[ed] to fight the blaze had told him there h[ad] been a lot of smoke, making it possi[ble] Snapp could not see where he was go[ing] as he sought to leave his home.

An autopsy was scheduled for lat[er] today at Memorial Medical Cen[ter]. Richter said an inquest will be co[n]ducted later. A time has not yet be[en] scheduled.

—*Predict low of zero*—

It'll be partly cloudy and very cold tonight with a low of zero. Thursday will be mostly sunny but cold with a high of 18. Details on page 55.

On the inside

Robert Walbaum

THE ONLY lawyer on the Sangamon County Board, Robert Walbaum, has resigned his position effective immediately. Al Manning, page 23.

WHY NOT have a "Merry, Merry Kitchen" too this holiday season? Heloise, page 29.

THE ALL-CITY girls' field hockey team is announced today by the State Journal-Register. Sports, page 49.

Comics	44	Financial	54	People	26-29
Editorials and Commentary	22-23	Hospital list	30	Sports	49-52
		Obituaries	55	Theaters	52

6 sections, 80 pages
including 2 advertising supplements

(If you did not receive these supplements, please call 525-0744. No supplements in mailed copies.)

a Copley Newspaper

Oldest Newspaper In Illinois

Our 145th Year — No. 37

Secrecy veils Senate's Angola aid discussion

WASHINGTON (UPI) — The Senate took up controversial U.S. aid to Angola today in one of its tightest secret sessions in memory. Everyone but the senators was excluded from the floor when classified reports were given on Russian and Cuban involvement in the African nation.

The fight centered on a move by liberal senators to cut off covert American aid to Angola, which has already totaled an estimated $50 million, on grounds that the African civil war may be a budding Vietnam.

The closed session began at 9:30 a.m. EDT and was scheduled for two hours. But it continued an hour longer after the staffers and even official congressional reporters — who record debate — were ushered from the chamber.

At the White House, a spokesman for President Ford said the United States has no military advisers in Angola and did not "contemplate any form of U.S. combat intervention there."

Deputy Press Secretary William Greener declined to spell out U.S. interest and action in Angola where, according to senior U.S. officials, the Soviets are airlifting arms and the Cubans have sent as many as 5,000 troops.

In the Senate, Sen. John V. Tunney, D-Calif., was leading the liberals' fight

Turn to page 3, col. 1

Stevens confirmed for high court post

WASHINGTON (AP) — The Senate today confirmed President Ford's nomination of Judge John Paul Stevens of Chicago to be a Supreme Court Justice.

Stevens will fill the vacancy left by the retirement of Justice William O. Douglas on Nov. 12 because of ill health.

Ford's first appointee to the nation's highest court, Stevens won the unanimous endorsement of the Senate Judiciary Committee after three days of hearings.

Stevens' confirmation by the Senate brings the Supreme Court to full strength for the start of its new term Jan. 12 when the constitutionality of the death penalty and the free press-fair trial controversy will be among the major issues confronting it.

House okay extension of tax cuts

WASHINGTON (UPI) — The Hou[se] today passed by voice vote a six-mo[nth] extension of 1975's recession-fighting [tax] cuts, setting up a veto showdown w[ith] President Ford.

The bill goes to the Senate, which a[l]... was expected to approve it and send [it] to the White House. Ford was expect[ed] to act with equal haste in vetoing [it].

Votes to override the veto could co[me] Thursday or Friday.

The Senate is expected to easily ov[er]ride the veto, but a close showdown v[ote] is expected in the House where Dem[o]crats failed by 22 votes to gain a t[wo-]thirds vote Tuesday night to speed House procedures and pass the [bill] quickly. A two-thirds vote also is need[ed] to override a veto.

One final Republican effort to op[en] the bill to a vote on the $395 billion fis[cal] spending ceiling failed 232-178. Num[er]ous procedural votes have been taken [on] the spending ceiling question, but the[re] never has been a direct up-or-do[wn] House vote on the spending ceili[ng]

Clare Luce Vs. Keating and Kennedy
N.Y. Conservative Party Says She's Willing to Run. Page 2.

WEATHER
Today:
Sunny, hot and very humid.
Tomorrow:
Warm humid, late showers.
Temperature Range:
Yesterday 65-92.
Today 72-95.
Humidity
Yesterday 4 P.M. 86.
Today 40-80.
Charts Details: Page 14.

The Sunday
Herald Tribune
ESTABLISHED 124 YEARS AGO. A EUROPEAN EDITION IS PUBLISHED DAILY IN PARIS
AUGUST 23, 1964

1

CITY EDITION

Vol. CXXIV No. 42,963 © 1964 NEW YORK HERALD TRIBUNE, INC. • 230 WEST 41st STREET, NEW YORK, 10036 N. Y. TEL. PENNSYLVANIA 6-4000   35c IN AREAS 50 MILES FROM NEW YORK CITY EXCEPT ON LONG ISLAND   *THIRTY CENTS*

IN THE NEWS THIS MORNING

3 Congo Yanks Safe: The Colonel's Story

Two American Army colonels and a U.S. diplomat emerged safe from the eastern Congo bush after three days of terror that included being machine-gunned by Congolese rebels and threatened with death by hostile villagers. From the United Nations, Herald Tribune correspondent Darius Jhabvala notes a surprising change of pace: the Russians are being rather agreeable over the Congo, an issue on which they used to break records for vituperation. The reports are on **Page 3.**

Tense Cease-Fire in Cyprus

The United Nations peace force on Cyprus was acting bolder yesterday in defense of a tense cease-fire—especially when it came to getting food to beleaguered Turkish Cypriots. In Athens, however, the Greek government has had trouble making up its mind just how bold to be in dealing with Greek Cypriot President Makarios—and its indecision threatens to push the nation's politics leftward, reports Seymour Freidin. **Page 23.**

Castro: The Tough Questions

What question is Fidel Castro most reluctant to answer about his regime? And what question makes him *see* Red in more ways than one? Barnard L. Collier asked them both during his seven-day running interview with the Cuban dictator. **Page 26.**

Coming Red Victory in Chile

Within two weeks Chile will hold a Presidential election in which the Communists cannot lose even if they are beaten; both the other candidates have been driven far to the Left by the Reds' appeal to the voters. Henry Lee reports. **Page 7.**

Old Nazis in the New Germany

West Germany's 20-year statute of limitations on Nazi war crimes expires next May, but hundreds of ex-Nazis are still at large and many are back in government. Werner H. Guttmann, who saw the Nazi movement's rise before he left Germany in 1933, analyzes the problem in an article on **Page 20.**

Reapportionment Nears Vote

The Supreme Court's sweeping reapportionment edict—designed to give urban and rural dwellers equal voice in public affairs—will be put to another crucial battle in Congress early next month. That's when Senate Minority Leader Everett Dirksen hopes to force a vote on a bill to thwart the court's decision. Ironically, however, reporter Andrew Glass finds that politicians are far more perturbed than voters over the reapportionment matter. **See Page 11.**

Howard Hughes' $1 Billion Empire

The bankroll behind Howard Hughes is a South-western tool company whose penchant for anonymity makes Greta Garbo appear to be a headline-hunter. But from this corporate head-water has come the millions of dollars that the brilliant and eccentric Hughes has used to spawn a billion-dollar empire. Dennis Duggan reports some little-known facts about the cornerstone of the Hughes complex on **Page 1, Section 3.**

Beauty & New York—By Bob Bird

National Correspondent Robert S. Bird take a penetrating look at places of beauty around New York. He begins at the Central Park Zoo, ends at Lincoln Center for the Performing Arts, and in between details New York's progress in making a fuller, richer life for us all. On **Page 18.**

—Index on Page 3—

Late TV-Radio Ratings—Page 33

Atlantic City: Democratic Sunshine and Shadows

- *People and Places and Problems in Boardwalk City. Page 8.*
- *Johnson's Choices for Vice-President. Page 8.*
- *White House 'to Run' Convention Electronically. Page 14.*
- *Platform Contrast — Justifiably Extreme. Page 14.*
- *Credentials Fight on Alabama, Mississippi. Page 14.*
- *Point by Point in Democratic Platform. Page 35.*

Boardwalk Bandwagon

It's Johnson's Convention

By David Wise
Washington Bureau Chief
ATLANTIC CITY.

This is, all the way, Lyndon B. Johnson's convention.

It was supposed to have been John F. Kennedy's.

That simple, delicate fact is everywhere, like the tang of the salt in the air. And the sea, that rolls in timelessly, is a reminder that all things human are fragile, even the "portraits of LBJ in indestructible metal" on sale in the lobby of the convention hall.

The truth is, President Johnson never wanted the convention here, in this land of salt-water taffy, frozen custard and pre-Cambrian plumbing.

Back in January, President Johnson explored the possibility of moving the 1964 national convention to Chicago, which he would have preferred. But he was told it could not be done.

President Kennedy had approved the Atlantic City convention site, and here it will take place.

Had it been as planned by the Democratic National Committee, this convention would have been a gay celebration of President Kennedy's renomination for a second term. The choice of a pleasure resort would have been in keeping with the occasion. But the occasion has changed.

Perhaps that is why Mr. Johnson tried to switch the convention to Chicago, although the reasons given for the White House discontent with Atlantic City had more to do with the alleged lack of hotel rooms and baths.

Delegates, alternates and the press are occupying 11,000 rooms. The Atlantic City Public Relations Bureau insists only 109 rooms are bathless. Because the convention is taking

It's a Johnson Convention with Kennedy in background...

Herald Tribune—UPI telephoto
... and Barry Goldwater on the Atlantic City boardwalk.

place nine months after the assassination of the President of the United States, Atlantic City seems even more tawdry than it might. Aged vacationers sit in the gloomy lobbies of cavernous Victorian hotels. They stare at the sea and at the aimless stream of people seeking carnival thrills along the boardwalk.

One reason that President Kennedy

approved Atlantic City as his renomination site was the $625,000 the city offered the national committee, along with free use of the Convention Hall. Miami Beach had offered more money, but in view of the civil rights issue and Miami's large Cuban exile population, it was thought wiser to come here.

On Thursday night, after the nomination of President Johnson, there will be a tribute to President Kennedy in the the form of a film called "A Thousand Days." White House officials said yesterday that Mrs. John F. Kennedy had talked with Mrs. Johnson yesterday by phone and "felt she could not watch" the movie about her husband's life and the scenes showing him with their two children.

Mrs. Kennedy has told convention officials she would rather enter the hall after the film, about fifteen minutes before President Johnson arrives to accept the cheers of 17,000 persons in Convention Hall.

Earlier that day, Mrs. Kennedy will receive all 5,300 delegates and alternates at a tea at the Deauville Hotel given by Under Secretary of State W. Averell Harriman "to thank the delegates who supported" John F. Kennedy at the 1960 convention in Los Angeles.

But none of this can take away the fact that this is LBJ's convention. Mounted behind the speaker's platform in the great, empty hall yesterday there were three small photographs—of Franklin D. Roosevelt, John F. Kennedy and Harry S. Truman. Beneath them and dwarfing them in size were two Orwellian photographs of President Johnson, each 60 feet high. And there are also the new President's words:

"Let us continue . . ."

A View Within CIA: Can't Win in Viet

By Laurence Barrett
Of The Herald Tribune Staff
WASHINGTON

A ranking Central Intelligence Agency official believes there is "serious doubt" that the Communist rebellion in South Viet Nam can be quelled and says a "prolonged stalemate" might be all the West can hope for.

This conclusion, reached in a scholarly paper called "Trends in the World Situation," promises to set off a political explosion because of Sen. Barry Goldwater's determination to make the Vietnamese war a major campaign issue. The Republican Presidential candidate accuses the Administration of being timid and feckless in dealing with Communists.

Although the CIA was prepared to allow publication of the entire paper in a scholarly journal, the Administration became concerned when it learned that one newspaper—the Chicago Tribune—had acquired a copy. The newspaper was understood to be planning a story on the document today.

The State Department took the unusual step of

attempting to reduce the impact of the story by making the paper available to a small group of State Department reporters Friday night. At the same time, Secretary of State Dean Rusk reportedly said the document did not represent the Administration's viewpoint.

Mr. Rusk was said to have emphasized that the paper was the work of one man only—the author, Willard Matthias—and that it had no official status. Other sources said the paper was not an official appraisal by CIA's Board of National Estimates, even though Mr. Matthias is a member of that important body and even though other board members saw the report and concurred in it in general terms.

The 68-page paper, dated June 9, 1964, touched on virtually every aspect of the cold war. Its controversial section on South Viet Nam consisted of these lines:

"The guerrilla war in South Viet Nam is in its fifth year and no end appears in sight. The Viet Cong in the South, dependent largely on their own resources but under direction and control of the

Communist regime in the North, are pressing their offensive more vigorously than ever. The political mistakes of the Diem regime inhibited the effective prosecution of the war, which is mainly more of a political contest than a military operation, and led to the regime's destruction.

"The counter-guerrilla effort continues to flounder, partly because of the inherent difficulty of the problem and partly because Diem's successors have not yet demonstrated the leadership and inspiration necessary.

"There remains serious doubt that victory can be won, and the situation remains very fragile. If large-scale United States support continues, and if further political deterioration within South Viet Nam is prevented, at least a prolonged stalemate can be attained. There is also a chance that political evolution within the country and developments upon the world scene could lead to some kind of negotiated settlement based on neutralization."

For other developments in Viet Nam, and a report on how Americans are fighting there, see Page 21.

Figure 16–1 [OPPOSITE]. Story at top is dominant because of position and border. [*Courtesy Illinois State Journal-Register.*]

Figure 16–2 [ABOVE]. Dominating stories on front page. Note the dramatic emphasis given these stories in a total design concept page.

343

Wife's anguish

Friends try to comfort Mrs. Edward Fonville as Mrs. Fonville watches ambulance attendants and police work to free her husband, trapped between his car and a garage wall after a freak accident yesterday afternoon. Fonville died in the hospital this morning from the accident injuries.—News-Dispatch photo, Jack Meyer

Freak accident takes man's life

EDWARD FONVILLE, 48, 907 Elston St., died this morning from injuries suffered in a freak accident in his garage yesterday afternoon.

Fonville was injured at 4 p.m. when his parked car suddenly slipped into gear as Fonville was outside. The car jumped forward and crashed into the garage wall, trapping Fonville between the car fender and the wall, which fell down.

FONVILLE'S WIFE, who witnessed the accident, said her husband had gotten out of the car to move some garbage cans from the garage entrance. The car was standing in the garage driveway when it jumped into gear.

The car spun its tires and threw back dirt for about 10 feet after crashing into the garage wall. The garage is owned by Ray Hall, 601 W. 10th St.

Before taking Fonville out of the garage, LaPorte County Ambulance Service attendants Don Daily and Dan Jenkins worked to relieve Fonville's suffering by dressing the wound and applying a splint to one of his legs.

FONVILLE SUFFERED multiple fractures to both legs, as well as broken ribs and extensive cuts. He underwent six hours of surgery in St. Anthony Hospital, but died in the intensive care unit at about 9 a.m. today. Mrs. Fonville, who coincidentally is employed in the hospital, was notified this morning.

Policemen Theodore Stantz and Arthur Gumns, who assisted the ambulance attendants, commended Daily and Jenkins for their efforts.

Funeral services are pending at Coleman-Williams Funeral Home.

Sirica: Give Nixon written questions

WASHINGTON (AP) — U.S. District Judge John J. Sirica proposed today that written questions be submitted to former President Richard M. Nixon in lieu of having him testify at the Watergate cover-up trial.

Sirica opened the day's court session by asking attorneys for the five defendants whether they had any objection to his contacting the doctors who examined Nixon last week to ask whether the former president is well enough to answer written questions.

The court-appointed panel of three doctors had reported that Nixon would not be well enough to appear even at a question-and-answer session in his home in California until Jan. 6. That would be well beyond the expected conclusion of the trial.

None of the lawyers had any objection to making an inquiry of the panel and Sirica sent his law clerk to contact Dr. Charles A. Hufnagal, the chairman of the panel.

But chief prosecutor James F. Neal expressed reservations about allowing Nixon to answer written questions, saying "we have had a number of statements about Watergate from the former president, none of which was satisfactory."

He did not, however, express any opposition to calling the doctors.

The judge's suggestion came as H. R. Haldeman returned to the stand for a second day of cross-examination.

Haldeman said Monday that orders from Nixon prevented his telling the Watergate grand jury that the White House had a clandestine taping system.

"You didn't mention tapes and you hoped they wouldn't be revealed," said assistant prosecutor Richard Ben-Veniste Monday as he began to cross-examine Haldeman at the Watergate cover-up trial. The questioning was to continue today.

"I was under orders from the President of the United States that it would not be disclosed," said Haldeman. "It was not a matter of my hopes, it was my instructions."

But Ben-Veniste noted that Haldeman had resigned as Nixon's chief of staff two weeks before his May 14, 1973 grand jury appearance.

"I still considered myself subject to orders given to me during the term of my service to the President of the United States," Haldeman replied.

The 48-year-old Haldeman is charged with John N. Mitchell, John D. Ehrlichman, Robert C. Mardian and Kenneth W. Parkinson of conspiring to derail official investigations into the Watergate break-in.

Only a tight handful of White House aides, including Haldeman, knew about the White House taping system until Alexander P. Butterfield disclosed it during Senate Watergate testimony on July 16 last year.

Ben-Veniste had brought out that Haldeman told the grand jury that he wanted to be "candid, volunteering and help out" but that he said there were no records he could provide except his telephone logs.

"I think you testified there were no other records on the face of the earth that would reflect contacts with other people," said Ben-Veniste. "But you didn't mention tape recordings, did you Mr. Haldeman?"

"No sir," was the reply.

Ben-Veniste, a persistent cross-examiner who drew frequent rebukes from the judge for interrupting the witness, asked Haldeman whether he and the President had not discussed "a way you could evade giving truthful answers to the Senate (Watergate) committee."

"No sir," said Haldeman.

Ben-Veniste asked if he didn discuss the use of "I don't recall as a device to duck toug questions.

"I don't recall," said Haldeman

The prosecutor read from transcript of a conversatic Haldeman had with Nixon ar John W. Dean III on March 21, 19 when Haldeman said, "You ca refuse to talk ...you can say yc forgot, too, can't you?"

Dean agreed that could be don running the risk of being accused perjury and Nixon added: "That right, just be damned sure you sa I don't remember, I can't recall."

The jury had heard the tape that crucial conversatio Haldeman said he remembered t reference but explained: "Th was not a discussion of evadi telling the truth, it was questioni on my part as for giving testimo at various forums."

The weather

Clear tonight. Low in upper tee to mid-20s. Morning fog tomorro Clearing in late morning a afternoon. High in the upper 3 and low 40s. High yesterday 44, l 37.

Death record

Zurry Belles, 69, 904 Fifth S LaPorte.

Louise Ehmke, 95, S Bernardino, Calif.

Edward Fonville, 48, 907 Elst St.

Irene Gunter, 67, McLeansbo Ill.

Wayne Peeples, 67, Kingsbury.

Jennifer Sample, 2 months, 3 West U.S. 20, LaPorte.

(Details on Pages 1 and 5)

Allen traded to Atlanta

NEW ORLEANS (AP) — The Atlanta Braves acquired controversial slugger Dick Allen from the Chicago White Sox in a deal completed today at baseball's winter meetings.

The Braves sent cash and a player to be named later to the White Sox-contingent upon Allen's ending his announced retirement and reporting to Atlanta for the 1975 season.

City police have a John Dough case

Police this morning were attempting to determine the identity of a man found wandering on E. Michigan Boulevard early today with $3,000 in crisp $100-bills in his hands.

The man was picked up at about 6 a.m. near E. 11th Street after police saw him walking in the middle of the street. He was taken to the police station to get him out of the cold, and after he got to the station police discovered t money.

The man this morning refused tell police who he is or why he w in the street. Police said the $ bills must have come from a bar as they were number consecutively.

The man appears to be in early 20s and had part of a tr ticket to Chicago in his pock police said.

City hall, convention center termed keys

Retiring redevelopment commissioner Harriet Miller told fellow commissioners yesterday that construction of a new city hall and a convention center are key factors to successful redevelopment of the Beachway urban renewal area.

Mrs. Miller said the new city hall should be built now rather than in the future. She called the Beachway area an ideal convention center location at the gateway to Dunes National Lakeshore.

The retiring commissioner said a member of the Indiana Board of Realtors told her the board feels there is a need for a third convention center in Indiana aside from Indianapolis and French Lick. She said the member describes Michigan City as a good site for a convention center.

"If we spend money to bring developments into the city, it will bring more money back into the city," Mrs. Miller said. "Unless we're willing to put some money into the area, we won't get anything out of it."

Mrs. Miller also complimented the library board for selecting a Beachway site for the proposed new library. The library board purchased the site at Michigan Boulevard and Franklin and Fourth Streets.

The retiring commissioner has served the past six years on the commission and the previous four years as a redevelopment trustee. The redevelopment department's board of trustees in a meeting earlier chose downtown businessman Michael Lernihan, 4230 Cleveland Ave., to replace Mrs. Miller, effective Jan. 1. Commissioners John Garrettson, Daniel Slocum, Robert Rose and Donald Missal, were elected to serve another term next year.

Lernihan is an officer of Michigan City Interiors.

In other redevelopment busine the commission authorized t leases for nominal sums. T commission leased the Tonn Blank property boat docks alo the south bank of Trail Creek to t port authority for 1975. It a leased Second Street prope directly across from the pol station to the city for parking spa for persons using the building.

The commission authoriz acting redevelopment direct Charles Oberlie to negotiate t appraisal contracts for the Tonn Blank property. One contract w be with Ralph Lauver for review land disposition appraisals. T other contract will be with Jo Shanahan for the updating of earlier land disposition appraisa

The commission also authoriz the hiring of attorneys Claren Sweeney and O.J. Winski to ser the redevelopment department.

Ford says agreement allows buildups of nuclear weapons

WASHINGTON (AP) — The new U.S.-Soviet strategic arms agreement allows both countries to continue costly nuclear weapons buildups over the next decade, President Ford has acknowledged.

In a news conference Monday night, Ford said the accord, worked out last week in Siberia with Soviet Communist Party Leader Leonid I. Brezhnev, allows each country 2,400 long-range missiles and bombers.

Of that quota, both nations can place multiple warheads — MIRVs — on 1,320 missiles.

Although the President said this agreement "put a cap on the arms race," he described a situation in which both countries have great flexibility in increasing the number of MIRV missiles as well as the lifting power of each missile — "throw-weight" in military-diplomatic jargon.

For instance, the Soviet Union has about 2,200 long-range missiles, none of which is believed to carry multiple warheads. Moscow can and is expected to install MIRV warheads on up to the 1,320-missile limit.

The United States already has 822 of its 1,710 offensive missile force carrying multiple warheads. Ford made it clear Monday night the United States will push its MIRV program to the limit.

"We do have an obligation to stay up to that ceiling," he said of the figures worked out at the Vladivostok summit. "The budget that I will recommend will keep our strategic forces either up to or aimed at that objective."

Ford opened the news conference by segregating topics into two categories. He dealt first with the strategic arms question and then turned to domestic matters, primarily the economy.

He repeated his assertion that inflation remains the nation's worst enemy, although acknowledging that a recession "is a serious threat that already has hurt many citizens and alarms many more."

Still, Ford challenged a growing belief among congressional Democrats that the recession should be fought by recharging the economy, possibly by increased spending.

"Our greatest danger today is to fall victim to the more exaggerated alarms that are being generated about the underlying health and strength of our economy," Ford said.

Since in his mind inflation is the "deadly, long-range enemy," Ford asked Congress to act before it adjourns later this month to cut the fiscal 1975 budget by $4.6 billion, while providing $2.6 billion for public service jobs to offset rising unemployment.

The question of costs also involved the arms agreement. Ford said, "We will probably have to increase our military budget next year just to take care of the costs of inflation."

Griffin wins Heisman

NEW YORK (AP) — Archie Griffin, a speedy and powerful tailback who weaved his way to a national rushing record as the leader of Ohio State's crunching ground attack, was named winner of the 1974 Heisman Trophy today.

Pioneer 11 makes closest approach to planet Jupiter

Story, pictures on Page 13

Figure 16–3. Page divided into 3:3 ratio. The division tends to affect the appearance of a unified page.

page horizontally. Instead, he is probably trying to separate two large elements. But although accomplishing one goal, he inadvertently is destroying another (unity). Sometimes the white space runs vertically, dividing the page from left to right rather than from top to bottom. Either way is undesirable.

3. Alignment of elements. Makeup editors sometimes have trouble noticing the effect of too many different alignments occurring on a contemporary front page. Alignment means placing elements on a page so that they form an imaginary straight line. In traditional makeup, alignment was easy because every story had to fit into a column structure, and columns were straight. In contemporary makeup, stories and pictures may have different widths and be positioned differently. If they do not align, at least to some extent, the reader is faced with a ragged, unattractive appearance. Too many things seem to be vying for attention because there are too many different starting places. The goal, therefore, is to deliberately bring about more alignment without having all elements align. A little off-center placement adds a dash of interest and excitement to the page. A lot of the same thing becomes unattractive. Most alignment should take place on the left side so that the reader's eyes always return to the same position when reading. For example, it is not as easy to read a column of type set flush left, ragged right as it is one set flush on both sides. The perfect alignment on the type set flush both sides brings about an orderly arrangement of lines, and readers know from experience where to find the next line. But flush left, ragged right is much easier to read than having both sides set ragged, as is sometimes done in advertisements. The design of type set with varying alignments presents an obstacle to reading. Lack of alignment on a page is something to be avoided.

Inside Page Makeup

Almost any page on which advertisements have been placed presents makeup problems. The only space for news is whatever remains after the advertisements have been dummied. Often the person who dummies advertisements does not consider the problems of the news makeup man. Other times, the advertising man simply cannot find enough pages on which to place advertising without increasing the total number of pages in the newspaper. So he may cram the advertisements into most of the available space, leaving the news makeup man with design problems. Modern techniques of contemporary makeup, therefore, are hard to apply on inside pages.

Some tabloid newspaper editors partially solve the problem by keeping the first few inside pages free of advertising. This practice gives the makeup man more opportunities to create attractive and readable inside pages. But larger-sized newspapers may not have the space to free such pages for news alone. To do so might result in other pages filled with so much advertising that neither the advertisements nor the news can be read easily. If the management, however, feels that it can spare the space, then a policy can be made that keeps advertising from the first few pages.

Editorial Pages

The editorial page is usually better designed than most other pages in a newspaper. Editorials are often set in larger types and in wider column widths. Sometimes, column rules have been eliminated from this page even though they are used on all other pages. The effect of these makeup practices would seem to result in an attractively designed editorial page. Such is not always the case, however.

One reason that such pages are not attractive is that the type lines are not leaded. When larger typefaces (than used for body type) are set solid, they may not be as easy to read, and they certainly do not look as attractive as they might be if leaded. The appearance of these editorials is like a mass of letters crammed into paragraphs. The value of setting larger-sized type in wider column widths may be lost because of lack of white space between the lines of type. Research on the amount of leading needed for maximum legibility of type is indeterminate, but common sense should tell the makeup editor that when there is more white space between the lines the mass effect becomes easier to look at and it may be easier to read. Therefore, type lines used in editorials should be leaded anywhere from a minimum of 2 to 4 points a line, depending on the amount of white space within the individual letters. Paragraphs, too, should receive more white space through the addition of a bit more leading than between lines. This gives the reader a fraction of a second to pause before proceeding. Presumably this will aid reading and certainly will enhance the appearance of the editorials.

Some editors use the same size of body type and column widths for editorials as they do for regular news. The effect is to make the page appear to be simply another news page. It is not as inviting as pages where larger type and wider column widths are used. If the policy of the newspaper is such that editorials cannot be set in different sizes and widths, then the least that the makeup editor can do is to urge that more leading be placed between the lines of type. Although the result is not as dramatic as the above-mentioned procedure, it is better than treating editorials in the same typographical manner as news.

Page Structure

Although much attention has been given to the makeup of editorials themselves, less has been given to the structure of the editorial page. Because editorial pages carry such diverse items as cartoons, guest columnists, letters to the editor, news and sometimes advertisements, the remainder of the page often tends to become a catchall for material not included on news pages.

Some editors use an editorial page makeup that never varies from day to day. The main advantage of a nonvarying makeup is that it provides the reader with a familiar page. But that page can often appear boring, especially if the editorials are not especially noteworthy. It is therefore reasonable to vary editorial page makeup. Perhaps three or four alternative designs should be prepared beforehand, and alternated from time to time. On the other hand, too much variety would have no particular advantages.

But the concept of editorial page makeup should be based on the desirability of utilizing full makeup control, coupled with a desire to personalize the page better than any other page. Editors have complete control over the contents of the editorial page, something they do not have in the makeup of front pages. Front page makeup is often affected by the nature of the news, which results in designs that are a compromise between what is desired and what is most practical. But the editor does not have this problem on the editorial page. Furthermore, the nature of editorial material is personal. Editorials are personal messages from the editor to readers whereby opinions of the newspaper are expressed. Guest columnists tend to be personal in their approach to opinion or interpretation, and letters to the editor also reflect readers' personal opinions. The concept of editorial page makeup, therefore, should be based on a more personalized design than used for any other page in the newspaper. A personalized style of makeup is warm, appealing and simple (Figures 16–4a and 16–4b). The effect of such design is to make the page *See pages 348 and 349.* inviting. A complex and cold-looking page tends to make readers hesitate to read it. Because research has shown that readership traffic of editorial pages is often 50 per cent less than on front pages, there is an urgent need to make the page more readable and increase traffic there. Presumably the editors have something important to say and readers need help to read what has been written. Some newspapers have done remarkably well in executing this concept; many have not.

The masthead (often incorrectly called the nameplate) is a **Other Makeup** small body of type in which the name of the newspaper, the top **Techniques for** editorial and business officers and, sometimes, the philosophy **Editorial Pages** of the paper are given. The masthead is often placed at the top of editorial columns, apparently to relate the name of the newspaper and its staff with the opinions shown below. Sometimes when the editorial page is placed within the first five pages of an issue, it serves as the source of necessary postal information for second-class matter. There is, however, a good reason for not placing the masthead at the top of editorial columns.

Editorial pages usually are found near the front of the newspaper, in the left-hand column of a left-hand page. The upper-left corner of this page, therefore, is the most important position on the page, perhaps the most important position in the entire issue. It should be devoted to the most significant piece of in-

editorials . . . what we think... After hours problems . . . Do-it-yourself . . .

Trouble for police

A concerned effort of local tavern operators and their supporters to extend hours past 1 a.m. in the city should be defeated in City Council.

Supporters of the move make much of the fact that the city may well be the last in the county to maintain the 1 a.m. closing hours.

This, they say, is driving tavern business out of the city to communities with more liberal limititations.

We say "good riddance!"

The early morning swiggers don't do a community any good, anyway.

Our limited police department has enough difficulty regulating taverns during what hours they have.

And that drags them away from street patrols which could be concentrated on discouraging burglaries and other crimes in the community.

Years ago, when the move to liberalize tavern hours began in the south end of the county, and in St. Clair, we predicted it eventually would end up on our doorstep.

Any open tavern is a law enforcement problem.

No community needs an extension to their operating hours.

Anti-crime fighters

Nobody's blown "Retreat" yet.

But it appears a couple of drive-in waitresses at Godfrey may have made an important discovery:

Nothing confuses a nervous holdup man as much as laughter.

They laughed their wouldbe holdup man right out of his business with them.

Again, we remind that law enforcing authorities don't generally encourage such tactics. They'd rather save lives and promote good health on the part of holdup victims.

But the number of instances where the intended victims have been successful in driving off their assailants has been increasing over the past week.

As the denouement for another, the youth whom East Alton jeweler Don Ott drove out of his store by grabbing at a suspected fake gun and throwing it at him was picked up by police and identified as a Pere Marquette Youth Camp escapee, after being picked up by police.

And Alton police over the week-end rounded up three juveniles to solve at least one of six burglaries reported during that period.

Sometime in the next decade people may be faced with the question of whether to give in to crime, or whether life is worthwhile in a civilization so infested with it.

Pinpointing services

Another move is under way to improve coordination of public services to persons with disabilities.

The Illinois State Advisory Planning Council on Developmental Disabilities has announced a forthcoming survey in a seven-county area of such persons, with a view to determining what services they are receiving, and what agencies are giving it to them.

W. B. Fisher, chairman of the local planning committee for the seven counties, says aim of the survey is to determine what services are already being provided and to whom, with a view of finding gaps in the service and making adjustments to fill them in.

We would suggest that the survey attempt to uncover overlapping of services, as well.

Included in the list to be surveyed are agencies providing medical, psychological, educational, residential, transportation, among other things. "Developmental disabilities" served are mental retardation, cerebral palsy, epilepsy, and autism.

In view of the county's recent sharp reduction in appropriations for organizations providing services to the handicapped, we believe the new district monitoring program may well be needed in the area.

Efforts of Specialized Services, Inc. the Alton Mental Health Center, and the Quad Cities Mental Health Center to protest those reductions in their budgets by the county should stress the need for having available a better examination of all their functions and services. We hope these can be included in the state survey.

Our principal apprehension over it is that the program may be merely a new expansion of state personnel under the current program pressed by Governor Dan Walker to build up his political patronage organization.

We would be extremely naive if we failed to express the hope that the new survey's work remains in effective and legitimate channels.

Paul S. and Stephen A. Cousley

what YOU think...

Robbing schools to pay 'pols'

Can you imagine this headline in a metropolitan paper: "Waste in Illinois Aid Put at $151 million"?

The story was written from Washington, D.C. by Robert L. Joiner and appeared in a newspaper outside Illinois.

The basis for the account was testimony by James L. Trainor before a Senate subcommitte. Trainor stated that his figures were supplied by the Department of Health, Education, and Welfare. He was commenting on testimony last month by John Goff, a former employe of the Department of Public Aid in Illinois.

Goff charged that he was ordered not to cancel payments to 3,000 welfare recipients, fraudulently receiving aid in Chicago, until after the Democrat primary.

He also testified that personnel in the office of Governor Dan Walker attempted to recruit state public aid employes to work in political campaigns in Chicago — violating the Hatch Act.

Further, Goff testified that the Illinois Department of Public Aid wasted about $250 million in fiscal 1975 on payments to ineligible persons.

Although much of the Goff testimony was denied by Trainor, he did acknowledge that welfare payments were made to ineligible recipients.

In 1974 cards were sent out by the former director, Joel Edelman, to 208,000 aid recipients to determine whether they were still eligible to receive the payments.

About 9,000 failed to return the cards. Some 3,000 of these were found to be ineligible, but continued to receive payments when they were left on the rolls because of the political situation.

It is disturbing to find such waste. There is every reason to help those in need, but this political ploy to keep ineligibles on the rolls is a disgrace.

Think how this wasted money could have made possible full funding of school aid that was voted by the General Assembly, but vetoed by Gov. Walker!

JOHN E. BYRNES,
Box 428,
Brighton

Epidemic stimulant

The rule at Alton High School is that students with three or more excused absences have to take final examinations.

Really, only those with unexcused absences should have to take the exams.

When our daughter got a severe strep throat, the doctor put her on medication, told her to go to bed, and not even talk. She missed four days of school.

She wanted to go to school very ill, and with temperature, because of this rule. I'm sure a lot of children go to school very ill under such pressure — and that may contribute to spread of illness through the school.

Our daughter is an honor roll student — and this is the recognition she gets for keeping an outbreak of strep throat out of the school!

The rule doesn't reward the student, but it does reward the school through state aid. The aid is based on daily attendance figures.

I sincerely believe the only fair rule is excuse from exams for those with a doctors written excuse for illness.

PATRICIA A. GROSS,
78 E. Elm St.

Who can snoop?

When the late Sen. Long, D-Mo., conducted hearings on the Internal Revenue Service and its use of paid informers to snoop into the private lives of our citizens, I do not recall one Congressman or member of the Justice Department coming to the defense of the victims.

But subtle effort to replace the Senator was effective. Sen. Long, until then held in high esteem by his collegues, lost the election.

Sen. Fullbright, chairman of the Foreign Relations Committee, conducted hearings on the tax exempt foundations and the registration of foreign agents. The information from these hearings never made the news.

Fullbright expressed grave concern that privileges granted tax exempt foundations and foreign agents provide a conduit for large sums of money to flow from the United States for use in undermining our domestic and foreign policies.

Fullbright, a power in the Senate for more than 20 years, suddenly became a marked man. Like Sen. Long, he, too, was defeated. The lickspittles were a bit bewildered in view of his liberal record, but the sages knew.

Now it is difficult to understand how Congress can become so exorcised over the treatment our adversaries are getting from the FBI and CIA, whose job it is to investigate and report.

Perhaps information made available on the background of Attorney General Levi would be helpful.

LOIS PETERSEN,
1217 Central Ave.

Bang! bang!

In Knightstown, Ind. a casket company is observing the national Bicentennial by offering a red, white, and blue burial casket — complete with miniature flags.

It reports having sold 400 of them already.

I wonder what would be the extra cost of a 20-gun salute.

WILLIAM A. CRIVELLO,
349 Bluff St.

What YOU think:

The Telegraph welcomes prose expressions of its readers' own opinions to What YOU think. Writers' names and addresses must be published with their letters. The writer's telephone number will add to our convenience in re-checking. Contributions should be concise, preferably not exceeding 150 words, and are subject to condensation.

Conservatives are mediators

By John Roche

"National Review," the conservative weekly edited by my old sparring partner William F. Buckley Jr., has just celebrated its 20th anniversary. As a close student of political theory, I'm still not sure what American conservation is except a wide selection of "No-Noes." But as a practicing journalist, I feel impelled to congratulate Bill and the "National Review." It is unquestionably the best political magazine in the nation — every time I read an issue, I wish that we liberals had a remotely comparable journal.

The 20th Anniversary edition (12/5/75) contains a remarkably sensitive analysis of the "Conservative Intellectual Movement in America since 1945" by George H. Nash, which may go some distance in explaining why traditional liberalism is, for all intents and purposes, voiceless. Although he doesn't mention it, conservatives over the past 30 years have had a great deal more leisure time to engage in meditation than liberals, who by the very nature of their commitment were engaged in political activism. The basic aspirations of the liberals were therefore voiced in political forums ("fora" would, I suspect, be "National Review" usage) by politicians such as Harry Truman, Adlai Stevenson, Estes Kefauver, John F. Kennedy and Lyndon Johnson.

SPOKESMEN TOGETHER — But Nash emphasizes another development which I think is equally important, though I disagree with his essential judgment. He argues that there has been a movement away from liberalism, a confluence of old liberal sopkesmen such as Irving Kristol, Norman Podhoretz, Daniel Bell and Daniel Patrick Moynihan with the new conservatives.

He suggests that this arose because of the breakdown of the liberal polity, the riots and demonstrations which forced liberal intellectuals to revise their premises. Liberalism, as "National Review" has defined it for 20 years, involves creating an "open society" in which everybody does his "own thing" and "lets it all hang out." Thus, to complete Nash's elegantly written brief, liberals have repudiated John Stuart Mill and returned to the classical concept that a society, in order to avoid Hobbes' "state of nature," must enforce certain fundamental values.

I find this argument fundamentally flawed because it describes a liberalism which is decidedly a historical. Mill, who is the prize target, was no advocate of "letting it all hang out." While writing his essay on "Liberty" with one hand, he ran India with the other. And he specifically excluded from the category of those exercising liberty any who are not capable of intelligent discussion. For them, he said, the ideal form of government is "despotism."

But Mill aside, the founders of this Republic and its liberal tradition never designed a progressive kindergarten. Just over 200 years ago the Continental Congress recommended that the provincial legislatures "arrest and secure every person . . . whose going at large may in their opinion endanger the safety of the colony, or the liberties of America." A number of conservatives found this had a "chilling effect."

CONSERVING WHAT? — Liberals, in other words, have never thought that everything was up for grabs, but they have insisted that authority be rationally justified and exercised in a fashion neither arbitrary nor capricious. The interesting thing is that conservatives have never made up their minds what precisely they are conserving — unless it is this liberal tradition! I would therefore argue that over the past quarter of a century American conservatives, formerly noted for their eccentricities, have moved towards the standard of traditional liberalism. As I told Bill Buckley once on "Firing Line," there will always be a light in the window.

Of course, the activities of the whirling dervishes of the New Left have presented "National Review" with a strawman: They call this inane clamor "liberalism" and then beat hell out of it. But rhetorically this is the equivalent of liberals identifying "National Review" with the John Birch Society. At any rate, however deficient their historical knowledge may be, congratulations to the editors of "National Review" — they consistently enliven my week and I hope continue to do so. Lively Error is much preferable to dull exhortations to the True Faith.

Albert has Moon girl

By Jack Anderson with Les Whitten

WASHINGTON — In the past year, Speaker Carl Albert has acquired a new friend.

She is Susan Bergman, a smiling young follower of the Korean religious-political cultist, Reverend Sun Myung Moon.

The hazel-eyed Ms. Bergman sits in the House gallery, often in a special section reserved for Congressmen's families, where she watches the Speaker in action almost every day.

Earlier in the day, she usually greets him in the hallway outside his office and presents him with flowers. Often she brews him Ginseng tea in the small kitchen just down the hall from the Speaker's ornate office where the two of them spend many pleasant hours.

Albert has also been seen on the cocktail circuit with other young women from his office, two of them exotic Oriental beauties. He arranged a special visa so one of them, Grace Chen, could work in his office. Not long afterward, he turned up in his own car to help her move to a new apartment.

The Speaker brought three office girls — Iris Adams, Verneil English and Kathryne Prewitt — to keep him company on his recent trip to Russia.

And four lovelies — Iris Adams, Loise Butler, Kathleen Kwock and Helen Newman — accompanied him to China.

In those gossip circles that thrive on the bons mots, the pouts, the whims and the blunders of Washington bigwigs, the Speaker's relationship with his attractive office help has stirred titillating talk.

Several associates of the Speaker say he looks upon the women on his staff in more than a fatherly fashion. Albert claims no more than a mildly paternal attitude toward the women he employs. He admitted having a stormy argument, however, with a former staff member about her social life. According to Albert, "I told her I didn't want my staff going with married Congressmen."

The fading, freckled firebrand, who at five-foot-four was once known as the mighty mite of Capitol Hill, is indignant over the gossip. He insists that he has never behaved improperly with his female employes. "I'm just friendly with them," he told us.

Susan Bergman was once seen making a hasty exit from his private office when the Speaker's wife, Mary Isabelle, arrived in the outer reception area. The Moon proselyte departed hurriedly through a side door as Mrs. Albert entered the front door.

The Speaker told us he couldn't remember any such incident. Anyway, he said, Mrs. Albert knows Sue Bergman and "knows she's a nice girl."

Albert described his new friend as "just a nice girl, a very nice girl, a Jewish girl from New York. She got all hepped up on the Lord Jesus, and she just wants to share it. I think that's a nice thing . . . She's trying to convert me."

The friendship, he said, is perfectly innocent. "Why, I'm 67 years old. She's just a girl. She doesn't have any crush on me. She just brings me flowers. She just walks in here and sits down and chats. Sometimes she'll walk in and sit down while I'm working. I don't pay her no mind."

When Egypt's President Anwar Sadat spoke to Congress, Albert kindly gave the Moon girl one of his two gallery passes so she could watch the historic moment. He also introduced her to some of the astronauts at a reception for the Russian-American space team.

He may have given her an occasional ride, too, in his Speaker's limousine, he acknowledged. "I've got no apologies for it!"

The Reverend Moon, who claims to have talked with Jesus, preaches a mixture of fundamentalist Christianity, anti-communism and self-deification. In the Spring of 1974, his disciples blitzed Capitol Hill begging Congressmen to forgive and forget any transgressions then-President Nixon may have committed.

Speaker Albert insists his favorite Moon girl has never lobbied him on this or any other political issue. "She knew how I felt about that," he said sternly.

The Speaker leaned back in his padded chair and propped a foot on his massive desk. Behind him, stacked among congressional directories and other standard reference books, was a black-covered, gold-trimmed copy of Moon's catechism, "Divine Principle."

"I've told her," said Albert, "I thought it (the Moon movement) was stupid."

TELEGRAPH of YESTERYEAR News from 25 and 50 years ago

DECEMBER 16, 1950

President Truman proclaimed a state of national emergency, summoning the nation to marshal its strength against the threat of "Communist world conquest." The White House released a long list of laws, carrying extraordinary powers, which it said automatically became effective upon signing of the declaration.

Approximately 5,400 hourly-paid and salaried employes of Olin Industries, Inc., East Alton plant, would receive extra compensation checks. The announcement of the special payment was made by the Olin board of directors and included the East Alton employes of the Western Cartridge Co. division, Western Brass Mills division and Equitable Powder Manufacturing Co, an affiliate.

Harvey Miller, 38, a farmer of southeast of Jerseyville, was injured in the runaway of a team of horses at his farm. Following the accident, he was brought by his wife to the home of her parents, Mr. and Mrs. Ray Harris of 606 Porter St., and from there was taken by Harris to Alton Memorial Hospital where he was treated for shoulder and leg injuries.

Firemen extinguished a blaze in the rear compartment of a truck that had been parked in the basement of the Eagle Home Conditioning Co., 91 Henry.

Albert Favre took office as president of Alton Municipal Band at the annual meeting of the organization. He succeeded George M. Brooks.

After crashing through the guard railing in a skid, a 1½-ton truck of Godfrey Elevator Co., operated by Herbert Kraushaar, hung with the front wheels projecting from the Alby-Humbert bridge over the G. M. & O. railroad until the vehicle was extricated from its perilous position by one of the Haper tow-trucks.

DECEMBER 16, 1925

President Coolidge was deferring a decision on sending representatives to the international arms limitation conference at Geneva pending a further study of the project by the State Department.

Japan dispatched troops from Korea to Mukdan, capital of Manchuria, and declared no fighting would be permitted around that city. The Japanese order was directed at Marshal Chang Tso Lin, dictator of Manchuria, and his former henchman, Gen. Kuo Sun Lin, who had become Chang's principal adversary in factional fighting.

Forced air ventilation for the new high school building was decided upon by the board of education after extensive investigation of both that and natural systems (by window) which took both board members and Superintendent W. R. Curtis out of town on several observation trips.

Permission to operate a bus system between Alton and East St. Louis was sought from the Illinois Commerce Commission by Receiver W. H. Sawyer in behalf of the Alton, Granite & St. Louis Traction Co., operator of an electric transit system between here and St. Louis. R. F. Allen, local manager for the line, said the bus service would not compete with the electric traction system that operated fast "limiteds" over the area, but would provide more local service for points between. J. J. Reilley, operator of the Wood River bus line, said he would file a protest.

Five hundred children between the ages of 5 and 19 were to be guests of organizations affiliated with the Alton Community Council at a series of Christmas dinners and entertainments. The Shurtleff College YWCA was to lead off because of the approaching holidays for students.

Figure 16–4a. Contemporary design of an editorial page. [*Courtesy Alton Illinois Telegraph.*]

The Brandon Sun

No Man is an Island, entire of itself: Every Man is a piece of the continent, a part of the main
Never send to know for whom the bell tolls; it tolls for thee.
—Donne

WEDNESDAY, DECEMBER 4, 1974

Who bombed in Quebec?

Fans of Progressive Conservative Leader Robert Stanfield will sympathize with his openly stated expression of disappointment last weekend of his failure to win Quebec's confidence. But it's not the sort of thing any Conservative leader can afford to dwell upon. Nobody could have done better under the circumstances.

Mr. Stanfield had the built-in disadvantage of getting himself elected just when the party was splitting apart. Two clear-cut factions emerged and the result has been a reformist leader trying his utmost to reform a party which did not particularly want to be reformed.

Mr. Stanfield's proposals for a guaranteed annual income policy thus got him nowhere. His wage and price control policy took him backward, and his identification with the "dump Diefenbaker" movement has been as painful a thorn in his side as has the former chief himself. But nowhere has the existence of Conservative factionalism made its presence more clearly felt than in its Quebec policy.

The policy was officially based on the recognition that Canada was made up of two founding cultures. And while Stanfield was committed to the working out of this policy, many members of the party caucus, particularly in the west were not. Nor, to be truthful, were their constituents. Assimilation remains as an ideal that is basic to many Conservative outlooks. It deserves expression, of course. But it is unfortunate for Mr. Stanfield that it was expressed so forcefully by members of his own party.

That Mr. Stanfield wasn't able to resolve the factions within his party is not surprising. Perhaps his successor — whoever that may be — will do better. But until the issue is settled once and for all, it is almost certain that to those Quebecers for whom culture and language remain priority concerns, the Conservative party will retain the image of an alien force. And nobody wants to vote for that.

Mad hatter

It might have happened to anybody. But, alas, it was a defence department functionary who ordered 100,000 winter caps — 75,000 of them too small. And it's the defence department that's taking the lumps; just as it has taken its lumps in the past for having horses on the payroll, aircraft carriers made out of money, and people doing odd, well-paying jobs that had little relation to defence.

Granted, there's a lot of waste that should be eliminated. But let's be fair. And before Canadians get the idea that the armed forces are a wanton lot indeed, it may be useful to reflect on the fact that the defence department is also the largest government department going. While its wastage is going to be proportionately large, so are its savings. Name another department that's still making do with 20- and 30-year-old vehicles. For that matter, name another department that is likely to hold onto the small winter caps until every last one of them finally gets issued.

The Brandon Sun

An Independent Newspaper Serving Western Manitoba Since 1882
Published daily except Sunday and holidays by The Sun Publishing Company, Limited, 501 Rosser Ave., Brandon, Manitoba. Member of The Canadian Press, Audit Bureau of Circulations, The Canadian Daily Newspaper Publishers Association, Inland Press Association and International Press Institute.
Second Class Mail Registration Number 0309

LEWIS D. WHITEHEAD
Editor and Publisher

ROLF H. PEDERSEN
Editorial Page Editor

GARTH STOUFFER
Associate Editor

by Richard Gwyn

Social indicators may be coming into fashion

Are you happy? Are you happier than a year ago? Are you a great deal happier; a little bit happier; about the same; a little less happy; totally and thoroughly miserable?

The formal name for happiness measurement is "social indicators." No pollster, ever, will come around asking you questions as ridiculous as those (happiness is in the eye of the sufferer) but a fascinating, an potentially important, movement has just begun to develop measures, qualitative as well as quantitative, of our society's health, wealth in other than money terms, accomplishments and satisfactions.

"We are trying," explains Chief Statistician Sylvia Ostry, "to get people away from their fixation with the standard indicators — the Gross National Product, unemployment, the cost of living."

In other words, to put some reality into that after-dinner platitude about there being more - to - life - than - the - Gross National Product, namely the "quality of life," and to develop ways to test whether the real quality of our life is on the rise or the decline.

Perspective Canada, a recent report by Statistics Canada, pulls together for the first time all available statistics that measure the ups and downs of social trends; the criminal offence rate, 1962-70, has almost doubled; the quality of housing on Indian reserves has declined, from 1963 to '71; office workers put in 37.6 hours a week, no different from their 37.7 hours a week 10 years ago.

There's a compulsive, did - you - know quality of the Guiness Book of Records to Perspective Canada. Did you know, for instance, that immigrant families earn almost $1,000 more a year than Canadian - born families. Did you know that while the rate of cigarette smoking has dropped among young men it is increasing rapidly among young women?

Notoriously, social indicators are hard to establish. Definitions of good and bad are the first difficulty. A decade ago, say, any increase in the divorce rate would have been widely accepted as an indicator of social problems. Social attitudes have changed. Divorce has become a less traumatic event and some argue that a high divorce rate shows that couples now have the courage, and opportunity, to correct their mistakes.

Almost all social statistics are suspect in themselves. The criminal offence rate, for example, reflects not only the extent of crime but also the size and competence of the police force. Also, recent studies have shown that the real offence rate is much higher than the official rate, because of the enormous number of unreported burglaries, assaults, rapes, family crimes.

Finally, social indicators are not yet taken seriously by the decision - makers. Politicians jump at an increase in the unemployment or inflation figures but yawn at claims that the quality of life is up or down.

The Economic Council of Canada in its annual report published this week makes the first attempt to link social indicators to public policy. The French are ahead of us; also the Japanese who a couple of years ago came up with a "national welfare index."

The familiar housing indicators are average prices and the number of units built each year. The Economic Council has developed a new, "crowding" index. Allowing for kitchens and bathrooms, there should be one person per room. One fifth of Canadians, the council found, are overcrowded. Sudbury, Ont., is the worst-off city, and Victoria, B.C. is the best.

A sound housing indicator developed by the council is the proportion of their income that Canadians pay for each room they occupy. Here the trend is bleak: Canadians paid only 3.7 per cent of their income for each room in 1961, but 4.2 per cent today.

The council also studied health and found, for example, that Canada's infant mortality rate is one of the highest in the world: 17.5 per 1,000 live births compared to 11.1 in Sweden and Holland.

Social indicators are in their infancy in Canada. The council's findings about overcrowding, poor medical treatment, and also about pollution, caused it to make only general recommendations to government, essentially for further study. Statistics Canada this week holds a two-day conference to find out where it should go from here.

An important first step, though, has been taken. And in the process we are learning something about ourselves. Did you know that as many Canadians go to live theatre, classical music performances, art galleries and museums (26 per cent of the population) as watch sports events (23.4 per cent).

Even if you believe that happiness never can be measured you can still be the first on your block to know facts like that.

(Copyright 1974. Toronto Star Syndicate)

HAVE A GOOD DAY SIR.
AND AN EQUALLY GOOD DAY TO YOU SIR!
NUCLEAR HEADS' SUMMIT

by Harold Greer

The bagmen will know no constraints

TORONTO — Should big business be prohibited from giving money to political parties and politicians?

In its report on political fund-raising and election campaign expenses, the commission on the Ontario legislature chaired by Dalton Camp says no. But its reasons for coming to this opinion are hardly such as to settle the controversy forever, or even for a day.

One reason is that the costs of election campaigns being what they are and the dependency of the Liberal and Conservative parties on corporate giving being what it is (the commission estimates 90 per cent of their campaign expenses come from business donations), then big business money is necessary if the party system is to be maintained "adequately" and in a position to wage "effective" campaigns.

Well, now, that all depends on what is meant by "effective" campaigns. Electioneering has become a multi-million dollar proposition largely because of the huge sums spent on media advertising; sad to say, elections can be won with intensive, slick advertising, as the Ontario Conservative party has demonstrated time after time.

To adman Camp, this may be "effective" campaigning but to most people it is safe to say that it is a corruption of the political process, because it simply means that the party with the most money can mount the most propaganda and thereby sway the most votes. If political parties were limited or prohibited in this direction, elections would be a lot more honest and the need for big business money would be greatly diminished.

As for maintaining the party system "adequately" between elections, the Camp commission takes the orthodox view that political parties are the "root and branch" of the parliamentary system and perform "a crucial, vital service" for society. One could also argue, and come closer to the truth, that political parties are the curse of the parliamentary system. In any event, a party which cannot maintain itself financially through its membership without dependency on big business ought to be allowed, surely, to wither away.

A second reason advanced by the Camp commission is that a prohibition on corporate contributions would discriminate against the Liberals and Conservatives unless the trade unions were also prohibited from giving to the NDP.

The answer to that, of course, is that they should be. Trade unions cannot vote any more than corporations can. The decision of a union executive to give to the NDP gets as much membership scrutiny and approval as the shareholders are able to give to a corporation's decision to give to the other parties — which is to say, none. One wonders, indeed, where the authority for such donations comes from in either case and why there has never been a legal action for conversion.

The main reason for allowing corporate contributions, however, is that, according to the Camp commission, a prohibition would be too difficult to enforce. It points out, correctly, that such a prohibition was written into the Canadian Election Act in 1908 and it was simply ignored by all concerned. It points that corporate contributions are illegal in the United States (federally-speaking) but that it has become common practice for companies to "bonus" senior executives who then donate the money as individuals. It points out that corporate contributions can be channelled through non-profit associations and "fronts."

But the answer to all these difficulties is simply to prohibit all financial contributions to political parties and candidates for election expenses and to pay for such expenses on a formula basis from the public treasury.

Provided the nomination requirements of the election laws are changed to eliminate frivolous candidates (in Ontario, one needs only 100 nominators now), it would be no great chore to limit campaign costs, both on a constituency and party level, to so much per voter for each candidate and party. The new federal election law, which will apply next time round, has such a scheme although the limits on what a party can spend are ridiculously generous. But the federal law does not prohibit or even limit private contributions.

The Camp commission goes the other way of limiting contributions but not expenditures, which is no great improvement, and it does propose public funding of candidates' expenses up to $7,500 according to a formula which, it is claimed, will act as an incentive to hold total spending down and make candidates less dependent on private fund-raising.

But for some reason which is not quite explained in its report, the commission cannot bring itself to go all the way in respect of public funding. It suggests public funding would eliminate "independent" candidates, which is simply not necessarily so, and it frets that if all recognized political parties are treated the same in the apportioning of public funds, then minority parties would be favored at the expense of major ones — an apparently intolerable objection.

This is a pity, because the alternative is to continue the present reliance on big business in the case of the Conservatives and the Liberals, and on big labor in the case of the NDP, which is surely more intolerable.

It is intolerable because in a democracy the ideal ought to be equality where a person's opinion is equal to his vote and not to his money. Where a sector of society can influence elections or the decisions and attitudes of politicians by giving money, the ideal is vitiated.

The standard defence, of course, is that this does not happen, that politicians are not influenced by where the money comes from, and that corporate donors are simply practising good citizenship. One may then wonder why the corporations do not give to the NDP, or why the trade unions do not give to the Conservatives or Liberals.

Perhaps in this respect the comments of Sen. John Godfrey, the chief fund-raiser for the federal Liberal party, are as instructive as any. Speaking on the new election expenses bill last January, Sen. Godfrey said, amongst other things:

"I have never seen the slightest evidence that any member of the government is the least bit interested in, or concerned about, whether or not anything the government does will influence the amount of money the party can raise.

"I have encouraged this attitude and have told members of the government that the members of the business community were, on the whole, highly responsible in this area, and that while they may make loud noises and breathe fire and thunder from time to time, when the chips are down, no matter what the government or the opposition did, they would continue to provide reasonable financial support to the two major free enterprise parties."

Yes, indeed.

Report on Britain

IRA ban will not help, say Irish

by GEORGE BAIN

LONDON — As an anti-terrorist measure, the Irish Republican Army is about to be declared illegal in England. Belonging to it, or supporting it with money or carrying its banners, will be punishable by fines or prison terms.

Home Secretary Roy Jenkins made the announcement in the House of Commons yesterday.

About the time that Jenkins was preparing to speak, Kevin, one of the barmen in Biddy Mulligan's, the Pride of Kilburn, was going around the rooms there bawling: "All right then. Time now, lads."

That was at 3 in the afternoon and the lads were putting up the pint jars from which they'd been drinking mostly Guinness and their smaller glasses of Hennessey brandy.

Biddy Mulligan's, an Irish pub in northwest London, is in the Sacred Heart parish of Kilburn where there are between 10,000 and 12,000 souls. The ramshackle Biddy Mulligan's, along with the church, is one of their centres.

It's a reputed Republican hangout. The Daily Telegraph had written of leaflets displayed on the bar for the Prisoners Aid Committee, which asked for 2,000 pounds to get a "revolutionary fighter for the freedom of Ireland" out of an English jail.

There were no Republican leaflets on the bar yesterday, or anything more menacing than a couple of hollow plastic figures inviting drinkers to drop in their spare coins to help crippled children. And, according to Kevin's pinch-faced and sturdily anonymous colleague behind the bar, there never had been.

"It was all bullshit," he said.

The few clients of Biddy Mulligan's who were willing to talk about terrorism, Birmingham, and what the home secretary might do about them didn't think that banning the IRA would do much good.

If people believed in a cause and were prepared to help it with money or in other ways, making it illegal wouldn't deter them.

That wasn't an opinion confined to the perhpas Irish Republican precincts of Biddy Mulligan's after Jenkins made his announcement. In fact Jenkins himself, who had previously taken the view that declaring an organization illegal might only drive it underground, didn't seem to have shed those doubts entirely.

But what has been apparent since Thursday night's bombing of two pubs in Birmingham, when 19 people were killed and many maimed for life, is that public opinion demanded that nothing be left untried.

Consequently, Jenkins has acted against his own previously stated reservations, and proposed penalties of up to five years in prison for belonging to the IRA.

And he has resorted to such other measures — "unprecendented in peacetime," he said — as permitting police to arrest suspects without warrant and to hold them for up to five days, more stringent immigration procedures, and provisions for expelling those considered undesirable.

The Commons is expected to pass these measures on Thursday.

But looking around Biddy Mulligan's — certainly Irish if not Republican Irish — it woul be hard to say that such measures will affect anything much.

If funds for Republican causes were being openly solicited there on Sunday, they could as easily have been unnoticed yesterday. And a sympathizer with no membership card in anything could presumably plant a bomb as well as anyone with one.

In fact, the textbook example of ineffective tough measures is Northern Ireland itself, where there are checkpoints on the streets at which shoppers are frisked, rules against parking cars unattended, summary arrest procedures, and internment without trial. But still the terrorism goes on.

The London police, although cautious about what they say, admit that more powers don't necessaril guarantee anything. A spokesman says they've a bomb squad that goes into action whenever they receive a warning, but "there's not much we can do . . ."

George Bain is London correspondent of The Toronto Star.

Letter

Step beyond abortion

If we look at our nation and society almost everything we do and all our efforts are such that emphasize 'life' and the living of that life to its fullest potential.

Much money is spent to insure our old people of a decent living. Doctors spend many hours, at a great cost to the family, on a patient who is dying, just to keep him alive or prolong his life for a few more hours or days.

Many hours of dedicated work is spent with our disabled, crippled, blind and deaf to help them realize life with all its meaning.

We spend millions on our retarded children and adults to help them become useful citizens and find their place in the sun.

Our hearts are moved when we see a starving child and we spend millions more to feed those in other countries who are dying of hunger and disease.

At great cost, we even give the convicted criminal, who is a real threat to our own life, a chance to live and change and become whole again.

It can't be because all these are invaluable to our society, that they are such a great asset in terms of production and usefulness. It must be because we value life — no matter how poor or depraved it is. Is life **more** than just our physical being? A preparation for something higher? Eccl. 12:7, "Then shall the dust return to the earth as it was; and the spirit shall return unto God who gave it."

A few astronauts are stranded. What an enormous amount of effort and money is spent to insure their safety.

The bottom falls out of our life when someone we know and love is killed in a traffic accident. We raise a great hue and cry about our dreadful road conditions, etc. What a tragic waste of human life!

Our little boy or girl is lost — the neighbors stand ready to search, we call the police with their squad cars, the army with their helicopters, everybody wants to find that child **alive!** What makes these lives "wanted."

The strength of a nation lies in its youth! Children have the greatest potential for the future, the yet unborn, the **unwanted.** Why then do we kill off our greatest hope for the future, our greatest asset? Why not invest some of our money here? Insure the birth of these young lives and give them surroundings that will allow them to become the persons they were meant to be.

Actually we don't take this concept of abortion FAR enough. There is a sickness worse than death amongst us and we refuse to recognize it. The Lord God give His ancient people a remedy for this disease. Deut. 22:22, "If a man is found lying with the wife of another man, both of them shall die; so you shall purge the evil from Israel." This would really eradicate the "unwanted" lives.

MRS. L. KLASSEN
27 Balsam Crescent
Brandon

Figure 16–4b. Another contemporary design of an editorial page. [*Courtesy Brandon, Canada, Sun.*]

formation on the page, which is not the masthead. Editorials are much more significant and demand top position. There is little justification for wasting a key position. If the masthead is attractively designed, as many are, it will not matter where it is placed on the page. The best placement, therefore, is in the lower-right corner because in that position it can achieve readership without distracting from any other feature on the page.

Another editorial page feature that could well be buried is the editorial cartoon. As research has indicated, a cartoon will achieve readership no matter where it is located on a page. That being the case, why take one of the most crucial positions (top center) and place the cartoon there? If the position of the cartoon is fixed because of tradition, there is little that can be done. But attempts should be made to move it to the bottom, where it will still achieve readership and yet free the top position for more significant editorial material.

Although larger type, wider columns, more white space bebetween the columns and a cleaner page are the result, the editorial page often lacks drama because there is too much type on the page and relatively few illustrations. Occasionally a small portrait of a columnist may appear somewhere on the page, but that plus the cartoon is the extent of decorative material. One key editorial or an important column may be boxed each day as a means of dominating the page. Sometimes editorials, although important, are not long enough to receive dramatic treatment. But often a columnist's material is. Even then, the same individual may not have an exciting column each day. But some other columnist may have material worthy of being boxed. The makeup editor might select some story, editorial or column to be given a dramatic treatment each day.

Finally, large initial letters are sometimes used for the first letter of each editorial as a means of making the page look more attractive. Their use is debatable. On the one hand, they sometimes look attractive if not too many of them are placed on the page. They are decorative devices. But they pose problems for the composing room. Sometimes they break off in stereotyping. Other times they take too long to be cut in by printers. Perhaps the most significant factor in their use should be whether they enhance or detract from the editorials. When they are too bold or too large, they may detract. If there is not enough space around them, they may not look attractive. Therefore, the use of large initial letters as a desirable makeup device must be considered of indefinite value.

Women's Pages

The proper concept of women's pages makeup generally has not been clear. The basic idea was to present news and features of interest to women in a distinctly feminine makeup style. To implement that idea, a style of makeup was devised that used lighter typefaces for headlines and body copy and perhaps a bit more space between the columns. Column rules were sometimes eliminated on these pages to help lighten the page. This concept, however, was really inadequate to fulfill the need for feminine design because the result was nothing more than lighter-appearing pages. The only change from the makeup of other pages in the same issue was the lightness of the pages. But lightness is hardly the most significant dimension needed for communicating with women who are often sensitive to good design. Women's facial makeup, hair, clothes, homes and gardens all express sensitivity to some or large proportions of contemporary design. In other words, there is still a need to change women's pages makeup radically to be more in line with the contemporary frame of reference in which women tend to think.

The use of lightface types for headlines often can result in rather ugly pages. Simply because a typeface is lightface rather than boldface does not make it feminine. Furthermore, the widespread use of italic, script or cursive typefaces on women's pages is intended to bring about a feminine appearance. But some of these typefaces are so grotesque they defeat the goal. For example, Lydian Cursive, Brush Script, Coronet or Mandate are types that, although different from roman faces, are not necessarily attractive on women's pages. They are too ornate and are more suited for advertising. Ultra Bodoni Italic, Bodoni Book Italic, Cheltenham Light or Medium Italic and Century Italic also are not feminine. Garamond or Caslon Italic are feminine, but they lack charm in bolder versions and neither is a contemporary type style. Contemporary styles are noted for their extended appearance and their use of ultrafine serifs coupled with contrasting heavier elements (Figure 16–5). Although headline types can help achieve some femininity, more than typeface selection is needed.

A number of newspapers, mostly the larger ones, have understood the need for change and have designed women's pages that make them radically different from what they were before. They have adopted a newer concept, which is to make the page appear not only feminine but chic, charming and dramatic as well (Figures 16–6 and 16–7). A page may appear feminine and yet may be in poor taste or lack charm. The newer concept has been implemented with bold and imaginative planning.

The most important means of implementing this new concept is to design, rather than make up, pages. In other words, pages are not dummied as pages have been traditionally—they are designed with the total page concept in mind. Because much of the material appearing on women's pages is advance or time copy that can be set before the current news is set, there is usually time to design a page rather than build it piece by piece. But the task of designing is of such major importance that sometimes newspapers hire persons with strong commercial art backgrounds to create the lead women's page. Unless the makeup editor is capable of creating a dramatic, imaginative

Traditional Typefaces

HEADLINE GOTHIC
ABCDEFGHIJK | 12345

GARAMOND BOLD
ABCDEFGHIJKLMNOPQRSTUVWS
abcdefghijklmnopqrstuvwxyz | 123456

BODONI BOLD
ABCDEFGHIJKLMNOPQRSTUVW
abcdefghijklmnopqrstuvwxy | 12345

FUTURA BOLD
ABCDEFGHIJKLMNOPQRSTUVWXJ
abcdefghijklmnopqrstuvw | 12345

GOUDY EXTRA BOLD
ABCDEFGHIJKLMNOPQRS
abcdefghijklmnopqrstu | 12345

CHELTENHAM BOLD CONDENSED
ABCDEFGHIJKLMNOPQRSTUVWXYZ
abcdefghijklmnopqrstuvwxyz | 123456789

STYMIE BOLD
ABCDEFGHIJKLMNOPQRST
abcdefghijklmnopqrstu | 12345

CENTURY BOLD
ABCDEFGHIJKLMNOPQRSTU
abcdefghijklmnopqrstuvw | 12345

Contemporary Typefaces

CLARENDON BOOK (CRAW)
ABCDEFGHIJKLMNOPQR
abcdefghijklmnopqr | 12345

CHISEL (Reduction)
ABCDEFGHIJKLMNOPQRS
abcdefghijklmnopvr | 123456

FORTUNE LIGHT
ABCDEFGHIJKLMNOPQRS
abcdefghijklmnopqrstuv | 12345

FOLIO MEDIUM EXTENDED ITALIC
ABCDEFGHIJKLMNOPQRSTUV
abcdefghijklmnopqrstuv | 12345

MODERN ROMAN NO. 20
ABCDEFGHIJKLMNOPQRSTU
abcdefghijklmnopqrstuvwxy | 12345

WEISS ROMAN
ABCDEFGHIJKLMNOPQRSTUVWXY
abcdefghijklmnopqrstuvwxyz | 12345678

TORINO ROMAN
ABCDEFGHIJKLMNOPQRSTUVWX
abcdefghijklmnopqrstuvwxyz | 12345

HELLENIC WIDE
ABCDEFGHIJKLMNI
abcdefghijklm | 12345

Figure 16–5. Traditional versus contemporary type faces.

design, it should be left to experts. Young persons who are now becoming makeup editors may have the kind of sensitivity and ability to design such pages.

Other than use of a total page design concept of dramatic appearance, some papers use four-color printing to further enhance the page. But color added to unimaginative design does not achieve the goal of the newer concept. In fact, it calls the inadequacy of design to the attention of readers.

Conclusions on Special Page Makeup

The principles of makeup discussed apply to other special pages within the newspaper, even though there are some differences between these sections. The differences, for makeup purposes, however, are not that important. To a great extent the makeup of these pages is affected by the dummying of advertisements. Rarely are they free of advertisements. The goal of makeup editors should be to salvage a page whose design may have been distorted by the shape and positioning of the ads. Every attempt should be made to simplify these pages to the extent possible. It is virtually impossible to create the same kind of dramatic format required on the front, editorial and women's pages. Therefore, the following check points are offered with the goal of helping the makeup editor work within the built-in limitations of advertising to achieve the maximum amount of readability and aesthetic appearance.

The question is often raised about whether standing headlines such as **Sports, Financial,** or **Feature Section** should be buried somewhere in the middle of the page, thereby freeing top space for news. The answer: If such headlines can be buried, why use them at all? Will it not be obvious to an individual that he is reading the sports page or the financial page (Figure 16–8)? It would take only a little while to learn from either the headlines or the pictures on a page. Therefore, the function of standing headlines is to keep readers from having to study other headlines or pictures to learn which section they are reading. Furthermore, if an index appears on page 1 and it refers to a special page, then the standing headline serves as an advertisement to tell readers they have arrived at the correct section. Such labels, therefore, should not be buried.

Burying Standing Heads

Because the bottoms of inside pages lack news space, the makeup editor tends to allow that space to disintegrate. To whatever extent the bottoms of pages can be brightened, they should be. Pictures, horizontally made-up stories, and boxes can help accomplish the job if the space is there. Even when the only editorial space available is a "well" between two ads, the makeup editor can use a one-column picture at the bottom to help brighten the page.

Bottoms of Special Pages Need Brightening

Smaller newspapers often will allow odd-shaped advertisements to be used on inside pages. A flexform is one with an unusual shape. Less obtrusive are L-shaped advertisements. If the management allows such advertisements within its pages, the makeup editor will have a struggle to make a page appear attractive. The best procedure is to keep makeup display to a minimum on such pages and keep significant news for other pages. Any attempts to add display with a flexform advertisement may simply make the page confusing.

Flexforms and Other Odd-Shaped Advertisements

Occasionally, to offer the reader a change of pace in design, the editor will round off the corner of pictures or boxes. The effect is novel and interesting, if not overdone. When used occasionally, it tends to brighten the page. When overused, it loses whatever novelty it has and may be ignored by readers.

Boxes or Pictures with Rounded Corners

Traditionally, columnists' articles are positioned in the same section of the newspaper every day so that readers will know where they may be found. But they need not be placed in or near major sections. If the columnist has a loyal following, chances are that readers wll search for the column no matter where it appears. The main sports column is often placed in the most

Positioning of Columnists' Articles

family living
LERNER NEWSPAPERS

St. Peter's convent still home to 3 nuns

By ROSEMARY SAZONOFF
Lerner-Life Newspapers Correspondent

ON THE TOP floor of the cream aluminum-sided house at 8126 Niles Center in Skokie, a small chapel with delicately-carved altar and niches and medallion stained glass window inserts is used almost exclusively by one semi-retired nun.

The home, built more than 100 years ago and which once housed St. Peter's rectory, is the convent of the School Order of St. Francis, the sisters which staff St. Peter's school.

At its peak, in the early 60's, 20 sisters occupied the bedrooms on the first and second floor and an adjoining building and ate communally in a huge dining room remodeled from three rooms.

Today, three sisters (two of them blood relatives) reside in the large house; but they work together to keep it spotlessly clean and share the meeting room on the second floor and the recreation room in the basement with parish groups.

A passageway which once bridged two buildings has been closed off and is now used as a residence by the four-man maintenance crew for the church complex.

IF YOU WALK UP THE convent's broad front stairs, ringing the bell will bring the excited barking of Mac, the poodle-terrier watch dog pet of the nuns.

Mac seems to cotton to women. He sniffs, looks the visitor over carefully and then awaits direction from his mistresses. The residents say Mackie continues barking if it's a man.

"I guess he's more accustomed to women," says Sister Mary Claire Schulte who opened the door for the Lerner-Life reporter. She has been at St. Peter's for 15 years.

Her sister, Laureta, chose the move to the same convent two years ago. The decision was her own but permission was granted for the move by the region she came from—Milwaukee. Of 11 children in the Schulte family five became nuns.

SISTER MARY CLAIRE INVITES the visitor to some home-baked bread, one of her hobbies, and a fresh cup of coffee on the plastic covered over-sized dining room table. Plants are all around. The plastic protects a bright pink knit tablecloth, sewed by Sister Laureta. All the sisters use the second floor sewing room to make their own clothes.

The doorbell rings. It's a guppy salesman who has been asked to bring refills for a school fish tank Sister Mary Claire discovered long ago was soothing to some of her students in the sixth grade class room of the Catholic school next door.

A telephone rings. Sister Mary Claire excuses herself and Sister Laureta takes up the story. The discussion turns to habits.

Sister Laureta is in a neat pantsuit, Sister Mary Claire in a dress she made herself.

"I WAS IN THE HABIT FOR 40 years and when the change came I was happy I no longer had to wear and launder the habit," she says.

She points out the five-yard skirt was dangerous as well as uncomfortable as there were cases of sisters killed in accidents when skirts caught.

Sister Mary Amica Ries, who joined the order in 1917, enters also wearing a neat print dress and white sweater.

Sister Mary Amica, who only teaches slow learners on a part-time basis now, still wears the nun's veil. She says she, too, is happy with the change, but is somehow shy of being seen without the veil.

All three wear the Tau cross, the Greek symbol for Christ chosen by St. Fracnis in a chain around their necks. The order had to patent the cross, in order to keep it from being worn indiscriminately.

SISTER MARY AMICA is the early riser. She's up at 5 a.m., uses the convent chapel for priate prayers, has a light breakfast and at 6 a.m. opens up the church for the 6:30 a.m. mass

In addition to teaching, all three sisters are responsible for the care of the sanctuaries and sachristines. They wash the altar cloths, keep sanctuary lights burning, dust, vacuum and mop. They have help in doing the job. They prepare dinner together.

The sisters are paid a salary for the teaching jobs. The money goes into a common pot for their food, clothing and sundy needs. They are high in their praise of The Rev. Father Kenneth Close, who sees to other needs for the convent.

He feels they don't ask for enough parish funds to pay for the utilities. The sisters also contribute to the general assessment of their order. There is no mortgage on the buidling.

SISTER MARY CLAIRE is the driver. Shoppping is generally a weekly outing.

She also belongs to the parish council, is the mass song leader, handles the Bingo game; attends classes at St. Isaacs Joques; enjoys cooking stews and soups, paints, sews and earns money making candles, which she sends to her missionary sister in South America.

Sister Laureta teaches in the primary center. She, too, earns money for the missionary work by sewing and crocheting various items. In addition to church work in the chapel, she is distributes communion.

SHE ENJOYS TENDING THE plants amply displayed in garden bowers throughout the house.

The doorbell rings yet again. A very attractive former nun arrives to pick up Sister Mary Amica to take her to a birthday party dinner. When they leave, the sisters are reluctant to discuss the private affairs of the sister who left the order.

"Taking vows is not a sacrament; and our sisters may continue work even when they leave the order," says Sister Mary Claire, who mentions the former sister is still teaching in a Catholic school.

Asked if they had any doubts or regrets, both sisters declare firmly that they find life full and satisfying. They enjoy working, with the children, admit sometimes the current drug problems are difficult to solve and seek advice from a variety of sources.

They visit sick parihioners, lend a hand with church activities whenever requested.

"We picked blueberries and strawberries and freeze and can some of them, but we try to bring things to disabled people in our parish," says Sister Mary Claire. "Visiting them is a form of recreation for us."

SISTER LAURETA Schulte enjoys tending plants in the Skokie convent of the School Order of St. Francis at St. Peter's Church. Mac, the ever present watch dog, announces any visitors or noises.

RELAXING IN her room, Sister Mary Amica Ries checks reading material for slow learners in her part time classes at St. Peter's parochial school, next door to the convent of the School Order of St. Francis. Sister Mary Amica wears modern dress but still prefers the veil.

MASS is no longer held in the convent's top floor mini-chapel. Hand carved antique panels from the Potter Palmer mansion, and medallion stained glass windows offer space for quiet prayers by the three siseters in residence, from left, Sister Mary Claire Schulte, Sister Laureta Schulte and Sister Mary Amica Ries.

WOMAN of the MONTH

She helps Skokie residents watch where the dollars go

By JUDY BRAGINSKY

SHOPPERS DON'T complain enough, says Lori Velco, who's not shy about rending prepackaged plastic off two plump green peppers to separate them from a third shrunken brother.

"And when shoppers do get angry and frustrated about similar supermarket practices, they blurt out their feeling to the wrong person," adds the volunteer chairman of Skokie's Consumer Affairs Commission.

"If you call the store's headquarters and talk reasonably with a vice president, you generally will get some satisfaction. A reputable merchant wants to see his customers satisfied."

In the case of those green peppers, Mrs. Velco, 4325 Lee, took the severed sale items to be weighed, sans packaging, only to be told the peppers would cost her more in their naked state.

"I LEFT THE PEPPERS with the clerk," says the Life Woman of the Month.

"I hate prepackaging anyway; and if enough people break open these unasked-for fruit and vegetable containers and leave what they don't want, the store would eventually get the message.

"One has to have the same spirit shoppers did when boycotting sugar as prices skyrocketed.

354 "Stores are not doing you a favor when you buy an item. You are doing the store a favor and I think many consumers have forgotten this."

SUCH INTREPIDITY FROM the chairman, newly re-appointed to a second one-year term, has helped bring about changes to the consumer's good since the unit was formally established in 1973.

Tackling several well-chosen projects each year, the 14-member advisory group to village trustees includes such victories as laws upholding shoppers' rights to pricing on foodstuff items, clear plastic meat trays and display of total gasoline prices, when such pricing is put on view.

The commission also wrote a still-available condominium buyer's guide to help people know what to look out for with such purchases.

NEWER ITEMS UP THE commission's sleeve, she says, include a subcommittee on adult consumerism education and studying both what Congress is doing about natural gas pricing and the makeup of the Illinois Commerce Commission which approves telephone and utility rates.

"Yes, it is awfully hard for me to vaccuum and do my laundry," she says for, besides lengthy bouts on her telephone with commission business, she's also on advisory boards for both the Better Business Bureau and MONACEP at Oakton Community College in Morton Grove.

Two months ago, Mrs. Velco, a former guidance counselor in Chicago schools, became den mother for Boy Scout Troop 72, sponsored by Central Methodist Church.

Mrs. Velco admits it takes time for a consumer to save money, adding that one Harvard University study reports that only one-third of the people comparison shop at all.

"I REALIZE IT'S HARD to do so with one child climbing out of your cart and another tossing things in as once was the case with me," says the mother whose community involvement began with a toe-hold in the Skokie-Lincolnwood League of Women Voters, of which she is secretary.

"As my children—Jan, now 6, and Jimmy, 8,—grew older, I was able to do more. Consumerism was just something I jumped into; but one can learn an awful lot by just reading as I do all the time."

Mrs. Velco says persons should also realize that the supermarket isn't the only place they should be wary when spending their dollars.

"Consumerism is a tremendous area and also includes such questionable regions as utility, hospital and gasoline rates," she says.

"TOTALING MY BILLS at the end of last year, I discovered my gasoline bill doubled for our two cars and actually cost more than my electricity, heating gas and telephone bills combined.

"I think this says you pay an awful price for the convenience of a car; and we in the suburbs have not yet demanded good alternative transportation, even though the situation is going to get worse."

Eyeing hospital billings as equally "horrifying," Mrs. Velco cited one 26-day hsopital stay by her son, after which she says she was charged 60 cents for four baby aspirin as well as for extra unused bandaging and uneaten trays of food.

"People don't comparison shop hospitals or doctors and I think it would be a wise thing to do," she says.

"I know the area is an emotional and relatively untouched one, as is funeral services, but there's an awful lot of waste going on in all these areas and guess who's paying for it."

(Nominations for next month's Woman of the Month should be sent to Family Living Editor, Lerner Newspapers, 7519 N. Ashland, Chicago. Simply write and tell us in your own words why your candidate should be selected Woman of the Month. Include addresses and telephone numbers.)

WOMAN OF the Month Lori Velco, of Skok says shoppers are doing stores a favor, not v versa, when they make purchases. As vol teer chairman of Skokie's Consumer Affa Commission, she's always looking for ways uphold shoppers' rights.

She

DAY PUBLICATIONS

If snow is your thing, you're not alone. You're probably destined to become one of the one million snowmobile owners in the North American snow belt.

There's no need to give up fashion for warmth. Ski-Doo Sports, Ltd. has designed a wardrobe especially for snowmobilers. From head to toe you'll find warm accessories for everyone, even in apres snowmobiling attire.

A new fabric, Vistram, is used in this flattering one-piece snowmobile suit with fur-trimmed hood. Vistram looks like leather but doesn't become brittle in cold temperature. It's air permeable allowing it to breathe and maintain a suppliness at any temperature.

His and her one-piece nylon snowmobile suits with orlon fleece are the warmest thing on the snowmobilé trail.

These boots are definitely made for snow. T'NT snowmobile boots are ankle-padded and come in black with yellow racing stripes and a removable felt liner.

Colorful hip hugger sweaters, 100 per cent wool, are great before and after snowmobiling.

There's still more—fiber glass helmets; goggles; wool tuques; finger mitts; socks; thermal underwear; seal skin boots; mukluks; shearling boots; snow shoes; kidney belts; saddlebags and a duffle bag to put it all in.

Snow safariers can be found where the action is—and they're very warm and fashionable.

— marilyn helfers, editor

Fashions available at Sports Chalet
Rolling Meadows
Photos from Ski-Doo Sports, Ltd.

Figure 16–6 [OPPOSITE]. Attractive women's page because of its clean, light-appearing makeup. [*Courtesy Lerner Newspapers, Chicago, Illinois.*]

Figure 16–7 [ABOVE]. Sample of contemporary design on women's pages.

355

sports

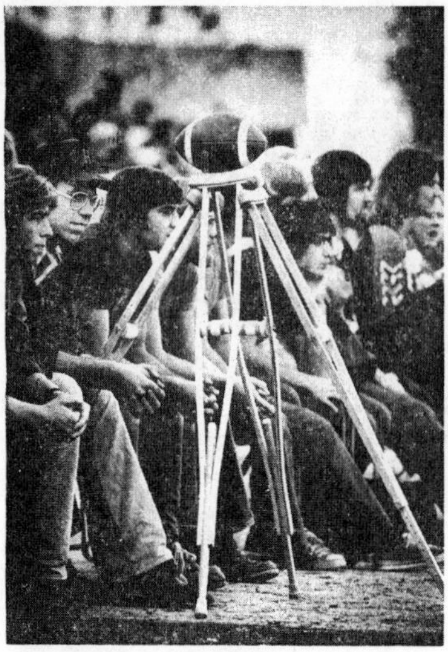

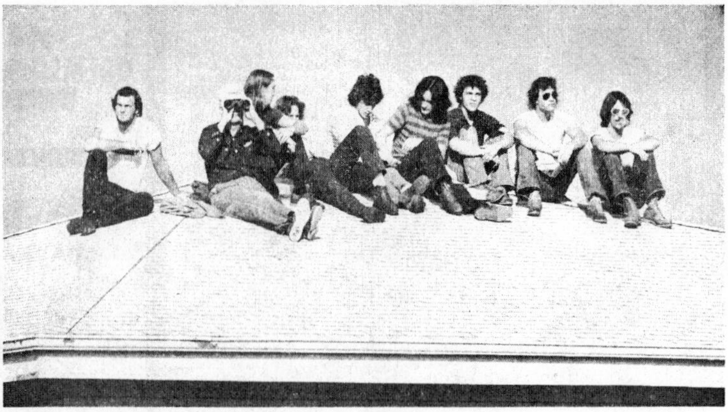

SPECTATOR COMFORT? The extremes of spectator viewing locations are shown here during Hersey's battle with Loyola in the state football tournament. The interested fans at left have sideline seats blocked only by a display of crutches, while the other spectators found a house roof just right for viewing the action. Over 6,000 fans lined the Hersey field to watch Loyola win a thriller, 10-3. (Photos by Dave Tonge)

Bob Frisk
Sports Editor

Idle thoughts for a Friday

TELEVISION TALK:

Have you been listening carefully to those Monday night television games? The man in the middle — blond, blue-eyed Frank Gifford — is a pretty funny guy. Maybe the funniest and smartest, of the three that handle the pro football telecasts.

I have had to learn to like Gifford's work. I resented his taking the place of Keith Jackson as the Monday night play-by-play man, a classic example of an ex-athlete, New York and all that, shoving an accomplished sportscaster out of the booth.

Times change and opinions change. You have to listen very carefully, for Gifford's humor is very subtle, but also very pointed. He knows what he

Frank Gifford

is up against — super star left, super star right — and he must tread carefully.

As more and more Monday nights pass, he becomes more of himself, a little bolder each week, and he is starting to come through as a very interesting man, a very aware man and one who is pretty honest.

You have to respect Gifford because he is handling a very difficult assignment in a very stylish way. He will outlast both Howard Cosell and Alex Karras because he is himself on the air while the others are "gimmick guys," and television eventually devours gimmicks, no matter how sensational they may seem at the moment.

• • •

HOCKEY TALK:

Why are there so many fights in hockey when there are so few in pro football, which is even more physical?

What makes hockey exciting is when there is that endless flow of action from one end of the rink to the other. But that requires great skill and apparently this is no longer possible in an era of expansion when the talent has been diluted so badly. So they brawl to make their headlines.

I don't mind a good fight — if it is spontaneous. Men always will fight when they're engaged in combat. But this business of barging into each other and brawling all over the place is a joke. What does it prove?

I buy the old theory that a man's more of man when he walks away from a fight rather than when he starts one. What skill is required to drop your gloves and start flailing away — or start swinging your hockey stick at the other guy?

Maybe the public likes it. I don't know but give me the Montreal Canadiens going from one end of the ice and making a great play on the net and then the Boston Bruins coming right back and making a great play at the other end of the ice.

That's what it is all about; or used to be anyway. Professional hockey bores me as it is played today.

• • •

FOOTBALL TALK:

Fremd High School product Jerry Finis had a good look last Saturday at the awesome offensive power of Ohio State, the nation's No. 1 team. Finis, an offensive guard through much of his career, was thrust into a starting defensive tackle role for the University of Illinois.

Was Finis, a former prep All-Stater, impressed after the Buckeyes buried Illinois, 40-3, wearing down a defensive unit that spent most of the day on the field?

"Their offensive line wasn't the kind that blew you out," Jerry reports. "They try to finesse block you, they're real quick off the ball.

"Green (quarterback Cornelius) is so quick. A couple times I was pursuing him and if it had been a normal quarterback, I would have gone right at him. But because it was Green I had to angle him. He's so fast.

"And Archie Griffin is phenomenal. He gets hit behind the line but he still gets his yardage."

Welcome, Jerry, to the club of defensive players who have been dazzled by the awesome Buckeyes. Now don't relax. Michigan comes to town Saturday.

• • •

BOOK TALK:

Watching the parents at high school sports events often can be as entertaining as watching the event itself.

That's why I was particularly anxious to read the book "My Son, The Jock," by Gerald Green. It is a middle-aged man's look at his son, a 17-year-old defensive football star. The son is a surprise athlete in a family without athletic accomplishments.

Green, who wrote "The Last Angry Man," followed his son during a high school football season, asking questions, reading the play book and cheering for him on the sidelines.

Throughout it all you learn a lot about Gerald Green's values, his love for his son and his reminiscences on American life.

When Green is writing of the rather pitiful team and explaining his son, who loves all sports but who also has other interests, he does well.

The author's word pictures of parents, coaches, players all crowding the sidelines anticipating defeat are good ones, and anyone whose son has participated in sports, particularly football, should enjoy the book.

Unfortunately, Green gets too carried away writing about himself, his own shortcomings, and this exercise in flagellation becomes tedious.

The book is worth reading if you skim the parts on the author's migraine headaches, his weak ankles, bad eyes and overprotective mother.

• • •

BASKETBALL TALK:

Believe it or not, the high school basketball season opens tonight.

I don't believe it.

Basketball season begins; Wheeling to host Addison

by KEITH REINHARD

With the oblong-shaped ball hardly deflated and the shoulder pads not even on the shelves long enough to gather a few specks of dust, basketball muscles its way to the forefront of the Herald area sports scene tonight at Wheeling's gymnasium.

Not bothering with any patsy or even a mediocre outfit for an opening tuneup, the Wildcats jump right into the thick of things when they entertain Addison Trail at approximately 8 p.m. It is one of the earliest cage starts in the history of the area.

And one of the most challenging. The Trail Blazers lost only three of 27 contests last winter and have a solid nucleus of returnees headed up by all-state candidate Scott Anderson. They have been ranked among the top 10 teams in the entire Chicagoland area.

The 'Cats figure to be no slouches themselves however. While coach Ted Ecker has only a pair of lettermen (and just one of them a starter) from the Wheeling squad which produced a fine 19-6 slate last season, the 'Cats have a tradition of roundball excellence and Ecker is optimistic about extending that tradition.

"We should have more quickness than we've had the past few years and I'm anticipating a good defensive season. . . . this looks to be one of the stronger facets of our game," the veteran Wildcat mentor observed. "Getting ready for competition this quickly has put some extra pressure on us, of course, but Addison Trail has the same thing to contend with."

The Blazers will also have to contend with veteran Keith Schildt (6-5), Wheeling's leading scorer and rebounder in '74-75 and Carl Krueger, a 6-3 ready reservist last year who promises to augment the 'Cat inside punch.

After that Ecker will be drawing chiefly from a jayvee unit that carved a solid 16-3 slate last season and produced the likes of 6-1 senior Al Begrowicz and 6-0 junior brother Brian, 5-10 senior Dave Schultz, 6-1 senior Glen Barry, 6-2 senior Rick McGowen and 6-4½ senior Tom Polster. The Begrowicz's, Schultz and Barry all saw limited action with the varsity last season.

Also figuring in Ecker's plans is Danny Larsen, a 6-0 sophomore. Rounding out the team are 5-11 junior Rick Heredia, 6-1 senior John Muno and 6-2 junior Keith Block, a transfer from nearby Hersey.

Mainstays for Addison Trail in addition to 6-7 Anderson are 6-6 Steve Long and 6-4 Mike Kalamiki. Anderson averaged 18 points and 10 rebounds a game last season while the Blazers lost only a pair of mid-season bouts to potent East Leyden and a sectional contest to powerful Proviso East.

Tonight's contest will be followed next weekend by a landslide of area openers with Arlington traveling to Proviso West, Palatine hosting Maine East, Hersey taking on visiting Crystal Lake, Buffalo Grove journeying to Cary Grove, Lake Park coming in to Forest View and Hoffman Estates welcoming in Fenton on Friday.

Next Saturday, Nov. 21, Schaumburg, Conant and Prospect follow suit with their lid-lifters, at home against Maine North, Fenton and Evanston respectively.

Corzine, Pancratz return home

DAVE CORZINE

by CHARLIE DICKINSON

Hersey High School basketball fortunes past and present will be on display in the Huskies' gym tonight when Roger Steingraber unveils his 1975-76 team in an intrasquad game to be followed by Ray Meyer's DePaul Blue Demons at eight o'clock.

The Demons, who finished 15-10 last year, are anchored by two former Hersey stars, senior Andy Pancratz and sophomore Dave Corzine.

The 6-11 Corzine, who was second in total rebounds last year, will continue to give the Demons board strength. As a freshman Corzine averaged 8.3 rebounds a game and demonstrated considerable poise for a first year man.

His strength, agility and soft shooting touch will make him a dominant force on the court this season.

Pancratz is the DePaul captain this year and the young Demons will need the leadership qualities this senior can provide. Expected to start at a forward, Pancratz has used his jumping ability and shooting accuracy to prove he can play with the best in major college basketball.

The Demons are a young team and lost seven lettermen from last year's team, including Bill Robinzine, who led the team to scoring and rebounding and was picked in the first round of the National Basketball Association draft by the Kansas City Kings.

The Demons also lost their starting guards, Greg Boyd and Jim Bocinsky.

Meyer is not without a surplus of players to fill the shoes of the departed, though.

Joe Ponsetto, a 6-7 forward who led Proviso East to the state championship two years ago, will provide muscle on the front line.

Fighting for the starting forward job alongside Pancratz will be 6-5 Curtis Watkins from Thornton High School, who was the South Suburban Player of the Year in 1975. He was the fourth player in Thornton history to top 1,000 points for a career.

The guard slots are up for grabs and Meyer has a wide variety of talented players to choose from.

The director of the offense, from his point guard position, figures to be Ron Norwood, who averaged 14.3 points a game last season to place second to Robinzine. Meyer thinks the 6-4 Norwood has All-America possibilities.

The wilds of New Jersey which provided Norwood for the DePaul program, may also supply a running mate for the Blue Demon senior.

His name is Gary Garland and as a senior at East Orange Scott High School last year, he popped for 29 points a game.

Other candidates for the starting guard position include 6-4 Emmett McGovern, a freshman from St. Pat's, juniors Randy Ramsey and Greg Coehlo and sophomore Randy Hook.

Hersey will return three starters from last year's 6-20 club including All-Conference forward Clyde Glass, junior Tom Frye and senior Tom Burzak.

Admission for the night is $1 for adults and 50 cents for students.

ANDY PANCRATZ

favorable position. It robs the more exciting sports stories because they must be placed in less conspicuous positions. The main columnist should be given a less favorable position to prevent this from happening. Readers will not avoid reading the column.

The following suggestions discuss ways in which the makeup man can improve the situation somewhat.

Datelines and Folios

One way to help modernize inside pages is to eliminate datelines, folios and accompanying rules that traditionally have appeared at the top of inside pages. They not only waste space, but they look old-fashioned. If the space occupied by the dateline (including the rule and some white space underneath) is 2 picas, as it often is, then multiplying that by 8 (for the eight-column page) equals 16 picas of space a page that is wasted. If that same issue has 84 pages in it, then it wastes 1344 picas (16×84) or 226 inches (almost a full page and a half each day.) Datelines cannot be eliminated entirely from pages where advertisements appear because they must be included in the tearsheets sent to the advertisers as proof of publication.

But datelines can be shortened into one- or two-column widths and condensed into not more than three lines. The top line may carry the page number; the second line, the newspaper's name; and the last line, the date. These three lines may be placed in the first column on left-hand pages and in the last column on right-hand pages. If there is no first or last column either because this is a full page advertisement or because an eight-column banner headline is used, then the three lines may be placed at the bottom of the page or run sideways, but both set in the margin. In some newspapers, the datelines are buried anywhere near the top of the newspaper in the most convenient place possible. After all, they can be circled when they appear on tearsheets. If the newspaper has an index, then the page number may be of considerable importance in helping readers find a page. In such cases, plans can be made to position the page numbers as close to the outside columns as possible.

Compartment Headlines

Newspapers of the future probably will have more compartmentalization of news than ever before. Compartmentalization is not new, but only recently has there been a determined effort to segment the news into smaller compartments as a convenience to the reader. The use of compartmentalization is well-known in news magazines, where it is one of the strongest features of such makeup. In newspapers, the makeup editor usually does not have the prerogative of deciding whether compartmentalization should be used. It is decided by the managing editor, most likely. But the makeup editor should strongly recommend its use as a means of keeping the design consistent with contemporary makeup.

Figure 16–8 [OPPOSITE]. Attractive sports page. [*Courtesy Arlington Heights, Ill., Herald.*]

In contemporary newspapers, compartmentalization requires the use of standing headlines that a reader is supposed to recognize immediately as an aid in finding a story. There is one exception to the use of compartmental heads. They need not be used for pages whose characteristics are so obvious that the reader does not need a headline to tell him he is reading that page. The editorial page and perhaps the sports pages are sometimes that obvious.

But to keep the newspaper makeup policy consistent, standing headlines may be developed for these and other sections. No matter how many such headlines are used, they should be designed in a consistent and contemporary manner. Consistency is needed to prevent the newspaper from becoming a hodgepodge of design. This does not mean that different typefaces cannot be used in the design for heads. A more feminine-appearing typeface may be appropriate for the women's page but not for a sports page. But there should be some common element in the shape and design of standing heads that gives the reader the feeling he is reading the same newspaper, only a different section. Often this consistency can be achieved through the use of a common size of type, a hairline border around each head, or a Ben Day background for each.

In terms of contemporary styles, the standing heads should not be set in old-fashioned typefaces. Other than the type selection, the design of such headlines should be entrusted to commercial artists or graphic designers—not the makeup man—to find the best possible design for the headline. At times, someone in the back shop, or perhaps the makeup editor himself, may try his hand at design. It probably would make more sense to entrust this kind of responsibility to a professional artist.

Picture Placement   There is a tendency to place pictures in the left corner of inside pages. This was traditional makeup practice in bygone years, but it is unsatisfactory today. It is unsatisfactory because a picture may not be the best news element to occupy such an important position. Formerly, pictures were placed in such positions to anchor the page. Anchoring was a means of providing stability to the makeup design. But a more reasonable approach, and one that will not affect page stability, is to place these pictures as low as possible on any given page. They will get high readership no matter where they are placed. Therefore, the most important positions (corners) should not be used for material that automatically receives high readership. Some kind of headline belongs in the corners: presumably, a headline and story of significance if possible. The objective is to get the story read. If the story is buried underneath the picture it may not be read because it is in a less attractive position. By giving a story an outstanding position, the editor may help the reader learn something significant. Meanwhile, the buried picture will brighten any position on the page (Figure 16–9). The bottom of pages, particularly, where there is a combination of advertisements

Figure 16–9. Buried picture on an inside page. [*Courtesy Cedar Falls Iowa Record.*]

359

and editorial materials, needs considerable brightening. Any effort to make this position more attractive not only benefits the reader, who finds the page better balanced, but the advertiser as well, who gets the reader to look at the bottom as well as the top of inside pages.

Advertising Placement

The makeup editor has little control over the placement of advertisements. But it may be wise to consult with the advertising department about the possibility of placing advertisements in positions that enhance the design of inside pages for the benefit of both readers and advertisers. Traditionally, ads have been pyramided diagonally from the lower left of a page to the upper right. The left side of the newspaper, therefore, received most of the editorial material. This is a reasonable approach to advertising placement in relation to editorial matter because it always frees the left side of the page for news. Because reading took place from left to right, it was assumed that all news material should align on the left as a means of making the page easy to read. Left- and right-hand pages were dummied in the same manner so that the pyramid faced the same direction on all pages (Figure 16–10).

See page 362.

It is also just as reasonable, however, to believe that the present system of dummying advertisements is not always logical. Most readers do not see only one page at a time. Instead, they open the paper so that both the left- and right-hand sides of the paper are visible at once. Obviously a person cannot read two pages at one time, but he may see the total design of two facing pages in his peripheral vision (Figure 16–11). Therefore, the makeup of a single page carrying advertisements should never be considered alone. The opposite page is also part of the total page design. Makeup editors traditionally have not conceived of two facing pages as a single entity because they dummy only one page at a time. But it is reasonable to consider the combined effect of the two facing pages. In such a situation, the left side of the paper ought to be dummied so that the advertisements are placed in the position opposite of their placement on right-hand pages (Figure 16–12). This means that the advertisements on the left side of the page are dummied with the diagonal running from the top left to the lower right. The right-hand page is dummied oppositely. As a result of this makeup procedure, all the news is concentrated in the center between the two facing pages in a concave shape.

See page 363.

See pages 364 and 365.

When pages are tightly dummied so that there is little room for news on the page, the arrangement just described will not work very well. In the latter situation, perhaps both pages should be dummied the traditional way; the makeup editor will have to live with a situation where there is little he can do to design an attractive page.

If he has at least one-quarter page of space available on each of two facing pages, he should then ask the personnel responsible for advertising dummying whether he can reverse the pyramid on the left-hand page. It is that simple. Where one page has about one quarter of the space for news and the other has much more or much less, the editor should ask that an advertisement be shifted to another page so that he can make up as many two facing page units as possible in an attractive design.

There are times when it is impossible to change the pyramid direction of advertisements, either because of the advertising department's policy or because there is little time left. Yet there is another approach to improving inside page design provided space is available for news. Perhaps there may be as much as one third or more of the space on a page for news. When that much space is available, the page may be considered to be "open." At that time a makeup procedure may be used whereby the space immediately adjacent to advertisements is filled completely so that the top of the news aligns across the page with the top of the highest-positioned advertisement. What remains, then, is a rectangle of white space that is also available for news (Figure 16–13). A rectangular space is relatively easy to use for creating an attractive page design. If the page were filled in the traditional manner, then the odd-shaped space may or may not provide the means of creating an attractive page. The rectangular approach may be used only when the pyramid advertisements do not extend much above the fold.

Open Inside Page Makeup

See page 366.

Many times the makeup editor is faced with so many advertisements on a page, or a few large advertisements, that there is little space for news. Either constitutes a *tight* page. In this situation, it is best to dummy a single long story in the remaining space than to use a number of short stories on the page (Figure 16–14). The long story may be wrapped from column to column until the space is filled. The reader should have no difficulty determining which story he is reading because there is only one story on the page. On the other hand, where many short stories are dummied on a tight page, wraps are necessary and may be confusing to the reader because a headline may not cover each of them. There may not be enough time to reset a one-column headline in a two-column width, or there may not be enough multiple-column heads to cover all raw wraps. Furthermore, when many short stories are used on a tight page it may be difficult to avoid tombstones. If there are no long stories available and shorter ones must be used on tight pages, there is the possibility that more than one headline will be positioned across the top of the page, usually an unsightly makeup procedure. If the placement of headlines in such positions cannot be avoided, then they should be alternated at the top to avoid tombstones. Perhaps a two-column headline can be alternated with a single-column head, or perhaps a headline set in a roman type can be alternated with one set in italics (Figure 16–15). Least effective from a makeup point of view is the use of headlines positioned

Tight Page Makeup

See page 367.

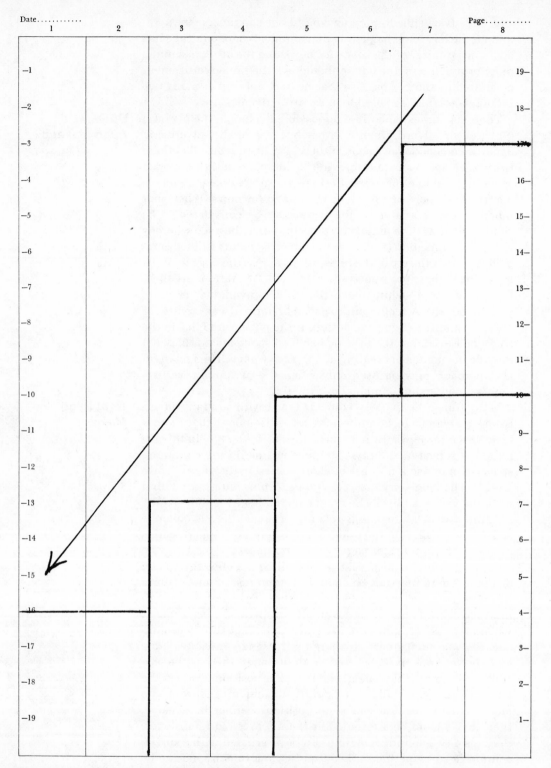

Figure 16-10. Pyramid style used for placing advertisements on both left- and right-hand pages.

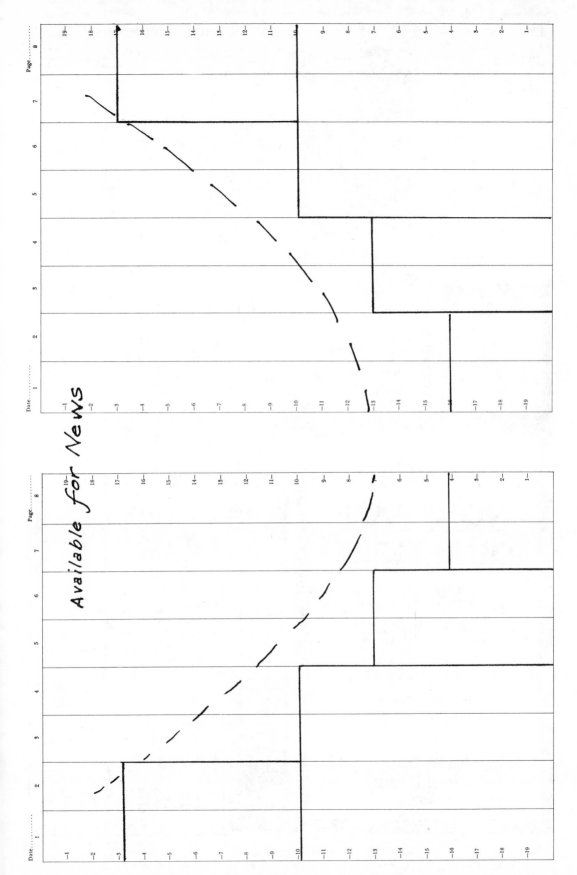

Figure 16–11. Two facing pages dummied with advertisements pyramided toward the center.

Section One—Page Two

LERNER NEWSPAPERS, WEEK OF DECEMBER 31, 1969

Housing

(Continued from page 1)

groups in the area whose members view proliferation of the buildings as a threat to neighborhood stability.

OUTLOOK for the Uptown Model Cities program is bleak. The program, which was heralded by former President Lyndon Johnson as the solution to the nation's urban ills, has failed to live up to its promise, especially in Chicago.

It is top-heavy in administration, uncreative in programming and incapable of involving the poor in the decision-making process. The program will roll on in Uptown and the city's three other Model Cities areas this year, but offers little hope of relief for the city's ills.

Some promise exists in the election of 20 members of the new 40-member model cities councils, but at present it appears that the cards are still stacked against community participation. Under the proposed rules for the election, the mayor makes his 20 selections either before or after—probably after—the elections are held.

LAKE VIEW may get some relief this year from the proliferation of four-plus-one buildings in its family residential areas. Ald. William Singer (44th), chief political spokesman for the community in its fight, said a few weeks ago that the city fathers are responding and may provide some changes to restrict development of the buildings.

Organizations in the Lake View area charge that the four-plus-one buildings are driving families from the community. Apartments in the buildings, which begin the first of five floors just below ground level, are primarily of the efficiency and one-bedroom types.

A few months ago, it appeared that Lake View would have an urban renewal program underway during 1970. However, the proposal may have to wait because of an impasse between community leaders and the Department of Urban Renewal over the naming of a Conservation Community Council.

The community has picked its own slate of 15 persons to pass on renewal plans for an area bounded by Broadway, Racine, Belmont and Diversey and demanded the city accept the slate before the area is tabbed for urban renewal. Thus far, the DUR has refused to accede to the demand.

West Lake View might see the erection of some portable college classrooms on the site of the old Riverview amusement park at Western and Belmont by September, 1970. The Chicago City College board has instituted condemnation procedings for the land, which is owned by the Arvey Corp.

However, a prolonged court battle could put the ax to college plans for 1970.

And the Lincoln Park Conservation Community council, whose meetings through most of 1969 were like search and destroy missions, may see relative calm in 1970. The decreasing supply of low-income housing units, which provided the rallying cry of protest in the last year, will diminish even more in 1970, due mainly to private housing rehabilitation in west Lincoln Park.

However, with the optimism that a new year and a new decade brings, we see more planning and less protest in the effort to get decent housing for the poor.

HENRY Hindin, 2616 Farwell, whose hobbies include playing first violin in the Evanston Symphony Orchestra, was named second vice-president of Exchange National Bank.

● Four generations celebrated Thanksgiving dinner in the Court of the Lions restaurant, 6935 N. Sheridan. Hostess was Mrs. Sophie Cohen, widow of the late Harry B. Cohen. Mrs. Cohen lives at Hollywood Towers, 5701 N. Sheridan Rd. Present were daughter, Aileen, and her husband, Harold D. Baum, 3900 Lyons, Skokie, and children David and Debbie. Third generation was represented by Mr. and Mrs. Lawrence Charles Silton. Fourth generation consists of Steven, 17 months,

● **Irwin W. Iroff**, of Rogers Park, has been named midwest regional sales manager for business equipment by Toshiba America, Inc.

WHOOPS!
Clean Sweep
CLEARANCE SALE!
STARTS SAT. JAN. 3rd
20% TO 50% OFF
ELMHURST, ILL., 164 N. YORK ST.
GLENVIEW, ILL., 1723 GLENVIEW RD.
WINNETKA, ILL., 932 LINDEN
CHICAGO, 2831 W. TOUHY
MILWAUKEE, WISC. 8716 N. PORT WASHINGTON

ACE
SHERIDAN BAZAAR
4654 BROADWAY ED 4-7146
WINTER'S HERE!
SNOW SHOVELS | COCOA MATS
ROCK SALT | WEATHER STRIP

JANUARY — MARCH
APRIL — JUNE
JULY — SEPTEMBER
OCTOBER — DECEMBER
INTEREST
NOW PAID
QUARTERLY
ON ALL
SAVINGS
ACCOUNTS
STARTING JANUARY 1, 1970
North Shore
National Bank
1737 W. HOWARD at the "L"
Chicago
SH 3-2112

Schools picture resembles play

(Continued from page 1)

Daley put the responsibility of school financial support on the state—where it legally rests.

So where last year the city's revenue from the state income tax bailed the school's out—in 1970 there is no hope of the city arriving on a white horse and "saving the schools."

Waiting for the state legislature has proven to be the same as waiting for Godot. The state has never responded to the crisis. The legislature has only reacted with token aid.

To relieve the crisis, the governor would have to call a special session of the state legislature. This seems highly unlikely since the legislature met in early fall and froze all possibilities of additional aid to Chicago schools.

WHAT DOES appear certain in 1970 is that the Board of Education members will have, at least, learned from the experience of 1969. They will not sign a contract they cannot fulfill as they did last year.

They will either cutback in areas which will not directly hurt the teachers or they will bring on a strike. And it is very possible that the board will provoke a strike—in the hopes that the state legislature will respond.

This brings us back to 1969. The teachers union is again crying that the board is using the teachers to bring about a response from the state legislature. "The board has never met its responsibility to lobby for state aid," a union official recently told the Lerner Newspapers.

THE ABSURDITY is that even with the $20 million the children of Chicago will still be the victims of a school system that denies them quality education.

Dr. Redmond recently highlighted the school's unmet needs for 1970. These totaled $139,456.767 plus the $20 million.

What they add up to is deficiences in every area of the educational and building program of the Chicago schools.

THE YEAR 1970 may see a bond issue to relieve the crisis in the building fund. This would help a school system top heavy with deteriorated buildings and antiquated teaching facilities.

But in areas of special education, reading improvement, bi-linqual programs, vocational training, and pupil personnel services—areas which are crucial to the present crop of students in Chicago—their will be no improvement. Some relief may come but only at the sacrifice of teachers and the creation of overcrowded classrooms.

It will be a year with more problems than solutions. School buildings will deteriorate more, mobiles will increase to relieve overcrowded facilities, many retarded children will find no classes for them, Spanish-speaking children will move farther behind because they don't speak English, high school students will continue to drop out, and children who cannot read will fall deeper behind.

THE NEW YEAR will undoubtedly be another year of student riots and racial trouble. A human relations program costing upwards of $6 million will be buried in the 1970 budget.

Undoubtedly, in 1970 there will be more community organization over school problems. This is especially true of the Spanish-speaking community which only began organizing last year.

In the light of past experience, it seems unlikely that the community groups will be able to bring the Chicago school system closer to the schools. Again they will meet with powerless district and area superintendents, and again they will discover a bureaucracy unable to cope with the needs of individual schools.

Ideally, 1970 should bring the state legislature to the point of commitment to fulfilling the unmet needs of Chicago schools. And ideally, the Board of Education would create an atmosphere where community participation in school decision making would be more than words.

Realistically, however, waiting for the state and the board to take such action could only duplicate the characters of an absurd play who sit around waiting for Godot.

Police

(Continued from page 1)

ence. If there's any major crime, it'll probably be in or around the bars of the deteriorating Lawrence-Kedzie business strip.

TOWN HALL (19TH) DISTRICT: Cmdr. John Fahey shares the problems of the Young Lords with the 18th district. Fahey runs a tolerably tight ship, although a lot of the old-line policemen sometimes cause him public relations problems.

Major problems in the district will come from the poor Latins and from the drug scene. Policemen will continue to be the target of the largely class-orientated resentments, and this is the other North Side district with a good potential for violence.

Much will depend on whether or not Fahey manages to face his challenge in such a way that he satisfies the law and order demands of the older faction without provoking the anti-police groups into some sort of armed confrontation.

The Latins build martyr images easily here, and, given a martyr and the excuse for confrontation, they could be explosive.

Crimes against persons will be on the upswing, despite aggressive patrol. This is one of the districts considered hazardous by those who are against one-man cars, and Fahey will probably be faced with a choice between the demands of the war on crime and the demands of some of his own policemen.

Police in general throughout the city will probably organize more and more into unions ("associations") to represent their views in discussion on everything from salaries to sin. Supt. James B. Conlisk will deplore the actions of the associations but won't risk his already shaky prestige in a direct confrontation.

● Karen Hope Johnson, 2654 Ainslie, is enrolled as a student at Wheaton college for the 1969-70 academic year. The daughter of Rev. and Mrs. Ernest Johnson, she transferred to Wheaton from Moody Bible Institute.

● **Steven A. Slor**, 930 Agatite, has joined the Allstate Insurance as a casualty claim supervisor.

For want ads that pull call BR 4-7100 and ask for a friendly Lerner ad-taker.

HAUL IT YOURSELF
RENT A TRAILER
SAVE $$$ SAVE $$$
OPEN EVENINGS AND SUNDAYS
MID-WEST TRAILER RENTAL
6025 N. CLARK ST.
AMbassador 2-6774

TO BE BRA-LESS
OR NOT TO BE BRA-LESS
These Days . . . That Is the Question
If your Bra problem is one of discomfort or improper fit DON'T GO BRA-LESS — GO PENNYRICH.
With sizes 28 thru 46 and 12 cup sizes per bra size, your problem is solved.
Also ideal for mothers-to-be and nursing mothers.
Take advantage of a free custom fitting. By private appointment or party plan, call 433-0728, or write to: JUDY, 585 County Line Road, Highland Park, Ill. 60035.

WISE
choice—for high value, low cost life insurance. Contact me today!
VERN COMISKEY
Jen Insurance Agency, Inc.
3413 IRVING PARK
IN 3-4343
STATE FARM
Life Insurance Company
Home Office: Bloomington, Illinois

DID YOU KNOW?
THAT OUR APPETIZING FOODS ESPECIALLY
LOX, SMOKED FISH
AND OUR
KOSHER MEATS
ARE THE FINEST!
CORNED BEEF $1.19 lb
PASTRAMI $1.49 lb
SHEL-MAR
FISHERY AND DELICATESSEN
2637 W. DEVON
AM 2-7810

AMERICAN GIRL SHOE SALE
20% OFF . . . Original prices! Save Many Dollars!
SHOE BOOTS
30% OFF . . . Original prices. Values to $30.00
Water-Proof Leather, Suede
HUSH PUPPIES (Special Group)
$7 & $8
Values to $16.00 • Discontinued Styles Only!
Not All Sizes in Every Style
SPECIAL GROUP! FAMOUS BRAND FLATS
Values to $16.00
Discontinued styles. Not all Sizes in every style.
$5
RED TAG CLEARANCE SALE!
20% OFF
ORIGINAL PRICES!
Deduct 20% Off The Price Tags During Our Red-Tag Sale!
Great Savings!
ALL SALES FINAL!
BOSTON SHOES
Your Red Cross and American Girl Store on Devon
2534 W. DEVON AVE. Phone 465-9421

 Figure 16–12. Two facing pages printed with advertisements pyramided toward the center.

Hope for state park on golf land may be fulfilled for NS in 1970

By LILY VENSON
Lerner Newspapers
Staff Writers

FOR THOSE who have long hoped for a public park on the beautiful Edgewater golf land, 1970 may be the year in which that dream could be fulfilled. Gov. Richard B. Ogilvie has committed himself to every effort to save the land for the people. He has joined a community cause and taken it all the way to the White House.

BUT THERE is much work ahead before the gateway to an innovative state park on the North Side opens.

It will be a time for lacing everyone together to create unanimity of purpose.

State Rep. Edward J. Copeland (R-10th), who introduced the bi-partisan state park legislation, is on the side of the people in their fight against "concrete canyons" and for precious open green spaces in the city.

Philip Krone, conservationist, has been the quiet

Forecast 1970

voice working behind the scenes to make the park a reality.

NO ONE NEEDS to be reminded of the role of Allied North Side Community Organizations (ANSCO), headed by Dr. James Barry and later by Laurence Warren.

ANSCO never gave up the public park goal for a moment, not even when prospects were so dismal, a weaker group would have disbanded at the brink of failure.

Ald. Jack I. Sperling (50th) has been saying the same thing over and over again for almost four years —"there are federal funds under the open spaces program to save the land for public park use."

THERE ARE MANY, many more people and organizations, too numerous to mention here, working unceasingly toward the park goal.

But those who must now be drawn into this crusade with sincere commitment are representatives of the various levels of local governmental agencies.

The year 1970 must be the time of cohesive, realistic working together.

The mayor, the City Council, the Chicago Park district headed by Dan Shannon (who some people believe has started a new era in park planning) must work with the community, the governor and the state Conservation department headed by William Rutherford.

IF THIS JOINT effort does not begin early in 1970, the whole park acquisition process could be slowed down.

Lastly, the private developers should remember that 1970 could be the year when all their patient waiting will mean a return of a very fair market value on their land. They will, no doubt, be disappointed that they could not erect their Edgewater Village on the golf land.

But when that day should come, when a pioneering state park in the city of Chicago is a reality, the private developers can rightly feel they had their thumb print on it if they negotiated amicably for the sale of the land.

We hope they will have the vision to do so in 1970. The people will remember them for it.

THERE IS ICE skating at Sam Leone Park, Touhy and Sheridan, and youngsters are taking advantage of this fact to become more proficient at figure skating. In the picture one ten year old girl has fallen, Kathleen Monahan, and her companion, Bridgid Donohue, also 10, tries to pick her up. The leg at left belongs to an unidentified adult, and our photographer got it in the picture for artistic effect.

(Photo by Charles Allen)

Urban Line

Resident points out dead elm

A NORTH Side resident recently complained to UR-BAN LINE about "a huge dead elm tree" at 2006 Arthur.

The complainant said that many calls have been made in an effort to get the tree removed and that large branches hanging over the sidewalk present a serious hazard to passers by. Some branches, he claimed, have fallen already.

URBAN LINE contacted Public Works Deputy Comr. Francis Patrick Kane, who promised that an inspector would be sent to investigate the situation during the first part of next week. Kane said that if the tree was found to be a hazard it would be removed immediately.

• • •

URBAN LINE received an acknowledgment from Mrs. Pearl Goldstone, 6253 N. Troy.

Mrs. Goldstone said that for the past three months the Forestry Bureau had failed to remove tree branches and other debris "that make the parkway in front of my home a danger to persons passing this area, and very unsightly to look at."

URBAN LINE contacted the Forestry department and the debris has been removed. Mrs. Goldstone sent in her vote of thanks.

Pollution hearings January 5

THE ILLINOIS House Air Pollution Study Committee will hold the second in a series of public hearings throughout the state at 10 a.m. Monday, Jan. 5, at the Illinois Commerce Commission, State of Illinois Building, 160 N. LaSalle.

State Reps. J. Theodore Meyer (R-28th), Chicago, chairman of the committee, and Harry Yourell (D-6th), Oak Lawn, chairman of the Metropolitan Chicago subcommittee, invite all civic and citizens organizations to offer their views with regard to the control of air pollution in the Metropolitan Chicago area.

Future hearings will be held in Chicago at which business, labor and the public will be invited to testify.

Those organizations planning to testify are urged to bring a written statement to submit to the Committee.

LERNER HOME NEWSPAPERS
A Lerner Newspaper
Published weekly by
The Myers Publishing Co.
7519 N. Ashland Avenue
Chicago, Ill. 60626
Classified Advertising
BR 4-7100
Display Advertising
Editorial and Other Offices
RO. 1-7200

LEO A. LERNER, 1907-1965
Editor and Publisher
LOUIS A. LERNER, Publisher
JOSEPH L. FIRSTL,
Executive Vice President
T. P. GORMAN,
Executive Editor
THEODORE MITAMURA,
Managing Editor

SECOND CLASS POSTAGE
PAID AT CHICAGO, ILL.
SUBSCRIPTION RATES
By Mail for Any
One of the Following
Newspapers, $2.50 Per Year
UPTOWN NEWS
NORTHTOWN NEWS
RAVENSWOOD-LINCOLNITE
ALBANY-NORTH PARK NEWS
ROGERS PARK-EDGEWATER NEWS
5¢ Per Year for Any One of the above listed Newspapers combined with the Sunday Star, Add $1.00 outside of Cook County.

Figure 16–12. Continued. [*Courtesy Lerner Newspapers, Chicago, Illinois.*]

365

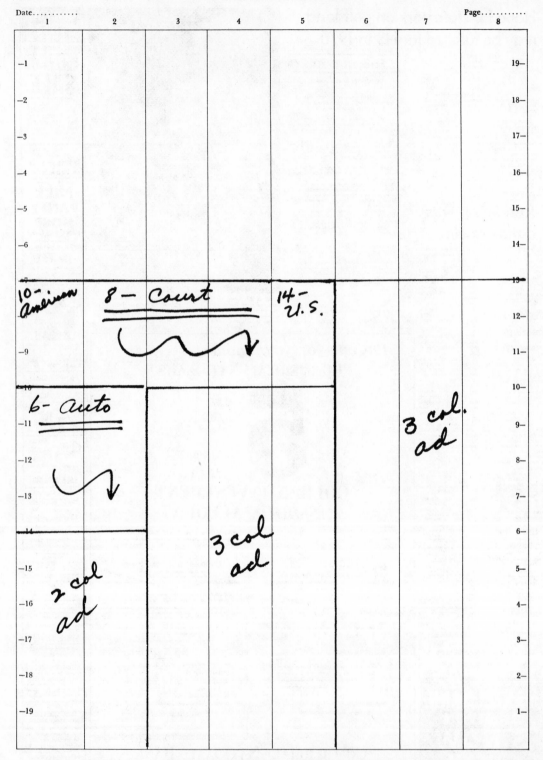

Figure 16-13. Rectangle of space remaining at top after the lower part of the page has been dummied to align with the top of the advertisements.

The Art of Editing

Cuts in Heart Aid Aired in Senate

WASHINGTON (UPI) — Sen. Warren G. Magnuson, D-Wash., Wednesday expressed amazement the Department of Health, Education and Welfare is phasing out the nation's only community heart disease and stroke control program.

Local volunteer physicians and others who organize the program last year at Savannah, Ga., believe they can discover why the Georgia coastal locality has the nation's highest incidence of heart disease and strokes.

Dr. James C. Metts Jr., a private physician heading Savannah's unique Community Cardiovascular Council, told Magnuson's Senate Appropriations Subcommittee HEW is phasing out its aid in two years.

"I hadn't heard they were

abolishing the heart disease control program," said Magnuson, who conducted a hearing on the administration's proposed sweeping cutbacks in its medical research programs.

Metts brandished a letter from a top HEW officials to prove his statement and added, "I don't think you can permit them to do this."

"We can only suggest that they not do it," Magnuson said. "If the administration won't spend the money there is nothing we can do about it. We can't put them in jail."

At another point Magnuson asked, "Why did they pick on you?"

Metts replied, "I don't think they knew what they were doing. I—".

"Well," Magnuson interrupted, "that's a sufficient answer." Metts said the project has received commitments of grants totaling $160,000, plus the loan of several career experts from the Public Health Service.

"We are not worried about the loss of the funds," Metts said.

Magnuson appeared amazed for a second time.

"I'll keep you here all day," he blurted, spoofing Metts. There was laughter in a hearing room jammed with groups who had come from across the nation to protest the loss of funds for various projects.

Metts explained that without the help of the HEW experts provided under the regional heart disease and stroke control program the Savannah project cannot continue, regardless of funds.

"I assure you," Magnuson said, "there will be more discussion about this in the committee."

Metts was accompanied by Rep. Elliott Hagan, D-Ga., Dr. John L. Elliott, a pioneer Savannah internist specialist, and Savannah Alderman Boyd Yarley Jr.

They advised Magnuson they had on hand a petition signed by an estimated 10,000 Savannah and Chatham County residents asking that the Savannah project be continued.

The Savannah project's unique feature is its method of evaluating causes of heart and stroke conditions that are related to the patient's life and environment.

Dr. Joseph A. Wilbur, director of the Georgia Health Department's Cardiovascular Disease Control Service, testified that other significant work in Geor-

gia is at stake. A 1961-62 venture in Evans County provided unique information about the distribution of high blood pressure and coronary disease in an entire bi-racial community, Wilbur said.

"This study showed that Negroes had much more high blood pressure and that whites had much more coronary heart disease," he said. "Diet did not seem to be a factor, but occupation and socio-economic factors

turned out to be very important." He said this community was rechecked in 1968-69 and the new data are still being analyzed.

In another project in Baldwin County, Ga., it was found that 20 per cent of the entire population over the age of 15 had high blood pressure," Wilbur said.

Belk advertisement (left)

As seen on TV

Belk

New! Chic!
Really waterproof
stretch boots by "totes".
Fit like a glove over
low heel shoes.
So light they fold
to take along.

Slip on, easy off "totes" shape to your shoes for a slim, slender look. Feel unbelievably trim and light as you walk. Made of soft pure rubber, "totes" are seamless, 100% waterproof. Non-skid soles. Black, sizes S (4-5½), M (6-7), L (7½-8½), XL (9-10½). With flowered satin purse-pouch ... **$5.95**

without pouch ... $4.95

totes

(LEASE SEND ME THE FOLLOWING LADIES "totes" STRETCH BOOTS)

NO. OF PAIRS	SIZE	PRICE

Charge ___
Check/M.O. ___
C.O.D. ___

Add 3% sales tax. Outside Greater Atlanta add 65c shipping, handling 1st item, 10c each additional.

NAME ___
ADDRESS ___
CITY ___
STATE ___ ZIP CODE ___

AT THESE 23 BELK STORES

Passport Scotch advertisement (right)

If you want your friends to visit you on New Year's, send them a Passport.

Passport Scotch is a blend of the finest whiskies Scotland has to offer. So when your friends receive it, and taste it, they'll know you've given the best.

What they won't know is that Passport Scotch is very reasonable. Thinking it's a very expensive Scotch they'll put it away for special occasions.

Then they'll start trying to think of places where they can drink Passport. Naturally, they'll think of your house first.

Passport Scotch.
Imported by Calvert

86 PROOF · 100% BLENDED SCOTCH WHISKY · IMPORTED BY CALVERT DISTILLERS CO., N.Y.C.

Belk

'State Pride' pillow e-x-p-l-o-s-i-o-n

A. Striped cut velvet, wool corner tassels. Zippered. Avocado, red or gold 6.00
B. Corduroy accent pillows with zip-off cover. Kapok-fill. Square, round or knife-edged square. Olive, red, gold ...... 2 for 5.00
C. Kapok-filled rayon and acetate antique satin. Green, crimson, gold. Round or square 3.50
D. Contemporary diamond-textured rayon tweed; rolled edge. Kapok fill. Avocado, red, gold 3.00
E. Kapok-filled rocker set in luscious cotton velveteen. Avocado, red, gold, pumpkin. 7.00
F. Tufted poly-foam filled rocker set in cotton corduroy. Olive, red, gold 7.00
G. 16" square cotton velveteen, edged with matching fringe. Green, red or gold. 3.00
H. Corduroy covered bedrest with zip-off cover; armrest sides with tuckaway pockets. Kapok-filled. Olive, red, gold 11.00
J. Jewel-tone cotton velveteen. Olive, scarlet or gold. Rounds or squares with zippered cover 4.50
With button tufting 5.00
K. Turk's hat pillow with button center. Luxurious cotton velvet in avocado, red or gold. Kapok filling 6.00

AT YOUR NEAREST BELK ... your happy shopping store

Figure 16–14. Single story on a tight page. Note the raw wrap at top right.

FIRST PRESBYTERIAN

Talented Soloist Does Justice to 3600-Pipe Organ

The new 3600-pipe organ of First Presbyterian Church was greeted in the first of several dedication recitals Sunday afternoon, with visiting organist Luigi Tagliavini as the strong and artistically convincing soloist.

The view from the loft is exciting, several open-ribbed wood casings for the imposing array of great and small pipes, the "positive" organ in a tri-arch casing suspended from the ceiling.

On first hearing it is a subtle instrument with a very quick response and a fine balance in

GALLERY AUDITORIUM

Sirens and Court Oaths, All in the Name of Music

By HERMAN TROTTER

It was another experiment in mind-expanding entertainment forms, Saturday evening, as the UB Creative Associates took over the auditorium of Albright-Knox Art Gallery for the latest edition of their "Evenings for New Music."

The most elaborate item was the premiere of visiting Slee Professor Istvan Anhalt's "Foci," presumably the plural of "focus," although one can't be sure these days.

It employed taped and live voices (several languages) and instruments, slides, and lighting effects to delineate its nine sections. To snippets of taped

movement around the hall, reaching a crescendo of pure "happening" and then receding. The text was from "Zettel" by Ludwig Wittgenstein, but it could just as easily have been the Yellow Pages.

* * *

THE HIGHLIGHT for this observer was a lovely, anonymous young thing who sat

KLEINHANS HALL

The Band Blends Country, Rock With Dazzling Versatility

The Band has its roots in layers of hard rock music and rich earthy country melodies, and its hybrid sound plucks the best of both genres.

Its sweet down-home style packed Kleinhans Music Hall Sunday. Usually rock concert crowds are a little more hepped up, a little more noisy and a little more demanding, but these followers seemed to reflect the music they had come to hear.

The Band's music isn't loud. It's balanced with a fine mixture of vocals and instrumentals. Performing these countrified, tight arrangements

Figure 16–15. Alternated heads.

next to each other at the top where two-line heads are alternated with three-line heads, especially when both are set in the same size and typeface. Alternation should be more contrasting.

Boxed Stories Brighten Inside Pages

Pictures invariably brighten inside pages, but they may not be available or they may be too large for the space. Another means of brightening inside pages is boxing one story on a page. (Figure 16–16). Only those stories whose contents are significant should be boxed. Assuming that there usually will be at least one such story per page, it should be boxed with a hairline rule. The size of the box should be at least two columns but preferably three columns wide. The reason is that only a box of sufficient size to be noticed can bring about dominant appearance. The effect of boxing a story is to enhance the appearance of the news portion of the page.

If there is any objection to the boxing process, it usually is that too much production time is taken. The type to be boxed may have to be reset to a narrower measure or a column of news may have to be eliminated to provide the space taken by the box, which is larger than regular column width. When a column of news is eliminated as described previously, the remaining columns will have to be respaced to odd-column measures, a procedure that usually is not appreciated in the back shop because it takes so much time. Yet, the makeup man will have to determine whether he really wants to improve the appearance of inside pages at the cost of extra production time or whether his role is one of forcing news to fit into inside pages regardless of the appearance. Inside pages of most newspapers seem to have been made up with the latter idea in mind.

A final problem relating to boxed stories and improving the appearance of inside pages concerns the practice of not dummying any more than a few large stories on such pages and allowing the makeup to be done by the printer. When this happens the page may show the lack of planning. The printer, plagued by the

Figure 16–16 [OPPOSITE]. Box brightens an inside page. [*Courtesy Lerner Newspapers, Chicago, Illinois.*]

The Art of Editing

the FASHION scene BY VALERIE LONG

New York spring previews result in 10 fashion tips

NEW YORK — The Big Apple is plagued with default worms and is no longer Fun City, but it still is the Fashion City as proved this week at the spring press previews of American designers.

The tight economy has forced designers to sharpen their designing pencils both from a price and liberated fashion point of view.

Designers are giving women a lot of style for their money in addition to giving them sexy clothes that are versatile, wearable, packable and know no season.

Although most women do not "think spring" until after the holidays, designers are shipping spring clothes now and style-savvy women will be on the lookout for certain trends that will update her spring, 1976 wardrobe and give it a look of today.

HERE ARE OUR TEN spring fashion commandments, which we have compiled after viewing hundreds and hundreds of Spring styles.

1. Thow shalt have a tunic ensemble whether its over a daytime dress or evening pajamas.
2. Thou shalt have a drawstring or shirred waist dress, evening gown or pajama.
3. Thou shalt have a dress or pants outfit in spring's most popular fabric, crepe de chine.
4. Thou shalt have a white outfit for spring or summer.
5. Thou shalt have an off-the-shoulder daytime or evening dress.
6. Thou shalt have a jump-suit in crepe de chine, matte jersey or nyesta.
7. Thou shalt have a blouson ensemble.
8. Thou shalt have an outfit in mauve, spring's most popular color.
9. Thou shalt have an evening dress in floating chiffon with a fringed stole or scarf.
10. Thou shalt cut thy hair short for spring, 1976.

WHEN I RETURN FROM covering fashion previews in New York, readers call and ask me three things. What skirt lengths are being shown? What's the new color? What about prices?

Spring skirt lengths are being shown at three inches below the knee but designers are encouraging women to find the length that suits them best. Important colors for spring begin with white, move through vanilla, pale pastels and into grey tones. The favorite beautiful colors are purples, especially mauve. Blues from ice to peacock and greens from Nile to jade were extensively used in the collections.

Red, white and blue is Bicentennially played up, as are bright red costumes. Navy, brown and black appear far more in evening than daytime clothes.

DESIGNERS ARE EXTREMELY price conscious, many holding the line or paring down prices during the economy stalemate. Designer Albert Capraro lit up the fashion world like a skyrocket when Betty Ford, the president's wife, (who is a size 6) chose some of his clothes and revealed his moderate prices. His daytime clothes run under a hundred dollars and his evening crepe de chine jumpsuits sell for $125 and look as fashionable as the haute couture (high fashion) designs that cost five times as much.

There's no doubt about it — style savvy women are demanding and getting more fashion for their money. More next week.

Every holiday a 'turkey' ... if one's unemployed

(Editor's Note: While many families will be sitting down to bountiful feasts next Thursday, to others the Thanksgiving festivities will only magnify their troubles and misfortunes. Lest we forget that many others are not as fortunate as we, a Lerner Newspapers staff writer, who wishes to remain anonymous, is sharing the events that have been happening in her home the past three months.)

(Aug. 20)

ONE WANT AD seeks a person who can write Benedictine script and speak Polish, another a belly dancer, still another a semi driver to run 38 states.

My husband, laid off from his architect job for two weeks now, fills none of these qualifications, but our four eyeballs duly scan every job opening.

How long can it take in the Cradle of the High Rise for another job with a busier firm to come along?

(Aug. 27)

It might take longer than expected. The recession, a topic once scanned in the newspapers and forgotten, has not only knocked at our door but walked right on in.

We have received a 40-pound box of food from my parents in Cleveland. We are surely stocked up beyond anyone's wildest dreams with both Jello and toilet paper.

Savings are another matter. Who has much squirreled away after plunking down the nest egg for a townhouse in Skokie in a marriage six years old with two youngsters?

Cats go on daily half rations. They're too fat anyway, I reason. Unemployment compensation, applied for three weeks ago, remains a stranger to our mailbox.

(Sept. 3)

Have moved all plants out of cats' reach. Also unhitch all toilet paper from bathrooms overnight. Hungry cats are munching up both in spite.

Calls to various creditors aren't that grim, though embarrasing. Am sure they've had a hike in calls asking OKs on $10 monthly payments.

Grumpy, house-bound husband is the worst part. Several dozen calls to architect firms in both Chicago and suburbs confirm the worst: nobody but nobody's hiring.

A neighbor whose husband is a supermarket manager has taken pity and generously brought over three large boxes of Raisin Bran whose tops were ripped off in unpacking. That's at least a month of free breakfasts, I figure, after offer of payment is refused.

(Sept. 10)

Newspapers announce a hotline number for sluggish unemployment checks. It is to be dialed forthwith and, from the other end, more patience is requested.

Husband continues grouchy and the kids are suddenly getting lots of fresh air from early morning escape walks. These are helping me keep awake since I am working extra hours at night.

We figure with my paycheck and unemployment, we should be able to squeak through most of the bills with about $5 to spare each month.

(Sept. 17)

Husband doesn't want his situation known by neighbors and am sure he's thought about carrying briefcase when emptying trash during the day.

Unemployment discovers the problem: husband's previous firm is fighting paying unemployment during the time severance was paid out. Several dozen other men have the same problem, we learn.

It is now six weeks with no unemployment check and nearly zilch in savings. Sunday want ad perusals continue late each Saturday night, mimeographed resumes at the ready.

Wanted are an anesthetist; a humanitarian; a stable hand, even a "slitter" supervisor, whatever the hell that is. Not wanted are architects.

Renewal membership notices for several animal groups are put in the back of the bill pile.

(Sept. 24)

Panic and depression set in. Leash-walking cat goes unwalked. She takes to the silent meow and sitting with nose to door. Five year old begins wetting bed at night.

(Oct. 1)

Early morning kid walks now including afternoons, tri-lingual husband attempting translation work. It keeps him busy, but he remains in the house, calling firms and teeth-gnashingly underfoot.

Grocery shopping becomes more and more depressing. Spending $35 a week for food is not too hard but magnifies awareness of all the women shopping nearby whose husbands are WORKING while mine is not.

Five year old returns home from kindergarten with a drawing of daddy for the first time. Daddy is holding two red apples marked 10 cents each and is reported to be selling them.

Where did my kid hear about the Depression?

(Oct. 8)

We receive two checks from unemployment in the mail. We go beserk with joy. Cats hide. Five year old asks for a new toy car.

(Oct.22)

We wait a week before paying bills, luxuriating in a beefed-up checking account. To celebrate, we pay six months' car insurance instead of by the usual 50-50 plan. Kids get $1.25 monster magazines and cats some Kal Kan.

Want ad perusals continue. They want a dog groomer and a doctor's assistant in nuclear medicine, and one architect firm seeking help wants a picture.

Husband cuts out a monster and sends it with a name-less resume.

(Nov. 5)

Want ads look for a watchspring maker, a black crow and a hot dog stand operator. Occasional resumes are dispatched with loving pats to a few architectural ads. One lone mimeographed regret comes back.

(Nov. 12)

It is now four weeks since last unemployment check. Thanksgiving will definitely be a non-turkey one.

Cats back on half rations and plants moved. Another call to unemployment is made. . .

EDITOR'S NOTE: We just received the news . . . the writer's husband got a job. Happy Thanksgiving!

family living LERNER NEWSPAPERS

MARY LEISTEN WINS GRANT

MARY Leisten, daughter of Mr. and Mrs. William Leisten, 1938 Fargo, won a freshman academic scholarship at Lewis University. A 1975 St. Scholastica High School graduate, Mary Catherine was a member of National Honor Society and Student Council, was Chairwoman of the Big Sister Committee and named an Illinois State Scholar.

LAMPSHADES
All Sizes Materials Colors & Styles
Bring In Your Lamp For Proper Fitting
ILLINOIS LAMP & SHADE CO.
RO 4-7020
2940 W. DEVON

Custom Refinishing to your choice of finishes
MASTERCRAFT REFINISHING Company
3140 W. CHICAGO AVE.
CALL SA 2-5730
Mastercraft Refinishing Co. can actually make your old furniture look like new again and so economically! Your furniture may be refinished in natural grain, various shades of fruitwood, decorator colors, pecan distressed, and ebony. We also refinish pianos like new. Special rates for hotels and offices. We also specialize in upholstery work.

CHANUKAH EVE. NOVEMBER 28th
MENORAHS Largest Selection On Devon
Wishing a HAPPY CHANUKAH to Our Good Friends...
• Dreidlach
• Records
• Decorations
• Books & Games
SCHWARTZ'S
GOODMAN BROS. HEBREW BOOK STORE
2611 DEVON BR 4-0286

Anthony Hair Stylists is NEW
(Formerly Anthony & Justin)
Young, exciting, with all the latest, most up to date Haircuts. Haircare with custom Hair-coloring by Dorothy & Lois. Get acquainted offer on Tuesday and Wednesday.
THERMAL PERMANENTS (Complete) with HAIRCUT $25.00
HAIRCUTS with THERMAL STYLING.......... $12.00
ANTHONY HAIR STYLISTS
3143 W. DEVON AM 2-2501

CARVELL'S TENNIS ACADEMY
HOLIDAY SPECIAL
4 LESSON SESSIONS STARTING DEC. 1st
$35.00 INCLUDES A NEW TENNIS RACKET
RAINBO SPORTS CENTER
4836 No. Clark St. Chicago 60640 275-5500

Community Calendar

YESHIVA WOMEN PLAN DESSERT TEA

YESHIVA Women of the Hebrew Theological College, 7135 N. Carpenter, Skokie, will hold a dessert tea at 12:30 p.m. Wednesday, Nov. 26, at Congregation Chesed L'Avrohom Nachlas David, 3135 Devon.

Ald. Sol Gutstein will speak on "Freedom—Torah's Contribution to American Law."

Program chairperson is Mrs. Colman Ginsparg. Mrs. Mitchell Macks is organization president.

ZIONA HADASSAH PLANS PARTY

ZIONA Hadassah will present a children's theater party for Youth Aliah at 1 p.m. Dec. 7 at Philbin's Little Theater, 2323 Devon. Presentation will be a musical "Beauty and the Beast." For further information, call 465-2839.

BOWLING LEAGUE SEEKS PLAYERS

BEN LEVIN Memorial for Retarded Children has openings for women in its bowling league which bowls at 9:15 p.m. Mondays at Gabby Hartnett's.

For further information, call president Gloria Biondo at 275-5252, or vice president Fran Gardberg at 743-4202.

AREA 2 IN 'PINAFORE'

SOUTH Commons Music Theater presents Gilbert and Sullivans' "Pinafore" at Sauers Restaurant, 311 23rd St.

Performers include Rogers Park area residents Pam Bork, 6631 N. Glenwood, a dancer in the production also doing costumes, and Jim Vandendorpe, 1622 Juneway, also president of the South Commons Music Theater group.

Mrs. Arthur Berman named fund official

MRS. ARTHUR BERMAN has been elected vice president of area development for the Women's Division of the Jewish United Fund at the group's recent annual meeting.

In her new position, Mrs. Berman, of Sherwin Avenue, will help coordinate and broaden the reach of the group's yearly programs of cultural, educational and fund-raising activities.

Mrs. Berman has been active with the Jewish United Fund for a number of years, and served in leadership roles with the group's young people's division before coming on the women's division board.

A partner in the public relations firm of Group One Associates, she is involved in the Illinois Arts Council and the Israel Bonds organization. She has also been active in philanthropic work with Little City.

MRS. ARTHUR BERMAN

Funds raised by the women's division will aid immigrants to Israel from the Soviet Union and other lands with health, welfare and educational programs; meet housing and other needs of immigrants from previous years and maintain operating budgets of Israel's seven universities.

JUF contributions also provide aid to Jews in the Soviet Union, in other Eastern European countries and Moslem lands. They also support the health, welfare and educational agencies of the Jewish Federation of Metropolitan Chicago, which face rising costs and new requirements for service by families, children, young people, the aged and the poor as well as Soviet refugees resettling in Chicago.

DO IT ★ YOURSELF
Rent a Steamex Carpet Cleaner
Call KE 9-6200 to reserve unit.
Chicago's Finest Professional Cleaners
RUBY DRIVE-IN CLEANERS
A Complete Quality Dry Cleaning Service
CORNER

UNDER SUPERVISION OF UNITED KASHRUTH COMMISSION
Shaevitz Kosher Meats & Sausage
2907 W. DEVON AVE. SH 3-9481
We Deliver
Our Meat is U.S.D.A. Choice
OPEN SUNDAYS 8:30 A.M. to 6 P.M.
PICKLED TONGUES 89¢ lb.
CHUCK STEAKS $1.19 lb.
KISHKIE 79¢ lb.
TURKEYS 79¢ lb.
Whole BOOK ROAST $1.49 lb.
TOP RIB $1.39 lb.
Whole or Cut-Up LAMB CHOPS (Shoulders) $1.39 lb.
RIB LAMB CHOPS $1.69 lb.
Whole BRISKETS $1.59 lb.
SHORT RIBS 98¢ lb.
WE MAKE OUR OWN SAUSAGE
SALAMI CHUBS $1.49 lb.
2 lb. CHUNKS BOLOGNA HOT DOGS $1.29 lb.
PASTRAMI $2.29 lb.
CORNED BEEF $3.59 lb.

Thanksgiving Specials
PASTRY TREATS
You will always get the mother-made it flavor in pastries and candies from SCHROEDER'S because we never skimp on time, care or ingredients.

Please Place Your Thanksgiving Orders in Advance
• Mince Pie
• Pumpkin Pie
• Fruit Cake
• Spumoni Rum Cake
• Anise Drops
• Peppernuts
• Cookies (Fancy gift-boxed)
• Salted Nuts
• Stollen
• European Tortes & Pastries
• Milk Chocolate (Ass't Home Made)
• Whipped Cream Cakes
• Strawberry Cheese Torts
SPECIAL CAKE With Thanksgiving Decorations, 8 inch size $3.40
SCHROEDER'S PASTRY SHOP
5635 N. LINCOLN LO 1-2707

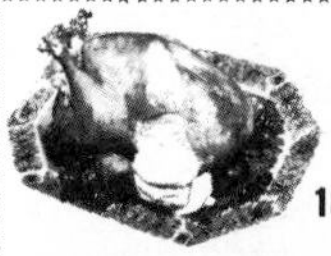

GRADE 'A' COUNTRY'S DELIGHT 18 TO 22 LBS.
TOM TURKEY 38¢ lb.
LIMIT 1
with the purchase of $17.50, excluding turkey, cigarettes and liquor.
OPEN THANKSGIVING DAY 9 A.M. TO 2 P.M.
ALL POULTRY U.S.D.A.
TREASURE ISLAND
6125 N. LINCOLN AVE. (LINCOLN VILLAGE SHOPPING CENTER)
3460 NORTH BROADWAY (PARKING FOR 100 CARS)
5245 NORTH BROADWAY (PARKING FOR 100 CARS)
1639 NORTH WELLS (PLENTY OF FREE PARKING)
2540 W. LAWRENCE (ONE BLOCK WEST OF WESTERN)
COUNTRYSIDE MALL SHOPPING CTR. (PALATINE NORTHWEST HWY. & BALDWIN RD.)
WILMETTE 911 RIDGE ROAD (STORE CLOSED SUNDAY)
Prices Good thru Wed.
We reserve the right to limit quantities.

necessity of speeding up production, usually takes the most traditional route toward finishing the makeup process. In fact, he is discouraged from even attempting new makeup procedures. Therefore, the remainder of such makeup is often less than the best. Even when the makeup editor stands next to the printer and directs him in filling undummied inside pages, the result is apt to look poor. The best technique is to tightly dummy the remaining space in the editorial office and take enough time to make the pages as attractive as possible.

17

Magazine Editing

For six days a week the staff of a metropolitan daily writes, edits, assembles and produces the daily paper. Then on the seventh day the giant emerges, the marvel of American journalism. This mighty tome is crammed with news and news summaries, interpretives and features, sports, business and finance, real estate, comics, classified and display advertising, advertising supplements and magazines.

The Sunday Special

Advertising probably claims 50 to 60 per cent of the Sunday paper's space. News and editorials, including interpretives and columns, may take roughly one fourth of the remaining space and magazine supplements nearly one half.

Unlike its daily counterpart, the Sunday edition has been days or weeks in the making. A closing deadline of four weeks before publication date is not unusual for a four-color rotogravure magazine page. Letterpress supplements may have a closing deadline of about a week.

Supplement sections have to be printed before the final run of the spot news, sports and markets. At one time some metropolitan dailies predated the Sunday edition. That is, they printed the entire Sunday paper in the middle of the week for delivery to outlying areas on Saturday or Sunday. Today, most run-of-press supplements have a one-week deadline. They are printed on the Friday before delivery.

Even with automation and high-speed presses, the production of the big Sunday edition is a week-long process involving the early closing of as many pages as possible. Copy for the Sunday paper bears the Sunday stamp and gets edited along with the regular daily copy. Copy for the supplements bears the name of the supplement and the date.

Locally Edited Magazines

One of the gems of the Sunday paper is the locally edited magazine, especially those printed by rotogravure. These magazines differ from the oldtime Sunday supplement, started shortly after the Civil War, in that they no longer aim to startle and titillate or to concern themselves with the famous and the infamous. Instead, today's magazine seeks to educate as well as to entertain and to portray real people close to the readers.

Although this weekly supplement is an integral part of the newspaper, it is distinctly a magazine. It is built like a magazine and printed like a magazine. It may be identified with its parent newspaper but it has a style and personality of its own.

The Sunday magazine is more carefully designed and edited than the hastily prepared news sections. And because readers tend to judge it as a magazine and not as just another section of the newspaper, the magazine editor is compelled to follow exacting standards of magazine presentation.

Although some newspaper magazines exhibit provincialism in both content and presentation, more are demonstrating that readers in all regions have common interests in topics such as medicine, science, psychiatry, economics, ecology and religion. Almost any topic may be associated in some manner with a particular area.

For example, why would the Denver *Post's Empire Magazine*, which bills itself as the voice of the Rocky Mountain empire, feature a story on the Alaskan oil rush? Because the oil rush in Alaska has some elements in common with the gold rush, a part of the heritage of the mountain states. Also, many of these states are engaged in the exploration and production of oil, especially Colorado, Wyoming and Utah with their oil shale deposits. Anyway, this particular story happened by chance. A free-lance photographer had brought in striking photos he had taken on a trip to the frozen North Slope of Alaska. But without an accompanying story the editor could not use the pictures. Then a professional writer offered a story based on material he had collected in the same area. The result was a well-written and well-illustrated piece for *Empire* readers.

Writing that goes beyond the reach of the routine feature writer and pictures that surpass those shot by a harried news photographer have made the newspaper magazine a favorite with readers. One survey has shown that 59 per cent of the women and 48 per cent of the men read the average inside page of a local magazine section, even topping the readership for a nationally syndicated supplement distributed with the same papers.

Magazine Characteristics

A magazine format does not necessarily make a magazine. Some newspaper executives who have taken over the job of editing a Sunday magazine or an independent magazine fail to produce a good magazine because newspaper techniques differ from magazine techniques. Even display advertising may not be the same in newspapers as it is in magazines.

A magazine differs from a newspaper in many ways, including:

1. A better grade of paper, or stock. The cover paper may be heavier than the paper for inside pages. Different grades and weights of paper may be used for inside pages. Tinted stock may be used.

2. Magazines use more color, not only in illustrations but in type and decorations as well.

3. Illustrations are more dominant in a magazine than in a newspaper. The illustrations may run (or bleed) off the page or extend into the fold.

4. Magazines breathe; they use air or white space to emphasize text and illustrations.

5 Magazines vary typefaces to help depict the mood or tone or pace of the story (Figure 17–1). They use initial capital letters to help readers turn to the message or to break up columns of type (Figure 17–2). They wrap type around illustrations (Figure 17–3).

6. Magazines may use reverse plates (white on black) or use display type over the illustration (overprinting) or use a mortise (portion cut out of a picture) for display headings or even text.

7. Magazines may vary the placement as well as the design of the headline (Figure 17–4).

"The first and singularly most difficult fact for many newspapermen to grasp about a Sunday newspaper magazine is that it is not a newspaper," said Henry Baker, special projects editor for the Fort Myers (Fla.) *News-Press.*

A true Sunday magazine never will carry material that could have run practically anywhere in the paper but just happened to wind up in the magazine.

A (cover story) should be able to pass three tests:

1. Does it feel big? Does it have relevance to the lives of many people, ask a question many people ask, deal with some area of common human experience?

2. Does it feel necessary? Can the reader be told why he should care about it right now? What's so important about it today?

3. Does it feel whole? Does it have a quality of compactness and unity; is it a single, solid thing, not a diffuse cloud?

This third test is largely a problem of focus, the key element to every successful magazine story. Any story that lacks a sharp focus on a theme, an individual or an event will never hold a reader.

Each issue would carry . . . articles of 1,000 to 2,500 words—a cover story and secondary stories. With occasional exceptions, the cover story would be the strongest, most important of the (stories)—a story with a loud ring of urgency about it for everyone in the state.

Secondary story could be of less vital interest and contain more of a (regional) slant.

Subject matter could be anything clean enough to have lying around

---

Magazine Editing   373

Elegance

Set in French Script
with Clearcut initial.

DIGNITY
Set in Forum type.

Antiquity

Satanick

UNUSUALNESS
Newfangle

Fluency

Mandate

Distinctiveness
Civilite

CIRCUS
Playbill

Figure 17–1. Mood typefaces.

A WILD Alaskan wolf yawns broadly as
he lolls in the warm sun of the arctic
spring. Trumpeter swans dabble in a small

There aren't any weekend beer parties
pus. No pep rallies. No homecoming ce
dormitories and no football team.

Figure 17–2. (Top) Two-line sunken initial cap. (Bottom) Upright initial cap.

the family living room—profiles, perspectives on a big newsstory, surveys of what's new in a field, trend stories, narratives, first-person or as-told-to stories, humor, travel, fashion—so long as it passed those

The path of time that
will lead us from today
through the 21st cen-
tury will be lined with
many new mechanical
and electronic marvels,
better energy sources, and
new construction materials and
methods.

Figure 17–3. Wraparound type.

three tests, could be narrowed to a sharp focus and dealt with (area) people, places and things.[1]

Unless an editor is also an artist he cannot hope to produce a superior publication. Magazine editing is essentially a joint endeavor, with the editor providing editorial excellence and the artist creating the visual image.

The Editing Process

Front pages of daily newspapers look distressingly alike. But the magazine comes in a distinctive wrapper or cover that reflects the nature of the publication, stresses a seasonal activity or merely directs readers to the "goodies" inside the magazine.

News, as we have seen, may be presented in many styles, but usually the traditional format of the summarized lead with details in descending order of significance prevails in the news department. In a magazine the space is likewise limited, but the writing style is more relaxed, more narrative and more personal. The pace of the magazine piece may be slower but certainly not less dramatic than the news story. Following is the beginning of a magazine feature:

In Chicago some middle-aged businessmen plan a skiing trip to Colorado. In Miami a middle-aged woman with high blood pressure seeks

[1] "Magazine not just an extension," Gannetteer, March 1976 (P.1 of "Editorially Speaking" section).

working together On the Job

Figure 17–4. Headline designs.

medical advice before leaving for Denver to visit her daughter. In Baltimore a family is cautioned against vacationing in Colorado because one of the children has a lung ailment.

All three of these examples involve a change from low to high altitude, and, owing to air travel, making the change in a relatively short period.

Coupled with exertion, cold temperatures and high altitude, won't the businessmen who have been sedentary for months be risking heart attacks? Won't the visiting mother experience even higher blood pressure? And won't high altitude aggravate the child's illness?

Not until later in the story does the angle that normally would be in the lead of a news story appear:

Contrary to the popular belief that reduced oxygen pressure at high altitude has an adverse effect on the coronary artery system, research indicates high altitude may be beneficial and even afford a degree of protection against coronary artery disease.[2]

So rigid are the style requirements of some magazine editors that they lean heavily on staff writers, use staff writers to reshape free-lance material or buy only from free-lancers who demonstrate they are acquainted with the magazine's requirements. Still, Sunday magazines may get more than half their material from free-lancers, a greater volume than is procured by the news sections.

Free-lance photographers likewise seek out the Sunday magazine market. One magazine editor remarked, "An exciting roto works like a magnet, drawing in talented free-lance contributors you never realized existed."

Article Headings

A newspaper uses illustrations to focus the readers' attention to a page. It relies on the headline to lure readers into the story. But in a magazine the whole page—headline, pictures, placement—is designed to stop the readers in their tracks. They may get part of the story from a big dramatic picture before they ever see the head. It is the combination of elements that must make readers say to themselves, "I wonder what this is all about."

The magazine editor is not confined to a few standardized typefaces for headings. He may select, instead, a face that will help depict the mood of the story. Nor is he required to put the heading over the story. He may place it in the middle, at the bottom or on one side of the page.

The heading may occupy the whole page or only part of a page. It may be accented in a reverse plate or in some other manner. It may be overprinted on the illustration. More often it will be below the illustration rather than above it. Almost invariably it is short, not more than one line. Frequently it is a mere tag or teaser. A subtitle then gives the details:

[2] Gerry Himes, "High altitude can be good," Denver Post *Empire*, p. 10 (March 28, 1976).

The Art of Editing

Oil from the Heart Tree
An exotic plant from Old China produces
a cash crop for the South

I Can HEAR Again!
This was the moment of joy, the rediscovering
heet...

nd

e basic ele-
out a third
white space
izing other

etween text
rately plans
gain extra

ers are told
of text and
ality of the
ure's value,
the reader
dequate but
atic appeal

at least one
le; and (3) a
ical device
ning of the
square fol-

**Magazine
Layouts**

lowed by a few words in all-capital letters. Or it may be an initial capital letter, either an inset initial (its top lined up with
the top of the indented small letter) or an upright or stick-up
initial (the bottom of the initial lined up with the bottom of the
other letters in the line). (See Figure 17–2.)

Simplicity is the keynote in effective page layout. An easy,
modular arrangement is more likely to attract readers than a
tricky makeup with odd-shaped art and a variety of typefaces.

Magazine Editing 377

Illustrations need not be in the same dimensions, but they should be in pleasing geometric proportions. Margins should be uniform or at least give the effect of being uniform. Usually the widest margin is at the bottom of the page, the next widest at the side, the third at the top and the narrowest at the inside or gutter. The content of the page is thus shoved slightly upward, emphasizing the eye level or optical center of a rectangle. The outside margin is larger than the gutter because the latter, in effect, is a double margin.

Kenneth B. Butler, author of a series of practical handbooks (published by Butler Typo-Design Research Center in Mendota, Ill.) treating the creative phases of magazine typography and layout, advises layout editors to touch each margin at least once, regardless of whether illustrations are used. He contends that the eye is so accustomed to the regular margin that even where the margin is touched only once, an imaginary margin is immediately formed by this treatment. If the illustration bleeds off the page, the margin on the bleed side may be widened to give more impact to the bleed device.

The art director must know the position of the page—whether left, right or double spread—and whether the page contains advertising. It would also help him if he knew the content and appearance of the advertising on the page to avoid embarrassing juxtapositon. If he is working on a one-page layout he should know the content and appearance of the facing page.

He tries to visualize what the page is supposed to say. From experience he has developed a feel for the magazine page, knowing in his mind's eye how it will look. The beginner may have to use trial and error to find an appropriate design. He may, for example, cut out pieces from construction paper to represent the black blocks, then juggle these blocks until he gets a usable design.

Layout is a means rather than an end in itself. If the reader becomes aware of the layout the chances are the layout is bad.

One danger most art directors seek to avoid is cluttering. This occurs when too many illustrations are attempted on the same page, when the pages are crowded because of lack of spacing or uneven spacing or when too many elements—dingbats, subtitles, boldface type—make the page appear busy. The primary goals of layout are to catch and direct the reader's attention and to make the pages easy to read.

Copy Fitting

Widths of magazine columns may vary with the number, shape and size of the ads or the size and shape of the illustrations. It is not unusual for a magazine story to be strung over four pages in four different widths. The editor must be able to estimate whether the story will fill despite these type changes.

The most accurate method of determining copy length is by

counting characters in the manuscript. The following steps are used:

Count the number of typewritten characters, including spaces between words and for indentions, in an average line of the manuscript. An average line can be determined visually or it can be measured by placing a ruler over most of the line endings and drawing a line down these endings.

Multiply the number of lines of copy by the number of characters to the average typewritten line. A line extending half the width of the line is counted as a full line.

Consult a type book to determine the characters per pica in a given body size and typeface. For example, Bodoni Book in Linotype in 10-point size gives 2.75 characters per pica. If the type line is to be 20 picas wide, then 55 typewritten characters will fill one line of type.

Divide the number of lines of type by the number of type lines per column inch. If the type is set in 10 point with 2-point spacing, the number of type lines per column inch is determined by dividing 72 by 12. This will show the number of column inches the manuscript will occupy.

The same figure can be obtained by multiplying the number of type lines by the point size (including leading or spacing between lines) of the typeface, then dividing the total points by 72 to find column inches. To convert into pica depth, the point total is divided by 12 (points per pica) rather than by 72.

For fitting copy into a specified space, the method can be used in reverse. Suppose the space to be filled is 6 inches deep and 24 picas wide. The type is to be 12 point. The type chart shows 2.45 characters per pica or 59 characters to the 24-pica line. Twelve-point type set 6 inches deep requires 36 type lines. Multiplying 59 by 36 gives 2,124 characters. If the manuscript lines average 65 characters, then 32 lines of the manuscript will be needed.

A simpler method can be used. Set the typewriter stops at 59 characters and retype 36 lines of the manuscript. Some editors used ruled sheets so that for a given typeface, size and measure the copy can be sent to the printer typed with the proper number of characters to the line. The proof will run practically line for line with the copy.

Placement of Advertising

The usual newspaper practice is to pyramid the ads on the right of the page. In a magazine the ads generally go on the outside of the pages or may appear on both outside and inside, leaving the *well* for editorial copy. The ads need not restrict editorial display, especially if the well is on a double spread.

On magazines where the advertising manager makes up the dummy of ad placement, there is a give and take between ad manager and editor. The editor may want to start a story in a certain part of the magazine, but there is a two-column ad on the most likely page. The editor then asks the ad manager if the ad can be moved to another page where perhaps another story can end.

Scheduling and Dummying

No story, heading or picture will leave the editor's desk until it has been properly slugged and scheduled. Sluglines relay information such as name of publication, the date the story is to be used, story identification and the number of the page on which the story is to appear. Other instructions placed on the copy may include the set (width of type line in picas), body type size and typographic indicators such as initial capitals or italics.

The headline copy likewise carries all the information needed for the desired style, size and set and a line to match the headline with the story.

Illustrations contain special instructions for the roto cameraman for effects such as cropping and mortising. Usually the photos are numbered consecutively through a story and also carry the number of the page on which the photo is to appear.

The schedule is simply a record to remind the editor of the copy that has been edited and sent on for processing. An important item in the schedule is a line showing the date and time the material was delivered to roto (Figure 17–5).

As he starts to plan for an edition, the editor first obtains a schedule for the issue, showing the pages on which ads have been dummied and whether the ads are in monotone, duotone or full-color. This schedule then tells the editor how much space he has available and the likely color positions. If the editor has control of the ad dummy he simply receives a schedule of the ads or he may receive ad proofs.

Closing deadlines regulate the priority of editing. A story may start toward the end of a run of monotone but spill over to a four-color page. This means the story will have to make the earlier deadline of the four-color pages rather than the later deadline of the monotone pages (Figure 17–6).

Imposition

This would suggest that the editor should know something about imposition, or the arrangement of pages for binding. This means the way the pages are positioned on the imposing stone or on the reproduction proof and not the way they will appear on the printed sheet. The printer can give the editor the imposition pattern or the editor can diagram the imposition himself provided he knows whether pages in the form are upright or oblong.

For a 16-page form, upright and printed work and turn, the editor makes three right-angle folds and numbers the pages. This will show page 1 opposite page 8, 16 opposite 9, 13 opposite 12, 4 opposite 5. The remaining eight pages will be in this order— 7 and 2, 10 and 15, 11 and 14, 6 and 3. For an oblong form, printed

EMPIRE MAGAZINE   ISSUE _July 27_ _____ PAGES _____

FORM	PAGE	SLUG	TO ROTO	TIME
	1	COVER	7-3	
	2	POST TIME-LETTERS		
	3	FRITO PG 4/C		
	4	CAROUSEL	7-7	3⁰⁰
	5	MAY CO.		
	6	TOSHI	7-7	2⁰⁰
	7	"	7-7	2⁰⁰
	8	GHOST	7-8	9⁰⁰
	9		7-8	9⁰⁰
	10	MAGEE PG 4/C		
	11	MAGEE PG 4/C		
	12	GHOST	7-8	9⁰⁰
	13	SLEEP PG. 4/C		
	14	LOMBARDI "	7-7	2⁰⁰
	15	HOMESTEAD PG 4/C		
32	16	DIGEST	7-7	3⁰⁰
33	17		7-7	3⁰⁰
34	18		7-7	3⁰⁰
35	19		7-7	3⁰⁰
36	20	DENVER DRY 20-32		
37	21			
38	22		7-8	8⁰⁰
39	23		7-8	8⁰⁰
40	24	HOUSE DOC	7-3	2³⁰
41	25	"	7-7	2⁰⁰
42	26	LIBRARY	7-7	2⁰⁰
43	27	"	7-7	2⁰⁰
44	28	FOOD	7-3	2⁰⁰
45	29	FOOD	7-3	2⁰⁰
46	30	JOHN	7-11	9⁰⁰
47	31			
48	32			
49	33	DIGEST	7-8	2⁰⁰
50	34	MOUSE	7-8	2⁰⁰
51	35	"	7-8	2⁰⁰
52	36	MAY CO PG 4/C		
53	37	MAY CO PG 4/C		
54	38	DANCERS	7-8	2⁰⁰
55	39	"	7-8	2⁰⁰
56	40			
57	41			
58	42			
59	43			
60	44			
61	45			
62	46			
63	47			
64	48			

Figure 17–5. A Sunday magazine schedule.

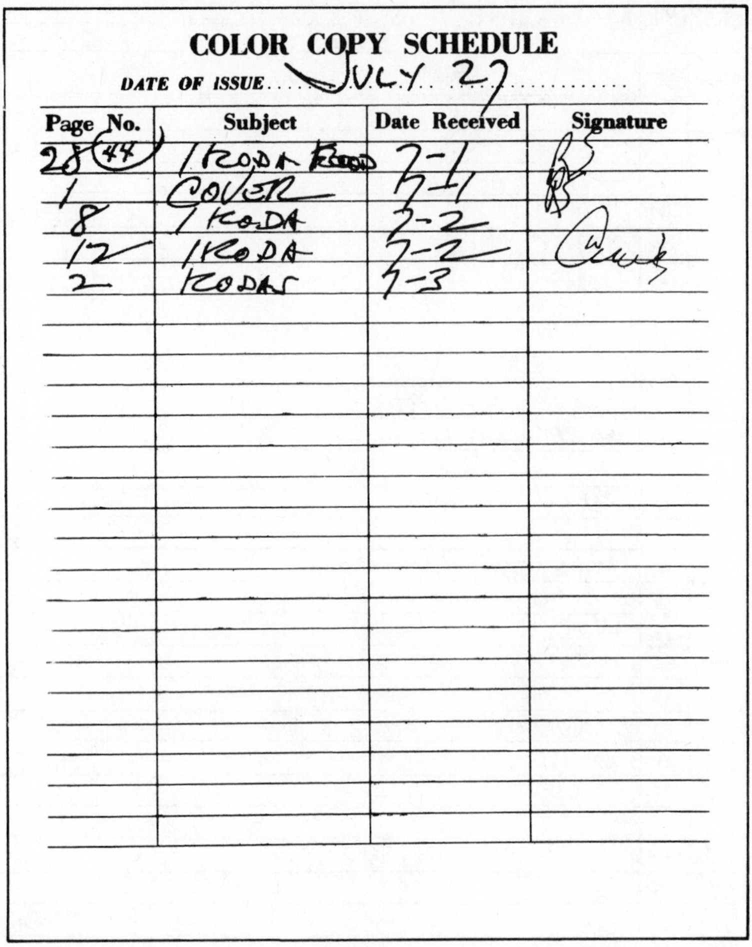

Figure 17–6. A color schedule for a Sunday magazine.

work and turn, the pattern is 1 and 16, 4 and 13, 5 and 12, 8 and 9, 15 and 2, 14 and 3, 11 and 6, 10 and 7. Again, the editor may make his own pattern by making three parallel or accordion folds and one right-angle fold. Or he may use the following formula: the size of the book, plus one page. Thus, in a 32-page section, page 4 is opposite 29 $(33 - 4)$ (Figure 17–7).

If the editor has a spread story, he tries to get the pages on the fewest forms possible to avoid tying up too many forms with one story. Knowing imposition also can help guide him in using color. If one page in a four-page form is in full color, four forms will be needed, one each for red, yellow, blue and black. The other three pages on the same form can accommodate color with little added expense.

Page layout usually starts with the preparation of a thumbnail or miniature dummy. The rough sketch shows pages blocked off in rectangles of facing pages (Figure 17–8).

The thumbnail dummy serves as the artist's working plan. It

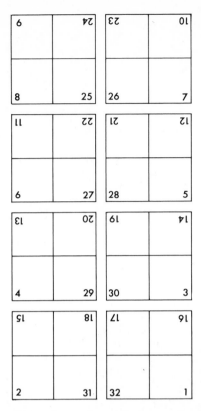

Figure 17-7. Imposition pattern for a 32-page section in 4-page forms. The pattern is obtained by gathering four quarter-sheets and making two right-angle folds. The facing pages total 33 (pages in the section plus one).

gives him the first image of the total publication. Using the thumbnail as a guide, the artist is ready to sketch the layout on full-sized sheets (Figures 17-9a, 17-9b, 17-9c).

First he receives proofs on newsprint for copy checking and correction. These are returned to the composing room for changes. Then the art director receives corrected proofs on slick paper, which he uses for the pasteup. All the elements in the pasteup are arranged precisely as they will appear in print. In a sense, the art director assumes the function of makeup editor and in arranging the proved material on the page makes sure flaws in magazine makeup are avoided. Among such flaws are leaving a widow or lone word at the top of the column, placing subheads near the feet of the columns or in parallel positions in columns or having the last line on the right-hand page of a continued story end with a period.

When the pasteup is completed it goes to the makeup department where a negative of the page materials is stripped in. Generally the art director insists on inspecting page proofs to be sure his makeup pattern has been followed.

Magazine Editing

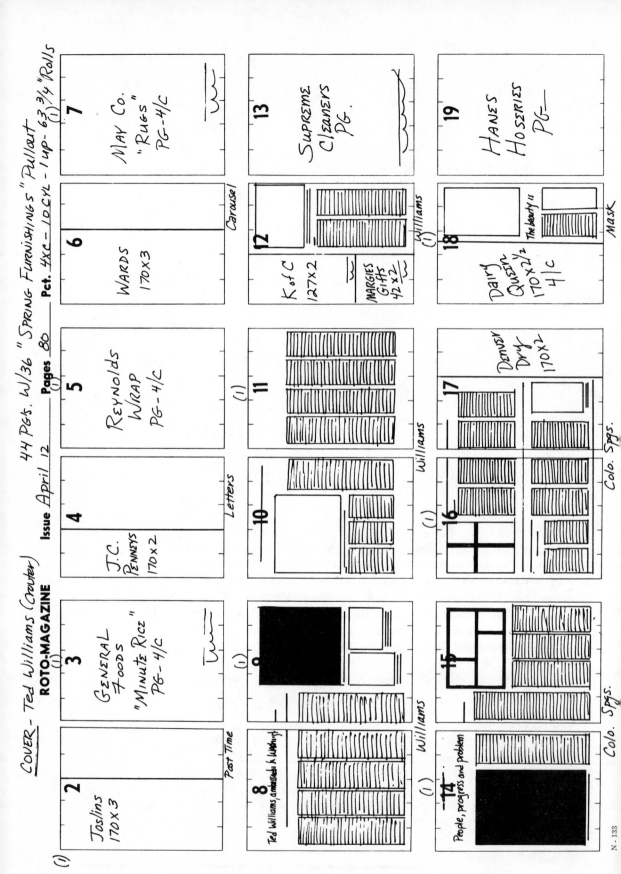

COVER – Ted Williams (Crouter) 44 Pgs. W/36 "Spring Furnishings "Pullout

ROTO-MAGAZINE   Issue April 12   Pages 80   Pct. 4xc – 10 cyl – 1 up – 63¾" Rolls

384

N – 133

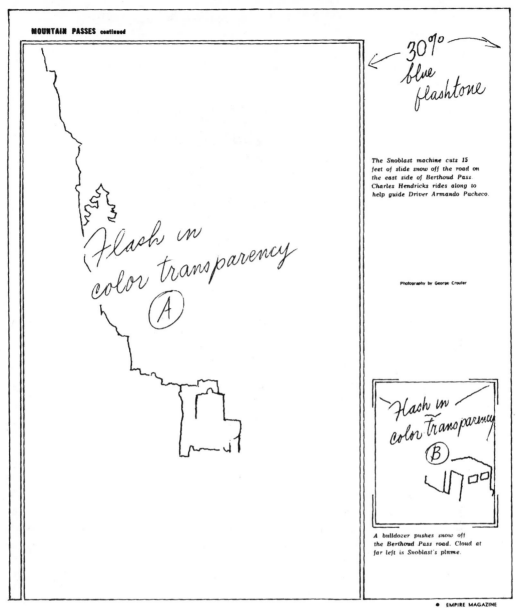

MOUNTAIN PASSES continued

30°% blue flashtone

Flash in color transparency Ⓐ

The Snoblast machine cuts 15 feet of slide snow off the road on the east side of Berthoud Pass. Charles Hendricks rides along to help guide Driver Armando Pacheco.

Photography by George Crouter

Flash in color Transparency Ⓑ

A bulldozer pushes snow off the Berthoud Pass road. Cloud at far left is Snoblast's plume.

● EMPIRE MAGAZINE

Figure 17–9a. Completed paste-up is ready for the roto cameraman. Note the instructions for flashing-in unattached photographs and for line and tone work, created for double-exposing the negative or positive.

On some magazines the editors receive duplicate sets of corrected proofs. One set is used to check further for errors; the other is used in a pasteup. Galley proofs used for this pasteup bear numbers on each paragraph corresponding with the galley number. This helps the makeup worker in the printing department locate the proper galley.

Figure 17–8 [OPPOSITE]. A sample of the thumbnail dummy roughing out the first pages of a 48-page magazine.

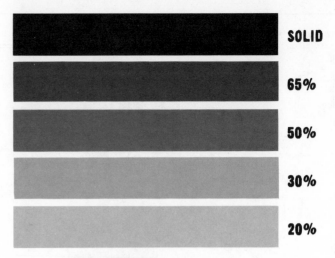

SOLID

65%

50%

30%

20%

FLASH TONES

Figure 17–9b.

Magazine Production

A magazine editor relies on an artist to help him attain editorial excellence. By the same token, he relies on a production expert, usually a printer, to help him produce the best possible publication within his budget.

The editor is responsible for providing the printer with complete specifications of the magazine, not only the size of the publication, the number of pages and the press run but the use and placement of color, the number and size of the illustrations, the type area, size of type and any items that will require special handling.

The editor can save money, and make his printer happy, by giving clear and adequate instructions, presenting clean copy, editing the copy thoroughly rather than making changes in proofs, reading and returning promptly all proofs, meeting copy deadlines and giving the printer time to do good-quality work.

Stock

An editor should have some acquaintance with the elementary principles of production. In addition to imposition there are two other key elements—stock and composition.

Paper comes in various sizes, weights and textures. Use of the stock and its appearance determine the class of paper used. One grade may be used for the cover, another for inside pages. One grade may be preferred for color, another if the pages are in black and white. Almost any grade of paper can be used in letterpress if halftones are not required. In offset printing the grade must be designed to accommodate moisture and other problems peculiar to offset printing. In roto printing the selection is de-

PAGE 9 (29) Roto-Mag Issue AVIATION Paste-up_____ Form No._____ Due at Plant_____

SLUG _____ Monotone _____ 4-Color _____ 2-Color _____

world

pleasure of it when I'm on the ground. And there is a cute little farm set, complete with the farmhouse, barn and outbuildings, a mirror for a pond and a nice assortment of animals. There's the farmer's truck and tractor, and look, he drives a school bus, too. He has plowed his fields, and the pasture land is starting to green up. The ground shows through in spots, like a carpet that is wearing out.

Here comes a train winding through the hills of a toy display in a department store. Will that little car on the road around the bend stop in time? Yes, the crossing gate is going down. At a little country airport a wee plane, like ours, is landing, and there's another one approaching in back of him—much too close. That second plane should have waited just a little longer, but it's all right now; they've both landed safely.

There's so much to oversee from up here. I just can't do everything at once. Now look at that factory belching reddish-brown smoke into the air. The sky ahead is completely filled with this ominous cloud. We'll have to do something about that. That has no place in this sparkling world of mine.

A lovely lake is nestled in the hills with some sailboats skimming over it, their wakes trailing through the water like knives cutting through the frosting on a cake. And back in that sheltered inlet is a fisherman, perhaps with a load of microscopic fish. Where have I seen that campground before, with the tents scattered through the woods where the little creek tumbles into the lake? Why, I know, that's the model Indian village we made for a display in grade school.

This miniature world of mine has everything you could possibly want. Wouldn't it be a delight to go down there and live? Back on earth again, the vantage point will be lower, but may I keep these pictures in my mind, and may I keep this joy in my heart.

Orin A. Seah

There's really no place in my personal kingdom for an ominous cloud. But that'll change soon.

Les Southern

There's a cute little farm set, complete with farmhouse and barn, and a mirror for a pond.

The Denver Post ●

9

Figure 17–19c. Full-sized page layout.

termined by the paper's ability to absorb the large amount of ink required in that process.

The magazine editor is concerned with only three of the many classifications of stock—newsprint, book and cover. Newsprint does not necessarily mean cheap paper. A good grade of newsprint takes halftones up to 85-line screen and in roto up to 150-screen. It is adequate for run-of-press color and ideal for full-color roto work.

The surface smoothness of book paper is determined by the degree of calendering or smoothing during the paper-making process. Antique or eggshell has a minimum of calendering—hence its resemblance to paper used in the early days of printing. More extensive calendering is used on machine finish, giving a smoother surface. English finish, next in the degree of calendering, is used primarily in letterpress. Supercalendered paper has the slickest surface of the uncoated book stocks.

Coating is a supplementary process giving the paper a surface suitable for fine-screened halftones. Coated finishes range from dull-coated, which is smooth but not glossy, to grades of glossy-coated, usually called enamel finish.

Paper weight is calculated on the basis* size of a ream (500 sheets) of a particular paper. For book paper, the basis size is 25×38 inches. Fifty-pound book paper is the weight of a ream of book paper in a sheet size of 25×38 inches. Sheet stock can be ordered in many sizes other than 25×38 inches. For web presses, stock is ordered by the roll. However the paper is packaged, the basic weight prevails.

For example: a booklet is 6×9 inches, 48 pages of 40-pound paper and a run of 25,000 copies: $\frac{25 \times 38}{6 \times 9} = 16 \times 2$ (both sides of sheet) $= 32 \times 500 = 16{,}000$ pages in one ream. That makes $48 \times 25{,}000 = \frac{240{,}000}{16{,}000} = 75$ reams; $75 \times 40 = 3{,}000$ pounds of paper.

The basis size of newsprint is 24×36. Most newsprint is 32 pounds basic weight. Some magazines use the same weight of paper on the cover as used on inside pages. Heavier cover stock may call for a different basis size, usually 20×26 inches.

The different weights of basic sheet sizes may cause confusion. The basic sheet size for bond paper, for instance, is 17×22 inches. But 20-pound bond is not the equivalent of 20-pound book paper. Each sheet of 20-pound bond would be the equivalent of approximately 50-pound book because of the differences in the basic sheet sizes.

An editor who intends to bleed pages of a magazine may run into a higher paper cost because trimming is needed on pages that bleed.

---

* This term generally is used in describing paper sizes and weights. The word may be interchanged with *basic.*

Composition

The editor need not know the cost basis of composition (the setting of type). The editor should realize, however, that straight matter can be composed more quickly and more economically than lines of small capitals, numbered lines, various indentions (See Figure 17–3) and initial capital letters.

Other Cost Items

Press-run costs reflect the time required to print the job. Here the printing process can determine the speed of the press run. Rotogravure is the fastest, then offset and finally letterpress. But gravure printing is limited to plants with roto presses and generally is more expensive than the other processes. Letterpress and offset costs differ primarily according to the number of illustrations used, with offset the cheaper when the ratio of illustrations to type is high and when the press run is higher.

The cost of ink depends on the total amount needed and this varies with the grade of paper, the printing process and other things Tint blocks and zinc etchings, for example, require extra ink. Cost of color ink includes, in addition to the ink itself, the cost of washing up rollers and fountains. If color is applied by sizing or by metallic powders, printers may charge the equivalent of two extra colors.

Printing in color entails the separation of the colors as well as plates or negatives for each color and an additional expense in makeup and press work.

18

Broadcast News Editing

Most of the techniques suggested for the presentation of news in newspapers apply as well to news by radio and television. Those responsible for news copy for any medium must have good news judgment, a feeling for an audience and the ability to handle the language.

Broadcast news differs from other news types in two major respects. Broadcasting must aim at the majority audience and cannot, as newspapers can, serve the interests of the minority. And because enough items must be packed into the newscast to give listeners and viewers the feeling they are getting a summary of the big and significant news of the moment, condensation is required.

A newspaper offers its readers a 1,000-word story, then lets the readers decide how much of the story, if any, they want to read. The broadcast audience has no such choice. If too much time is given to items in which listeners and viewers have only a mild interest, they can turn the dial.

Following are wire service accounts of the same story, one intended for the newspaper members, the other for radio and television stations:

MASSENA, N.Y. (AP)—Unarmed Canadian police scuffled with some 100 Mohawk Indians today and broke an Indian blockade of the international bridge that goes through Mohawk territory in linking the United States and Canada.

The Indians put up the human and automobile blockade after Canadian government officials refused to stop levying customs duties on Indians—duties the Indians say are illegal under the Jay Treaty of 1794.

The Indians had brought 25 automobiles into line at the center of the bridge linking the United States and Canada, and Indian women had thrown themselves in front of police tow trucks to hinder the clearing of the roadway.

There were no reports of serious injury. Forty-eight Indians were arrested—including most leaders of the protest—and taken into Canadian custody by police on Cornwall Island.

A spokesman for the Indians called for the other five nations of the Iroquois Confederacy to join the protest Thursday.

Figure 18–1a. Newsroom of a network-affiliated television station. [*Courtesy KMGH-TV, Denver.*]

Figure 18–1b. Assignment desk for a television news operation. The editor's telephone is a direct line to a radio station newsroom. Another telephone is used for emergency messages and a third connects with the station's mobile units. The panel in the background monitors police and fire calls. [*Courtesy KMGH-TV, Denver.*]

The Indians went on the blockade warpath after the Canadian government refused Tuesday to stop customs duties on Indians who live on the St. Regis Reservation, that includes parts of the United States and Canada.

Scattered fighting and shoving broke out among the Mohawks and police when officers tried to move in to clear away the automobile blockade. One automobile and two school buses were allowed over the international span around noon.

At least 50 words of this story might be trimmed by a copyeditor to make the story tighter and to eliminate the repetition. The story was pared to about 70 words for the radio wire round-up item:

(MASSENA, NEW YORK)—UNARMED CANADIAN POLICE HAVE ARRESTED 48 MOHAWK INDIANS. THE INDIANS HAD FORMED A HUMAN WALL AND BLOCKED THE INTERNATIONAL BRIDGE LINKING CANADA AND THE UNITED STATES NEAR MASSENA, NEW YORK, TODAY.

THE MOHAWKS ARE UP IN ARMS ABOUT CANADA'S INSISTENCE ON COLLECTING CUSTOMS DUTIES FROM INDIANS TRAVELING TO AND FROM THEIR RESERVATION ON THE BRIDGE. THEY SAY IT'S A VIOLATION OF THE 1794 JAY TREATY.

As an item in the news summary, it was cut even more:

FORTY-EIGHT INDIANS HAVE BEEN ARRESTED BY CANADIAN POLICE NEAR THE NEW YORK STATE BORDER. THE INDIANS BLOCKED THE BRIDGE, WHICH LINKS THE U-S AND CANADA. THEY CLAIM VIOLATION OF A 1794 TREATY. THE MOHAWKS SAY THEY PLAN NO BLOCKADE TOMORROW.

News is written and edited so that readers will have no trouble reading and understanding the item. Broadcast news has to be written so it can be read fluently by a reporter and so that it sounds right to the listeners. Broadcast news style must be so simple that listeners can grasp its meaning immediately. The language must be such that even casual listeners will feel compelled to give the story their full attention.

A reader's eyes may on occasion deceive him but not to the extent that the listener's ears deceive him. If the reader misses a point while reading he can go over the material again. If he loses a point in listening to news, he has lost it completely. All radio-television news manuals caution against clauses, especially those at the beginning of a sentence and those that separate subject and predicate. The AP Radio-Television News *Stylebook* uses this example: "American Legion Commander John Smith, son of Senator Tom Smith, died today." Many listeners will be left with the impression that Senator Tom Smith died.

The broadcast message is warm and intimate, yet not flippant or crude. The tone is more personal than that of the newspaper story. It suggests, "Here, Mr. Doe, is an item that should interest you."

The refreshing, conversational style of broadcast news writing has many virtues that might be studied by all news writers. The old International News Service was so adept at this style of presentation that a single wire served both newspaper and radio clients. Radio writing emphasizes plain talk. The newspaper reporter may want to echo a speaker's words, even in an indirect quote: "The city manager said his plan will effect a cost reduction at the local government level." Broadcast style calls for nickel words: "The city manager said his plan will save money for the city."

The newspaper headline is intended to capture the attention and interest of news readers. The lead on the broadcast news story has the same function. First, then, a capsule of the news item, then the details:

THE F-B-I SAYS THERE WAS AN OVER-ALL 19 PER CENT CRIME RATE INCREASE THE FIRST MONTHS OF THIS YEAR. AND THE CRIME WHICH INCREASED THE MOST WAS PURSE-SNATCHING —UP 42 PER CENT. . . .

THE NEW YORK STOCK MARKET TOOK A SHARP LOSS AFTER BACKING AWAY FROM AN EARLY RISE. TRADING WAS ACTIVE. VOLUME WAS 15 (M) MILLION 950-THOUSAND SHARES COMPARED WITH 16 (M) MILLION 740-THOUSAND FRIDAY. . . .

The newscast is arranged so that the items fall into a unified pattern. This may be accomplished by placing related items together or by using transitions that help listeners shift gears. Such transitions are made with ideas and skillful organization of facts and not with crutch words or phrases. Said UPI,

Figure 18–2. A television station news producer goes over a news service ratio wire. At his right is a news service picture receiver. [*Courtesy KMGH-TV, Denver.*]

"Perhaps the most overworked words in radio copy are MEAN-WHILE, MEANTIME and INCIDENTALLY. Forget them, especially 'incidentally.' If something is only 'incidental' it has no place in a tight newscast."

Broadcast copy talks. It uses contractions and, if necessary, fragmentary sentences. It avoids harsh, shrill or hissing sounds such as those produced in combinations like "Sing a song of sixpence." It dodges rhyming words that produce a singsong effect when spoken: "The boat passed the light on its way to Wight."

The present tense, when appropriate, or the present perfect tense is used in the broadcast message to create immediacy and freshness and to eliminate repetition of "today." Example:

AN AWESOME WINTER STORM HAS BLANKETED THE ATLAN-TIC SEABOARD—FROM VIRGINIA TO MAINE—WITH UP TO 20 INCHES OF SNOW. GALE FORCE WINDS HAVE PILED UP SIX-FOOT DRIFTS IN VIRGINIA, BRINGING TRAFFIC THERE AND IN WEST VIRGINIA TO A VIRTUAL HALT. SCHOOLS IN SIX STATES HAVE BEEN CLOSED.

TRAINS AND BUSES ARE RUNNING HOURS LATE. PENN-SYLVANIA AND MASSACHUSETTS HAVE CALLED OUT HUGE SNOW-CLEARING FORCES.

Copy Sources

Copy for the broadcast newsroom comes from the wires of a news-gathering association and from local reporters. The news agencies deliver the news package in these forms:

1. Spot summary, a one-sentence item:

(DENVER)—F-B-I sharpshooters have shot and killed a gunman who killed two hostages aboard a private plane at Stapleton International Airport in Denver.

2. Five-minute summary:

(DENVER)—F-B-I agents fatally shot a gunman early today as he boarded an airline jet at Denver Airport which he thought was to fly him to Mexico. The F-B-I said the gunman had his two hostages with him at the time of the shooting. He had held them on a small private plane for seven hours. Before he left the first plane, the gunman had told authorities over the radio "I'll tell you what. I'm still gonna have this gun right up the back of his (the hostage's) head, and it's gonna be cocked, and if anybody even budges me, it's gonna go off, you know that."
—DASH—

The chief of the Denver office of the F-B-I, Ted Rosack, said 31-year-old Roger Lyle Lentz, was killed shortly after midnight, ending an episode that began in Grand Island, Nebraska, and included two separate flights over Colorado aboard the commandeered private plane. Neither hostage was injured.

3. Takeout. This is a detailed, datelined dispatch concerning one subject or event.

4. Spotlights and vignettes. Both are detailed accounts, the latter usually in the form of a feature.

5. Flash. This is seldom used and is restricted to news of the utmost urgency. A flash has no dateline or logotype and is limited to one or two lines. It is intended to alert the editor and is not intended to be broadcast. The flash is followed immediately by a bulletin intended for airing.

6. Bulletin. Like the flash, it contains only one or two lines. A one-line bulletin is followed immediately by a standard bulletin giving details.

7. Double-spacers. This indicates a high-priority story but not as urgent as a bulletin. The double-spacing makes the item stand out on the wire and calls the item to the attention of news editors:

HOSTAGES (TOPS)
(DENVER)—AN F-B-I SPOKESMAN SAYS A GUNMAN WAS SHOT TO DEATH AFTER HE SEIZED A PRIVATE PLANE IN NEBRASKA, ORDERED THE PILOT TO FLY TO DENVER AND HELD TWO HOSTAGES FOR SEVEN HOURS. F-B-I SPOKESMAN TED ROSACK SAYS THE GUNMAN, 30-YEAR-OLD ROGER LENTZ OF GRAND ISLAND, NEBRASKA, WAS SHOT AND KILLED IN AN EXCHANGE OF GUNFIRE WITH F-B-I AGENTS ABOARD A CONVAIR 990 AT STAPLETON INTERNATIONAL AIRPORT.
ROSACK SAYS THE HOSTAGES WERE NOT HURT.

8. Special slugs—These include AVAILABLE IMMEDIATELY (corresponds to the budget on the news wire), NEW TOP, WITH (or SIDE BAR), SPORTS, WOMEN, FARM, WEATHER, BUSINESS, CHANGE OF PACE, PRONUNCIATION GUIDE, EDITORS NOTE, ADVANCE, KILL, CORRECTION, SUBS (OR SUBS PREVIOUS).

On some local stations the news is broadcast in the form it is received from the news agency. This may suggest that an announcer dashes into the newsroom, rips the latest summary off the machine and goes on the air with it. This may have been true in the early days and on the smaller stations. The practice is becoming increasingly rare because news has commercial as well as public service value. Furthermore, the many typographical errors in wire copy force the reporter to preread and edit for errors. Here is a fairly typical example:

A U-S DEPARTMENT OF AGRICULTURE OFFICIAL SAYS IN DENVER HE FEELS INSPECTION REPORTS OF COLORADO MEAT-PLANTING PACKS HAVE BEEN ACCURATE.

How about "packing plants"?

Most broadcast news today is handled by trained reporters who know how to tailor the news for a specific audience. This is done by "tacking up" items from several roundups and double-spacers to create the desired format. Increasingly, nearly all wire copy is rewritten before it is assembled for broadcast, giving the listener some variety in items that may be repeated several times during the broadcast period.

Some radio and television stations subscribe to the national newswire of a wire service as well as to the radio newswire. This gives an editor an opportunity to decide for himself what details to include. It also provides a greater number and variety of stories.

Preparation of Copy

All copy should be written double-spaced, preferably triple-spaced. Copy should be easier to read in capital and lower case than in all caps but because reporters are used to reading all-cap wire copy, some prefer the all-cap style. If a letter correction is to be made in a word, the word should be scratched out and the correct word substituted in printed letters. If word changes are made within sentences, the editor should read aloud the edited version to make sure the revised form sounds right. If the copy requires excessive editing it should be retyped before it is submitted to a narrator.

The type line in news copy averages 10 words a line. This makes it easy for the news editor to gauge the reading time of the item. A reporter's normal reading rate is 150 to 175 words a minute.

All editing of broadcast copy is done with the newscaster in mind. If a sentence breaks over from one page to another, the reporter will stumble. No hyphens should be used to break words from one line to the next.

Some news editors prefer to put each story on a separate sheet. This enables them to rearrange the items or to delete an item entirely if time runs short. A few briefs tacked near the end of the newscast help the reporter fill his allotted time.

Most reporters need pronunciation aids. A reporter can distinguish between *desert* and *dessert* but before the microphone he could easily falter over the phrase "his just deserts." The copyeditor can help him by adding phonetic spelling after the word ("dih-zurt'") or the reporter himself may underline the word or indicate the pronunciation.

Supplying the proper pronunciation, especially of regional place names, is part of the editing job. Words pronounced one way in one region may be pronounced differently in another. The Florida river in Colorado, for example, is pronounced "floor-ee'-duh." The Arkansas ("ar-kan-saw") river in Colorado is transformed into "Ar-kan'-sas" by the mere fact of flowing over the state line. Many Spanish place names have acquired a corrupted regional pronunciation: Monte Vista ("Mawn-tuh-vihs'-tuh.") The editors' and announcers' key is a state pronunciation guide.

The wire services provide a pronunciation list of foreign words and names appearing in the day's report. The guide is given in phonetic spelling (Gabon—Gaboon') or by indicating the rhyme

(Blough—rhymes with how; Likelike Highway—rhymes with leaky-leaky).

Phonetic Spelling System Used by Wire Services

A—like the "a" in cat
AH—like the "a" in arm
AW—like the "a" in talk
AY—like the "a" in ace
EE—like the "ee" in feel
EH—like the "ai" in air
EW—like the "ew" in few
IGH—like the "i" in time
IH—like the "i" in tin
OH—like the "o" in go
OO—like the "oo" in pool

OW—like the "ow" in cow
U—like the "u" in put
UH—like the "u" in but
K—like the "c" in cat
KH—gutteral
S—like the "c" in cease
Z—like the "s" in disease
ZH—like the "g" in rouge
J—like the "g" in George
SH—like the "ch" in machine
CH—like the "ch" in catch

Broadcast Style

No abbreviations should be used in radio-television news copy with these exceptions: **Abbreviations**

1. Common usage: Dr. Smith, Mrs. Jones, St. Paul.
2. Names of organizations widely known by their initials: U-N, F-B-I, G-O-P (but AFL-CIO).
3. Acronyms: NATO.
4. Time designations: A-M, P-M.
5. Academic degrees: P-H-D.

To indicate a pause where the newscaster can catch his breath, the dash or a series of dots are preferable to commas: The House plans to give the 11-billion-500-million dollar measure a final vote Tuesday . . . and the Senate is expected to follow suit—possibly on the same day. **Punctuation**

The hyphen is used instead of the period in initials: F-B-I. The period is retained in initials in a name: J. D. Smith. All combined words should have the hyphen: co-ed, semi-annual, de-segregation. (Spelling should also use the form easiest to pronounce: employee.)

Contractions are more widely used in broadcast copy than in other news copy to provide a conversational tone. Common contractions—isn't, doesn't, it's, they're—may be used in both direct and indirect quotes:

(SAN FRANCISCO)—MEMBERS OF THE TRANSPORT WORKERS UNION IN SAN FRANCISCO SAY IF THE MUNICIPAL STRIKE DOESN'T BEGIN LOOKING LIKE A GENERAL STRIKE BY THIS AFTERNOON, THEY'LL RE-CONSIDER THEIR SUPPORT OF THE WALKOUT. THE REFUSAL BY DRIVERS TO CROSS PICKET LINES SET UP BY STRIKING CRAFT UNIONS HAS SHUT DOWN MOST TRANSPORTATION IN THE CITY

A contraction should not be used if the stress is on the negative: "I do not choose to run." Or for emphasis: A U-S Air Force spokesman reported that several of the refugee islanders said they will never return to their homes.

Even in broadcast copy, contractions should not be overworked. Nor should the awkwardly contrived ones be attempted: they'd, he's, here's, they'll, that'll. The result would be something like this:

It's possible there's been a major air disaster in Europe.

A British airliner with 83 persons aboard disappeared during the day and is considered certain to've crashed in the Austrian Alps.

Apparently no search'll be launched tonight. There's no indication of where the aircraft might've gone down.

Quotation Marks   The listener cannot see quotation marks. If the reporter tries to read them into the script—"quote" and "end of quote"—the sentence sounds trite and stilted. It is easier and more natural to indicate the speaker's words by phrases such as "and these are his words," "what he called," "he put it in these words," "the speaker said." Direct quotes are used sparingly in the newscast. If quotes are necessary, they should be introduced casually:

(MOSCOW)—THE SOVIET NEWS AGENCY TASS SAID TODAY THAT SOVIET SCIENTISTS WERE AWARE OF AN IMPENDING EARTHQUAKE THIS MONTH IN CENTRAL ASIA FIVE DAYS BEFORE IT HAPPENED. . . .

THE NEWS AGENCY SAID "AT THAT TIME, A CONNECTION WAS FIRST NOTICED BETWEEN THE GAS-CHEMICAL COMPOSITION OF ABYSSAL (DEEP) WATERS AND UNDERGROUND TREMORS."

The source should always precede the quotation.

Quotation marks are placed around some names that would otherwise confuse the reporter.

IN ANSWER TO AN S-O-S, THE U-S COAST GUARD CUTTER "COOS BAY" ALONG WITH OTHER VESSELS STEAMED TO THE AID OF THE STRICKEN FREIGHTER. THE NORWEGIAN VESSEL "FRUEN" PICKED UP NINE SEAMEN FROM THE "AMBASSADOR" IN A TRICKY TRANSFER OPERATION IN THE TEMPEST TOSSED SEAS.

In this illustration the reporter is more likely to fumble "tempest tossed seas" than the names of the vessels.

Figures   Numbers are tricky in broadcast copy. "A million" may sound like "eight million." No confusion results if "one million" is used.

In most copy, round numbers or approximations mean as much as specific figures. "Nearly a mile" rather than "5,200 feet," "nearly a half" rather than "48.2 per cent," "just under two per cent" rather than "1.7 per cent."

An exception is vote results, especially where the margin is close. It should be "100-to-95 vote" rather than "100–95 vote." The writer or editor can help the listener follow statistics or vote tallies by inserting phrases such as "in the closest race" and "in a landslide victory."

Fractions and decimals should be spelled out: one and seven-eights (not $1\frac{7}{8}$), five-tenths (not 0.5).

Numbers under 10 and over 999 are spelled out and hyphenated: one, two, two-thousand, 11-billion-500-million, 15-hundred (rather than one-thousand-500), one-and-a-half million dollars (never $1.5 million). Despite the rules, some writers prefer to use figures whenever possible.

When two numbers occur together in a sentence the smaller number should be spelled out: twelve 20-ton trucks.

Any figure beginning a sentence should be spelled out.

Figures are used for time of day (4:30 p-m), in all market stories and in sports scores and statistics (65-to-59, 2:9.3). If results of horse races or track meets appear in the body of the story, the winning times should be spelled out: two minutes, nine and three-tenths seconds (rather than 2:9.3).

In dates and addresses the -st, -rd, -th and -nd are included. June 22nd, West 83rd street. Figures are used for years: 1910.

On approximate figures, writers sometimes say, "Police are looking for a man 50 to 60 years of age." This sounds like "52" to the listener. It should read, "Police are looking for a man between 50 and 60 years of age."

Titles

The identification prepares the ear for the name. Therefore, the identification usually precedes the name: Secretary of State Brown. If the title is long, break it with a comma: the President of the Marble Shooters' Union, John Kelley. Some titles are impossible to place before the name: The vice president of the Society for the Preservation and Encouragement of Barbershop Quartet Singing, Joe Doe. Use "Vice president Joe Doe of the Society for the Preservation and Encouragement of Barbershop Quartet Singing." Use "Police Chief Don Vendel" rather than "Chief of Police Don Vendel."

Some radio and television newsrooms insist that the President should never be referred to by his last name alone. It would be President Ford, the President, Mr. Ford.

Broadcast copy does not have the fetish of using middle initials and ages with all persons in the news. Some initials are well-known parts of names: John L. Lewis. Some persons prefer to use their middle name rather than their first name.

Ages may be omitted unless the age is significant to the story: "A 12-year-old boy—Mitchell Smith—was crowned winner," and so on. Ages usually appear in local copy to aid in identification. Place the age close to the name. It should not say, "A 24-year-old university student died in a two-car collision today. He was John Doe." Use "A university student died. . . . He was 24-year-old John Doe."

Obscure names need not be used unless warranted by the story. In many cases the name of the office or title suffices: "Peoria's police chief said," and so on. The same applies to little-known place names or to obscure foreign place names. If the location is important it may be identified by placing it in relation to a well-known place—"approximately one hundred miles south of Chicago." In local copy most names and places are important to listeners and viewers.

Where several proper names appear in the same story, it is better to repeat the name than to rely on pronouns unless the antecedent is obvious. Also, repeat the names rather than use *the former, the latter* or *respectively.*

Datelines The site of the action should be included in broadcast copy. The dateline may be used as an introduction or a transition: "In Miami." Or the location may be noted elsewhere in the lead: "The Green Bay Packers and the Chicago Bears meet in Chicago tonight in the annual charity football game."

In the newspaper wire *here* refers to the place where the listener is. Because radio and television may cover a wide geographical area, the word *here* should be avoided. Said a UPI radio news editor, "If the listener is sitting in a friendly poker game in Ludowici, Georgia, and hears a radio report of mass gambling raids 'here,' he may leap from the window before realizing the announcer is broadcasting from Picayune, Mississippi."

Time Angle In the newspaper wire story nearly everything happens "today." Radio copy breaks up the day into its component parts: "this morning," "early tonight," "just a few hours ago," "at noon today." The technique gives the listener a feeling of urgency in the news. Specific time should be translated for the time zone of the station's location: "That will be 2:30 Mountain Time."

Radio's use of the present and present perfect tenses helps to eliminate the time angle:

SEARCHERS HAVE FOUND THE WRECKAGE OF A TWIN-ENGINE AIR FORCE PLANE IN PUERTO RICO AND LOCATED THE BODIES OF SIX OF THE AIRCRAFT'S EIGHT CREWMEN. THE PLANE, MISSING SINCE SATURDAY, HAD GONE DOWN ON A PEAK 23 MILES SOUTHEAST OF SAN JUAN.

Taste Broadcast news editors should be aware of all members of their captive audience—the young and the aged, the sensitive and the hardened. Accident stories can be reported without the sordid details of gore and horror. Borderline words that may appear innocent to the reader carry their full impact when given over the more intimate instruments of radio and television. If spicy items of divorce and suicide are tolerated by the station, at least they can be saved until the late-hour news show when the young and infirm are abed.

The wire services protect the editor by prefacing the morbid or "gutsy" items with discretionary slugs:

(FOR USE AT YOUR DISCRETION)

(RAPE)

MIAMI, FLORIDA—POLICE IN MIAMI REPORT THEY SUSPECT JOHN DOE IN THE CRIMINAL ASSAULT (RAPE) OF AN 18-YEAR-OLD GIRL. DOE—27 YEARS OLD—WAS ARRESTED IN THE CITY MUSEUM AND CHARGED WITH STATUTORY ASSAULT (RAPE).

(END DISCRETIONARY MATTER)

References to physical handicaps or deformities are avoided unless they are essential to the story. Never say "Blind as a bat," "slow as a cripple" and the like. Similarly, unless they are essential, reference to color, creed or race should not be used.

Wire services handle items involving pertinent profanity by bracketing the profanity:

"GODFREY SAID—IT HURTS (LIKE HELL)."

The practice of including a humorous item, usually near the end, in a newscast has produced some unfunny stories such as the one about a man breaking his neck by tripping over a book of safety hints. A truly humorous item leavens the heavy news report. Invariably it needs no embellishment by the editor or reporter.

On many stations someone other than the news reporter gives the commercials. One reason, among others, for this practice is to disassociate the newsperson from the commercial plugger. Even so, the director or reporter should know the content of commercials sandwiched in news. If a news story concerns a car crash in which several are killed, the item would not be placed ahead of a commercial of an automobile dealer. Airlines generally insist that their commercials be canceled for twenty-four hours if the newscast contains a story of an airliner crash, a policy that is likewise applied to many metropolitan newspapers.

The sponsor does not control or censor the news. The story of a bank scandal might be omitted on a news program sponsored by a bank but it would be used on another newscast and would be heard on every newscast if it were of major importance. Similarly, a newspaper would be judicious enough not to place a bank scandal story next to a bank ad.

Attributions

Attribution is an important aspect of radio news writing. If an error is discovered, the station has an "out" if the item has official attribution. Example: "The state patrol said Smith was killed when his car overturned in a ditch" rather than "Smith was killed when his car overturned in a ditch." Attribution can also be vital in the event of any court action over a story written and aired by the news staff.

Should identification of accident victims be made before relatives have been notified? Some stations insist on getting the coroner's approval before releasing names of victims. If the release is not available, the tag would be, "The name of the victim is being withheld until relatives have been notified."

In stories containing condition reports on persons in hospitals, the report should not carry the same condition over from one newscast to another without a check with the hospital to find out whether there has been a change.

Tapes All news copy for radio and television should show the date, the time block, the story slug, the writer's name or initials, the story source and whether the story has a companion tape cartridge or a film segment. If there is more than one tape accompanying a story, the slug would indicate the number of tapes. A tape cartridge is simply a tape recording or audio tape from a news source.

If a tape is used, a cue line is inserted for each tape. Many stations use a red ribbon to type the out-cues or place red quotation marks around the cue line. At the end of the tape, the newscaster should again identify the voice used on the tape.

If several tapes are used in one newscast, the tapes should be spaced so that the same voices, or series of voices, are not concentrated in one part. The control room needs time to get the tapes ready for broadcast. (Figure 18–3).

Figure 18–3. Editing room for news film preparation. The editor uses a synchronizer to edit from a single reel or from a complex of picture reels and a sound track reel. [*Courtesy KMGH-TV, Denver.*]

The out-cues of the tape should be made in the *exact* words of the person interviewed. This will insure that the engineer will not cut off the tape until the message is concluded. The reporter should provide the engineer or boardman with a list of news cartridges to be used and the order in which the reporter intends to use them.

The same would hold true of telephone interviews, either taped or live.

The broadcast newsman also may have access to audio news services provided by networks, group-owned facilities and the wire services. These feeds, provided to the station on audio tapes, may be voiced reports or actuality situations. See Figure 18–4 for a wire service audio tape feed.

```
T
(SIXTH AUDIO ROUNDUP)
73 :12 A GREAT NECK, N.Y. (PATRICIA MEARNS, WIFE OF AIRMAN MISSING IN
    NORTH VIETNAM, WHO JUST RETURNED FROM PARIS TO PLEAD FOR NEWS OF
    HUSBAND) RESPONDS TO NORTH VIETNAMESE SUGGESTION THAT POW WIVES JOIN
    PEACE GROUPS TO WORK FOR END OF WAR (IN PEACE)
74 :26 A GREAT NECK (PAT MEARNS) DOESN'T BLAME U-S FOR HER PREDICAMENT
    (SITUATION)
75 :40 A GREAT NECK (PAT MEARNS) REFLECTS ON REASONS FOR TRIP TO PARIS
    (LOTS OF US)
76 :42 V WASHINGTON (GENE GIBBONS, FOR VACATIONING UPI FARM EDITOR
    BERNARD BRENNER) HOUSE INVESTIGATION OF MEAT PRICES OPENS WITH
    TESTIMONY FROM ANGRY HOUSEWIFE
77 :22 A SAN FRANCISCO (CHARLES O'BRIEN, CHIEF DEPT ATT GENERAL FOR
    CALIF) SAYS CALIFORNIA CONSIDERING SUEING CAR MAKERS FOR SMOG
    DAMAGE (CALIFORNIA)
78 :42 A WASHINGTON (SEN ALAN CRANSTON, D-CALIF) CONDEMNS RISING
    UNEMPLOYMENT AND NIXON ADMINISTRATION INFLATION FIGHT (UNACEPTABLE)
79 :33 V UNITED NATIONS (MORRISON KRUS) ARGREEMENTS NOT BE BE
    RENEWED FOR U-S BASES IN LYBYA
                        UPI/ AUDIO/NEW YORK
                                BA953PED..
```

Figure 18–4. A United Press International audio tape feed roundup. The roundup, called a billboard, shows the news editor the number of cut or selection and the length of the taped message. The first figure represents the number of the selection; the second shows the length of the tape in seconds. The letter A following the time indicates an actuality or a taped voice of a news source such as a governor. The letter V indicates a voicer or the voice of a wire service correspondent. V/A would indicate both an actuality and the correspondent's voice—an interview type. The words in the message itself provide an introduction to the tape by the newsman. The words in parentheses at the end of the selection are the out-cue words, showing the conclusion of the voice on tape. Out-cue words are not needed on voicers because the correspondents follow a standard out-cue, such as "This is Morrison Krus reporting for United Press International." Normally, six audio roundups are delivered daily.

Listeners with news tips frequently call the station newsroom. Such tips often lead to scoops. Those in the newsroom receiving such calls should try to get as much information as possible, including the caller's name and telephone number. If a telephoned message is to be used on the air, the reporter should get the caller's permission to use his voiced interview.

If something big arises, the reporter checks it out by telephone with the police department or sheriff's office before using it on the air. It is illegal to use information obtained from radio monitors. This prohibition, however, is flagrantly violated in times of emergency. During such times, police dispatchers are too busy to take calls from fifteen or twenty broadcasting stations. A reporter would be derelict in not warning the listeners of an oncoming flood or tornado merely because he couldn't reach a dispatcher to confirm what he was hearing on the police radio.

Television News

Newspapers communicate by sight, radio by sound and television by sight, sound and motion. Editing a television news or special event show involves all three levels. As described by Chet Huntley, one-time National Broadcasting Company news commentator, television news editing is the marriage of words to pictures, words to sound, pictures to sound and ideas to ideas.

Reuven Frank, former president of NBC News, contended that the highest power of television is to produce an experience. Television cannot disseminate as much information as newspapers, magazines or even radio. But in many instances it causes viewers to undergo an experience similar to what would happen if they were at the scene. One can read about napalmed civilians or the drowning of a child at a swimming pool and think, "Isn't that a shame." But watching the same thing on a television newscast is a wrenching, personal experience that gets people worked up and angry. Television is an instrument of power, not because of the facts it relates but because it conveys an experience to viewers.

Words speak for themselves to the newspaper reader. In radio, a newscaster voices the words for the listener. In television, the reporter is there, talking to the viewer about the news. He or she is the key actor and many a station has fallen behind in ratings for its news shows, not because the station did not have good reporters and cameramen or lacked a well-paced news format, but because competing stations had better newsroom talent.

In the early days of television, stations hired journalists to report and write the news, then handed the polished manuscript over to a good-looking announcer with pearl-shaped tones. Today more and more newscasters are men and women with journalistic background who may or may not sound like movie stars but who know what they are talking about. (Figure 18–5).

Television news editing, the sorting or processing of the news for television, requires more time than for radio. Producers and writers must spend hours reviewing, sifting and editing all the material available for a single, fifteen-minute newscast.

Figure 18–5. News, weather, sports. These have become the traditional pattern in television news. In this modern console the performers are able to view the show's progress. Behind every newscast is a team to support those behind the microphone. These include producer, director, assignment editor, reporters, photographers, camera operators, film editors and the like. [*Courtesy KMGH-TV, Denver.*]

They use these criteria in selecting items—the significance of the item, whether it is interesting, either factually or visually, and (sometimes) whether the item will bring a chuckle.

All local newsfilm must be examined before it is edited to determine which of the film will be used and how much each should be cut. Sometimes a film may have relatively little news value but is included because of its visual quality. A barn fire might not rate mention on a radio newscast but the film could be spectacular.

Network films also are examined. Late afternoon network news commentaries are reviewed to determine what can be lifted for the late evening local news show. The networks provide their affiliates with an afternoon news feed for their use as they see fit. This closed-circuit feed from New York consists of overset material not used on the network news. These feeds are recorded on video tape and usually include a half-dozen or more one- or two-minute films and perhaps standup reports on national and world events. These have to be monitored so the editor can decide which ones can be used.

Chain-owned stations maintain a Washington or New York bureau that sends member stations daily film reports. These, too, must be reviewed.

In addition to editing this considerable amount of film reports, the editor must also go over the vast amount of wire agency news and facsimile pictures, not to mention stories filed by station reporters. Having selected what to use, the editor's next job is to determine how and where it can be used within the few minutes allotted the news show.

In film editing the editor looks over the images on the film and directs a technician to delete (by cutting and splicing the film) the images the editor does not want to use. Before ordering the cutting of a video tape the editor must put the tape in a recorder where the tape can be stopped for cutting. An audio tape is edited by running the tape through a playback, cutting out the sounds not wanted or recording revised messages. Or, a tape may be edited by using duplicate recorders or a recorder and a tape cartridge. The original tape is placed in one recorder and fed into another. At points where material is to be deleted, the receiving recorder is stopped while the portions of the tape to be deleted are rolled through the playback recorder (Figure 18–3).

Filmed pictures are similar to those produced by movie cameras. They may be films with sound (sound-on-film or SOF), sound under (audible background sounds) or silent film (SIL), sometimes called "voice over" or VO film). A taped film or video tape (VTR for video-tape recording) is one that has been recorded electronically.

Still pictures may be the standard two by two transparencies, either in black and white or in color, which are projected. Or they may be photos or printed material that are placed before the studio camera. The still pictures used most commonly on a television newscast are wire service news pictures—or facsimile pictures printed on tissue-thin paper. These are first mounted on heavy cardboard, then placed in a horizontal raster, or a pattern of scanning lines covering the area upon which the image is projected in the cathode-ray tube, to fit the television screen. At some stations these facsimile pictures are colored in the newsroom by using felt-tip color pens.

In a two-camera operation the still pictures must be aired either singly or in odd-numbered sequences. One camera is on the newscaster (usually referred to as a *standup* in this situation) and the other lingers on the sideline to shoot closeups of the still pictures. At the appropriate moment the director punches from camera 1 to camera 2. This frees camera 1 to pivot and focus on the second picture. If the scene were to shift back to the newscaster, camera 2 could be used but it is out of position. If camera 2 could focus on a third picture, camera 1 could get back to the newscaster. The problem does not arise when a third camera is used.

Figure 18–6 is a condensed script used on a typical day by KMGH, Channel 7, Denver. This is from a 5:30 p.m. newscast devoted to local news. The underscored lines help alert the director and the newscaster to the impending use of film or video tape.

In the first item the reporter deleted the sentence referring to rape because the information adds little to the story and is in poor taste. In the second item the reporter added a thought and

VIDEO	AUDIO
PALMER ON CAMERA.....	Good Afternoon.
	Denver Detectives are busy this afternoon trying to gather facts in the murder of a 23-year-old secretary whose
FILM CUE: CUT TO FILM:	<u>body was found in her Capitol Hill</u> Apartment. The victim was Miss Lucille Martinez, of Trinidad, who came to Denver May 1st, to work ~~for~~ *with* the War-on-Poverty.
	The body was found in the living room of her apartment at 1330 Race Street this morning by a niece and two other women.
	Police said evidence indicated she'd been raped and stabbed to death with a paring knife.
	The women went to the apartment after Miss Martinez failed to show up for work in a week. She was last seen alive June 23rd
FILM ROLLING...	by the apartment manager--Mrs. C.M. Bostock. Mrs. Bostock said she'd heard no unusual noises in the apartment.... and other occupants of the building had
END FILM:	observed nothing suspicious. Police are trying to trace the girl's activities on June 23rd...the day it's assumed she was murdered.
	-0-
	Meanwhile....all days off have been cancelled for uniformed policemen through July 5th. Chief George Seaton says thousands of young people---including many hippies, and others---are still in Denver after attending a Summer Pop-Music Festival and are expected to

Figure 18-6.

	remain here through the 4th-of-July
	weekend. He wants all police officers
FILM CUE:	available in case of further trouble.
CUT TO FILM. . .	City crews began trying to clean up
	Mile High Stadium this morning, where
	last night, 5 policemen and one TV
FILM ROLLING . .	reporter suffered minor injuries at the
	final night of the festival. Some thirty
	young people were arrested as police
	tangled with gate crashers. The cleanup
	job ~~as you can see~~ is going to take *done at no expense to the city--*
BACK TO PALMER:	awhile. In the meantime...the city is
	still offering a campground near 6th and
	Federal...and providing bus transportation
commercial cue:	there after the city parks close at 11 p.m.
SPOT #1	COMMERCIAL
PALMER ON CAMERA ..	Mayor Bill McNichols is said *to be* resting
	comfortably at Rose Memorial Hospital...
	where he was admitted yesterday. A
	spokesman said the 59-year-old Denver
	Mayor suffered a return of the heart
	pains *he experienced during* ~~~~ a mild heart attack
	~~ suffered last month. Doctors say
	he'll probably be in the hospital for
	2 weeks while undergoing various tests
	and treatment.
	-O-
PALMER ON CAMERA . . .	Also in the hospital today is Gene
	Cervi, publisher of Cervi's Rocky
	Mountain Journal. The bombastic Denver
	editor was admitted to St. Joe's Saturday
	after what appears to have been a minor
	heart attack. His condition today is
FILM CUE:	listed as "fair."
	-O-
CUT TO FILM:	A group of between 50 and 75 people
	picketed the State Capitol in Denver this

Figure 18–6. (*Continued.*)

The Art of Editing

Figure 18-6. (Continued.)

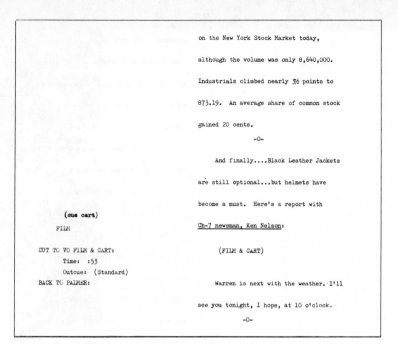

```
                                          on the New York Stock Market today,

                                          although the volume was only 8,640,000.

                                          Industrials climbed nearly 3½ points to

                                          873.19.  An average share of common stock

                                          gained 20 cents.
                                                          -0-

                                          And finally....Black Leather Jackets

                                          are still optional...but helmets have

                                          become a must.  Here's a report with
          (cue cart)
             FILM                          Ch-7 newsman, Ken Nelson:

      CUT TO VO FILM & CART:                    (FILM & CART)
          Time:  :53
          Outcue:  (Standard)
      BACK TO PALMER:                       Warren is next with the weather. I'll

                                          see you tonight, I hope, at 10 o'clock.
                                                          -0-
```

Figure 18–6. *(Concluded.)*

took out a needless phrase. In the item on picketing, the reporter had expected a complete story to go with the film. As newscast time neared he grabbed the story (first paragraph) then padded the account (second paragraph) to utilize all the film.

In the final item, Ch-7 is the reporter's abbreviation for Channel 7. CART means tape cartridge. In the video directions "cut to VO film & cart" tells the director to use voice over film with the tape cartridge. The film runs fifty-three seconds and has an obvious closing such as, "This has been Ken Nelson—Channel 7 —reporting."

Editing the television script conforms, in general, with the suggestions given for editing radio news copy. Because of the numerous cutbacks to pictures, the television news script contains more cue tips than the radio script and invites more mechanical problems. For instance, the newscaster would like to start off with two top stories. However, both are on video tape and only one video tape machine is available and the tapes have to be changed between something else. That means the newscaster can start with one of the video tapes, then shift to a story of lesser importance while the tape machine is being changed.

Again, if only one tape machine is available, the script cannot call for a video tape story immediately preceding a taped commercial. The engineer has to have time to recue the machine.

Similar problems arise with news film. Commercial films may be spliced between the news stories, requiring a few seconds of padding following a news film before introducing a commercial.

The script prepares the viewer for what he is about to see but avoids repeating what the viewer can see for himself. If the mayor has criticized the city's water supply and his statement has been recorded, the script merely sets up the statement with a brief introduction. The script may contain a description of what the picture omitted or may direct the viewer's attention to a significant detail but it should avoid phrases such as "we're now looking at" or "this picture shows."

Because most television newsrooms function with only a fraction of the staff found on a metropolitan daily, each reporter must be a jack of all trades—a writer and editor, an engineer, a public speaker and a movie producer. The ideal news worker can report adequately on any assignment, from the arrival of the President to a water controversy between the states. The reporter should be able to film the story with 16-millimeter silent or sound equipment, write and edit the script, record background sound on an audio tape machine, edit the film to fit, then voice the story on the air.

Both broadcast and newspaper news editors must have knowledge and talent if they are to perform the art of editing adequately.

Newspaper Style[1]

Abbreviations Readers easily recognize, common abbreviations such as U.N., FBI, AP, UPI, CBS, NATO and VISTA. Frequently, readers are more familiar with acronyms (names for words formed by combining initial letters or syllables of a series of words) than with the original combination of words. Examples: Alcoa (Aluminum Corporation of America), laser (light amplification through simulated emission of radiation), radar (radio detection and ranging), smog (smoke and fog), Socony (Standard Oil Company of New York).

A problem arises when the writer tries to force the reader to recognize unfamiliar abbreviations. The second paragraph in a story refers to the Naval Enlisted Scientific Education Program (NESEP). Eight paragraphs later, the organization is referred to by initials only. Will the reader remember what NESEP stood for? If he can't, will he go back to the second paragraph to find out?

Abbreviate	*Do Not Abbreviate*
Agencies that are recognized by their initials—AFL-CIO, VISTA, YMCA, TVA.	First mention of organizations, firms, agencies, groups; thereafter the abbreviations may be used—Distant Early Warning line (DEW line), Organization of American States (OAS).
Time zones, airplane designations, ships, distress calls, military terms—EDT, CST, MIG17, SOS, USS Iowa.	First mention of some military terms—Absent without leave (AWOL); he is not a deserter until absent 90 days.
Addresses—St., Ave. (or Av.), Blvd., Ter.: 16 E. 72nd St., 16 Gregory Ave. NW.	Point, Port, Circle, Plaza, Place, Oval, Road, Lane, or where there is no address—Main Street, Fifth Avenue.
Business firms—Warner Bros.; Brown Implement Co.; Amalgamated Leather, Ltd.	

[1] Style rules provide, at best, a general guide to usage. Such rules are arbitrary, frequently inconsistent and sometimes illogical. Style rules for newspapers differ from broadcast news style rules. Even within the same news operation, the style changes from department to department. Many of the style guides listed here have been adapted, with permission, from UPI *Stylebook,* rev. ed (1968), The AP *Stylebook,* rev. ed (1968) and some of the projected changes in the joint revision (1976).

Lower case abbreviations usually take periods; also if the letters without periods spell out words, use periods—c.o.d., f.o.b., a.m., p.m. Periods are not needed in 35 mm (film), 105 mm (armament), mph, mpg.	First mention of speed should be miles an hour (or miles per hour); thereafter—mph, rpm.
Versus as vs. (with period). In court citations—v.	
Most states and provinces that follow cities, towns, airbases, Indian agencies, national parks. So far, few newspapers have adopted the code for state abbreviations used by the Postal Service.	All states standing alone. The AP-UPI *Stylebook* has dropped abbreviations for Canadian provinces. Montreal, Ottawa, Quebec and Toronto stand alone in datelines; all other datelines have the name of the city and the name of the provinces spelled out. The *Stylebook* also specifies no abbreviations for Alaska and Hawaii and any continental state with five or fewer letters.
B.C. as abbreviation of Canadian province must be preceded by town name; B.C., the era, must be preceded by a date.	
U.S.S.R. (Union of Soviet Socialist Republics) and U.A.R. (United Arab Republic).	
United States and United Nations in titles and when used as nouns in texts or in direct quotations—U.S. Junior Chamber of Commerce, U.N. Educational, Scientific, and Cultural Organization (UNESCO).	When used as nouns.
UN and US may be used without periods in headlines, except in an all-capital headline.	
Religious, fraternal, scholastic or honorary degrees—A.B. degree, Ph.D.	
Titles before names but not after names—Mr., Mrs., Miss, Ms., M., Mlle., Dr., Sen., Rep., Asst., Lt. Gov., Gov., Gen., Atty. Gen. Do not abbreviate attorney in "The statement by defense attorney John Jones," etc.	When standing alone or after a name or as a descriptive term— he is a doctor; John Jones, governor of Ohio; the statement by defense attorney John Jones (false title). Avoid Mesdames at the head of a list in social items.
Most military titles preceding a name—Gen. Pershing, Lt. Jones.	Port, association, joint, detective, department, deputy, general manager, secretary-general, secretary, treasurer.
Months when used with dates— Oct. 12. Abbreviate months as follows: Jan., Feb., Aug., Sept., Oct., Nov., Dec.	October 1492. March, April, May, June, July and days of the week except in tabular or financial listings.
St. and Ste.—St. Louis, Sault Ste. Marie.	Saint in Saint John, N.B.
Names of mountains—Mt. Everest.	Mountain or mount when used as part of a city—Mount Vernon, Mountainview.
	Proper first names unless the person himself does so.

Capitalization

Capitalize	*Lower case*
Titles preceding a name—Secretary of State Richard Smith.	When standing alone or following a name—Richard Smith, secretary of state. Occupational or false titles—the deputy defense attorney John Jones.
Government officials when used with name as title—Queen Elizabeth.	When standing alone or following a name—Jones, ambassador to Finland; the ambassador; the queen, the president.
Pope and Dalai Lama and foreign religious leaders.	The general religious terms—the pontiff, the patriarch, the pope.
Union, Republic, Colonies referring to the United States—Republic of Korea, Fifth French Republic.	Long titles following a name—John Jones, executive director of the department.
The legislative building—the Capitol.	The city. The capital is Denver.
Full names of committees—Senate Judiciary Committee.	When standing alone—the committee; the subcommittee. Shortened versions of long committees —the rackets committee.
Courts—Supreme Court, Juvenile Court, 6th U.S. Circuit Court.	When standing alone—the court.
Governmental systems—Social Security.	General use—he was an advocate of security for old age.
Holidays, historic events, ecclesiastical feasts, special events, fast days, hurricanes, typhoons—Mothers Day, Labor Day, Battle of the Bulge, Good Friday, Easter, Passover, Christmas, Halloween, New Year's Day.	General terms—the holidays, the feast, the hurricane, the typhoon, the new year, the battle, the armistice, the cease-fire.
Regions or areas, political, or ideological—Antarctica, Arctic Circle, Middle East, Midwest, Upper Peninsula, Panhandle, Orient, Chicago's Loop, East-West, East Germany.	General—antarctic, arctic. Directions—western North Dakota, toward the east, traveled west, westerly winds. Seasons of the year—spring, summer, fall, winter.
Political parties and members—Democrat, Democratic, Republican, Socialist, Independent, Communist.	Systems or ideologies—democratic form of government, republican system, socialism, communism.
Names of fraternal organizations —B'nai B'rith, Ancient Free & Accepted Masons (AF&AM), Knights of Columbus (K. of C.), Order of the Eastern Star (O.E.S.), the Elks.	

All forms of the Deity—He, His, Him. Religious works—the Bible, Talmud, Koran, and books of the Bible and all confessions of faith and their adherents, and such terms as Satan and Hades.

Devil, hell. Religious philosophies —he is catholic in his views.

Wars—Civil War, Korean War, World War I, World War II.

General—The war in the Pacific; nations at war, the war to end all wars.

Species of livestock, animals and fowls—Airedale, Percheron, Hereford, Angus.

Common nouns—terrier, horse, whiteface, bantam.

Names of races and nationalities —Caucasian, Chinese, Negro, Indian, Afrikaans, Afrikander, Israeli, Filipino.

General—black, white, red, yellow. Do not use *colored* for Negro except in National Association for the Advancement of Colored People.

Names of flowers, including Latin generic names—Peace rose, Thea.

General—camellia, japonica, rose, hollyhock.

Common noun as part of formal name—Hoover Dam, Missouri River, Barr County Courthouse, Empire State Building, Blue Room, Carlton House (hotel), Wall Street, Hollywood Boulevard.

Proper names that have acquired independent common meaning— paris green, dutch oven, brussel sprouts, german measles.

General—dam, river, courthouse, Carlton house (home). Plurals— Broad and Main streets.

Titles of books, plays, hymns, poems, songs (and place in quotation marks)—"The Courtship of Miles Standish." Words such as *a, in, of,* etc., are capitalized only at the beginning or end of a title—"Of Thee I Sing," "All Returns Are In."

Titles of newspapers and magazines should follow the style used by the publication. The titles are not inclosed in quotes. Greensboro *Daily News, The Christian Science Monitor, Harper's, Time* magazine.

Names of planets, expositions, organizations—Boy Scouts, World's Fair, Venus.

Sun, moon and earth unless they are used in a series with capitalized planets.

Decorations, awards and degrees —Medal of Honor, Nobel Peace Prize, A.B. degree, Ph.D.

College degrees when spelled out —bachelor of arts, doctor of philosophy.

In general, spell below 10, and use numerals for 10 and above. Spell any number that starts a sentence.

Numerals

| *Use Numerals* | *Spell Out Numerals* |

In all tabular and statistical matter, records, election returns, times (3 o'clock or 3 p.m.), time sequences (2:30:21.6—hours, minutes, seconds, tenths). speeds, latitude and longitude, temper-

Fourth of July, July Fourth (or July 4).

Casual numbers—a thousand times no, Gay Nineties, mixed foursome, tenfold.

atures, highways (U.S. 301, Interstate 6), distances, dimensions, heights (the flag hung from a 10-foot pole), all ages, percentages, (3-year-old girl), ratios, proportions, military units (6th Fleet, 1st Army), political divisions (8th Ward), orchestral instruments, court districts or divisions (3rd district), handicaps, betting odds, dates, numbers (No. 1 boy), calibers (.38-caliber pistol).

Under 10 for inanimates—four-mile trip, four miles from center.

Fifth Avenue, Fifth Republic of France, Big Ten, Dartmouth eleven.

Plurals—twos, threes.

Money—$4 million (the $ is the equivalent of the second numeral). In a series—there are four 10-room houses, one 14-room house, 25 five-room houses, and 40 four-room houses.

Cents in amounts less than $1—seven-cent stamp.

In amounts of more than 1 million, round numbers take the dollar sign and *million*—$4 million. Decimalization is carried to two places—$4.35 million. Exact amounts would be $4,351,242. In less than 1 million—$500, $6,000. $650,000.

Pounds rather than the English pound symbol and convert into dollars.

In ranges—$12 million to $14 million, not $12 to $14 million.

Serial numbers are printed solid—A1234567.

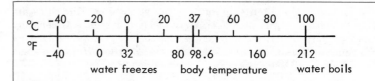

This scale converts temperatures from Fahrenheit to Celsius readings.

Sample Conversions

Nautical mile = approx. 6,076 feet
League = 3 miles
Furlong = 1/8 mile
Fathom = 6 feet

Peck = 8 quarts
Bushel = 4 pecks
Gross or long ton = 2,240 pounds

Centimeter = .3937 inches
Meter = 1.094 yards (39.37 inches). To convert feet to meters, multiply by .3048

Printer's measure:
    72 points = 1 inch
    6 (12 pt.) picas = 1 inch
    14 agate lines = 1 inch

For metric conversion, use
    2.5 centimeters = 1 inch (approx.)
    Or refer to a metric comparison rule

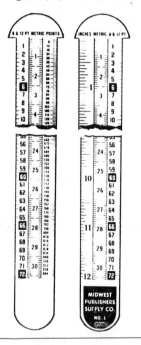

Kilometer = 3,280 feet or approx. 5/8 mile; 10 kilometers = $6\frac{1}{4}$ miles

Millimeter = .03937 inches
Centimeter = 10 millimeters
Decimeter = 10 centimeters
Meter = 10 decimeters
Dekameter = 10 meters
Hectometer = 10 dekameters
Kilometer = 10 hectometers

Square centimeter = .155 square inches
Square meter = 10.764 square feet
Square kilometer = .386 square miles (247 acres)

Cubic centimeter = .061 cubic inches
Cubic meter = 1.308 cubic yards

Newspaper Style   417

Liter = 1.057 liquid quarts
British Imperial gallon = 1.201 U.S. gallons

For current rates of foreign exchange or price of metals, consult a bank or a recent paper of record such as the *Wall Street Journal.*

Punctuation

Many authorities insist that the comma is the most troublesome of all punctuation marks. The use of commas cannot be learned by rule. Sir Ernest Gowers, a foremost British authority on style, wrote, in *The Complete Plain Words* (London: Her Majesty's Stationery Office, 1954), "The correct use of the comma—if there is such a thing as 'correct' use—can only be acquired by commonsense, observation and taste."

The Comma

Most news stylebooks are hostile to the comma and dictate that commas should be used sparingly. Roy H. Copperud, on the other hand, said, in the Editorial Workshop column in *Editor & Publisher* (May 5, 1956), "An examination of current newswriting shows that commas are more often omitted when required than used superfluously." Copperud, an arbiter of newspaper style, and stylebook compilers would agree that commas are required if they help make the passage clear. They should be omitted when they interrupt or slow down thought. H. W. Fowler's *A Dictionary of Modern English Usage* (New York: Oxford University Press, 1965) insists, "It may almost be said that what reads wrongly if the stops are removed is radically bad."

Note the role of the comma in the following examples:

"Erhard said the chancellor lacks the political sagacity required for the top government post." The sentence is absurd. It was the chancellor who said that Erhard lacked the political sagacity required for the top government post, a meaning made clear by inserting commas after *Erhard* and *chancellor.*

"No woman, whose attire makes her conspicuous, is well-dressed." Again absurd. This says that no woman is well-dressed. Both commas should be removed.

"We would walk out to the area where the animals roam free and talk for hours." This could mean that the animals talked for hours. Commas after *free* and before *where* make it clear who did the talking.

"I am going to Dublin perhaps with Murphy." This sentence needs a comma, but where? If placed after *Dublin,* the passage has one meaning. If placed after *perhaps,* it has another meaning.

The comma should not be used to perform the duty of a heavier stop such as a semicolon, a colon or a period. "I put my hand in the jar, this was a silly thing to do."

Commas generally are needed in the following:

To inclose words in apposition unless they are restrictive—"Richard Lamm, governor of Colorado, seconded the nomination." But "The Cunard liner Queen Mary has been sold."

To set off parenthetical elements—"The letter, however, was never delivered."

To set off adjectives when they equally modify the same noun—"She wore an old, faded dress." The dress was both old and faded. Commas are superfluous if the adjectives apply cumulatively to their nouns. "Ned was a balky old mule."

To set off nonrestrictive phrases or clauses—"Committee members, who had feared White House suppression of the report, were jubilant." This means that all the committee members were jubilant. Without the commas, only those who had feared White House suppression of the report were jubilant.

In places and dates—"Their first son, John, was born in Charleston, Ill., on July 2, 1910, and their second son, Robert, on Feb. 2, 1915." But, "The dam was completed in June 1970."

To set off a noun of address—"Here's to you, sir."

In attributions—"'While ditching the plane,' Hamphill said, 'the craft flipped over.'"

To indicate stress or nuance—"Ancient Ostia is near, but not on, the sea." "The president, finally, signed the measure." There is an implication that the president should have signed the measure long before he did. Such an implication is absent in "The president finally signed the bill."

Commas generally are not needed in the following:

Before Roman numerals, jr., sr., the ampersand and the dash; in street addresses, telephone numbers and serial numbers—Louis XIV; John Jones jr.; Smith & Col.; 443-1808; 12345 Oak St.; A1234567.

Before *of*—"Brown of Arkadelphia."

Before *and* and *or*—"The flag is red, white and blue." A comma is needed in this sentence: "Fish abounded in the lake, and the shore was lined with deer."

After adverbs and adverbial phrases at the beginning of sentences—"Sometimes I rode but usually I walked."

To introduce *that* clauses—"The Air Cav unit (,) that took such a battering Tuesday (,) made a helicopter landing in a jungle clearing."

The comma is optional in some sentences. If the stop does not clutter it should be retained. "When the man filed suit (,) the court held that he too was entitled to a television set." "Three miles to the east (,) 12 U.S. B52s dropped 360 tons of bombs on enemy base camps and supply depots."

ONE-LEGGED COMMA. The term "one-legged comma" was used by Copperud to describe construction that should have two commas or none at all. He gives these examples:

Newspaper Style   419

"Severe storms accompanied by hailstones up to three-quarters of an inch in diameter, pounded western Texas." Either two commas (one after *storms*) or none.

"All New Orleans schools were closed as a precaution but the storm, bringing winds of 64 miles an hour passed the city without causing much damage." A comma is needed after *hour* to bracket the clause.

Commas that clutter usually indicate that the sentence is too long, too jerky or in poor order. "A corporation, which is unique in the rubber industry, has been formed." One remedy is to recast the sentence—"A corporation unique in the rubber industry has been formed."

The Period The period is used in some abbreviations—U.S., U.N., c.o.d. It is not used in abbreviations such as KMOX (radio station), FTC, YMCA, USS Iowa, NW, mm, SOS.

The period is used after a question intended as a suggestion: "Tell how it was done."

The period is used for ellipsis: "The combine . . . was secure."

The period is sometimes dropped in headlines: OK, UN, US, OSU.

The Semicolon The semicolon separates phrases containing commas to avoid confusion and separates statements of contrast and statements too closely related:

The draperies, which were ornate, displeased me; the walls, light blue, were pleasing.

The party consisted of B. M. Jordan; R. J. Kelly, his secretary; Mrs. Jordan; Martha Brown, her nurse; and three servants.

The Apostrophe The apostrophe indicates the possessive case of nouns, the omission of figures, and contractions.

Usually the possessive of a singular noun not ending in "s" is formed by adding the apostrophe and "s"; the possessive of a plural noun is formed by adding the "s" and then the apostrophe: boys' wear.

The apostrophe also is used in the plural possessive "es"; Joneses' house.

The "s" is dropped and only the apostrophe is used in "for conscience' sake" or in a sibilant double or triple "s" such as Moses' tablet.

It is used in single letters: A's. But it is GIs for persons, and GIs' for the possessive.

Some reporters mistake *it's* for the possessive of *it*. By that reasoning, the possessive of *her* would be *her's* and of *their* would be *their's*.

The apostrophe is used in contractions—isn't—and in the omission of figures—'90s.

Copy should be free from contractions except in direct quotations: "Walt Disney's hired four of them." This is supposed to mean Disney has hired four of them. It does not.

The apostrophe is omitted in words that form part of a noun: Johns Hopkins University, State Teachers College, Actors Equity Association.

The Colon

The colon precedes the final clause summarizing prior matter; introduces listings, statements and texts; marks discontinuity; and takes the place of an implied "for instance":

The question came up: What does he want to do?

States and funds allotted were: Alabama $6,000, Arizona $4,000, etc.

The colon is used in Biblical and legal citations—Matt. 2:14; Missouri Statutes 3:245–260.

The Exclamation Point

The exclamation point is used to indicate surprise, appeal, incredulity or other strong emotion. It may also replace the question mark in rhetorical questions:

How wonderful! He yelled, "Come here!"

Was there ever a day like this!

The mark should not be used after ordinary statements such as "I didn't say that." Nor should two exclamation points ever be used.

The Question Mark

The question mark follows a direct question and marks a gap or uncertainty. In the latter use, it is enclosed in parentheses:

What happened to Jones?

It was April 13 (?) that I saw him.

Parentheses

Parentheses set off material or an element of a sentence: "It is not the custom (at least in the areas mentioned) to stand at attention."

When the parenthetical material ends a sentence, the period goes outside the final parenthesis. When the parenthetical material is a sentence in itself, the period goes inside the final parenthesis.

He habitually uses two words incorrectly (practical and practicable).

(The foregoing was taken from an essay.)

Several paragraphs of parenthetical matter start with the opening mark on each paragraph, and the final paragraph is ended with a closing parenthesis with the punctuation inside.

Parentheses are used where location identification is needed but is not part of the official name: "The Springfield (Ohio) Historical Society edition." It is not necessary to bracket "The Springfield, Ohio, area population."

Quotation Marks

Quotation marks enclose direct quotations; phrases in ironical uses; slang expressions; misnomers; titles of books, plays, poems, songs, lectures or speeches when the full title is used; hymns; movies; television programs and so on.

The comma and period are placed inside the quotation marks. Other punctuation is placed according to construction:

Why call it a "gentlemen's agreement"?

In multiple quotations, the sequence is as follows: "The question is 'Does his position violate the "gentlemen's 'post-haste' agreement" so eloquently described by my colleague as 'tommy-rot'?"

The Dash The dash indicates a sudden change and can be used instead of parentheses in many cases:

He claimed—no one denied it—that he had priority.

The monarch—shall we call him a knave or a fool?—approved it.

The Hyphen The general rule for hyphens is that "like" characters take the hyphen, and "unlike" characters do not: A-bomb, 20-20 vision, 3D, B60, MIG17, north-central (Exception: 4-H Club.)

Adjectival use must be clear: "The 6-foot man eating shark was killed" (the man was). "The 6-foot man-eating shark was killed" (the shark was).

Suspensive hyphenation: "The A- and H-bombs were exploded."

Ordinarily in prefixes ending in vowels and followed by the same vowel, the hyphen is used: pre-empt, re-elect. (Check a dictionary for exceptions such as cooperate, coed and coordinates.)

Hyphens should not be used with an adverb ending in *ly* or with the adverb *almost:* badly damaged, almost insuperable obstacle.

The hyphen serves to distinguish the meanings of similarly spelled words: recover, re-cover; resent, re-sent.

The hyphen separates a prefix from a proper noun: pre-Raphaelite, un-American.

The hyphen has been abandoned in newspaper usage in *week-end, worldwide, nationwide* and the like.

Plurals Most nouns form the plural by adding -s, or es: girls, 1930s, Joneses, churches.

An apostrophe is not used to form a plural except in single letters: He received all A's.

In some nouns ending in -f or -fe, the "f" changes to "v" and "es" is added: calves, leaves, knives.

Some nouns ending in -o add "es" and some merely add "o": cargoes, potatoes; broncos, pianos.

Proper names ending in -y generally add "s": Little Italys, Murphys; but Alleghenies, Rockies.

Some nouns ending in -y add only "s" to form plurals: boys, volleys, donkeys, moneys. Others change the "y" to "i" and add "es": berries, stories.

In compound nouns consisting of nouns and adjectives the plural is formed by adding "s" to the noun: attorneys general, courts-martial, bills of fare. The true noun takes the plural: major generals, judge advocates, mousetraps.

Latin plural endings are gradually giving way to Anglicized words: formulas (for formulae), stadiums (for stadia), gymnasiums (for gymnasia). Words of Latin and Greek-Latin origins form the plural by changing "i" to "e" (analysis, analyses; thesis, theses) or "um" to "a" (medium, media: bacterium, bacteria) or "us" to "i" (alumnus, alumni or alumnae).

All nouns of capacity or measurement ending in -ful are pluralized by adding "s": armfuls, cupfuls, roomfuls.

Few agree as to the correct use of compound words—whether compounds are one word, two words or hyphenated words. A safe rule is to use the form that will not confuse the reader, even if the usage is not logical or consistent. The following list demonstrates some of these variations.[2] Copyeditors should adhere to the newspaper's stylebook. If one is lacking, editors can refer to a dictionary or a manual of style, such as the *Government Printing Office Style Manual*.

Compounds

Able—able-bodied.
Above—above-mentioned.
Absent—absent-minded.
After—afterbeat, afterdeck, after-dinner.
Aide—aide-de-camp (aides-de-camp).
Air—airborne, air-condition, air conditioning, airdrop, airfield, air base, air mail, air raid (n.), airman, airlines, airplane, Alitalia Airlines, Bonanza Air Lines, Japan Air Lines.
All—all-star, all-America (team).
Ante, anti—antebellum, antislavery, anti-American, antichrist, anti-Christian, antifreeze, antilabor, antipoverty, antisocial, antitrust, anti-imperialistic.
Arch—archbishop, archduke, archenemy, arch-Protestant.

Baby—baby-sit, baby sitter, baby-sitting.
Back—back room (n.), back-room (adj.), back seat, back stairs (n.), backstairs (adj.), backyard, backstroke, backfire, comeback.
Ball—ballplayer, ball park.
Bath—bathhouse, bath mat, bathroom, bath towel.
Battle—battle-ax, battlefield, battle front, battle cry, battleground, battleship.
Best—best-dressed, best seller, best-selling, best man, best-known.
Bi—bicameral, bicentennial, bifocal, bistate, biweekly, bipartisan.
Black—blackjack, blacklist, blackmail, blackout, black race.

[2] Adj. = Adjective, n. = noun, v. = verb.

Boat—boathouse, boat race.

Book—bookcase, bookstore.

Bound—eastbound, snowbound, Africa-bound, vacation-bound.

Box—box office (n.), box-office (adj.).

Brand—brand-new.

Business—businesswoman, small-business man.

By—byline, by-election, bylaw, bypass (n. and v.), bypath, byplay, by-product, bystander, byword.

Center—centerboard, center field.

Church—churchgoer.

City—city council, city-born, citywide.

Class—classmate, class day, classroom.

Clean—clean-cut, cleanup (n.).

Club—clubhouse.

Co—co-op, cooperate, copilot, coauthor, co-defendant, coequal, coexist, coordinate, copartner, cooperative (n. and adj.), co-star, co-worker.

Coast—Coast Guard, Coast Guardman (if member of U.S. Coast Guard).

Commander—commander in chief.

Counter—counterargument, counterfoil, counterattack.

Court—court-martial (courts-martial), courtroom, courthouse.

Crack—crackup.

Cross—crosscurrent, crossroad, cross reference, cross-examine.

Cut—cut back (v.), cutback (n.).

Death—deathbed, death's-head, death knell, death rate.

Down—downcast, downstroke, touchdown.

Drive—drive-in.

Drop—dropouts.

Electro—electrolysis.

En—en route.

Ex, extra—ex-champion, ex post facto, extracurricular, extra-fine, extraterritorial, ex officio, ex-Waldorf waiter, ex-serviceman.

Far—far-fetched.

Farm—farmhouse.

Father—father-in-law, father love.

Feather—featherweight.

Fire—fire escape, firetrap.

First—first-rate.

Fist—fistful, fistfight.

Fold—twofold, threefold, manifold.

Frame—frame-up (n.).

Full—full-scale (adj.), full-time (adj.), full time (n.), [Also with part time (n.), and part-time (adj.), but pastime.]

The Art of Editing

Give—giveaway.
Go—go-between, go-getter.
Good—good-natured, good will (n.), goodwill (adj.).
Great—great-uncle.
Gun—gunfire, gun-shy.

Hair—hairdresser, hair shirt, red-haired, hairdo, hairdos.
Half—half-staff, half-mast, halfback, halfway, half dollar.
Hold—holdup.
Home—home run, homecoming, homemade, homeowner, home rule (n.), home-rule (adj.), homework, home town (n.).
Horse—horseplay, horse race.

In—insufferable, stand-in, inbound, in-law.
Infra—infrared.
Inter, intra—interstate, intrastate, intramural.

Law—law-abiding, lawbreaker, lawmaker, lawsuit.
Long—long shot, longtime.

Mid—mid-American, midday, mid-ocean, midwife, midship, midstream, midsummer, midtown.
Middle—middle-aged, middle-of-the-road (adj.), Middle Ages.
Multi—multimillion, multifaced, multicolored, multilateral.

Night—nightclub, nighttime.
No—no-hitter, no-trump.
Non—nonfarm, nonpartisan, non sequitur, nonprofit.

Open—open house, openhanded.
Out—out-box, out-talk, out-and-out, outboard, outdoor, out-of-doors (adj.).
Over—overabundant, overcome, pushover.

Place—place name, place kick.
Post—postwar, post-mortem, postnuptial, postmaster, post office, post card (postal card indicates the card is already stamped), post-Civil War, postgraduate.
Pre—predetermined, predawned, pre-empt, prejudge, prewar, preadolescent, pre-Roman.
Pro—pro-Arab, proclassical, pro-slavery.
Push—pushover.

Quarter—quarter-deck, quarter horse.
Quasi—quasi comfort, quasi-judicial.

Rain—raincoat, rainfall, rain-soaked, rainstorm.
Re—reappear, re-elect, re-enter, reopen, reinstated. Punctuation distinguishes between recover and re-cover, re-creation and recreation, re-treat and retreat.

Newspaper Style 425

Right—right wing, right-wing (adj.), right-hander, right field, right fielder, right-of-way, right-to-work, birthright, birth rate.
Round—round trip (n.), round-trip (adj.).
Run—run-off.

Safe—safe-conduct, safe-cracker, safeguard.
Self—self-respect, selfsame, self-service, self-defense, self-control.
Semi—semiannual, semi-invalid, semiofficial, semiyearly.
Sit—sit-down.
Store—storehouse, storekeeper, cigar store, drugstore.
Sub—subzero.
Super—superabundant, super-Republican, superman, superbomb, supermarket.

Take—takeoff.
Trade—trademark, trade name.
Trans—trans-American, transatlantic, trans-Canada, transcontinental, transoceanic, transpacific, trans-Siberian.
Tri—tricolor, trifocal.

Ultra—ultraviolet.
Un—un-American (Un-American Activities Committee), unshaven, unnecessary.
Under—underdog, underground, undersecretary, undersold, under way.
Uni—unicolor.
Up—up-to-date.

Vice—vice chairman, vice president.

War—warlike, warpath, warship.
Water—waterway, watercolor.
Weight—weightlifting.
Wheel—wheelchair.
Wide—worldwide, nationwide, wide-awake, wide-brimmed, wide-eyed.
Wire—wiretapping.
Work—workaday, workhouse, workout (n.), workshop.

Spelling The first preference in spelling is the short version in *Webster's New World Dictionary of the American Language* with exceptions as given in this section; the U.S. Postal Guide: the U.S. Board of Geographic Names and the National Geographic Society with exceptions as given in this section. The news services have agreed on some spellings where authorities do not agree. The following list includes agreed spellings:

Algiers	Antwerp	Athens	Bangkok
Antioch	Archangel	Bagdad	Basel

Bayreuth	Formosa Strait	Macao	Saint John, N.B.
Beirut	Frankfurt	Madagascar	St. John's, Nfld.
Belgrade	Genoa	Marseille	Salonika
Berchtesgaden	Goteborg	Mt. Sinai	Sofia
Bern	Gulf of Riga	Mukden	Taipei
Brunswick	The Hague	Munich	Tehran
Bucharest	Hamelin	Naples	Thailand
Cameroun	Hanover	North Cape	Tiflis
Cape Town	Hong Kong	Nuremberg	Turin
Coblenz	Jakarta	Peking	Valetta
Cologne	Katmandu	Pescadores I.	Mt. Vesuvius
Copenhagen	Kingston	Prague	Vietnam
Corfu	Kurile	Rhodes	Warsaw
Corinth	Leghorn	Romania	Wiesbaden
Dunkirk	Lisbon	Rome	Zuider Zee
Florence			

Where old and new names are used, or where quoted material uses a different form, one is bracketed: Formosa [Taiwan], Gdansk [Danzig] and so on.

Words Frequently Misspelled

accede	busses (kisses)	drunkenness
adherence		dumfounded or
admissible	caliber	dumbfounded
advertent	Canada geese	
advertise	candelabra	eked
adviser*	caress	embarrass
accommodate	cave-in	emphysema
accordion	chaperon	employe* (employee)
accumulate	chieftain	exhilarating
all right	cigarette	
alleged	clue	fallout
allotted, allotment	coconut	feud
anyone	commitment	fidgeted
appall	consensus	firefighter
Asian flu	consistent	fraudulent
asinine	consul	fulfill
ax	controversy	
	copter	gaiety
balloon	council	gaily
baritone	counsel	gauge
battalion		goodby* (good-by)
bellwether	demagogue	grammar
benefiting	descendant	Gray Lady
berserk	desiccate	greyhound
bettor	dietitian	grisly
blond (male)	diphtheria	guerrilla
blonde (female, hue)	disastrous	
Borse (German ex-	disc	hangar (aircraft
change)	dismantle	shelter)
Bourse (French ex-	dissension	hanger (hanging
change)	divisive	device)
boyfriend	drouth or	haranguing
buses (vehicle)	drought	harass

* Preferred spelling. Words in parentheses also indicate common newspaper usage.

Newspaper Style

hemorrhage
hieroglyphics
hitchhiker
homicide

idiosyncrasy
impostor
impresario
incredible
indestructible
indispensable
inflammable
innocuous
inoculate
insurer
ionosphere
irresistible
isotope

judgment*
jukebox

kamikazes
kidnaped*
kimono

lambastes
largess
legionnaire
liaison
lightning
likeable
liquefy
logjam

mantel (shelf)
mantle (covering)
marijuana
marshal
medieval
mementos
metallurgical
miniature
minuscule or (min-
   iscule)
missile
mold
monocle

naphtha
nerve-racking

occasion
occurred

old-timer

panicked
pantomime
papier-mache
parallel
paraphernalia
parasol
pastime
penicillin
per cent (percent)
percentage
peremptory
permissible
persistent
personnel
phony
picnicking
pinscher
playwright
politicking
pompons
preceding
presumptuous
princesse (dress)
principal (main)
principle (concept)
privilege
procedure
propeller
prostate
publicly

quandary
Queensberry (Mar-
   quis of)
questionnaire
queue

rarefy
recommend
reconnaissance
restaurant
restaurateur
Rigsdag (Danish par-
   liament)
Riksdag (Swedish
   parliament)
rock 'n' roll (rock-and-
   roll)

sacrilegious
schoolteacher
seize

separate
siege
sizable
skillful
soothe
soybean
specter
stanch (verb)
stationary (not mov-
   able)
stationery (writing
   material)
staunch (adj.)
straitjacket (straight
   jacket)
strait-laced
strict
strong-arm
subpoena
summonses
supersede
swastika
syrup*

teen-age (adj.)
teenager (noun) or
   (teen-ager)
theatre* or theater
thrash (punish)
thresh (grain)
townhouse
trampolin (general)
Trampoline (trade
   name)
tumultuous

vacuum
Veterans Day
veterinarian
vice versa
vichyssoise
vilify
violoncello

warranted
weird
whisky* (whiskey, ex-
   cept for Scotch)
wield
wondrous

X ray (noun)
X-ray (adj.)

Place Names

Albuquerque
Allegany (county in New York and Maryland)

* Preferred spelling. Words in parentheses also indicate common newspaper usage.

The Art of Editing

Alleghany (county in Virginia)
Allegheny Mountains
Arapaho (Indians, National Forest, peak)
Arapahoe (city, county, street, basin)
Arctic
Argentina (Argentines—people; Argentine—adj.)
Aroostook
Ascension (island)
Asuncion, Paraguay

Banff
Berkeley
Bosphorus (omit Strait; likewise with Dardanelles—but, Strait of Gibraltar, Straits of Florida)

Canon City, Colo.
Canyon, Texas
Charleston, S.C., W. Va.
Charlestown, Mass. (navy yard)
Cheboygan, Mich.
Coeur D'Alene

Edinburg, Texas
Edinburgh, Scotland
Eglin (Fla.) Air Force base

Guadalupe Hidalgo, Mex.
Guadeloupe, W.I.
Guiana
Guinea

Harpers Ferry
Hudson Bay (Hudson's Bay Co.)
Huntingdon—Pa. and Tenn.
Huntington—W.Va., Ind., Mo., Ore., Ark., Utah

Kearney, Neb.
Kearny—N.J. and Kan.
Kootenai River (U.S.)
Kootenay River (B.C.)

Lorain, Ohio
Loraine, Fr.

Macalester (College)
Mackenzie River
Manila
Matamoras, Pa.
Matamoros, Mex.
Meriden, Conn.
Meridian, Miss.
Middle East (not Near East)
Monterey, Calif.
Monterrey, Mex.
Murfreesboro
Muscogee, Ga.
Muskogee, Okla.

New Castle, Pa.
Newcastle, Eng.

Oahu
Ogallala, Neb.
Oglala (Indians)
Okeechobee

Paterson, N.J.
Philippines (Filipino—male, Filipina—female)
Pittsburg, Kan.
Pittsburgh, Pa.
Poughkeepsie
Puebla, Mex.
Pueblo, Colo.

Rio, Ho and Kiang mean river—Rio Grande, Hwang Ho (or Hwang River), Yangtze Kiang (or Yangtze River)

Saguache, Colo.
Saint John, N.B.
St. John's, Nfld.
St. Johns, Que.
Santa Ana
Saranac
Schenectady
Scotts Bluff (county)
Scottsbluff, Neb.
Sequoia
Shansi, Sensi (Chinese provinces)
Sheboygan, Wis.

Taos

Uncompahgre River

Westminster

Yugoslavia (Yugoslav—person and adj.)

Proper Names

Jane Addams
Mark Antony
Jane Austen
Dr. Christiaan Barnard
Phineas T. Barnum
Jakob Ludwig Felix Mendelssohn-Bartholdy
Ludwig van Beethoven
Sarah Bernhardt
Otto Bismarck
Sam Browne (belt)
Anthony J. Celebrezze
Julius Caesar
Moss Ceaser
Lady Chatterley
Katharine Cornell
Frederick Douglass
Fitzsimons (general hospital)
Phileas Fogg
Mohandas K. (or Mahatma) Gandhi
Hapsburg or Habsburg
Ernest Hemingway

Katharine Hepburn
Adolf Hitler
A. E. Housman
Court of St. James's; St. James Palace
Ben Jonson
Julliard (music school)
Kublai Khan
Nikita Khrushchev
Lillie Langtry
Nikolay Lenin (Vladimir Illich Ulianov)
Charles Lindbergh
Walter Lippmann
Lloyd's (insurance)
Lloyds (bankers)
Clare Boothe Luce
Macmillan (book publisher)
Ignace Jan Padrewski
August Piccard
Procter and Gamble
Richard Rodgers (American composer)
Cesar Romero (actor)
Artur Rubenstein
George Santayana
Arthur Schopenhauer
Franz Schubert
Ernestine Schumann-Heink
Alexander Solzhenitzin
Herbert Spencer (philosopher)
Edmund Spenser (poet)
Oscar Straus (Austrian composer)
Johann Strauss (Austrian composer)
Richard Strauss (German composer)
Barbra Streisand
Tutankhamen
Arthur Vandenberg
Stephen Van Rensselaer
Josiah Wedgwood (potter)
Flo Ziegfeld

Proofreading

Proofs have several uses other than that of indicating typographical errors.

Copyeditors, as we have seen in Chapters 3 and 4, use a galley proof as a marker to show where insertions and new leads go.

Copyeditors also may be assigned the task of updating overset matter and stories that made the later editions but not the earlier ones. On some papers such stories are called *pork*. Before the forms are torn up at the end of the press run, a makeup editor or his equivalent goes over the paper, circling items that should be retained for future use. Proofs of the circled stories go to the desk for updating. Proofs of overset material likewise go to the desk for updating.

On larger papers a dozen or so proofs may be pulled from each galley or strips of type. A set goes to each department head, including the desk chief, and to the wire service of which the paper is a member or client.

Duplicate sets of revised proofs go to the makeup editor on offset papers and to editors of out-of-office publications for paste-up dummies. When the dummies are returned, type is assembled in pages and page proofs go to the respective editors.

When the page has been assembled, a makeup editor or some other executive should scan the page to note the following:

Whether the date, the issue number and the page number in the folio are correct.

Whether the headlines have been placed over the right stories.

Whether the pictures are right side up.

Whether the sluglines have been removed.

Whether the jump-line information is accurate.

Whether a makeup change is properly noted in the index.

Thorough editing should be done on the story before the copy ever reaches the typesetter or the tapecutter. A proof is no place to make editing judgments. Printing companies charge the customer for all changes except typographical ones, basing the charge on time unit composition costs.

The Proofreader

Misspelled words and names, factual errors, grammatical errors and libelous statements have to be changed even though the errors should have been caught in the editing. But minor or nit-picking errors usually are allowed to remain. The reason is a matter of cost. One change in a line of type may result in the resetting of a paragraph of type. Sometimes, where a word replacement is desired, a word of similar character length can be used, thus averting the resetting of more than one line.

If the proofreader suspects a number of broken letters or uneven margins, he may ask for a set of cleaner proofs. The proofreader may or may not mark uneven spacing between words—but at least he might call the uneven spacing to the attention of the composing room foreman. Similarly, if wrong fonts, improperly aligned letters or lines that are indistinct in the upper or lower half of the line occur, the foreman should be notified. These errors would indicate that typesetting machines need attention.

One of the irritating flaws, and one that may or may not be corrected on proofs, is improper division of words at the end of the type line. Here are a few taken at random from several galleys of type: "reci-pient" for *recip-ient,* "opera-te" for *oper-ate,* "pal-aver" for *pa-laver,* "ne-bula" for *neb-ula,* "reven-ue" for *reve-nue,* "obes-ity" for *obesi-ty,* "implac-able" for *implaca-ble,* "child-ren" for *chil-dren.*

Even in computerized typesetting, where rules, rule exceptions and tables can be applied, word division accuracy can never be reliable because of ambiguities, dual meanings, different hyphenations for identically spelled words and different hyphenations in different usages.

In newspaper composition one hyphenization occurs in every seven lines of text, depending on the type size and line length. Roughly 15 per cent of these hyphenations will be in error. Some newspapers manually reset the incorrect broken lines after the type has been set. Some do not, as already indicated in the examples given of words incorrectly divided.

When 8-point type is set in 12-pica measure, line-ending breaks average one for every five lines. When 8-point type is used on 15-pica lines, hyphenation drops to one for every 12 lines.

The same is true for unjustified line composition. To speed composition, the Denver *Post* began using unjustified lines. The editors expected reaction from readers who were used to reading justified lines but got none. In the 11-pica columns the ragged lines (sometimes lacking 12 points of filling the line) occur about once every four lines. In 14-pica columns the ragged line endings virtually disappear.

Broken lines can be eliminated by adding space between words to justify lines. This is being done increasingly by newspapers using automated typesetters. In one experiment, a group of newspaper executives were handed a printed sheet containing no hyphens. No one seemed to miss the hyphens. Too much word spacing, of course, wastes page space and causes rivers of space in the text column, making it relatively difficult for the eye to read. But the time may come, in newspapers at least, when readers will be spared all word breaks.

Typesetters are expected to follow copy. Some hew to this rule so closely that they faithfully reproduce misspelled words. Others take it upon themselves to make corrections. If the copyeditor suspects that a compositor will try to second-guess him, he indicates that the spelling as written is correct no matter what the typesetter thinks. If the name is Billi, the copyeditor or reporter marks *cq* after the spelling so that it will not come out as Billie.

Typesetters, like other humans, look at one word but see another. Errors that spell a word are harder to catch than a misspelling. So, costumer comes out as customer, miliary as military, eclectic as electric, exorcise as exercise, diary as dairy, collage as college, calvary as cavalry, model as motel, farce as force, defective as detective, morality as mortality, bottle as battle, conservation as conversation, winch as wench.

Few typesetters can compose type without errors. A glance at first-edition stories that have been railroaded, that is, not proofread, will confirm this.

The proofreader, therefore, catches errors made in composition as well as the errors that should have been caught by copyeditors. It was a proofreader, not a copyeditor, who wondered why a bomber should be christened "Shadow Theory." (It was supposed to be Chateau-Thierry.) A proofreader wondered why a ship that had escaped many misfortunes should be renamed "Lucy." (It turned out to be "Lucky.")

Proofreading is an exacting task. Those who can do it well, in Dr. George P. Atwater's view, are real artists: "They must watch a dozen diverse things at once. They must look for errors of sense, uniformity of capitalization, punctuation, spelling, disarrangement of paragraphs, the use of wrong fonts of type, broken letters, letters upside down, incorrect page references, incorrect spacing and many other difficulties."[1]

Among other difficulties is lack of consistency. Are words, particularly names, spelled the same throughout the text? Are facts consistent, say, in compiled stories? Does the writer use one style in one paragraph and another in a later paragraph? In numbered series, are the numbers in order?

[1] Rhoda A. Porte, *Proofreading* (Salt Lake City: The Porte Press, 1944), p. 11.

Even the best proofreaders in the trade will not catch all errors. In the larger publishing houses where proofs may be read by several persons, including the author, errors still occur—and this despite the fact that proofreaders have a chance to catch errors in galley proofs, again in revised proofs, in page proofs and perhaps in revised page proofs.

Ideally, two persons should read proofs. One, the copyholder, reads the copy aloud while the other follows the reading on the proof. Or, the process may be reversed with the proofreader reading the proof aloud to the copyholder. If only one person reads proof he would do well to place a ruler under the line of type, then concentrate on syllables rather than on words and sentences.

Copy should accompany proofs to the proof room. Even though the proofreader may not have to refer to the copy, he has the copy available in case he questions a construction. Also, by having copy available he does not have to mark on the proof "out—see copy."

Proofreading Methods

Two methods are used in marking proofs. One is the formal or book method in which two marks are used—one, within the line, to indicate the offender and the other, in the margin, to indicate the correction. If only one error appears in the line, the correction is noted in the left margin. If more than one error occurs, the corrections are in the right margin, each correction being separated by a slash mark (Figure II–1).

The second method is the guideline system, probably used in the majority of newspapers. Here a line is drawn from the error within a line to the nearest margin. If several errors appear within the same type line, the guidelines may be drawn to both margins. Care is taken not to obliterate the place in the type line where the error occurs (Figure II–2).

In neither system is the correction made inside the type line or between lines of type.

If more than one error appears in the same word, the word should be circled and the correct word printed in the margin. Also, it is usually safer to rewrite a figure in the margin than to indicate changes in the figure by proof symbols.

If a line of type is upside down the proofreader not only makes this fact known in the margin notation but turns the proof around and reads the topsy-turvy line to be sure no typos occur in the reversed line. Similarly, typos should be sought out in transposed lines.

Using Proof Symbols

If an entire line of type appears to be missing, the proofreader should read farther down the proof for the missing line before rewriting the line. The line could be transposed rather than omitted.

If several lines have to be inserted, it is better to type the lines and show on the proof where they are to be inserted rather than

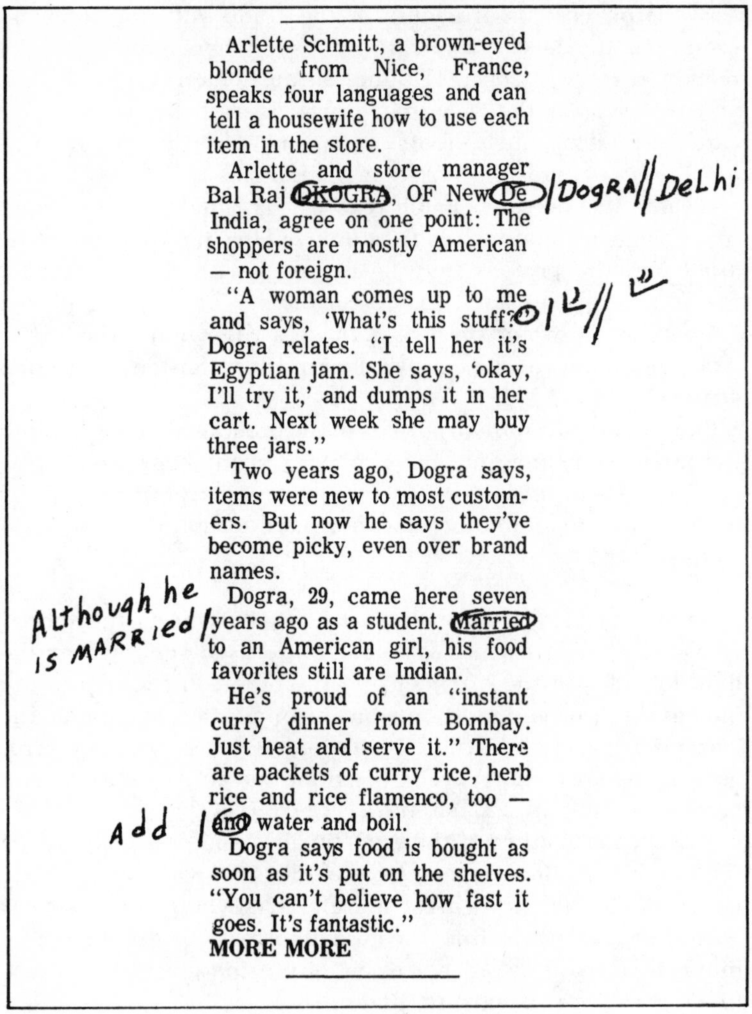

Arlette Schmitt, a brown-eyed blonde from Nice, France, speaks four languages and can tell a housewife how to use each item in the store.

Arlette and store manager Bal Raj QKOGRA, OF New De India, agree on one point: The shoppers are mostly American — not foreign.

"A woman comes up to me and says, 'What's this stuff? Dogra relates. "I tell her it's Egyptian jam. She says, 'okay, I'll try it,' and dumps it in her cart. Next week she may buy three jars."

Two years ago, Dogra says, items were new to most customers. But now he says they've become picky, even over brand names.

Dogra, 29, came here seven years ago as a student. Married to an American girl, his food favorites still are Indian.

He's proud of an "instant curry dinner from Bombay. Just heat and serve it." There are packets of curry rice, herb rice and rice flamenco, too — and water and boil.

Dogra says food is bought as soon as it's put on the shelves. "You can't believe how fast it goes. It's fantastic."

MORE MORE

Figure II–1. Formal method of marking proofs.

to attempt to write the lines in longhand on the margin of the proof.

Proof symbols are used to indicate typographical changes (Figure II–3) and editorial changes (Figure II–4).

Joyce on Film-Gal 2
Adv for Sunday, Nov. 6

"I'm afraid the essence of this picture must challenge him — if it's done honestly."

He made one of his long pauses again.

"All I can do is to say I think this is a fair approximation of what Joyce intended. I think it would almost be fairer to call the film 'Homage to Joyce,' or 'Homage to Ulysses,' than to call it 'Ulysses.'

"I've gotten what I consider is the main line of the story. I want to give the audience a special thing that relates to Joyce's vision. If I can do that, then I'll be in great shape. We hope" — he emphasized the word — "to have the cooperation of the censor in Britain."

Strick must get "Ulysses" past the British censor, John Trevelyan. To get the $840,000 necessary to make the movie in Dublin — using Joyce's actual locations — he had to promise to get the censor's O.K.

"We don't have to cooperate with the censor in America," said the producer-director, who with associate producer Fred Haines, is filming in Ireland, "because the censor doesn't really exist in the United States."

No censorship in America?

"There are only two general territories in the United States, I believe, that require pre-censorship. They are Chicago and the state of Maryland.

"The only viable censorship in America rests in the hands of the police who are entitled to terminate the performance of any show or screen exhibit. But they've got to say, 'This is deleterious to the public and we're going to end it.'

The more than 700-page book, first published in a limited edition in 1921, is about one day in the life of a Dublin Jew, Leopold Bloom.

"It is, I believe," said Stric, "the central literary work of the century, concerning itself with the affirmation of life, the search of a father for a son, and of a son for a father.

Strick looks on Bloom as the most fully developed character in fiction. He wanted an actor of stature to play such a part and he says he is sure he found him in the Dublin actor, Milo O'Shea. With the exception of the English actress, Barbara Jefford, who has the role of Molly, Scotland's Maurice Reeves, a n d Englishman Graham Lines, the cast is Irish.

Figure II–2. Informal or newspaper method of marking proofs.

Proofreading

437

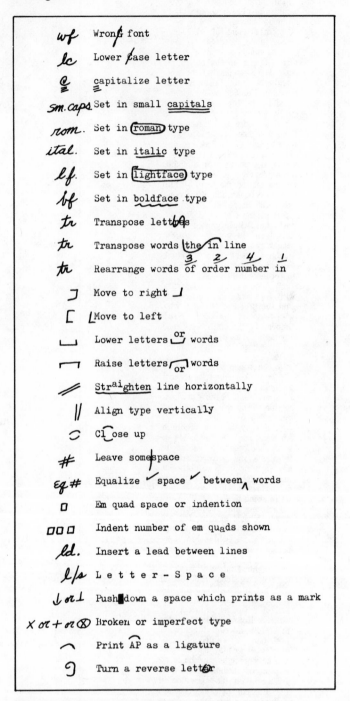

Figure II–3. Standard proofreading symbols and how they are applied.

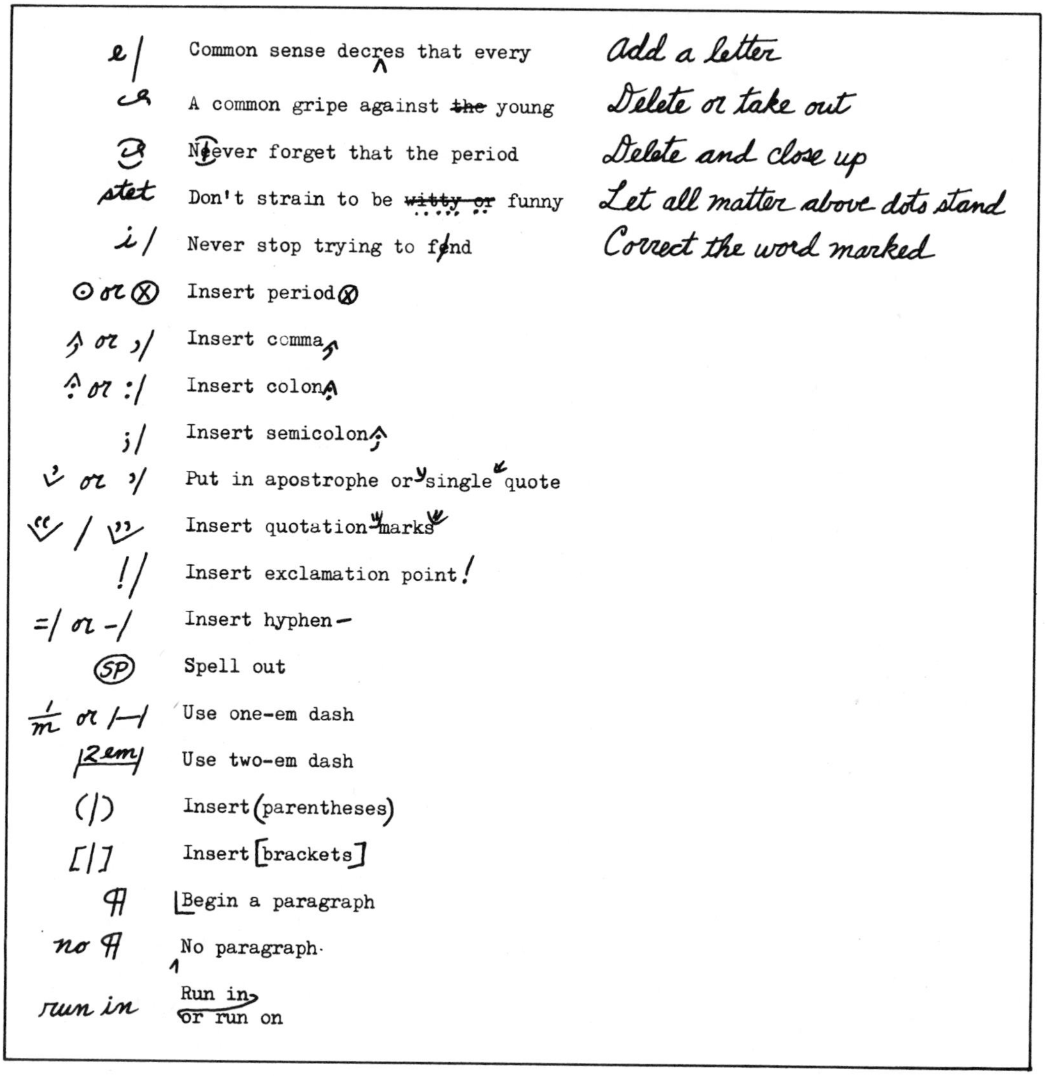

Figure II–4. Standard proofreading symbols.

Glossary

Accordion fold—parallel folds on sheet of paper to determine an imposition pattern.

Acetate—transparent sheet placed over art in mechanical color separation.

Ad—short for advertisement.

Ad alley—section in mechanical department where ads are assembled.

Add—material to be added to news story, usually with a number and slug: add 1 fire.

Add end—addendum to a story after it has been apparently closed.

Ad lib—unscripted comment made before a microphone.

Ad-side—advertising department as distinguished from editorial department.

Advance—story sent out in advance of the scheduled publication date.

Agate—name of a type size, e.g., agate type, or type that is $5\frac{1}{2}$ points high. Advertising is also sold on the basis of agate lines, or 14 agate lines to an inch.

Air—white space.

Align—to place adjacent to an even base line on a horizontal plane.

Alley—portion in composing room devoted to special sections, such as ad alley, Linotype alley.

All in hand—all available copy has been sent to composing department.

All up—all copy has been set into type.

A.M.—morning edition.

Angle—special aspect of a story; a slant.

Antique—rough-surfaced paper resembling old handmade papers.

AP—short for Associated Press, a major news agency.

Art—newspaper or magazine illustrations.

Astonisher—same as exclamation point.

Attribution—source of the material in a story.

Audio tape—tape on which sound has been transcribed.

A wire—usually the main wire of a news agency.

Back room—mechanical section as distinguished from front office. Also back shop.

Back timing—timing of a script so that it ends strong and clean.

Back up—printing the reverse side of a sheet.

Bad break—bad phrasing of a headline; bad wrapping of headline type; bad arrangement of type in columns, giving the reader the impression a paragraph ending is the end of the story.

Bank—cabinet or bench where type is kept; the lower portion of a headline (deck).

Banner—usually a headline stretching across all columns of a newspaper.

Barker—reversed kicker in which the kicker is in larger type than the lines below it. Also called a hammer.

Bastard type—type that varies from the standard point system.

Beeper—telephone interview recorded on audio tape.

Ben Day—a pattern of lines or dots to give a shaded effect as background for type or illustrations.

Binder—inside page streamer; head that binds together two or more related stories.

Black and white—reproduction in one color (black).

Black Letter—text or Old English style of type.

Blanket head—headline over several columns of type or over type and illustration.

Bleed—running an illustration off the page.

Blooper—any embarrassing error in print or broadcast.

Body—main story or text; body type is the size of type used for the contents.

Boil—to trim or reduce wordage of a story.

Boiler plate—syndicated material in mat or plate form.

Boldface—type that is blacker than normal typeface; also black face. Abbreviated bf.

Book—sheet of paper (usually half-sheet) on which a story is written. A basic category of printing paper.

Book number—number assigned to each item in a wire service report.

Box—unit of type inclosed by a border.

Brace—type of makeup, usually with a banner headline and the story in the right-hand column. A bracket.

Break—point at which a story turns from one column to another. An exclusive story.

Glossary   **441**

Break over—story that jumps from one page to another.

Brightener—short, amusing item.

Broadside—large sheet printed only on one side.

Broken box—splitting the lines of a box to accommodate words or pictures. Also split box.

Broken heads—headlines with lines of different widths.

Broken rule—rule that has been broken or nipped so that it does not print. Also busted rule.

Bug—type ornament; a logotype; a star or other element that designates makeovers.

Bulldog—an early edition of a newspaper.

Bulletin—last-minute story of significance; a wire service designation of a story of major importance, usually followed by bulletin matter. Abbreviated bun.

Bullets—large periods used for decoration, usually at the beginning of paragraphs.

Bumper—two elements placed side by side or one immediately beneath the other. A bumped headline is also called a tombstone.

Butted slugs—composition that requires two or more slugs to make the desired width.

Byline—credit given to the author.

Canned copy—copy released by press agents or syndicates.

Canopy head—streamer headline from which two or more readout heads drop.

Caps—short for capital letters or upper-case letters.

Caption—display line over a picture or over the cutline. Also used as a synonym for a cutline. Also called an overline.

Cartridge—holder for audio tapes. Also a staccato lead.

Case—type cabinet.

Casting box—receptacle used to make or cast stereotype plates.

Centered—type placed in the middle of a line.

Center spread—two facing pages made up as one in the center of a newspaper section; also called double truck.

Chase—metal frame in which forms are locked before printing or stereotyping.

Chaser—fast, urgent replate.

Cheesecake—slang for photographs emphasizing women's legs. Also called leg art.

Circumlocution—wordy, roundabout expressions. Also redundancy.

Circus makeup—flamboyant makeup featuring a variety of typefaces and sizes.

City room—main newsroom of a newspaper. The city editor presides over the city desk.

Ck—short for *can kill* (usable but not important).

Clean copy—copy with a minimum of typographical or editing corrections. Clean proof is proof that requires few corrections.

Clips—short for clippings of newspaper stories.

Clipsheet—publicity material printed on a sheet so that each item may be cut out and used.

Closeup—photo showing head or head and shoulders or an object seen at close range.

Closing—time at which forms are closed. Also ending.

Cloze—method of testing readability. Respondents are asked to fill in words in blank spaces.

Col.—abbreviation for column.

Cold type—reproduction of characters composed photographically.

Color page—page on which color is used.

Color story—biased account or a feature story.

Column inch—unit of space measurement; one column wide and one inch deep.

Column rule—printing units that create vertical lines of separation on a page.

Combination cut—engraving that includes both halftone and line work.

Combo—short for combination, pictures of the same subject used as a single unit.

Compose—type is set or composed in a composing room by a compositor.

Composition—all typesetting.

Compre—same as standalone or without story.

Computer terms—see glossary at end of Chapter 3.

Constant—element used regularly without change. Also called standing or stet material.

Copy—words typewritten by reporters or editors from which type is set. Printers set copy.

Copy cutter—composing room worker who distributes copy among compositors.

Copy fitting—editing copy to fit a required space.

Copyholder—person who reads manuscript while another person marks the proof.

Copyreader—same as copyeditor, one who edits copy and writes headlines.

Cq—symbol or word is correct; folo (follow) copy.

Credit line—same as byline.

Crop—to eliminate unwanted portions of a photograph. Marks used to show the elimination are called crop marks.

Crossbar—printing press attachment to guide or turn print paper.

Crossline—headline composed of a single line.

Cue—signal given to announcer; a line in a script indicating a change.

Cut—illustration or engraving. Or, a direction to trim or shorten a story.

Cut-in—may refer to an initial letter beginning a paragraph or to a side head that is set into the opening lines of a paragraph.

Cutline—explanatory material, usually placed beneath a picture. Also called underline, legend and caption.

Cutoff—hairline that marks the point where the story moves from one column to another or to separate boxes and cuts from text material or to separate a headline from other elements.

Cx—short for correction. Indicates that corrections are to be made in type. Also called fix.

Dangler—short for dangling participle or similar grammatical error.

Dash—short line separating parts of headlines or headline and story.

Dateline—opening phrase of story showing origin, source and sometimes date of story. Also the publication date at the top of each page.

Dead—newspaper copy or type that is no longer usable.

Deadline—the shutoff time for copy for an edition.

Deck—section of a headline.

Delete—take out. The proofreader uses a symbol for a delete mark.

Desk—standing alone, usually the copydesk. Also city desk, sports desk, etc.

Dingbat—typographic decoration.

Display—term given to a type of advertising that distinguishes it from classified advertising. Display lines are those set in larger sizes than regular body type.

Dissolve—in broadcasting, a smooth transition from one image to another.

Dog watch—late shift of an afternoon paper or early shift of a morning paper. Also lobster trick.

Double chain—film story on two reels going through two projectors simultaneously.

Double spacer—term used on radio news wire to designate a story of unusual significance. Extra space is used between copy lines to alert the editor to the story.

Double truck—two pages at the center of a section made up as a single unit.

Down style—style using a minimum of capital letters.

Drop line—headline in which each line is stepped. Also called step line.

Dub—transfer of film or tape.

Dummy—diagram outlining the makeup scheme. A rough dummy has little detail; a paste-up dummy is created by pasting page elements on a sheet of paper the actual size of the page.

Dupe—short for duplicate or carbon copy.

Dutch break—breaking body type from one column to another not covered by the display line. Also called dutch turn or raw wrap.

Ears—small box on one or both sides of the nameplate carrying brief announcements of weather, circulation, edition and the like.

Edition—one of several press runs such as city edition and late home edition.

Electrotype—engraving duplicate made by electroplating a waxed impression.

Em—measurement of type that is as wide as it is high. A pica em is 12 points wide. Some printers still refer to all picas as ems. Ems are sometimes referred to as mut or mutton.

En—one-half em. Mostly used to express space. If the type is in 10 points, an indention of an en would equal 5 points. Sometimes referred to as a nut.

Endmark—symbol (such as # or 30) to indicate the close of the story. An end dash (sometimes called a 30 dash) is used at the end of the story in type.

Etching—process of removing nonprinting areas from a relief plate by acid.

Etch proof—name given to a proof of type on a special paper on which the printing is photographed. Also called reproduction proof.

Extra—special edition published to carry an important news break.

Eyebrow—another name for a kicker head.

Face—style or cut of type; the printing surface of type or of a plate.

FAX—short for facsimile or transmission by wire of a picture.

Family—as applied to type, all the type in any one design. Usually designated by a trade name.

Fat head—headline too large for the space allowed for it.

Feature—to give special prominence to a story or illustration. A story that stresses the human interest angle.

Feed—story or program electronically transmitted to other stations or broadcast to the public.

Filler—short items, usually set in type in advance and used to fill out space in a column of type. Also called briefs or shorts.

Fingernails—parentheses.

Fix—to correct or a correction.

Flag—title of paper appearing on page 1. Also nameplate, logo, name line.

Flash—brief announcement by a wire service of urgent news. Usually followed by a bulletin.

Flat—group of pictures engraved on a single unit. Also group of shots on one negative.

Flimsy—carbon copy.

Flip—to turn a story from last column of first page to first column of second page.

Float—ruled side bar that may go anywhere in a story. To center an element in space that is not large enough to fill.

Glossary

445

Floorman—printer.

Flop—illustration reversed in engraving.

Floss—overwritten.

Flush—even with the column margin. Type aligned on one side. Alignment may be either on left or right side.

Folio—lines showing the newspaper name, date and page number. Generally, however, the page number only.

Follow—related matter that follows main story. Abbreviated folo.

Followup—second-day story.

Follow copy—set the story as sent; disregard seeming errors.

Form—type and engraving assembled in a chase, ready for the press.

Format—physical form of a publication.

Foundry type—metal type cast in a type foundry and used for hand-set type.

Frame—top or cabinet or case rack upon which the compositor works.

Frame makeup—vertical makeup.

Freaks—devices that depart from normal indented body and headline type, etc.

Frontispiece—illustrated leaf preceding a book's title page.

Fudge box—device, usually a clamp, inserted in a press plate allowing the paper to carry line scores and the like after the edition has gone to press.

Fullface—same as boldface.

Furniture—spacing material placed around type area to lock it into a chase.

Future book—record kept by the city desk of future events.

FYI—for your information

Gain—sound level.

Galley—metal tray used to hold type.

Galley proof—print of the assembled type, used in proof-reading.

Gatekeeper—one who decides whether to pass a news story along. The account of an event goes through many gatekeepers before it reaches the reader.

Gathering—process of assembling all the signatures (or groups of pages) into a complete booklet.

Glossy—photograph with a hard, shiny finish.

Gobbledygook—editor's slang for material characterized by jargon and circumlocution. Also spelled gobbledegook.

Gothic—sans serif type. Also called block letter.

Graf—short for paragraph.

Gravure—process of photomechanical printing. Also roto-gravure or intalgio (printing ink is transferred to paper from areas sunk below the surface) printing.

Grease pencil—type of pencil used to make crop marks on pictures.

Guideline—instructions on copy to direct a printer. Usually includes slug, edition, section etc.

Gutter—vertical space that separates one page from another on two facing pages. Also, long unbroken space between two columns of type.

Hairline—finest line available in printing. Often used for rules between columns.

Hairspace—thin space.

Half stick—matter set in one half column measure. A depth one half of the column width.

Halftone—photoengraving. A dot pattern gives the illusion of tones.

Hammer—see Barker.

Handout—release story from a public relations firm.

Hanger—headline that descends from a banner. Also called readout.

Hanging indention—headline style in which the top line is set full measure and succeeding lines are indented from the left.

Hard copy—original copy, distinguishing it from monitor copy or carbon copy. Also a glossy photographic print as contrasted to facsimile.

Hard news—spot news or news of record as contrasted to features and background material.

Head count—number of letters and spaces available for a headline.

Headlinese—overworked short words in a headline, such as *cop, nab, hit, set.*

Head shot—photo of person's head or head and shoulders. Also called face shots and mug shots.

HFR—hold for release.

Highlight—white or light portions of a photograph. Also the high point of a story.

Hold for release—copy that is not to be used until a specified time.

Holdout—portion held out of a story and placed in the overset.

Hood—border over the top and both sides of a headline.

Horseshoe—copydesk, once shaped like a horseshoe.

Hot metal—line-caster slugs as opposed to cold type or type set photographically.

HTK—headline to come. Also HTC.

Hugger mugger—newspaper lead crammed with details.

Imposition—process of placing type and illustrations in pages.

Impression—any printing of ink on paper. Also appearance of the printed page. Also the number of times a press has completed a printing cycle.

Index—newspaper's table of contents, usually found on page 1.

Initial (Initial cap)—first letter in a paragraph set in type larger than the body type.

Glossary

447

Insert—addition to a story placed within the story.

Intertype—line-casting machine.

Intro—short for introduction. Opening copy to film or tape.

Inverted pyramid—news story structure in which the parts are placed in a descending order of their importance. Also a headline in inverted pyramid shape.

Issue—all copies produced by a newspaper in a day.

Italics—slanted letter form. Shortened form is itals.

Jargon—language of a profession, trade or group. Newspaper jargon.

Jim dash—short centered line between decks of a headline or between head and story. Also designated as 3-em or 4-em dashes.

Jump—to continue a story from one page to another.

Jump head—headline over the continued portion of a story.

Jump lines—continuation lines: continued on page X.

Justify—spacing out a line of type to fill the column; spacing elements in a form so form can be locked up.

Kicker—overline over a headline. Also eyebrow.

Kill—to discard copy, type, mats and so on.

Label head—dull, lifeless headline. Sometimes a standing head such as **News of the World.**

Layout—pattern of typographic arrangement. Similar to dummy.

Lead—beginning of a story or the most important story of the day (pronounced "leed").

Lead—piece of metal varying from 1 to 3 points placed between lines of type for spacing purposes (pronounced "led").

Leaders—line of dots.

Leading—process of placing leads (leds) between lines of type.

Lead out—to justify a line of type.

Legend—information under an illustration. Also cutline.

Letterpress—technique of printing from raised letters. Ink is applied to the letters, paper is placed over the type and impression implied to the paper, resulting in printing on paper.

Library—newspaper's collection of books, files and so on. Also called morgue.

Ligature—two or more letters on a type character: fi, ffi.

Light pencil—device resembling a small flashlight used to edit copy displayed on a television screen. A light eraser is used in the same manner, but to delete unwanted portions.

Line-caster—any keyboarded machine that casts lines of type.

Line cut—engraving without tones. Used for maps, charts and so on.

Line gauge—pica rule or a ruler marked off in pica segments.

Linotype—line-casting machine.

Lock up—process of tightening a form.

Logotype—single matrix of type containing two or more letters commonly used together: AP, UPI. Also a combination of the nameplate and other matter to identify a section. Also an advertising signature. Commonly abbreviated logo.

Lower case—small letter as distinguished from a capital letter. Abbreviated lc.

Ludlow—machine to cast slugs from hand-set matrices.

Magazine—part of a typesetting machine that holds the matrices.

Makeready—process of aligning elements on the page to assure a uniform impression.

Makeover—to change page content or layout.

Makeup—design of a newspaper page. Assembling elements in a page.

Marker—proof or tearsheet used to show where inserts are to go after story has been sent to the composing room or other instructions for guidance of printers and makeup editors.

Masthead—informational material about a newspaper, usually placed on the editorial page.

Mat—short for matrix or mold for making a stereotype. The mat of a page is made of papier-mâché. In typesetting machines, the matrix is made of brass.

Measure—length of a line of type.

Monitor copy—tearsheet copy or copy produced electronically. A monitor is also a television or radio receiver. To monitor is to watch or time a radio or television program.

Monotype—line-casting machine that casts one letter at a time.

Montage—succession of pictures assembled to create an overall effect. Usually a single photograph using several negatives.

Morgue—newspaper reference library or repository for clippings.

Mortise—cutaway section of an engraving into which type is inserted.

Mug shot—same as closeup or face shot.

Must—matter that someone in authority has ordered published.

Nameplate—name of newspaper displayed on page 1. Also called flag, title or line.

Newshole—space left for news and editorial matter after ads have been placed on pages.

Newsprint—low-quality paper used to print newspapers.

NH—slug on copy indicating new head.

NL—slug on copy and notation on a marker indicating new lead.

Obit—abbreviation for obituary.

Offset—method of printing differing from letterpress. A photograph is taken after the page has been assembled. The negatives are placed over a light-sensitive printing plate and light is exposed through the open spaces of the negative. The result is that the letters are hardened and the nonprinting surface is washed away. The method of printing involves inking the printed plate with water and then with ink. The water resides only on the nonprinting surface, whereas the ink resides on the printing surface. The inked letters are then printed on a rubber blanket, which in turn prints (or offsets) on paper.

Offsetter copy—Associated Press copy prepared for papers using offset printing.

Op. ed—page opposite the editorial page.

Optional—matter that may be used without regard to the time element. Also called time copy, grape and AOT (any old time).

Out-cue—cue telling a news director or engineer that a film or tape is near the end.

Outlined cut—halftone with background cut out. Also silhouette.

Overline—display head over a picture or over a cutline. Also called caption.

Overset—type in excess of amount needed.

Pad—to make a story longer with excess words.

Page proof—proof of an entire page.

Parameter—symbol in computer programming indicating a constant such as a figure.

Parens—short for parentheses.

Photocomposition—type composed photographically.

Photolithography—printing process such as offset where the impression is transferred from a plate to a rubber roller and to paper.

Pi—to jumble type hopelessly. Type is pied.

Pica—linear measure in 12 points. A pica em is a standard measure but only 12-point type can be a pica em.

Pickup—material in type that is to be used with new material such as a new lead.

Pix—short for pictures. The singular may be pic or pix.

Pixel—small picture element to denote gray or color values for computer storage.

Planer—block or mallet used to even a printing surface or to pound an impression on a page proof.

Plate—stereotyped page ready for the press.

Play—prominence given a story, its display. Also the principal story.

Plug—filler copy. Also time copy, grape, pork.

Point—unit of printing measurement, approximately $\frac{1}{72}$ inch. Actually .01384 inches. Also any punctuation mark.

Pork—matter saved from one edition and printed in another or matter taken from one day's final edition and used in the next day's early edition.

Pos.—positive film image.

Precede—material such as a bulletin or an editor's note appearing at the top of a story.

Predate—edition delivered before its announced date. Usually a Sunday edition delivered to outlying areas.

Printer—machine that produces copy by telegraphic impulses. A Teletype machine. Also a person who prepares composition for imprinting operations.

Printout—visual copy produced by a computer, usually for proofreading. Same as master copy or tear sheet.

Process color—method of printing that duplicates a full-color original copy.

Proof—print of type used for proofreading purposes.

Proofreader—one who corrects proofs.

Prop—an object used during a newscast to give credence to an item.

Puff—personal publicity story.

Pull-out—a special section within a paper but designed to be removed from the main portion.

Put to bed—to lock up forms for an edition.

Pyramid—arrangement of ads in half-pyramid form from top right to lower left.

Quad—short for quadrat, a blank printing unit for spacing.

Quadrant—layout pattern in which the page is divided into fourths.

Query—brief message outlining a story. Also a question put to a news source.

Quoins—metal wedges used to hold printing elements in a chase. The wedges are locked with a quoin key.

Quotes—short for quotation marks.

Race—classification of type, such as roman, text, script.

Rack—cabinet in which composition is kept.

Railroad—to rush copy to the printer before it is edited; to rush type to press without proofreading. Also a term for a headline type.

Reader—machine used with a computer to read copy or tape and record a justified tape.

Read in—to omit the rule.

Readout—secondary head accompanying a main head.

Rear projection—projection of a film, photo, map or graph placed on a screen behind the newscaster.

Regional split—interruption in the main radio wire to permit the transmission of regional news.

Register—alignment of plates to get true color reproduction.

Release copy—copy to be held until a specified release time. Same as advance copy.

Reperforator—machine that produces tape for automatic typesetting.

Replate—to make a page over after an edition has gone to press.

Reproduction—another name for an etch proof. Abbreviated as repro.

Retouch—to alter a photograph by painting or airbrushing.

Reverse plate—reversing the color values so that white letters are on a black background.

Revised proof—second proof after corrections have been made.

Ribbon—another name for a banner or streamer headline.

Rim—outer edge of a copydesk. Copyeditors are known as rimmen or rim-person.

Ring—to draw a circle around a word or symbol to indicate a different form.

Ring bank—composing room stands where corrections are made in type. A ring person is an operator who makes corrections in type on a line-caster or ring machine.

Rip and read—derogatory expression applied to radio newspersons who simply read the latest summary from the radio wire without careful editing.

Rising initial—initial capital letter that aligns with the body type at the base line.

Rivers—streaks of white space caused by uneven typesetting.

ROP—run of the paper. Stories or art that do not demand up-front position. Ads that may appear anywhere in the paper. Color printed in a newspaper without the use of special presses.

Rotogravure—means of printing from recessed letters. One of the major printing techniques (along with letterpress and offset). Used mostly in catalogs, magazines and fine color work.

Rough—may be applied to a dummy that gives little or no detail or to an uncorrected, unjustified proof.

Roundup—compilation of stories.

Routing—removing nonessential parts from a plate.

Rules—any line that is printed. Lines are cast in type metal form. Hairline rules are often used in newspaper work. The underscore of the preceding is a type rule.

Run—reporter's beat.

Runaround—method of setting type around a picture.

Run-in—to incorporate sentences or lists into one paragraph.

Running story—story handled in takes or small segments. Each take is sent to the composing room as soon as it is edited.

Runover—portion of a story that continues from one page to the next. Also a jump story.

Sans serif—typeface without serifs.

Sc—proofreader's mark meaning "see copy."

Schedule—list of available stories and pictures; desk's record of stories edited.

Scoop—to get an exclusive story. Also a beat.

Screen—to view film or video tape.

Script—in broadcast news, the arrangement of news, together with an opening and closing and leads to commercials.

Second front page—first page of the second section. Also called a split page.

Section page—first page of a pull-out section.

Sectional story—same as running story where copy is handled in takes.

Serifs—the fine cross strokes at the top and bottom of most styles of letter.

Set solid—lines of type without extra spacing between lines.

Shirt tail—slang for a follow story.

Short—brief item of filler.

Side bar—brief story with a special angle that goes with the main story.

Signature—group of pages printed on one sheet. Also an advertiser's name displayed in an ad.

Silhouette—form of halftone with the background removed. Same as outline cut.

Skeletonize—copy sent by wire where unnecessary words are omitted. Same as cablese.

Skyline—headline across top of page over nameplate. Also called over-the-roof head.

Slant—angle of a story. A story written a certain way for policy reasons.

Slug—label identifying a story. Same as guideline or catchline. Also a piece of metal used for spacing. Also used to designate line-caster slugs.

Soc—short for society page material.

Sound-on-film—film carrying its own sound track. Abbreviated SOF.

Sound under—audio level where background sounds may be heard.

Space out—direction to the printer to add space between lines until the story fills the space allotted for it.

Split page—first page of the second section of a newspaper.

Split run—making a change in part of a press run of the same edition.

Spot news—news obtained firsthand; fresh news.

Spread—story prominently displayed, often over several columns and with art.

Squib—short news item or filler.

Standalone—a picture without an accompanying story.

Standing box—type box kept on hand for repeated use. Likewise with standing head.

Standing type—similar to standing boxes and heads; type kept standing for future use.

Standupper—television report at the scene with the camera on the reporter.

Step lines—headline with successive lines indented; same as dropline.

Glossary

Stereotype—process of casting a plate from a papier-mâché mold.

Stet—let it stand. Disregard correction.

Stick—typeholder. A story as long as a column width.

Sticker—refers to a page that will undergo no makeup changes from edition to edition.

Stinger—another term for kicker or eyebrow.

Stock—paper used for any printing job.

Stone—table on which type for the paper is assembled.

Straight matter—copy set in one size of type for the main reading matter of a page. Also called body type.

Streamer—another name for a banner or a ribbon headline.

String—clippings of stories, usually from a correspondent.

Stringer—correspondent paid on space rate. In television news, a free-lance cameraman.

Strip-in—to insert one illustrative element into another.

Sub—short for substitute. Sub bomber means a new story for a story slugged bomber.

Subhead—one- or two-line head used within the body of a story in type. Also called column break.

Summary—may be a news index or a news roundup. A summary lead gives the gist of the facts in the story.

Super card—in television, white lettering on a black card.

Supplemental service—syndicated service in addition to major wire service.

Swash cut—picture cut on the edges to give the effect of broken glass.

Tabloid—newspaper format, usually five columns wide and approximately 16 inches deep. Also refers to a sensational style of news presentation.

Take—small part of a running story. Also the part of a story given to a compositor.

Tape—perforated paper used in Teletype or Teletypesetter.

Tear sheet—sheet or part of a sheet used for corrections. Also copy produced by a computerized copy follower.

Tease—news announcement before the station break with details to follow the break.

Telephoto—UPI system of transmitting pictures by wire. UPI Unifax transmits facsimile pictures.

Teletype—automatic printer used to send and receive wire copy.

Teletypesetter—device attached to a line-caster so that the typesetting is controlled by perforated tape. Abbreviated TTS—copy (and tape) for papers with Teletypesetters.

Thirty dash—endmark.

Thumbnail—half-column portrait. Also a rough sketch or dummy.

Tie-back—part of a story providing background material.

Tight paper—paper containing so much advertising there is limited space for news.

Time copy—copy that may be used anytime. Also called grape, plug copy and so on.

Toenails—quotation mark or apostrophe. Also parentheses.

Tombstone—to place headlines of the same type side by side. Such adjacent heads are called bumped heads.

Tr—short for turn rule. A turned rule (upside-down slug) shows a printer where an insert is to be placed. Also refers to heavy rules used in an obituary of an outstanding person.

Turn story—same as jump story (continues from last column on one page to first column on the next page).

Trunk—main news wire of a news agency.

Typo—short for typographical error.

Undated—story without a dateline (but usually a credit line) summarizing related events from different origins.

Underline—same as cutline.

Unisetter—UPI service for papers using offset.

UPI—short for United Press International, a major news agency.

Up-date—to bring a story up to date or to give it a timely angle.

Up style—newspaper style using a maximum of capital letters.

Video tape—tape that projects pictures.

Vignette—halftone with a fading background. Also a feature story or sketch.

Visible—tape perforations arranged so that they spell words or symbols.

Visual—anything seen on a television screen.

Viz—short for vismo, a rear projection process.

VTR—short for video-tape recording.

Wf—short for wrong font or type of a different size or style from that used in the text.

Wicket—kicker-like element placed to one side of a headline.

Widow—one or two words appearing at the end of a paragraph and on the last line. It is unsightly because of the excessive white space appearing after the widow, particularly at the top of a column.

Wirephoto—AP system of transmitting pictures by wire. The AP facsimile system is called Fotofax.

Without—picture that does not go with a story. See Standalone and Compre.

Wooden head—one that is dull and lifeless.

Wrap around—ending the top line of a headline with a preposition, conjunction or the like, or splitting words that are properly a unit.

Wrapup—complete story. Wire services use a wrapup to contain in one story all elements of the same story sent previously.

Zinc—metal used for a photoengraving; zinc etching or a cut without a halftone screen.

Index

A

Index